ALVIS

A CENTURY OF DRIVERS

SOCIETY

Also from Veloce Publishing:

Those Were The Days ... Series
Alpine Trials & Rallies 1910-1973 (Pfundner)
American ½-ton Pickup Trucks of the 1950s (Mort)
American ½-ton Pickup Trucks of the 1960s (Mort)
American 'Independent' Automakers – AMC to Willys 1945 to 1960 (Mort)
American Station Wagons – The Golden Era 1950-1975 (Mort)
American Trucks of the 1950s (Mort)
American Trucks of the 1960s (Mort)
American Woodies 1928-1953 (Mort)
Anglo-American Cars from the 1930s to the 1970s (Mort)
Austerity Motoring (Bobbitt)
Austins, The last real (Peck)
Brighton National Speed Trials (Gardiner)
British and European Trucks of the 1970s (Peck)
British Drag Racing – The early years (Pettitt)
British Lorries of the 1950s (Bobbitt)
British Lorries of the 1960s (Bobbitt)
British Touring Car Racing (Collins)
British Police Cars (Walker)
British Woodies (Peck)
Buick Riviera (Mort)
Café Racer Phenomenon, The (Walker)
Chevrolet ½-ton C/K-Series Pickup Trucks 1973-1987 (Mort)
Don Hayter's MGB Story – The birth of the MGB in MG's Abingdon Design & Development Office (Hayter)
Drag Bike Racing in Britain – From the mid '60s to the mid '80s (Lee)
Dune Buggy Phenomenon, The (Hale)
Dune Buggy Phenomenon Volume 2, The (Hale)
Endurance Racing at Silverstone in the 1970s & 1980s (Parker)
Hot Rod & Stock Car Racing in Britain in the 1980s (Neil)
Mercedes-Benz Trucks (Peck)
MG's Abingdon Factory (Moylan)
Motor Racing at Brands Hatch in the Seventies (Parker)
Motor Racing at Brands Hatch in the Eighties (Parker)
Motor Racing at Crystal Palace (Collins)
Motor Racing at Goodwood in the Sixties (Gardiner)
Motor Racing at Nassau in the 1950s & 1960s (O'Neil)
Motor Racing at Oulton Park in the 1960s (McFadyen)
Motor Racing at Oulton Park in the 1970s (McFadyen)
Motor Racing at Thruxton in the 1970s (Grant-Braham)
Motor Racing at Thruxton in the 1980s (Grant-Braham)
Superprix – The Story of Birmingham Motor Race (Page & Collins)
Three Wheelers (Bobbitt)

Great Cars
Austin-Healey – A celebration of the fabulous 'Big' Healey (Piggott)
Jaguar E-type (Thorley)
Jaguar Mark 1 & 2 (Thorley)
Jaguar XK A Celebration of Jaguar's 1950s Classic (Thorley)
Triumph TR – TR2 to 6: The last of the traditional sports cars (Piggott)
Volkswagen Beetle – A Celebration of the World's Most Popular Car (Copping)

General
1½-litre GP Racing 1961-1965 (Whitelock)
AC Two-litre Saloons & Buckland Sportscars (Archibald)
An Austin Anthology (Stringer)
An Austin Anthology II (Stringer)
An English Car Designer Abroad (Birtwhistle)
An Incredible Journey (Falls & Reisch)
Anatomy of the Classic Mini (Huthert & Ely)
Anatomy of the Works Minis (Moylan)
Armstrong-Siddeley (Smith)
Art Deco and British Car Design (Down)
Automotive A-Z, Lane's Dictionary of Automotive Terms (Lane)
Automotive Mascots (Kay & Springate)
Bentley Continental, Corniche and Azure (Bennett)
Bentley MkVI, Rolls-Royce Silver Wraith, Dawn & Cloud/Bentley R & S-Series (Nutland)
Bluebird CN7 (Stevens)
BMC, The Cars of (Robson)
BMC Competitions Department Secrets (Turner, Chambers & Browning)
British at Indianapolis, The (Wagstaff)
British Cars, The Complete Catalogue of, 1895-1975 (Culshaw & Horrobin)
BRM – A Mechanic's Tale (Salmon)
BRM V16 (Ludvigsen)
Classic British Car Electrical Systems (Astley)
Classic Engines, Modern Fuel: The Problems, the Solutions (Ireland)
Coventry Climax Racing Engines (Hammill)
Daily Mirror 1970 World Cup Rally 40, The (Robson)
Dorset from the Sea – The Jurassic Coast from Lyme Regis to Old Harry Rocks photographed from its best viewpoint (also Souvenir Edition) (Belasco)
Draw & Paint Cars – How to (Gardiner)
Drive on the Wild Side, A – 20 Extreme Driving Adventures From Around the World (Weaver)
Driven – An Elegy to Cars, Roads & Motorsport (Aston)
East German Motor Vehicles in Pictures (Suhr/Weinreich)
Essential Guide to Driving in Europe, The (Parish)

Fast Ladies – Female Racing Drivers 1888 to 1970 (Bouzanquet)
Fate of the Sleeping Beauties, The (op de Weegh/Hottendorff/op de Weegh)
Formula 1 - The Knowledge 2nd Edition (Hayhoe)
Formula 1 All The Races - The First 1000 (Smith)
Formula One – The Real Score? (Harvey)
Formula 5000 Motor Racing, Back then ... and back now (Lawson)
France: the essential guide for car enthusiasts – 200 things for the car enthusiast to see and do (Parish)
The Good, the Mad and the Ugly ... not to mention Jeremy Clarkson (Dron)
Great British Rally, The (Robson)
GT – The World's Best GT Cars 1953-73 (Dawson)
Immortal Austin Seven (Morgan)
Inside the Rolls-Royce & Bentley Styling Department – 1971 to 2001 (Hull)
Jaguar - All the Cars (4th Edition) (Thorley)
Jaguar from the shop floor (Martin)
Jaguar E-type Factory and Private Competition Cars (Griffiths)
Jaguar, The Rise of (Price)
Jaguar XJ 220 – The Inside Story (Moreton)
Jaguar XJ-S, The Book of the (Long)
The Jowett Jupiter – The car that leaped to fame (Nankivell)
Land Rover Design - 70 years of success (Hull)
Land Rover Emergency Vehicles (Taylor)
Land Rover Series III Reborn (Porter)
Land Rover, The Half-ton Military (Cook)
Land Rovers in British Military Service – coil sprung models 1970 to 2007 (Taylor)
Lea-Francis Story, The (Price)
Lotus 18 Colin Chapman's U-turn (Whitelock)
Lotus 49 (Oliver)
Lotus Elan and +2 Source Book (Vale)
Lotus Elite – Colin Chapman's first GT Car (Vale)
Lotus Evora – Speed and Style (Tippler)
Making a Morgan (Hensing)
Maximum Mini (Booij)
Meet the English (Bowie)
MG, Made in Abingdon (Frampton)
MGA (Price Williams)
MGB & MGB GT– Expert Guide (Auto-doc Series) (Williams)
MGB Electrical Systems Updated & Revised Edition (Astley)
MGB – The Illustrated History, Updated Fourth Edition (Wood & Burrell)
The MGC GTS Lightweights (Morys)
Mini Cooper – The Real Thing! (Tipler)
Mini Minor to Asia Minor (West)
Montlhéry, The Story of the Paris Autodrome (Boddy)
Morgan Maverick (Lawrence)

Morgan 3 Wheeler – back to the future!, The (Dron)
Morris Minor, 70 Years on the Road (Newell)
Motor Movies – The Posters! (Veysey)
Motor Racing – Reflections of a Lost Era (Carter)
Motor Racing – The Pursuit of Victory 1930-1962 (Carter)
Motor Racing – The Pursuit of Victory 1963-1972 (Wyatt/Sears)
Motor Racing Heroes – The Stories of 100 Greats (Newman)
Motorhomes, The Illustrated History (Jenkinson)
Motorsport In colour, 1950s (Wainwright)
Preston Tucker & Others (Linde)
RAC Rally Action! (Gardiner)
Racing Colours – Motor Racing Compositions 1908-2009 (Newman)
Roads with a View – England's greatest views and how to find them by road (Corfield)
Rolls-Royce Silver Shadow/Bentley T Series Corniche & Camargue – Revised & Enlarged Edition (Bobbitt)
Rolls-Royce Silver Spirit, Silver Spur & Bentley Mulsanne 2nd Edition (Bobbitt)
Rover P4 (Bobbitt)
Russian Motor Vehicles – Soviet Limousines 1930-2003 (Kelly)
Russian Motor Vehicles – The Czarist Period 1784 to 1917 (Kelly)
Schlumpf – The intrigue behind the most beautiful car collection in the world (Op de Weegh & Op de Weegh)
Singer Story: Cars, Commercial Vehicles, Bicycles & Motorcycle (Atkinson)
Sleeping Beauties USA – abandoned classic cars & trucks (Marek)
Standard Motor Company, The Book of the (Robson)
Steve Hole's Kit Car Cornucopia – Cars, Companies, Stories, Facts & Figures: the UK's kit car scene since 1949 (Hole)
Tales from the Toolbox (Oliver)
Taxi! The Story of the 'London' Taxicab (Bobbitt)
This Day in Automotive History (Corey)
To Boldly Go – twenty six vehicle designs that dared to be different (Hull)
Triumph & Standard Cars 1945 to 1984 (Warrington)
Triumph Cars – The Complete Story (new 3rd edition) (Robson)
Triumph TR6 (Kimberley)
Volvo Estate, The (Hollebone)
You & Your Jaguar XK/XKR – Buying, Enjoying, Maintaining, Modifying – New Edition (Thorley)
Which Oil? – Choosing the right oils & greases for your antique, vintage, veteran, classic or collector car (Michell)
Works MGs, The (Allison & Browning)
Works Minis, The Last (Purves & Brenchley)
Works Rally Mechanic (Moylan)

www.veloce.co.uk

First published in August 2022 by Veloce Publishing Limited, Veloce House, Parkway Farm Business Park, Middle Farm Way, Poundbury, Dorchester DT1 3AR, England. Fax 01305 268864 / e-mail info@veloce.co.uk / web www.veloce.co.uk or www.velocebooks.com. ISBN: 978-1-787114-73-9 UPC: 6-36847-01473-5

ALVIS

A CENTURY OF DRIVERS

SOCIETY

David Culshaw

VELOCE PUBLISHING
THE PUBLISHER OF FINE AUTOMOTIVE BOOKS

CONTENTS

"I had seen much, and I had thought much upon what I had seen; I had something of a habit of investigation, and a disposition to reduce all that I had observed and felt in my own mind, to method and system."
– Discourse by Sir Joshua Reynolds to the Royal Academy, 1790.

A maxim that has guided the author throughout the preparation of this work

FOREWORD

It is a great privilege to write a foreword for this magnificent book, as it represents the coming together of two great masters of their chosen craft.

Alvis has always been a true master of automobile design and manufacture. Similarly, the author is a renowned aficionado on all aspects of automotive history, so to bring the two together in this one tome is a remarkable achievement.

I have known the author almost as long as I have known Alvis cars, and over that time he has never failed to help me with whatever I have needed. He possesses a combination of two exceptional skills; his meticulous approach to research guarantees the facts are reliable with the added bonus that his work is always entertaining and engaging for the reader – a truly rare combination.

The book itself represents a real 'first' by including every car that Alvis made. No previous Alvis book has listed every individual chassis manufactured, where each batch sanctioned is identified by its model. There are short biographies of some of the more notable people who bought and drove the cars, along with a wealth of previously unseen photographs and original works material.

It is particularly fitting that it should be published 100 years after the very first Alvis car emerged from the production line in Coventry. Who could have imagined that from such modest beginnings would evolve one of the most famous and most innovative British car manufacturers.

I am confident this authoritative book will be acclaimed both now and by future generations of enthusiasts as the definitive work on Alvis cars.

The Alvis Car Company is proud to have been associated with such an outstanding publication.

Alan Stote
Chairman – The Alvis Car Company

INTRODUCTION

The historical background to this story, whilst harrowing, is most pertinent.

The Great War of 1914-1918 had just ended, a conflict with unprecedented loss of life, which was summarised by Ernest Hemingway in *A Farewell to Arms* as "the most colossal, murderous, mismanaged butchery."

With over 17 million human beings dead, their skills and talents perishing with them, there was a void in all trades and professions, not least of which were in the realm of engineering and transportation. It had been a conflict, let us not forget, where mechanised warfare was in its infancy. A quarter of a million horses had been pressed into service, and even an elephant had been deployed in a Sheffield steelworks before being returned to the circus in 1918. Flight, too, was comparatively new, with the Atlantic only recently having been conquered. In fact, defence – by air, land and sea – is never far from this story. There were gaps to be filled, rebuilding to be done, trading to be resumed. People who had mercifully survived would apply themselves diligently to the national recovery.

A literary comparison comes to mind. During that same postwar period the Sicilian dramatist Luigi Pirandello was just putting the finishing touches to his experimental play *Six Characters in Search of an Author*, whilst in Britain, a similar number of characters, seeking to further their careers in the new order, would fortuitously come together over a short period of time and thus bring about the furtherance of an engineering operation that would become a synonym for excellence, and thereby generate some remarkable enthusiasm amongst the general public for the varied products which were to follow.

Thus, it is that the first of our characters – prime mover, catalyst and magnet, without whom there would be no story to tell – is the notable figure of Thomas George John. Born in 1880 in Pembroke Dock and highly distinguished academically (as indeed were his two brothers), John acquired a multitude of significant, wide-ranging qualifications, encompassing those of naval architect and civil engineer. The former would take him to the Vickers Shipyard in Barrow-in-Furness until 1914, prior to a move to Siddeley-Deasy, which was then engaged in aircraft engine development and production. The Siddeley-Deasy operation was based in Coventry, hence the appointment would later have considerable geographical significance. Rare amongst engineers, John was also well qualified in accountancy, and his business acumen will become increasingly apparent as this story unfolds.

As the Great War came to an end, John – correctly perceiving that military demands would diminish, at least for a while – took the bold decision to further his career individually, independent of previous employers. This decision was undoubtedly facilitated by the timely availability of the former Holley Brothers carburettor factory in Hertford Street, Coventry. So it was, then, that with the financial backing of friends and family from his native Wales, John took over said factory. The

Thomas George John, 1880-1946.
Founder of the Alvis company.

official date of this transaction, and the emergence of T G John Ltd, is thus recorded as March 13, 1919. Whilst this was the first official company title, contemporary advertisements (whether for employers or to promote services) would often bear the suffix 'Engineers.'

It has been said that at this very early stage, John had no specific plan as to what he wanted to make, and it is clear that, initially, contracts were sought from a variety of places; amongst them, the best known ones were the Hillman Electra stationary engine, the Stafford Pup scooter, the Arden motorcycle engine, and the Buckingham cyclecar.

It is against this general background that the next significant figure appears, this being Geoffrey P H de Freville, born in 1883 in Chartham, Kent. A versatile individual (and erstwhile poultry farmer), he had not only made his mark in the motor trade as an importer of French and American products, but also (and more significantly) in the development of aluminium pistons, which would eventually supersede the cast iron ones then commonplace.

De Freville was something of a polymath, being multi-lingual, inventive, a keen driver, and a former employee of W O Bentley during the days of the DFP car's importation. He was thus familiar with the French Buchet car, a factor which will be shown to be especially relevant. He is also credited in some sources as renewing his association with Alvis in 1938, as interpreter during the Gnome-Rhône aero engine negotiations. As late as 1957, at the age of 74, this remarkable man had translated Hermann Oberth's book *Menschen im Weltraum* (on rocket propulsion) for the British market, published by Weidenfeld and Nicolson. A number of writers, including Hull and Johnson in *The Vintage Alvis*, have drawn attention to the similarities between the Buchet car, and the light car that de Freville was in the process of designing (ie same bore and stroke, wheelbase, gearing and tyre size etc). Be that as it may, de Freville succeeded in interesting T G John in the series production of his concept, which included the trademark 'Alvis,' which had been used for the aforesaid pistons. So it was, then, that production of this vehicle, named the 10/30 Alvis, began in March 1920 (qv 'The 6000 Series').

Our next character, and the one (at least up to now) having enjoyed the lowest profile, is George Hope Tattersall, a forthright Lancastrian born in Oldham in 1883, and one of T G John's most trusted and long-serving employees. He had commenced his career with Vickers (who also made some of the early Alvis chassis); if, as has often been said, Claude Johnson was the hyphen in Rolls-Royce, then Tattersall was the Araldite that brought adhesion to the sometimes difficult circumstances of those early days. Equally respected by management, the workforce and the competition drivers, he was always there as mechanic, navigator, tuner, facilitator and team management, taking every opportunity to advance the new product. It has also been recorded that G H Tattersall was

personally involved with the acquisition of that Buchet car, which he dismantled for examination and subsequently rebuilt – probably an early case of industrial espionage. His service to the marque continued until his retirement in 1947, thereafter remaining in residence in Coventry until he died in his nineties.

Arguably the greatest 'genius' of the Alvis story is Captain George Thomas Smith-Clarke, born in Bewdley, Worcestershire in 1884. He had worked, after leaving school at the age of 13, in a chemist's shop and as a bus conductor. He joined the Great

A significant example of early works advertising, showing the triangle in its original position.

Western Railway Company in 1902, progressing to the post of chief draughtsman. Outbreak of war saw him appointed as a captain in the Royal Flying Corps, and, when it ended, a post of assistant works manager at Daimler beckoned. It was in 1922 that he joined the T G John team as chief engineer, giving him virtually a free hand to implement some of his advanced engineering thinking. His first success was the development of the 12/50 model, but it is for his pioneering design work for the front-wheel drive that he is best remembered today, though his work on the classic Alvis products of the '30s, together with the increasingly important aeronautical and military lines, was much more of a commercial success.

In, what appears to be, the little spare time that he had, Smith-Clarke was an amateur astronomer and radio communications expert. He was also a great humanitarian and his contribution to medical science and hospital administration became legendary. Notable in this particular area was his redesigning of the 'iron lung,' and his long time chairmanship of the Coventry and Warwickshire hospitals. Upon retirement from Alvis Ltd in 1949, he was presented with the third prototype 3-Litre Alvis, and thereafter he took on a consultative post with Standard-Triumph, being allocated a number of its products, including two Triumph Mayflowers (KRW 147 and LHP 129), and the second prototype Standard Pennant, WWK 207. He died in March 1960, an active thinker and motivator until the very end.

A short, though especially significant, contribution of the early T G John days would be that of Leopold Adams, who was appointed as the first sales manager in 1920. He had served in the Dorset Yeomanry, transferring, upon the outbreak of war, to the Royal Flying Corps, where he was injured. By 1922, he had built up an impressive network of agencies, and duly established widespread advertising by bringing in the Heritage Peters Company. His pastimes included horse-riding (like John), and the comparatively new amateur cinematography. He was a notable and persuasive orator and had served as a Coventry Rotary Club president. He sadly died when only 47, in August 1933, after returning from a holiday in Egypt, where he had contracted a form of toxaemia, possibly connected with his WWI injury. His legacy was the company's enviable marketing system, and the memorial fund set up after his death raised substantial funds for his favourite charity, the Coventry and District Crippled Children's Guild.

Last, but far from least in this listing of some of the original personalities is William M Dunn, born in 1894 in Annan, Dumfries. He had served an initial engineering apprenticeship with Milburn's, Workington between 1908 and 1914, before wartime saw him serving as a marine engineer, and thereafter joining Daimler as a draughtsman – where Smith-Clarke had also served. Dunn was taken on by T G John in 1922, under Smith-Clarke, with whom most of the classic Alvis designs of the '20s and '30s came to fruition. Dunn concentrated

on the military side of the business after 1936, but, in the lead up to Smith-Clarke's retirement in 1949, he designed the all-new successor to the 'Fourteen,' namely the 3-litre model that entered production in 1950 (qv 23803-on). Upon Dunn's own retirement in 1962, he was succeeded by an equally distinguished engineer – his own son Mike Dunn, who would continue to hone the 3-Litre concept through various metamorphoses until the end of car production with the TF 21 in 1967.

At this point, another literary comparison comes to mind. All the above were 'eminent Victorians,' not perhaps in the same genre as those in Lytton Strachey's 1918 biography of that name, but were certainly role-models with regards to engineering excellence and innovation. Apart from the aeronautical and military production (outside the scope of this volume), these pioneers have handed down to us an authentic record of some 21,250 motor cars that gave pleasure to the original buyers, the experience of which was redoubled whenever they changed hands. This, then, is *their* story – the buyers and users of these charismatic devices, ranging from a king to a serial killer – with a few epic travelogues thrown in for good measure.

That this story can be told at all is largely due to the generally good condition and completeness of the extant factory records, which include guarantee cards (often giving the names of owners), and 'build sheets,' which confirm the specification of each individual chassis. The exception is pre-June 1925, for when no guarantee cards have survived, and deciphering the sales ledgers, affected by rust, dust, damp and even mice, had the author particularly empathising with the late Professor J M Allegro's notable work on the Dead Sea Scrolls. Seldom, though, do factory records quote original registration numbers, but this has been rectified by collective research into extant County Record Office files, to which Dr Bernard Nield has made a major contribution. Thanks are also due to John Fox for translating elements of my Master Register into the clearly readable tables, plus the input from Wayne Brooks (USA), John Burnell and Dr Tony Cox. All dyed-in-the wool Alvis enthusiasts with whom I have been exchanging data for many decades.

Captain George Thomas Smith-Clarke, inventor, astronomer, radio ham, and chief engineer of the company. Seen here with an example of his most significant contribution to automobile engineering: the front wheel drive concept. This, the racing version of 1927.

PART 1

▼

1919-1932

THE '6000' SERIES

March 1920 to September 1921
6001-6342
342 cars
All 10/30 models, sometimes referred to
as '10.5 hp'

Consisting of coachbuilders:

Morgan Zephyr	91
Charlesworth	51
Cross & Ellis	43
Midland	10
Louth	2
Carbodies	1
Coombe	1
Riley	1
Other (chassis-only deliveries), mostly undeclared or indecipherable	142
Total	342

Chassis	Reg	Chassis	Reg	Chassis	Reg	Chassis	Reg	Chassis	Reg	Chassis	Reg
6001	HP 1665	6039	- - - - - -	6078	- - - - - -	6115	- - - - - -	6185	- - - - - -	6255	- - - - - -
6002	HP 3075	6040	- - - - - -	6079	- - - - - -	6116	- - - - - -	6186	- - - - - -	6256	MA 7668
6003	HP 2436	6041	HP 2075	6080	HP 2442	6117	TB 6943	6187	- - - - - -	6257	HP 3071
6004	- - - - - -	6042	- - - - - -	6081	CP 2145	6118	- - - - - -	6188	HP 2433	6258	- - - - - -
6005	- - - - - -	6043	HP 2654	6082	- - - - - -	6119	HP 2317	6189	GA 8564	6259	- - - - - -
6006	- - - - - -	6044	- - - - - -	6083	- - - - - -	6120	HP 2313	6190	HP 2444	6260	- - - - - -
6007	HP 2440	6045	- - - - - -	6084	- - - - - -	6121	- - - - - -	6191	GA 8620	6261	GA 9442
6008	- - - - - -	6046	- - - - - -	6085	- - - - - -	6122	- - - - - -	6192	- - - - - -	6262	- - - - - -
6009	- - - - - -	6048	DD 1071	6086	- - - - - -	6123	- - - - - -	6193	- - - - - -	6263	- - - - - -
6010	- - - - - -	6049	- - - - - -	6087	- - - - - -	6124	- - - - - -	6194	- - - - - -	6264	- - - - - -
6011	EA 1021	6050	HP 2434	6088	- - - - - -	6125	CR 5865	6195	HP 2437	6265	- - - - - -
6013	- - - - - -	6051	GA 8257	6089	- - - - - -	6126	- - - - - -	6196	- - - - - -	6266	HP 2446
6015	DU 609	6052	- - - - - -	6090	- - - - - -	6127	- - - - - -	6197	- - - - - -	6267	HP 3072
6016	- - - - - -	6053	- - - - - -	6091	- - - - - -	6128	HP 2311	6198	- - - - - -	6268	- - - - - -
6017	- - - - - -	6054	- - - - - -	6092	- - - - - -	6129	- - - - - -	6199	- - - - - -	6269	- - - - - -
6018	HP 1910	6055	- - - - - -	6093	- - - - - -	6130	- - - - - -	6200	- - - - - -	6270	- - - - - -
6019	- - - - - -	6056	- - - - - -	6094	HP 2319	6131	- - - - - -	6201	- - - - - -	6271	- - - - - -
6020	TB 3006	6057	- - - - - -	6095	- - - - - -	6132	- - - - - -	6202	- - - - - -	6272	- - - - - -
6021	- - - - - -	6058	- - - - - -	6096	HP 2314	6133	- - - - - -	6203	- - - - - -	6273	- - - - - -
6022	DD 142	6059	- - - - - -	6097	- - - - - -	6134	- - - - - -	6204	- - - - - -	6274	- - - - - -
6023	- - - - - -	6060	- - - - - -	6098	- - - - - -	6135	- - - - - -	6205	- - - - - -	6275	- - - - - -
6024	- - - - - -	6061	- - - - - -	6099	- - - - - -	6136	- - - - - -	6206	- - - - - -	6276	TB 8780
6025	- - - - - -	6062	- - - - - -	6100	- - - - - -	6137	- - - - - -	6207	- - - - - -	6277	- - - - - -
6026	- - - - - -	6063	- - - - - -	6101	SA 5316	6138	- - - - - -	6208	- - - - - -	6278	GA 8868
6027	- - - - - -	6064	HP 2318	6102	- - - - - -	6139	- - - - - -	6209	- - - - - -	6279	- - - - - -
6028	- - - - - -	6065	- - - - - -	6103	- - - - - -	6140	- - - - - -	6210	- - - - - -	6280	- - - - - -
6029	- - - - - -	6066	- - - - - -	6104	- - - - - -	6141	- - - - - -	6211	HP 2438	6281	HP 2443
6030	- - - - - -	6068	- - - - - -	6105	- - - - - -	6142	- - - - - -	6212	- - - - - -	6282	HP 3070
6031	- - - - - -	6069	- - - - - -	6106	HP 2447	6143	- - - - - -	6213	- - - - - -	6283	- - - - - -
6032	- - - - - -	6070	- - - - - -	6107	- - - - - -	6144	- - - - - -	6214	- - - - - -	6284	HP 2449
6033	- - - - - -	6071	BO 2481	6108	- - - - - -	6145	- - - - - -	6215	- - - - - -	6285	- - - - - -
6034	DU 4820	6072	- - - - - -	6109	- - - - - -	6146	- - - - - -	6216	- - - - - -	6286	- - - - - -
6035	- - - - - -	6073	XE 8436	6110	- - - - - -	6147	- - - - - -	6217	- - - - - -	6287	- - - - - -
6036	- - - - - -	6074	HP 2243	6111	- - - - - -	6148	- - - - - -	6218	- - - - - -	6288	- - - - - -
6037	- - - - - -	6075	HP 2320	6112	- - - - - -	6149	HP 2439	6219	- - - - - -	6289	- - - - - -
6038	- - - - - -	6076	MA 7050	6113	- - - - - -	6150	- - - - - -	6220	- - - - - -	6290	- - - - - -
		6077	CR 5794	6114	HP 2312	6151	HJ 16	6221	- - - - - -	6291	EN 1859
						6152	- - - - - -	6222	- - - - - -	6292	- - - - - -
						6153	- - - - - -	6223	- - - - - -	6293	- - - - - -
						6154	- - - - - -	6224	HP 2450	6294	- - - - - -
						6155	- - - - - -	6225	TC 1969	6295	- - - - - -
						6156	- - - - - -	6226	DK 1617	6296	- - - - - -
						6157	- - - - - -	6227	- - - - - -	6297	- - - - - -
						6158	- - - - - -	6228	- - - - - -	6298	- - - - - -
						6159	- - - - - -	6229	- - - - - -	6299	- - - - - -
						6160	- - - - - -	6230	- - - - - -	6300	- - - - - -
						6161	- - - - - -	6231	- - - - - -	6301	- - - - - -
						6162	- - - - - -	6232	HP 2441	6302	- - - - - -
						6163	- - - - - -	6233	- - - - - -	6303	- - - - - -
						6164	GA 8448	6234	- - - - - -	6304	- - - - - -
						6165	TB 5164	6235	GA 9125	6305	- - - - - -
						6166	- - - - - -	6236	HP 2445	6306	- - - - - -
						6167	- - - - - -	6237	GA 9408	6307	- - - - - -
						6168	GA 8620	6238	- - - - - -	6308	- - - - - -
						6169	- - - - - -	6239	GA 9005	6309	- - - - - -
						6170	HP 2431	6240	- - - - - -	6310	- - - - - -
						6171	- - - - - -	6241	- - - - - -	6311	- - - - - -
						6172	- - - - - -	6242	- - - - - -	6312	- - - - - -
						6173	NL 2068	6243	- - - - - -	6313	- - - - - -
						6174	- - - - - -	6244	TB 9750	6314	- - - - - -
						6175	- - - - - -	6245	GA 9367	6315	- - - - - -
						6176	- - - - - -	6246	- - - - - -	6316	- - - - - -
						6177	HP 2315	6247	HP 1821	6317	- - - - - -
						6178	- - - - - -	6248	- - - - - -	6318	- - - - - -
						6179	GA 8240	6249	- - - - - -	6319	- - - - - -
						6180	- - - - - -	6250	- - - - - -	6320	- - - - - -
						6181	EE 3220	6251	- - - - - -	6321	- - - - - -
						6182	HP 2435	6252	- - - - - -	6322	- - - - - -
						6183	GA 8662	6253	- - - - - -	6323	- - - - - -
						6184	- - - - - -	6254	- - - - - -	6324	- - - - - -

6325	- - - - - -	6332	- - - - - -	6338	- - - - - -
6326	- - - - - -	6333	- - - - - -	6339	- - - - - -
6327	- - - - - -	6334	- - - - - -	6340	- - - - - -
6328	- - - - - -	6335	- - - - - -	6341	- - HP 3410
6330	- - - - - -	6336	- - - - - -	6342	- - - - - -
6331	- - - - - -	6337	- - - - - -		

Often asked is why this chassis sequence, apparently randomly commencing at 6001, was allocated to the very first Alvis production run. One has to remember that in these pioneering days T G John Ltd was primarily a general engineering company, seeking contracts from whatever source; examples of this included the Hillman Electra stationary engine, the Kenilworth and Stafford motor scooters, and the Buckingham cyclecar. Research has established that the chassis numbers allocated to the latter included batches commencing at 2001 and 7001, thus the 'in between' allocation of 6001 for the new product is entirely logical.

The new and rather more ambitious project came about from the purchase of Geoffrey de Freville's design for a light car, combined with the purchase, for evaluation, of an example of the French Buchet car, which was dismantled and elements of it copied and incorporated into the finalised 10/30.

Initially, it was intended to lay down a pilot run of 500 cars, with related engine numbers also numbered 6001 and on. For some reason, as yet unknown to us, the first run terminated at 6342 in September 1921, and a new sequence initiated with a starting point of 1000 and on. The engines, however, had all been numbered by this point, so engines numbered 6343 to 6500 turn up in the first 150 or so cars of the successor 1000 Series. All, that is, except engine 6461, which was spirited away by Captain D M K Marendaz and utilised in a Marseel car registered HP 3337 on December 12, 1921.

The company lost no time in promoting the 10/30 in competition events, in which both de Freville and T G John himself personally took part. Much favourable publicity was thereby generated, with the result that this new marque was very soon to be talked about and sought after.

HP 1665

6001

Works development car
The first Alvis car, finally released March 31, 1920.

EA 1021

6011

Competition car
One of the first competition appearances of the

THE ACCELERATION TEST. The scene at Sunrising, on the Edge Hill range, and on the Stratford-on-Avon to Banbury main road. No. 6, H. J. Evans (10-20 h.p. Alvis), after rounding the abrupt bend in last Saturday's Midland Light Car Club Trial.

6011: This car, identified as EA 1021, was immortalised in a remarkable drawing by F Gordon Crosby during the Midland Light Car trial of 1921, and published in *Autocar* of May 7, 1921.

new Alvis car was in the hands of one H J Evans. There are several photographs of it in the motoring journals of the time, but more importantly it was immortalised in a painting by the famous artist F Gordon Crosby (1895-1943) who would, much later on, design the leaping Jaguar mascot.

DU 609

6015

Works development car
Much photographed works hack. Most probably the subject of Geoffrey de Freville's letter in the

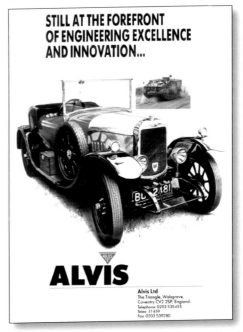

STILL AT THE FOREFRONT OF ENGINEERING EXCELLENCE AND INNOVATION...

ALVIS

Alvis Ltd
The Triangle, Walsgrave,
Coventry CV2 2SP. England.
Telephone: 0203 535455
Telex: 31459
Fax: 0203 539280

6071: The company has frequently used its first production in advertising features, as here in the course of an earlier anniversary.

Automotor Journal of May 20, 1920, about his drive from London to Coventry on May 11. The Coventry registration authority would quite often, at this time, re-issue marks that had previously lapsed. DU 609 is one such, having first been deployed in 1904.

6120

Competition car

A successful early competition car used by one J R Oliver on the Land's End Trial. Oliver also used this car on the London-Edinburgh Trial, gaining a silver medal, as a photograph in *Autocar* of May 28, 1921, page 971, confirms.

6151

Competition car

Campaigned by one Maitland Keddie, he of an enthusiastic Southend motoring family. Well recorded in hillclimb events of the day.

– –

Lt F Bridgland

Bridgland, an army officer residing in Rustington, West Sussex, had lost a leg and part of another when serving in WWI. Even this, like Douglas Bader many years later, did not stop his determination to drive. Ingeniously, he developed a modification to this Alvis, combining the clutch and brake pedal in such a way that the first half of travel operated the clutch and the remainder, the brake.

– –

David Scott-Moncrieff

Scott-Moncrieff (1907-1987), also known as 'Bunty,' was educated at Eton and Cambridge, and will always be known as the 'Purveyor of Horseless Carriages to the Nobility and Gentry.' He was also a respected writer with books like *Vintage and Edwardian Motor Cars* (Batsford, 1955) and *The Three-Pointed Star* (Cassell, 1955). Also recommended reading is his *Cars I Have Owned* in *Motor Sports*' regular series – issue of August 1950, pages 381 to 383.

6247

Sir Arthur Whitten-Brown

Having but recently accomplished the first

6151: Maitland Keddie in his 10/30 in a competition in July 1921. (Courtesy John Warburton)

transatlantic flight with John Alcock, one would like to think that Whitten-Brown made a bee-line to Alvis because of the engineering quality. The explanation, however, is rather more mundane, as his employer (Vickers Ltd) was also contracted to build Alvis chassis at the time.

NEW 1000 SERIES

September 1921 to August 1923
1000-2087
1087 cars
All side-valve cars of the 10/30, 11/40, 12/40 type often undeclared or indecipherable

Consisting of coachbuilders:

Cross & Ellis	478
Carbodies	414
Midland	19
Cubitt	10
Robinson	16
Wilton	16
Charlesworth	4
Connaught	1
Coombe	1
Grose	1
Other (chassis-only deliveries)	
Mostly undeclared or indecipherable	127
Total	1087

Chassis	Reg				
1000	- - - - - -	1003	- - HP 3076	1007	- - - - - -
1001	- - - - - -	1004	- - - - - -	1008	- - - - - -
1002	- - - - - -	1005	- - - - - -	1009	- - - - - -
		1006	- - - - - -	1010	- - - - - -

No.	Code	No.	Code	No.	Code	No.	Code	No.	Code	No.	Code
1011	- - - - - - -	1081	- - - GB 51	1151	- - - GB 229	1221	- - - - - -	1291	- - - - - -	1361	- - GB 1598
1012	- - - - - - -	1082	- - - - - -	1152	- - - - - -	1222	- - - - - -	1292	- - AT 6600	1362	- - - - - -
1013	- - - - - - -	1083	- - - - - -	1153	- - - - - -	1223	- - TB 9576	1293	- - - - - -	1363	- - - - - -
1014	- - - - - - -	1084	- - - - - -	1154	- - - - - -	1224	- - - - - -	1294	- - - - - -	1364	- - - - - -
1015	- - HP 3680	1085	- - - - - -	1155	- - - - - -	1225	- - TB 9941	1295	- - - GB 849	1365	- - HP 3690
1016	- - - - - -	1086	- - - - - -	1156	- - - - - -	1226	- - - - - -	1296	- - - - - -	1366	- - - - - -
1017	- - - - - -	1087	- - - - - -	1157	- - - - - -	1227	- - - - - -	1297	- - - - - -	1367	- - - - - -
1018	- - - - - -	1088	- - - - - -	1158	- - - - - -	1228	- - - - - -	1298	- - - - - -	1368	- - - SA 5637
1019	- - - - - -	1089	- - - - - -	1159	- - - - - -	1229	- - - - - -	1299	- - - - - -	1369	- - - - - -
1020	- - - GB 68	1090	- - CR 6498	1160	- - - MB 78	1230	- - - - - -	1300	- - SG 5453	1370	- - - - - -
1021	- - - - - -	1091	- - AT 7269	1161	- - - - - -	1231	- - - - - -	1301	- - - - - -	1371	- - - - - -
1022	- - - - - -	1092	- - - - - -	1162	- - - - - -	1232	- - MA 9748	1302	- - - - - -	1372	- - FU 1076
1023	- - - - - -	1093	- - - - - -	1163	- - - GB 150	1233	- - - - - -	1303	- - - - - -	1373	- - HP 4159
1024	- - - - - -	1094	- - - - - -	1164	- - - - - -	1234	- - - - - -	1304	- - - - - -	1374	- - - - - -
1025	- - - - - -	1095	- - HP 3557	1165	- - - - - -	1235	- - SR 3008	1305	- - - - - -	1375	- - - - - -
1026	- - - - - -	1096	- - - - - -	1166	- - - - - -	1236	- - - - - -	1306	- - - - - -	1376	- - - - - -
1027	- - - - - -	1097	- - - - - -	1167	- - - - - -	1237	- - - - - -	1307	- - HP 3682	1377	- - - - - -
1028	- - - - - -	1098	- - HP 3080	1168	- - - - - -	1238	- - - - - -	1308	- - NP 997	1378	- - - - - -
1029	- - - - - -	1099	- - HP 3079	1169	- - PC 6395	1239	- - - - - -	1309	- - HP 3681	1379	- - - - - -
1030	- - - - - -	1100	- - NM 1504	1170	- - - - - -	1240	- - - - - -	1310	- - - - - -	1380	- - NM 2345
1031	- - - - - -	1101	- - - - - -	1171	- - - - - -	1241	- - GB 1173	1311	- - - - - -	1381	- - GB 2735
1032	- - - - - -	1102	- - PC 6624	1172	- - - - - -	1242	- - - - - -	1312	- - HP 3676	1382	- - - MB 72
1033	- - - - - -	1103	- - - - - -	1173	- - - - - -	1243	- - - - - -	1313	- - AT 6791	1383	- - HP 4164
1034	- - - GB 105	1104	- - SG 5353	1174	- - HP 3678	1244	- - - - - -	1314	- - - - - -	1384	- - KS 1910
1035	- - HH 1257	1105	- - - - - -	1175	- - BK 6510	1245	- - - - - -	1315	- - - - - -	1385	- - SG 6565
1036	- - FD 1877	1106	- - - - - -	1176	- - - - - -	1246	- - - - - -	1316	- - - - - -	1386	- - - - - -
1037	- - - - - -	1107	- - HP 3675	1177	- - - - - -	1247	- - - - - -	1317	- - - - - -	1387	- - HP 4162
1038	- - - - - -	1108	- - - - - -	1178	- - - - - -	1248	- - NM 2649	1318	- - - FA 1361	1388	- - AT 7059
1039	- - HP 3077	1109	- - - - - -	1179	- - - - - -	1249	- - - - - -	1319	- - - - - -	1389	- - HP 4155
1040	- - - - - -	1110	- - HP 3683	1180	- - - - - -	1250	- - - - - -	1320	- - - - - -	1390	- - - - - -
1041	- - - - - -	1111	- - - GB 480	1181	- - - - - -	1251	- - - - - -	1321	- - - - - -	1391	- - - - - -
1042	- - - - - -	1112	- - - - - -	1182	- - - - - -	1252	- - - - - -	1322	- - - - - -	1392	- - - - - -
1043	- - - - - -	1113	- - - - - -	1183	- - - - - -	1253	- - - - - -	1323	- - HP 4158	1393	- - - - - -
1044	- - TB 7854	1114	- - - - - -	1184	- - AT 6599	1254	- - - - - -	1324	- - - - - -	1394	- - - - - -
1045	- - - GB 794	1115	- - TB 9208	1185	- - - - - -	1255	- - GB 1831	1325	- - - - - -	1395	- - - - - -
1046	- - - - - -	1116	- - - - - -	1186	- - - - - -	1256	- - - - - -	1326	- - - - - -	1396	- - - - - -
1047	- - HP 3074	1117	- - BD 6216	1187	- - SG 5497	1257	- - - - - -	1327	- - - - - -	1397	- - - - - -
1048	- - - - - -	1118	- - - - - -	1188	- - HP 3549	1258	- - - - - -	1328	- - - - - -	1398	- - - - - -
1049	- - - - - -	1119	- - HP 3078	1189	- - - NN 635	1259	- - - - - -	1329	- - - - - -	1399	- - - - - -
1050	- - - - - -	1120	- - - - - -	1190	- - - - - -	1260	- - - - - -	1330	- - HP 4151	1400	- - - - - -
1051	- - - - - -	1121	- - - - - -	1191	- - SG 5082	1261	- - - - - -	1331	- - - - - -	1401	- - - - - -
1052	- - NM 1447	1122	- - HP 3683	1192	- - - - - -	1262	- - AT 6815	1332	- - - - - -	1402	- - - - - -
1053	- - - - - -	1123	- - SG 5529	1193	- - - - - -	1263	- - - - - -	1333	- - - - - -	1403	- - - - - -
1054	- - - - - -	1124	- - HP 3552	1194	- - - - - -	1264	- - - - - -	1334	- - - - - -	1404	- - - - - -
1055	- - - - - -	1125	- - - - - -	1195	- - HH 1352	1265	- - - - - -	1335	- - - - - -	1405	- - - - - -
1056	- - - - - -	1126	- - - - - -	1196	- - - - - -	1266	- - AT 6914	1336	- - - - - -	1406	- - - - - -
1057	- - - - - -	1127	- - - - - -	1197	- - - - - -	1267	- - - - - -	1337	- - - - - -	1407	- - - - - -
1058	- - - - - -	1128	- - - - - -	1198	- - - - - -	1268	- - - - - -	1338	- - - - - -	1408	- - - - - -
1059	- - - - - -	1129	- - - - - -	1199	- - MA 9461	1269	- - - - - -	1339	- - - - - -	1409	- - - - - NZ
1060	- - - NP 569	1130	- - - - - -	1200	- - - - - -	1270	- - HP 3679	1340	- - - - - -	1410	- - HP 4160
1061	- - - - - -	1131	- - - - - -	1201	- - TB 9002	1271	- - - - - -	1341	- - HP 4157	1411	- - - - - -
1062	- - - - - -	1132	- - - - - -	1202	- - NM 1862	1272	- - GB 1341	1342	- - - - - -	1412	- - - - - -
1063	- - - - - -	1133	- - - - - -	1203	- - - - - -	1273	- - HP 4154	1343	- - HP 4149	1413	- - - - - -
1064	- - - - - -	1134	- - - - - -	1204	- - - - - -	1274	- - - - - -	1344	- - - - - -	1414	- - - - - -
1065	- - - - - -	1135	- - - - - -	1205	- - HP 3550	1275	- - - - - -	1345	- - HP 4156	1415	- - - CX 5225
1066	- - - - - -	1136	- - - - - -	1206	- - - - - -	1276	- - HP 4153	1346	- - HP 4156	1416	- - - TC 788
1067	- - - - - -	1137	- - CP 2335	1207	- - - - - -	1277	- - - - - -	1347	- - - - - -	1417	- - - - FU 36
1068	- - HH 1339	1138	- - - - - -	1208	- - - GB 744	1278	- - - - - -	1348	- - - - - -	1418	- - HP 4169
1069	- - - - - -	1139	- - - - - -	1209	- - - - - -	1279	- - - - - -	1349	- - - - - -	1419	- - DU 4463
1070	- - - - - -	1140	- - - - - -	1210	- - - GB 513	1280	- - - - - -	1350	- - - - - -	1420	- - - - - -
1071	- - CR 6444	1141	- - - - - -	1211	- - - - - -	1281	- - - - - -	1351	- - - - - -	1421	- - - - - -
1072	- - - - - -	1142	- - - - - -	1212	- - - - - -	1282	- - - - - -	1352	- - HP 4150	1422	- - HP 4581
1073	- - - - - -	1143	- - - - - -	1213	- - - NP 869	1283	- - SG 5647	1353	- - - - - -	1423	- - - - - -
1074	- - - - - -	1144	- - - - - -	1214	- - - GB 632	1284	- - - - - -	1354	- - - - - -	1424	- - - - - -
1075	- - - - - -	1145	- - - - - -	1215	- - - - - -	1285	- - - - - -	1355	- - HP 4161	1425	- - - - - -
1076	- - - - - -	1146	- - EE 3632	1216	- - - - - -	1286	- - - - - -	1356	- - - - - -	1426	- - - - - -
1077	- - - - - -	1147	- - - GB 507	1217	- - HP 3677	1287	- - - - - -	1357	- - NO 7223	1427	- - - - - -
1078	- - - - - -	1148	- - - - - -	1218	- - CR 6575	1288	- - HP 3689	1358	- - - - - -	1428	- - - - - -
1079	- - - - - -	1149	- - - - - -	1219	- - HH 1383	1289	- - CX 5142	1359	- - - MB 38	1429	- - HP 4602
1080	- - - - - -	1150	- - HP 3073	1220	- - - GB 803	1290	- - DB 3364	1360	- - - - - -	1430	- - - - - -

1431 - - -MB 353	1501 - - - - - -	1571 - - - - - -	1641 - - - - - -	1711 - - HP 4841	1781 - - - - - -
1432 - - - - - -	1502 - - - - - -	1572 - - - - - -	1642 - - - - - -	1712 - - - - - -	1782 - - - - - -
1433 - - - - - -	1503 - - - - - -	1573 - - - - - -	1643 - - - - - -	1713 - - NP 2226	1783 - - - - - -
1434 - - - - - -	1504 - - - - - -	1574 - - - - - -	1644 - - MB 1098	1714 - - - - - -	1784 - - - - - -
1435 - - - - - -	1505 - - HP 4582	1575 - - - - - -	1645 - - - - - -	1715 - - - - - -	1785 - - - - - -
1436 - - - - - -	1506 - - - - - -	1576 - - - - - -	1646 - - - - - -	1716 - - HH 1712	1786 - - - - - -
1437 - - - - - -	1507 - - - - - -	1577 - - - - - -	1647 - - - - - -	1717 - - - - - -	1787 - - - - - -
1438 - - HP 4163	1508 - - HT 6185	1578 - - - - - -	1648 - - HP 4831	1718 - - GB 2801	1788 - - - - - -
1439 - - - - - -	1509 - - - - - -	1579 - - HP 4828	1649 - - GB 2435	1719 - - - - - -	1789 - - - - - -
1440 - - - - - -	1510 - - - - - -	1580 - - GB 2611	1650 - - MB 1366	1720 - - HP 4836	1790 - - HP 6150
1441 - - - GB 850	1511 - - - GB 850	1581 - - DN 4672	1651 - - AT 7761	1721 - - HP 4838	1791 - - - - - -
1442 - - - - - -	1512 - - MB 1265	1582 - - - - - -	1652 - - NO 7821	1722 - - - - - -	1792 - - - - - -
1443 - - - - - -	1513 - - BC 6419	1583 - - - - - -	1653 - - - - - -	1723 - - - - - -	1793 - - HH 1796
1444 - - HP 4591	1514 - - - - - -	1584 - - - - - -	1654 - - DD 2002	1724 - - GB 2984	1794 - - - - - -
1445 - - - - - -	1515 - - DN 4512	1585 - - HH 1632	1655 - - - - - -	1725 - - - - - -	1795 - - - - - -
1446 - - - - - -	1516 - - - - - -	1586 - - - - - -	1656 - - - - - -	1726 - - - - - -	1796 - - XN 6563
1447 - - - - - -	1517 - HP 4823	1587 - FU 1175	1657 - - - - - -	1727 - - HP 4842	1797 - - - - - -
1448 - - - - - -	1518 - NP 2262	1588 - - - - - -	1658 - - CX 5495	1728 - - - - - -	1798 - - - - - -
1449 - - NO 7976	1519 - - - - - -	1589 - - - - - -	1659 - - - - - -	1729 - - NP 2493	1799 - - - - - -
1450 - - - - - -	1520 - - - - - -	1590 - -MB 826	1660 - SG 6833	1730 - - - - - -	1800 - - HP 5414
1451 - - HP 4168	1521 - - - - - -	1591 - BD 7133	1661 - - - - - -	1731 - - - - - -	1801 - - - - - -
1452 - - HP 4166	1522 - - - - - -	1592 - - - - - -	1662 - CR 7478	1732 - - TC 3411	1802 - - WA 7863
1453 - - - - - -	1523 - - HP 4588	1593 - CP 2853	1663 - - - AUS	1733 - - - - - -	1803 - - - - - -
1454 - - HP 4167	1524 - - - - - -	1594 - TC 3928	1664 - - - AUS	1734 - - - - - -	1804 - - NP 2631
1455 - - - - - -	1525 - - HP 4593	1595 - - - - - -	1665 - - - AUS	1735 - - - - - -	1805 - - - - - -
1456 - - - - - -	1526 - - - - - -	1596 - - - - - -	1666 - - - AUS	1736 - - CP 2809	1806 - - - - - -
1457 - - HP 3691	1527 - - - - - -	1597 - - HP 4823	1667 - - - AUS	1737 - - HP 4844	1807 - - - - - -
1458 - - HP 4165	1528 - - HP 4586	1598 - - - - - -	1668 - - - AUS	1738 - - - - - -	1808 - - - - - -
1459 - - - - - -	1529 - - - - - -	1599 - - - - - -	1669 - - - AUS	1739 - - - - - -	1809 - - - - - -
1460 - - HP 4584	1530 - - - - - -	1600 - - HP 4596	1670 - - - AUS	1740 - - - - - -	1810 - - - - - -
1461 - - - - - -	1531 - - - - - -	1601 - - HP 4171	1671 - - - AUS	1741 - - - - - -	1811 - - - - - -
1462 - - - - - -	1532 - - - - - -	1602 - - - - - -	1672 - - - AUS	1742 - - - - - -	1812 - - - - - -
1463 - - HP 4170	1533 - - - - - -	1603 - - - - - -	1673 - - - AUS	1743 - - HP 4833	1813 - - HP 5417
1464 - - - - - -	1534 - - - - - -	1604 - - - - - -	1674 - - - AUS	1744 - - - - - -	1814 - - - - - -
1465 - - - - - -	1535 - - - - - -	1605 - - - - - -	1675 - - - - - -	1745 - - TC 3640	1815 - - - - - -
1466 - - - - - -	1536 - - - - - -	1606 - - HP 4595	1676 - - HP 4837	1746 - - - - - -	1816 - - - - - -
1467 - - - - - -	1537 - - HP 4824	1607 - - HP 4594	1677 - - HP 4829	1747 - - GB 3690	1817 - - - - - -
1468 - - - - - -	1538 - - HP 7246	1608 - FE 5576	1678 - - - - - -	1748 - - - - - -	1818 - - - - - -
1469 - - - - - -	1539 - - HP 4590	1609 - - HP 4603	1679 - CA 5840	1749 - - - - - -	1819 - - - - - -
1470 - - HP 4587	1540 - NP 1746	1610 - - - - - -	1680 - HP 4830	1750 - - - - - -	1820 - - - - - -
1471 - - - - - -	1541 - AT 6728	1611 - - - - - -	1681 - - - - - -	1751 - - - - - -	1821 - - HH 1839
1472 - - HP 4582	1542 - - - - - -	1612 - - - - - -	1682 - - - - - -	1752 - - - - - -	1822 - - XN 7168
1473 - - HP 4172	1543 - - -MB 803	1613 - - - - - -	1683 - - - - - -	1753 - - - - - -	1823 - - - - - -
1474 - - - - - -	1544 - - - - - -	1614 - - - - - -	1684 - - - - - -	1754 - - - - - -	1824 - - YA 5620
1475 - - MB 1336	1545 - - - - - -	1615 - - - - - -	1685 - - - - - -	1755 - - HP 4839	1825 - - - - - -
1476 - - - - - -	1546 - - HP 4589	1616 - - - - - -	1686 - - - - - -	1756 - - - - - -	1826 - - - VS 842
1477 - - - - - -	1547 - - - - - -	1617 - - - - - -	1687 - - - - - -	1757 - - - - - -	1827 - NT 2589
1478 - - - - - -	1548 - - - - - -	1618 - - - - - -	1688 - - - - - -	1758 - - - - - -	1828 - - AT 7810
1479 - - - - - -	1549 - HP 4592	1619 - - - - - -	1689 - - - - - -	1759 - - - - - -	1829 - - - - - -
1480 - - NP 2003	1550 - - - - - -	1620 - - - - - -	1690 - - HP 4834	1760 - - - - - -	1830 - - - - - -
1481 - - - - - -	1551 - - - - - -	1621 - - HP 4821	1691 - - - - - -	1761 - - - - - -	1831 - - - AUS
1482 - SR 3192	1552 - AT 7213	1622 - - - - - -	1692 - - HP 4835	1762 - - - - - -	1832 - - - - - -
1483 - - - - - -	1553 - EE 4087	1623 - - - - - -	1693 - - - - - -	1763 - - - - - -	1833 - - - AUS
1484 - - - - - -	1554 - - - - - -	1624 - - - - - -	1694 - - - - - -	1764 - - HP 5409	1834 - - - AUS
1485 - - - - - -	1555 - CP 2688	1625 - - HP 4826	1695 - GB 2575	1765 - - - - - -	1835 - - - - - -
1486 - - - - - -	1556 - - - - - -	1626 - - - - - -	1696 - - - - - -	1766 - - - - - -	1836 - - - - - -
1487 - - BD 6963	1557 - - - - - -	1627 - - - - - -	1697 - GB 2662	1767 - - HP 5413	1837 - - - AUS
1488 - - TC 1251	1558 - - - - - -	1628 - - - - - -	1698 - - - - - -	1768 - - - - - -	1838 - - - - - -
1489 - - - - - -	1559 - - - - - -	1629 - - - - - -	1699 - - - - - -	1769 - - MB 2061	1839 - - - - - -
1490 - - BT 5594	1560 - HP 4604	1630 - - - - - -	1700 - - - - - -	1770 - - HP 5419	1840 - - - AUS
1491 - - - - - -	1561 - - ER 368	1631 - - GB 2381	1701 - - - - - -	1771 - - HP 4840	1841 - - - AUS
1492 - - -MB 499	1562 - - - - - -	1632 - NP 2011	1702 - - - - - -	1772 - - - - - -	1842 - - - AUS
1493 - - - FU 275	1563 - - - - - -	1633 - GB 2576	1703 - - - - - -	1773 - - - - - -	1843 - - - AUS
1494 - - - - - -	1564 - - - - - -	1634 - GB 2333	1704 - - - - - -	1774 - - - - - -	1844 - - - AUS
1495 - - - - - -	1565 - - FU 276	1635 - - - - - -	1705 - - - - - -	1775 - - - - - -	1845 - - - AUS
1496 - - - - - -	1566 - - - - - -	1636 - - HP 4827	1706 - - - - - -	1776 - - - - - -	1846 - - HP 5415
1497 - - - - - -	1567 - - - - - -	1637 - - - - - -	1707 - - FC 5255	1777 - - - - - -	1847 - - - - - -
1498 - - - - - -	1568 - - - - - -	1638 - - HP 4598	1708 - - - - - -	1778 - - ER 9926	1848 - - TC 4297
1499 - - GB 1988	1569 - - - - - -	1639 - - - - - -	1709 - - - - - -	1779 - - NO 9564	1849 - - - AUS
1500 - - - - - -	1570 - - HP 4597	1640 - - BT 5742	1710 - - HP 4843	1780 - - TC 3335	1850 - - - - - -

1851 - - GB 2738	1921 - - - - - -	1991 - - - - - -	2061 - - - - - -	2070 - - - - - -	2079 - - GB 4501
1852 - - - - - -	1922 - - - - - -	1992 - - - - - -	2062 - - - - - -	2071 - - - - - -	2080 - - - - - -
1853 - - - - - -	1923 - - - - - -	1993 - - - - - -	2063 - - - - - -	2072 - - - - - -	2081 - - - - - -
1854 - - - - - -	1924 - - - - - -	1994 - - HP 6149	2064 - - - - - -	2073 - - - - - -	2082 - - - - - -
1855 - - - - - -	1925 - - - - - -	1995 - - - - - -	2065 - - - - - -	2074 - - - - - -	2083 - - HP 6904
1856 - - - - - -	1926 - - TA 7007	1996 - - HP 6152	2066 - - - - AUS	2075 - - - - - -	2084 - - - - - -
1857 - - - - - -	1927 - - - - - -	1997 - - - - - -	2067 - - - - - -	2076 - - - - - -	2085 - - - - - -
1858 - - - - - -	1928 - - - - - -	1998 - - - - - -	2068 - - - - - -	2077 - - - - - -	2086 - - - - - -
1859 - - - - - -	1929 - - - PR 718	1999 - - - - - -	2069 - - - - - -	2078 - - - - - -	2087 - - - - - -
1860 - - - - - -	1930 - - - - - -	2000 - - - - - -			
1861 - - - - - -	1931 - - - - - -	2001 - - GB 4596			
1862 - - - - AUS	1932 - - GB 3654	2002 - - - - - -			
1863 - - - - AUS	1933 - - HP 5738	2003 - - - - - -			
1864 - - - - AUS	1934 - - - - - -	2004 - - TA 6956			
1865 - - - - AUS	1935 - - - - - -	2005 - - - - - -			
1866 - - - - AUS	1936 - - HP 5741	2006 - - HP 6155			
1867 - - - - - -	1937 - - - - - -	2007 - - HP 6145			
1868 - - HP 5734	1938 - - - - - -	2008 - - - - - -			
1869 - - - - - -	1939 - - - - - -	2009 - - - - - -			
1870 - - - - AUS	1940 - - - - - -	2010 - - - - - -			
1871 - - - - AUS	1941 - - AT 8261	2011 - - - - - -			
1872 - - - - - -	1942 - - - - AUS	2012 - - - - - -			
1873 - - - PR 650	1943 - - - - AUS	2013 - - - - - -			
1874 - - KU 2224	1944 - - - - AUS	2014 - - - - - -			
1875 - - - - - -	1945 - - - - AUS	2015 - - - OL 330			
1876 - - AT 7881	1946 - - - - AUS	2016 - - CX 5775			
1877 - - - - AUS	1947 - - - - AUS	2017 - - HP 6160			
1878 - - - - - -	1948 - - - - AUS	2018 - - HP 6159			
1879 - - CD 7795	1949 - - NL 4813	2019 - - - - - -			
1880 - - - - AUS	1950 - - - - - -	2020 - - - - - -			
1881 - - - - - -	1951 - - - - - -	2021 - - - - - -			
1882 - - - - AUS	1952 - - NP 2696	2022 - - - - - -			
1883 - - - - AUS	1953 - - NP 2696	2023 - - TA 7523			
1884 - - HP 5416	1954 - - - - - -	2024 - - - - - -			
1885 - - - - - -	1955 - - - - - -	2025 - - HP 6156			
1886 - - - - - -	1956 - - - - - -	2026 - - - - - -			
1887 - - - - - -	1957 - - - - - -	2027 - - - - - -			
1888 - - ND 1448	1958 - - TA 7207	2028 - - TA 7217			
1889 - - AT 7992	1959 - - - - - -	2029 - - - - - -			
1890 - - - - - -	1960 - - HP 6146	2030 - - - - - -			
1891 - - - - - -	1961 - - - - - -	2031 - - - - - -			
1892 - - - - - -	1962 - - - - - -	2032 - - - - - -			
1893 - - GB 3679	1963 - - - - - -	2033 - - - - - -			
1894 - - - - - -	1964 - - - - - -	2034 - - FU 1185			
1895 - - HP 5733	1965 - - - - - -	2035 - - - - - -			
1896 - - GB 3426	1966 - - HP 6148	2036 - - - - - -			
1897 - - - - - -	1967 - - - - - -	2037 - - - - - -			
1898 - - - - - -	1968 - - - - - -	2038 - - HP 6154			
1899 - - HP 6147	1969 - - - - - -	2039 - - - - - -			
1900 - - GB 4088	1970 - - - - - -	2040 - - - - - -			
1901 - - - - - -	1971 - - - - - -	2041 - - BD 8079			
1902 - - HP 5730	1972 - - - - - -	2042 - - - - - -			
1903 - - - - - -	1973 - - - - - -	2043 - - GB 4500			
1904 - - HP 5735	1974 - - - - - -	2044 - - - - - -			
1905 - - - - - -	1975 - - - - - -	2045 - - HP 6157			
1906 - - - - - -	1976 - - - - - -	2046 - - HP 6158			
1907 - - - - AUS	1977 - - DD 3100	2047 - - - - - -			
1908 - - - - AUS	1978 - - DN 4949	2048 - - - PU 100			
1909 - - - - AUS	1979 - - - - - -	2049 - - - - - -			
1910 - - - - AUS	1980 - - - - - -	2050 - - - - - -			
1911 - - - - AUS	1981 - - - - - -	2051 - - - - - -			
1912 - - - - AUS	1982 - - - - - -	2052 - - - - - -			
1913 - - - - - -	1983 - - - - - -	2053 - - ND 2345			
1914 - - - - - -	1984 - - - - - -	2054 - - - - - -			
1915 - - DD 3084	1985 - - HP 6151	2055 - - AT 8225			
1916 - - - - PD 2	1986 - - GB 3685	2056 - - MB 3212			
1917 - - - - - -	1987 - - - - - -	2057 - - - - - -			
1918 - - - - - -	1988 - - TA 7030	2058 - - - - - -			
1919 - - - - - -	1989 - - HP 6144	2059 - - - - - -			
1920 - - - - - -	1990 - - - - - -	2060 - - - - - -			

These are all side-valve cars, with the 10/30 being continued, initially using up engines 6343 to 6500 which had already been earmarked and numbered for the 6000 Series, and before the new engine numbering of 1501 onwards. The type is progressively improved, with an 11/40 being built alongside the 10/30 from chassis 1060 (circa November 1921), and then the first 12/40 making its appearance at chassis 1558 (circa October 1922).

Works records of this period do not always state which model designation applied to which chassis, and in any case, legibility is often a problem.

A further complication for the researcher relates to the introduction of an additional engineering number from March 1923. This is the 'car number' (often misconstrued by registration authorities as the chassis number). Commencing at 7001, it was generally allocated only after a chassis had been returned from the coachbuilder concerned, and 'signed off' by the works. The only exception to this practice was where 'chassis-only' orders from the Antipodes were allocated a 'car number' prior to shipment. At this time, there is also the increasing use of type letters as well as the fiscal horsepower. In general, the prefix 'S' implies 'Sporting' and 'T,' 'Touring,' though there are overlaps and inconsistencies.

Unfortunately, not specifically identifiable by chassis number or type, are the pair of cars from this sequence, purchased by the famous science fiction writer H G Wells, from Henly's London agency. Wells wrote enthusiastically about the service that he had received, and the letter concerned was used in a Henly's advertisement appearing in the *Autocar* of April 27, 1923.

1098   HP 3080
Iliffe Publications Ltd

It was in late August 1921 that the works changed its chassis numbering system from the 6001 and up of the very first 10/30s, to the 1000 and up system, which would run with only minor deletions until 1967. An early car to use the new system was 1098,

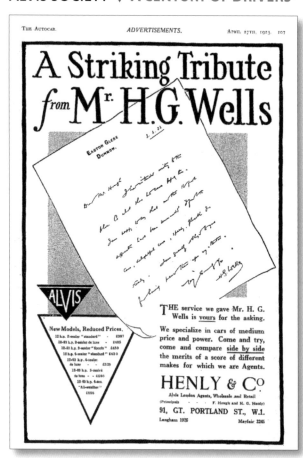

In this very early example of Alvis advertising. The Henly's dealership quotes novelist H G Wells, the father of science fiction, on his two Alvis cars. Not specifically identified, but certainly in the 1000 Series.

1098: One of very few surviving 10/30 models, the one-time *Autocar* road test car hp 3080 is seen here just after its painstaking restoration by Alan Stote. (Author's collection)

submitted to *Autocar* and published in the issue of April 8, 1922, pages 586 and 587. It is headed as 'A trial through ten counties embracing three well-known and difficult hills,' and receives an excellent report. One of the earliest Alvis cars to survive, it spent some time in a museum before being privately exported to the USA, where it joined the Southern California collection of that enthusiast for the Graham Hollywood model, Fred Jungles. Subsequently repatriated and fully restored at Red Triangle.

1409
1506
First works exports

I have connected these two deliveries for good reason. 1409 was the first export to New Zealand, and 1506 the first to Australia, the former as a

standard duckback, the latter as a chassis. Exports to the Antipodes would become comparatively numerous, and prove to be among the works most popular destinations, and for the next 40 years the initials TKM would appear regularly in records. These letters stood for 'Tozer, Kemsley and Millbourn,' who were the shippers in almost every case, sometimes handling cars for intermediate destinations, like India, as well. The ability of the Alvis product to cope with extreme conditions is quoted several times elsewhere in the book, and, of course, the 'chassis-only' option played a significant part in these exports, to be bodied locally by such well-known firms as Martin & King.

1487   BD 6963

2041   BD 8079

2118   BD 8363

Sears Family (Northampton)

This is a most familiar name in motoring circles and has been for many years. The most prominent member was Stanley Sears (1905-1989), a manifestly dyed-in-the-wool enthusiast. Who else, when still a teenager, could persuade his mother that the purchase of one of the Parry Thomas-designed Leyland eight-cylinder cars would be a good idea, and, moreover, to have it bodied locally by the Grose company, who were also Alvis agents? The aforesaid Leyland was the 15th such, and registered RP 1966. The three cars above were purchased in fairly quick succession, 2041 also being bodied by Grose. Other Alvis cars would later join the Sears stable (qv 4957, 5758, and 10899).

Stanley's infectious enthusiasm would lead to him, in due course, becoming president of the Veteran Car Club, when custodianship of three 1914 cars is notable: a Mercedes, the TT Sunbeam, and the GP Opel. Enthusiasm was obviously inheritable, as one takes into account Stanley's son 'Gentleman' Jack Sears, a co-organiser of the 1968 London to Sydney Marathon, and fifth place at the 1963 Le Mans 24-hour race. Nearly as memorable was the win, also in 1963, with the formidable 7-litre Ford Galaxie (Touring Car Championship). To prove the point, Stanley's grandson, David, continues to uphold the family name in competitions.

Jack Sears also rallied a 3.5-litre model (qv 13087).

1638
HP 4598
Iliffe Publications Ltd
Autocar, issue of March 2, 1923, page 359, carries a report of a body subsequently found to have been constructed by Cross & Ellis Ltd, specifically for camping/touring purposes. It is similar to the four/five-seater tourers built by that company, but has only two doors and an ingenious method of folding seats. It was a special commission from one Major Urwick, of Dringhouses, Yorkshire, who was about to embark upon a tour of France and Italy. A later photograph has emerged, which suggests that by 1932 the vehicle had returned to the ownership of Alvis Ltd, in use in van format at the London Service Department.

1687
Ambrose Shardlow Ltd
Probably the first of at least four company cars supplied to the Sheffield-based forgemaster, producer of crankshafts for many motor manufacturers under the 'Ambrosia' trade name (qv 3085, 5905, and 8423 for the others).

1720
HP 4836

1824: A happy couple, with dog, are accompanied by the very first overhead-valve 12/40 to be produced.

(Courtesy Ernest Shenton collection)

1721
HP 4838
Iliffe Publications Ltd
Publishers of the weekly *Autocar*, Iliffe had a number of other titles, including the *Midland Daily Telegraph*. The above are part of an order for three suitably liveried newspaper delivery vans, all bodied locally by Robinsons, who had other contracts with Alvis, including some two-seater bodies (qv 3012 for the third MDT van).

1824
YA 5620

1852
HP 6145

2007
Competition cars
Very closely related to the works racing cars (which immediately follow), of the above, 1824 is designated as the very first 12/40 SA sports, whilst 1852 was allocated to H H Brayshaw of Leicester, who, like Charles Follett and Frank Hallam later on, combined race driving with an Alvis agency. Brayshaw used 1852 in the Brooklands 200-mile race, finishing eighth, to Major Harvey's first. 2007 is shown as allocated to Harvey, but annotated as being 'wrecked,' but as the works wasted nothing, its components were most probably recycled.

2088-4919

August 1923 to February 1927
2831 cars

Consisting of models:

SA	70
SB	163
SC	178
SD	15
TC	571
TD	276
TE	840
TF	36
TG	353
TH	9
Undeclared	320
Total	**2831**

Consisting of coachbuilders:

Cross & Ellis	1678
Carbodies	977
Cubitt	54
Midland	23
Albany	5
Hoyal	2
Robinson	2
Plus one each of Egerton, Grose, Vanvooren, Vincent,	4
Other (chassis-only deliveries) Mostly undeclared	86
Total	**2831**

Chassis	Reg	Chassis	Reg	Chassis	Reg
2088	- - - - - -	2106	- - - - - -	2125	- - - - - -
2089	MB 3375	2107	- - - - - -	2126	- - - - - -
2090	- - - - - -	2108	- - - - - -	2127	NP 3754
2091	HP 6161	2109	- - - - - -	2128	- - - - - -
2092	KS 2311	2110	AT 8304	2129	- - - - - -
2093	- - - - - -	2111	- - - - - -	2130	- - - - - -
2094	- - - - - -	2112	BR 2833	2131	- - - - - -
2095	- - - - - -	2113	- - - - - -	2132	KU 2830
2096	- - - - - -	2114	FU 1299	2133	- - - - - -
2097	- - - - - -	2115	- - - - - -	2134	- - - - - -
2098	- - - - - -	2116	- - - - - -	2135	FY 6080
2099	- - - - - -	2117	- - - - - -	2136	- - - - - -
2100	- - - - - -	2118	BD 8363	2137	ER 1575
2101	AT 8330	2119	GB 4349	2138	HP 6561
2102	- - - - - -	2120	- - - - - -	2139	- - - - - -
2103	HP 6887	2121	HP 6886	2140	- - - - - -
2104	- - - - - -	2122	- - - - - -	2141	- - - - - -
2105	- - - - - -	2123	- - - - - -	2142	- - - - - -
		2124	CR 8372	2143	- - - - - -

Chassis	Reg	Chassis	Reg	Chassis	Reg
2144	- - - - - -	2214	- - - - - -	2284	- - - - - -
2145	- - - - - -	2215	- - - - - -	2285	- - - - - -
2146	- - - - - -	2216	- - - - - -	2286	- - - - - -
2147	- - - - - -	2217	- - - - - -	2287	- - - - - -
2148	- - - - - -	2218	HP 6889	2288	- - - - - -
2149	- - - - - -	2219	HP 6892	2289	- - - - - -
2150	- - - - - -	2220	- - - - - -	2290	TC 5746
2151	- - - - - -	2221	- - - - - -	2291	MB 3252
2152	- - - - - -	2222	- - - - - -	2292	- - - - - -
2153	- - - - - -	2223	- - - - - -	2293	- - - - - -
2154	- - - - - -	2224	- - - - - -	2294	- - - - - -
2155	- - - - - -	2225	XP 5660	2295	BD 8496
2156	- - - - - -	2226	HP 6890	2296	OR 2851
2157	- - - - - -	2227	- - - - - -	2297	HP 6897
2158	- - - - - -	2228	- - - - - -	2298	TA 8155
2159	- - - - - -	2229	- - - - - -	2299	- - - - - -
2160	TA 7712	2230	- - - - - -	2300	- - - - - -
2161	- - - - - -	2231	HR 9745	2301	BR 2927
2162	- - - - - -	2232	GB 4639	2302	GB 5841
2163	HH 1970	2233	GB 4921	2303	- - - - - -
2164	- - - - - -	2234	PU 2446	2304	- - - - - -
2165	AT 8331	2235	- - - - - -	2305	- - - - - -
2166	- - - - - -	2236	ND 3133	2306	XT 5887
2167	AUS	2237	- - - - - -	2307	NL
2168	AUS	2238	HP 6901	2308	- - - - - -
2169	- - - - - -	2239	- - - - - -	2309	AUS
2170	AUS	2240	- - - - - -	2310	- - - - - -
2171	- - - - - -	2241	HP 6900	2311	TA 8335
2172	- - - - - -	2242	-HU 249	2312	- - - - - -
2173	- - - - - -	2243	HP 6899	2313	MB 3852
2174	- - - - - -	2244	HP 6893	2314	- - - - - -
2175	- - - - - -	2245	HP 6896	2315	- - - - - -
2176	- - - - - -	2246	HP 6895	2316	NZ
2177	- - - - - -	2247	- - - - - -	2317	AT 8891
2178	- - - - - -	2248	- - - - - -	2318	- - - - - -
2179	- - - - - -	2249	HP 6898	2319	- - - - - -
2180	- - - - - -	2250	- - - - - -	2320	- - - - - -
2181	MB 3585	2251	- - - - - -	2321	- - - - - -
2182	- - - - - -	2252	- - - - - -	2322	TA 8763
2183	- - - - - -	2253	TA 9717	2323	HP 6902
2184	HP 6894	2254	BC 8449	2324	- - - - - -
2185	- - - - - -	2255	HP 8126	2325	AT 8704
2186	FU 2030	2256	- - - - - -	2326	AUS
2187	- - - - - -	2257	- - - - - -	2327	- - - - - -
2188	MB3640	2258	- - - - - -	2328	- - - - - -
2189	HP 6885	2259	HP 6891	2329	- - - - - -
2190	MB 3625	2260	- - - - - -	2330	E
2191	GB 4331	2261	- - - - - -	2331	HP 6903
2192	AUS	2262	GB 4689	2332	- - - - - -
2193	AUS	2263	- - - - - -	2333	- - - - - -
2194	- - - - - -	2264	- - - - - -	2334	- - - - - -
2195	- - - - - -	2265	- - - - - -	2335	PD 3649
2196	HP 6888	2266	- - - - - -	2336	- - - - - -
2197	- - - - - -	2267	- - - - - -	2337	- - - - - -
2198	- - - - - -	2268	SG 8638	2338	CD 8450
2199	GB 4505	2269	- - - - - -	2339	CP 3754
2200	- - - - - -	2270	- - - - - -	2340	- - - - - -
2201	- - - - - -	2271	BD 8504	2341	AUS
2202	- - - - - -	2272	- - - - - -	2342	AUS
2203	- - - - - -	2273	- - - - - -	2343	AUS
2204	- - - - - -	2274	- - - - - -	2344	AUS
2205	- - - - - -	2275	- - - - - -	2345	AUS
2206	- - - - - -	2276	- - - - - -	2346	NU 2148
2207	- - - - - -	2277	AT 8435	2347	- - - - - -
2208	- - - - - -	2278	MR 762	2348	HP 6805
2209	HP 7248	2279	- - - - - -	2349	- - - - - -
2210	- - - - - -	2280	TC 8809	2350	FU 1507
2211	- - - - - -	2281	TC 7688	2351	HP 6906
2212	- - - - - -	2282	- - - - - -	2352	- - - - - -
2213	- - - - - -	2283	- - - - - -	2353	- - - - - -

No.	Code	No.	Code	No.	Code	No.	Code	No.	Code	No.	Code
2354	- - - - - -	2424	- - DD 4633	2494	- - - - - -	2564	- - - - - -	2634	- - - - TT 7	2704	- - -BR3220
2355	- - HP 7247	2425	- - - - - -	2495	- - - - - -	2565	- - - - - -	2635	- - - - - -	2705	- - SG 9404
2356	- - - - - -	2426	- - - - - -	2496	- - - - - -	2566	- - -GB5322	2636	- - - - - -	2706	- - - - - -
2357	- - - - - -	2427	- - - - - -	2497	- - - - - -	2567	- - CD 8434	2637	- - HP 7798	2707	- - - - - -
2358	- - - - - -	2428	- - - - - -	2498	- - - - - -	2568	- - - - - -	2638	- - KU 3539	2708	- - - - - -
2359	- - - - - -	2429	- - - - - -	2499	- - - - - -	2569	- - - - - -	2639	- - HP 7811	2709	- - - - - -
2360	- - - - AUS	2430	- - HP 7258	2500	- - HP 7263	2570	- - - - - -	2640	- - HP 7805	2710	- - GB 6145
2361	- - - - AUS	2431	- - - - - -	2501	- - - - - -	2571	- - XX 7194	2641	- - MB 5418	2711	- - - - - -
2362	- - - - AUS	2432	- - KS 2399	2502	- - GB 5139	2572	- - SR 3836	2642	- - - - - -	2712	- - - - - -
2363	- - - - AUS	2433	- - HP 7253	2503	- - TA 8722	2573	- - AT 8531	2643	- - - - - -	2713	- - - - - -
2364	- - - - AUS	2434	- - - - - -	2504	- - - - - -	2574	- - NL 7898	2644	- - HP 7804	2714	- - - - - -
2365	- - - - - -	2435	- - - - - -	2505	- - FC 6208	2575	- - - - - -	2645	- - NL 6817	2715	- - - - - -
2366	- - - - - -	2436	- - - - - -	2506	- - - - - -	2576	- - - - - -	2646	- - - - - -	2716	- - HP 7818
2367	- - - - - -	2437	- - - - - -	2507	- - - - - -	2577	- - HP 7267	2647	- - - - - -	2717	- - HC 4217
2368	- - - VS 866	2438	- - GB 5021	2508	- - SG 9338	2578	- - - - - -	2648	- - - - - -	2718	- - - - - -
2369	- - - - - -	2439	- - - - - -	2509	- - HP 7260	2579	- - - - - -	2649	- - - - - -	2719	- - - - - -
2370	- - - - - -	2440	- - - - - -	2510	- - - AUS	2580	- - - - - -	2650	- - - - - -	2720	- - - - - -
2371	- - SG 8996	2441	- - HP 7256	2511	- - - - - -	2581	- - - - - -	2651	- - - - - -	2721	- - - - - -
2372	- - PU 1236	2442	- - - - - -	2512	- - - - - -	2582	- - BT 6861	2652	- - - - - -	2722	- - - - - -
2373	- - - - AUS	2443	- - GB 4932	2513	- - NP 4660	2583	- - - - - -	2653	- - - - - -	2723	- - - - - -
2374	- - - - AUS	2444	- - HP 7250	2514	- - - - - -	2584	- - - - - -	2654	- - - - - -	2724	- - - - - -
2375	- - - - - -	2445	- - - AUS	2515	- - KU 3321	2585	- - SG 9066	2655	- - - - - -	2725	- - - - AUS
2376	- - AT 8530	2446	- - - AUS	2516	- - - - - -	2586	- - TC 6810	2656	- - - - - -	2726	- - - - - -
2377	- - - - - -	2447	- - - AUS	2517	- - - - - -	2587	- - - - - -	2657	- - AT 9372	2727	- - DD 4420
2378	- - - VS 532	2448	- - - AUS	2518	- - - - - -	2588	- - - - - -	2658	- - HP 7816	2728	- - - - AUS
2379	- - SG 8966	2449	- - - - - -	2519	- - HP 7262	2589	- - - - - -	2659	- - HP 7808	2729	- - - - - -
2380	- - - - - -	2450	- - - - - -	2520	- - - VS 879	2590	- - - - - -	2660	- - - - - -	2730	- - - - - -
2381	- - HP 6907	2451	- - - - - -	2521	- - HP 7265	2591	- - HP 7266	2661	- - - - - -	2731	- - - - - -
2382	- - - - - -	2452	- - - - - -	2522	- - - - - -	2592	- - MB 5972	2662	- - - - - -	2732	- - - - - -
2383	- - NP 3672	2453	- - - - - -	2523	- - SG 9145	2593	- - - - - -	2663	- - TS 4433	2733	- - HP 8829
2384	- - - - - -	2454	- - - - NL	2524	- - - - - -	2594	- - - - - -	2664	- - - - - -	2734	- - - AUS
2385	- - - - - -	2455	- - - - - -	2525	- - -SS 1804	2595	- - - - - -	2665	- - - - - -	2735	- - - - NZ
2386	- - - AUS	2456	- - - - - -	2526	- - HH 2106	2596	- - - - - -	2666	- - - - - -	2736	- - - - - -
2387	- - - - - -	2457	- - HP 7252	2527	- - GB 5137	2597	- - - - - -	2667	- - - - - -	2737	- - - - - -
2388	- - - - - -	2458	- - - - - -	2528	- - SA 6866	2598	- - - - - -	2668	- - - - - -	2738	- - - - - -
2389	- - HP 6908	2459	- - BD 8765	2529	- - - - - -	2599	- - - - - -	2669	- - - - - -	2739	- - - - - -
2390	- - - - - -	2460	- - - - - -	2530	- - - AUS	2600	- - - - - -	2670	- - - - - -	2740	- - - - - -
2391	- - - - - -	2461	- - MR 111	2531	- - CTH 887	2601	- - - - - -	2671	- - CD 9101	2741	- - - - - -
2392	- - - - - -	2462	- - HP 7251	2532	- - SG 9084	2602	- - - - - -	2672	- - HP 7810	2742	- - - - - -
2393	- - - - - -	2463	- - - - - -	2533	- - - - - -	2603	- - - - - -	2673	- - - - - -	2743	- - DN 6248
2394	- - - - - -	2464	- - - - - -	2534	- - - - - -	2604	- - HP 7797	2674	- - - - - -	2744	- - HP 7813
2395	- - - AUS	2465	- - - AUS	2535	- - - - - -	2605	- - - - - -	2675	- - - - - -	2745	- - HP 7815
2396	- - - AUS	2466	- - BR 2993	2536	- - - - - -	2606	- - HP 7800	2676	- - - - - -	2746	- - -BD9377
2397	- - AT 8632	2467	- - - - - -	2537	- - - - - -	2607	- - - - - -	2677	- - - - - -	2747	- - - - - -
2398	- - - - - -	2468	- - HP 7257	2538	- - AT 8771	2608	- - - - - -	2678	- - HP 7809	2748	- - - - - -
2399	- - TA 8513	2469	- - HP 7807	2539	- - CD 8492	2609	- - - - - -	2679	- - BD 9215	2749	- - - - - -
2400	- - DD 3829	2470	- - EE 4825	2540	- - GB 5113	2610	- - - - - -	2680	- - - - - -	2750	- - - - - -
2401	- - - - - -	2471	- - - - - -	2541	- - HH 2088	2611	- - AT 8806	2681	- - HP 7799	2751	- - - - - -
2402	- - GB 4876	2472	- - XR 7839	2542	- - - - - -	2612	- - BR 3053	2682	- - - - - -	2752	- - - - - -
2403	- - MO 2502	2473	- - - - - -	2543	- - HP 7264	2613	- - - - - -	2683	- - - - - -	2753	- - - - - -
2404	- - HP 7255	2474	- - GB 5033	2544	- - TA 8999	2614	- - - - - -	2684	- - - - - -	2754	- - - - - -
2405	- - - - - -	2475	- - HP 7259	2545	- - - - - -	2615	- - - AUS	2685	- - HP 7801	2755	- - HP 7806
2406	- - - - - -	2476	- - - - - -	2546	- - SG 9771	2616	- - - - - -	2686	- - HP 7801	2756	- - - - - -
2407	- - NP 4550	2477	- - - - - -	2547	- - GB 5226	2617	- - - - - -	2687	- - - AUS	2757	- - - - - -
2408	- - - AUS	2478	- - - - - -	2548	- - - - - -	2618	- - - - - -	2688	- - - - - -	2758	- - -FC6625
2409	- - - - - -	2479	- - HP 7254	2549	- - - - - -	2619	- - -SS 1930	2689	- - - - - -	2759	- - KU 3899
2410	- - - AUS	2480	- - - - - -	2550	- - - - - -	2620	- - - - - -	2690	- - - - - -	2760	- - - AUS
2411	- - XR 1856	2481	- - - - - -	2551	- - GB 5676	2621	- - - - - -	2691	- - - AUS	2761	- - - - - -
2412	- - - - - -	2482	- - - - - -	2552	- - NP 3828	2622	- - HP 7268	2692	- - HP 7803	2762	- - KU 3540
2413	- - - - - -	2483	- - AT 8660	2553	- - - - - -	2623	- - - - - -	2693	- - - - - -	2763	- - - - - -
2414	- - - - - -	2484	- - BD 8754	2554	- - - - - -	2624	- - - - - -	2694	- - - - - -	2764	- - - - - -
2415	- - - - - -	2485	- - - - - -	2555	- - - - - -	2625	- - - - - -	2695	- - - - - -	2765	- - - - - -
2416	- - HP 7249	2486	- - HP 7261	2556	- - ER 1987	2626	- - - - - -	2696	- - HP 7802	2766	- - HP 7812
2417	- - - - - -	2487	- - - - - -	2557	- - - - - -	2627	- - - - - -	2697	- - - - - -	2767	- - - - - -
2418	- - - - - -	2488	- - BR 3234	2558	- - - - - -	2628	- - - - - -	2698	- - - - - -	2768	- - - - - -
2419	- - DN 6115	2489	- - - - - -	2559	- - BR 3148	2629	- - - - - -	2699	- - - - - -	2769	- - - - - -
2420	- - MB 3804	2490	- - - - - -	2560	- - AT 8810	2630	- - KS 2452	2700	- - - - - -	2770	- - HP 7820
2421	- - DD 6721	2491	- - TA 8904	2561	- - - - - -	2631	- - - - - -	2701	- - - - - -	2771	- - - - - -
2422	- - - - - -	2492	- - - - - -	2562	- - - - - -	2632	- - KU 3538	2702	- - - - - -	2772	- - - - - -
2423	- - - - - -	2493	- - MB 4436	2563	- - GB 5208	2633	- - SR 3931	2703	- - AT 8939	2773	- - - - - -

No.	Reg.	No.	Reg.	No.	Reg.	No.	Reg.	No.	Reg.	No.	Reg.
2774	- - - - - -	2844	- - - - - -	2914	MB 4087	2984	- - - - - -	3054	- - - - - -	3124	- - - - - -
2775	FC 6638	2845	HP 8851	2915	MB 4089	2985	- - - - - -	3055	GB 6717	3125	- - - - - -
2776	- - - - - -	2846	MR 1159	2916	AUS	2986	- - - - - -	3056	TT 1682	3126	AUS
2777	- - - - - -	2847	- - - - - -	2917	- - - - - -	2987	HP 8840	3057	MB 6740	3127	- - - - - -
2778	- - - - - -	2848	TC 8901	2918	- - - - - -	2988	- - - - - -	3058	- - - - - -	3128	AUS
2779	- - - - - -	2849	CO 6835	2919	DD 4873	2989	- - - - - -	3059	- - - - - -	3129	GB 7454
2780	- - - - - -	2850	- - - - - -	2920	- - - - - -	2990	- - - - - -	3060	- - - - - -	3130	- - - - - -
2781	- - - - - -	2851	GB 6286	2921	- - - - - -	2991	- - - - - -	3061	HP 8848	3131	MB 7424
2782	- - - - - -	2852	- - - - - -	2922	- - - - - -	2992	- - - - - -	3062	NL 8400	3132	- - - - - -
2783	TT 152	2853	BR 6317	2923	- - - - - -	2993	- - - - - -	3063	- - - - - -	3133	GB 7286
2784	- - - - - -	2854	-XU 362	2924	HP 8832	2994	- - - - - -	3064	- - - - - -	3134	- - - - - -
2785	- - - - - -	2855	- - - - - -	2925	HP 8831	2995	- - - - - -	3065	- - - - - -	3135	- - - - - -
2786	AUS	2856	MR 1054	2926	- - - - - -	2996	- - - - - -	3066	- - - - - -	3136	HH 2497
2787	- - - - - -	2857	- - - - - -	2927	- - - - - -	2997	- - - - - -	3067	GB 6574	3137	RW 3866
2788	- - - - - -	2858	BR 3291	2928	- - - - - -	2998	- - - - - -	3068	HP 8841	3138	- - - - - -
2789	- - - - - -	2859	AUS	2929	-RW 1	2999	- - - - - -	3069	- - - - - -	3139	- - - - - -
2790	- - - - - -	2860	- - - - - -	2930	RW 13	3000	- - - - - -	3070	- - - - - -	3140	AUS
2791	- - - - - -	2861	- - - - - -	2931	RW 12	3001	AUS	3071	- - - - - -	3141	AUS
2792	AUS	2862	HH 2223	2932	- - - - - -	3002	- - - - - -	3072	- - - - - -	3142	HP 8852
2793	AUS	2863	- - - - - -	2933	- - - - - -	3003	HP 8843	3073	- - - - - -	3143	AUS
2794	TD 1899	2864	HP 8897	2934	- - - - - -	3004	- - - - - -	3074	AT 9646	3144	AUS
2795	- - - - - -	2865	- - - - - -	2935	- - - - - -	3005	TT 590	3075	- - - - - -	3145	MO 4325
2796	- - - - - -	2866	- - - - - -	2936	- - - - - -	3006	- - - - - -	3076	- - - - - -	3146	AT 9743
2797	TC 7624	2867	GB 6675	2937	HP 8837	3007	-JF 1181	3077	-RW 141	3147	- - - - - -
2798	- - - - - -	2868	- - - - - -	2938	NZ	3008	- - - - - -	3078	NL	3148	AUS
2799	- - - - - -	2869	DD 4705	2939	- - - - - -	3009	- - - - - -	3079	- - - - - -	3149	AT 9906
2800	- - - - - -	2870	- - - - - -	2940	- - - - - -	3010	HP 9871	3080	- - - - - -	3150	NL 8234
2801	- - - - - -	2871	- - - - - -	2941	HP 8847	3011	NL	3081	- - - - - -	3151	- - - - - -
2802	XT 2998	2872	BD 9534	2942	RM 228	3012	HP 8846	3082	- - - - - -	3152	GB 6916
2803	AUS	2873	- - - - - -	2943	HP 8850	3013	- - - - - -	3083	- - - - - -	3153	- - - - - -
2804	- - - - - -	2874	- - - - - -	2944	- - - - - -	3014	- - - - - -	3084	- - - - - -	3154	VS 920
2805	- - - - - -	2875	GB 7278	2945	HP 8839	3015	- - - - - -	3085	- - - - - -	3155	- - - - - -
2806	HP 7817	2876	- - - - - -	2946	- - - - - -	3016	- - - - - -	3086	- - - - - -	3156	- - - - - -
2807	KL 199	2877	AUS	2947	- - - - - -	3017	- - - - - -	3087	- - - - - -	3157	HP 9873
2808	- - - - - -	2878	AT 8998	2948	- - - - - -	3018	- - - - - -	3088	HP 9868	3158	- - - - - -
2809	- - - - - -	2879	KU 4441	2949	NL 7646	3019	- - - - - -	3089	- - - - - -	3159	- - - - - -
2810	- - - - - -	2880	- - - - - -	2950	- - - - - -	3020	NL	3090	- - - - - -	3160	- - - - - -
2811	- - - - - -	2881	- - - - - -	2951	KS 2600	3021	- - - - - -	3091	- - - - - -	3161	- - - - - -
2812	- - - - - -	2882	TC 8177	2952	GB 6274	3022	- - - - - -	3092	NZ	3162	- - - - - -
2813	- - - - - -	2883	-KL 599	2953	- - - - - -	3023	- - - - - -	3093	TC 9034	3163	- - - - - -
2814	AUS	2884	- - - - - -	2954	SG 9859	3024	BR 3415	3094	- - - - - -	3164	- - - - - -
2815	AUS	2885	- - - - - -	2955	- - - - - -	3025	- - - - - -	3095	- - - - - -	3165	AUS
2816	AUS	2886	- - - - - -	2956	HP 8838	3026	- - - - - -	3096	AUS	3166	- - - - - -
2817	AUS	2887	- - - - - -	2957	- - - - - -	3027	- - - - - -	3097	- - - - - -	3167	- - - - - -
2818	AUS	2888	GB 6261	2958	BR 3423	3028	BR 3501	3098	- - - - - -	3168	- - - - - -
2819	HP 7814	2889	- - - - - -	2959	- - - - - -	3029	- - - - - -	3099	- - - - - -	3169	AUS
2820	AUS	2890	- - - - - -	2960	HP 8834	3030	- - - - - -	3100	AUS	3170	AUS
2821	- - - - - -	2891	- - - - - -	2961	HP 8833	3031	- - - - - -	3101	- - - - - -	3171	GB 6883
2822	- - - - - -	2892	- - - - - -	2962	TC 8529	3032	FU 2697	3102	NP 5034	3172	AUS
2823	AUS	2893	- - - - - -	2963	- - - - - -	3033	- - - - - -	3103	- - - - - -	3173	AUS
2824	AUS	2894	MB 5637	2964	- - - - - -	3034	SF 198	3104	- - - - - -	3174	AUS
2825	NP 6908	2895	- - - - - -	2965	HP 8836	3035	- - - - - -	3105	- - - - - -	3175	AUS
2826	- - - - - -	2896	- - - - - -	2966	SF 147	3036	- - - - - -	3106	YA 9005	3176	AUS
2827	- - - - - -	2897	- - - - - -	2967	- - - - - -	3037	-XW 5448	3107	HP 8842	3177	AUS
2828	- - - - - -	2898	HP 8830	2968	- - - - - -	3038	- - - - - -	3108	HP 8849	3178	AUS
2829	AUS	2899	- - - - - -	2969	- - - - - -	3039	- - - - - -	3109	PY 1974	3179	AUS
2830	- - - - - -	2900	RM 147	2970	- - - - - -	3040	- - - - - -	3110	BR 3553	3180	AUS
2831	- - - - - -	2901	- - - - - -	2971	MB 7077	3041	- - - - - -	3111	AUS	3181	AUS
2832	- - - - - -	2902	- - - - - -	2972	- - - - - -	3042	- - - - - -	3112	AUS	3182	AUS
2833	- - - - - -	2903	SR 4117	2973	AUS	3043	- - - - - -	3113	AUS	3183	AUS
2834	- - - - - -	2904	- - - - - -	2974	AUS	3044	- - - - - -	3114	HP 9861	3184	RP 596
2835	AUS	2905	- - - - - -	2975	AUS	3045	- - - - - -	3115	- - - - - -	3185	AUS
2836	- - - - - -	2906	RM 152	2976	AUS	3046	- - - - - -	3116	- - - - - -	3186	- - - - - -
2837	KL 351	2907	- - - - - -	2977	AUS	3047	- - - - - -	3117	- - - - - -	3187	AUS
2838	TT 83	2908	GB 6504	2978	HP 8835	3048	TC 9416	3118	- - - - - -	3188	AUS
2839	- - - - - -	2909	- - - - - -	2979	TD 2514	3049	- - - - - -	3119	AUS	3189	AUS
2840	- - - - - -	2910	- - - - - -	2980	HP 9864	3050	BR 3474	3120	AUS	3190	AUS
2841	HP 7819	2911	- - - - - -	2981	HP 8844	3051	- - - - - -	3121	AUS	3191	AUS
2842	- - - - - -	2912	- - - - - -	2982	RM 335	3052	- - - - - -	3122	- - - - - -	3192	AUS
2843	- - - - - -	2913	- - - - - -	2983	- - - - - -	3053	TT708	3123	- - - - - -	3193	- - - - - -

3194 - - HP 9863	3264 - - - - - -	3334 - - - - - -	3404 - - DD 6592	3474 - - - - - -	3544 - - - - - -
3195 - - - - - -	3265 - XW 4483	3335 - - - KH 85	3405 - - - - - -	3475 - - - - - -	3545 - - - - - -
3196 - - - - - -	3266 - - - - - -	3336 - - - - - -	3406 - - - RR 146	3476 - - - - - -	3546 - - NP 6222
3197 - - - - - -	3267 - - - - - -	3337 - - - - AUS	3407 - - HP 9879	3477 - - KU 6294	3547 - - - - - -
3198 - - - - AUS	3268 - - - - - -	3338 - - - - - -	3408 - - - - - -	3478 - - HP 9884	3548 - - - - - -
3199 - - - - AUS	3269 - - - - - -	3339 - - -SF 1442	3409 - - - - - -	3479 - - GB 8601	3549 - - - - - -
3200 - - - AUS	3270 - - - - - -	3340 - - - - AUS	3410 - - - - - -	3480 - - - - - -	3550 - - RW 2421
3201 - - - AUS	3271 - - - - - -	3341 - - GB 7384	3411 - - - - AUS	3481 - - - - - -	3551 - - - - - -
3202 - - - AUS	3272 - - - - AUS	3342 - - - - - -	3412 - - - - - -	3482 - - - - - -	3552 - - RW 2417
3203 - - - - - -	3273 - - - - - -	3343 - - - - AUS	3413 - - BR 3994	3483 - - - - - -	3553 - - - - - -
3204 - - - - - -	3274 - - - - - -	3344 - - - - - -	3414 - - DN 6857	3484 - - RW 2423	3554 - - - - - -
3205 - - - - - -	3275 - - - - - -	3345 - - - - - -	3415 - - TT 2470	3485 - - BR 4102	3555 - - - - - -
3206 - - - - - -	3276 - - - - - -	3346 - - BR 3779	3416 - - MR 3222	3486 - - - AUS	3556 - - - - - -
3207 - - - - - -	3277 - - - - - -	3347 - - - - AUS	3417 - - - AUS	3487 - - - - - -	3557 - - - - - -
3208 - - - - - -	3278 - - - - NL	3348 - - - - - -	3418 - - - - - -	3488 - - - - - -	3558 - - -SS 2322
3209 - - - - - -	3279 - - - - - -	3349 - - - - - -	3419 - - HP 9877	3489 - - TD 4005	3559 - - CP 4564
3210 - - - - - -	3280 - - - - - -	3350 - - - - NL	3420 - - - AUS	3490 - - - - - -	3560 - - - AUS
3211 - - - - - -	3281 - - - - - -	3351 - - - - - -	3421 - - MB 8006	3491 - - - - - -	3561 - - - - - -
3212 - - - - AUS	3282 - - - - AUS	3352 - - - - AUS	3422 - - - - - -	3492 - - - - - -	3562 - - GB 9248
3213 - - - - AUS	3283 - - - - AUS	3353 - - - - AUS	3423 - - - - - -	3493 - - SL 9879	3563 - - NE 2580
3214 - - - - AUS	3284 - - - - - -	3354 - - GB 8977	3424 - - - - - -	3494 - - - AUS	3564 - - RW 2424
3215 - - - - AUS	3285 - - - - - -	3355 - - -XX 306	3425 - - - - - -	3495 - - - - - -	3565 - - TD 2813
3216 - - - - AUS	3286 - - MB 7123	3356 - - - - - -	3426 - - - - - -	3496 - - OR 7293	3566 - - - - - -
3217 - - - - AUS	3287 - - - - - -	3357 - - - - - -	3427 - - - - - -	3497 - - - - - -	3567 - - - - - -
3218 - - - - - -	3288 - - - - - -	3358 - - - - - -	3428 - - - - - -	3498 - - RW 7327	3568 - - TD 2518
3219 - - AT 9905	3289 - - - - - -	3359 - - - - - -	3429 - - - - - -	3499 - - - - - -	3569 - - - - - -
3220 - - - - - -	3290 - - HP 9869	3360 - - - - - -	3430 - - - - - -	3500 - - RW 2416	3570 - - RW 3870
3221 - - - - - -	3291 - - - - - -	3361 - - - - - -	3431 - - KU 6793	3501 - - - - - -	3571 - - - - - -
3222 - - - - - -	3292 - - - - - -	3362 - - - - AUS	3432 - - - - - -	3502 - - -RR 725	3572 - - - - - -
3223 - - HP 9872	3293 - - - - - -	3363 - - HP 9874	3433 - - BR 4011	3503 - - - - - -	3573 - - - - - -
3224 - - - - - -	3294 - - -RW 481	3364 - - - - - -	3434 - - - AUS	3504 - - - AUS	3574 - - - - - -
3225 - - - - - -	3295 - - - - - -	3365 - - - - - -	3435 - - - - - -	3505 - - - AUS	3575 - - - - - -
3226 - - -XX 610	3296 - - HP 9878	3366 - - - - - -	3436 - - - - - -	3506 - - - - - -	3576 - - - - - -
3227 - - - - AUS	3297 - - SF 912	3367 - - KH 1306	3437 - - - - - -	3507 - - - AUS	3577 - - - - - -
3228 - - - - AUS	3298 - - BT 7819	3368 - - - - - -	3438 - - - - NL	3508 - - - - - -	3578 - - CD 9788
3229 - - - - - -	3299 - - - - - -	3369 - - - - - -	3439 - - GB 8731	3509 - - HP 9883	3579 - - - AUS
3230 - - - - - -	3300 - - - - - -	3370 - - HH 2473	3440 - - - - - -	3510 - - - - - -	3580 - - - - - -
3231 - - - - - -	3301 - - - - - -	3371 - - HP 9881	3441 - - - - - -	3511 - - - - - -	3581 - - - - - -
3232 - - NL 7185	3302 - - - - - -	3372 - - - - - -	3442 - - - - - -	3512 - - EW 4092	3582 - - GB 9501
3233 - - - - - -	3303 - - - - - -	3373 - - - - - -	3443 - - - - - -	3513 - - - AUS	3583 - - BR 4426
3234 - - HP 9862	3304 - - - - - -	3374 - - - - - -	3444 - - - - - -	3514 - - - AUS	3584 - - RW 2420
3235 - - - - - -	3305 - - - - - -	3375 - - - RU 504	3445 - - - FG 104	3515 - - - - - -	3585 - - - AUS
3236 - - - - AUS	3306 - - - - AUS	3376 - - - - - -	3446 - - - - - -	3516 - - GB 8734	3586 - - - - - -
3237 - - - - - -	3307 - - - - AUS	3377 - - - - - -	3447 - - MB 7425	3517 - - - - - -	3587 - - - - - -
3238 - - - - - -	3308 - - - - AUS	3378 - - - - - -	3448 - - - AUS	3518 - - - - - -	3588 - - RP 1217
3239 - - - - AUS	3309 - - - - - -	3379 - - GB 8192	3449 - - - AUS	3519 - - HP 9883	3589 - - - - - -
3240 - - - - AUS	3310 - - - - - -	3380 - - - AUS	3450 - - - - - -	3520 - - - - - -	3590 - - - - - -
3241 - - GB 7350	3311 - - - TD 518	3381 - - - - - -	3451 - - - - - -	3521 - - - - - -	3591 - - RW 2418
3242 - - - - AUS	3312 - - - - - -	3382 - - XX 4901	3452 - - - - - -	3522 - - HP 9880	3592 - - - - - -
3243 - - - RP 150	3313 - - - - - -	3383 - - - - - -	3453 - - GB 8810	3523 - - RW 3877	3593 - - - - - -
3244 - - - - - -	3314 - - - VS 527	3384 - - - - - -	3454 - - - - - -	3524 - - - - - -	3594 - - - - - -
3245 - - - - - -	3315 - - - - - -	3385 - - HP 9882	3455 - - HP 9867	3525 - - - - - -	3595 - - BR 4208
3246 - - - - - -	3316 - - - - AUS	3386 - - - - AUS	3456 - - - - - -	3526 - - - - - -	3596 - - TR 582
3247 - - AT 9904	3317 - - - - - -	3387 - - - - - -	3457 - - DN 6943	3527 - - RW 2419	3597 - - - - - -
3248 - - - - - -	3318 - - - - NL	3388 - - MB 7843	3458 - - - - - -	3528 - - - - NZ	3598 - - RW 2422
3249 - - HP 9870	3319 - - - - - -	3389 - - XX 4065	3459 - - - - - -	3529 - - - - - -	3599 - - - - - -
3250 - - - - - -	3320 - - - - - -	3390 - - - AUS	3460 - - - - - -	3530 - - - - - -	3600 - - - - - -
3251 - - - - - -	3321 - - - - - -	3391 - - - - AUS	3461 - - - AUS	3531 - - GB 9645	3601 - - - - - -
3252 - - - - - -	3322 - - - - - -	3392 - - - - - -	3462 - - RW 2657	3532 - - - - - -	3602 - - - - - -
3253 - - - - - -	3323 - - YK 3711	3393 - - - - - -	3463 - - - AUS	3533 - - MB 7499	3603 - - RW 3875
3254 - - - - - -	3324 - - - - - -	3394 - - - - - -	3464 - - - AUS	3534 - - - - - -	3604 - - NL 9801
3255 - - - - - -	3325 - - - - AUS	3395 - - - - - -	3465 - - - - - -	3535 - - - - - -	3605 - - - - - -
3256 - - HP 9866	3326 - - - - - -	3396 - - GB 9504	3466 - - - - - -	3536 - - - - - -	3606 - - - - - -
3257 - - - - - -	3327 - - - - AUS	3397 - - KU 5488	3467 - - HP 9875	3537 - - - AUS	3607 - - - - - -
3258 - - - - - -	3328 - - - - - -	3398 - - - - - -	3468 - - - - - -	3538 - - - - - -	3608 - - - - - -
3259 - - - - - -	3329 - - - - - -	3399 - - - - - -	3469 - - XX 9278	3539 - - HH 2695	3609 - - - - - -
3260 - - HH 2404	3330 - - - - AUS	3400 - - MR 2991	3470 - - - - - -	3540 - - - - - -	3610 - - - AUS
3261 - - - - - -	3331 - - BR 3743	3401 - - RW 3874	3471 - - - - - -	3541 - - RW 3865	3611 - - - AUS
3262 - - MB 7012	3332 - - - - - -	3402 - - MB 7907	3472 - - - - - -	3542 - - - - - -	3612 - - MB 9577
3263 - - HP 9865	3333 - - - - - -	3403 - - NP 5613	3473 - - - - - -	3543 - - NL 9639	3613 - - KU 6645

No.	Reg.	No.	Reg.	No.	Reg.	No.	Reg.	No.	Reg.	No.	Reg.
3614		3684		3754	AUS	3824		3894		3964	TU 834
3615		3685	RW 2427	3755		3825		3895		3965	RW 3792
3616	NL	3686	RW 3879	3756		3826		3896	AUS	3966	
3617	FC 8740	3687		3757		3827		3897		3967	NL
3618	GB 9650	3688		3758	YL 6224	3828		3898	RW 5161	3968	
3619		3689		3759	TU 498	3829		3899	TU 1593	3969	TR 3669
3620	AUS	3690	AUS	3760		3830		3900		3970	
3621		3691	AUS	3761	YR 2992	3831	RM 2032	3901		3971	NZ
3622	RW 2426	3692		3762		3832		3902		3972	
3623		3693		3763		3833	DB 6390	3903		3973	GD 1315
3624		3694		3764	RM 1984	3834		3904		3974	AUS
3625	AUS	3695	RW 3867	3765		3835		3905		3975	MB 4931
3626		3696		3766		3836	YL 9560	3906		3976	TT 6660
3627		3697	AUS	3767	AUS	3837		3907	BR 4518	3977	AUS
3628		3698		3768		3838	NU 8114	3908		3978	AUS
3629		3699		3769	BR 4475	3839	BT 9031	3909	EM 1868	3979	AUS
3630		3700		3770	RW 3885	3840		3910	YM 990	3980	
3631		3701		3771	AUS	3841		3911		3981	
3632	NL	3702		3772		3842		3912	SM 5482	3982	TD 4462
3633		3703		3773		3843	RM 2083	3913		3983	
3634	AUS	3704	AUS	3774		3844	CO 9044	3914	UM 3208	3984	RW 4932
3635		3705		3775		3845		3915	RW 3888	3985	AUS
3636		3706		3776		3846		3916		3986	
3637		3707	RW 3873	3777		3847		3917	SB 2481	3987	
3638	AUS	3708	RW4926	3778		3848		3918		3988	
3639	RW 3871	3709		3779		3849		3919		3989	
3640		3710		3780	AUS	3850	DD 8366	3920		3990	TW 1226
3641		3711		3781	AUS	3851		3921		3991	GD 1314
3642	TR 698	3712	RW 3881	3782		3852		3922	Ceylon	3992	
3643	CX 7619	3713	YL 169	3783	TU 472	3853	PE 7330	3923		3993	
3644	AUS	3714		3784	TU 437	3854		3924	NL	3994	RR 42
3645	DN 8055	3715		3785	TU 437	3855		3925		3995	
3646		3716		3786	AUS	3856		3926		3996	
3647	AUS	3717		3787	DF 697	3857	RW 4928	3927	RW 4929	3997	KH 2396
3648		3718		3788		3858	AUS	3928		3998	
3649	AUS	3719		3789		3859	MB8333	3929		3999	
3650		3720	YL 6225	3790		3860	AUS	3930		4000	
3651		3721	GD 429	3791		3861		3931	RW 4927	4001	PE 8486
3652		3722	RM 1957	3792	AUS	3862	EN 2684	3932	RM 2123	4002	
3653		3723	AUS	3793	DH 4704	3863		3933		4003	
3654	NL 732	3724	KU 6573	3794	RW 3887	3864		3934		4004	
3655	RW 3872	3725		3795		3865		3935	AUS	4005	
3656		3726		3796	MR 5334	3866	FA 2355	3936	AUS	4006	GD 1463
3657		3727	RW 3882	3797		3867	TT 6237	3937		4007	
3658	RW 3868	3728		3798		3868	ER 4970	3938		4008	
3659		3729	RW 3884	3799		3869		3939	AUS	4009	
3660	KU 7759	3730		3800		3870	CA 8516	3940	AUS	4010	AUS
3661	NZ	3731		3801		3871		3941	NL	4011	NZ
3662	RW 3869	3732	RW 3883	3802	GD 433	3872		3942	AUS	4012	
3663		3733		3803		3873		3943	AUS	4013	AUS
3664		3734	RW 3886	3804	HH 2893	3874		3944		4014	
3665		3735		3805		3875		3945	RW 4930	4015	
3666		3736		3806		3876	KU 7476	3946	GD 990	4016	AUS
3667	RW 3880	3737		3807	RW 5101	3877		3947		4017	AUS
3668	AUS	3738		3808	DX 5638	3878		3948		4018	AUS
3669		3739		3809		3879	TW 879	3949	SF 3993	4019	
3670		3740		3810		3880		3950		4020	
3671	AUS	3741		3811		3881	RF 1254	3951		4021	YM 9785
3672	IK 8437	3742	NE 3249	3812		3882		3952		4022	
3673	RW 3878	3743		3813	UF 507	3883		3953		4023	
3674		3744		3814		3884	YL 8743	3954		4024	SM 5564
3675		3745		3815	FU 4914	3885		3955		4025	
3676	AUS	3746		3816		3886		3956		4026	
3677		3747		3817		3887		3957		4027	RW 4933
3678		3748		3818		3888		3958	BR 4575	4028	
3679	AUS	3749	AUS	3819	GD 432	3889	DN 8269	3959	AUS	4029	NE 4515
3680		3750	MB 8332	3820		3890		3960		4030	
3681	AUS	3751		3821	NE 3253	3891		3961		4031	
3682		3752		3822		3892	YM 998	3962		4032	RW 4934
3683		3753		3823	FY 8701	3893	MR 8931	3963		4033	

4034 - - - - - -	4104 - - RW 4938	4174 - - - - - -	4244 - - YO 4582	4314 - - - - - -	4384 - - - - - -
4035 - - - - - NZ	4105 - - - - - -	4175 - - - - - -	4245 - - - - - -	4315 - - GD 2416	4385 - - - - - -
4036 - - - - - -	4106 - - - - - -	4176 - - - - - -	4246 - - - - AUS	4316 - - - - - -	4386 - - - - - -
4037 - - - - - -	4107 - - - - - -	4177 - - - - - -	4247 - - - - AUS	4317 - - - - - -	4387 - - - - - -
4038 - - - - - -	4108 - - - - AUS	4178 - - TW 2524	4248 - - - - - -	4318 - - - - - -	4388 - - - - - -
4039 - - - - - -	4109 - - - - - -	4179 - - - - - -	4249 - - - - - -	4319 - - - - - -	4389 - - - - - -
4040 - - - - - -	4110 - - - - - -	4180 - - - - - -	4250 - - RW 4940	4320 - - - - - -	4390 - - - - - -
4041 - - - - - -	4111 - - GD 1647	4181 - - - - NL	4251 - - - - - -	4321 - - RW 7329	4391 - - - - - -
4042 - - - - - -	4112 - - - - - -	4182 - - - - - -	4252 - - - - - -	4322 - - - - - -	4392 - - - - - -
4043 - - - - - -	4113 - - FB 5104	4183 - - - - - -	4253 - - - - - -	4323 - - -DJ 2805	4393 - - - - - -
4044 - - - - - -	4114 - - - - - -	4184 - - KU 8370	4254 - - RW 4943	4324 - - - - - -	4394 - - - - - -
4045 - - - - - -	4115 - - - - - -	4185 - - KH 2532	4255 - - - - - -	4325 - - UM 4815	4395 - - - - - -
4046 - - - - - -	4116 - - - - - -	4186 - - - - - -	4256 - - GD 2413	4326 - - - - AUS	4396 - - - - AUS
4047 - - GD 1416	4117 - - - - - -	4187 - - - - - -	4257 - - - - - -	4327 - - - - - -	4397 - - - - - -
4048 - - - - NZ	4118 - - GD 1648	4188 - - - - - -	4258 - - - - - -	4328 - - RR 4208	4398 - - - - - -
4049 - - PT 7127	4119 - - - - - -	4189 - - - - - -	4259 - - GD 2414	4329 - - - - - -	4399 - - - - - -
4050 - - - - - -	4120 - - - - - -	4190 - - - - - -	4260 - - RW 4942	4330 - - - - - -	4400 - - - - - -
4051 - - - - - -	4121 - - - TY 847	4191 - - - - - -	4261 - - BR 5058	4331 - - RW 7328	4401 - - - - - -
4052 - - - - AUS	4122 - - - - - -	4192 - - - - AUS	4262 - - - - - -	4332 - - TD 6395	4402 - - - - - -
4053 - - DB 6446	4123 - - ET 3995	4193 - - PT 7270	4263 - - - - - -	4333 - - - - AUS	4403 - - - - - -
4054 - - - TY 732	4124 - - - - - -	4194 - - RW 4939	4264 - - - - - -	4334 - - TD 6394	4404 - - - - - -
4055 - - HH 3005	4125 - - - - AUS	4195 - - DB 6801	4265 - - ON 5940	4335 - - - - - -	4405 - - - - - -
4056 - - - - AUS	4126 - - - - - -	4196 - - - - - -	4266 - - - - - -	4336 - - RW 7332	4406 - - - - - -
4057 - - - - - -	4127 - - - - - -	4197 - - - - - -	4267 - - - - - -	4337 - - - - - -	4407 - - YO 8649
4058 - - - - - -	4128 - - - - - -	4198 - - RW 4944	4268 - - - - AUS	4338 - - - - - -	4408 - - - - - -
4059 - - KU 8657	4129 - - - - - -	4199 - - KM 5265	4269 - - - - - -	4339 - - - - - -	4409 - - - - - -
4060 - - - - - -	4130 - - RW 1469	4200 - - - - - -	4270 - - TD 6388	4340 - - - - - -	4410 - - TU 2638
4061 - - BN 9688	4131 - - - - - -	4201 - - - - - -	4271 - - - - - -	4341 - - YO 4599	4411 - - - - - -
4062 - - - - AUS	4132 - - - - NZ	4202 - - - - - -	4272 - - RP 2852	4342 - - RP 2852	4412 - - KS 3421
4063 - - GD 1546	4133 - - - - - -	4203 - - - - - -	4273 - - - - AUS	4343 - - - - - -	4413 - - - - - -
4064 - - KU 9604	4134 - - - - - -	4204 - - - - - -	4274 - - NU 9360	4344 - - HH 3238	4414 - - - - - -
4065 - - -FA 2410	4135 - - - - - -	4205 - - RM 2541	4275 - - - - AUS	4345 - - PT 7995	4415 - - CA 9283
4066 - - - - - -	4136 - - RW 4935	4206 - - - - - -	4276 - - - - - -	4346 - - - - - -	4416 - - - - - -
4067 - - - - - -	4137 - - - - - -	4207 - - DB 6686	4277 - - KM 4596	4347 - - TD 5895	4417 - - - - AUS
4068 - - - - - -	4138 - - - - - -	4208 - - - - - -	4278 - - - - - -	4348 - - RW 7331	4418 - - - - - -
4069 - - - - AUS	4139 - - - - - -	4209 - - RW 6673	4279 - - RD 2564	4349 - - - - - -	4419 - - - - AUS
4070 - - - - - -	4140 - - - - - -	4210 - - - - - -	4280 - - - - - -	4350 - - PT 7849	4420 - - - - - -
4071 - - - - AUS	4141 - - NP 7904	4211 - - - - - -	4281 - - KU 8746	4351 - - - - - -	4421 - - YR 2992
4072 - - - - - -	4142 - - - - - -	4212 - - - - - -	4282 - - - - - -	4352 - - - - - -	4422 - - - - AUS
4073 - - - - - -	4143 - - - - - -	4213 - - - - AUS	4283 - - - - - -	4353 - - - - AUS	4423 - - -SF 6550
4074 - - - - - -	4144 - - - - - -	4214 - - - - - -	4284 - - - - - -	4354 - - - - AUS	4424 - - - - - -
4075 - - - YN 803	4145 - - - - - -	4215 - - GD 2282	4285 - - - - AUS	4355 - - RW 7343	4425 - - YO 8042
4076 - - - - - -	4146 - - - - - -	4216 - - KU 8371	4286 - - - - - -	4356 - - - - - -	4426 - - - - - -
4077 - - - - - -	4147 - - - - - -	4217 - - - - - -	4287 - - - - - -	4357 - - - - - -	4427 - - - - - -
4078 - - - - NZ	4148 - - - - - -	4218 - - - - - -	4288 - - - - - -	4358 - - TD 6992	4428 - - GD 3088
4079 - - - - - -	4149 - - - - AUS	4219 - - - - - -	4289 - - CO 9783	4359 - - - - AUS	4429 - - YP 5021
4080 - - - - AUS	4150 - - TU 2033	4220 - - - - - -	4290 - - - - - -	4360 - - - - AUS	4430 - - RW 7333
4081 - - CH 5956	4151 - - GD 3269	4221 - - - - - -	4291 - - - - - -	4361 - - - - - -	4431 - - RW 8744
4082 - - RM 2381	4152 - - - - - -	4222 - - - - - -	4292 - - - - - -	4362 - - - - - -	4432 - - - - - -
4083 - - GD 1830	4153 - - - - - -	4223 - - - - - -	4293 - - - - - -	4363 - - TW 3090	4433 - - - - AUS
4084 - - DH 4916	4154 - - - - - -	4224 - - DD 9526	4294 - - - - - -	4364 - - - - - -	4434 - - YP 2116
4085 - - GD 1417	4155 - - - - - -	4225 - - - - - -	4295 - - TT 9632	4365 - - - - AUS	4435 - - - - AUS
4086 - - - - - -	4156 - - YN 5608	4226 - - - - - -	4296 - - GD 2574	4366 - - - - - -	4436 - - - - - -
4087 - - TT 7010	4157 - - - - - -	4227 - - RW 4941	4297 - - PR 6971	4367 - - - - - -	4437 - - - - AUS
4088 - - HH 3015	4158 - - CO 9545	4228 - - - - - -	4298 - - - - - -	4368 - - - - - -	4438 - - - - - -
4089 - - - - - -	4159 - - RW 4937	4229 - - - - AUS	4299 - - - - - -	4369 - - DD 9881	4439 - - - - - -
4090 - - TR 1853	4160 - - - - AUS	4230 - - GD 2571	4300 - - - - - -	4370 - - - - - -	4440 - - - - - -
4091 - - - - - -	4161 - - - - AUS	4231 - - - - - -	4301 - - - - - -	4371 - - GD 2935	4441 - - - - - -
4092 - - - - - -	4162 - - - - - -	4232 - - - - - -	4302 - - - - - -	4372 - - - - - -	4442 - - SR 5643
4093 - - - - NL	4163 - - - - AUS	4233 - - - - - -	4303 - - - - - -	4373 - - GD 3466	4443 - - - - - -
4094 - - FG 1123	4164 - - - - - -	4234 - - YN 9612	4304 - - YO 4586	4374 - - - - - -	4444 - - - - - -
4095 - - - - - -	4165 - - TT 7623	4235 - - - - AUS	4305 - - - - - -	4375 - - - - - -	4445 - - - - - -
4096 - - - - - -	4166 - - RW 4936	4236 - - YN 9610	4306 - - TT 8518	4376 - - - - - -	4446 - - OT 2106
4097 - - - - - -	4167 - - - - - -	4237 - - - - - -	4307 - - YO 6994	4377 - - - - ZA	4447 - - RW 7337
4098 - - - - - -	4168 - - BR 4775	4238 - - - - AUS	4308 - - MR 6766	4378 - - DN 8643	4448 - - - - - -
4099 - - - - - -	4169 - - ET 3961	4239 - - - - AUS	4309 - - - - - -	4379 - - - - - -	4449 - - - - - -
4100 - - RW 7326	4170 - - - - - -	4240 - - - - - -	4310 - - - - - -	4380 - - - - AUS	4450 - - - - - -
4101 - - - - - -	4171 - - TU 1986	4241 - - - - - -	4311 - - RW 7330	4381 - - - - - -	4451 - - - - - -
4102 - - MR 6082	4172 - - CX 9182	4242 - - - - - -	4312 - - - - - -	4382 - - - - - -	4452 - - - - - -
4103 - - - - - -	4173 - - - - - -	4243 - - - - - -	4313 - - - - - -	4383 - - - YO 622	4453 - - - - - -

No.	Reg	No.	Reg	No.	Reg	No.	Reg	No.	Reg	No.	Reg
4454		4524		4594		4664	CA 9617	4734	YR 9934	4804	
4455		4525	BN 9688	4595	RW 8746	4665		4735	MR 8316	4805	
4456	RW 7335	4526		4596		4666		4736		4806	
4457		4527	GD 4059	4597		4667		4737		4807	
4458	RW 7334	4528	RW 7342	4598	GD 4299	4668		4738	YR 7238	4808	
4459	GD 3465	4529		4599	GD 4590	4669		4739		4809	
4460	YP 5013	4530	CX 8520	4600		4670	DB 7442	4740		4810	
4461		4531	DR 929	4601		4671		4741		4811	PT 8752
4462		4532		4602	RA 651	4672		4742		4812	
4463		4533		4603		4673		4743		4813	
4464	RW 7339	4534		4604	SF 6699	4674		4744		4814	
4465	RM 2943	4535		4605	AUS	4675		4745		4815	
4466	OP 1383	4536	RW 7344	4606	AUS	4676		4746	HH 3461	4816	
4467	NR 9008	4537		4607		4677		4747		4817	
4468	DR 771	4538		4608		4678		4748		4818	
4469	MR 7826	4539		4609	RW 8743	4679		4749	DX 6078	4819	
4470		4540	RW 8739	4610		4680		4750		4820	WK 111
4471		4541	YP 7894	4611	TY 1897	4681	RW 8749	4751		4821	
4472		4542	KU 9724	4612		4682		4752		4822	
4473	GD 3468	4543	CA 9500	4613	YE 4560	4683	DR 987	4753	CA 9684	4823	
4474	GD 3843	4544	TW 5932	4614	CA 9616	4684		4754		4824	
4475	RM 2991	4545	NZ	4615		4685		4755		4825	RF 2693
4476	KM 7129	4546		4616	CM 6911	4686	CA 9660	4756	RW 9376	4826	
4477		4547		4617		4687		4757	UO 3934	4827	
4478	AUS	4548		4618	YX 6888	4688	DH 5540	4758	SU 2095	4828	
4479		4549		4619		4689	UO 227	4759	RW 8754	4829	
4480		4550		4620		4690	CX 9079	4760		4830	TD 8498
4481		4551		4621	RW 8750	4691	AUS	4761		4831	
4482		4552	RW 7341	4622		4692		4762		4832	CA 9817
4483		4553	AUS	4623		4693	SF 6891	4763		4833	WF 122
4484	RW 7338	4554	RW 8742	4624	MR 8047	4694	RW 8751	4764		4834	TX 2177
4485		4555		4625	NZ	4695		4765	WL 1398	4835	RW 9380
4486	TY 1895	4556		4626	KM 8429	4696		4766		4836	
4487	RW 7336	4557		4627	TY 2081	4697	UD 480	4767	GD 4594	4837	AUS
4488	GD 3842	4558	DX 6144	4628		4698		4768		4838	
4489		4559	AUS	4629		4699	RW 9375	4769	BR 5351	4839	RW 9378
4490		4560	AUS	4630	GD 4301	4700		4770	PT 8674	4840	RF 2635
4491		4561	OP 1383	4631		4701	ER 6912	4771		4841	
4492	NF 1094	4562		4632		4702	AUS	4772		4842	
4493		4563	GD 4297	4633	YR 4429	4703		4773		4843	AC 70
4494		4564		4634		4704		4774		4844	
4495		4565		4635		4705		4775	RM 3331	4845	
4496	RF 2127	4566		4636	DR 1100	4706	OT 3017	4776		4846	
4497		4567		4637	RW 8747	4707		4777		4847	RW 9379
4498		4568		4638		4708		4778	PR 7999	4848	RW 9377
4499		4569	TT 9818	4639		4709		4779	YP 9325	4849	
4500		4570		4640	OT 2744	4710	RW 9373	4780		4850	YE 4563
4501		4571		4641	RW 8745	4711		4781	GD 534	4851	HU 4563
4502		4572	PY 6077	4642		4712		4782	FU 6691	4852	HH 3513
4503		4573	YR 9318	4643		4713		4783	RL 5878	4853	
4504		4574	PY 6092	4644		4714		4784	NR 9917	4854	
4505		4575	RW 8738	4645		4715		4785	HD 3008	4855	FU 6759
4506	RW 7340	4576	YR 2872	4646	YR 2868	4716	HH 3444	4786	SR 5871	4856	
4507		4577		4647		4717		4787		4857	
4508		4578	GD 4300	4648		4718		4788	GD 991	4858	AUS
4509		4579		4649		4719	PF 5534	4789		4859	
4510	AUS	4580		4650		4720	RW 8753	4790		4860	KH 4045
4511	AUS	4581		4651	DH 5426	4721		4791		4861	
4512	AUS	4582		4652		4722		4792		4862	
4513	AUS	4583		4653		4723		4793	WM 47	4863	
4514		4584		4654		4724		4794		4864	ED 4435
4515		4585		4655	KA 5281	4725	RW 9852	4795	RP 4485	4865	
4516	YP 7880	4586	DH 5417	4656	RW 8748	4726	RW 9374	4796	RP 3552	4866	
4517		4587		4657		4727	RW 9383	4797		4867	UH 2203
4518		4588	DF 858	4658	NH 7276	4728		4798		4868	AUS
4519		4589		4659		4729	AUS	4799		4869	
4520		4590		4660		4730	AUS	4800		4870	WK 123
4521	AUS	4591		4661		4731	AUS	4801	TD 8257	4871	
4522	AUS	4592	TD 7753	4662		4732		4802		4872	
4523	SM 5971	4593		4663	PF 5573	4733	RW 8755	4803		4873	GD 5127

4874 - - GD 9148	4890 - - RW 9381	4906 - - - - - -
4875 - - - - - -	4891 - - - - - -	4907 - - - - - -
4876 - - - - AUS	4892 - - - - - -	4908 - - - - - -
4877 - - - - - -	4893 - - - - - -	4909 - - RW 9382
4878 - - HH 3564	4894 - - - - - -	4910 - - - - - -
4879 - - - - - ZA	4895 - - SM 6162	4911 - - - - - -
4880 - - - - - -	4896 - - - - - -	4912 - - - - - -
4881 - - - - - -	4897 - - - - - -	4913 - - - - - -
4882 - - - - - -	4898 - - - - - -	4914 - - - - AUS
4883 - - - - - -	4899 - - - - - -	4915 - - - - - -
4884 - - SM 6161	4900 - - - - - -	4916 - - KH 3972
4885 - - - - - -	4901 - - -SF 8054	4917 - - YE 4541
4886 - - - - - -	4902 - - - - - -	4918 - - - - - -
4887 - - - - - -	4903 - - TR 3245	4919 - - - - - -
4888 - - - - - -	4904 - - - - - -	
4889 - - - - - -	4905 - - - - - -	

2091 seen here with long-time owner Jack Linnell. (Courtesy Alvis Archive Trust)

The appearance of the first production overhead-valve car at chassis 2088 marks the beginning of a new and most successful era. The 12/50, as it would be known, would become one of Britain's best known and most popular light cars, and would appear in eight forms during the period mentioned above. It soon earned a reputation for sturdiness and reliability, which is reflected in the sales figures quoted earlier. Competition events, as ever, played a significant part in this, with London agent Henly's organising a number of events, particularly at Brooklands.

The side-valve cars, however, remained in demand for some time, with the final TC being built in March 1925, and the final TD in October of the same year.

1925 was also the year when the company's first experiments with the front-wheel drive system came to the fore, using a 12/50 engine turned round in a 'sprint' chassis, with spectacular results.

Exports, especially to Australia and New Zealand, gathered momentum at this time, whilst significant numbers would also find a niche market in The Netherlands.

2124: A fine example of one of the few remaining 12/40 models. The TD 21 in the background is 27001. (Courtesy Alvis Archive Trust)

2091
2206
2207
Competition cars
Designated as Racing Cars No 1, No 2, and No 3 in works records, this must be assumed to be for the 1923 season, as there were earlier works cars of the type. Of these, 2091 is easily the best known, being the winner of the Brooklands 200-mile race, driven by Major Harvey. In 1924, it was bought by A J Linnell, who kept it until his death in 1983, whereupon it was taken over by his friend Robert Wicksteed of the 147-acre Wicksteed Park at Kettering – the historic leisure complex founded by

Unitarian minister Charles Wicksteed (1810-1885). The other two cars have not survived and were probably scrapped or recycled.

Robert Wicksteed also owned a Speed 25 model (qv 14488).

2346 NU 2148
William Boddy
The long-time editor of *Motor Sport* has, on numerous occasions, referred to his occasional Alvis ownership in his columns. However, his most detailed account of this actually appeared as a contribution to *Autocar* in the issue of March 7, 1952, pages 304 and 305, being No 346 in its *Talking of Sports Cars* series. An especially useful

account, containing as it does, a number of 12/50 maintenance tips.

2556   ER 1987
Betty Haig

Betty Lindsey-Haig (1906-April 30, 1987) was a great-niece of field marshal Earl Haig KG, GCB, OM, and one of the most successful women drivers of all time. For an account of her life and cars, look no further than William Boddy's interview with her in the January 1965 issue of *Motor Sport*, pages 28 to 35. Well over 60 cars (mostly campaigned) had been owned by then. Too numerous to quote in full, however, but highlights must include her Singer (the only car to have been awarded an Olympic gold medal back in 1936) and her Ferrari drive with Mme Simon at Le Mans in 1951, finishing 15th overall. Also, in 1951 she had bought the 2556 above and painstakingly restored it.

(See text)   XR 6979
Competition car

A young man by the name of Paul Baddeley once wrote how, having the ambition to compete in a national trial, he borrowed £50 from his mother, purchased, early in 1926, a grey and black 12/50 sports (1924) from Henly's London stock, for £250. An entry was duly made for the MCC London-Land's End Trial, with his younger brother as navigator. There were no fewer than 15 Alvis-driving competitors in this event, including the notable W Urquhart-Dykes, whose time up the Porlock Hill section Paul managed to better by just over a minute. Five of the 15 Alvis were successful in obtaining a gold medal, including Paul, who was justifiably well pleased with his first competition appearance. As to the actual car, there were three grey, and one grey/black 12/50 tourers allocated to Henly's at about the time of the issue of the known registration mark. The writer's apportionment of the car at this point in the sequence is, of necessity, approximate.

2571   XX 7194
Movie car

2571 starred alongside Peter O'Toole and Petula Clark in the 1969 remake of the popular story *Goodbye Mr Chips*. Robert Donat and Greer Garson had been the 'role' models in the original version of 1939.

2571: As featured in the movie *Goodbye Mr Chips* and driven by Petula Clark, who has also been photographed with a much later Alvis (qv 25120). (Courtesy Metro-Goldwyn-Mayer and Alvis Archive Trust)

2852   XU 362
L T C Rolt

It would be difficult indeed, if not impossible, to find examples where any nation has had aspects of its engineering history researched and expounded in as comprehensive a way as was done by Lionel Thomas Caswell Rolt (February 11, 1910-May 9, 1974. In his comparatively short lifetime, a canon of some forty books – some histories, some biographies, some travelogues – would explore facets of British industry which up to then had been largely overlooked. His accounts of the lives of Brunel and of Newcomen most readily spring to mind, as does his championing of the return to use of the nation's inland waterways. Cars were but a small fraction of his interests, and he will forever be associated with his two Alvis cars, the earlier (above) being bought second-hand, and the later (qv 3850) having been purchased new by his father.

2929   RW 1

2930   RW 13

2931   RW 12
Works competition cars

The history of the 1924 team cars is quite well

documented. After the notable Brooklands 200-mile race appearances, 2929 was sold, being collected from the factory by P G (Phil) Garlick, and taken to Australia for racing events. Tragically, Garlick lost his life in it during an accident at Maroubra in 1927. The car was rebuilt, using first a Hudson, then a Mercury engine, but is being put back to 'standard.' 2930, the single seater of the trio was used by Harvey and Miller to take some under 1500cc records at Brooklands, whilst 2931 was allocated first to Dunlop's for tyre testing purposes. Later raced by a number of individuals (and re-registered as NF 7788 in September 1927), this is the only one of the three to survive in largely original form.

HP 8835

2978
Movie car
Henry Alfred Kenneth Russell (July 3, 1927 to November 27, 2011), mostly known just as 'Ken,' was a most versatile and sometimes flamboyant film director. One of his specialities was covering the lives of the great composers, resulting in a series of five: Elgar, Delius, Tchaikovsky, Mahler and Liszt. It was in the filming of the Elgar topic, which took place in Worcestershire in 1962, that the locally domiciled Alvis 2978 came to be used, giving rise to the speculation that Sir Edward Elgar had owned such a car. Exhaustive searches of the county registration records have not produced evidence of this, but an extant photograph suggests that he favoured the slightly more local Wolseley at that time.

HP 8849

3012
Iliffe Publications Ltd
The above is the later of three suitably liveried newspaper delivery vans for Iliffe's *Midland Daily Telegraph*, all bodied locally by Robinsons (qv 1720 and 1721 for the earlier).

Four years later, a fourth van would be ordered, this time based on a TG 12/50 chassis (qv 6791).

HP 8841

3068
C C Wakefield & Co Ltd
Maker of that much-lauded lubricant Castrol, Wakefield featured an Alvis in its 1932 advertising, appearing in *Motor*, *Autocar*, and *Light Car* in the spring of that year. It quotes a letter from owner W P Stone, to Alvis Ltd, attributing the 99,500 miles covered by his two-seater, then approaching eight years old without ever having the head removed – to the use of the recommended Castrol XL. Subsequent research has established that Mr Stone's car had been 3068 – a works-supplied SA 12/50.

3085
Ambrose Shardlow Ltd
The Sheffield-based forgemaster, who made crankshafts by the million for the motor industry under the 'Ambrosia' trade name, would replace this TE 12/50 with an early example of new six-cylinder 14.75hp model in due course (qv 5905), and later still, replace that with a 16.95hp Silver Eagle TB (qv 8423). Probably the very first Shardlow-supplied Alvis, however, was 1687, back in March 1923.

HP 9863

3194
R M V Sutton
Engineer and racing driver Roland Manners Verney Sutton was born in December 1895 and was educated at Harrow. He was a cousin of the ninth Duke of Rutland and first became interested in Alvis after following Major Harvey's exploits in the 200-mile race car, and duly bought an example of the new 12/50 sports from the stand at the 1923 Olympia Show (car unidentified but circa 2250). This was campaigned with some success, sometimes with works support, and led to the purchase of another, being the 3194 above. After a spell, when he would occasionally join the works team, Sutton took a position as tester at Lea-Francis, which was only one of many significant jobs held within the motor industry. By 1948 he had joined Jaguar as a tester, and will probably be best remembered for the record-breaking run of 132.6mph of May 30, 1949 in the new XK120. Known to colleagues as 'Soapy,' he penned an account of his fascinating career in the *Motor Sport* issue of November 1956, pages 696-702. Written with consummate professionalism, erudition, and humour, it is a story well worth reading. After the employment of Jaguar, Sutton returned to Alvis as tester on the fighting vehicles series FV 601 et seq, and remained there until his death in 1957, at the age of 62.

NP 5613

3403
C C W Dyson Perrins FRAS
Full details recorded with the next Perrins Alvis car (qv 7960).

4013 still on its New South Wales plates after the epic drive from Australia. Here is Rob and Ann Gunnell's 'old smokey': Crystal Palace 1961. (Courtesy the late Peter Cameron-Clarke collection)

3537 OSU 629
Competition car
One of six standard-bodied 12/50 cars shipped to Australia in May 1925, 3537 underwent substantial changes in the postwar years, mostly done by Alan Griffin. The chassis was shortened, and the bore increased to 72mm. It is known in competition circles as the MacJob special, and was shipped back to England in the 1980s, and campaigned by P Owen and J Campbell. It was allocated the anachronistic mark 'OSU 629' upon re-importation, which DVLA deem age-related, though the first authentic three letter mark would not appear until October 1932.

3720 YL 6225
Movie car
This car's chief claim to fame is that it starred in the 1948 Ealing Studios' *Another Shore* alongside Robert Beatty, Moira Lister, Stanley Holloway, and Wilfred Brambell (he of Steptoe & Sons fame). An interesting account of events both during and after filming may be found in Bill Boddy's *Vintage Veerings* in the *Motor Sport* issue of January 1950, page 13. 3720 can also lay claim to competition car status, being accorded, in 1959, the VSCC 1500 Trophy for the best performance by a 1.5-litre car in that year's events, ably campaigned by Julian Berrisford.

3850 DD 8366
L T C Rolt

Revered writer and engineer Rolt is particularly associated with two Alvis cars. 3850 is the later. For further details see 2852.

4013 7885 RW
Rob Gunnell
A particularly significant and ambitious Alvis journey was that undertaken by Australian Rob Gunnell and his wife Ann, driving from Bombay to London over 1960/1961. This honeymoon holiday in a car that had cost £12, took them through India, the Khyber Pass, Afghanistan, Turkey, Greece, Spain and Finland, finally clocking up some 29,000 miles. Rob, an industrial radiographer by profession, sought employment in the Midlands for a while, in order to finance the somewhat less adventurous shipping back to Australia. This had necessitated 'Old Smokey' being registered in England for a while. Thus, the mark '7885 RW' was allocated (perfect for a TD 21, but anachronistic for a 12/50 unless reversed, as RW **** was indeed current when 4013 was new).

4039
Shiell Racing
4039 left the factory in standard form for the Belfast agent Stanley Motors, in February 1926, but it was not until three months later that the car was reported sold, annotated 'for racing' to A Shiell. The extent of this racing has not yet come to light.

4081 CH 5956
Paul Redfern and Fred Basnett
One of the best-recorded epic Alvis journeys is that undertaken in 1961 by the pair above. The first leg was the shipment from Tilbury to Gothenburg, and thence to Trondheim, Narvik, Helsinki and Leningrad. On the way from there to Moscow, some time was lost when replacing a broken connecting rod. Russian red tape also intervened, necessitating a freight train passage between Tbilisi and Azerbaijan, before returning to London via Iran, Turkey, Bulgaria and Yugoslavia, and France. It is related that on the day of return to the same London pub where the journey had started, some low-life stole the hare mascot. This memorable trip is more than adequately chronicled in the book *Travels of a Capitalist Lackey*, published in 1965 by Allen & Unwin, and later by The Companion Book Club. It is an entertaining read, not just for

4081: Immortalised on the cover of Fred Basnett's remarkable travelogue.

4321: Miss E V Watson in action at Shelsley Walsh hillclimb. (Courtesy Alvis Archive Trust)

the motoring, but for the political commentary. The late Lord Montagu is especially deserving of mention, since it was he who loaned the car.

4194   RW 4939
6th Earl of Cottenham
Alvis racing driver Mark Pepys owned a number of Alvis cars. 4194 would be followed by a 12/50 TG (qv 4250) and a Speed 25 (qv 14457 for bio).

4321   RW 7329
Competition car
Miss E V Watson was a well-known driver in competitions during the 1920s, and was particularly successful with this car in the Shelsley Walsh events of 1926 and 1927. She would later obtain another works-registered Alvis (qv 6864).

4369   DD 9881
Sprung wheel experiments
The concept of a sprung (sometimes known as

a resilient) wheel goes back at least 1827, and possibly even to Leonardo. Basically, it was an attempt to increase adhesion at the tyre tread by allowing the road wheel to fractionally depart from its normal circular pattern. Numerous firms and individuals have toyed with the concept, and one such saw a design produced by the North British Company, using the 12/50 TE as a test bed. A works record for this car is annotated 'axles damaged,' perhaps unsurprisingly in the circumstances.

4421   YR 2992
Denis Knowles
One of several Alvis cars owned by Denis Knowles (1895-1979), a much travelled Alvis enthusiast (qv 7909 for details).

4423   SF 6550
Movie car
At one time a very familiar car on the Scottish motoring scene, 4423 has appeared in that well-remembered series *Dr Finlay's Casebook*, particularly the episode entitled 'Kate and Robert,' where it was driven by its intrepid owner Pop Brown (A W Brown MBE).

4433
Steve Denner
4433 was originally shipped to Australia as a

4423: Patinated, but still very much in use, this star of the small screen is seen here on a Scottish competition outing. (Courtesy Alvis Archive Trust)

chassis and bodied there. By 1973 it had become dilapidated. Steve Denner then bought it and shipped it back to England for restoration to be completed. In November 1977 he began a 10,000-mile drive back to Australia, arriving just in time for the 1978 FIVA Rally in NSW and Queensland. The route taken went through Luxembourg, Germany, Austria, Hungary, Romania, Turkey, Iran, Pakistan and India. There were sea passages between Madras and Penang, and between Kuala Lumpur and Fremantle. Melbourne was reached on February 2. A truly epic drive, with no serious fault developing, in a car which was then over 50 years old.

4434 — YP 2116
Bulmers Cider Ltd
The Hereford-based maker of the nationally popular libation purchased this TE 12/50 second-hand in July 1927. It must have proved satisfactory, as at least two other Alvis cars would follow, a Silver Eagle (qv 12628) and a TD 21 Series II (qv 26876).

4497 — RF 2127
Iliffe Publications Ltd
Autocar issue of February 13, 1931, page 302, has a photograph of 4497 competing in that year's Colmore Trial, with driver Price of Stourbridge.

4540 — RW 8739
Viscount Hinchingbrooke
Alexander Victor Edward Paulet Montagu (May 22, 1906-February 25, 1995) was educated at Eton

and Trinity College Cambridge, and served in the Northamptonshire Regiment. He sat as MP for the South Dorset constituency between 1941 and 1962, and was seen as a reforming politician. However, he had to relinquish the seat upon inheriting a peerage, but later disclaimed that when new legislation made it possible.

4556
A E Dobell
Fuller details of this most interesting Alvis owner will be found later (qv 8223), when listing his well-documented Silver Eagle. 4556, a 12/50, preceded this by some years and may have been purchased second-hand. The registration number remains to be identified, but given the location of the supplying dealer, was most probably in Cheshire's 'TU' series.

4618 — YX 6888
Phillip Runciman
Phillip Runciman (1875-June 6, 1953) was a shipping magnate, probably best known for his management of Anchor Line. A serial Alvis owner (4618 was probably the first), he enjoyed competing with them, and was a friend of racing driver and Alvis agent Charles Follett. For details of the other known Runciman cars see 5752, 7727, 8845, and 9548 for a bio. A well-known figure in his day, there is an image of Runciman in the National Portrait Gallery.

4709
Rosewarne family
4709 is just one of this prominent Cornish family's considerable sequence of Alvis cars (qv 6776, 7349, 10687, 13309, 13390 for bio, 14457, and 23987).

4719 — PF 5534
Major-General Sir Edward Northey
Sir Edward would replace 4719, bought second-hand in January 1930, with a new Crested Eagle (qv 13753 for biography).

4758 — SU 2095
Iliffe Publications Ltd
In 1930, weekly magazine *Autocar* commenced a series aimed at the used car buyer, and specifically looking at three-year-old vehicles. The very first

Works driver Bill Urquhart-Dykes, with, inset, the logo of his patent attorney company, Urquhart-Dykes & Lord. (Courtesy Alvis Ltd)

4793: With Ruth Urquhart-Dykes at Brooklands 1927. (Courtesy Alvis Archive Trust)

of this series, in the issue of April 4, took 4758 as its starting point – a car borrowed from Henly's London stock, though originating in Glasgow when it was new.

4793

WM 47

Competition car

Most vintage cars have ups and downs in their fortunes, and a noteworthy example of this is the story of 4793, rejected by its first owner in Southport and returned to the factory because of its alleged lack of 'go.' There, it was seen by Bill and Ruth Urquhart-Dykes, accomplished amateur competition drivers with a number of makes, and already owners of a much-campaigned 12/50 two-seater, with registration number MF 4557 (chassis no circa 2250). It was duly bought, and within a matter of weeks had formed part of the victorious Alvis team in the 1927 Brooklands six-hour race (Essex Motor Club). The dust had hardly settled on this event when, at Henly's Alvis Day, again at Brooklands, Ruth took 4793 to victory in the three-lap scratch race at a speed of 83mph. There would be many other successes, too numerous to mention in this limited space, but for further reading these

are chronicled in great detail within William Boddy's *History of the Brooklands Motor Course*, and Hull and Johnson's *The Vintage Alvis*.

4859
Edwin Richard Foden

Edwin Foden: a lorry magnate, and serial Alvis owner (qv 13641 for bio, and 14676).

4891
Professor Norman Dott

Professor Dott: a distinguished neurosurgeon and serial Alvis owner (qv 11923 and 14810 for bio).

4920-6000

February 1927 to March 1928
1080 cars

Consisting of models:

TG	790
TA	207
SD	75
TH	6
Undeclared	2

Consisting of coachbuilders:

Cross & Ellis	539
Carbodies	505

Albany	13
Other	
(Chassis-only deliveries)	
Mostly undeclared but including	
one each from Egerton, Martin Walter	23

Chassis	Reg
4920	- - WK 122
4921	- - - - - -
4922	- - - - - -
4923	- - - - - -
4924	- - - - - -
4925	- - PY 6419
4926	- - TD 8666
4927	- - - - - -
4928	- - - - - -
4929	- - - - - -
4930	- - - - - -
4931	- - - - - -
4932	- - OP 3290
4933	- - - WO 82
4934	- - - - - -
4935	- - - UT 249
4936	- - - - - -
4937	- - UO 1125
4938	- - KW 627
4939	- - - - - -
4940	- - GD 5554
4941	- - - - - -
4942	- - - - - -
4943	- - - - - -
4944	- - SN 3921
4945	- - - - - -
4946	- - - - - -
4947	- - - - - -
4948	- - - - - -
4949	- - - - - -
4950	- - - - AUS
4951	- - - - AUS
4952	- - - - - -
4953	- - RM 3507
4954	- - GD 5556
4955	- - - - - -
4956	- - DH 5637
4957	- - RP 3671
4958	- - - - - -
4959	- - WW 224
4960	- - BA 6474
4961	- - - - - -
4962	- - - - - -
4963	- - YE 4109
4964	- - KH 5523
4965	- - - - - -
4966	- - - - - -
4967	- - - - - -
4968	- - - - - -
4969	- - - - - -
4970	- - WO 185
4971	- - - - - -
4972	- - - - - -
4973	- - ET 4522
4974	- - TR 3223
4975	- - - - - -
4976	- - - - - -
4977	- - WK 128
4978	- - RW 9384
4979	- - GD 5948

Chassis	Reg
4980	- - WK 124
4981	- - - - - -
4982	- - - - - -
4983	- - - - - -
4984	- - - - - -
4985	- - - - - -
4986	- - - - - -
4987	- - HS 4585
4988	- - RP 3862
4989	- - - - - -
4990	- - WK 129
4991	- - - - - -
4992	- - - - - -
4993	- - - - - -
4994	- - WK 125
4995	- - - - - -
4996	- - HH 3614
4997	- - TD 9031
4998	- - WK 877
4999	- - - - - -
5000	- - - - AUS
5001	- - - - - -
5002	- - - - - -
5003	- - KW 824
5004	- - - - - -
5005	- - - - - -
5006	- - WK 1141
5007	- - MR 8941
5008	- - - - - -
5009	- - - - - -
5010	- - - - - -
5011	- - - - - -
5012	- - - - - -
5013	- - TU 4634
5014	- - YE 8743
5015	- - - - - -
5016	- - - - - -
5017	- - - - - -
5018	- - TW 7670
5019	- - - - - -
5020	- - GD 5946
5021	- - CY 9876
5022	- - - - - -
5023	- - - - - -
5024	- - KW 646
5025	- - GD 5740
5026	- - MR 8951
5027	- - EE 7016
5028	- - GD 5945
5029	- - - - - -
5030	- - - - - -
5031	- - - - - -
5032	- - - - - -
5033	- - RU 4926
5034	- - NF 4154
5035	- - - - - -
5036	- - RU 5040
5037	- - - - - -
5038	- - - - - -
5039	- - - - - -
5040	- - - - - -

Chassis	Reg
5041	- - WK 127
5042	- - - - - -
5043	- - - - - -
5044	- - - - - -
5045	- - - - - -
5046	- - - - - -
5047	- - WK 131
5048	- - - - - -
5049	- - GD 5744
5050	- - - - - -
5051	- - - **6413
5052	- - - - - -
5053	- - - - - -
5054	- - - - - -
5055	- - WK 126
5056	- - ML 2685
5057	- - OP 5694
5058	- - BR 5611
5059	- - TD 9538
5060	- - - - - -
5061	- - GD 5742
5062	- - KW 940
5063	- - - - - -
5064	- - - - - -
5065	- - CP 5584
5066	- - - - - -
5067	- - - - - -
5068	- - - - - -
5069	- - - - - -
5070	- - - - - -
5071	- - - - - -
5072	- - - - - -
5073	- - - - - -
5074	- - - - - -
5075	- - RP 4034
5076	- - KW 823
5077	- - GD 5741
5078	- - GD 5949
5079	- - - - - -
5080	- - PT 9298
5081	- - UE 3471
5082	- - RM 3714
5083	- - - - - -
5084	- - RL 5437
5085	- - - - - -
5086	- - VS 1283
5087	- - WK 677
5088	- - - - - -
5089	- - - - - -
5090	- - MR 9124
5091	- - FB 5959
5092	- - - - - -
5093	- - - - - -
5094	- - OU 3931
5095	- - - - - -
5096	- - - - - -
5097	- - - - - -
5098	- - - - - -
5099	- - - SF 8005
5100	- - EE 7083
5101	- - DB 7757

Chassis	Reg
5102	- - - - - -
5103	- - - - - -
5104	- - WK 132
5105	- - GD 5950
5106	- - KW 938
5107	- - - - - -
5108	- - RY 4479
5109	- - - - - -
5110	- - KO 1745
5111	- - - - - -
5112	- - WK 142
5113	- - - - - -
5114	- - - - - -
5115	- - OP 6779
5116	- - - - - -
5117	- - EN 3251
5118	- - - - - -
5119	- - - - - -
5120	- - - - - -
5121	- - - - - -
5122	- - PT 9386
5123	- - - - - -
5124	- - - - - -
5125	- - - - - -
5126	- - - SF 9367
5127	- - - FA 2898
5128	- - WK 1203
5129	- - KW 1783
5130	- - GD 6771
5131	- - WK 1144
5132	- - - - AUS
5133	- - - - - -
5134	- - - - - -
5135	- - - UT 811
5136	- - - - - -
5137	- - - - - -
5138	- - - - - -
5139	- - TD 9637
5140	- - NF 4156
5141	- - WN 410
5142	- - GD 6776
5143	- - - - - -
5144	- - - - - -
5145	- - - - - -
5146	- - - - - -
5147	- - - - - -
5148	- - - - - -
5149	- - - - AUS
5150	- - GD 7599
5151	- - - - AUS
5152	- - SH 2798
5153	- - - - - -
5154	- - - - - -
5155	- - - - - -
5156	- - GD 6485
5157	- - TU 5206
5158	- - - - - -
5159	- - - - - -
5160	- - BR 5674
5161	- - - - - -
5162	- - - - - -
5163	- - - - - -
5164	- - - - - -
5165	- - TY 2437
5166	- - TW 5371
5167	- - - - - -
5168	- - - - - -
5169	- - - - - -
5170	- - - - - -
5171	- - WK 1145

Chassis	Reg
5172	- - WK 1147
5173	- - FR 8098
5174	- - BR 5802
5175	- - - - - -
5176	- - - - - -
5177	- - - - - -
5178	- - SR 6176
5179	- - KW 1271
5180	- - - - - -
5181	- - - - - -
5182	- - GD 6488
5183	- - - - - -
5184	- - - - - -
5185	- - - - - -
5186	- - - - - -
5187	- - - - - -
5188	- - GD 6876
5189	- - - - - -
5190	- - - - - -
5191	- - PP 8189
5192	- - WK 1149
5193	- - - - - -
5194	- - - - - -
5195	- - - - - -
5196	- - - - - -
5197	- - NF 6196
5198	- - WK 1143
5199	- - GD 6877
5200	- - - - - -
5201	- - - - - -
5202	- - GD 7061
5203	- - - - - -
5204	- - - - - -
5205	- - KW 2248
5206	- - - - - -
5207	- - PR 8803
5208	- - - - - -
5209	- - - - - -
5210	- - - - - -
5211	- - - - - -
5212	- - - - - -
5213	- - - - - -
5214	- - - - - -
5215	- - WK 1938
5216	- - - - - -
5217	- - - - - -
5218	- - - - - -
5219	- - WK 1151
5220	- - - - - -
5221	- - WK 2441
5222	- - - - - -
5223	- - TW 6000
5224	- - - - - -
5225	- - - - - -
5226	- - GD 6878
5227	- - - - - -
5228	- - YF 7640
5229	- - OT 4800
5230	- - - DT 318
5231	- - - - - -
5232	- - DF 2615
5233	- - - - - -
5234	- - - - - -
5235	- - WK 1148
5236	- - - - - -
5237	- - - - - -
5238	- - - - - -
5239	- - - - - -
5240	- - - - YF 3
5241	- - - - - -

Chassis	Reg
5242	- - - - - -
5243	- - - - - -
5244	- - - - - -
5245	- - CF 7634
5246	- - - - - -
5247	- - - - - -
5248	- - - - - -
5249	- - - - - -
5250	- - - WF 649
5251	- - - - - -
5252	- - GD 7062
5253	- - - - - -
5254	- - - - - -
5255	- - - - - -
5256	- - UF 2093
5257	- - - - - -
5258	- - - - - NL
5259	- - - - - -
5260	- - - - - -
5261	- - PY 7191
5262	- - - - - -
5263	- - - - - -
5264	- - - - - -
5265	- - - - - -
5266	- - - - - -
5267	- - BR 5764
5268	- - - - - -
5269	- - CY 9977
5270	- - TU 5559
5271	- - KW 2036
5272	- - - - - -
5273	- - - - - -
5274	- - - - - -
5275	- - - - - -
5276	- - NF 5996
5277	- - - - - -
5278	- - NF 5143
5279	- - WL 3213
5280	- - - - - -
5281	- - - - - -
5282	- - - - - -
5283	- - NF 6166
5284	- - - HW 76
5285	- - - - - -
5286	- - WK 1150
5287	- - - - - -
5288	- - - - - -
5289	- - WK 1152
5290	- - MR 9818
5291	- - - - - -
5292	- - TY 3028
5293	- - MR 9801
5294	- - - - - -
5295	- - KH 4960
5296	- - - - - -
5297	- - - - - -
5298	- - - - - -
5299	- - - - - -
5300	- - - - - -
5301	- - - - - -
5302	- - - WN 30
5303	- - TR 4296
5304	- - - - - -
5305	- - - TE 379
5306	- - - - - -
5307	- - - - - -
5308	- - YH 6339
5309	- - - - - -
5310	- - - - - -
5311	- - - - - -

No.	Code	No.	Code	No.	Code	No.	Code	No.	Code	No.	Code
5312	- - GD 7530	5382	- - WM 862	5452	- - UO 3646	5522	- - UC 6631	5592	- - GD 8279	5662	- - UO 4284
5313	- - WM 859	5383	- - WK 2442	5453	- - - - - -	5523	- - YT 8753	5593	- - - - - -	5663	- - - - - -
5314	- - WK 2449	5384	- - KS 3788	5454	- - KW 2186	5524	- - OX 1671	5594	- - VS 1321	5664	- - TR 5516
5315	- - - - - -	5385	- - - AUS	5455	- - - - - -	5525	- - - - - -	5595	- - GD 8280	5665	- - - - - -
5316	- - - - - -	5386	- - - - - -	5456	- - - - - -	5526	- - - - - -	5596	- - - - - -	5666	- - - - - -
5317	- - - - - -	5387	- - GD 7066	5457	- - WK 3177	5527	- - WK 3176	5597	- - - - - -	5667	- - - - - -
5318	- - UO 2978	5388	- - - - - -	5458	- - - - - -	5528	- - - - AUS	5598	- - - - - -	5668	- - SC 1216
5319	- - GD 7301	5389	- - TR 3996	5459	- - YT 4667	5529	- - KW 2423	5599	- - WK 3533	5669	- - KW 2583
5320	- - - - - -	5390	- - NF 6792	5460	- - - - - -	5530	- - - - - -	5600	- - - - - -	5670	- - - - - -
5321	- - - - - -	5391	- - - - - -	5461	- - TE 1392	5531	- - VS 1326	5601	- - - - - -	5671	- - - - - -
5322	- - - - - -	5392	- - - - - -	5462	- - FR 9025	5532	- - YT 8742	5602	- - - - - -	5672	- - - - - -
5323	- - - - - -	5393	- - - - - -	5463	- - - - - -	5533	- - GD 7990	5603	- - - - - -	5673	- - TU 7069
5324	- - GD 7598	5394	- - - - - -	5464	- - - - - -	5534	- - UO 3971	5604	- - - - - -	5674	- - - - - -
5325	- - - - - -	5395	- - - - - -	5465	- - - - - -	5535	- - TU 6583	5605	- - - - - -	5675	- - - - - -
5326	- - - - - -	5396	- - - - - -	5466	- - - - - -	5536	- - - - - -	5606	- - UY 1825	5676	- - - - - -
5327	- - BR 5823	5397	- - - YT 428	5467	- - - - - -	5537	- - - - - -	5607	- - - - - -	5677	- - - - - -
5328	- - - - - -	5398	- - - - - -	5468	- - RF 3552	5538	- - GD 7993	5608	- - WK 3196	5678	- - - - - -
5329	- - - - - -	5399	- - - - - -	5469	- - - - - -	5539	- - - - - -	5609	- - - - - -	5679	- - FG 3522
5330	- - GD 7304	5400	- - - - - -	5470	- - - - - -	5540	- - - - - -	5610	- - - - - -	5680	- - - - - -
5331	- - BR 5840	5401	- - - - - -	5471	- - GD 7988	5541	- - YT 7393	5611	- -WM 1370	5681	- - - - - -
5332	- - WK 2443	5402	- - GD 7600	5472	- - - - - -	5542	- - - - - -	5612	- - SC 1651	5682	- - WK 3569
5333	- - - - - -	5403	- - - - - -	5473	- - WK 3180	5543	- - - - - -	5613	- - - - - -	5683	- - WL 3210
5334	- - - - - -	5404	- - - - - -	5474	- - - - - -	5544	- - - - - -	5614	- - - - - -	5684	- - KW 2737
5335	- - - - - -	5405	- - - - - -	5475	- - - - - -	5545	- - - - - -	5615	- - - - - -	5685	- - - - - -
5336	- - - - - -	5406	- - - - - -	5476	- - - - - -	5546	- - - - - -	5616	- - NF 7791	5686	- - RP 7046
5337	- - BA 6627	5407	- - - - - -	5477	- - - - - -	5547	- - - - - -	5617	- - - - - -	5687	- - GD 8495
5338	- - WK 2452	5408	- - - - - -	5478	- - YT 4672	5548	- - YU 2867	5618	- - - - - -	5688	- - - - - -
5339	- - MR 9857	5409	- - - - - -	5479	- - - - - -	5549	- - RM 4411	5619	- - - - - -	5689	- - - - - -
5340	- - - - - -	5410	- - - - - -	5480	- - BR 5976	5550	- - - - - -	5620	- - - - - -	5690	- - - - - -
5341	- - - - - -	5411	- - YT 2219	5481	- - - - - -	5551	- - - - - -	5621	- - GD 8904	5691	- - YU 5870
5342	- - - - - -	5412	- - WK 3157	5482	- - TR 4197	5552	- - - - - -	5622	- - - - - -	5692	- - WK 3198
5343	- - WK 2444	5413	- - - - - -	5483	- - WK 2451	5553	- - - - - -	5623	- - - - - -	5693	- - - - - -
5344	- - - - - -	5414	- - - - - -	5484	- - RA 3794	5554	- - RM 4412	5624	- - - - - -	5694	- - - - - -
5345	- - - - - -	5415	- - - - - -	5485	- - GD 7601	5555	- - - - - -	5625	- - - - - -	5695	- - UF 3275
5346	- - - - - -	5416	- - - - - -	5486	- - NF 7098	5556	- - - - - -	5626	- - - - - -	5696	- - - - - -
5347	- - - - - -	5417	- - NF 6195	5487	- - - - - -	5557	- - - - - -	5627	- - - - - -	5697	- - - - - -
5348	- - - - - -	5418	- - - - - -	5488	- - WK 3173	5558	- - - - - -	5628	- - GD 8281	5698	- - - - - -
5349	- - - - - -	5419	- - - - - -	5489	- - - - - -	5559	- - - - - -	5629	- - - - - -	5699	- - TR 4872
5350	- - - - - -	5420	- - - - - -	5490	- - - - - -	5560	- - UO 4068	5630	- - KO 5404	5700	- - - - - -
5351	- - - - AUS	5421	- - - - - -	5491	- - EF 3605	5561	- - - EY 567	5631	- - UT 1830	5701	- - - - - -
5352	- - WK 2447	5422	- - - - - -	5492	- - KW 2493	5562	- - - - AUS	5632	- - - - - -	5702	- - - - - -
5353	- - - - - -	5423	- - ER 7839	5493	- - ET 4806	5563	- - - - - -	5633	- - - - - -	5703	- - GD 8903
5354	- - - - - -	5424	- - -SF 9365	5494	- - - - - -	5564	- - GD 8493	5634	- - - - - -	5704	- - - - - -
5355	- - RF 3428	5425	- - PP 8956	5495	- - YT 7391	5565	- - TE 1734	5635	- - - - - -	5705	- - - - - -
5356	- - - - - -	5426	- - - - - -	5496	- - - - - -	5566	- - - - - -	5636	- - KD 3452	5706	- - - - - -
5357	- - - - - -	5427	- - - - - -	5497	- - KW 2397	5567	- - - - - -	5637	- - - - - -	5707	- - KW 3044
5358	- - WK 2445	5428	- - KO 3990	5498	- - KW 2185	5568	- - - - - -	5638	- - - - - -	5708	- - - - - -
5359	- - - TE 849	5429	- - - - - -	5499	- - YT 7295	5569	- - UO 3965	5639	- - - - - -	5709	- - - - - -
5360	- - - - - -	5430	- - - - - -	5500	- - - - - -	5570	- - - - - -	5640	- - VH 1710	5710	- - TU 6994
5361	- - - - - -	5431	- - - - - -	5501	- - WL 3073	5571	- -MW 2438	5641	- - - - - -	5711	- - - - - -
5362	- - - - - -	5432	- - KW 2085	5502	- - - - - -	5572	- - - - - -	5642	- - - - - -	5712	- - DF 3815
5363	- - - - - -	5433	- - - - - -	5503	- - - - - -	5573	- - - - - -	5643	- - SN 3921	5713	- - - - - -
5364	- - - - - -	5434	- - - - - -	5504	- - - - - -	5574	- - WK 3178	5644	- - BA 8098	5714	- - DR 2832
5365	- - - - - -	5435	- - YT 8787	5505	- - WL 3204	5575	- - YT 8775	5645	- - - - - -	5715	- - - IND
5366	- - WK 2446	5436	- - WK 2450	5506	- - - - - -	5576	- - - - - -	5646	- - - - - -	5716	- - - - - -
5367	- - - - - -	5437	- - GD 7989	5507	- - WK 3174	5577	- - YU 6721	5647	- - XY 6923	5717	- - UO 4448
5368	- - UT 1309	5438	- - KH 5389	5508	- - - - - -	5578	- - - - - -	5648	- - WK 3197	5718	- - - - - -
5369	- - GD 7615	5439	- - YT 2217	5509	- - FG 3454	5579	- - - - - -	5649	- - - - - -	5719	- - - - - -
5370	- - - - - -	5440	- - - VJ 425	5510	- - - - - -	5580	- - - - - -	5650	- - ER 8419	5720	- - - - - -
5371	- - - - - -	5441	- - BR 5977	5511	- - - - - -	5581	- - RM 4784	5651	- - YC 1041	5721	- - - - - -
5372	- - - - - -	5442	- - - - - -	5512	- - TY 3606	5582	- - - - - -	5652	- - - - - -	5722	- - NF 8358
5373	- - DR 2294	5443	- - - - - -	5513	- - - - - -	5583	- - - - - -	5653	- - - - - -	5723	- - KA 9761
5374	- - WK 2651	5444	- - - - - -	5514	- - KA 8908	5584	- - YU 2867	5654	- - - - - -	5724	- - ER 8585
5375	- - - - - -	5445	- - - - - -	5515	- - - - - -	5585	- - CH 5152	5655	- - - - - -	5725	- - - - - -
5376	- - PM 8942	5446	- - - - - -	5516	- - - - - -	5586	- - WK 3179	5656	- - WK 4427	5726	- - - - - -
5377	- - KW 2035	5447	- - YT 2220	5517	- - - - - -	5587	- - WK 3195	5657	- - TE 4581	5727	- - MW 911
5378	- - - - - -	5448	- - - - AUS	5518	- - HH 3932	5588	- - - - - -	5658	- - - - - -	5728	- - VU 4727
5379	- - - - - -	5449	- - - - - -	5519	- - - - - -	5589	- - - - - -	5659	- - UT 1875	5729	- - - - - -
5380	- - WK 2448	5450	- - WK 2448	5520	- - - - - -	5590	- - - - - -	5660	- - - - - -	5730	- - UO 4519
5381	- - - - - -	5451	- - YT 4666	5521	- - - - - -	5591	- - MW 688	5661	- - - - - -	5731	- - OX 3609

Chassis	Reg	Chassis	Reg	Chassis	Reg
5732	BR 6160	5802	EK 6628	5872	HC 8541
5733	-WE 790	5803	- - - - - -	5873	RL 7058
5734	- - - - - -	5804	- - - - - -	5874	WK 3580
5735	- - - - - -	5805	WK 3572	5875	- - - NL
5736	VJ 554	5806	YU 4746	5876	DH 6345
5737	TO 9842	5807	- - - - - -	5877	- - - - - -
5738	YC 5511	5808	- - - - - -	5878	VJ 574
5739	- - - - - -	5809	- - - - - -	5879	- - - - - -
5740	- - - - - -	5810	WK 3575	5880	- - - - - -
5741	- - - - - -	5811	PY 7974	5881	- - - - - -
5742	- - - - - -	5812	RF 4020	5882	- - - - - -
5743	WK 3571	5813	UO 4681	5883	- - - - - -
5744	-SC 99	5814	- - - - - -	5884	- - - - - -
5745	TE 2855	5815	- - - - - -	5885	- - - - - -
5746	- - - - - -	5816	OT 7144	5886	-WW 5055
5747	- - - - - -	5817	- - - - - -	5887	- - - - - -
5748	- - - - - -	5818	EW 5363	5888	DH 6335
5749	PH 5184	5819	YU 7125	5889	OT 7214
5750	- - - - - -	5820	HF 5239	5890	GD 9146
5751	- - - - - -	5821	GD 9145	5891	- - - - - -
5752	- - - - - -	5822	RX 1898	5892	FB 6571
5753	- - - - - -	5823	YU 7129	5893	- - - - - -
5754	RY 5750	5824	- - - - - -	5894	WK 4429
5755	- - - - - -	5825	WK 3574	5895	- - - - - -
5756	DB 8392	5826	- - - - - -	5896	- - - - - -
5757	- - - - - -	5827	- UL 706	5897	- - - - - -
5758	RP 5296	5828	- - - - - -	5898	AUS
5759	- - - - - -	5829	- - - - - -	5899	- - - - - -
5760	- - - - - -	5830	- - - - - -	5900	BR 6227
5761	- - - - - -	5831	WK 4428	5901	TN 6572
5762	- - - - - -	5832	- - - - - -	5902	- - - - - -
5763	- - - - - -	5833	- - - - - -	5903	- - - - - -
5764	- - - - - -	5834	- - - NL	5904	- - - - - -
5765	- - - - - -	5835	CM 7821	5905	WE 1143
5766	- - - - - -	5836	RY 5944	5906	-KD 381
5767	GD 9114	5837	DH 6855	5907	- - - - - -
5768	GD 8901	5838	- - - - - -	5908	- - - - - -
5769	-MW 1014	5839	WL 4728	5909	ET 4951
5770	- - - - - -	5840	- - - - - -	5910	- - - - - -
5771	- - - - - -	5841	- - - - - -	5911	TY 3610
5772	KH 6045	5842	- - - - - -	5912	FJ 5370
5773	KA 9731	5843	- - - - - -	5913	UP 633
5774	- - - - - -	5844	- - - - - -	5914	FE 9924
5775	FR 8693	5845	- - - - - -	5915	WK 3579
5776	- - - - - -	5846	WK 3578	5916	- - - - - -
5777	SY 3455	5847	- - - - - -	5917	WK 4430
5778	- - - - - -	5848	TR 4721	5918	- - - - - -
5779	WK 3577	5849	DF 4228	5919	- - - - - -
5780	- - - - - -	5850	WK 3573	5920	- - - - - -
5781	WK 3570	5851	DF 4040	5921	- - - - - -
5782	UX 1694	5852	YU 8745	5922	TU 7599
5783	- - - - - -	5853	BR 6323	5923	NF 9485
5784	- US 9	5854	- - - - - -	5924	- - - - - -
5785	AV 1342	5855	KS 3883	5925	TU 7630
5786	YU 8724	5856	DR 3082	5926	SM 6797
5787	NF 8733	5857	TR 4783	5927	GD 9147
5788	- - - - - -	5858	KW 2920	5928	- - - - - -
5789	GD 8904	5859	- - - - - -	5929	- - - - - -
5790	UK 4543	5860	OX 4291	5930	- - - - - -
5791	YU 7131	5861	- - - - - -	5931	- - - - - -
5792	GD 8902	5862	TU 7196	5932	- - - - - -
5793	- - - - - -	5863	- - - - - -	5933	EN 3558
5794	BR 6157	5864	WK 3576	5934	- - - - - -
5795	- - - - - -	5865	- - - - - -	5935	- - - - - -
5796	BX 8429	5866	HH 4108	5936	- - - - - -
5797	- - - - - -	5867	- - - - - -	5937	AUS
5798	AG 2506	5868	- - - - - -	5938	KW 3349
5799	- - - - - -	5869	- - - - - -	5939	- - - - - -
5800	- - - - - -	5870	DR 2979	5940	- - - - - -
5801	- - - - - -	5871	- - - - - -	5941	- - - - - -

Chassis	Reg	Chassis	Reg	Chassis	Reg
5942	TU 7602	5962	- - - - - -	5982	-MW 1407
5943	- - - - - -	5963	AUS	5983	YU 4723
5944	- - - - - -	5964	- - - - - -	5984	TS 7075
5945	- - - - - -	5965	- - - - - -	5985	WK 5493
5946	- - - - - -	5966	HH 4151	5986	- - - - - -
5947	- - - - - -	5967	- - - - - -	5987	- - - - - -
5948	KW 3199	5968	- - - - - -	5988	- - - - - -
5949	KW 3359	5969	- - - - - -	5989	DF 5131
5950	- - - - - -	5970	WK 4435	5990	- - - - - -
5951	-EJ 2236	5971	- - - - - -	5991	- - - - - -
5952	- - - - -	5972	UC 3272	5992	WK 6150
5953	AUS	5973	SH 3020	5993	AUS
5954	AUS	5974	WK 4437	5994	- - - - - -
5955	- - - - - -	5975	- - - - - -	5995	WK 6147
5956	- - - - - -	5976	- - - - - -	5996	- - - - - -
5957	- - - - - -	5977	- - - - - -	5997	WK 4438
5958	HL 3834	5978	- - - - - -	5998	WK 6151
5959	WK 4432	5979	- - - - - -	5999	- - - - - -
5960	- - - - - -	5980	- - - - - -	6000	NF 9909
5961	- - - - - -	5981	TU 8087		

This sequence commences with the appearance of the company's first six-cylinder car. This was of 14.75hp fiscal rating and mounted in the TG Series 12/50 chassis of the day. The new model had a somewhat slow start. Whilst obviously smoother than the four, it came with the penalty of increased weight, and it has frequently been said that a spiritedly-driven 12/50 could run rings around the 14.75.

Within only a year, this anomaly had become addressed with the development of a new cylinder block with a bore of 67.5mm instead of the earlier 63mm, giving 16.95hp fiscal rating.

Instances abound of the company most generously allowing owners who desired this useful upgrade to have it done 'in-house,' so examples of the original 14.75hp specification are now comparatively rare. The first 'official' example of the larger version is understood to have been 5978, with the model name 'Silver Eagle' being applied for the first time, and using the appropriate radiator mascot, whilst the 14.75s continued to use the hare mascot, as on a 12/50.

Readers of a mathematical disposition will probably have noted that as the chassis number 6000 was reached, it would inevitably clash with the initial 6000 10/30 series of 1920. This was addressed by 'leap-frogging' over that sequence, hence the next chronological sequence recommences at 6501.

Note: Chassis numbers 6343 to 6500 inclusive are not deployed on any Alvis model.

4920

Works development car

This is an especially significant car in Alvis history,

being the very first 'Six,' and a design which would evolve into the ultimate 4.3-litre model produced until 1940. This particular prototype, as with the second prototype (qv 4900), started life in TG 12/50 format. After the usual development process, it was transferred to Henly's London stock and sold as 'shopsoiled.'

DH 5637

4956
William Preston MP
Details are under Preston's next Alvis purchase, 7620.

RP 3671

4957
Sears family (Northampton)
For the quite numerous series of Alvis cars owned by one of Britain's best-known motoring families, see 1487 et seq.

4985
Bishop of St David's
Educated at Llandovery, then Keble College Oxford, and a prominent Welsh Anglican churchman, David Lewis Prosser (June 10, 1865-February 28, 1950), took delivery of this 12/50 TG just after being consecrated in the office of bishop. He would later progress to become Archbishop of Wales between 1944 and 1949, though retaining the St David's title until his death.

WK 129

4990
Works development car
Starting life as a TG 12/50, this car became the second prototype for the new six-cylinder 14.75hp engine. Initially, it was for T G John's own personal use, but was later sold in the Pembroke Dock area (qv 4920 for the first prototype).

5015
'Eugster'
The works record for this car merely has it allocated to a Mr Eugster. It is probably safe to assume that this was the E J P Eugster of Henly's London branch, who, along with D Watson, would be involved in the much reported 'Blue Train' escapade (qv 7857).

RU 4926

5033

RU 5040

5036
H E Beale Esq
Herbert Beale was a key figure in the then family-owned chain of Bournemouth-based department stores. He was a serial Alvis owner, with at least five such to his credit, these two being unusual in that he bought them direct from the factory on the same day, April 8, 1927. It is, however, his earlier cars which provide the greater interest, as he wrote detailed travelogues of his continental tours.

Probably the first of his purchases was his 12/40 two-seater, registered as EL 7272 (chassis number as yet unapportioned but circa chassis 1600). Beale took this car on a 2500-mile tour of the continent, and his account of the trip appeared in *Autocar*, entitled *An Alvis in the Alps*, in two parts: the first was in the issue of November 28, 1924, pages 1093-1096, with the second part a week later, on December 5, pages 1147-1150.

He was then inclined to change this car for an overhead valve 12/50 model, which was then just coming on stream. Initially, this car seems to have been something of a 'Friday afternoon' model, with Beale complaining most eruditely to the factory about its inferior performance compared with the earlier 12/40, and notably its propensity for breaking valve springs. The works must have conscientiously attended to these warranty matters, because the car, registered RU 504 (qv tables page 20, entry 3375), was whisked off to the Dolomites for a 3500-mile round trip, similarly reported upon in *Autocar* issue of November 27, 1925, page 1047-1051. This was followed, equally successfully, the next year with a 3800-mile excursion *Into the Heart of Spain* – again, in *Autocar*, issue of December 31, 1926. All the above were two-seaters, but additionally, Beale is known to have taken on a four-seater tourer, chassis 4742, on November 12, 1926, but no details of its registration have thus far surfaced.

- - 6413

5051
Judge R W H Davies
A Light Car Odyssey is the title of a travelogue written by Judge Davies, relating a drive from his posting in Belgaum, India, back to his home near Tewkesbury. The book was reviewed by Bill Boddy in the *Motor Sport* issue of July 1966, page 616. A photograph confirms the registration digits to have been 6413, but the letters are concealed. However,

given that the car was purchased from Henly's London operation, it is highly likely that they accorded with the 'YE' sequence used by Henly's at this time. Davies replaced this car with another Alvis (qv 9027).

5132
Roy Bulcock
The popularity of Alvis cars in the Antipodes is due in no small measure to the advocacy of Bulcock, who, at the age of only 24, with the above car bought as a chassis and bodied locally, was entered in a Queensland RAC's Endurance Trial in 1928. After giving an excellent account of itself in this event, Bulcock drove it, with limited stops, the 813 miles from Brisbane to Sydney in just 24 hours and 57 minutes. The enduring popularity of the marque to this day in that part of the world is largely due to the reputation gained in coping admirably with arduous conditions, well in excess of those encountered in the country of its birth.

5170
Sir Walter Runciman
Walter Runciman (July 6, 1847-August 13, 1937) was clearly a larger than life character: he had run away to sea at the age of 11, had qualified as a master mariner at the age of 21, and founded a shipping line. He was the author of several seafaring books, and learned discourses on historical topics. He had also progressed to become Liberal MP for Hartlepool between 1914 and 1918. Whilst prosperous, he was not profligate, buying this Alvis second-hand from Henly's London stock, when it was some six months old.

5219 WK 1151
Winifred Pink
This was the car campaigned vigorously by Miss Pink in a number of competitions, including the Shelsley Walsh Hillclimbs (qv 10598 and 13812 for her subsequently owned Alvis cars).

5240 YF 3
6th Earl of Cottenham
Alvis racing driver Mark Pepys owned a number of Alvis cars. This one is known to have been preceded by 4194 and succeeded by 14457 (qv 14457 for bio).

The car was featured in *Autocar*, issue of June 17, 1927, page 1060.

5235: The Alvis car has always been favoured by service personnel, as evidenced by this TG 12/50, seen here in wartime use by officer Kenneth Banks. (Courtesy the late Mrs Hazel Buck)

5250 WF 649
Lady May Mellanby
Lady Mellanby (née Tweedy) (1882-March 5,1978) was educated at Bromley High School and Girton College Cambridge, and her hugely significant medical research deserves to be better known. She entered a world then almost entirely dominated by men. Dentistry was a field of special interest and she controversially challenged the then prevalent view that oral hygiene was the only way of combatting the problem of cavities. Diet, she would successfully argue, especially the intake of Vitamin D, was also paramount. A view initially dismissed by her peers, it was not until research conducted on the remote island of Tristan da Cunah, where the inhabitants, of necessity, had a high Vitamin D intake (and the best teeth of any peoples on the planet), that her view prevailed. A respected contributor to a host of learned periodicals like *The Lancet*, and those of the BMA, her very numerous research papers are now housed in the Wellcome Library, on London's Euston Road.

5534

UO 3971

Commander A H Maxwell-Hyslop GC RN
Alexander Henry Maxwell-Hyslop (May 25, 1895-August 28, 1978) was educated at Rottingdean, Osborne Naval School, and Dartmouth Naval College. He had a most distinguished career, serving in both WWI and WWII, which, in the case of the former, included serving on four airships. He received the Albert Medal (later George Cross) for bravery when a serious explosion occurred on HMS Devonshire in July 1929, at a time when some test firing was taking place. Following retirement he took an active part in Cornwall's civic activities, and maintained a nautical connection as vice-commodore of the Fowey Yacht Club. The reader is referred to 11167 for notes relating to his other Alvis, an SB Speed 20 model.

5586

WK 3179

Jonas Woodhead & Co Ltd
This Leeds-based manufacturer of suspension components subsequently bought a front-wheel drive model (qv 7301 for further details).

56**

YU 4746

Denis Knowles
This was one of several Knowles Alvis cars (qv 7909 for further details). The chassis dating of 56** given here is approximate, pending further research. Knowles used the above car for a tour of Europe in 1930/31, covering Berlin, Dresden and Prague. He shipped the car to New Zealand in 1932, where its registration number was changed to Y103 809 6. Car not heard of since 1935.

5618

London Motor Show 1927
Recorded in the works guarantee cards as an Olympia Show entry.

5622

George Duller
By the time champion jockey Duller (January 26, 1891-June 6, 1962) had taken delivery of this TG 12/50 in October 1927, he had already ridden well over 300 winners. It was presumably with this Alvis that he was summonsed in February 1928, accused of failing to stop after an accident involving a woman on a bicycle. A driving ban of some months

resulted. Duller had turned to motor racing, and had become a familiar figure at Brooklands with a variety of makes, but particularly Bentley and Sunbeam. The Alvis that he will mostly be associated with, however, is the straight-eight Grand Prix racing car, mentioned elsewhere (qv 7529 et seq).

5648

WK 3197

Tangye Ltd
This was a company car (direct sale ex-Alvis works) for the Birmingham based engineering group noted for its hydraulics, pumps, and indeed steam engines. Its long history goes back to 1856, when it was founded by Richard Trevithick Tangye, and includes the proud fact that it was Tangye lifting jacks that helped to launch Isambard Kingdom Brunel's 'Great Eastern.'

5752

Philip Runciman
One of quite a number of Alvis cars supplied to this enthusiastic owner and competitor, including 4618, 7727, 8845, and 9548 for bio.

5758

RP 5256

Sears family (Northampton)
The Sears family have been connected with Alvis cars right from the earliest days of the company (qv 1487 et seq). 5758 is interesting in that it is one of those originally built in 14.75hp form, but quite early in its life upgraded to 16.95hp form, a procedure that it seems the works most generously carried out in a number of instances.

5770

Lord de la Warr GBE, PC, JP, DL
The ninth Earl of this title, Hebrand Edward Dundonald Brassey Sackville (June 20, 1900-January, 28 1976)was educated at Magdalen College Oxford. Perhaps less well-known as a former Mayor of Bexhill-on-Sea, he also enjoyed a number of governmental positions including that of Lord Privy Seal, and, under Winston Churchill's 1952 administration, that of Postmaster General. The de la Warr Pavilion in Bexhill-on-Sea, a Grade I listed building since 1986 and named after him, came about as a result of a competition in the *Architects' Journal* of 1934, and remains very much in use as an art gallery and conference centre.

5860 on product testing. (Courtesy Dunlop Rubber Company and Alvis Archive Trust)

5860
Dunlop Rubber Co Ltd

This car was used by Dunlop to promote the introduction of a product somewhat less well known than its tyres. This was a spiked mat designed to stop speeding or stolen vehicles. Intended to be used in pairs across each half of a carriageway, the device folded up, pantograph-style into a box bearing a 'HALT' sign. Modern versions of this concept remain in use by police forces internationally, to this day, but are generically known as 'stingers,' and unfurl rather like a rolled up carpet.

5905
Ambrose Shardlow Ltd

A company car for the Sheffield-based forgemaster who made crankshafts under the 'Ambrosia' trade name. Previously owned a 12/50 TE model (qv 3085), and later a 16.95hp Silver Eagle TB (qv 8423).

5946
Marquess Of Waterford

John Charles de la Poer Beresford (January 6, 1902-May 25, 1934), the seventh to bear this title, served in the Royal Regiment of Horse Guards. His career ended somewhat prematurely due to an accident in the gun room at the family seat of Curraghmore.

5969
Sir Cedric Hardwicke

Actor and serial Alvis owner (qv 10877 for a bio, and also 7367, 8549, 8524 and 10737).

5998
Rev Charles H S Gmelin

This remarkable individual was born in 1872 in

5974: Seen here with an early example of the 14.75hp model, somewhere in St Andrews, is Keith Elliot, who was a major force in the Galt's of Glasgow dealership, which sold Alvis cars for four decades. (Courtesy Ernest Shenton collection)

Bengal, to missionary parents. He was educated in England at Magdalen College School and thence on a scholarship to Keble College, Oxford. It was in 1896, whilst at the latter, that there was the revival of the Olympic Games movement, and as a notable athlete he found himself in Athens in April of that year. He entered the 400-metre race and finished third. This significant, though largely unsung achievement, would make Charles Gmelin Britain's very first Olympic medal winner. Returning to his studies, he duly took up holy orders and teaching, eventually becoming headmaster of Freshfields School, Oxford, where he died in October 1950. His Alvis car was a TA 14.75 Mk 2 Alvista saloon, bought July 25, 1928. It was a works-registered car, though supplied via the F E Wootten, Oxford dealership.

6501-8423

March 1928 to December 1930
1922 cars

Consisting of models:

TA	766
TB	315
TG	358
TH	3

SA	150
SB	36
SD	114
FA	29
FB	22
FC	1
FD	40
FE	58
F8/15	10
Other (experimental, or redesignated)	20

Consisting of coachbuilders:

Cross & Ellis	926
Carbodies	920
Other	
(Chassis-only deliveries) Mostly undeclared, but known examples from: Brigden, Egerton, Grose, Hoyal, Lancefield, Morgan, Salmon, Swallow, and James Young	76
Total	**1922**

Chassis	Reg
6501	- - - - - -
6502	- - - - - -
6503	- - GD 9850
6504	- - KW 3239
6505	- - WK 4431
6506	- - BR 6317
6507	- - - - - -
6508	- - - - AUS
6509	- - - - - -
6510	- - - - - -
6511	- - - - - -
6512	- - TU 8919
6513	- - WK 4433
6514	- - - - - -
6515	- - - - - -
6516	- - YV 3819
6517	- - - - - -
6518	- - RM 4816
6519	- - - - - -
6520	- - - - - -
6521	- - - - - -
6522	- - - - - -
6523	- - - - - -
6524	- - - - - -
6525	- - KW 3195
6526	- - KH 6214
6527	- - - TK 361
6528	- - KW 3097
6529	- - - SC 567
6530	- - - - - -
6531	- - - - - -
6532	- - TY 4326
6533	- - - - - -
6534	- - BA 7134
6535	- - - - - -
6536	- - CP 6473
6537	- - - - - -
6538	- - WK 9646
6539	- - OT 7704

6540	- - - - - -
6541	- - - - - -
6542	- - TM 2763
6543	- - UX 2847
6544	- - YV 2273
6545	- - - - - -
6546	- - - - - -
6547	- - TM 2603
6548	- - - - - -
6549	- - GD 9419
6550	- - UC 6641
6551	- - - - - -
6552	- - YV 3832
6553	- - BR 6473
6554	- - - - - -
6555	- - - - - -
6556	- - TM 2325
6557	- - WK 4434
6558	- - - - - -
6559	- - - - - -
6560	- - - KP 38
6561	- - WK 5482
6562	- - - - - -
6563	- - GD 9681
6564	- - - GE 187
6565	- - - - - -
6566	- - - - - -
6567	- - - - - -
6568	- - - - - -
6569	- - - - - -
6570	- - YV 1289
6571	- - - - - -
6572	- - OX 6854
6573	- - - - - -
6574	- - - - - -
6575	- - - - - -
6576	- - TY 4325
6577	- - - - - -
6578	- - - - - -
6579	- - - - - -

6580	- - - - - -
6581	- - - - - -
6582	- - - - - -
6583	- - BR 6957
6584	- - EC 8113
6585	- - - - - -
6586	- - WK 4436
6587	- - - - - -
6588	- - - - - -
6589	- - - - - -
6590	- - - -G 364
6591	- - - OX 7014
6592	- - - - - NZ
6593	- - - - - -
6594	- - SM 6980
6595	- - - - - -
6596	- - DF 6450
6597	- - UN 1218
6598	- - - - - -
6599	- - - GE 805
6600	- - KW 3971
6601	- - WK 6945
6602	- - - - - -
6603	- - - - - -
6604	- - - - - -
6605	- - TU 8386
6606	- - WK 5489
6607	- - - - - -
6608	- - KW 4739
6609	- - - - - -
6610	- - - - - -
6611	- - WL 4780
6612	- - - - - -
6613	- - - - - -
6614	- - - - - -
6615	- - - - - -
6616	- - RU 7045
6617	- - PN 2225
6618	- - TR 5018
6619	- - - - - -

6620	- - - - - -
6621	- - VA 7705
6622	- - KW 3747
6623	- - - - - -
6624	- - - - - -
6625	- - - - - -
6626	- - - - - -
6627	- - - - - -
6628	- - TY 4323
6629	- - VM 1106
6630	- - - - - -
6631	- - - TK 595
6632	- - UF 3429
6633	- - UP 2126
6634	- - - - - -
6635	- - WK 8952
6636	- - - - - -
6637	- - - - - -
6638	- - SB 3102
6639	- - - - - -
6640	- - - - - -
6641	- - TE 4017
6642	- WK 7360
6643	- - - - - -
6644	- - - - - -
6645	- HW 2184
6646	- - - - - -
6647	- - KH 6245
6648	- - - - - -
6649	- - - - - -
6650	- - - - - -
6651	- - YC 1341
6652	- - - - - -
6653	- - - - NL
6654	- - - - - -
6655	- - WK 5486
6656	- - - - - -
6657	- - WK 5494
6658	- - WK 5487
6659	- - WK 4439
6660	- - - - - -
6661	- - - - - -
6662	- - YC 3006
6663	- - HS 5065
6664	- - - - - -
6665	- - FU 9136
6666	- - - - - -
6667	
- - - - YW 7126
6668	- - YV 6955
6669	- - - - - -
6670	- - - - - -
6671	- - - - - -
6672	- - WK 6152
6673	- - - OU 167
6674	- - OX 6383
6675	- - - - - -
6676	- - - - - -
6677	- - VT 1478
6678	- - BR 6541
6679	- - - - - -
6680	- - - - - -
6681	- - YC 3335
6682	- - - - - -
6683	- - - - - -
6684	- - - - - -
6685	- - - - - -
6686	- - WK 5774
6687	- - YW 1609
6688	- - - - - -

6689	- - - - - -
6690	- - WK 5488
6691	- - UT 3045
6692	- - TU 8909
6693	- - WK 6157
6694	- - - - - -
6695	- - UY 4123
6696	- - WK 6951
6697	- - - - - -
6698	- - KW 3848
6699	- - - - - -
6700	- - - - - -
6701	- - - RG 216
6702	- - - - - -
6703	- - - - - -
6704	- - - - - -
6705	- - - - - -
6706	- - SR 6700
6707	- - - - - -
6708	- - - - - -
6709	- - WK 6149
6710	- - - - - -
6711	- - - - - -
6712	- - FU 9507
6713	- - - - - -
6714	- HW 4092
6715	- - - - - -
6716	- - - - - -
6717	- - - - - -
6718	- - - - - -
6719	- - - - - -
6720	- - - - - -
6721	- - YV 9835
6722	- - WK 5485
6722	- - WK 7349
6723	- - - - - -
6724	- - - - - -
6725	- - - - - -
6726	- - - - - -
6727	- - - - - -
6728	- - UT 4078
6729	- - - - - -
6730	- - - - - -
6731	- - TM 3130
6732	- - - -RG 3
6733	- - - - - -
6734	- - - - - -
6735	- - WK 5495
6736	- - - - - -
6737	- - - - - -
6738	- UO 6497
6739	- - - - - -
6740	- - WK 6159
6741	- - WK 6941
6742	- - WK 6941
6743	- - - - - -
6744	- - - - - -
6745	- - WK 6148
6746	- WM 2142
6747	- - - - - -
6748	- - WK 6160
6749	- - BR 6828
6750	- - - - - -
6751	- - - - - -
6752	- - - - - -
6753	- - - - - -
6754	- - UY 3694
6755	- - DR 3561
6756	- - - - - -
6757	- - RA 5925

6758	- - RF 5251
6759	- - JM 1250
6760	- - - - - -
6761	- - TN 8687
6762	- - UK 7019
6763	- - - - - -
6764	- - WK 6155
6765	- - - - - -
6766	- - - - - -
6767	- - - - - -
6768	- - - - - -
6769	- - - - - -
6770	- - - - - -
6771	- -MW 2262
6772	- - - GE 190
6773	- - SC 2113
6774	- - WK 6857
6775	- - WK 6963
6776	- - - - - -
6777	- - - - - -
6778	- - WK 6952
6779	- - - - - -
6780	- - - - - -
6781	- - KW 4206
6782	- - - - - -
6783	- - RM 5146
6784	- - - - - -
6785	- - - - - -
6786	- - - - - -
6787	- - YW 8577
6788	- - CM 8204
6789	- - - - - -
6790	- - WK 5496
6791	- - WK 6158
6792	- - - - - -
6793	- - WK 5491
6794	- - WK 5492
6795	- - WK 5490
6796	- - YW 7166
6797	- - - - - -
6798	- - - - - -
6799	- - YW 3821
6800	- - - - - -
6801	- - - - - -
6802	- - - - - -
6803	- - YW 1984
6804	- - KP 1131
6805	- - - - - -
6806	- - - - - -
6807	- - VH 1497
6808	- - TR 5992
6809	- -MW 2238
6810	- - - - - -
6811	- - VM 6439
6812	- - - - - NL
6813	- - - - - -
6814	- - - - - -
6815	- - TN 8065
6816	- - - - - -
6817	- - -FF 2808
6818	- - -FXF 42
6819	- - DR 3709
6820	- - - - - -
6821	- - - - - -
6822	- - TR 5562
6823	- - - - - -
6824	- - - - - -
6825	- - - - - -
6826	- - - - - -
6827	- - KW 4143

Chassis	Reg.	Chassis	Reg.	Chassis	Reg.	Chassis	Reg.	Chassis	Reg.	Chassis	Reg.
6828	------	6898	------	6968	------	7038	XV 2050	7108	YC 4752	7178	------
6829	DP 9888	6899	YW 8788	6969	DR 4097	7039	------	7109	------	7179	LG 38
6830	------	6900	------	6970	------	7040	------	7110	------	7180	MW 3341
6831	------	6901	YX 1085	6971	WK 7348	7041	------	7111	UO 8586	7181	SO 3441
6832	------	6902	------	6972	------	7042	------	7112	------	7182	------
6833	GE 1559	6903	------	6973	------	7043	GE 7114	7113	------	7183	VR 2720
6834	------	6904	KW 4444	6974	YX 9047	7044	------	7114	TE 7745	7184	------
6835	------	6905	------	6975	AUS	7045	------	7115	WM 2734	7185	------
6836	YX 2294	6906	------	6976	AUS	7046	------	7116	------	7186	------
6837	------	6907	UO 7918	6977	------	7047	------	7117	UL 3593	7187	GC 6836
6838	WK 6154	6908	WK 7354	6978	WK 6950	7048	------	7118	------	7188	------
6839	------	6909	------	6979	GE 2313	7049	BR 8095	7119	WK 7359	7189	------
6840	------	6910	YX 2296	6980	------	7050	SR 6921	7120	AUS	7190	AUS
6841	------	6911	WK 8046	6981	------	7051	------	7121	SC 2780	7191	GN 8586
6842	UN 1654	6912	BR 6691	6982	------	7052	------	7122	KW 4863	7192	XV 2995
6843	------	6913	------	6983	------	7053	------	7123	------	7193	GE 3582
6844	------	6914	------	6984	TY 4933	7054	KW 5388	7124	------	7194	AZ 1713
6845	MW 2643	6915	------	6985	WK 7353	7055	VC 5065	7125	UY 4296	7195	WK 8053
6846	------	6916	RF 4826	6986	------	7056	JK 645	7126	UU 8283	7196	------
6847	------	6917	LG 54	6987	------	7057	------	7127	WK 8044	7197	TU 9888
6848	------	6918	------	6988	------	7058	US 158	7128	XV 2990	7198	DF 6294
6849	AUS	6919	------	6989	UL 3593	7059	PN 3146	7129	KW 5388	7199	------
6850	------	6920	------	6990	WK 7352	7060	------	7130	------	7200	UD 2527
6851	YW 8610	6921	WK 7346	6991	------	7061	------	7131	DJ 4397	7201	DF 6437
6852	AUS	6922	WK 7347	6992	AUS	7062	------	7132	------	7202	------
6853	WK 6156	6923	------	6993	UT 3976	7063	------	7133	------	7203	------
6854	AUS	6924	------	6994	------	7064	------	7134	------	7204	EK 6945
6855	------	6925	------	6995	UO 8913	7065	------	7135	------	7205	------
6856	------	6926	------	6996	------	7066	YC 6068	7136	HW 4959	7206	EY 3460
6857	HS 5150	6927	WK 6943	6997	------	7067	------	7137	------	7207	GE 4988
6858	------	6928	------	6998	------	7068	------	7138	------	7208	GU 5138
6859	------	6929	VP 1387	6999	TU 9531	7069	------	7139	XV 2382	7209	------
6860	AUS	6930	------	7000	UY 4161	7070	KX 1369	7140	XV 2957	7210	AUS
6861	------	6931	------	7001	BX 9100	7071	------	7141	------	7211	------
6862	------	6932	------	7002	------	7072	------	7142	RF 5221	7212	GU 539
6863	------	6933	KW 4382	7003	PN 2650	7073	------	7143	HW 3890	7213	NL
6864	WK 6153	6934	YX 3502	7004	WK 7345	7074	PN 5195	7144	------	7214	------
6865	FR ?	6935	WK 7343	7005	KW 4723	7075	KW 4864	7145	OU 123	7215	------
6866	YX 2262	6936	WK 6948	7006	DY 5211	7076	WK 7358	7146	------	7216	VY 1528
6867	------	6937	WK 7342	7007	------	7077	------	7147	------	7217	------
6868	WK 6942	6938	YX 6424	7008	------	7078	UE 7697	7148	VC 4366	7218	------
6869	TM 3347	6939	WK 7344	7009	AUS	7079	SC 3330	7149	------	7219	------
6870	------	6940	WK 7341	7010	------	7080	CM 8395	7150	------	7220	HS 5322
6871	------	6941	------	7011	------	7081	SR 6951	7151	------	7221	AUS
6872	------	6942	------	7012	------	7082	------	7152	WN 2030	7222	AUS
6873	TU 9712	6943	------	7013	AUS	7083	------	7153	IL 1574	7223	AUS
6874	------	6944	------	7014	DF 7638	7084	BR 6924	7154	VP 3711	7224	AUS
6875	VJ 986	6945	HC 1	7015	------	7085	RM 5522	7155	------	7225	------
6876	YC 3334	6946	RM 5278	7016	WK 7355	7086	------	7156	------	7226	WL 5771
6877	HC 9493	6947	------	7017	------	7087	------	7157	KP 3421	7227	------
6878	------	6948	DF 6018	7018	------	7088	------	7158	------	7228	KP 3634
6879	WK 6944	6949	UN 1842	7019	------	7089	KW 5130	7159	FW 450	7229	BR 7099
6880	------	6950	YX 6396	7020	UR 1834	7090	WK 8042	7160	------	7230	------
6881	HB 3271	6951	------	7021	------	7091	------	7161	OU 92	7231	AUS
6882	YW 8608	6952	------	7022	------	7092	------	7162	------	7232	------
6883	YX 1083	6953	XV 2081	7023	WF 1175	7093	------	7163	WK 8041	7233	------
6884	GE 1898	6954	FG 4394	7024	------	7094	WK 9994	7164	------	7234	CP 7052
6885	YX 3782	6955	KW 4577	7025	PY 9319	7095	TR 6441	7165	WK 8049	7235	MW 4044
6886	VM 3517	6956	------	7026	WK 7356	7096	------	7166	HW 4520	7236	LG 1149
6887	UX 3038	6957	WK 6949	7027	------	7097	------	7167	------	7237	DV 659
6888	WK 6947	6958	TY 4327	7028	WK 7357	7098	------	7168	------	7238	------
6889	------	6959	------	7029	------	7099	------	7169	------	7239	------
6890	WK 7350	6960	------	7030	------	7100	MW 4626	7170	------	7240	------
6891	------	6961	WK 8043	7031	TK 1552	7101	RM 5523	7171	VM 5060	7241	US 12
6892	WK 8209	6962	PN 2244	7032	RY 7343	7102	------	7172	UL 369	7242	------
6893	------	6963	------	7033	MW 3270	7103	KD 3683	7173	------	7243	WK 8954
6894	------	6964	WK 7351	7034	------	7104	------	7174	------	7244	------
6895	------	6965	TE 7572	7035	AUS	7105	------	7175	UO 9663	7245	------
6896	------	6966	------	7036	HC 9797	7106	------	7176	DH 6880	7246	------
6897	------	6967	RG 115	7037	------	7107	US 176	7177	------	7247	------

No.	Code	No.	Code	No.	Code	No.	Code	No.	Code	No.	Code
7248	- - - - - -	7318	- - UL 6429	7388	- - - - - -	7458	- - - - - -	7528	- - GE 4844	7598	- - - - - -
7249	- - - - - -	7319	- - - - - -	7389	- - BR 7101	7459	- - - - - -	7529	- - - - - -	7599	- - - - - -
7250	- - - - - -	7320	- - KW 5466	7390	- - - - - -	7460	- - - - - -	7530	- - - - - -	7600	- - - - - -
7251	- - KW 5022	7321	- - UL 5405	7391	- - - - - -	7461	- - - AUS	7531	- - UA 8000	7601	- - DR 5294
7252	- - - - - -	7322	- - VM 6570	7392	- - - - - -	7462	- - - AUS	7532	- - GU 1785	7602	- - - - - -
7253	- - - - - -	7323	- - VC 1218	7393	- - - - - -	7463	- - SW 3215	7533		7603	- - VY 1103
7254	- - SC 2959	7324	- - - - - -	7394	- - VH 2101	7464	- - VC 449	7534		7604	- - TX 7332
7255	- - - - - -	7325	- - UL 2393	7395	- - - IA 7913	7465	- - - - - -	7535		7605	- - HW 5737
7256	- - CK 9999	7326	- - WK 8950	7396	- - - - - -	7466	- - - - - -	7536		7606	- - RP 7967
7257	- - WK 8052	7327	- - WK 8057	7397	- - - - - -	7467	- - KW 6245	7537	- - US 192	7607	- - - - - -
7258	- - - - - -	7328	- - - - - -	7398	- - GE 3794	7468	- - VE 1596	7538	- - - - - -	7608	- - - - - -
7259	- - - - - -	7329	- - - - AUS	7399	- - - - - -	7469	- - DC 8822	7539	- - - - - -	7609	- - GU 7087
7260	- - FR 9876	7330	- - - - - -	7400	- - SN 4635	7470	- - - - - -	7540	- - - - - -	7610	- - - - - -
7261	- - - - - -	7331	- - - - - -	7401	- - - - - -	7471	- - - - - -	7541	- - TF 582	7611	- - KW 6454
7262	- - VH 1949	7332	- - VC 4364	7402	- - KH 8902	7472		7542	- - SN 4699	7612	- - UN 2893
7263	- - WK 9991	7333	- - - TV 100	7403	- - KD 5139	7473		7543		7613	- - - - - -
7264	- - - - - -	7334	- - YC 5513	7404	- - DF 7087	7474		7544		7614	- - VC 451
7265	- - - - - -	7335	- - UK 6567	7405	- - VC 1297	7475		7545	- - VC 7	7615	- - EK 6964
7266	- - - - - -	7336	- - - - - -	7406	- - TY 6040	7476		7546	- - - - - -	7616	- - UU 666
7267	- - - - - -	7337	- - BR 7057	7407	- - DF 7352	7477		7547	- - - - - -	7617	- - - - - -
7268	- - WK 8050	7338	- - - - - -	7408	- - - VC 263	7478	- - HS 5469	7548	- - DV 1106	7618	- - SV 858
7269	- - TE 6596	7339	- - SC 3819	7409	- - WK 8059	7479	- - - - - -	7549	- - - - - -	7619	- - - - - -
7270	- - WK 8051	7340	- - - - - -	7410	- - - - - -	7480	- - DV 4908	7550	- - - - - -	7620	- - DH 7341
7271	- - - - - -	7341	- - UL 6433	7411	- - TY 7949	7481		7551	- - - - - -	7621	- - RY 8348
7272	- - - - - -	7342	- - PK 6539	7412	- - SC 3671	7482	- - - - - -	7552	- - - - - -	7622	- - KW 7052
7273	- - WF 2520	7343	- - - - - -	7413	- - WK 8953	7483	- - PN 3187	7553	- - UU 3504	7623	- - - CDN
7274	- - WK 8045	7344	- - - - - -	7414	- - PN 4697	7484		7554	- - HS 5544	7624	- - - - - -
7275	- - WK 8047	7345	- - - - - -	7415	- - GF 6168	7485	- - KW 6211	7555	- - - - - -	7625	- - - - - -
7276	- - - - - -	7346	- - GU 1753	7416	- - - - - -	7486	- - PN 3793	7556	- - - - - -	7626	- - - - - -
7277	- - - - - -	7347	- - - - - -	7417	- - - - - -	7487	- - GE 5356	7557	- - VC 19	7627	- - - - - -
7278	- - - - - -	7348	- - - - - -	7418	- - VC 1572	7488	- - TY 6036	7558	- - - - - -	7628	- - - OF 688
7279	- - - - - -	7349	- - DR 4734	7419	- - - - - -	7489	- - WK 9992	7559	- - WK 8958	7629	- - VK 27
7280	- - TK 1906	7350	- - WK 8055	7420	- - VA 8701	7490	- - - - - -	7560	- - - - - -	7630	- - UU 3526
7281	- - WK 8048	7351	- - - - - -	7421	- - UX 4242	7491	- - - - - -	7561	- - - - - -	7631	- - GE 5588
7282	- - - - - -	7352	- - - - - -	7422	- - - - - -	7492	- - SC 4054	7562	- - VE 8566	7632	- - - - - -
7283	- - KW 6155	7353	- - KX 1871	7423	- - WK 8951	7493	- - RF 5625	7563	- - VC 262	7633	- - OU 2217
7284	- - - - - -	7354	- - - - - -	7424	- - - - - -	7494	- - HW 5028	7564	- - VH 2260	7634	- - UA 7518
7285	- - CM 8479	7355	- - - - - -	7425	- - UT 4538	7495		7565		7635	- - - - - -
7286	- - - - - -	7356	- - CH 8145	7426	- - TE 7521	7496		7566		7636	- - - - - -
7287	- - UY 4749	7357	- - - - - -	7427	- - - - - -	7497		7567	- MW 4807	7637	- - DF 8287
7288	- - - - - -	7358	- - DF 8296	7428	- - TE 6926	7498		7568	- - WK 8957	7638	- - TR 7060
7289	- - VP 8911	7359	- - LG 2734	7429	- - CM 8651	7499	- - TE 7469	7569	- - WK 8959	7639	- - CM 8926
7290	- - GO 1591	7360	- - HW 4681	7430	- - VM 8657	7500	- - - - - -	7570	- - - - - -	7640	- - - VC 266
7291	- - GU 1728	7361	- - SC 3778	7431	- - PN 3306	7501	- - - - - -	7571	- - VC 18	7641	- - GE 5357
7292	- - - - - -	7362	- - WK 8058	7432	- - - - - -	7502		7572	- - - - - -	7642	- - FV 261
7293	- - YC 4823	7363	- MW 3670	7433	- - - - - -	7503		7573		7643	- - - - - -
7294	- - - - - -	7364	- - - - - -	7434	- - - - - -	7504		7574	- - UO 8888	7644	- - - - - -
7295	- - KH 8022	7365	- - - - - -	7435	- - - - - -	7505		7575	- - - - - -	7645	- - - - - -
7296	- - WK 8054	7366	- - - - - -	7436	- - PN 3186	7506	- - WK 8955	7576	- - - - - -	7646	- - DV 1547
7297	- - - - - -	7367	- - - - - -	7437	- - GU 5140	7507	- - PN 3390	7577	- - - - - -	7647	- - LG 2185
7298	- - - - - -	7368	- - - - - -	7438	- - GE 4296	7508	- - - - - -	7578	- - - - - -	7648	- - KH 9107
7299	- - AG 3606	7369	- - - - - -	7439	- - - - - -	7509	- - VR 55	7579	- - DX 8021	7649	- - DV 1264
7300	- - UO 9307	7370	- - WK 8060	7440	- - EY 3578	7510	- - - - - -	7580	- - KH 8801	7650	- - KD 6660
7301	- - WK 8056	7371	- - - - - -	7441	- - - - AUS	7511		7581	- - WK 9996	7651	- - - - - -
7302	- - TY 6399	7372	- - TK 2426	7442	- MW 4001	7512		7582		7652	- - - - - -
7303	- - XV 7408	7373	- - - - - -	7443	- - - - - -	7513	- - TE 7644	7583	- - VC 261	7653	- - VC 1574
7304	- - - - - -	7374	- - UX 4206	7444	- - - - - -	7514	- - CB 9083	7584	- - - - - -	7654	- - - - - -
7305	- - - - - -	7375	- - - - - -	7445	- - TN 8690	7515	- - US 193	7585	- - TY 5226	7655	- - - - - -
7306	- - UW 2017	7376	- - KP 8085	7446	- - - - - -	7516	- - - - - -	7586	- - - - - -	7656	- - UU 8244
7307	- - - - - -	7377	- - - - - -	7447	- - HH 4766	7517	- - UR 2928	7587	- - WK 9993	7657	- - - - - -
7308	- - - - - -	7378	- - SC 3922	7448	- - - - - -	7518	- - DV 2510	7588	- - WK 9995	7658	- - - VC 265
7309	- - - - - -	7379	- - - VR 859	7449	- - SM 7523	7519	- - WK 8956	7589	- - - - - -	7659	- - OU 2416
7310	- - PL 9088	7380	- - - - - -	7450	- - TN 9229	7520	- - - - - -	7590	- - VC 264	7660	- - - - - -
7311	- - - - - -	7381	- - - - - -	7451	- - - - AUS	7521	- - WK 9171	7591	- - - - - -	7661	- - UU 6339
7312	- - TE 6467	7382	- - - - - -	7452	- - - - - -	7522	- - - - - -	7592	- - VC 766	7662	- - SS 3014
7313	- - VP 7564	7383	- - IO 2993	7453	- - - - - -	7523		7593	- - VC 17	7663	- - RA 8962
7314	- - - - - -	7384	- - UO 9713	7454	- - WE 4497	7524		7594	- WM 3326	7664	- - - - - -
7315	- - UL 5456	7385	- - WK 8949	7455	- - - - - -	7525		7595		7665	- - - - - -
7316	- - GU 5129	7386	- - KS 4290	7456	- - - - - -	7526	- - KD 6077	7596	- - KD 6077	7666	- - - - - -
7317	- - VC 4363	7387	- - - - - -	7457	- - - AUS	7527	- - TE 7437	7597	- - DF 8276	7667	- - - - - -

No.	Reg.	No.	Reg.	No.	Reg.	No.	Reg.	No.	Reg.	No.	Reg.
7668		7738		7808	UA 9808	7878	KR 2142	7948		8018	
7669	GE 5939	7739		7809	AUS	7879		7949		8019	KW 7538
7670	TS 8100	7740		7810		7880		7950	VC 2673	8020	VC 2670
7671		7741		7811	AUS	7881		7951	VC 2948	8021	AZ 4064
7672	YC 6510	7742	UV 1613	7812	AUS	7882	WL 9723	7952		8022	OF 6922
7673		7743	VC 1577	7813	GE 6423	7883		7953	KW 7702	8023	
7674	VC 454	7744		7814	AUS	7884	VC 1907	7954		8024	
7675		7745		7815	VE 2211	7885	AUS	7955	VC 3853	8025	VC 2942
7676		7746		7816	DV 3065	7886	LJ 640	7956	VC 2671	8026	
7677		7747	VC 1580	7817	SR 7420	7887	GC 2309	7957		8027	
7678		7748	FM 5799	7818		7888	VC 1906	7958		8028	
7679	TK 3079	7749	YC 7404	7819	AUS	7889	VA 9316	7959	WE 6965	8029	DV 3657
7680	GE 5789	7750		7820	UA 9936	7890	HW 7640	7960	UY 6978	8030	OU 4309
7681	UX 4998	7751	HW 7208	7821	KX 3587	7891	OF 5683	7961		8031	HA 6282
7682	DF 8330	7752	VC 1579	7822		7892		7962	DV 3361	8032	
7683	VC 762	7753	UA 9122	7823	VC 1902	7893		7963		8033	
7684	CP 7717	7754		7824	ZA	7894		7964		8034	TY 5875
7685		7755	VC 1912	7825		7895		7965		8035	
7686	SV 4959	7756		7826	ZA	7896	UW 5779	7966		8036	
7687	GE 5358	7757		7827	VC 3854	7897	OU 3931	7967		8037	
7688		7758		7828		7898	KW 8394	7968		8038	VC 2672
7689	VC 453	7759	UR 6348	7829		7899	VC 2951	7969		8039	
7690		7760	VC 1571	7830		7900		7970		8040	
7691		7761		7831		7901		7971		8041	VC 2952
7692	ZA	7762	SX 2951	7832		7902		7972	UY 7164	8042	MW 6488
7693		7763		7833		7903	DR 6084	7973	SC 6156	8043	
7694		7764	VC 763	7834		7904	KW 7229	7974		8044	VC 2945
7695	VC 450	7765		7835	RH 2706	7905	VC 2402	7975	VC 2669	8045	
7696		7766		7836	UT 6212	7906	VC 2949	7976		8046	
7697	DV 1544	7767		7837		7907	WM 4380	7977		8047	VC 4367
7698		7768		7838	UD 3433	7908		7978	KR 3147	8048	
7699		7769	UV 8063	7839	VC 1910	7909	VC 2405	7979		8049	
7700		7770		7840	UW 7246	7910		7980		8050	
7701	GE 6709	7771	GE 6709	7841		7911	UW 7212	7981		8051	
7702	KW 8289	7772	WX 1710	7842		7912		7982		8052	
7703	VC 761	7773		7843	GC 6414	7913		7983	RH 361	8053	
7704	VC 764	7774	DF 8676	7844	VC 1909	7914	UW 7251	7984		8054	
7705	GE 5940	7775	BR 7606	7845	GE 7012	7915		7985	VC 3584	8055	
7706	UY 6219	7776		7846	VC 1904	7916		7986	MW 6406	8056	KS 4646
7707	VC 452	7777	WM 4114	7847		7917		7987	KW 7730	8057	
7708		7778		7848		7918	DV 4153	7988	LG 3360	8058	
7709		7779	CV 830	7849		7919	GE 7462	7989		8059	SW 3456
7710		7780	VC 1901	7850		7920		7990		8060	
7711		7781		7851		7921	LG 2427	7991		8061	TF 564
7712	UV 2648	7782		7852	KW 7402	7922		7992	DF 9520	8062	VC 2674
7713	DV 2204	7783		7853	GH 4904	7923		7993		8063	TY 6831
7714		7784	UV 6717	7854	GC 321	7924		7994		8064	TR 8649
7715		7785	GE 6710	7855	KS 4651	7925	VC 2950	7995		8065	VC 2403
7716	MW 5302	7786	GE 6856	7856	VC 1905	7926		7996	GF 1354	8066	
7717	DF 8681	7787		7857	GC 326	7927		7997		8067	
7718		7788	GE 6711	7858	RA 9963	7928	DV 4988	7998		8068	DV 4398
7719	HW 6391	7789		7859	KW 7277	7929	JK 800	7999	LG 3680	8069	GC 5170
7720		7790		7860		7930		8000		8070	
7721	VC 1573	7791		7861		7931	DV 5086	8001		8071	HH 5225
7722		7792	DV 2582	7862	VC 1908	7932	DF 9208	8002	VC 3585	8072	LG 3674
7723	WE 5977	7793		7863	VA 9234	7933	SC 6073	8003	VC 3855	8073	
7724		7794		7864	OU 4730	7934		8004	HW 7505	8074	DV 4555
7725		7795	VC 1903	7865	VC 2946	7935	VL 1869	8005	UB 306	8075	TR 8480
7726	VC 765	7796	DF 8911	7866	VC 1911	7936	MW 6611	8006		8076	RX 6479
7727		7797	EK 7845	7867		7937	DF 9631	8007	GC 2280	8077	KW 8240
7728		7798		7868	GE 7013	7938	TE 9969	8008		8078	
7729		7799	VC 1578	7869		7939	VC 2406	8009		8079	
7730		7800		7870	VC 2941	7940		8010		8080	
7731	VO 2305	7801	GE 7014	7871	UY 6839	7941		8011		8081	
7732		7802		7872	VC 2944	7942	UW 8934	8012	VC 2404	8082	
7733		7803		7873	GE 7411	7943	VC 2943	8013		8083	
7734		7804		7874	GE 7417	7944		8014		8084	VC 2947
7735		7805		7875	OU 4127	7945		8015		8085	GJ 2156
7736	VC 1575	7806	VA 9185	7876	MW 5851	7946	DV 8897	8016		8086	
7737	KW 7036	7807		7877	VC 2401	7947	DV 8372	8017	HW 7717	8087	

No.	Reg.	No.	Reg.	No.	Reg.	No.	Reg.	No.	Reg.	No.	Reg.
8088	- - - - - -	8158	- - TF 1968	8228	- - - - - -	8298	- - VC 5347	8340	- - - - - -	8382	- - SN 5139
8089	- - DV 4835	8159	- - UB 2937	8229	- - - - - -	8299	- - OU 6121	8341	- - - - - -	8383	- - - - - -
8090	- - - - - -	8160	- - - - - -	8230	- - - - - -	8300	- - - - - -	8342	- - - - - -	8384	- - - - - -
8091	- - VR 7119	8161	- - - - - -	8231	- - - - - -	8301	- - - - - -	8343	- - OU 6390	8385	- - GG 1941
8092	- - - - - -	8162	- - - - - -	8232	- - VC 5342	8302	- - RB 2302	8344	- - - - - -	8386	- - - - - -
8093	- - - - - -	8163	- -MW 7226	8233	- - VC 5345	8303	- - - - - -	8345	- - - - - -	8387	- - - -BR 1
8094	- - -FJ 6925	8164	- - VC 3856	8234	- -MW 7230	8304	- - GH 4904	8346	- - VC 6426	8388	- - VC 5708
8095	- - -GJ 6032	8165	- - VC 3857	8235	- -WE ****	8305	- - SC 8125	8347	- - UW 5779	8389	- - - - - -
8096	- - VC 3583	8166	- - VC 3858	8236	- -WE ****	8306	- - - - - -	8348	- - - - - -	8390	- - KW 8978
8097	- - DV 4070	8167	- - VC 3581	8237	- - - - - -	8307	- - - - - -	8349	- - FH 7007	8391	- - SC 8679
8098	- - TY 7001	8168	- - - - - -	8238	- - - - - -	8308	- - - - - -	8350	- - VC 6720	8392	- - VC 5704
8099	- - - - - -	8169	- - - - - -	8239	- - - - - -	8309	- - -LJ 3059	8351	- - - - - -	8393	- - VC 5709
8100	- - - - - -	8170	- - TF 1537	8240	- - OG 1598	8310	- - - - - -	8352	- - VU 1115	8394	- - KS 4988
8101	- - GC 5151	8171	- - - - - -	8241	- - - - - -	8311	- -WO 4456	8353	- -KW 9043	8395	- - - - - -
8102	- - - - - -	8172	- - - - - -	8242	- -KW 8022	8312	- - RX 7272	8354	- - - - - -	8396	- - - - - -
8103	- -HW 8182	8173	- - - - - -	8243	- - - - - -	8313	- - -GG 490	8355	- -WO 5355	8397	- - - - - -
8104	- - VC 4080	8174	- - SC 8595	8244	- - VC 5346	8314	- - VC 5607	8356	- - -GG 795	8398	- - - - - -
8105	- -MW 6711	8175	- - - - AUS	8245	- - - - - -	8315	- - VH 3184	8357	- - UB 3723	8399	- - -KY 863
8106	- -HW 8191	8176	- - - - - -	8246	- - - - - -	8316	- - - - - -	8358	- - TF 3016	8400	- - - - - -
8107	- - - - - -	8177	- - - - AUS	8247	- - - - - -	8317	- - - - - -	8359	- - VC 5703	8401	- - LG 7580
8108	- - -LJ 1111	8178	- - - - - -	8248	- - - - - -	8318	- - - - - -	8360	- - VC 5348	8402	- - - - - -
8109	- - LG 3480	8179	- - UX 6784	8249	- - - - - -	8319	- - - - - -	8361	- - - - - -	8403	- - GG 1401
8110	- - - - - -	8180	- - VH 3062	8250	- - FS 424	8320	- - - - - -	8362	- - - - - -	8404	- - - - - -
8111	- - TF 1910	8181	- - - - AUS	8251	- - -GH 778	8321	- - - - - -	8363	- -WX 6691	8405	- - -YD 817
8112	- - GF 2641	8182	- - VC 4368	8252	- - VH 3161	8322	- - UB 3952	8364	- - VC 5712	8406	- - - - - -
8113	- - - - - -	8183	- - ET 6848	8253	- - - - - -	8323	- - ET 6430	8365	- - VC 7010	8407	- - DR 8016
8114	- - VC 4365	8184	- - - - - -	8254	- - - - - -	8324	- - -KY 908	8366	- - GK 5287	8408	- - VC 7008
8115	- - HH 5185	8185	- - FG 5949	8255	- - - - - -	8325	- - - - - -	8367	- - SC 9450	8409	- - RH 2888
8116	- - - - - -	8186	- - VC 5063	8256	- - - - NZ	8326	- - VC 5706	8368	- - - - - -	8410	- - KX 7200
8117	- - - - - -	8187	- - VC 5343	8257	- - - - - -	8327	- - VC 5711	8369	- - - - - -	8411	- - - - - -
8118	- - - - - -	8188	- - - - - -	8258	- - - - ZA	8328	- - - - - -	8370	- - - - - -	8412	- - - - - -
8119	- - AZ 4247	8189	- - VN 1787	8259	- - - - - -	8329	- - PL 1452	8371	- - LG 5253	8413	- - - - - -
8120	- - - - - -	8190	- - - - - -	8260	- - - - - -	8330	- - - - - -	8372	- - - - - -	8414	- - RX 7232
8121	- - - - - -	8191	- - GE 9642	8261	- KW 8704	8331	- - - - - -	8373	- - - - - -	8415	- -WX 5463
8122	- - - - - -	8192	- - - - - -	8262	- - - - - -	8332	- - GG 1451	8374	- - UP 5152	8416	- - - - - -
8123	- - - - - -	8193	- - - - - -	8263	- - UY 8254	8333	- - - - - -	8375	- - - - - -	8417	- - - - - -
8124	- - - - - -	8194	- - VC 5064	8264	- - VC 5701	8334	- - - - - -	8376	- - VC 5705	8418	- - VC 6423
8125	- - - - - -	8195	- - - - - -	8265	- - TY 7100	8335	- - - - - -	8377	- - SC 9449	8419	- - - - - -
8126	- - UB 3724	8196	- - - - - -	8266	- - - - - -	8336	- - GG 1942	8378	- -WX 5678	8420	- - - - - -
8127	- - - - - -	8197	- - -GJ 2196	8267	- - - - - -	8337	- - - - - -	8379	- - HY 1194	8421	- - TF 3445
8128	- - - - - -	8198	- - - - - -	8268	- - - - - -	8338	- - - JF 532	8380	- - GG 1255	8422	- - OU 7420
8129	- -MW 6646	8199	- -HW 9854	8269	- -HW 9824	8339	- - TY 7590	8381	- - -OW 99	8423	- - VC 6421
8130	- - - - - -	8200	- - -GV 269	8270	- - - - - -						
8131	- - - - - -	8201	- - BR 8287	8271	- - VC 5068						
8132	- - DV 4068	8202	- - - - - -	8272	- - GH 1288						
8133	- - - - - -	8203	- - - - - -	8273	- - VC 5344						
8134	- - UT 6823	8204	- - - - - -	8274	- - - - - -						
8135	- - - - - -	8205	- - RB 2753	8275	- - BR 8300						
8136	- - DV 4184	8206	- -KW 8647	8276	- - - - - -						
8137	- - VX 4492	8207	- - - - - -	8277	- - - - - -						
8138	- - PO 1846	8208	- - DV 5914	8278	- - RM 7243						
8139	- - LG 3616	8209	- - BR 8218	8279	- - - - - -						
8140	- - - - - -	8210	- - - - - -	8280	- -HW 9910						
8141	- - GF 8509	8211	- - - - - -	8281	- - VC 5702						
8142	- - TY 7006	8212	- - VC 5062	8282	- - - - - -						
8143	- - VC 3582	8213	- - -GJ 6036	8283	- - - - - -						
8144	- - WF 3127	8214	- - VX 6430	8284	- - - - - -						
8145	- - VC 3586	8215	- - - - - -	8285	- - RB 2260						
8146	- - - - - -	8216	- - LG 4787	8286	- - - - - -						
8147	- - - - - -	8217	- - SN 5076	8287	- - -YD 600						
8148	- - - - - ZA	8218	- - VC 5066	8288	- - -WJ 285						
8149	- - VC 5067	8219	- - CF 9882	8289	- - GH 1058						
8150	- - - - - -	8220	- - - - ZA	8290	- - -LJ 2592						
8151	- - - - - -	8221	- -WX 5071	8291	- - TF 2190						
8152	- - - - - -	8222	- - -GJ 5508	8292	- - - - - -						
8153	- - - - - -	8223	- - OG 1580	8293	- - - - - -						
8154	- - - - - -	8224	- - - - - -	8294	- - - - - -						
8155	- - RF 7329	8225	- - - - - -	8295	- - LG 4788						
8156	- - SC 6502	8226	- -KW 9069	8296	- - - - - -						
8157	- - GF 2680	8227	- - - - - -	8297	- - - - - -						

This was a particularly significant period in the history of the company, not only from the standpoint of production, but also that of design. Whilst the 14.75hp model continued to be available until March 1929 for the TA, and April 1929 for the TB, the larger 16.95hp derivatives were clearly in the ascendancy, and indeed, for the above period, for the first time, production of six-cylinder cars well exceeded that of all the fours put together.

Of rather more significance, however, from the historical point of view, is that after some three years of concentrated development work, the first British car to deploy front-wheel drive in series production, entered the market. Whilst the production may have fallen short of expectations, it is undeniable that this Alvis design was very many years ahead of its time and would influence automotive thought for many years to come.

It will be observed that whilst the Coventry-based coachbuilder Carbodies, together with Cross & Ellis, continued to clothe most of the Alvis production, the larger six-cylinder chassis was beginning to attract the attention of some specialist makers a little further afield.

6572 | OX 6854
Charles Meisl

Czechoslovakian-born Meisl really deserves a full biography to do justice to his remarkable career. Versatility would be an understatement. Coming to England in the mid-1930s, he saw service with the RAF, flying in Wellingtons as radar operator and gunner. Postwar he was involved in the hot air balloon 'Bristol Belle' (G-AVTL) project of 1970, and was also known for conducting an HRG with some verve. He was also a most astute businessman, becoming MD of Britover (Continental) Ltd, which was, amongst other activities, a concessionaire for the Cibie range of lighting systems. It is, however, for his journalistic and linguistic skills that enthusiasts owe him the most, being the remarkable translator of at least three major works of scholarship: *History of Skoda, Laurin & Klement* (Margolius), *Speed was my Life* (Neubauer) and *Porsche, the Man and his Cars* (von Frankenberg).

For further insight into Meisl, the reader is referred to the *Motor Sport* issue of October 1976, page 1188.

6695 | UY 4123
Morgan Motor Company

Famous for its charismatic three-wheelers, Morgan did not commence four-wheel car manufacture until 1935. Prior to this, on at least two occasions, choice of family transport fell upon Alvis cars. The above was ordered in chassis form and was bodied by Morgan itself in tourer format, and for a while it bore its Hispano-like stork as a mascot instead of the usual Alvis hare. Most interestingly, H F S Morgan took this Alvis on a trip to Cannes via the Alps, and wrote up his quite eventful trip in an issue of *The Light Car* and *Cyclecar* in 1929. The next foray into Alvis-owning would come with a somewhat more luxurious Speed 20 SB saloon (qv 11255).

6722 | WK 5485
Alvis Works Car

This is an especially significant entry for not only is it the first example of the front-wheel drive Alvis to enter series production, but also it is the first example of any such British car to so enter series production. It was the culmination of many experiments that had gone on since 1925, and the works continued to play with this 'first-off.' It was re-engined and rebuilt after only five months of in-house usage, and re-registered as WK 7349 before being sold to a Southampton customer.

6740 | WK 6159
Pytchley & Co Ltd

This Northampton company specialised in the construction of sliding roof systems for a large number of manufacturers. These could take the form of initial equipment, or indeed specialised conversions. It was truly the 'Webasto' of its day.

6746 | WM 2142
J A Cooper

John Arthur Cooper was born in Leicester, 27th November 1916, and was initially apprenticed to the Alvis Company in 1933, remaining with it until the commencement of WWII. He subsequently worked with a number of motoring's big names like Raymond Mays, Peter Berthon and Sir Roy Fedden. He also did two 'Montes' with Stirling Moss and Desmond Scannell.

In 1949, he took up journalism, succeeding that other Alvis-driving figure Sammy Davis as sports editor of *Autocar*. Cooper owned at least three Alvis, cars and the above example is described in some detail in the *Motor Sport* issue of February

6722: The very first Alvis front wheel drive production model. (Courtesy Alvis Ltd collection)

Alvis assembly line around 1927.

1975, page 134, by a later owner who notes some of the mods, which included dividing the chassis amidships and reversing the rear portion so as to give an underslung arrangement. Maybe a bit drastic, but the works did the same sort of thing on the 12/70 and the TA 14. Cooper had also written up his Alvis experiences in *Autocar*'s *Talking of Sports Cars* series, no 128, issue of November 27, 1942.

Though obviously an Alvis man through and through, John will be especially remembered for his Healey Silverstone, registration number JAC 100, which he did not live to enjoy to the full, being killed in an accident in March 1955 – at the age of only 38.

At one time the Brooke Bond Tea Company issued a series of 50 small cards marking the history of the motor car, which could be collected and mounted in an album obtainable from your local grocer for sixpence. The front wheel drive Alvis naturally figured in this selection as number 31. The image is obviously based on the 1928 Le Mans team cars (6793/4).

6765
London Metropolitan Police
Scotland Yard's purchase of this 14.75hp model evidently proved quite satisfactory, as other orders would follow (qv 7742 and 8079).

6776
Rosewarne family
An early example of this prominent Cornish family's considerable sequence of Alvis cars (qv 7349, 10867, 13390 for bio, 13309, 14457 and 23987).

6791
Iliffe Publications Ltd
The above is the fourth of the Alvis vans despatched to Iliffe's *Midland Daily Telegraph*, all finished in that firm's livery and logos (qv 1720, 1721 and 3012 for the others).

6793

6794
Competition cars
Arguably one of the company's finest moments, first and second in the 1.5-litre class at the Le Mans 24 Hour Race of 1928, with a sixth and ninth in the general classification, and only beaten there by six-cylinder cars of three times the engine size, despite only running in unsupercharged mode. Harvey and Purdy drove the first car, Davis and Urquhart-Dykes the second.

6795
Works development car
Immediately sequential to the Le Mans cars in chassis number, 6795 was the first production example of the FB front-wheel drive type, ie the long chassis version.

6798
A W Ketèlbey
Albert William Ketèlbey (August 9, 1875-November 26, 1959) was an incredibly prolific and successful composer and arranger of light music, with a canon of well over 200 works. He was also a multi-instrumentalist and conductor. At a time when the wind-up gramophone was

That doyen of motoring journalists (and Alvis driver) Sammy Davis was accorded honours at an RAC reception in 1976. This programme cover records that occasion.

Composer Albert W Ketèlbey in studious mode. (Courtesy biographer John Sant, from Bosworth sources)

becoming widespread family entertainment, few households would be without the 78rpm disc by Columbia, with *In a Monastery Garden* on one side, and *In a Persian Market* on the other. Sheet

music sales of the former had topped the million mark by 1924, making this Alvis easily affordable. Sadly, he bent it in an accident in February 1930, but his increasing prosperity would see him upgrading to a Silver Ghost and a Chrysler. Could it be that his motoring enthusiasm led to him composing a piece entitled *Dance of the Merry Mascots* in 1932? (I am greatly indebted to Ketèlbey's biographer, John Sant, for these and other details. His book is ISBN 0-9538058-0-8 – Manifold Publishing.)

6815   TN 8065
Super Gran

This car, one of the late 14.75hp models, appeared in one of the 27 episodes of a popular Tyne-Tees television series screened between 1985 and 1987, starring Gudrun Ure.

6838   WK 6154
Dr H C Wright

'Cam' Wright was a scientist employed at the Royal Naval Physiological Laboratory in Gosport, Hampshire. One of the research studies at the time was into the concussive effects of a detonating mine upon divers and frogmen. Alvis historian and former colleague, Dr Adrian Lloyd tells us that one such experiment involved Cam wading out into Stokes Bay, where a series of mines would be detonated upon his signal. A 'safe' distance would thereby be arrived at depending on the effect upon the observer in the water. This was, of course, long before health and safety regulations were applied, and plainly, in this case, the borderline between bravery and foolhardiness had become somewhat blurred.

6850
Sir Malcolm Campbell

Famous speed record breaker on both land and water, Campbell was born August 11, 1885 and died December 31, 1948. He had apparently considered a political career at one stage, having stood unsuccessfully for Parliament in 1935. His company's purchase of a front-wheel drive FB chassis saloon came about at a time when it was reported that he was hoping to interest the Alvis Car & Engineering Company in constructing and sponsoring a land speed record car based on the innovative FWD principle. Whilst this idea came to nought, Campbell was already on record as an advocate of Alvis engineering and its team of drivers, if a letter in *Motor* magazine, issue of October 4, 1927, is anything to go by.

6864 **WK 6153**
Competition car
Miss E V Watson's mount at the 1929 Shelsley Walsh event, winning the 1.5-litre class. For her previous Alvis competition car, see 4321.

6865 **FR - - - -**
William Lyons
Before the SS (later to become Jaguar Cars) operation was transferred to Coventry, it had been well established in Blackpool. The Swallow Sidecar was a popular product, and the firm expanded to produce some light car bodies of a distinctive style, probably best known on the Austin Seven chassis. Other makes of chassis were also used, of which this 12/50 TG Alvis is one. The only known photograph of this clearly shows the Blackpool registration letters 'FR' on its number plate, but unfortunately the numerals are concealed. After the move to Coventry, Lyons bought another TG 12/50 car; strangely not this time in chassis form, but a standard Carbodies saloon (qv 7323).

6892 **WK 8209**
Captain E C Nottingham M C
Eric Cato Nottingham, born 1897, was initially an army officer with service during WWI in France, Flanders, Egypt and Gallipoli. After hostilities ceased, he joined the Nigerian police force in 1919 and became acting deputy commissioner. In 1938, he transferred to a similar position in the Gold Coast.

His interesting personal papers are now lodged at the Bodleian Library, Oxford.

6935 **WK 7343**

6936 **WK 6948**

6937 **WK 7342**

Most probably works driver George A Willday is seen here with one of the 1928 team cars (6935). His female companion on this occasion could very well be Ruth Urquhart-Dykes. (Courtesy Ernest Shenton collection)

6938 **YX 6424**

6939 **WK 7344**

6940 **WK 7341**
Competition cars
This interesting block of identically-bodied FA Series front-wheel drive cars had been laid down specifically with works or works-supported competition entries in mind. Typically from this set, 6935 had been used by Leon Cushman in the TT, and by Maurice Harvey in the Boulogne Trials; 6936 was similarly campaigned by H W Purdy, whilst 6938 was entered by Commander Rooper in the Brooklands August bank holiday event, where he achieved a lap at 96mph, but was unfortunately unplaced.

6957 **WK 6949**
T B Andre Ltd
A front-wheel drive saloon on the FB chassis for this London-based maker of automotive suspension components. Some four years later, the company would also purchase an SA Speed 20 (qv 9854).

6978 **WK 6950**
Tokutura Hama
Hama was the first president of the Classic Car Club of Japan, and bought this FB Series front-

wheel drive saloon from a dealer on Great Portland Street, London, second-hand in 1935. It still survives, but not quite in its original form.

7010
7012
7045
7055
7057
7082
7083
London Motor Show 1928
The above is a list of the vehicles known to have been prepared for the Olympia Show, covering the works stand, coachbuilders' stands, and the London distributor Henly's demonstrators. The first five are Silver Eagles, and the two remaining are one example each of the revised front-wheel drive types now designated FD (short chassis) and FE (long chassis). With all the London registration number records having been destroyed, apportionment is virtually impossible. All that can be said is that Henly's were known to be using the 'UL,' 'UU,' and 'XV' sequences at this time.

7070 KX 1369
Lord Hailsham
The first Lord Hailsham, Douglas McGarel Hogg PC, KC (February 28, 1872-August 16, 1950) was educated at Cheam, Eton, and served in the Boer War. He was called to the Bar in 1902 and held governmental positions under three monarchs: George V, Edward VII and George VI.

There is further Alvis connection concerning his son, Quintin Hogg, second Lord Hailsham (qv 9619).

7127 WK 8044
Baron Takakimi Mitsui
A Japanese tycoon who was once one of his country's richest men. He had this TT-type two-seater delivered to his Park Lane, London address, but it was subsequently taken to Japan, and in 1934 rebodied as a saloon. It is understood that post-WWII, the Baron lost most of his not inconsiderable fortune, and the car was unfortunately scrapped about the time of the Korean War.

7128 XV 2990

7306 UW 2017
Iliffe Publications Ltd
This pair of front-wheel drive cars – one a short chassis FD, the other a long chassis FE, belonged to Austin Partridge, an exponent of the genre. They were written up in two entries of *Autocar*'s *Talking of Sports Cars* series: no 96, issue of April 17, 1942, and no 158, issue of June 15, 1943.

7168
Works development car
This is the one-off single-seater front-wheel drive car built with Brooklands endurance record attempts in mind, but not so used. It is the only FWD car to be allocated the 'FC' designation.

7273 WF 2520
The Burney Streamline car
There is arguably no more bizarre use of Alvis components than when front-wheel drive chassis 7273 was purchased new from Henly's London, and shipped up to Howden in Yorkshire, where Sir Dennistoun Burney and his team were working on the R100 Airship project, but evidently found time to develop what was described as an R100

7273: This patinated tax disc is of considerable historical significance, relating as it does to the Alvis front-wheel drive components that became the very first Burney Streamline car. Whilst the disc has miraculously survived, the Burney did not.

on wheels. The Alvis engine and transmission was hung out to the rear, Volkswagen-style, with the steering gear locked out, and a second set of steering gear placed at the front in a new aerodynamic frame, initially clad in balloon fabric but later panelled by Carlton Coachworks. Thus was born the prototype Burney car, the production versions of the very few made, using Beverley Barnes, Armstrong Siddeley, Lycoming, and Crossley engines. The enterprising Burney had evidently observed that the use of these parts had, by accident, given the potential for four-wheel steering, and promptly took out a patent thereto, but never used it. Another member of the Howden team at the time was novelist Nevil Shute, who, in his book *The Rainbow and the Rose* has a character, Captain Pascoe, who uses an unidentified Alvis car.

For further reading: *The Burney Car* by Dr Bernard Nield, published 2008, Howden Civic Society, ISBN 978-0-9557145-0-4.

7274

WK 8045

Competition car

This front-wheel drive car enjoyed much exposure when it was new, including an entry in the 1928 London-Exeter Trial, driven by S C H (Sammy) Davis, and also written up by him in *Autocar,* issue of February 22, 1929. Also the subject of a full road test by *Motor*, in April of the same year.

7291

GU 1728

John Wild MA, MMB

Nowadays, some patients attending hospitals will be quite familiar with the practice of ultrasound scans. That the technique not only became possible, but is now ubiquitous is largely down to one man: John Julian Cuttance Wild (August 11, 1914-September 18, 2009) who was educated at Merchant Taylors School and Downhill College, Cambridge. He graduated in medicine, and became a surgeon, initially during the final stages of WWII assisting injured military personnel. After WWII he emigrated to the USA, taking up a position at the University of Minnesota. Here, he continued his earlier experiments into ultrasound with a device that had been used to detect any flaws in the armour of tanks. He discovered that if the operating range of said device could be raised to 15 megacycles, it could 'see' through human tissue.

Subsequently, Wild was able to hone this virtually chance discovery into the advance of the medical practice that it is today. Wild's obituary, written by Phil Davison, and published in the *Financial Times* of October 2, 2009, was aptly headed: "The ingenious surgeon who could see through his own body." Wild retained his front-wheel drive Alvis until his death at the age of 95. It is the only surviving four-door saloon type.

7301

Jonas Woodhead & Co Ltd

This Leeds-based company, with roots going back to 1850, was a manufacturer of automotive springs and shock absorbers. Alvis Ltd was, of course, one of its clients, and it is quite possible that this works-registered Silver Eagle was part of a reciprocal arrangement, given that the firm had previously purchased a 12/50 TG (qv 5586).

7308

Hudson Motor Car Company

It is not unusual for car manufacturers to buy an example of another make for evaluation purposes, and it must have been the technical innovation of the Alvis front-wheel drive that led to 7308 being purchased via the London agent and shipped to Detroit. It was reported that at some point during Hudson ownership, the car was involved in an accident with a pedestrian, and thereafter languished at the factory. Interestingly, the building in which it was housed was taken over by the Bendix Corporation, who had the ambition to produce a Bendix car in competition to the major US manufacturers of the day. The Alvis came with the purchase of said building, and it is most intriguing that the single prototype of the Bendix SWC that was made, incorporated front-wheel drive, and bore a superficial resemblance to the Chrysler Airflow. The Alvis was subsequently disposed of, recommissioned privately, but was sadly involved in a further fatality in 1949.

A full account of the Bendix SWC connection appears in *Hemmings Classic Car*, issue of October 2008.

7316

Rob Walker/Tony Gaze

7316 has passed through the hands of these two notable owners. Rob Walker (August 14, 1917-April

2002) was heir to the eponymous whisky distiller, and became one of Britain's best-known racing drivers and team managers. Similarly, Frederick Anthony Owen Gaze, DFC (February 3, 1920-July 29, 2013) was an Australian educated at Geelong Grammar School and Queens College Cambridge, was a distinguished WWII flying ace, especially with Spitfires, and postwar had a versatile driving career, which included Formula 1 appearances with an HWM, Le Mans with a Frazer Nash, and the Monte Carlo Rally with a Holden. The advanced front-wheel drive system of this Alvis clearly had an equal appeal to both of these rabid car enthusiasts.

7323 — VC 1218
William Lyons

Interestingly, before becoming a serious competitor to Alvis Ltd with the manufacture of his own SS and Jaguar cars, Lyons bought this TG 12/50 Carbodies saloon via the London agent rather than the works. Equally interesting, is that in August 1928, when Lyons was still based at Blackpool, another TG 12/50 had been purchased in chassis form (qv 6865), and was duly bodied in the familiar Swallow coachwork style.

7332 — VC 4364
Competition car

Amateur racing driver F Taylor-Downes bought this front-wheel drive two-seater from the works to race, particularly on the Southport sand events. He was an old boy of Rydal School, in Colwyn Bay, and was well known locally, both as a sidesman at St John's Methodist Church, and as a Boy Scout leader. He was known to his peers as 'Hefty.' Later, becoming more adventurous, he bought, also from the works, one of the first series of straight-eight sports/racing Alvis (qv 7557) and campaigned that as well.

7349 — DR 4734
Rosewarne family

One of this prominent Cornish family's considerable sequence of Alvis cars (qv 4709, 6776, 10687, 13309, 13390 for bio, 14457, and 23987).

7356 — CH 8145
W A Robotham

Robotham was an esteemed Rolls-Royce engineer,

initially employed as an assistant to Ernest Hives, and known as 'Rumpty' to the team at the Belper operation. He was involved with chassis design, but progressed to the design work on the Meteor tank engine. Later still, he was instrumental in getting the B-Series of engines into production, which, it may be recalled, existed in four-, six-, and eight-cylinder forms, the latter being the version that powered the range of Alvis fighting vehicles, ie types FV 601 (Saladin) onwards, and its derivatives. Robotham was not the only Rolls-Royce engineer to appreciate the Alvis ethos (qv Ivan Waller and 7858).

Robotham's 7356 started life as a standard saloon, but still exists today in the form of a 'special.'

7357
Arthur Farrar-Hockley

A journalist who had worked both in Coventry, and in London, particularly for Temple Press, publishers of the magazine *Motor*. He was the father of General Sir Anthony Farrar-Hockley, distinguished army officer and a well-respected military historian, who would have been just five years of age when the above Silver Eagle was delivered.

7367
Sir Cedric Hardwicke

Actor and serial Alvis owner (qv 10877 for bio, 5969, and also 8549, 9524 and 10737).

7356 is seen here in its later 'special' guise, driven by Roy Heath. (Courtesy the late Julian Collins)

7371
Lord Hotham
Probably the first of Lord Hotham's series of Alvis cars (qv 8318 and 13137 for bio).

7397
Daily Mirror
A staff car supplied to this national daily newspaper.

DF 7352

7407
Movie car
A popular television series of the 1970s was the BBC's *Ripping Yarns*, the presenter of which was the famous actor and humourist Michael Palin. 7407 appeared in at least one of the nine episodes that were first screened between 1976 and 1978.

VM 8657

7430
Motor Sport
The regular column *Vintage Veerings*, in the issue of March 1950, page 133, contains an account of the above 12/50, which had then covered upwards of 200,000 miles, mostly in the hands of its second owner, Vivian Buck, who had bought it in 1934. In 1950, new cars were still scarce, and it was not unusual for older cars like the 12/50 to be in use every day for commuting, and to be used for minor competitive events at weekends. There is arguably no better account of the model's longevity, reliability, and sheer motoring fun as that described most eruditely by the owner.

7529

7557   VC 19

7558

7571   VC 18

7592   VC 766

7593   VC 17
Works development cars
The first manifestation of the pioneering Alvis front-wheel drive system had, of course, been in 1925, and had led to a limited run of four-cylinder production cars. The above, however, represent

7407: A particularly fine example of a TG 12/50, with Cross & Ellis tourer body. (Courtesy the late Peter Cameron-Clarke collection)

the far more ambitious straight-eight versions, consisting of six sports/racing cars and a grand prix car. All were the subject of much in-house experimentation, and 7571, 7592 and 7593 were 1929 TT Race entries. 7558 and 7571 found favour respectively with racing drivers W Mansell and L Cushman.

For the second batch of front-wheel drive, eight-cylinder production of a further four cars, see 8359-on.

Also see 7332, a four-cylinder front-wheel drive car supplied to amateur racing driver F Taylor-Downes, of Colwyn Bay, who also purchased the above 7557, competing with it at Southport and elsewhere.

VY 1103

7603
F H Sheppee Ltd
York-based engineering company and user of several Alvis cars (qv 8752 for details).

DH 7341

7620
William Preston MP
William Preston (August 1874-November 22, 1941) was a prominent Walsall businessman who had also played cricket for Staffordshire. He stood for Parliament in 1924 and was elected, but the result was initially overturned on the grounds that his business was a contractor to the Government. With the matter duly resolved, a by-election was held in which he stood again, and won again, retaining the seat until 1929. Previously owned an Alvis 12/50 TG (qv 4956).

7706

Terry & Sons Ltd

See 8263 for the other Silver Eagle supplied to this acclaimed manufacturer of automotive valve springs.

7712 UV 2648

Prince George, Duke of Kent

Prince George (December 20, 1902-August 25, 1942), was the younger brother of King Edward VIII, Duke of Windsor (qv 9018 and 27259) and of King George VI. He died when on active service in 1942 when a Short Sunderland flying boat that he was travelling on crashed into a hillside in Caithness. His Silver Eagle was specially bodied for him by Lancefield Coachworks, and a feature about it appeared in *The Automobile*, issue of December 1993, page 44.

7727

Philip Runciman

One of several Alvis cars ordered by Runciman (qv 4618, 5752, 8845 and 9548).

7741
8079

London Metropolitan Police

A pair of Silver Eagle models supplied to Scotland Yard. The earlier is interesting in that it is the only one of the very many Alvis cars ordered by various police forces, to be specified in 'chassis only' form. The works record does not mention a maker. This gives rise to the hypothesis that this could have been a van of the 'Black Maria' type used for custodial purposes. At about the same time, the London firm of Du Cros was constructing very similar ambulance vehicles for the Talbot company.

7807
7828
7829
7830
7831
7832
7839 VC 1910

London Motor Show 1929

The above represent the Alvis exhibits at the 1929 Olympia Show, covering works, and various coachbuilders' stands.

Note: the caveat concerning London registration numbers is explained under 7010 et seq.

7810

7845 GE 7012

7873 GE 7411

7874 GE 7417

7880

7889 VA 9316
7908

Scottish Motor Show 1929

A listing of works cars known to have been prepared for the 1929 Kelvin Hall show. All these cars were sold in Scotland after the show, except 7880 which was re-allocated to the Birmingham agent.

7838 UD 3433

Competition car

One of the first new Silver Eagle sports models to be delivered to a member of the public, 7838 first found favour with one W Budd, a resident of Caversham, who kept it until March 1934 when he sold it to Antony Powys-Lybbe for £130. Powys-Lybbe had already developed an Alvis special based upon a 12/60 (qv 8988), and set about modifying 7838 for competition, initially for the 1934 TT, using a 15.7hp two-litre cylinder block borrowed from his friend Michael May's 'Green' car (qv 8101). It has become known as the 'Black' car in order to differentiate it from its peers. The 1935 competition season found the car further uprated using a Speed 20 2.5-litre block. Some interest was shown by the Alvis works in Powys-Lybbe's developments, as it loaned such items as wheels, a 4.11 rear axle, and a special camshaft.

7854 GC 321

Iliffe Publications Ltd

By this time a much-used second-hand car, it was chosen by *Autocar*, from Henly's stock, to feature in its *Used Cars on the Road* series, no 78, in the issue of July 8, 1932, page 74.

7857

GC 326

The Blue Train car

Whilst maybe not quite as prestigious as the Orient Express, the Blue Train express service between Calais and St Raphael was a popular travel route, and there had been several well-publicised attempts to beat the schedule by car, notably in a Bentley and a Rover. Such an exercise took place in March 1930, with two staff members of the Henly's dealership, E J P Eugster and D Watson, conducting an example of the new Silver Eagle Sports from St Raphael to Calais, beating the train by three hours and 15 minutes. For many years the actual car involved remained unidentified, but this mystery has now been solved. It turns out to have been the same car that was heaped with praise by Edgar Duffield in the *Automotor Journal*, issue of February 7, 1930. Eugster's own detailed account of the trip also appears in *Autocar*, issue of March 7, 1930, page 442. The car is also mentioned in *Motor Sport*, issue of June 1930. After these quite strenuous outings, the car was sold second-hand to Lord Acton, a then-22 undergraduate of Trinity College, Cambridge.

7858

RA 9963

Competition car

A particularly notable example of the genre is the Waller Special, purchased new as a standard car by Ivan Waller (father of Peter Waller of ERA R9B fame), a production engineer at Rolls-Royce Ltd, Derby. With a confidence typical of a hands-on engineer, Waller modified his new car at a very early stage: lowered it by 2in, axle ratio raised from 4.77 to 4.33, and compression ratio up from 5.8 to 6.4 to one. Many competition appearances ensued, Shelsley Walsh in September 1931, and the Monte Carlo Rally of 1932, starting from Budapest (disqualified for returning an average speed higher than that allowed). Amply making up for this rebuff, however, was winning the Senior Handicap Race at Phoenix Park, Dublin, in September 1932, at an average speed of 77.87mph, and receiving the Wakefield Trophy. See *The Vintage Alvis*, page 356, by Hull and Johnson, for a more detailed account.

7876

MW 5851

Major C H Delmege

A serial Alvis owner (qv 10738 for bio, also 8476, 9479, 12052 and 1224).

7858: The Waller Special. (Courtesy Tom Grainger)

7903

DR 6084

Whitney Straight CBE, MC, DFC

This motoring legend (November 6, 1912-April 5, 1979) needs little in the way of introduction. American-born, but became a British citizen in 1935, following education at Dartington School and Trinity College, Cambridge. A notable figure at Brooklands, especially with his Maserati, he was also a pilot, joining the RAF and progressing to Air Commodore. Taken prisoner during WWII and afterwards becoming managing director of BOAC, and deputy chairman of Rolls-Royce.

7903's subsequent owner was, equally distinguished, the novelist Henry Williamson (December 1, 1895-August 13, 1977). Author of well over 40 books, mostly in the rural vein, Williamson is arguably one of the best chroniclers of the rural way of life since William Cobbett. Though probably best remembered for his *Tarka the Otter* of 1927, *Goodbye West Country* of 1937 must be mentioned, as it features his Alvis. Numbered amongst his friends were T E Lawrence, and the rather more controversial Sir Oswald Mosley.

Williamson's son, Richard, also caught the Alvis bug, owning three of the TA 14 model: 20977, 22318 and 22388. Of these, 20977, a 'woody' version had been owned previously by another serial Alvis owner, Dr Lancelot Ware.

7909

VC 2405

Denis Knowles Esq

Denis Knowles had been a very early devotee of

Whitney Straight, the first owner of 7903, was one of a number of racing drivers to be caricatured by the cartoonist 'Sallon' (Rachmiel David Zelon 1899-1999). His work, and that of other cartoonists is held at the British cartoon archive at the University of Kent, CT2 7NZ (01227 764000), to which enquiries for copies should be addressed.

In 1932, when still at Cambridge, a young American burst upon the motor racing scene. WHITNEY STRAIGHT was his name and, first with an M.G. and later a Maserati, he won many classic races. With Hugh Hamilton and Buddy Featherstonhaugh in his team the Straight equipe did much to revive Britain's interest in Continental racing.

7917: The WE Lewis Motor Engineering Works, pictured in the early 1930s. The principal, Mr Edward Lewis, is pictured standing by the driver's door of the Alvis in the foreground. (*Western Telegraph* press cutting discovered by Iwan Parry Esq)

the marque, purchasing new a 12/40 two-seater XN 5949 in April 1923 (unapportioned, but circa chassis 1750). Serial ownership ensued with at least six Alvis cars owned. The above Silver Eagle is the fourth, and was purchased second-hand in 1935 when on leave in the UK, used for a major tour of Europe and subsequently taken to New Zealand where it was sold in Wellington in 1937. Knowles finally returned to the UK in 1938 and is known to have used a tired Speed 20 SA saloon (unidentified) before WWII, and a 12/70 drophead coupé (unidentified) during the 1950s and 1960s. (For earlier Knowles references see 4421.)

I am much indebted to Martin Knowles (son of Denis) for these pertinent extracts from his father's detailed travelogues.

7917   - - - 5788
W E Lewis, Motor Engineering Works

The accompanying photograph, though of indifferent quality, is relevant in that it was taken only a short distance from Alvis founder T G John's birthplace at Pembroke Dock, and celebrates the delivery of a Silver Eagle to the proprietor. The entire workforce appears to have turned out to witness this notable event. Whilst the registration number '5788' is visible enough, the stem letters are unfortunately obscured, which has thus far prevented a complete identification.

7960   UY 6978
C W Dyson Perrins FRAS

Charles William Dyson Perrins (May 25, 1864-January 29, 1859) merits a mention on two distinct levels: his directorship of the Royal Worcester porcelain factory, and perhaps more obviously, the manufacture of that famous culinary addition Lea and Perrins Worcestershire Sauce. He was, self-evidently, a notable local figure, becoming Mayor of Worcester in 1891, and notable as an art collector beyond his immediate field of porcelain. He had been educated at Charterhouse and Queens College, Oxford, and served in the Highland Light Infantry. Many institutions benefited from his philanthropy during his lifetime and bequests after his death, including The British Library, the Victoria & Albert Museum, and the National Gallery. Previously owned a 12/50 model (qv 3403).

8005   UB 360
Viscount Castlereagh

Edward Charles Stewart Robert Vane-Tempest-Stewart (November 18, 1902-October 17, 1955) was educated at Eton. He was a page boy at the coronation of King George V in 1911, and subsequently became MP for County Down from 1931 to 1945. He was also a director of Arsenal Football Club from 1939 to 1946. Known also under his later title of Marquess of Londonderry.

8022   OF 6922
Docker Brothers Ltd

This Birmingham based company was a paint specialist, and supplier of that type of product to a whole host of British companies, of which Alvis Ltd was but one. Many years later, it would take over another Alvis car for the use of a director, the third prototype 3-litre car, numbered 3L3.

8025
Alvis Works car
Specifically recorded in the works archive as a 'press' car, which most probably meant a fairly hard life.

8050
Major General Sir Edward Northey
This car preceded Sir Edward's ownership of a Crested Eagle model, about which rather more is known (qv 13753 for bio).

8055
Competition car
This much travelled and well used car started life as a standard saloon, and the personal property of the Taunton Alvis agent, H H Sweet-Escott, who seemingly retained its original mark before passing the car on to an H L Garnham of Ashford, Kent. In 1949 it was privately exported to Malaya, and extensively raced there throughout the 1950s. 1962 saw it taken to Ontario, Canada, where it continued to be used in minor forms of competition. 1998 saw it returned to the UK and given the sort of sympathetic restoration that it deserved after over half a century of hard usage.

8058
Alvis publicity material
A fascinating story concerns the booklet put out by the factory in 1930, entitled *The Silver Eagle in the Alps*, written by the enthusiastic owner of just such a device, who relates, of the journey: "We started at the western end of the Alps, and went their whole length, finally leaving them at their eastern end for Hungary. We went over the plains of Hungary, round Lake Balaton, and then north for Budapest, and home via Vienna and Munich." Subsequent research reveals this owner to have been one H J Northcott, who resided at 1 Chester Place, Regents Park, (where incidentally he would have had as a neighbour, another Silver Eagle owner – actor Sir Cedric Hardwicke (qv 7367 and 8549), who lived at number 20).

Interestingly, the designer of the aforesaid booklet's cover turns out to be one Rowland Emett

(1906-1990), the famous cartoonist and constructor of all manner of strange mechanical devices. A very similar Silver Eagle Alpine journey would be undertaken later by one Denis Knowles, in a slightly older car (qv 7909).

8065

8084
Works development car
This pair of interesting experimental cars took the form of overhead camshaft 3-litre, straight-eight engine configuration. Both were of rear-wheel drive layout and maroon in colour, one a van, the other a saloon car. The engine design, though not proceeded with for production, may have had a spin-off with the four-cylinder experimental 'ACE' car (qv 9130).

8101
Competition car
The above represents the original form of one of the best-known Alvis racers, the 'Green Car' of Michael (MWB) May. Though initially using one of the very few 15.7hp (65mm) blocks to bring the unit within the 2-litre competition class, the car has undergone more metamorphoses than Ovid, being re-chassied and highly modified. Its fascinating, lengthy and highly detailed history is beyond the scope of this volume, but May's own account of it can be found in Hull and Johnson's *The Vintage Alvis*, pages 366-376 (ISBN 0-9525334-0-5).

Another first-hand account of the car is that written by William Boddy, in the June 1941 issue of *Motor Sport*, page 365.

8108
Henken Widengren
A Silver Eagle closed coupé supplied to the Swedish (but English-domiciled) racing driver. He would subsequently purchase two further Alvis cars, both with specially commissioned bodies from Bertelli (qv 9268 and 13105 for a bio).

8111
Barkers Brewery Ltd
The Barker family, of Lancaster, were serial Alvis

owners, and the above example immediately preceded a special order from them to Alvis Ltd (qv 9124).

8162
Sir Michael Nairn
See under 9384 and 10918 for subsequent Alvis cars owned.

8163 **MW 7226**
Sir Gordon Richards
Sir Gordon Richards (May 5,1904-November 10 1986) was one of Britain's best known and most successful jockeys, with some 4870 winners to his credit.

It is recorded that he presented a cup, in 1929, for a race for front-wheel drive Alvis cars, though exact details of this are elusive.

8164 **VC 3856**

8156 **VC 3857**

8166 **VC 3858**
Works development car
This interesting trio of SD Silver Eagles were specially built for competition purposes, with engines of a bore reduced to 65mm, giving a displacement for conformity with the 2-litre class. Never a company to waste anything, Alvis Ltd recycled two of the above, dismantling them entirely, with 8165 becoming the first TJ 12/50 (8393), and 8164 the second of that type (8424). The 8166 car remained relatively intact, but only a few months later was uprated from the unusual 15.7hp specification above, to the more usual 67.5mm bore 16.95hp. Only two other cars of 15.7hp rating are known to have been made, these being 8258 and 8260.

8170 **TF 1537**
Iliffe Publications Ltd
It has never been quite clear why 8170 was brought back from the Wigan agent Timberlakes, to take part in an *Autocar* road test. This was published as no 49 in that series, issue of May 16, 1930, pages 969-970.

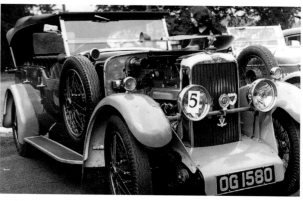

8223: Though of a type very popular with police forces, the Silver Eagles have always been in private hands. (Courtesy Alvis Archive Trust)

8223 **OG 1580**
A E Dobell
Clearly an enthusiast of some stature, having competed six times in the Monte Carlo Rally, A E Dobell (born October 7, 1907) was known to have served in the RAF, at least between 1930 and 1935. His 1934 Monte Carlo entry was in an Alvis, but whether or not it was the above is uncertain. He was Lagonda-mounted for the 1935, '36 and '37 events, and Railton for the 1938 and '39. Little is known of him given the secretive nature of his occupation, which included serving at Bletchley Park during WWII, and thereafter at GCHQ, Cheltenham. 8223 was subsequently acquired by Scottish enthusiast Eddie Chilcott and found fame on screen with the 1980s TV series *Bonnie and Clyde*, and also in the 1994 remake of *Dr Finlay's Casebook*. The car is still with the Chilcott family at the time of writing. Previously owned a 12/50 TE model (qv 4456).

8235
8236
Sheffield Police
The registration numbers allocated to this pair of SD Silver Eagles tourers have so far escaped detection, but are most likely to have been within that borough's 'WE' series current at the time. They were part of a larger contemporary order (qv 8719, 8728, 8780 and 8782).

8263 **UY 8254**
Terry & Sons Ltd
This long-established Redditch company manufactured valve springs by the million for most

of Britain's car makers, including Alvis Ltd. This above example was for the personal use of Cyril Terry, and had been preceded by another Silver Eagle (qv 7706).

8272 GH 1288
Viscount Lymington

The 9th Viscount of that line, and born May 16, 1898 as Gerald Vernon Wallop, he was educated at Winchester College, and at Balliol, before serving in WWI with the second Life Guards. The family were in possession of Isaac Newton's original papers, which were in due course committed to auction.

Author of at least five books, of which one, *A Knot of Roots* (1965), is an autobiography. He was also known as the 9th Earl of Portsmouth, and died September 28, 1984.

8318
Lord Hotham

7th Baron of that line, he would subsequently change this Silver Eagle model for a Mayfair-bodied 3.5-litre (qv 13137 for bio). Preceded by another Silver Eagle (qv 7371).

8336 GG 1942

8385 GG 1941
Glasgow City Police

A pair of identically specified Silver Eagle TB tourer patrol cars for this Scottish force.

8359 VC 5703

8360 VC 5348

8376 VC 5705

8392 VC 5704
Works competition cars

The above represent the second batch of straight-eight competition cars, best remembered for their remarkable performance in the 1930 Ulster TT, scoring a first, second and third in Class F, and fourth, sixth and seventh in the general

THE SECOND INTERNATIONAL ALVIS TOUR OF DENMARK 1990

Clearly inspired by the team of four 1930 straight-eight cars, this is a Danish Alvis club's interpretation of their undoubted charisma. (Courtesy Ernest Shenton collection)

classification, only being beaten here by blown Alfa Romeos of a somewhat larger capacity. The Alvis drivers were Cyril Paul, H W Purdy, Leon Cushman, and Maurice Harvey (qv 7529-on for the earlier batch of straight-eight competition cars).

8323 ET 6430
Iliffe Publications Ltd

The *Farmer and Stockbreeder* is a sister journal to the Iliffe group's better known (to us) *Autocar*. Unusually, perhaps as a pre-Christmas relaxation, *F&S* featured a road test of 8323 in the issue of December 3, 1968, on pages 123-124, written by R Giles-Browne. At least, that is my guess. Surely they did not think that the Silver Eagle was agricultural?

8366 GK 5287
Iliffe Publications Ltd

One of several Alvis cars featured in *Autocar*'s *Talking of Sports Cars* series. This is no 271 of that series, from the issue of October 12, 1945.

8367 | SC 9450

8377 | SC 9449

Edinburgh City Police

A pair of identically specified Silver Eagle TB touring patrol cars for this Scottish force.

8374 | UP 5121

8474 | UP 5113

8492 | UP 5107

Durham Police

This police fleet was slightly different to the usual order in that, whilst almost visually identical – all with four-seater touring bodies, 8374 was a Silver Eagle six-cylinder chassis, whilst the other two were of the TJ 12/50 four-cylinder type.

8424-9455

September 1930 to April 1932
1031 cars

Consisting of models:

TA	21
TB	25
TC	203
TD	17
SD	12
SB	36
SD	114
SE	2
TJ	538
TK	75
TL	23
SA 20	26
X-FD	1
'ACE'	1

Consisting of coachbuilders:

Cross & Ellis	436
Carbodies	533
Mayfair	40

Vanden Plas	9
Charlesworth	2
Batley	1
Bertelli	1
Carlton	1
Corsica	1
Other (Unrecorded)	7
Total	**1031**

Chassis	Reg	Chassis	Reg	Chassis	Reg
8424	VC 5707	8480	GH 765	8537	- - - - - -
8425	FM 6325	8481	GK 5267	8538	VK 3440
8426	- - - - - -	8482	TF 3224	8539	VC 6754
8427	- - - - - -	8483	TK 6200	8540	GV 343
8428	DS 21	8484	VU 1294	8541	- - - - - -
8429	BR 8433	8485	GK 6623	8542	- - - - - -
8430	YU 7125	8486	UP 6571	8543	- - - - - -
8431	- - - - - -	8487	GG 2704	8544	- - - - - -
8432	JK 1452	8488	PN 7594	8545	- - - - - -
8433	GK 2568	8489	VC 7387	8546	UU 3139
8434	- - - - - -	8490	VT 5478	8547	- - - - - -
8435	- - - - - -	8491	RG 1703	8548	- - - - - -
8436	KW 9650	8492	UP 5107	8549	VC 6753
8437	VT 5810	8493	- - - - - -	8550	- - - - - -
8438	- - - - - -	8494	- - - - - -	8551	DV 9849
8439	- - - - - -	8495	RV 1573	8552	- - - - - -
8440	- - - - - -	8496	- - - - - -	8553	- - - - - -
8441	MW 8216	8497	VH 3961	8554	VC 9604
8442	GG 3029	8498	WM 5641	8555	GG 1582
8443	HX 2003	8499	VC 6424	8556	- - - - - -
8444	VC 5710	8500	- - - - - -	8557	APH 811
8445	GG 13	8501	- - - - - -	8558	VT 6085
8446	VC 6422	8502	GK 2594	8559	VC 6425
8447	SC 9695	8503	RX 7663	8560	UX 7854
8448	- - - - - -	8504	- - - - - -	8561	- - - - - -
8449	GG 6581	8505	GG 1441	8562	GG 2053
8450	- - - - - -	8506	WX 5814	8563	- - - - - -
8451	PN 6738	8507	LG 6024	8564	GN 7735
8452	KS 4975	8508	GK 4033	8565	DG 3474
8453	- - - - - -	8509	- - - - - -	8566	VC 7011
8454	AV 4716	8510	TR 9590	8567	- - - - - -
8455	V 219	8511	TK 5950	8568	GG 1500
8456	GG 492	8512	VE 5476	8569	RF 7880
8457	HY 1132	8513	- - - - - -	8570	VK 3858
8458	GN 3489	8514	- - - - - -	8571	DV 7884
8459	BR 8672	8515	- - - - - -	8572	- - - - - -
8460	GG 1411	8516	UY 9100	8573	DV 7362
8461	- - - - - -	8517	KW 9085	8574	- - - - - -
8462	WJ 713	8518	- - - - - -	8575	- - - - - -
8463	RB 2920	8519	GK 6341	8576	- - - - - -
8464	- - - - - -	8520	- - - - - -	8577	TF 3762
8465	WV 847	8521	WV 836	8578	VC 7388
8466	DG 1482	8522	KW 9473	8579	MW 8806
8467	RT 7292	8523	JB 64	8580	VC 6755
8468	HS 6132	8524	GK 4031	8581	AV 4315
8469	GG 1431	8525	GN 2261	8582	GG 1886
8470	AUS	8526	BR 8550	8583	- - - - - -
8471	- - - - - -	8527	RX 7774	8584	GG 2415
8472	- - - - - -	8528	VC 6719	8585	- - - - - -
8473	- - - - - -	8529	- - - - - -	8586	GG 1926
8474	UP 5113	8530	PO 4574	8587	TK 5579
8475	FS 837	8531	- - - - - -	8588	- - - - - -
8476	MW 8037	8532	- - - - - -	8589	KW 9805
8477	MW 8562	8533	YD 1564	8590	DG 1671
8478	UR 8142	8534	VC 6718	8591	- - - - - -
8479	- - - - - -	8535	VR 6231	8592	- - - - - -
		8536	LG 5729	8593	SC 8910

8594 - - - - - -	8664 - -WM 6124	8734 - - - - - -	8804 - - GG 4051	8874 - - TF 5272	8944 - - VC 8957
8595 - - EY 4012	8665 - - BR 8709	8735 - - RD 2564	8805 - - BR 8806	8875 - - VU 5353	8945 - - -NV 438
8596 - - VH 3419	8666 - - - - - -	8736 - - - - - -	8806 - - VU 3957	8876 - - - - - -	8946 - - GO 5774
8597 - - HY 1778	8667 - - -GO 242	8737 - - GN 8884	8807 - - -WP 41	8877 - - - - - -	8947 - - - - - -
8598 - -MW 8673	8668 - - UB 5736	8738 - - VC 8794	8808 - - - - - -	8878 - - -KY 538	8948 - - GG 4139
8599 - - -OY 294	8669 - - VC 7007	8739 - - - - - -	8809 - - VK 4918	8879 - - - - - -	8949 - - VC 8956
8600 - - VC 6756	8670 - - HL 4984	8740 - - - - - -	8810 - - RX 8732	8880 - - TM 9057	8950 - - - - - -
8601 - - LG 6290	8671 - - VU 3145	8741 - - YD 1848	8811 - - - - - -	8881 - - VC 8422	8951 - - - - - -
8602 - - TG 1074	8672 - - - - - -	8742 - - GG 3034	8812 - - VC 8055	8882 - - VC 8574	8952 - - SN 5429
8603 - - - - - -	8673 - - WX 6535	8743 - - - - - -	8813 - - MY 8765	8883 - - VC 8573	8953 - - - - - -
8604 - - - - - -	8674 - - - - - -	8744 - - BR 8905	8814 - - LG 6595	8884 - - VU 6236	8954 - - TF 6129
8605 - - VK 4198	8675 - - -OD 1116	8745 - - - - - -	8815 - - - - - -	8885 - - OV 3239	8955 - - VC 8793
8606 - - GM 1713	8676 - - WX 6536	8746 - - VU 3139	8816 - - - FS 376	8886 - - - - - -	8956 - - EK 8839
8607 - - -GO 246	8677 - - GN 1944	8747 - - - - - -	8817 - - - KJ 658	8887 - - GP 7199	8957 - - - FS 912
8608 - - UF 7068	8678 - - GO 3457	8748 - - VC 7391	8818 - - BR 8823	8888 - - GG 3722	8958 - - - US 351
8609 - - -LJ 3355	8679 - - - - - -	8749 - - VC 7392	8819 - - WG 388	8889 - - KY 441	8959 - - - - - -
8610 - - OU 8057	8680 - - GO 5769	8750 - - - - - -	8820 - - - - - -	8890 - - RF 8573	8960 - - -FS 1288
8611 - - EK 8068	8681 - - GO 4125	8751 - - - - - -	8821 - - GO 7094	8891 - - - - - -	8961 - - - - - -
8612 - - - - - -	8682 - - GN 3876	8752 - - - - - -	8822 - - VU 3939	8892 - - - - - -	8962 - - GG 4140
8613 - - RP 9662	8683 - - - - - -	8753 - - -GO 245	8823 - - - - - -	8893 - - DV 9451	8963 - - GT 4435
8614 - - VS 1932	8684 - - PL 7192	8754 - - PL 7192	8824 - - LG 6998	8894 - - PN 7795	8964 - - - - - -
8615 - - - - - -	8685 - - - - - -	8755 - - GP 3300	8825 - - - - - -	8895 - - - - - -	8965 - - GO 5778
8616 - - VC 7012	8686 - - TF 4272	8756 - - GO 4232	8826 - - VG 3596	8896 - - - - - -	8966 - - GG 4052
8617 - - VC 8424	8687 - - - - - -	8757 - - - - - -	8827 - - GG 3930	8897 - - VK 4438	8967 - - -KY 738
8618 - - - - - -	8688 - - - - - -	8758 - - - - - -	8828 - - TF 5505	8898 - - WD 2428	8968 - - - - - -
8619 - - - - - -	8689 - - - - - -	8759 - - - - - -	8829 - - GO 5433	8899 - - HY 2980	8969 - - GP 5043
8620 - - VC 7009	8690 - - - - - -	8760 - - DV 8744	8830 - - VC 8056	8900 - - TF 5461	8970 - - - - - -
8621 - - - - - -	8691 - - GG 1943	8761 - - GO 5762	8831 - - TF 5116	8901 - - GO 6999	8971 - - - - - -
8622 - - BR 8585	8692 - - - - - -	8762 - - MY 8766	8832 - - TS 9202	8902 - - - FS 865	8972 - - VU 6239
8623 - - - - - -	8693 - - -VD 242	8763 - - - - - -	8833 - - - - - -	8903 - - - FS 557	8973 - - EK 8292
8624 - - -LJ 2971	8694 - - - - - -	8764 - - VN 2702	8834 - - GO 5767	8904 - - BR 8912	8974 - - LG 7057
8625 - - - - - -	8695 - - VC 8057	8765 - -WM 6315	8835 - - GG 3480	8905 - - OW 526	8975 - - -KY 462
8626 - - -OW 65	8696 - - OD 8426	8766 - - GO 2619	8836 - - GO 5780	8906 - - GY 1420	8976 - - OV 2227
8627 - - RX 8146	8697 - - - - - -	8767 - - GO 4883	8837 - - VE 5158	8907 - - - - - -	8977 - - RX 9113
8628 - - EN 4795	8698 - - - - - -	8768 - - SC 9865	8838 - - VC 8059	8908 - - BR 9087	8978 - - - - - -
8629 - - - - - -	8699 - - - - - -	8769 - - GP 3301	8839 - - -WP 106	8909 - - OW 611	8979 - - VC 8668
8630 - - ET 6666	8700 - - - - - -	8770 - - VC 7389	8840 - - HB 4013	8910 - - - - - -	8980 - - - - - -
8631 - - YD 1443	8701 - - UT 8899	8771 - - GG 3089	8841 - - - FS 304	8911 - - HY 3849	8981 - - SK 1774
8632 - - - - - -	8702 - - - - - -	8772 - - GG 3393	8841 - - -KY 285	8912 - - - - - -	8982 - - -RC 5
8633 - - - - - -	8703 - - GG 3498	8773 - - - - - -	8843 - - FS 352	8913 - - - - - -	8983 - - - - - -
8634 - - BR 8837	8704 - - -GO 248	8774 - - KR 9940	8844 - - - - - -	8914 - - DM 7577	8984 - - -KV 191
8635 - - - - - -	8705 - - - BG 48	8775 - - - - - -	8845 - - GP 7196	8915 - - - - - -	8985 - - VC 9461
8636 - - - - - -	8706 - - WX 6729	8776 - - LG 6525	8846 - - - - - -	8916 - - VC 8669	8986 - - GT 5535
8637 - - -KY 713	8707 - - VN 2451	8777 - - - - - -	8847 - - - - - -	8917 - - VC 8575	8987 - - - GT 587
8638 - - UR 8508	8708 - - VN 2452	8778 - - TY 8432	8848 - - - - - -	8918 - - KX 7074	8988 - - GO 5777
8639 - - KX 6317	8709 - - VN 2453	8779 - - DH 8767	8849 - - GG 3723	8919 - - LG 6817	8989 - - -KY 748
8640 - - - - - -	8710 - - TY 8227	8780 - - WJ 1277	8850 - - DG 2476	8920 - - -KY 689	8990 - - GG 4668
8641 - - - - - -	8711 - - TY 8144	8781 - - FW 2192	8851 - - EN 4903	8921 - - GP 7191	8991 - - VU 6176
8642 - - LG 6136	8712 - - KF 4505	8782 - - WJ 1278	8852 - - LG 6795	8922 - - GP 4994	8992 - - - - - -
8643 - - BA 9737	8713 - - SK 1728	8783 - - GS 2496	8853 - - VC 8446	8923 - - GP 5256	8993 - - - - - -
8644 - - YC 1314	8714 - - UT 8589	8784 - - - - - -	8854 - - - - - -	8924 - - - - - -	8994 - - FG 7059
8645 - - KW 9558	8715 - - - - - -	8785 - - - - - -	8855 - - - - - -	8925 - - - TM 8	8995 - - VC 8795
8646 - - - - - -	8716 - - - - - -	8786 - - - - - -	8856 - - FB 9257	8926 - - SY 4534	8996 - - WD 2524
8647 - - - - - -	8717 - - - - - -	8787 - - -DJ 5020	8857 - - VV 689	8927 - - - - - -	8997 - - KF 6055
8648 - - - - - -	8718 - - KR 9574	8788 - - -KY 326	8858 - - - - - -	8928 - - - - - -	8998 - - - - - -
8649 - - GG 2703	8719 - - -WJ 671	8789 - - - - - -	8859 - - - - - -	8929 - - - - - -	8999 - - - - - -
8650 - - - - - -	8720 - - GG 2790	8790 - - - - - -	8860 - - VC 8444	8930 - - VC 8670	9000 - - VC 9603
8651 - - - - - -	8721 - - - - - -	8791 - - - - - -	8861 - - - - - -	8931 - - - HX 28	9001 - - - - - -
8652 - - LG 5840	8722 - - VC 7390	8792 - - -KY 122	8862 - - GP 2046	8932 - - VE 3858	9002 - - -LJ 4140
8653 - - FB 8966	8723 - - VC 8058	8793 - - BR 8814	8863 - - - - - -	8933 - - - - - -	9003 - - UH 9906
8654 - - - - - -	8724 - - VC 8060	8794 - - -KY 121	8864 - - VC 8445	8934 - - - - - -	9004 - - HS 6375
8655 - - - - - -	8725 - - - - - -	8795 - - -LJ 3762	8865 - - DX 9466	8935 - - GG 4107	9005 - - GG 4282
8656 - - GN 3790	8726 - - - - - -	8796 - - PL 7782	8866 - - VC 8423	8936 - - UB 7254	9006 - - GP 8243
8657 - - GG 1661	8727 - - VC 9272	8797 - - RT 7753	8867 - - - - - -	8937 - - - - - -	9007 - - GP 8059
8658 - - - - - -	8728 - - -WJ 670	8798 - - - - - -	8868 - - -KJ 1267	8938 - - - - - -	9008 - - OV 2873
8659 - -VU 2446?	8729 - - TS 9137	8799 - - WJ 2494	8869 - - - - - -	8939 - - GG 3929	9009 - - VT 6761
8660 - -VU 2445?	8730 - - TS 9138	8800 - - - - - -	8870 - - CP 9257	8940 - - -LJ 4018	9010 - - TY 8435
8661 - - - - - -	8731 - - - JO 941	8801 - - -KY 188	8871 - - AG 6601	8941 - - BV 800	9011 - - -SS 3382
8662 - - - - - -	8732 - - GG 3262	8802 - - - - - -	8872 - - -JK 1907	8942 - - -JK 1907	9012 - - - - - -
8663 - - GN 6815	8733 - - LG 6435	8803 - - LG 6605	8873 - - VU 4738	8943 - - OV 2047	9013 - - PN 8026

No.	Reg.	No.	Reg.	No.	Reg.	No.	Reg.	No.	Reg.	No.	Reg.
9014	GO 5779	9084	OW 905	9154	RV 999	9223	WJ 2675	9293	DT 3466	9363	KV 199
9015	—	9085	—	9155	VK 5329	9224	—	9294	KV 286	9364	GW 84
9016	UF 7927	9086	—	9156	WM 7154	9225	KV 44	9295	KV 663	9365	KV 200
9017	—	9087	—	9157	—	9226	UF 8638	9296	TV 5784	9366	TG 2984
9019	VC 8923	9088	—	9158	—	9227	—	9297	KV 195	9367	UX 9900
9020	—	9089	VC 9270	9159	—	9228	—	9298	GG 5653	9368	SY 4653
9021	YD 3040	9090	GP 7195	9160	FS 1285	9229	—	9299	VN 3508	9369	GG 5980
9022	—	9091	GT 368	9161	—	9230	FS 2939	9300	GG 5377	9370	JU 313
9022	—	9092	KY 1287	9162	VC 9883	9231	VU 7675	9301	KV 197	9371	EY 4436
9023	—	9093	VU 6682	9163	KY 1675	9232	GX 8252	9302	RH 5150	9372	DX 9815
9024	HY 3376	9094	OW 906	9164	—	9233	RF 9091	9303	DG 3710	9373	FS 2713
9025	—	9095	—	9165	—	9234	GT 7943	9304	KV 2757	9374	HY 5866
9026	GP 47	9096	WX 8588	9166	—	9235	—	9305	GG 5375	9375	VU 9637
9027	VC 9032	9097	WV 188	9167	GG 8030	9236	—	9306	—	9376	—
9028	—	9098	OD 178	9168	VC 9716	9237	—	9307	WM 7165	9377	KV 703
9029	WM 6682	9099	HH 5897	9169	—	9238	—	9308	—	9378	VU 9642
9030	—	9100	LG 7568	9170	—	9239	DX 9693	9309	—	9379	—
9031	VU 6237	9101	KS 5304	9171	UF 8103	9240	WJ 2674	9310	LG 9081	9380	KV 702
9032	KG 71	9102	—	9172	—	9241	GG 5212	9311	—	9381	—
9033	—	9103	OW 1177	9173	VT 7052	9242	KY 1200	9312	GG 5156	9382	AUS
9034	KY 730	9104	—	9174	WJ 2592	9243	WX 9511	9313	WX 9700	9383	GG 5657
9035	SN 5404	9105	—	9175	KV 42	9244	JK 2121	9314	UB 8680	9384	FG 7503
9036	—	9106	JS 4061	9176	KY 1912	9245	—	9315	GW 4133	9385	—
9037	—	9107	RX 9226	9177	HY 4107	9246	—	9316	VU 9778	9386	—
9038	—	9108	GG 4953	9178	KX 8260	9247	—	9317	—	9387	—
9039	AG 7023	9109	—	9179	YD 4060	9248	NV 788	9318	—	9388	GY 5511
9040	VC 8925	9110	—	9180	VC 9855	9249	KV 41	9319	GW 4138	9389	OV 9778
9041	LJ 4284	9111	WV 421	9181	—	9250	NJ 323	9320	KV 193	9390	HY 4881
9042	—	9112	—	9182	GV 724	9251	KV 190	9321	GG 5941	9391	—
9043	GG 4284	9113	WV 310	9183	GG 5104	9252	FG 7358	9322	KV 45	9392	LV 561
9044	—	9114	HS 6411	9184	KV 1577	9253	WD 3379	9323	KV 704	9393	—
9045	VC 9463	9115	BR 9108	9184	VC 9605	9254	—	9324	WJ 3163	9394	LG 8511
9046	YD 2808	9116	—	9185	VC 9715	9255	JH 1520	9325	OD 1238	9395	FS 2206
9047	—	9117	JF 152	9186	—	9256	—	9326	GG 5376	9396	LG 8721
9048	WJ 2287	9118	—	9187	KV 1077	9257	OD 852	9327	HS 6565	9397	—
9049	KV 192	9119	TY 8437	9188	FS 2556	9258	—	9328	KV 1069	9398	TF 7957
9050	WD 3035	9120	—	9189	LJ 4689	9259	—	9329	—	9399	GG 5659
9051	—	9121	TM 9306	9190	—	9260	KV 700	9330	UB 9393	9400	FV 2600
9052	VK 5333	9122	AZ 8320	9191	KY 1806	9261	—	9331	SW 3907	9401	GW 4135
9053	UN 5061	9123	—	9192	—	9262	—	9332	GW 7157	9402	—
9054	AXX 106	9124	TF 6467	9193	—	9263	SN 5515	9333	—	9403	OV 7398
9055	KY 820	9125	VC 9369	9194	WX 9106	9264	VH 4162	9334	—	9404	OV 8066
9056	—	9126	—	9195	FS 1481	9265	—	9335	GX 3453	9405	—
9057	—	9127	—	9196	FM 7025	9266	—	9336	AG 7232	9406	KV 707
9058	OV 3333	9128	DG 3541	9197	—	9267	JK 2111	9337	—	9407	KV 198
9059	—	9129	KY 1045	9198	UN 5365	9268	VC 9453	9338	KF 8008	9408	KV 1070
9060	—	9130	VC 9368	9199	—	9269	OV 5738	9339	VK 6262	9409	—
9061	YD 2857	9131	—	9200	—	9270	VN 3419	9340	—	9410	KV 1570
9062	KY 974	9132	VC 9714	9201	GG 5658	9271	KF 7582	9341	GW 60	9411	KV 706
9063	AZ 8188	9133	GW 3726	9202	—	9272	HY 4412	9342	—	9412	—
9064	VC 8924	9134	TF 7437	9203	KY 1252	9273	TY 8947	9343	VU 8311	9413	—
9065	RG 2370	9135	PJ 1489	9204	KV 222	9274	—	9344	OV 6438	9414	GW 4131
9066	FS 968	9136	—	9205	FS 1462	9275	—	9345	LG 8198	9415	KV 1073
9067	—	9137	—	9206	JH 942	9276	—	9346	JU 172	9416	—
9068	ST 6690	9138	HB 4039	9207	—	9277	GT 7945	9347	PN 8715	9417	KV 710
9069	RF 8787	9139	GG 4789	9208	GG 5154	9278	DG 3666	9348	JS 4136	9418	—
9070	TY 8867	9140	FS 1444	9209	—	9279	UF 8179	9349	—	9419	GG 6086
9071	VC 9367	9141	—	9210	KV 46	9280	VC 9884	9350	VL 3750	9420	—
9072	SR 8034	9142	GG 5155	9211	—	9281	VK 5779	9351	—	9421	KY 2268
9073	RT 8091	9143	RB 5877	9212	—	9282	PO 4798	9352	KY 2254	9422	—
9074	VC 9271	9144	KY 1644	9213	KV 194	9283	VU 7678	9353	—	9423	OV 7706
9075	UT 9429	9145	GT 5533	9214	WV 1295	9284	TY 9050	9354	—	9424	KV 701
9076	LG 7295	9146	KV 699	9215	FV 2360	9285	KV 43	9355	—	9425	RH 4986
9077	OW 909	9147	LG 9855	9216	—	9286	DH 9089	9356	—	9426	KV 709
9078	SO 4270	9148	—	9217	LG 7919	9287	—	9357	TY 9288	9427	KV 1071
9079	TK 6900	9149	—	9218	VK 5774	9288	—	9358	AUS	9428	—
9080	KY 1194	9150	VC 9462	9219	—	9289	RH 5538	9359	KV 705	9429	WJ 4967
9081	UT 9609	9151	—	9220	BR 9343	9290	—	9360	KV 196	9430	KV 1068
9082	—	9152	KY 1174	9221	GW 311	9291	FG 7961	9361	—	9431	FS 2601
9083	—	9153	—	9222	MV 3568	9292	MV 9106	9362	UG 947	9432	GG 6085

9433	- -	KY 5089	9441	- -	BR 9769	9449	- -	KV 1576
9434	- -	- - - -	9442	- -	DG 4488	9450	- -	- - - -
9435	- -	WO 6281	9443	- -	LG 9039	9451	- -	KV 1076
9436	- -	FS 3419	9444	- -	KV 1074	9452	- -	- - - -
9437	- -	GX 3458	9445	- -	KV 1072	9453	- -	KY 2000
9438	- -	XJ 1191	9446	- -	- - - -	9454	- -	SB 4005
9439	- -	KV 1079	9447	- -	GX 4729	9455	- -	GX 4979
9440	- -	FG 7599	9448	- -	- - - -			

The ascendancy of the six-cylinder Alvis, referred to in the previous section, was briefly curtailed during the sequence above. The 12/50, by this time, was looking a little staid, but had, however, such an enviable reputation that it would not go quietly. Although successors were being considered, such as the 'ACE' (qv 9130), market demand necessitated that in the interim there just had to be a 'revival' of the four-cylinder line. The result was the TJ 12/50, which, together with the TK and TL 12/60s, would keep the company's position alive in that sector of the market until the advent of the Firefly.

This period too, where there was a perceived demand for a sports version of the Silver Eagle saw this idea morph into the pre-production examples of the soon-to-be-legendary line. Perhaps equally noteworthy was the chief designer's refusal to give up entirely on the front-wheel drive concept. The solitary example of a six-cylinder FWD Alvis (qv 8770) is testimony to this. It was also the largest, being based on 19.82hp Silver Eagle engine components mounted within what appears to be a derivative of the FA 8/15 racing chassis.

8432
Olympia Motor Show 1930
A sales ledger for this car's supplying agent, Caffyn's of Eastbourne, is annotated with the note 'Show Car' and certainly the date concerned is compatible with that year's London event.

8449
India Tyre Co Ltd
The Glasgow agent Galt's supplied this car to this well-known tyre maker, though whether for tyre testing purposes or merely executive use is not known. There was already evidence of rival company Dunlop using Alvis cars for testing purposes (qv 2931, 5860, and later 9212).

8539: A TJ 12/50 special, subject of a picture postcard. See text for possible availability.

8464
Kilmarnock Police
A TJ 12/50 saloon patrol car for this Scottish force supplied, unusually, by Henly's London agency.

8531
Sunderland Police
A TJ 12/50 saloon patrol car for this Durham force.

8539
Alvis works car
Starting life as part of a works demonstration fleet, this car subsequently had a fairly hard life, which included towing a caravan somewhat larger than itself. Later still, it was converted from a saloon to a tourer and then was used as the subject of a picture postcard. The publisher of this was Bamforth & Company, of Holmfirth, West Yorkshire, and maybe the product is still available.

8549
Sir Cedric Hardwicke
An actor and serial Alvis owner, Sir Cedric subsequently bought another Silver Eagle (qv 9524), a Crested Eagle (qv 10737) and a Speed 20 (qv 10877 for bio). *Autocar* magazine, issue of January 16, 1931, has a photograph of Hardwicke and his wife taking delivery of 8549, which replaced an earlier Silver Eagle saloon (qv 7367).

8563
Dewsbury Police
A saloon patrol car for this West Yorkshire force.

8595: A TJ 12/50 in the body style known as 'wide two-seater' seen here with hood erected. (Courtesy Alvis Archive Trust, Vivian Family, and PG Rains)

8595   EY 4012

Vivian (Family)

This is the family name of the successive Earls of Swansea, Welsh landowners. 8595 was supplied to a Bangor-residing member in December 1930, the Hon HH Vivian. The accompanying photograph is a nice period shot of a typical TJ 12/50 wide two-seater.

8597   HY 1778

David Humpherson

Beginning with an uneventful life with a first owner in Bristol, 8597 most certainly made up for this in the postwar years. By the mid-1950s, it had passed into the hands of one John Evetts. Along with his friend Dave Humpherson, it was decided to take the Alvis on a seven-month, 17,000-mile lap of the Mediterranean, which took place in 1967. John then emigrated to Canada, taking the car with him, but in 1981 decided to sell it to Dave and Sian Humpherson, who flew out to collect it, driving it, most ambitiously, from Vancouver to New York for shipment. Their adventures en route, though fascinating, are too lengthy to reproduce here, but worth mentioning is the fact that the leg of the journey between Chicago and New York covered almost exactly the same ground as that undertaken by BBC correspondent Edward Ward in a TB 14 in the summer of 1950 (qv 23500), though that had been east to west, whilst 8597's had, of course, been west to east, culminating in a voyage on the QE2, back to the UK. Few problems with these epic trips,

save for a puncture, and the not unusual vintage Alvis fibre coupling 'trait.'

8611   EK 8068

Wigan Police

A four-seater TJ 12/50 tourer patrol car for this Lancashire force.

8613   RP 9662

Northampton Police

A four-seater TJ 12/50 four-seater tourer for the borough force.

8624   LJ 2971

N Douglas Simpson

First Alvis of the pioneering botanist. More information under his second Alvis, a Silver Eagle (qv 9560).

Simpson took 8624 to Ceylon in September 1930 in the course of a colonial office assignment, where it remained until September 1932.

8624: Botanist Douglas Simpson's wide two-seater TJ 12/50 at Col de Tirourda, Algeria, 1937, during an expedition. (Courtesy Alvis Archive Trust)

8635

Earl of Jersey

The 9th Earl of that line, George Francis Child-Villiers (February 15, 1910-August 9, 1998) was also known as Viscount Grandison. His second wife was the American actress Virginia Cherrill, who had

8659/8660: One of a pair of Silver Eagle tourers supplied to the Manchester City police force. (Courtesy Local Studies Archive, Manchester Central Library)

8664: The second, and perhaps better-known of the 'Bianchi' specials. (Courtesy the late Julian Collins)

been 'discovered' by Charlie Chaplin. She had previously been married to actor Cary Grant. After WWII had ended, the Earl gave the family seat of Osterley Park, in Middlesex, to the nation.

8639
KX 6317
Aylesbury Police
A four-seater TJ 12/50 patrol car for this Buckinghamshire force.

8659
VU 2444/5

8660
VU 2445/4
Manchester City Police
A pair of identically specified Silver Eagle four-seater tourers for this (then Lancashire) force. Unfortunately, the record does not show precisely which registration number applied to which chassis.

8664
WM 6124
Competition car
Starting life as a mechanically standard Silver Eagle, 8664 was delivered to Wigan agent Timberlakes in chassis form only, and it has not yet been established who exactly constructed the body. In the postwar years, however, it was highly modified and put to competition use, being known as the Tony Bianchi special. It remains arguably the fastest ever 'vintage' Alvis, assisted by its Speed 25 engine (no 15150 ex-chassis 14665).

8668
UB 5736
Leeds City Police
A Silver Eagle four-seater tourer for this Yorkshire force.

8670
HL 4984

8673
WX 6535

8676
WX 6536

8679
Yorkshire (West Riding) Police
This quartet of identically specified TJ 12/50 four-seater tourers was delivered to the County Police HQ in Wakefield. 8670 bears a Wakefield Borough mark, whilst 8673 and 8676 bear West Riding marks. The mark that was allocated to 8679 remains to be identified.

8690
Dumbarton Police
A Silver Eagle two-seater for this Scottish force.

8697
Earl of Rosebery KT DSO MC PC
Albert Edward Harry Meyer Archibald Primrose (January 8, 1882-May 31, 1974) was the 6th Earl of that line. He was educated at Eton and Sandhurst, serving in WWI and in the Palestine campaign under General Allenby. As Harry Primrose, he had served as Member of Parliament for Midlothian

between 1906 and 1910. Prior to this he was equally well-known as a cricketer, playing for Middlesex, and captaining Surrey for the 1905 to 1907 seasons. His tally included a total of over 3500 runs, and two centuries. The name is also familiar in horse racing circles, one of the colours here being congruent with the family name of Primrose. One source suggests that the above Alvis was two-toned, with the lower colour in the same hue.

8707 VN 2451

8708 VN 2452

8709 VN 2453
Thirsk Police
A trio of identically-specified TJ 12/50 saloons for this Yorkshire, North Riding force.

8711 TY 8144
Morpeth Police
A patrol car for this Northumberland force.

8713 SK 1728
Caithness Police
A patrol car for this Scottish force.

8719 WJ 670/I

8728 WJ 671/0
Sheffield Police
A pair of identically specified TJ 12/50 two-seater tourers for a regular customer of Alvis Ltd. Unfortunately, the record does not show precisely which registration number applied to which chassis. Two Silver Eagle cars were supplied to this force at about the same time (qv 8780 and 8782).

8752
F H Sheppee Ltd
This York-based engineering company had been established in 1904, initially producing steam-powered commercial vehicles and, in 1912, a pair of steam-powered private cars. The above was at least the fourth Alvis car to be obtained by the

company, being preceded by 7603, 4378 and (most probably) 2899. In 1924, the firm was listed as making non-skid chains for vehicles, but in more recent years branched out into washing machines and vacuum cleaners. At the time of writing, Sheppee International still exists, and still operates in the York area.

8765 WM 6315
Sir George Burton CBE, DL
It was as Lieutenant Burton that Sir George had his 12/60 Beetleback featured in *Autocar*'s wartime series *Talking of Sports Cars* (no 148, issue of April 16, 1943). He was a serial Alvis owner (qv 9384, 13011, 13334, 13501, 14630, 25870 and 27382 for a bio).

8766 GO 2619
A F Rivers-Fletcher
An interesting account of Rivers-Fletcher's experiences with this 12/60 Beetleback forms the basis of *Autocar*'s *Talking of Sports Cars* no 282 (issue of February 8, 1946). His more ambitious Speed model specials are enumerated elsewhere (qv 11298, 11859, and 14456 for a bio).

8770 VC 7389
Works experimental car
Arguably one of the most remarkable cars ever produced by the company, 8770 was the last FWD car made, and the only six-cylinder version.

8770: Unique six-cylinder fwd car, used a derivative of the eight-cylinder racing chassis, but with a 20hp Silver Eagle engine. Employee Bill York is seen with the car. (Courtesy the York family)

Whereas the preceding FWD's had all been 1.5-litre models of four- and eight-cylinders, with a distinctly sporting bias, here was a much larger experiment involving the turning round of a 19.82hp, 2.5-litre Silver Eagle engine and mounting it in a chassis which apparently owed much to late eight-cylinder practice. This roomy saloon was used personally by T G John, who tested it in Spain. It was thinly disguised by the use of a radiator shell that resembled a horsecollar (John was known to favour equestrian pursuits). Sadly, all details of its specific construction were withdrawn from works records, so it remains an enigma.

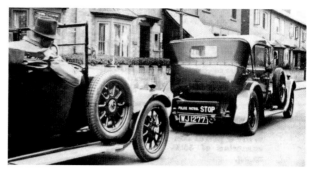

8780/8782: One of a pair of Sheffield police patrol Silver Eagles, testing a new 'Stop' system. The 12/50 Alvis astern of it is almost certainly one of the two TJs delivered at the same time (qv 8719/8728).

8776 LG 6525

8852 LG 6795

8974 LG 7057

Cheshire County Police

A fleet of three identical two-seater patrol cars. Police records of the day indicate that 8776 was based at Heswall, 8852 at Wilmslow, and 8974 at the divisional headquarters in Chester.

8780 WJ 1277/8

8782 WJ 1278/7

Cheshire County Police

A pair of identically specified Silver Eagle four-seater tourers for a regular customer of Alvis Ltd. Unfortunately, the record does not show precisely which registration number applied to which chassis. Two four-cylinder cars were supplied to this force at about the same time (qv 8719 and 8728).

8832 TS 9202

Dundee Police

A two-seater patrol car for this Scottish force.

8833 GO 247

Movie car

One of the several Alvis cars offered by enterprising dealer Charles Follett for stage and screen productions, this car featured prominently in

the 1931 Paramount British Production of *These Charming People*, based on a story by Michael Arlen. Leading lady was Nora Swinburne, and the actors visible in the accompanying 'still,' are Anthony Ireland and Cyril Maude.

8833: On the set of the 1931 movie *These Charming People*. (Courtesy Alvis Archive Trust)

8845 GP 7196

Philip Runciman

An entry in the RAC Rally of 1932 by a serial Alvis owner. Featured in *Motor*, issue of March 6,1932, page 243 (qv 9548 – a Runciman Monte Carlo Rally entry).

Previously owned another Silver Eagle (qv 7727), and prior to that, a 12/50 TG model (qv 4618), and a 14.75 (qv 5752).

8860 VC 8444

Harry Wragg

Harry Wragg (June 10, 1902-October 18, 1985) was a notable jockey, clocking up 1762 wins in his career, including three Epsom Derbys. He was known as 'The Head Waiter' on account of his patient riding strategy. Alvis owning was evidently a family trait, with younger brothers Arthur (qv 10847) and Samuel (qv 11307) both owning Alvis cars. Both were also successful jockeys.

8923 GP 5256

GP 5101

Movie cars

Two memorable movies, both of 1969 release, featured Alvis cars, and indeed owners. *Battle of Britain* featured GP 5256, and actors Harry Andrews (qv 26814 and 27182), Trevor Howard (qv 23467), and Ralph Richardson (an as yet unidentified front-wheel drive car).

GP 5101 is also as yet unidentified, but is known to have appeared in *Monte Carlo or Bust*, which also starred Tony Curtis (qv 27327) and Jack Hawkins (qv 24627).

8943 OV 2047

Iliffe Publications Ltd

Featured in *Autocar*'s *Used Cars on the Road* series (no 24, issue of January 18, 1952).

8982 RC 5

Derby Police

A distinctly-registered Silver Eagle for Derby's chief constable, and supplied by the Birmingham Alvis agent (and racing driver) Frank Hallam. Not long after this, there would be another Alvis delivery to the Derby force (qv 10369).

8987 GT 587

Iliffe Publications Ltd

Featured in *Autocar*'s popular series *Talking of Sports Cars* (no 72, issue of November 7, 1941), and again in no 200 of that same series, issue of April 14, 1944.

8988 GO 5777

Competition car

One of the more instantly recognisable Alvis racing cars, 8988 was bought new as a standard 12/60 TK Beetleback by Anthony Powys-Lybbe, a product of the Royal Military Academy, who, over the years, extensively modified and lightened the car, racing it at such venues as Donington and Brooklands throughout the 1930s. Inevitably, it is always referred to as the Powys-Lybbe car. 8988 has thankfully survived, and many postwar appearances have resulted.

9018 VC 8923

A royal visit

The *Automotor Journal* of August 7, 1931 has a photograph of the then Prince of Wales being chauffeur-driven in 9018 through Llanelli, on his way to open the Royal Welsh Show. It would be many years later, as the Duke of Windsor, following the abdication crisis, that he would purchase his own Alvis (qv 27259).

9021

Fox's Glacier Mints Ltd

A company car for this well-known Leicestershire firm whose trademark was that of a polar bear atop a clear block of its popular confection.

9027 VC 9032

Judge R W H Davies

In his book, A Light Car Odyssey, Judge Davies had related adventures encountered when driving his previous Alvis (qv 5051) from Belgaum, India back to England. The earlier car had been bought from Henly's in London, but the above directly from the Alvis works.

9068 ST 6690

Ronnie Aldrich

Ronnie Aldrich (February 15, 1916-September 30, 1993) was a hugely talented musician, enjoying success at many levels and in many genres, as a composer, arranger, conductor and performer. The discography of his work is quite enormous. He is probably best remembered as leader of that wartime-founded, morale-boosting orchestra known as The Squadronaires, whose popularity continued well into peacetime. He also produced music for such TV classics as *The Benny Hill Show*. Upon retiring to the Isle of Man, 9068 went with him but had to be re-registered with the Manx '1385 MN' plate.

9071 — VC 9367
Temple Press Ltd
A dual claim to fame here, as not only was 9071 used as a road test car in the November 24, 1931 issue of *Motor*, page 811, but also featured as a lead car in the 1933 movie *The King's Cup,* which had an aeronautical story line. This film was directed by Herbert Wilcox and starred Chili Bouchier.

9079 — TK 6900
Col H Pomeroy Bond DL
A prominent figure in Dorset life, Colonel Bond's purchase of Silver Eagle 9079 preceded that of his uniquely-bodied Silver Crest (qv 13931 for bio).

9101 — KS 5304
Duke of Roxburghe
Henry John Innes-Ker (July 21, 1876-September 29, 1932), the eighth Duke of that name, was educated at Eton and Sandhurst, and saw service with the Argyll and Sutherland Highlanders as second Lieutenant in both the Boer War and WWI. He was a first cousin of Winston Churchill. Unfortunately, he was only able to enjoy 9101 for rather less than a full year.

9117 — JF 152
John Fenwick
John Fenwick is listed as the first owner of 9117, and, given his address in Newcastle-upon-Tyne, one wonders if he was the same John Fenwick of department store fame that would purchase a TE 21 model many years later (qv 27100). The 'JF' mark seems to be an early example of a personalised application, originating in Leicester, rather than the London supplying agent Charles Follett. This car is much travelled as a subsequent owner, a Professor N P W Moore, took it to India, where it was in use for a number of years before being repatriated to the UK, fortunately retaining its original and distinctive registration mark.

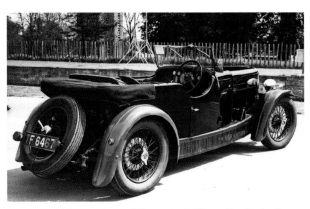

9124: The unique 'TA 19.82' Silver Eagle built specially to the order of the Baker family. (Courtesy Alvis Archive Trust)

9124 — TF 6467
Works Special Order
This unique vehicle, specially constructed to order for the Barker brewing family of Lancaster, basically consisted of infusing a 19.82hp engine of the current Silver Eagle type, into a chassis of the shorter 12/60 dimensions, but with a special four-seater tourer body. Perhaps unkindly described as a 'parts bin' job, it is, however, an obvious antecedent of the imminent first Speed 20 (only 60 chassis numbers later), which was being developed at the same time (qv 8194).

The Barkers had previously owned a standard Silver Eagle tourer, 8158.

9130 — VC 9368
The Alvis 'Ace'
This enigmatic experimental car was devised by Willie Dunn at a time when chief engineer G T Smith-Clarke was absent due to illness. A possible replacement for the 12/50, it had an advanced overhead camshaft engine. It was disguised by having a Lea-Francis fabric body and a Morris radiator with an emblem like an Iron Cross bearing the letters 'ACE,' an acronym for Alvis Car and Engineering. It was not approved of when Smith-Clarke returned, and was merely deployed as a factory hack and loan car for quite a few years. In 1971, employee E Roland Fox (later of Vanden Plas Ltd) waxed lyrical of its performance, and Arthur Varney (designer of the famous Alvis all-synchromesh gearbox) wrote of it in 1989: "The car was eventually sold to an Englishman said to have taken part in the murder of the

Russian monk, Rasputin." From separate sources we know one individual to have been Oswald T Rayner (1888-1961), an Oxford educated Army officer, fluent in French, German and Russian, who worked for MI6. The car seems to have been returned to the factory, and was last heard of with one D Blair (another Alvis employee?) in Birmingham, March 1939.

9131

9132 VC 9714

9133 GW 3726

9134 TF 7437

9135 PJ 1489

9147 LG 9855

9149
London Motor Show 1931
Quite an Alvis 'raid' on Olympia in 1931, with at least seven examples of the marque on works and various coachbuilders' stands.

9163 KY 1675
Scottish Motor Show 1931

9232 GX 8252
Two known exhibits at the 1931 Kelvin Hall Show by agents J H Galt Ltd.

9212
Dunlop Rubber Company
As supplier of most of the Alvis company's tyre requirements at this time, Dunlop would also occasionally take Alvis cars for tyre testing purposes. 9212 was one of these (qv 2931 and 5860 for two of the others).

9240 WJ 2674
Sheffield Police
A patrol car for a regular Alvis customer.

9365: Ornithologist Elsie Pemberton-Leach's TJ 12/50, pictured at a Stoneleigh Park event in 1970. The author is seen speaking with subsequent owner Roger White. The accompanying Speed 20 is SA 10098, which was owned at that time by Peter Mitchell, then Keeper of Industry at the Herbert Museum, Coventry. (Courtesy, via Wayne Brooks, Colonel Phil Adair, USAF (qv 14316))

9294 KV 286
Coventry Transport Museum
This archetypal example of a 12/60 TL Beetleback has been an exhibit at the CTM for many years, its original condition making it a benchmark for restorers of the model. Appropriately Coventry-registered too.

Also appeared in *Autocar*'s *Talking of Sports Cars* series, no 182 of December 10, 1943.

9320 KV 193
Harry Weston MBE
A notable figure in the industrial and civic life of the city of Coventry, Weston, Harry Weston (1896-1989) owned a company, Modern Machine Tools Ltd, that produced such things as lathes, and smaller engineering items. He became both Lord Mayor, and Alderman of the city, and stood, unsuccessfully, in the 1945 general election. His personal papers are lodged at the University of Warwick.

9365 KV 200
Elsie Pemberton-Leach MBE
Elsie Pemberton-Leach (June 30, 1888-May 9, 1968) was born in Plymouth, the younger daughter of General Sir Edward Pemberton-Leach VC. Between 1937 and 1963 she did a prodigious amount of

work researching bird migration, especially the practice of ringing them. She kept meticulous records, which made a major contribution to ornithology.

9372 — DX 9815
Charles Whitfield King

Almost as familiar a name in the world of philately as Stanley Gibbons, Whitfield King would, in due course, replace his TJ 12/50 with a rather more ostentatious 3.5-litre model (qv 13132).

9438 — XJ 1191
Brian Trueman

Born May 16, 1932, and well known as a writer and TV presenter having worked for both the BBC (on such programmes as *Screen Test*) and for ITV on *Granada Reports*. He also worked for Cosgrove Hall Films, contributing to at least 13 of its productions. Of these, perhaps *Dangermouse* and *Count Duckula* will be most familiar to readers of a certain age.

SILVER EAGLE
TB, TC, TD

1932 to 1933
130 cars
9456-9585

Consisting of models:

TB 19.82	23
TC 19.82	30
TD 16.95	68
Unrecorded	9

Consisting of coachbuilders:

Mayfair (various)	38
Carbodies (various)	26
Cross & Ellis (various)	53
Unrecorded	13

Chassis	Reg	Chassis	Reg	Chassis	Reg
9456	- - KY 2682	9460	- - - - - -	9465	- - TF 8790
9457	- - - - - -	9461	- - - - - -	9466	- - - - - -
9458	- - - - - -	9462	- - KV 2255	9467	- - -FS 4096
9459	- - WP 1937	9463	- - -FS 3222	9468	- - - - - -
		9464	- - - - - -	9469	- - - - - -

Chassis	Reg	Chassis	Reg	Chassis	Reg
9470	- - GY 7673	9509	- - - - - -	9548	- - KV 2870
9471	- - NV 1429	9510	- - - - - -	9549	- - KV 3825
9472	- - MV 2504	9511	- - - - - -	9550	- - - - - -
9473	- - KV 2168	9512	- - GG 8511	9551	- - - - - -
9474	- - HY 6018	9513	- - - - - -	9552	- - GG 9022
9475	- - KY 2422	9514	- - YD 5582	9553	- - - YG 2
9476	- - - - - -	9515	- - - - - -	9554	- - - - - -
9477	- - WN 4769	9516	- - - - - -	9555	- - YS 7552
9478	- - KV 2169	9517	- - KV 2861	9556	- - - - - -
9479	- - WV 1952	9518	- - - - - -	9557	- - WJ 6036
9480	- - - - - -	9519	- - - - - -	9558	- - KV 3822
9481	- - - - - -	9520	- - -YS 156	9559	- - WV 2579
9482	- - - - - -	9521	- - -US 418	9560	- - -LJ 7368
9483	- - - - - -	9522	- - GG 8220	9561	- - KY 3627
9484	- - - - - -	9523	- - - - - -	9562	- - - - - -
9485	- - - - - -	9524	- - - - - -	9563	- - - - - -
9486	- - - - - -	9525	- - UN 6098	9564	- - - US 665
9487	- - - - - -	9526	- - KY 3300	9565	- - - JR 65
9488	- - - - - -	9527	- - LV 2270	9566	- - -YS 166
9489	- - - - - -	9528	- - - - - -	9567	- - US 1116
9490	- - VD 1893	9529	- - KV 2509	9568	- - -GL 461
9491	- - KV 2507	9530	- - VV 1706	9569	- - VD 2549
9492	- - - - - -	9531	- - KV 2868	9570	- - GG 9870
9493	- - GY 1859	9532	- - - - - -	9571	- - - - - -
9494	- - HY 6395	9533	- - GG 9401	9572	- - - US 616
9495	- - -JA 2809	9534	- - - - - -	9573	- - - - - -
9496	- - KV 2172	9535	- - GG 9656	9574	- - KV 3826
9497	- - KV 2506	9536	- - EK 9011	9575	- - - - - -
9498	- - - - - -	9537	- - KY 4080	9576	- - - - - -
9499	- - - - - -	9538	- - -JX 499	9577	- - KV 5379
9500	- - KV 2165	9539	- - - - - -	9578	- - - - - -
9501	- - BR 9771	9540	- - GG 9066	9579	- - - - - -
9502	- - - - - -	9541	- - - - - -	9580	- - - - - -
9503	- - OD 3340	9542	- - -JU 1617	9581	- - KV 9773
9504	- - - - - -	9543	- - KV 2867	9582	- - - JR 607
9505	- - - - - -	9544	- - GG 8512	9583	- - WV 2921
9506	- - - - - -	9545	- - KV 3823	9584	- - - - - -
9507	- - - - - -	9546	- - SM 9753	9585	- - - - - -
9508	- - - - - -	9547	- - GG 9015		

Whilst technically the true 'Vintage' designation ended on December 31,1930, the final batch of Alvis TB, TC, and TD Silver Eagles built up to 1933 were identical with the 1930 examples of the genre, and are thus officially VSCC-recognised. The logical successor to this large type of six-cylinder would be the Crested Eagle model of chassis number 10651 onwards. However, the Silver Eagle model name would be shortly revived with chassis number 11351 onwards, but this was completely different to its earlier namesake, being a six-cylinder derivative of the new Firefly model.

9479 — WV 1952
Major C H Delmege

A serial Alvis owner by any standards (qv 7876, 8476, 10738 for bio, 12052 and 12244).

9511
Laura Henderson

Laura Henderson (December 6, 1863-November

Whilst no image of Laura Henderson's actual car has survived, this piece of contemporary works advertising shows a virtually identical model.

9546 was one of the Glasgow police force's Silver Eagles, seen here in a somewhat patinated state, postwar, long lost after decommissioning. (Photo taken with kind permission of Martin Emslie)

9524
Sir Cedric Hardwicke
Actor and serial Alvis owner, first of an earlier Silver Eagle (qv 8549). Subsequently a Crested Eagle (qv 10737) and a Speed 20 (qv 10877 for bio).

9520	YS 156
9521	US 418
9522	GG 8220
9540	GG 9006
9546	SM 9753
9547	GG 9015
9552	GG 9022

Scottish Police
Concentrated advertising in the Police Gazette of the availability of certain Alvis models to a high performance specification did result in a substantial number of orders for over a decade. There is no better example of this than the accompanying closely-related cars despatched to Scotland via agent Galt of Glasgow.

29, 1944) will forever be remembered as the founder of London's Windmill Theatre, a vaudeville establishment whose trademark description was, "we're never closed" (but sometimes rendered as 'never clothed'). It was a mecca during the war years for servicemen on leave, and continued for quite a while in the same genre in peacetime. When WWII broke out, Laura was 76 years of age, and engaged a manager, Vivian Van Damm (father of rally driver Sheila Van Damm) to run the business. This partnership, and remarkable aspect of show business, inspired a BBC drama film in 2005 entitled *Mrs Henderson Presents,* with Judi Dench as Henderson, and Bob Hoskins as Van Damm. A decade later this was turned into a musical with Tracie Bennett and Ian Bartholemew in the respective roles. Henderson left the Windmill to Van Damm when she died in 1944, and Van Damm left it to his daughter when he died in December 1960. However, the theatre as a vaudeville venue closed in October 1964, but the name has continued in other entertainment formats.

All of these were for the Glasgow force, except 9546 which was for Dumfries, and all were open touring cars except 9552 which was a limousine, perhaps for the chief constable's official use, or maybe custodial transport. After decommissioning from police work in 1940, 9546 was taken over by the Governor of Greenock Prison, J G Monteath.

9548 — KV 2870
Monte Carlo Rally 1933
This was a works-prepared car driven in the above event by Philip Runciman (1875-1953), a director of the Anchor Shipping Line, and a friend of Charles Follett. There is an image of Runciman in the National Portrait Gallery, and one of the cars in *Motor,* issue of January 24, 1933, page 1120. Clearly an enthusiastic Alvis driver, Runciman had previously owned several of the marque (qv 4618, 5752, 7727 and 8845).

9560 — LJ 7368
N Douglas Simpson
Simpson (September 23, 1980-August 29, 1974) was educated at Clifton College, Bristol, and Trinity College Cambridge, reading Botany, Zoology and Natural Sciences. He served in WWI with the Army Transport Corps, retiring as Captain. His lifetime's work in the field of Botany has already been referred to in the account of his Alvis 12/50 (qv 8624) and his collecting of specimens for his Herbarium is now legendary, travelling widely in pursuit of this specialised knowledge, sometimes in the 12/50, and sometimes in the above Silver Eagle, which he inherited from his father in 1936. His legacy continues with his Sudan, Egypt and Jordan collections being deposited at Kew, and the rest to the Natural History Museum. His botanical books were presented variously to the Cambridge Botany School, Reading University as well as to the aforementioned Kew, and NHM.

9581 — KV 7993
Alvis works car
Described in the factory records as a service loan car, it began life as a 19.82hp TC, but was converted to 16.95hp TD specifications. It would seem to have been the subject of some development work as its despatch date is much later than its immediate

peers, and the body maker has never been recorded.

9585
Hartwells (coachbuilder)
Research suggests that this, the last 16.95hp TD Silver Eagle made, was the one-off Hartwell body described in *Autocar,* issue of July 14, 1933, page 69. Sold to a Mrs F Wells of Eastbourne.

9586 — KV 1080
Works development car
The final Silver Eagle chassis frame laid down was actually endowed with an experimental four-cylinder engine, and became a development 'hack' for what would become the Firefly model (qv 9901 onwards for the eventual series production of that model).

Chassis numbers 9587-9600 were not used.

12/50 12/60
TJ, TK, TL

1932 only
199 cars
9601-9800

Consisting of models:

TJ 12/50	106
TK 12/60	1
TL 12/60	92

Consisting of coachbuilders:

Carbodies (various)	91
Cross & Ellis (various)	107
Salmon Tickford	1

Chassis	Reg	Chassis	Reg	Chassis	Reg
9601	- - - - - -	9613	- - -GX 493	9626	- - BR 9363
9602	- - - - - -	9614	- - JO 4421	9627	- - - -MJ 62
9603	- - OV 8760	9615	- - VY 3333	9628	- - - - - -
9604	- - FG 7717	9616	- - EV 4162	9629	- - UN 5645
9605	- - - - - -	9617	- - - - - -	9630	- - DT 3764
9606	- - - - - -	9618	- - -PJ 3915	9631	- - -KJ 5767
9607	- - GG 6820	9619	- - - UG 83	9632	- - DG 5193
9608	- - CP 9755	9620	- - - - - -	9633	- - - - - -
9609	- - WJ 3492	9621	- - -JB 127	9634	- - - - - -
9610		9622	- - CN 5148	9635	- - KV 1075
9611	- - RN 1875	9623	- - KV 1121	9636	- -KJ 6098
9612	- - KF 8626	9624	- - -KV 708	9637	- - KF 9140
		9625	- - GG 5981	9638	- - OY 2659

9639 - - SM 9330	9694 - - KY 2294	9749 - - OJ 2646
9640 - - - - - -	9695 - - - - - -	9750 - - WJ 4911
9641 - - KV 1067	9696 - - PN 9546	9751 - - TF 8636
9642 - - - - - -	9697 - - TG 3474	9752 - - - - - -
9643 - - RG 2830	9698 - - PN 9454	9753 - - VT 8213
9644 - - - - - -	9699 - - OD 2554	9754 - - DG 4675
9645 - - - - - -	9700 - - GY 3447	9755 - - NG 3638
9646 - - TF 8181	9701 - - - - - -	9756 - - - - - -
9647 - - OV 9081	9702 - - WJ 4334	9757 - - -JK 2433
9648 - - - - - -	9703 - - - - - -	9758 - - VS 2247
9649 - - - JU 597	9704 - - - -JU 718	9759 - - - - - -
9650 - - - - - -	9705 - - YD 4828	9760 - - - -LV 50
9651 - - - - - -	9706 - - -FS 3096	9761 - - - - - -
9652 - - VK 6260	9707 - - SM 9467	9762 - - NG 2965
9653 - - - -JY 67	9708 - - KF 9571	9763 - - -FS 3425
9654 - - - - - -	9709 - - - JU 786	9764 - - KV 1578
9655 - - BZ 1221	9710 - - - - - -	9765 - - KV 2174
9656 - - KV 1078	9711 - - KV 1571	9766 - - KY 2735
9657 - - GG 6684	9712 - -WM 7914	9767 - - CV 6910
9658 - - -FS 2947	9713 - - - - - -	9768 - - UG 1111
9659 - - - OJ 154	9714 - - - -YG 998	9769 - - MV 3177
9660 - - XG 1529	9715 - - GY 3979	9770 - - - - - -
9661 - - -LJ 5529	9716 - - - - - -	9771 - - XJ 2151
9662 - - - - - -	9717 - - TF 8544	9772 - - - - - -
9663 - - - - - -	9718 - - GY 3981	9773 - - - - - -
9664 - - OJ 2130	9719 - - -KJ 7785	9774 - - - - - -
9665 - - -JM 155	9720 - - - - - -	9775 - - - - - -
9666 - - - - - -	9721 - - EV 6485	9776 - - KV 2163
9667 - - -PJ 4543	9722 - - TY 9679	9777 - - GG 8294
9668 - - KV 1541	9723 - - - - - -	9778 - - KV 2141
9669 - - - - - -	9724 - -WM 8174	9779 - - KV 2862
9670 - - KY 2507	9725 - - GX 8150	9780 - - RG 3120
9671 - - LG 9418	9726 - - KY 2508	9781 - - GY 7593
9672 - - XJ 1214	9727 - - KV 1573	9782 - - DX 9999
9673 - - VE 7550	9728 - - - - - -	9783 - - - JY 680
9674 - - CG 1279	9729 - - KV 2096	9784 - - -LJ 6232
9675 - - - CZ 277	9730 - - KV 2280	9785 - - GX 9788
9676 - - - OJ 866	9731 - - - - - -	9786 - - MV 9120
9677 - - DW 7932	9732 - - EV 6485	9787 - - - JC 893
9678 - - - - - -	9733 - - - - - -	9788 - - - UJ 639
9679 - -WM 7780	9734 - -WM 8364	9789 - - GG 7095
9680 - - -FS 3568	9735 - - OJ 1830	9790 - - - - - -
9681 - - TS 9939	9736 - - WJ 4968	9791 - - - - - -
9682 - - - - - -	9737 - - - - - -	9792 - - KY 3672
9683 - - KV 1574	9738 - - KV 1580	9793 - - -JU 1450
9684 - - FW 3054	9739 - - KV 2164	9794 - - MV 3503
9685 - - KF 9355	9740 - - VH 4524	9795 - - -JY 1031
9686 - - - - - -	9741 - - TY 9056	9796 - - GG 8018
9687 - - TV 6614	9742 - - TK 8222	9797 - - TY 9796
9688 - - TG 3682	9743 - - - - - -	9798 - - - - - -
9689 - - GX 1990	9744 - - - - - -	9799 - - - - FB 1
9690 - - - - - -	9745 - - - - - -	9800 - - VE 7821
9691 - - - - - -	9746 - - GY 5928	
9692 - - GG 6990	9747 - - OJ 1921	
9693 - - AZ 7617	9748 - - HY 6285	

9619: 'Bonzo dog car' – Vernon Nowell's TJ 12/50. This view would certainly have qualified for the late William Boddy's *Vintage Tailpiece* series. (Courtesy Alvis Archive Trust)

9609 ‖ WJ 3492 ‖

Iliffe Publications Ltd

One of many Alvis cars featured in *Autocar*'s wartime series *Talking of Sports Cars*, no 194 in the issue of March 3, 1944. This feature describes an

9659: Most probably a posed photograph, apparently taken on a Bolton Street, date not recorded, but probably in winter if the radiator muff is anything to go by. The officer on the left is known to be one PC Henry Birkin, whose daughter, Mrs Ridyard, kindly supplied the photograph.

Whilst technically the true 'Vintage' designation ended on December 31,1930, the final batch of Alvis TJ, TK, and TL cars built during 1932 were identical to the 1930 examples of the genre and are thus officially VSCC-recognised. It had been intended to phase out this four-cylinder line but continuing demand kept it in production, hence this final series. Plans were already well in hand for its successor, the Firefly (qv 9901-on).

ambitious, though apparently successful conversion to six-cylinder Silver Eagle power.

9619   UG 83

Vernon Nowell

Vernon Dudley Bohay Nowell was a lecturer at Goldsmiths College, London, and a key member of the quaintly-named Bonzo Dog Doo Dah Band, playing banjo and double bass. The band was hugely popular for a while with well-remembered hits like *Urban Spaceman*. One of its discs, *Gorilla*, had its launch somewhat delayed following objections from Quintin Hogg MP, to his name being mentioned on it. There is an unusual coincidence here in that Hogg's father, Douglas, the first Lord Hailsham, was also an Alvis owner (qv 7070).

9659   OJ 154

Police in action?

Most probably a posed photograph, the accompanying one was apparently taken on a Bolton Street, date unrecorded, but probably in winter if the radiator muff is anything to go by.

9701   NPP 2

Competition car

A racing 12/60 TL specially constructed to the order of Charles Follett, with a lightweight body by Cross & Ellis (no B192). Confined to track use and not registered for road use until July 1950 in Buckinghamshire, hence the apparently anachronistic mark.

9777   GG 8294

Dr A W Maclennan

Comparatively little is known of 9777's first owner, save that he was a pioneering surgeon in the field of what has become known as plastic reconstructions. His work took on great significance when working with injured pilots who had suffered horrific burns in action during WWII. He died in 1959, and, interestingly, a subsequent owner of 9777 was an RAF Officer, Flt Lt George Stephen Bliss, DFC and Bar, Navigation Leader of 21 Squadron, mainly flying Mosquitos.

9800   VE 7821

The last 12/50

The end of an era was marked with the unceremonious despatch, of the final 12/50 chassis sanctioned, to a customer in Cambridgeshire, who most probably remained unaware of the significance of the purchase. At this time (July 1932), examples of the successor Firefly model were already beginning to filter out (qv 9901-onwards for this development).

PART 2

▼

1932-1940

9408	9414	9423	9424	9425
9426	9427	9431	9432	9433
9435	9436	9437	9447	9454
9455				

SPEED 20 SA

1931 to 1933
351 cars

9184-9455 mixed	26
9801-9900	100
10001-10200 (see page 79)	200
10601-10625 (see page 86)	25

Consisting of:

Charlesworth saloons numbered variously between 12092-12699	96
Vanden Plas saloons, coupés, tourers numbered variously between 1753-1999 and 3012-3-23	130
Cross & Ellis tourers numbered variously between 30206-30265	60
Mayfair various	10
Remainder: independent makers	

Sporting versions of the Silver Eagle had done very well in many forms of competition, but by 1931 their high stance on the road was of diminishing appeal, and thoughts turned to pure performance-led derivative. Thus it was that a new dropped chassis frame was developed, wider than hitherto and utilising the larger of the two available Silver Eagle engines. Indeed, when the first promotional example appeared at the Kelvin Hall Show in 1931, it still bore the escutcheon 'Silver Eagle' upon its radiator. The reaction was extremely positive, demand exceeding expectations, and a new name 'Silver Dart' was considered, but finally 'Speed 20' was chosen, with 26 pre-production examples being laid down. These have a flat radiator, but when proper series production commences at chassis 9801, the more familiar vee radiator has been adopted for what would become an iconic line.

The Speed 20

Unlike the 'production' Speed 20s, which were built in easily identified batches, the initial 26 pre-production examples had chassis numbers allocated randomly with other models such as the 12/50, 12/60 and Silver Eagle.

This is a definitive listing of the 26 chassis built:

9184	9268	9335	9336	9364
9383	9384	9385	9406	9407

Now extracted from the above listing are some of the more memorable examples, commencing with 9184 – the prototype that started the famous 'Speed Model' series, which would run until 1940.

9184 **VC 9605**
Works development car

The very first pre-production example of a new model was bound to cause a stir. Hurriedly prepared just in time for Glasgow's Kelvin Hall show of 1931, even the works people were uncertain what to call it. The name 'Silver Dart' had been mooted, but when exhibited it bore a 'Silver Eagle' escutcheon upon its radiator – a model with which it shared underpinnings. Much development work ensued following the show appearance. The Cross & Ellis body was in due course discarded, to be replaced by a Charlesworth coupé version, with the new assemblage being re-registered as KV 1577.

9268 **VC 9453**
Henken Widengren

The second pre-production example of the new model, which was now being promoted as the 'Speed 20,' was allocated to Swedish racing driver Henken Widengren, who commissioned a most attractive fixed-head coupé body for it from Bertelli. Widengren had previously owned a Silver Eagle (qv 8108) and, four years later, would order a 3.5-litre Alvis (qv 13105) which would also be bodied by Bertelli.

9383 **GG 5657**
RAC Rally 1932

An entry in the above event, I Fraser-Marshall.

9384 **FG 7503**
Sir Michael Nairn

First owner Nairn did not keep 9384 very long, changing it for an SB model shortly after its announcement (qv 10918 for bio). Much later on, 9384 would pass into the hands of that most serial of Alvis owners, Sir George Burton (qv 27382 for bio).

9384: A very early, flat radiator, pre-production speed 20 SA. Owned first by Sir Michael Nairn, and later by Sir George Burton. (Author's collection)

9406 **KV 707**

RAC Rally 1932

A 'works' car entered in the above event by Frank Hallam, who was the Alvis agent for Birmingham.

9414 **GW 4131**

RAC Rally 1932

An entry in the above event by Mrs C Booth-Hardcastle.

9432 **GG 6085**

Iliffe Publications Ltd

Autocar's *Talking of Sports Cars* series, no 228, featured in the issue of November 10, 1944, relates how Captain D G Newman of the Royal Engineers had, for reasons of economy, replaced the original six-cylinder engine of 9432 with a four-cylinder unit emanating from a 12/60 model. Not altogether a successful merger it would appear. Maybe the Captain was unaware that the works had carried out a similar exercise in May 1932, with chassis 9586, infusing an experimental four-cylinder engine into what amounted to Speed 20 underpinnings. That experiment served as a test bed for the forthcoming Firefly model.

For the next Speed 20 sequence see batch 9801 to 9900.

Chassis numbers
9801-9900
(Speed 20 SA – first batch)

Chassis	Reg	Chassis	Reg	Chassis	Reg
9801	- - GX 3457	9834	- - - - - -	9868	- - KV 1579
9802	- - -PJ 4888	9835	- - OW 2150	9869	- - -PJ 7539
9803	- - - YY 15	9836	- - - - - -	9870	- - GY 3986
9804	- - GX 7800	9837	- - GY 3980	9871	- - VE 8937
9805	- - - - - -	9838	- - GG 7094	9872	- - - - - -
9806	- - - - - -	9839	- - GY 3977	9873	- - KS 5546
9807	- - EV 6024	9840	- - - - - -	9874	- - GY 6949
9808	- - GN 3394	9841	- - RN 2005	9875	- - GY 6967
9809	- - GX 1751	9842	- -AWB 401	9876	- - - - - -
9810	- - - - - -	9843	- - -OJ 690	9877	- -WM 8100
9811	- - GX 8143	9844	- - VE 7424	9878	- - GY 7063
9812	- - -KJ 7069	9845	- - - - - -	9879	- - - - - -
9813	- - GY 741	9846	- - GY 4083	9880	- - OJ 1922
9814	- - - MJ 1	9847	- - - - - -	9881	- - - - - -
9815	- - OJ 1358	9848	- - HY 6195	9882	- - LG 9464
9816	- - KV 1572	9849	- - GY 3982	9883	- - KV 1577
9817	- - KV 1569	9850	- - -US 407	9884	- - RH 7401
9818	- - GG 6989	9851	- - - - AUS	9885	- - GY 7177
9819	- - GG 7592	9852	- - - - - -	9886	- -KJ 8452
9820	- - XJ 1031	9853	- - - - - -	9887	- - - - - -P
9821	- - KY 4387	9854	- - KV 2288	9888	- - YY 2583
9822	- - - - - -	9855	- - - - - -	9889	- - GY 7178
9823	- - - OJ 100	9856	- - JO 4690	9890	- - - - - -
9824	- - - - - -	9857	- - WJ 4318	9891	- - GY 2543
9825	- - KY 2370	9858	- - KV 1575	9892	- - - - - -
9826	- - - - - -	9859	- - GY 6969	9893	- - - - - -
9827	- - GY 7179	9860	- - WJ 4499	9894	- - YY 2582
9828	- - GX 3459	9861	- - - - - -	9895	- - OJ 1555
9829	- - LV 1530	9862	- - GY 9593	9896	- - OJ 1556
9830	- - - - - -	9863	- - RH 6076	9897	- - - - - -
9831	- - SR 8270	9864	- - KV 2173	9898	- - - - - -
9832	- - KV 2277	9865	- - WV 1644	9899	- - KV 2510
9833	- - KF 9570	9866	- - KV 2166	9900	- - - JJ 3233
		9867	- - - - - -		

9809 **GX 1751**

Sir Roland Gunter

A prominent racing driver, the 3rd Baronet (March 8, 1904-January 27, 1980) was a familiar figure at Brooklands, Le Mans, and indeed the Monte Carlo Rally. Whilst there is no evidence that 9809 was ever used for competition, his purchase of it lies chronologically midway between the Le Mans appearances with Bentley, and the later ones with Lagonda.

9814

Dunham family

The company Dunham & Haines of Luton, had been an Alvis agent virtually from the inception of the marque. Chassis 9814 was, however, for Dunham family use and was, either by accident or design, fortuitously registered with the above mark, which would appear on a succession of Dunham cars. Whilst the original car had been lost sight of, Dunham's removed its engine (no 10264) and some years later recycled it into the 12/70 racing chassis that had been bought from the works (qv 15620).

9827 GY 7179
RAC Rally 1933
An entry in the above event, driver Miss Audrey Sykes.

9844 VE 7424
Viscount Newport TD, DL, JP
Subsequently owned a Speed 25 tourer (qv 14353 for bio).

9854 KV 2288
T B Andre Ltd
London-based manufacturer of automotive suspension components, the company bought this early Speed 20 in chassis form, and bodied it itself. It had previously owned a front-wheel drive saloon (qv 6957).

9862 GY 9593
Temple Press Ltd
9862 was a special commission for the managing director, Roland E Dangerfield, of *Motor*'s publisher. It was a drophead coupé by the Mayfair Carriage Company Ltd, and was comprehensively written up in that periodical's issue of August 23, 1932, pages 145 and 146.

9863 RH 6076
Robert Blackburn
Aviation pioneer and serial Alvis owner (qv 10855 and 12097 for bio).

9874 GY 6949
Lt Cdr BH Clinkard RN
A larger than life character in the Alvis world, 'Clink,' as he was known to his many friends, was not only an engineer and competition driver, but also a raconteur and wit. He has written amusingly elsewhere as to how 9874 came to be transported from New Zealand back to the UK on the deck of a destroyer, and how its subsequent journey

from Portsmouth to Macclesfield was fraught with technical and meteorological problems. Upon retirement, he set up a spares 'emporium' at Assington, Colchester where he would leave no stone unturned to help any genuine Alvis enthusiast. Callers would most likely be invited to share a libation at The Shoulder of Mutton before departing. This worthy and useful service took a knock when some stubble burning in a nearby field got out of hand, and destroyed some of the cars. 9874, however, has miraculously survived, and became a Brooklands Museum exhibit.

9876
Gertrude Lawrence
Gertrude Lawrence (July 4, 1989-September 6, 1952) was a popular star of at least 22 stage and nine movie productions, and it has been said that she spent far more than she earned, resulting in an official receiver seizing her cars, flat, and indeed wardrobe in 1935. Of her many roles worth mentioning is that of Eliza Doolittle, in Shaw's *Pygmalion*, a character which, to a degree, uncannily mirrored her own background. She also appeared opposite Yul Brynner in the original stage production of *The King and I*.

9877 WM 8100
Arthur Mulliner Ltd, Northampton
The commission for a drophead coupé to be constructed by the above coachbuilder came from the Alvis agents Bamber, who had operations in both Southport and Sheffield. It got a lot of publicity when new, appearing in both *Autocar* and *Motor* during September 1932. Even many years later, following a private exportation to the United States, the car continued to attract attention, with a comprehensive feature in the *Road and Track* issue of January 1959. Interestingly, 1932 was the year that the Meccano company launched its Car Constructor Kit Number One – a clockwork toy with two easily interchangeable bodies. The coupé version bore an astonishing resemblance to 9877, and the roadster version to the Earl of March Alvis 10869. Both of these cars had been constructed by Mulliner, giving strength to the possibility that there may have been a connection. Volume 9, no 5 of *International Association of Automotive Modellers* (Sept/Oct 1959) carries a coachbuilder's drawing of 9877 which had been located by Tim McLaughlin, then President of the IAAM.

9900: The Birkin special returns to the factory in the course of an event. (Courtesy Ernest Shenton collection)

9882 **LG 9464**

Fodens of Sandbach

The Cheshire lorry maker was a regular customer of Alvis Ltd (qv 13641 and 14676).

9885 **GY 7177**

Works car

Unusually sourced from Charles Follett's London stock upon completion, 9885 was despatched back to Coventry, being initially allocated to engineering staff member Percy Joseland. Shortly afterwards, it was re-allocated to the Earl of Shrewsbury. Later still, in March 1936, a re-registration took place as BDD 834, the mark GY 7177 being transferred to an SC Speed 20, chassis 12772.

9891 **GY 2543**

Iliffe Publications Ltd

Autocar's long-running series *Talking of Sports Cars* carried a feature on 9891 (no 210 in the issue of June 23, 1944, page 449). The car was then domiciled in Poona, India, and appears to have stood up remarkably well, so far from ideal conditions.

9900 **JJ 3233**

Sir Henry (Tim) Birkin

Birkin (July 26, 1896-June 22, 1933) was a highly esteemed racing driver, having won at Le Mans on two occasions (1929 and 1931) in Bentleys. He specially commissioned this competition version of the SA Speed 20, but died as the result of a serious burn incident sustained at Tripoli, before he could actually race it. Its efficient styling has been much emulated by special builders (typically see 13134). Birkin is less well known as a novelist, with titles such as *Full Throttle*, last reprinted in 1948 by G T Foulis Ltd, but turned into a TV drama in 1995, starring Rowan Atkinson as Birkin.

For the next Speed 20 sequence see batch 10001 to 10200

FIREFLY SA

1932 to 1933
601 cars

9586 (prototype)	1
9901-10000	100
10201-10600	400
10751-10850	100

Consisting of:	
Cross & Ellis saloons numbered variously between 147-471	302
Cross & Ellis coupés numbered variously between 1091-1177	87
Cross & Ellis tourers numbered variously between 53483-53544	63
Carbodies saloons numbered 7826-7850	24
Carbodies (other)	3
Charlesworth saloons numbered variously between 12636-12800	72
Remainder chassis only or unidentified	

Conceived as a 'junior' version of the Speed 20 SA, with the same design philosophy and sharing a number of common components, the Firefly was intended to occupy the slot in the market previously occupied by the 12/50 and 12/60, but it was somewhat larger than these two, yet having the same size of engine was not really quite as 'sporting.' It was, however, quite a good seller for the company, with a good variety of coachwork. The works considered a six-cylinder 'Sixteen' version and actually built a derivative on chassis 10301, but this development would actually morph into the Silver Eagle SF type (qv 11351-on).

Chassis numbers
9901-10000
(Firefly SA – first batch)

Chassis	Reg	Chassis	Reg	Chassis	Reg
9901	KV 2167	9934	- - - - - -	9968	XJ 4710
9902	- - - - - -	9935	WV 2247	9969	- - - - - -
9903	OJ 3618	9936	-JV 1619	9970	KV 3381
9904	LG 9896	9937	RV 2665	9971	NJ 382
9905	KV 2669	9938	- - - - - -	9972	- - - - - -
9906	- - - - - -	9939	EV 8295	9973	XJ 3260
9907	VV 2655	9940	YY 5889	9974	HY 9120
9908	YY 2589	9941	HS 6811	9975	-FS 4512
9909	-FS 4233	9942	APH 310	9976	YJ 672
9910	- - - - - -	9943	YG 2521	9977	-JU 1478
9911	- - - - - -	9944	- - - - - -	9978	VK 7643
9912	YY 1281	9945	-JA 3321	9979	YW 2846
9913	- - - - - -	9946	- - - - - -	9980	- - - - - -
9914	-JY 1093	9947	- - - - - -	9981	JJ 10
9915	KY 3030	9948	US 735	9982	YD 6044
9916	-TJ 2269	9949	- - - - - -	9983	- - - - - -
9917	- - - - - -	9950	DG 7538	9984	TY 9800
9918	- - - - - -	9951	YY 6624	9985	- - - - - -
9919	GG 8559	9952	- - - - - -	9986	- - - - - -
9920	- - - - - -	9953	- - - - - -	9987	BR 9840
9921	KY 3159	9954	KV 3517	9988	YG 3087
9922	- - - - - -	9955	KV 3516	9989	-JU 1479
9923	- - - - - -	9956	- - - - - -	9990	KV 2872
9924	US 2532	9957	- - - - - -	9991	EW 7614
9925	LG 9933	9958	- - - - - -	9992	LV 1705
9926	VO 9036	9959	KV 3964	9993	OD 4271
9927	-FS 4131	9960	GG 9145	9994	LV 1786
9928	- - - - - -	9961	- - - - - -	9995	- - - - - -
9929	OD 4468	9962	- - - - - -	9996	KV 4026
9930	OJ 3617	9963	- - - - - -	9997	VN 4573
9931	KV 2619	9964	- - - - - -	9998	- - - - - -
9932	- - - - - -	9965	- - - - - -	9999	APA 275
9933	- - - - - -	9966	AKE 385	10000	- - - - - -
		9967	- - - - - -		

9901   KV 2167

9901   KV 2669

Works press cars
9901 was of course the very first example of a new 'Firefly' model devised to replace the long-running 12/50, which to some had become old-fashioned. Whilst vintagents initially resented the interloper, the Firefly was still streets ahead of its competitors in construction, albeit slower than its predecessor.

However, in marketing terms it was probably more 'user friendly.' 9905 was another press car, and will be found featured in *Motor*, issue of March 7, 1933, page 157, and in *Light Car*, issue of January 3, 1933.

9971   NJ 382
RAC Rally 1933
An entry in the above event by C E Harrington. The name Harrington will be familiar as constructors of coach bodies, and, of course, much later, of the Harrington Le Mans Sunbeam Alpine.

For the next Firefly sequence see batch 10201 to 10600.

Chassis numbers
10001-10200
(Speed 20 SA – second batch)

Chassis	Reg	Chassis	Reg	Chassis	Reg
10001	- - - - - -	10042	- - - - - -	10084	-JX 478
10002	-YY 924	10043	YY 5582	10085	- - - - - -
10003	- - - - - -	10044	- - - - - -	10086	- - - - - -
10004	YY 2585	10045	OJ 7199	10087	TJ 324
10005	YY 2991	10046	- - - - - -	10088	ARF 330
10006	- - - - - -	10047	- - - - - -	10089	KV 2866
10007	-LV 579	10048	- - - - - -	10090	SH 4203
10008	OJ 3	10049	KV 2863	10091	- - - - - -
10009	- - - - - -	10050	- - - - - -	10092	WJ 6462
10010	- - - - - -	10051	- - - - - -	10093	WJ 6496
10011	- - - - - -	10052	KV 2170	10094	ARF 471
10012	NV 1768	10053	KV 2865	10095	KV 3984
10013	OJ 2357	10054	AUS	10096	TJ 132
10014	- - - - - -	10055	YY 5588	10097	- - - - - -
10015	TF 9355	10056	US 1034	10098	LV 2200
10016	KY 3595	10057	MV 6348	10099	- - - - - -
10017	KV 2171	10058	YY 4945	10100	- - - - - -
10018	FV 3098	10059	KV 3893	10101	- - - - - -
10019	AUS	10060	- - - - - -	10102	KV 2869
10020	VH 4973	10061	- - - - - -	10103	AGC 818
10021	KV 2508	10062	- - - - - -	10104	-LJ 6969
10022	XJ 3404	10063	YY 5586	10105	APB 964
10023	- - - - - -	10064	OJ 6066	10106	FV 3267
10024	- - - - - -	10065	- - - - - -	10107	ZA
10025	YY 5618	10066	- - - - - -	10108	KV 4025
10026	YY 2581	10067	XJ 6396	10109	JJ 6963
10027	-FS 4232	10068	JJ 3231	10110	- - - - - -
10028	YY 2588	10069	UJ 903	10111	VD 2319
10029	YY 5581	10070	MJ 1444	10112	ZA
10030	- - - - - -	10071	- - - - - -	10113	JJ 6961
10031	YY 2586	10072	JJ 4679	10114	- - - - - -
10032	- - - - - -	10073	- - - - - -	10115	KY 3600
10033	UF 9613	10074	MG 2269	10116	-JV 1850
10034	YY 2584	10075	EV 8741	10117	JR 8
10035	HY 7278	10076	- - - - - -	10118	- - - - - -
10036	YY 5582	10077	- - - - - -	10119	AUS
10037	- - - - - -	10078	KV 2864	10120	- - - - - -
10038	YY 2920	10079	KY 3600	10121	- - - - - -
10039	-JX 285	10080	- - - - - -	10122	KV 4129
10040	ALU 453	10081	JJ 5608	10123	AGF 476
10041	YY 2337	10082	-JJ 66	10124	TK 8784
		10083	FG 8357	10125	FV 7278

10126 - - - - - -	10151 - - ALA 670	10176 - - -JB 2251
10127 - - AGT 325	10152 - - OJ 8431	10177 - - AGX 708
10128 - - -LJ 6967	10153 - - SO 4673	10178 - - - - - -
10129 - - - - - -	10154 - - -AAL 55	10179 - - US 2058
10130 - - - - - -	10155 - - XJ 7974	10180 - - - JJ 7193
10131 - - OJ 6804	10156 - - - - - -	10181 - - - - - -
10132 - - - - - -	10157 - - KG 2417	10182 - - - AJJ 585
10133 - - KV 5341	10158 - - AGU 241	10183 - - - - - -
10134 - - - - - -	10159 - - KY 4741	10184 - - - AJJ 577
10135 - - - - - -	10160 - - WD 5465	10185 - - VY 4668
10136 - - - - - -	10161 - - OJ 9053	10186 - - AGY 232
10137 - - - - - -	10162 - - - - AUS	10187 - - ALE 634
10138 - - - - - -	10163 - - AGT 388	10188 - - VE 8937
10139 - - WJ 6593	10164 - - KV 5141	10189 - - - - - -
10140 - - - - - -	10165 - - - - - -	10190 - - - AGT 9
10141 - - ALE 246	10166 - - - - - -	10191 - - AGT 368
10142 - - - - - -	10167 - - -JK 2779	10192 - - - AJJ 584
10143 - - LV 3066	10168 - - - - - -	10193 - - CG 4871
10144 - - VD 3261	10169 - - AGT 364	10194 - - TV 8700
10145 - - - GR 92	10170 - - CZ 2309	10195 - - ALD 879
10146 - - KV 4844	10171 - - ACD 449	10196 - - - - - -
10147 - - - - - -	10172 - - ALA 369	10197 - - - - - -
10148 - - - - - -	10173 - - -AJJ 578	10198 - - - - - -
10149 - - XJ 7063	10174 - - LV 4199	10199 - - - - NL
10150 - - KV 4842	10175 - - AGY 291	10200 - - - - AUS

10008

RAC Rally 1933 and 1934

A four-door saloon, specially prepared by Charlesworth, and incorporating a number of individual exterior and interior features. The customer was one Alan W F Smith – a friend of Alvis agent, Frank Hallam, who supplied the car. Correspondence has come to light which shows that Smith had intended it for the Monte Carlo Rally, but it was not quite ready for his exacting standards, though it made up for it in the two RAC events noted above. Sadly, at some stage, a later owner thought fit to part it from its very distinctive original registration mark, so it now wears JSJ 742.

10014

Viscount Clanfield

Arthur William Ashton Peel (May 29, 1901-September 22, 1969) was Lord Lieutenant of Lancashire between 1948 and 1951. He was the great-grandson of former Prime Minister, Sir Robert Peel, whose name, as Bobby, became attached to members of the police force, the very first of which he is credited with forming.

10021

Motor Sport magazine

An excellent photograph of 10021 appeared in the above periodical, issue of August 1950, page 407.

10026

Lord Inverclyde K St J

One of at least three Alvis cars owned (qv 13001 and 14645 for bio).

10029

Olympia Motor Show 1932

10029 was an exhibit on the Vanden Plas stand at the above event. Subsequently underwent two re-registrations, first as AOC 18, and then as YY 6484.

10031

Lord Waleran

Lord Waleran was born in 1905 as William George Hood Walrond, as he is probably better known in Lagonda circles for his notable drive (with Lord Selsdon) in the 1939 Le Mans 24-hour race, with the V12 Team Car. He had previously owned the above SA Speed 20. This car is presumably the one listed as an entry for the RAC Rally of 1933, to be driven by Lady Patricia Waleran, but was recorded as a non-starter. During WWII, Lord Waleran served as a Wing Commander with the RAFVR.

10040

Captain C B Wilson MC

Captain Wilson apparently decided to retain the above short registration mark allocated to 10040 when he disposed of it in favour of a later Alvis model, whereupon 10040 became 'ALU 453' (qv 10891 and 11218 for bio).

10041

Jimmy Nervo

Nervo (January 2, 1895-December 5, 1975) was part of the original 'Crazy Gang' stage performers, along with Teddy Knox. Especially versatile, his career had started in the circus – appearing as an acrobat and juggler before becoming extremely popular on the music hall circuit. Also made a number of films between 1926 and 1960.

10052 KV 2170

Competition car

Originally a standard works-registered Cross & Ellis tourer, 10052 was turned into a 'special' by Harold

10041: The Jimmy Nervo Speed 20 SA.
(Courtesy the late Tim Harding, via Richard Mitchell)

Barr, and successfully campaigned by him in VSCC and similar events. Highly modified and one of the fastest of its type.

10055   YY 5588
RAC Rally 1933
An entry in the above event by 'regular,' Charles Follett. A useful photograph of agent Follett with this car appeared in *Classic & Sportscar,* issue of September 2014, page 171.

10057   MV 6348
Betty Streather
Competition driver; used 10057 in the RAC Rally of 1933, later purchasing an SC type Speed 20 model which was also rallied (qv 11941 for biog). Many years later, in retirement, she also purchased a TD 21 (qv 26991).

10072   JJ 4679
Dorothy Patten
Prominent competition driver and Alvis enthusiast. Previously owned another SA Type Speed 20 (qv 9432) and later, an SB (qv 11190 for bio).

10074   MG 2269
Competition car
Campaigned quite prominently in some postwar club-type events by one L S Richards, 10074 was also featured in magazine *Motor,* issue of April 30, 1947, page 293.

10089   KV 2866
Alvis works car
Cars from the works press and demonstration fleet were popular, and often supplied to favoured customers. One such was 10089, which went to A J Linnell of Northampton, who, nearly a decade earlier, had purchased from them the ex Major Harvey Racing Car No 1 (qv 2091).

10099
Iliffe Publications Ltd
Originally supplied by Charles Follett to a London client, 10099 was taken to Sweden around 1936 and apparently used successfully in some competitions there. In 1942 it was acquired by Swedish enthusiast Tom Brahmer, who, due to the shortage of petrol at the time, fitted it with an Ello Producer Gas unit. Brahmer's account of this conversion is most amply written up in *Autocar*'s *Talking of Sports Cars,* no 237 of January 12, 1945, page 35. Later still, Brahmer also bought racing driver Henken Widengren's 3.5-litre Bertellibodied Alvis (qv 13105).

10112
Duke of Westminster
Evidently satisfied with this SA Speed 20 model, the Duke purchased an SB type about a year later (qv 11288 for bio).

10120
Competition car 'Thor'
Formerly a standard Charlesworth saloon, during the late 1970s a lot of money was spent converting it into a very professional-looking track car. It was known as the 'THOR' special at the time, but seems to have gone to ground.

10114
Sir Gomer Berry
Sir Gomer Berry (May 7, 1883-February 6, 1968) was a newspaper magnate. He was created Viscount Kemsley in 1945. An unusual claim to fame is that he had a 0-6-0 locomotive (no 1859) named after him.

10149   XJ 7063
1st Earl of Swinton CH MC PC
The 1st Earl of Swinton (May 1, 1884-June 27, 1972) was educated at Winchester and University

10158: The actor Lester Matthews' Speed 20 SA two-seater. (Courtesy Ernest Shenton collection)

College Oxford, and served as Member of Parliament for Hendon between 1918 and 1935, before the creation of the title.

10158 **AGU 241**
Lester Matthews
Matthews (June 6, 1900-June 5, 1975) was a highly successful movie actor, with well over 150 appearances. Too numerous to mention all, but typically *Werewolf of London* and *The Prince and the Pauper.*

10163
Steve Donoghue
Famous jockey Donoghue would replace the SA Type Speed 20 above with an SC model (qv 12087 for bio).

10176 **JB 2251**
Squire Car Company
The earlier of two Alvis Speed 20 cars supplied to Squire before taking up small scale car manufacture itself (qv 11837 for bio and the other). Later, it was somewhat lightened, turned into a competition car, and re-registered as MKR 740.

10177 **AGX 708**
Iliffe Publications Ltd
The first owner of 10177 had been the Hon A E

Winn, born January 4, 1909, who was killed in the WWII conflict, and was buried in the El Alamein cemetery on October 26, 1942.

The next owner was flying officer R Dunston-Carey, who took the car out to Africa where it served him well, standing up to the most arduous conditions. His adventures with the car are written up in two *Autocar* features, *Talking of Sports Cars* (no 172 of the series, issue of October 1, 1943, page 114), and then *Fast Work in Africa,* issue of August 25, 1944, pages 60 to 61.

10180 **JJ 7193**
Iliffe Publications Ltd
10180 was the subject of magazine *Autocar*'s *Used Cars on The Road* series, no 18, of October 26, 1951.

10182 **AJJ 585**
Dr Harold Dearden
Dr Dearden (November 13, 1883-July 6, 1962) was one of Britain's most eminent criminologists, and

Criminologist Harold Dearden – a portrait by photographer Otto Hope (1878-1972). (Courtesy Alvis Archive Trust)

wrote numerous books on the subject, including *Mind of a Murderer* (1930), *Death under the Microscope* (1934), *Devilish But True* (1948), and *Aspects of Murder* (1952).

10185 | VY 4668
Earl Castle Stewart
The 7th Earl of that line (August 6, 1899-November 5, 1961) was Member of Parliament for Market Harborough from 1929 to 1933, before inheriting the title.

10191 | AGT 368
RAC Rally 1934
A specially constructed, one-off Carlton bodied two-door saloon, entered in the above event by Mrs A M Damer-Priest.

10198
Major Oscar Guest MP
The Major replaced this car with a later SC Speed 20 model (qv 11890 for bio).

10199
Ruhaak & Co
An export to the Netherlands where it was apparently used competitively by the purchasers. After WWII the car was repatriated to the United Kingdom, and registered in November 1950 in the London Borough of East Ham as EHV 976.

For the next Speed 20 sequence see batch 10601 to 10625.

Chassis numbers
10201-10600
(Firefly SA – second batch)

Chassis	Reg
10201 - - - YS 160
10202 - - VK 8185
10203 - - ALG 316
10204 - - KY 3856
10205 - - KV 2871
10206 - - WD 6135
10207 - - - - - -
10208 - - - - - -
10209 - - - - - -
10210 - - -VJ 4913
10211 - - ALG 171
10212 - - FG 8253
10213 - - - - - -
10214 - - GG 8717
10215 - - -FS 4860
10216 - - - - - -
10217 - - - - - -
10218 - - XJ 5249
10219 - - AKE 773
10220 - - UG 2895
10221 - - - - - -
10222 - - UF 9534
10223 - - AKE 748
10224 - - -LJ 6953
10225 - - - - - -
10226 - - -XJ 5148
10227 - - -FS 4519
10228 - - BR 9841
10229 - - - JJ 3232
10230 - - OY 6788
10231 - - WJ 5768
10232 - - KY 3560
10233 - - - PV 333
10234 - - - - - -
10235 - - - JJ 3239
10236 - - - - - -
10237 - - AGU 225
10238 - - HS 6935
10239 - - - - - -
10240 - - - - - -
10241 - - MG 2204
10242 - - - - - -
10243 - - - - AUS
10244 - - OC 2301
10245 - - GG 9739
10246 - - DG 5866
10247 - - -IL 2068

10248 - - FV 3269	10318 - - - - - -	10388 - - - - - -
10249 - - TG 4585	10319 - - EV 9802	10389 - - -NJ 1171
10250 - - KV 3382	10320 - - - US 612	10390 - - KV 4027
10251 - - BAA 107	10321 - - - - - -	10391 - - KV 4651
10252 - - - - - -	10322 - - - -FM	10392 - - AMA 634
10253 - - KV 3849	10323 - - BG 1277	10393 - - XJ 6786
10254 - - - - - -	10324 - - - - - -	10394 - - - - - -
10255 - - WV 2712	10325 - - - YS 163	10395 - - -JY 1552
10256 - - - JJ 9312	10326 - - GG 9402	10396 - - -JU 2091
10257 - - - - - -	10327 - - - - - -	10397 - - - - - -
10258 - - - - - -	10328 - - - - - -	10398 - - - - - -
10259 - - - - - -	10329 - - - - - -	10399 - - JW 2932
10260 - - - - - -	10330 - - - - - -	10400 - - - - - -
10261 - - - - - -	10331 - - - - - -	10401 - - AGT 332
10262 - - GG 9146	10332 - - HS 7053	10402 - - -VJ 5100
10263 - - - - - -	10333 - - VO 9394	10403 - - YD 6851
10264 - - AKJ 139	10334 - - EX 3186	10404 - - - - - -
10265 - - -FS 4937	10335 - - KV 3895	10405 - - LV 3480
10266 - - YG 2795	10336 - - WD 5122	10406 - - RG 3535
10267 - - KV 3515	10337 - - - - - -	10407 - - RM 9475
10268 - - LV 2260	10338 - - - - - -	10408 - - - - - -
10269 - - - - - -	10339 - - VT 9087	10409 - - KY 4517
10270 - - - - - -	10340 - - UF 9658	10410 - - - - - -
10271 - - - - - -	10341 - - - - - -	10411 - - -NJ 1660
10272 - - -JF 4033	10342 - - - AJJ 589	10412 - - KV 4134
10273 - - ALG 524	10343 - - VT 9577	10413 - - HS 7097
10274 - - - - - -	10344 - - OD 4974	10414 - - US 664
10275 - - KV 3965	10345 - - - JJ 8761	10415 - - US 1115
10276 - - - - - -	10346 - - GG 9766	10416 - - RG 3759
10277 - - - - - -	10347 - - - - - -	10417 - - KY 4876
10278 - - - - - -	10348 - - - - - -	10418 - - - - - -
10279 - - - - - -	10349 - - - - - -	10419 - - AGK 1
10280 - - OY 5253	10350 - - - - - -	10420 - - - - - -
10281 - - KV 3963	10351 - - UF 9657	10421 - - US 1033
10282 - - KV 3821	10352 - - GG 9767	10422 - - - - - -
10283 - - AKJ 275	10353 - - - JR 388	10423 - - -WM 8878
10284 - - - - - -	10354 - - WP 3406	10424 - - KV 4131
10285 - - - - - -	10355 - - VN 4605	10425 - - KV 4132
10286 - - YD 6506	10356 - - KY 4231	10426 - - -JU 2128
10287 - - - TJ 510	10357 - - VN 4493	10427 - - - - - -
10288 - - - - - -	10358 - - VN 4517	10428 - - - - - -
10289 - - - - - -	10359 - - - - - -	10429 - - - - - -
10290 - - - - - -	10360 - - YJ 495	10430 - - KY 4255
10291 - - - -JR 76	10361 - - - - - -	10431 - - - - - -
10292 - - - - - -	10362 - - KY 3899	10432 - - - - - -
10293 - - - - - -	10363 - - - - - -	10433 - - - - - -
10294 - - - JJ 5603	10364 - - - - - -	10434 - - KV 4130
10295 - - - - - -	10365 - - JW 2912	10435 - - - AJJ 579
10296 - - - - - -	10366 - - - - - -	10436 - - - - - -
10297 - - CZ 1601	10367 - - - - - -	10437 - - OD 5565
10298 - - - - - -	10368 - - LV 2737	10438 - - ARF 822
10299 - - -GR 380	10369 - - RB 7864	10439 - - RG 3500
10300 - - - - - -	10370 - - - - - -	10440 - - -TJ 1214
10301 - - KY 4232	10371 - - - - - -	10441 - - - - - -
10302 - - OJ 7847	10372 - - RB 8205	10442 - - - - - -
10303 - - -FS 5120	10373 - - - - - -	10443 - - WV 4324
10304 - - - - - -	10374 - - - - - -	10444 - - - - - -
10305 - - - - - -	10375 - - - - AUS	10445 - -AHW 896
10306 - - KY 3788	10376 - - WD 5050	10446 - - -GR 109
10307 - - - - - -	10377 - - - - - -	10447 - - -JU 4567
10308 - - - - - -	10378 - - CZ 2272	10448 - - - - - -
10309 - - RN 2397	10379 - - WF 5572	10449 - - US 1663
10310 - - - JJ 5604	10380 - - -JU 1935	10450 - - KY 4495
10311 - - - - - -	10381 - - -LJ 7349	10451 - - - - - -
10312 - - AKK 127	10382 - - - - - -	10452 - - - - - -
10313 - - - - - -	10383 - - US 663	10453 - - - - - -
10314 - - VT 9253	10384 - - -FS 5550	10454 - - - - - -
10315 - - - - - -	10385 - - KY 4040	10455 - - AAL 280
10316 - - - - - -	10386 - - AGK 819	10456 - - - - AUS
10317 - - KY 3816	10387 - - - - - -	10457 - - KV 4574

Chassis	Reg		Chassis	Reg		Chassis	Reg
10458	—		10506	KV 4845		10554	—
10459	—		10507	ABH 352		10555	—
10460	—		10508	—		10556	VJ 5339
10461	US 1229		10509	XJ 8386		10557	FS 6429
10462	AAL 16		10510	—		10558	JO 7454
10463	—		10511	—		10559	WJ 7284
10464	AAL 47		10512	—		10560	—
10465	KV 5053		10513	LV 4197		10561	SR 8629
10466	—		10514	—		10562	KY 4861
10467	KY 5095		10515	UJ 1658		10563	RB 8772
10468	—		10516	TJ 1958		10564	NG 4989
10469	—		10517	—		10565	BG 1575
10470	—		10518	FS 5792		10566	—
10471	—		10519	—		10567	—
10472	AXE 246		10520	—		10568	—
10473	PO 8118		10521	AJJ 581		10569	OC 1179
10474	AOF 777		10522	AJJ 772		10570	PV 651
10475	BPB 1		10523	—		10571	LV 5447
10476	—		10524	ALD 346		10572	—
10477	YG 3877		10525	GM 2024		10573	AMA 662
10478	—		10526	CG 4684		10574	—
10479	—		10527	—		10575	US 2286
10480	—		10528	—		10576	TG 6067
10481	—		10529	WJ 7006		10577	JG 3655
10482	NV 3422		10530	—		10578	—
10483	—		10531	KY 4539		10579	—
10484	KG 2670		10532	LV 2260		10580	JH 5459
10485	KV 4843		10533	AKL 850		10581	—
10486	—		10534	—		10582	AUS
10487	—		10535	—		10583	US 2046
10488	KV 5075		10536	—		10584	KY 4971
10489	VT 9294		10537	KV 6330		10585	JU 2704
10490	KV 4133		10538	—		10586	VJ 5390
10491	ARF 896		10539	XJ 8390		10587	KV 4846
10492	—		10540	FT		10588	OD 6226
10493	MN 8719		10541	LJ 7778		10589	—
10494	HS 7140		10542	AAL 99		10590	AMA 830
10495	—		10543	AKL 704		10591	—
10496	—		10544	RB 8984		10592	—
10497	—		10545	—		10593	—
10498	—		10546	—		10594	—
10499	LJ 7947		10547	AKM 510		10595	TJ 2542
10500	AGU 464		10548	VV 2096		10596	—
10501	—		10549	—		10597	—
10502	—		10550	KY 4885		10598	—
10503	KV 5157		10551	VV 2116		10599	—
10504	AKL 335		10552	BG 1547		10600	—
10505	—		10553	LJ 8215			

10280 — OY 5253

Grenfell Special

Starting life as a standard Firefly saloon, like many of its type, 10280 found favour as the basis of a special. This is an especially well-known and successful example.

10283 — AKJ 278

Captain H B Sears DSO

Harold Baker Sears (September 15, 1880-May 9, 1959) was educated at Oundle, and the RNEC, Devonport. Served during WWI, mainly in destroyers. For a short period around 1928 he was Captain of HMS Hood, the vessel that was sunk in 1941 with catastrophic loss of life during the Battle of Jutland. He replaced his Firefly 10283 with a Firebird model (qv 12312).

10301 — KY 4232

Works development car

There were a number of ideas to extend the Firefly appeal (a handful of very late examples having been equipped with the 13.22hp Firebird engine). A 'Firefly Sixteen' was briefly promoted in the motoring press, but only a solitary example was made, the 10301. The idea, however, remained and morphed into a new generation of Silver Eagles commencing at chassis 11351. The solitary Sixteen was used for various purposes around the factory before being sold on as 'used,' and despatched to the Bradford agency of Waterhouse Ltd.

10322

Sultan of Selangor GCMG, KCVO

The fifth Sultan of Selangor (September 11, 1863-March 31, 1938), he was knighted by the British in 1912. 10322, a tourer, was delivered to the royal household in March 1933, but it seems there's been little trace of it following the Japanese occupation of 1942-1945. However, there was also an as yet unidentified tourer of the 12/70 model type, which was also supplied to the royal household, and this is believed to have survived.

10341

Jack Warner OBE

A popular actor (October 24, 1895-May 24, 1981), and brother to comediennes Elsie and Doris Waters (aka 'Gert and Daisy'), Warner is probably best remembered for his role in the movie *The Blue Lamp*, which, following its release in 1950, would spawn the television series *Dixon of Dock Green*, which ran from 1955 to 1976. Less well known is the fact that he had initially studied automobile engineering, and been employed by the Sizaire-Berwick company prior to WWI. The 1930s found him working as a salesman for London Alvis agent Charles Follett. The accompanying photograph shows him precisely in this role, demonstrating the versatility of one of the handful of Firefly tourers to be bodied by Ranalah (John Charles Ltd). Descriptions of this rare style of coachwork can be found in *Autocar*, issue of

10341: Actor Jack Warner in his previous role as one of Charles Follett's car salesmen, demonstrating the roominess of the Ranalah-bodied firefly tourer. (Courtesy Alvis Archive Trust)

May 1933, page 748, and *Motor*, issue of May 9, 1933, page 572.

10355 VN 4605

10357 VN 4493

10358 VN 4517
North Riding Police
A trio of identical Charlesworth-bodied saloon patrol cars for this Yorkshire force.

1042 KV 4132
Captain Russell MC
No doubt an interesting story (outside the scope of this volume) remains to be told as to how or why a works-registered Firefly coupé came to be exported to Tibet for a number of the British Legation based at Gyantse, which lies midway between Mount Everest and Lhasa. An expedition on Mount Everest had taken place only a couple of months earlier involving an Alvis owner (qv

12298), and all this at a time of some political uncertainty in the region, somewhat exacerbated by the death of the thirteenth Dalai Lama later in the same year.

10360 RB 7864
Derby Police
A patrol car for the city force.

10462 AAL 16
Newark Police
A patrol car for this Nottinghamshire force.

10475 BPB 1
Horstmann's of Bath
Probably the first of several Alvis cars bought by the family firm of car makers (qv 12362 for bio, 15446, and 15748).

10476 ALA
Rosemary Heath
Rosemary Heath was born in 1928 in Brentwood, Essex and attended Cheltenham Ladies College from 1944 to 1946. After this, she took up a position with the British Council in London, owning, in succession, a 1929 Austin Seven and an as yet unidentified Firefly saloon. In 1959, she was offered a posting with the British Council in Belgrade, and her friend, Dr Lancelot Ware, of MENSA fame, and a serial Alvis owner himself (qv 10708 for bio), was instrumental in obtaining the above Firefly drophead coupé for her, accompanying her on the fairly arduous journey overland to Yugoslavia. Upon her return to the UK, the car remained in that country, miraculously survived, and, at the time of writing, is in a Belgrade Museum.

10482
Northampton Police
A tourer-bodied Firefly for the above force.

10494 HS 7140
RSAC Rally 1933
An entry in the above event, with driver W A Scott-Brown.

10506

Light Car

Featured in the above magazine, July 7, 1933.
Evidently a works press car.

10540 FT- - - - -

Newcastle-Upon-Tyne Police

This car, a tourer, had not been long delivered
when it was involved in an accident sadly resulting
in the death of an officer. It would be replaced a
few weeks later with another Firefly – this time a
saloon (qv 11069).

10598

Winifred Pink

Competition driver, previously owned a 12/50
model (qv 5219) and later a Silver Crest (qv 13812
for biog)

10549 seen here in a much earlier incarnation.
(Courtesy Ernest Shenton collection)

Chassis numbers
10601-10625
(Speed 20 SA – third batch)

Chassis	Reg				
10601	- - KG 2812	10609	- - ALU 457	10618	- - ALR 782
10602	- - AKL 335	10610	- - OC 3230	10619	- - OC 4422
10603	- - RV 3774	10611	- - ALE 844	10620	- - KV 5159
10604	- - ALP 543	10612	- - KV 5299	10621	- - ALR 781
10605	- - - - - -	10613	- - BG 1523	10622	- - - - AUS
10606	- - - AJJ 588	10614	- - ALR 783	10623	- - ALR 783
10607	- - - - - E	10615	- - TK 9627	10624	- - RB 9158
10608	- - ALR 783	10616	- OW 3563	10625	- - KV 5815
		10617	- - ALK 228		

10609 ALL 694

R B Walpole

A descendant of a well-known family dynasty
that had produced Britain's first prime minister,
a couple of novelists, and several military men,
Walpole was the second owner of 10609, taking
it over in 1945, and giving his address as 87, New
Bond Street, London, then, as now, a prestigious
business location. Shortly after this he retired to the
family seat of Mount Usher in Wicklow, engaging
in equine pursuits. As late as 1967, he was writing
in the *Carriage Journal* (Vol 5, No 2) on the subject
of that highly specialised conveyance known as
the Irish Jaunting Car. Mount Usher had been
developed, rather like Kew Gardens, as virtually
a living museum of both native and foreign tree
species, and other flora. The establishment was sold
to Madeleine Jay in 1979, and is still maintained
by the Jay family as one of Southern Ireland's key
tourist attractions.

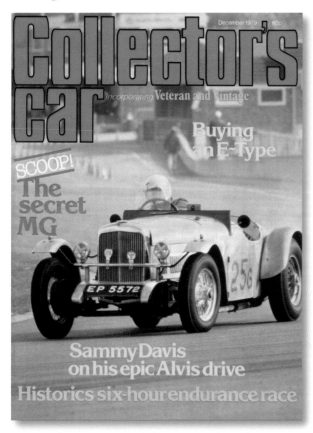

10549: On the cover of *Collector's Car* in December
1979 during some circuit racing. Owner the late
Dick Gilbert was equally at home on the judicial
circuit.

10610 OC 3230

J C (Jock) Stephen

By profession a serving officer with the London

10610: Jock Stephen with his rapid 4.3-litre-engined SA Speed 20. Jock's driving skills were undoubtedly honed during his day job as a London Metropolitan Police traffic cop.

Metropolitan Police Flying Squad, Jock not only used his skills with competitive driving in VSCC and similar events, but personally prepared 10610 to his own exacting standards. Whilst the bodywork was little altered save for the addition of cycle type front wings, the car had been endowed with a later 4.3-litre engine, making it one of the faster track cars of its day.

NB: Chassis numbers 10626 to 10650 were not used for any model. For the next Speed 20 sequence see batch 10851 to 10950.

CRESTED EAGLE

1933 to 1940
602 cars

10651-10751 TD, TE		100
10951-11050 TD, TE		100
11616-11710 TE, TE		85
12886-12985 TF, TG		100
13186-13285 TF, TG		100
13696-13701 TK		6
13746-13775 TA, TB		30
13876-13895 TA, TB		20
14496-14545 TA, TB		50
14949-14959 TC, TD		11

Consisting of:

Charlesworth saloons numbered variously between 12772 – 14509	322
Charlesworth, other	30

then:

Mayfair various (no body numbers recorded)	187

Remainder: independent markers

Whilst generally perceived as being the most staid of Alvis models, the Crested Eagle was in fact quite innovative, seeing the first application of the massive transverse leaf independent front suspension, and the remarkable all-synchromesh gearbox. Certainly though, the slant was formal saloons and limousines, and over the years improvements ran in parallel to those of the 'Speed' models, mostly using the same parts bin. There were some open versions but these were very few in number; being much heavier, they were not as nimble as their 'Speed' stablemates.

Chassis numbers
10651-10750
(Crested Eagle TD, TE, first batch)

Chassis	Reg				
10651 - - KV 3824	10677 - - KV 5158	10704 - - YG 5577
10652 - - - - - -	10678 - - - - - -	10705 - - - - - -
10653 - - SR 8650	10679 - - - - - -	10706 - - -US2850
10654 - - - - - -	10680 - - - - - -	10707 - - KV 5819
10655 - - - - - -	10681 - - AWA 827	10708 - - KV 6536
10656 - - ANO 854	10682 - - - - - -	10709 - - KV 8001
10657 - - AOK 646	10683 - - KV 5160	10710 - - - - - -
10658 - - - - - -	10684 - - SH 4330	10711 - - - LJ 8633
10659 - - - - - -	10685 - - - - - -	10712 - - - - - -
10660 - - - - - -	10686 - - - - - -	10713 - - - - - -
10661 - -AMA 780	10687 - - - - - -	10714 - - - - - -
10662 - - US 2045	10688 - - - - - -	10715 - - ALE 465
10663 - - KY 5025	10689 - - - - - -	10716 - - - - - -
10664 - - - - - -	10690 - - - - - -	10717 - - NV 2941
10665 - - KV 5142	10691 - - - - - -	10718 - - - - - -
10666 - - - - - -	10692 - - - - - -	10719 - - WP 5322
10667 - - - - - -	10693 - - KV 6296	10720 - - -NJ 2207
10668 - - -GR 236	10694 - - AUC 957	10721 - - JO 8770
10669 - - - - - -	10695 - - - - - -	10722 - - - - - -
10670 - - ALE 850	10696 - - - - - -	10723 - - -JU 2915
10671 - - - - - -	10697 - - KV 5817	10724 - - US 3853
10672 - - - - - -	10698 - - - - - -	10725 - - - - - -
10673 - - AMB 950	10699 - - - - - -	10726 - - KV 7062
10674 - - - - - -	10700 - - - - - -	10727 - - YD 7875
10675 - - - - - -	10701 - - - - - -	10728 - - - - - -
10676 - - - - - -	10702 - - - - - -	10729 - - KY 5287
	10703 - - KV 6533	10730 - - - - - -

10731 - - - - - -	10738 - - WV 4305	10745 - - AAT 189
10732 - - - - - -	10739 - - - - - -	10746 - - - - - -
10733 - - US 2553	10740 - - - - - -	10747 - - - AUV 2
10734 - - - - - -	10741 - - - - - -	10748 - - - - - -
10735 - - - - AUS	10742 - - WH 4950	10749 - - KY 6445
10736 - - - - AUS	10743 - - - - - -	10750 - - - - - -
10737 - - - - - -	10744 - - - - - -	

10651 — KV 3824
Alvis works car

The very first production example of the new Crested Eagle model, which, though staid in appearance, marked two important innovations: the massive transverse leaf independent front suspension, and the now famous all-synchromesh gearbox. Involved, naturally, in promotional work, it is interesting to have a drawn version of it instead of the usual photograph. An historic car that, sadly, seems to have ended its days around 1947 as the hack for a Salisbury garage.

10684 — SH 4330
Captain H H Liddell-Grainger DL

Henry Hubert Liddell-Grainger (1886-November

10651: The very first production Crested Eagle was the subject of an artistic impression used in initial promotions.

3, 1935) served during WWI with the Scots Guards. He later became Deputy Lieutenant and a Justice of the Peace for Berwickshire. In due course replaced 10684 with a Speed 20 SC model (qv 11903).

10708 — KV 6536
Dr Lancelot Ware OBE

Lance Ware (June 15, 1915-August 15, 2000) was educated at Steyning Grammar School and Imperial College, initially studying Science, and in due course found work with Boots of Nottingham and at the Government Research Centre at Porton Down. After WWII, he had a change of direction, returning to the academic life to study Law at Lincoln College Oxford, before being called to the Bar in 1949. A chance meeting with Australian Barrister Roland Berrill led to their founding, in 1946, what was initially called the High IQ Club, but later became MENSA, and grew to over 100,000 members. Lance Ware was a serial Alvis owner, of which 10708 was probably the first, being re-registered at ODH 416 following a rebuild into an estate car format (for the other Ware Alvis cars see 11535, 12023, 14308, 20977 and 22510). He was also instrumental in preparing a Firefly coupé for his friend Rosemary Heath's British Council posting to Belgrade, where the car has survived as a museum exhibit (qv 10476).

Dr Lancelot Ware OBE, co-founder of MENSA.
(Courtesy Alvis Archive Trust, via Martin Boothman)

10687
Rosewarne family
A prominent Cornish family based near Hayle had a series of Alvis cars, of which 10687 may have been the first (qv 13390, 14457 and 23987. Notes under 13390).

10737
Sir Cedric Hardwicke
Actor, and serial Alvis owner (qv Silver Eagles 8549 and 9524, also Speed 20 SB 10877 for bio).

10738 WV 4305
Major C H Delmege
Serving in WWI with the 21st Lancers, Major Delmege must rank as one of the most prolific of Alvis owners (qv 7876, 8476, 9479, 12052 and 12244). 10738 is of particular interest on two counts; firstly because of having a unique body by the REAL company, and secondly on account of an appearance in the 1935 movie *Car of Dreams*, driven by Rivers-Fletcher, and starring a young John Mills. Writing in the *Old Motor* issue of January 1980, Rivers renders an interesting account of an aspect of the film's production, where the storyline called for a procession of a couple hundred cars to be driven sedately around the Brooklands track. Apparently, the first two takes developed into an unofficial race and it was only on the third that the director's intentions were adhered to. This occasion was also reported upon in *Autocar* issue of May 24, 1935 and has a bird's eye view of this remarkable assembly on page 911. It is just possible to discern the presence of 10738, right of centre.

10738: On the set of the 1935 Gainsborough movie *Car of Dreams*. (Courtesy Rivers-Fletcher collection)

10747 AUV 2
William Henry Buffum
A descendant of the family firm that had made cars (and indeed boats) at Abington, Massachusetts between 1901 and 1907, and clearly an anglophile, W H Buffum gave his address as The Royal Yacht Club, when taking delivery of 10747. A prestigious club, founded in 1775 on London's Knightsbridge, it was frequented by some other notable Alvis owners at about this time, including the Earl of Inchcape (qv 11843), the architect J J Joass (qv 13004 and 13182) and one K G Poland (qv 11205), of whom little is known. Many years later HRH Prince Philip (qv 26600) would become the club's patron.

Chassis numbers
10751-10850
(Firefly SA – third batch)

Chassis	Reg	Chassis	Reg	Chassis	Reg
10751	UG 6271	10784	KV 6329	10818	- - - - - -
10752	ACD 535	10785	ALT 336	10819	ALN 928
10753	- - - - - -	10786	RB 9194	10820	ABB 453
10754	- - - - - -	10787	US 2938	10821	KV 6538
10755	ASM 81	10788	KV 5816	10822	- - - - - -
10756	- - - - - -	10789	- - - - - -	10823	- - - - - -
10757	- - - - - -	10790	AKN 877	10824	- - - - - -
10758	BLG 999	10791	AUL 735	10825	- - - - - -
10759	OY 6472	10792	RB 9416	10826	VH 6158
10760	- - - - - -	10793	-TJ 3187	10827	- - - - - -
10761	ALO 410	10794	MG 3106	10828	US 2939
10762	US 2421	10795	FP 2649	10829	WJ 9287
10763	- - - - - -	10796	ATA 221	10830	OW 5088
10764	KY 5299	10797	-LJ 8598	10831	GV 2050
10765	-JR 80	10798	-IE 2105	10832	-FS 7532
10766	- - - - - -	10799	- - - - - -	10833	-JU 3276
10767	AMA 878	10800	- - - - - -	10834	- - - - - -
10768	- - - - - -	10801	- - - - - -	10835	- - - - - -
10769	AMA 953	10802	KY 5645	10836	- - - - - -
10770	AAE 7	10803	- - - - - -	10837	DG 7741
10771	KY 5183	10804	- - - - - -	10838	- - - - - -
10772	- - - - - -	10805	TV 9454	10839	AYV 989
10773	- - - - - -	10806	AEH 205	10840	ABP 935
10774	-JN 3399	10807	- - - - - -	10841	GL 1719
10775	-FS 7254	10808	ALT ???	10842	- - - - - -
10776	JI 5755	10809	- - - - - -	10843	DT 5814
10777	-AUV 30	10810	PV 808	10844	WJ 8701
10778	YD 7867	10811	TK 9997	10845	- - - - - -
10779	- - - - - -	10812	- - - - - -	10846	JO 8413
10780	ABB 261	10813	- - - - - -	10847	- - - - - -
10781	KV 5818	10814	VH 5746	10848	- - - - - -
10782	CZ 6100	10815	- - - - - -	10849	ALX 381
10783	KV 6087	10816	- - - - - -	10850	YG 5223
		10817	- - - - - -		

10755 ASM 81
Dumfries Police
A tourer-bodied patrol car for this Scottish force.

10789 53
'Jackie' Brown

Jackie Brown (November 29, 1909-March 15, 1971) was a successful flyweight boxer from Manchester. *Autocar*, issue of October 27, 1933, page 827, has a photograph of him taking delivery of 10789 from Henly's. Unfortunately, all but the final '53' of the number plate is obscured. At this very time, Manchester was on the cusp of changing from two-letter to three-letter marks. Research from contemporary sources suggests that the mark allocated to 10789 lies somewhere between XJ 9*53 and ANA *53. Within a few weeks of taking delivery, Brown ran over and fatally injured a female pedestrian. Records also show that by September 1935 he had accumulated over 20 motoring offences. Evidently, he was one who was, as Kenneth More said during the filming of *Genevieve*, "... intoxicated by the exuberance of his own velocity."

10808 ALT
Frank Smythe

Distinguished mountaineer, and a member of the 1933 Everest expedition. Serial Alvis owner (qv Firefly 10256 and Firebird 12298 for bio). There was also an as yet unidentified SA Speed 20 Charlesworth saloon.

10812
Dr Rowley Richards MBE, ACM

Privately exported to Australia c1937 by Newcastle-

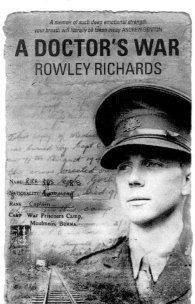

Dr Rowley Richards' remarkable autobiography.

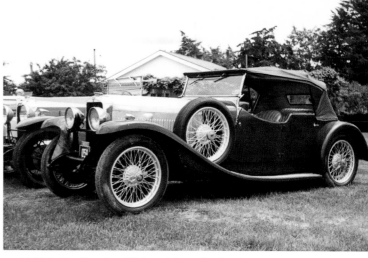

10812: Dr Rowley Richards' car in the hands of subsequent owner Adrian Palmer, pictured at Joadja, New South Wales, c1985.
(Courtesy Chris Edwards)

upon-Tyne resident Gilbert Howarth, 10812 subsequently came into the ownership of a most remarkable hero of WWII. Rowley Richards was born in Sydney, June 8, 1916, and graduated in medicine from the university there in 1939, whereupon he joined the 2nd Australian Imperial Force, becoming RMO of the 2/15th Field Regiment. Active service began in July 1941, bound for Singapore. With the fall of Singapore there came, for multitudes, the start of ordeals and privations which, though having passed into history, will never be forgotten. Richards, who witnessed all this, attended injured servicemen both in Malaya, and, after having been torpedoed, in Japan itself. Following the surrender of Japan, Richards was liberated back to Sydney on October 13, 1945. Very shortly after this, he bought the above Firefly tourer, with deferred pay. His autobiography, *A Doctor's War* (ISBN 0-7322-8009-5, Harper Collins Australia), is a fascinating military history 'must.' He died February 26, 2015, just short of his 99th birthday.

10831 GV 2050
RAC Rally 1934, 1935, 1936

The entrant and driver on each of these occasions was one H W Henshall of Bury St Edmunds. The accompanying photograph, however, relates to a rather more ambitious (holiday?) drive to Budapest, and features some local people.

10831: The Henshall family pictured with friends in Budapest, July 21, 1936. (Courtesy Bruce Dowell)

10847
Arthur Wragg
One of three famous brothers involved in the training and riding of racehorses. All three were Alvis owners (qv 8860 and 11307). Whilst perhaps not as overtly successful as his brothers, Arthur (1912-1954) still made it to sixth place in the jockey's championship of 1944.

SPEED 20 SB

1933 to 1934
375 cars

10851-10950	100
11151-11350	200
11801-11875	75

Consisting of:

Charlesworth saloons numbered variously between 12689-13490	137
Charlesworth coupés numbered variously between 12774-13388	23
Charlesworth (others)	2
Cross & Ellis tourers numbered variously between 30266-30304	41
Cross & Ellis (other)	3
Vanden Plas saloons, coupés, tourers numbered variously, between 3095-3246	130
Remainder: independent makers	

By 1933, the Speed 20 had deservedly carved itself a niche in the market, having been conspicuous in competition and a notable basis for specialised coachwork. Never a company to rest on its laurels, this position had to be preserved, a process that would be achieved by two highly significant improvements, resulting in the SB derivative of October 1933. This took the form of grafting on that innovative transverse leaf independent front suspension, first introduced on the Crested Eagle model some six months earlier. The other improvement was the adoption of the four-speed all-synchro gearbox – well ahead of its time, a joy to use, and robust enough to cope, a few years later, with the conditions of armoured car usage. These features would make the SB the most popular, in production figures, of the four Speed 20 types. An especially significant SB was 11263, where the wheelbase was extended to 11ft, 3in in order to accommodate Lancefield's 'Parallite' body.

Chassis numbers
10851-10950
(Speed 20 SB – first batch)

Chassis	Reg	Chassis	Reg	Chassis	Reg
10851	KV 5155	10884	- - - - - -	10918	FG 8989
10852	APK 354	10885	GJ 73	10919	- - - - - -
10853	ACD 481	10886	- - - - - -	10920	AXC 407
10854	ALR 75	10887	- - - - - -	10921	VD 3013
10855	RH 8274	10888	- - - - - -	10922	WJ 8350
10856	NG 7011	10889	ALU 458	10923	JT 187
10857	- - - - - -	10890	- - - - - -	10924	- - - - - -
10858	- - - - - -	10891	AXE 244	10925	- - - - - -
10859	- - - - - -	10892	PO 8473	10926	- - - - - -
10860	- - - - - -	10893	- - - - - -	10927	ACD 844
10861	RB 9292	10894	- - - - - -	10928	BU 7802
10862	AXK 279	10895	- - - - - -	10929	- - - - - -
10863	ALU 460	10896	- - - - - -	10930	BGW 595
10864	AUC 356	10897	ALR 784	10931	- - - - - -
10865	YD 8020	10898	KV 5300	10932	ANB 589
10866	OC 4424	10899	KV 7061	10933	CV 9453
10867	AUW 40	10900	VV 2409	10934	- - - - - -
10868	AUW 33	10901	- - - - - -	10935	ACD 948
10869	AXA 137	10902	LJ 9174	10936	- - - - - -
10870	AUC 392	10903	- - - - - -	10937	- - - - - -
10871	KV 6331	10904	KV 6534	10938	JO 8929
10872	- - - - - -	10905	YS 2	10939	- - - - - -
10873	- - - - - -	10906	- - - - - -	10940	KV 5820
10874	ST 7470	10907	- - - - - -	10941	AXE 329
10875	WP 608	10908	HF 9419	10942	- - - - - -
10876	YS 1	10909	TJ 3079	10943	VO 9923
10877	BPC 298	10910	- - - - - -	10944	KV 6951
10878	- - - - - -	10911	FS 7531	10945	OD 8054
10879	YY 15	10912	KV 6669	10946	UN 6771
10880	GR 213	10913	- - - - - -	10947	KY 5678
10881	KY 5286	10914	BCD 204	10948	VD 3079
10882	- - - - - -	10915	FG 9271	10949	- - - - - -
10883	JF 5206	10916	KV 6535	10950	NV 3322
		10917	NJ 2448		

10847 RH 8274

Robert Blackburn

Pioneer aviator and constructor. Previously owned an SA Speed 20 model (qv 9863), and later on an SC Type (qv 12097 for bio).

10866 OC 4424

RAC Rally 1938

An entry in the above event, driven by I P Grant.

10868 AUW 33

Competition car

This is one of the first Vanden Plas tourer bodies for the new, independently-sprung SB chassis, and was extensively used by Charles Follett for the purpose of demonstration, publicity, and competition.

10869 AXA 137

Earl of March

The Earl of March (February 5, 1904-November 2, 1989) was educated at Eton and Christ Church Cambridge, and, showing an early aptitude for engineering, it was as 'Freddie Settrington' that he joined Bentley Motors as an apprentice, progressing to the sales department, there encountering Rivers-Fletcher where the two became great friends. After leaving Bentley, he formed his own company and designed bodies for a number of different makes, of which the above Alvis is one, built for his own use by Mulliner of Northampton, and driven by him in the 1934 RAC Rally. There would later be another Alvis association when the company Kevill Davies & March would build a few estate car bodies on the TA 14 chassis. It is under his subsequently inherited title of the 9th Duke of Richmond and Gordon, and as developer of the Goodwood Circuit that he will be mainly remembered. As Rivers-Fletcher wrote in the obituary of his friend, "He was universally popular and will always be remembered for his contribution to the world of motor racing." A later owner of 10869 was the comedian Al ('Right Monkey') Read (1909-1987).

10871 KV 6331

Motor Sport

A works car borrowed by the above magazine for a road test published in the issue of February 1934.

10875: The imposing frontal aspect of the Watkinson family rally car. (Courtesy Ernest Shenton collection)

10875 WP 608

RAC Rally, 1934, 1935, 1936, 1937

Obviously one of the more determined competitors in this annual event, W E C Watkinson of Malvern would transfer his allegiance to an Alvis 12/70 Anderson tourer for the 1938 event, and to a 4.3-litre Vanden Plas tourer for the 1939. 10875's success is amply covered in *Motor*, issues of March 20, 1934, page 314, and March 27, page 49.

10876 BOL 229

Lands End Trial 1938

An entertaining account written by J R Thompson about his entry in the above event appears in the late Donald Cowbourne's definitive book, *British Trials Drivers, Their Cars and Awards*, pages 12 to 14, ISBN 1-85825-107-9. Originally registered by Galts as YS 1.

10877 BPC 298

Sir Cedric Hardwicke

A famous and versatile actor (February 19, 1893-August 6, 1964), he was hugely successful in both stage and screen productions. One of his specialities involved a number of plays written by his friend George Bernard Shaw, who is reported to have said of him that he was his fifth favourite actor, after the Marx Brothers. Hardwicke's other Alvis owning friends included Sir Barry Jackson and Sir Ralph Richardson. There had also been other Alvis cars in the Hardwicke household (qv Silver Eagles 8549 and 9524, and Crested Eagle 10737).

10877 was also featured in the August 1960 issue

of *Veteran and Vintage*, an article that includes much useful technical information for the driver of a Speed 20.

10891 AXE 244
Captain C B Wilson MC
One of Captain Wilson's three Alvis cars (qv SA Speed 20 10040, and SB Speed 20 11218 for bio). The above 10891 was the subject of a major feature in the *Automobile* issue of October 1996, by Brian Heath, pages 53 to 59.

10899 KV 7061
Sears family
The Sears family were serial Alvis owners and 10899 was supplied to Jack Sears as a chassis. Whilst the maker of the coachwork was not formally identified there is a precedent in Sears' use of the local company Grose of Northampton for this purpose.

10897 ALR 784
Captain Peter Black
Captain Peter Black (May 5, 1915-June 13, 1998, was a truly larger-than-life character in the world of Alvis cars. Peter's initial qualifying as a Chartered Engineer was a logical preliminary to commission into the Royal Tank Regiment when war broke out in 1939. His war service included the repairing and maintenance of tanks all over North Africa and the Middle East. Along with his second wife Marianne, married in 1948, who had been a participant in the French Resistance movement, he was a colourful character in automotive circles, particularly in East Anglia. After retirement, the couple moved to Provence, where he established the small but energetic Alvis Club de France. Thereafter, visitors to Peter's establishment, aptly named 'Chateau Vilbrequin' would receive a generous libation, which had frequently emanated from the winery of his friend Comte Audoin de Dampierre (one-time owner of a 3.5-litre Alvis see 13129). Several times a year the 'faithful' would be treated to an edition of *World Alvis News* which consisted of a batch of unnumbered undated Alvis-related press cuttings and information culled from sources all over the planet. That Peter was murdered in 1998 in the course of a bungled burglary, when he had still so much knowledge (and dry humour) to impart to supporters, remains a major tragedy.

10911 FS 7531
Motor Sport
This magazine's issue of June 1953 carries a photograph of the above.

10912 KV 6669
Monte Carlo Rally 1934
An entry in the above event, driven by K W B Sanderson. Featured in the issue of magazine *Motor* of February 6, 1934. Sanderson also used this car to compete in the RAC Rallies of 1934 and 1935.

10915 FG 9271
Olympia Motor Show 1933
10915 was initially exhibited as a polished chassis at the above exhibition. After the show it was despatched to Charlesworth's, where it was bodied as a drophead coupé. Upon completion, it was sold to one Andrew Blyth, who successfully competed with it in the 1934 RSAC Rally.

10918 FG 8989
Arthur Moore
Whilst the first owner of 10918 had been Sir Michael Nairn, 2nd Baronet, of the Fifeshire family noted for their linoleum products, it is the subsequent owner's biography which perhaps provides the wider interest. Arthur Moore (1887-January 20, 1949) became interested in wireless transmission early and was a key figure in its development. It was he, when working in the loft of Gelligroes Mill near Blackwood, at the age of 26, detected, in the early hour of April 15, 1912, a faint distress signal from the RMS Titanic. When passing on this news to the authorities, initially he was not believed, but the enormity of the disaster was soon to emerge. Moore's pioneering work in radio transmission would lead to employment with the Marconi Company, where he would develop, and patent, in 1932, an early form of sonar – the Echometer. He retired in 1947, but by then 10918 had been loaned back to Alvis Ltd, where it was used, following careful dismantling, to prepare new blueprint drawings lost in the Blitz, of major components, which would greatly facilitate their availability right through to the present day.

10921 `BU 7802`

RAC Rally 1934

An entry in the above event by Oldham businessman G E Stott. For some as yet unknown reason, the car was later re-registered as XG 9405. Stott also used this car in the RSAC Rally of the same year.

10945 `OD 8054`

Lord Carrington

One of three Alvis cars owned by this famous politician (qv 13637 for bio and 14396).

For the next Speed 20 sequence see batch 11151 to 11350

Chassis numbers
10951-11050
(Crested Eagle TD, TE – second batch)

Chassis	Reg	Chassis	Reg	Chassis	Reg
10951	-JV 3137	10984	- - - - - -	11018	KV 8002
10952	- - - - - -	10985	-JB 3216	11019	- - - - - -
10953	WJ 8131	10986	- - - - - -	11020	CG 7489
10954	VH 5797	10987	- - - - - -	11021	KS 6184
10955	DG 7639	10988	- - - - - -	11022	AYN 12
10956	-LJ 8818	10989	DG 8353	11023	-TJ 4683
10957	- - - - - -	10990	FG 9633	11024	OD 9029
10958	- - - - - -	10991	- - - - - -	11025	- - - - - -
10959	- - - - - -	10992	- - - - - -	11026	- - - - - -
10960	KV 6568	10993	LV 9113	11027	- - - - - -
10961	AMB 354	10994	YG 5669	11028	RC 1931
10962	VD 2975	10995	-TJ 4835	11029	- - - - - -
10963	HS 7294	10996	CRF 585	11030	AUS
10964	- - - - - -	10997	YG 5757	11031	- - - - - -
10965	KV 6332	10998	- - - - - -	11032	KV 9001
10966	- - - - - -	10999	- - - - - -	11033	- - - - - -
10967	KY 6199	11000	US 4682	11034	- - - - -
10968	- - - - - -	11001	-JY 7515	11035	US 7599
10969	- - - - - -	11002	- - - - - -	11036	- - - - - -
10970	CN 5854	11003	- - - - - -	11037	-JR 1595
10971	YD 8503	11004	US 5158	11038	JX 1599
10972	- - - - - -	11005	- - - - - -	11039	- - - - - -
10973	-TJ 3347	11006	- - - - - -	11040	- - - - - -
10974	YG 5506	11007	- - - - - -	11041	- - - - - -
10975	- - - - - -	11008	- - - - - -	11042	- - - - - -
10976	- - - - - -	11009	- - - - - -	11043	- - - - - -
10977	US 3433	11010	- - - - - -	11044	VV 2981
10978	- - - - - -	11011	ANN 777	11045	- - - - - -
10979	- - - - - -	11012	- - - - - -	11046	WP 6117
10980	OD 7441	11013	KY 6358	11047	OD 9476
10981	- - - - - -	11014	- - - - - -	11048	- - - - - -
10982	-JK 3400	11015	KV 7893	11049	- - - - - -
10983	-AYN 16	11016	US 4832	11050	RV 5089
		11017	OW 4519		

11010

Philip Fotheringham-Parker

Fotheringham-Parker's career as a competition driver will be found outlined with his Silver Eagle

(the 'Green Car') under chassis 8101. The rather more staid Crested Eagle above was purchased from Charles Follett (no mean competition driver himself) on February 14, 1934.

11046 `WP 6117`

Sir Barry Jackson

Barry Jackson (September 6, 1879-April 3, 1961) was a towering and dynamic force in many aspects of English Theatre. He is most famous for founding an institution which has been described as the University of the Stage, namely the Birmingham Repertory Theatre, in 1913. His influence extended to the London theatre scene also, managing the court and Kingsway theatres, and receiving his knighthood in 1925. He also, along with playwright, George Bernard Shaw, founded the Malvern Festival, and it was to his address in that town that this Crested Eagle was delivered in May 1934. Many actors trekked to Malvern in order to benefit from Jackson's influence and some, like Cedric Hardwicke, Ralph Richardson, and Laurence Olivier became personal friends. The Alvis influence was strong here, as Hardwicke owned several of these cars, and Richards, a front-wheel drive model. 11046 was disposed of in October 1938 and was taken over, perhaps as an official car, by Alcester Rural District Council.

FIREFLY SB

1933 to 1934
275 cars

11051-11150	100
11452-11615	165
11876-11885	10

Consisting of:

Cross & Ellis saloons numbered variously between 472-660 and 7000-7013	145
Cross & Ellis coupés numbered variously between 1174-1225	43
Cross & Ellis tourers numbered variously between 53531-53569	23
Cross & Ellis two-seaters (60, 93)	2
Holbrook saloons numbered variously between 2791-2282	38

Remainder chassis only, or unconfirmed
The availability of the ENV type 110 preselector gearbox, succeeding the type 75 that had been used as an alternative to Alvis's own 'crash' box, necessitated a repositioning of the brake cross-shaft on the chassis, giving rise to the 'SB' designation. Otherwise, the formula was much as before, with body styles continued. The only minor diversions during the course of this model's run occurred at the end of its production, with a handful of the final chassis being fitted with the enlarged engine of 1842cc, which was a mainstay of the imminent Firebird model that was to be the replacement.

Chassis numbers
11051-11150
(Firefly SB – first batch)

Chassis	Reg				
11051	AUW 36	11084	- - - - - -	11118	OD 8298
11052	KV 6537	11085	AXA 580	11119	- - - - - -
11053	- - - - - -	11086	VH 5903	11120	-JA 4183
11054	- - - - - -	11087	- - - - - -	11121	AHT 518
11055	- - - - - -	11088	- - - - - -	11122	- - - - - -
11056	-FS 8359	11089	KY 5777	11123	WG 2268
11057	- - - - - -	11090	- - - - - -	11124	- - - - - -
11058	WJ 8377	11091	TV 9828	11125	- - - - - -
11059	BRF 759	11092	AFY 850	11126	KV 7177
11060	- - - - - -	11093	BPB 997	11127	- - - - - -
11061	GR 1264	11094	- - - - - -	11128	- - - - - -
11062	CG 6000	11095	- - - - - -	11129	- - - - - -
11063	- - - - - -	11096	- - - - - -	11130	ANC 581
11064	ALL 997	11097	- - - - - -	11131	-JK 4112
11065	KY 5837	11098	PV 1296	11132	AHT 624
11066	- - - - - -	11099	- - - - - -	11133	- - - - - -
11067	- - - - - -	11100	OC 5677	11134	- - - - - -
11068	- - - - - -	11101	AYF 511	11135	JH 6847
11069	FT 3320	11102	KY 5985	11136	- - - - - -
11070	GV 2206	11103	FW 4374	11137	YD 8809
11071	- - - - - -	11104	- - - - - -	11138	-TJ 3557
11072	MG 2936	11105	- - - - - -	11139	US 4297
11073	- - - - - -	11106	US 3434	11140	- - - - - -
11074	AMB 622	11107	- - - - - -	11141	FV 4343
11075	- - - - - -	11108	ATV 860	11142	OC 7430
11076	AUW 573	11109	KV 7390	11143	- - - - - -
11077	- - - - - -	11110	-LJ 8960	11144	-TJ 4847
11078	-LJ 8787	11111	XS 3266	11145	- - - - - -
11079	-LJ 8865	11112	-TJ 3547	11146	KV 7436
11080	JO 8572	11113	AVK 214	11147	US 4299
11081	YD 8519	11114	- - - - - -	11148	-BPD 88
11082	-LJ 9429	11115	US 5919	11149	- - - - - -
11083	AWL 33	11116	KV 7063	11150	- - - - - -
		11117	DG 8355		

11069
Newcastle-Upon-Tyne Police
A patrol car (saloon), replacing a tourer supplied to the same force in June 1933, but written off in particularly tragic circumstances (qv 10540).

11072
Earl Cadogan MC DL
The 6th Earl of that name (February 13, 1914-July 4, 1997) was educated at Eton, and served in WWII (Middle East) as Captain in the Coldstream Guards, before becoming Mayor of Chelsea in 1964.

11101
Movie promotion
On a joint visit to Britain, two of Hollywood's most famous actors – George Raft (1895-1980) and James Cagney (1899-1986) – were taken on a tour of London in the above Firefly coupé. The driver was one Archie Summers.

Chassis numbers
11151-11350
(Speed 20 SB – second batch)

Chassis	Reg				
11151	AXB 850	11191	-AAU 80	11232	ANN 695
11152	KV 6334	11192	AMB 929	11233	- - - - - -
11153	-AYX 94	11193	KV 7175	11234	VG 6282
11154	AXH 434	11194	- - - - - -	11235	US 4833
11155	OC 7616	11195	- - - - - -	11236	-JJ 339
11156	KV 7174	11196	-FS 8069	11237	VH 6049
11157	- - - - - -	11197	- - - - - -	11238	LV 7000
11158	AND 333	11198	- - - - - -	11239	KV 7781
11159	- - - - - -	11199	-TJ 3420	11240	DG 8403
11160	- - - - - -	11200	AXV 329	11241	WJ 9104
11161	AXF 616	11201	AUW 38	11242	KV 7434
11162	OC 6633	11202	- - - - - -	11243	- - - - - -
11163	- - - - ZA	11203	-JR 1235	11244	KP 71
11164	VN 5502	11204	AXF 666	11245	WJ 9808
11165	AKR 249	11205	- - - - - -	11246	-AYN 17
11166	- - - - - -	11206	- - - - - -	11247	AUS
11167	OC 6428	11207	- - - - - -	11248	KV 7064
11168	KV 5892	11208	- - - - - -	11249	AUS
11169	- - - - - -	11209	-AXW 898	11250	- - - - - -
11170	AKP 579	11210	HS 7447	11251	US 4924
11171	AXV 325	11211	AYV 420	11252	VD 3232
11172	AXV 324	11212	- - - - - -	11253	YG 6780
11173	AEH 551	11213	- - - - - -	11254	- - - - - -
11174	-AYF 91	11214	WJ 8740	11255	WP 5642
11175	JH 6736	11215	- - - - - -	11256	-JU 3834
11176	AXV 323	11216	AXL 707	11257	ANE 477
11177	- - - - - -	11217	AHT 641	11258	- - - - - -
11178	AKR 21	11218	YY 96	11259	JT 668
11179	OC 5679	11219	AXK 1	11260	LV 9363
11180	- - - - - -	11220	- - - - - -	11261	- - - - - -
11181	JX 1334	11221	AYF 92	11262	AXV 321
11182	FV 5269	11222	ANN 569	11263	AYH 577
11183	CG 6512	11223	ET 8052	11264	BGN 942
11184	WG 2264	11224	- - - - - -	11265	RV 4715
11185	AYN 278	11225	-FF 4027	11266	-AXW 807
11186	- - - - - -	11226	KV 7176	11267	- - - - - -
11187	OC 5676	11227	- - - - - -	11268	ATU 781
11188	- - - - - -	11228	-JR 1419	11269	LV 7703
11189	- - - - - -	11229	- - - - - -	11270	- - - - - -
11190	AXE 635	11230	UD 5871	11271	ATU 991
		11231	AXU 635	11272	AUS

11273 - - BGO 904	11299 - - -NJ 3504	11325 - - - - - -
11274 - - - - - -	11300 - - WV 6071	11326 - - - - AUS
11275 - - - - AUS	11301 - - -FS 9596	11327 - - - - - -
11276 - - - AYF 93	11302 - - - - - -	11328 - - - AUS
11277 - -AXX 335	11303 - - KV 8302	11329 - - WF 6626
11278 - - - - - -	11304 - - AAO 324	11330 - - - - - -
11279 - - - - - -	11305 - - AOA 315	11331 - - RV 5063
11280 - - - - - -	11306 - - US 5620	11332 - - - - - -
11281 - - KV 8827	11307 - - - - - -	11333 - - KY 7036
11282 - - AYN 892	11308 - - - - - -	11334 - - VH 6690
11283 - - AXU 864	11309 - - - - - -	11335 - - - - - -
11284 - - - - - -	11310 - - AYR 674	11336 - - - - - -
11285 - - - - - -	11311 - - - - - -	11337 - - NG 7165
11286 - - BMF 323	11312 - - - CS 380	11338 - - KV 9005
11287 - - -AYN 14	11313 - - KV 9003	11339 - - - - - -
11288 - - -AYN 15	11314 - - - - AUS	11340 - - - - - -
11289 - - - - - -	11315 - - - - - -	11341 - - - - - -
11290 - - - - - -	11316 - - - CS 231	11342 - - - IND
11291 - - AFY 325	11317 - - KV 8303	11343 - - - - - -
11292 - - - - - -	11318 - - - - - -	11344 - - - - - -
11293 - - MJ 4070	11319 - - AYM 820	11345 - - - - - -
11294 - - AXT 87	11320 - - MG 3388	11346 - - BLB 794
11295 - - BGH 572	11321 - - - - - -	11347 - - BGT 581
11296 - - - - - -	11322 - - - - - -	11348 - - - AUS
11297 - - -AOE 44	11323 - - - YS 200	11349 - - VY 5442
11298 - - ANE 269	11324 - - - - - -	11350 - - HS 7710

11176 – Published in *Autocar*, November 22, 1946, immediately after the air speed record success, this photo shows Group Captain Donaldson collecting AXV 322 from a Nottingham garage, following an overhaul.

11165 — AKR 249
Lord G St V Harris CBE, MC, DL

Lord Harris, (September 3, 1889-October 16, 1984) was educated at Eton, and Christ Church College Oxford, and served in WWI with the Royal East Kent Yeomanry. He was appointed Justice of the Peace from 1919, succeeding to the Barony in 1932, and became Deputy Lieutenant for Kent in 1936. Awarded Master of Arts degree by Christ Church College in 1968.

11167 — OC 6428
Commander A H Maxwell-Hyslop GC RN

A summary of Commander Hyslop's distinguished naval career will be found under the entry for his previous Alvis (qv 12/50 model 5534). In *Motor Sport* of November 1954, page 646, he eulogised on the superb service that he had received from Alvis Ltd with this car, despite it then being 20 years old, and he serving in the outpost of BAOR.

11176 — AXV 323
Temple Press Ltd

Purchased as a staff car, and mainly used by *Motor* magazine's esteemed technical editor, Maurice Platt, 11176 figures quite prominently in a number of his erudite articles. These included features on *Touring in France* (July 9, 1935), *Steering* (December 31,

1935), *Wheelspin* (February 18, 1936). One of the most interesting of these exercises was when 11176 was specially equipped with a Zoller Supercharger by Michael McEvoy at Derby, for *Motor*'s tests (November 5, 1935 and May 12, 1936 refers). The association of 11176 with speed would continue after WWII, when it passed into the hands of Wing Commander A W Donaldson, who, at the time the accompanying photograph was taken, had just become the fastest man on the planet, having, in 1946, taken the World Air Speed Record at 610mph in a Gloster Meteor.

11179 — OC 5679
Iliffe Publications Ltd

Featured in magazine *Autocar*'s popular *Used Cars on The Road* series, no 73, in the June 11, 1934 issue.

11189
Lord Conyers MC

Sackville Pelham (December 17, 1888-December 7, 1948) was also the 5th Earl of Yarborough. He served in both WWI and WWII, initially with the 11th Hussars and subsequently with the Nottinghamshire Yeomanry, retiring as Lieutenant-Colonel. His choice of Alvis was one of very few (believed five) of the marque to be bodied by the company Freestone and Webb.

11190 — AXE 635
Dorothy Patten

An accomplished competition driver, Miss Patten

campaigned 11190 in the 1934 Alpine Trial (qv report in *Motor*, August 14, 1934, page 68) and also in the Monte Carlo Rally of 1935.

She was also known as Baroness Dorndorf, but does not appear to have ever used that title competitively.

11201 AUW 38
Hon Brian Lewis

Brian Lewis (December 7, 1903-July 18, 1978) was educated at Malvern, and Pembroke College Cambridge. He was a well-known motor racing figure of the 1930s with notable appearances at such events as Le Mans and Donington. A somewhat milder form of motoring was his entry in the 1934 RAC Rally, with the above Speed 20 saloon scoring a first in class in the Coachwork Competition. Report and photograph in *Motor* magazine of March 20, 1934, page 313, followed by a full page advertisement just one week later by Charles Follett, who supplied the car. Brian Lewis succeeded to the title of Lord Essendon in 1944.

11214 WJ 8740
Stage production

Featured in a production of *Ghost Train* at the Buxton Opera House starring those well-known actresses Nyree Dawn Porter and Kate O'Mara.

11216 AXL 707
Colonel P H Hordern DSO, OBE

Peter Hordern (July 13, 1916-October 17, 2006)

was educated at Marlborough, Sandhurst, and joined the Royal Tank Corps in 1936, and upon his retirement in 1967 became curator of the Tank Museum, Bovington. Outside his distinguished military career, he was councillor of the NSPCC, life governor of the RNLI, life member of the National Trust, freeman of the City of London, and liveryman of the Armourers and Brasiers Company. Peter was probably the first person to start cataloguing and researching all the Alvis cars known to have survived the WWII years, and his pioneering work in this regard is preserved with the Alvis Archive Trust.

11218 NG 8267
Captain C B Wilson MC

Born December 28, 1885, he was an early participant in the circumstances surrounding the development of aviation in Britain, obtaining one of the first Aviation Certificates. He became a director of the London Aeroplane Club and committee member of the Royal Aero Club. Was also involved with the Royal Thames Yacht Club. Appointed High Sheriff of Norfolk in 1942. Previously owned another SB Speed 20 Alvis (qv 10891) and before that, an SA model (qv 10040).

After leaving Captain Wilson's ownership, 11218 was shipped out to Singapore by L Bainbridge-Hawker – an RAF officer. It caught fire at Changi Airport a year later, and its Vanden Plas saloon body was written off. Rebuilt as a 'special' and subsequently acquired by the remarkable Henry Stonor (1926-2005) – rubber planter, jazz musician, car collector, clock repairer, baker (and friend of the famous test pilot, Brian Trubshaw).

11214: Actress Kate O'Mara (1939-2014) is seen here at the wheel of the Speed 20, along with the cast of *Ghost Train*. (Courtesy Chris Taylor)

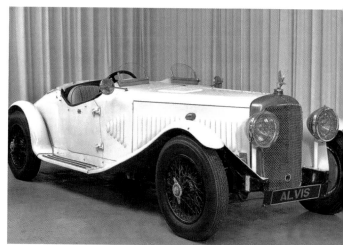

11218: The 'Stonor' special. (Courtesy Alan Stote)

11231 | AXU 635

Sir Cecil Beaton CBE

Beaton (January 14, 1904-January 18, 1980) was educated at Harrow, and St John's College Cambridge. He was a society photographer, artist, stage designer of considerable reputation, contributing to many periodicals. The Royal family, prominent politicians and movie stars were numbered amongst his clients. Whilst photography is what he is perhaps best known for, costume design also figured prominently, typically his work for the productions, *My Fair Lady* of 1956, *Gigi* of 1958, and *On a Clear Day You Can See Forever* of 1970.

11238 | LV 7000

RAC Rally 1934

An entry in the above event, and driven by R H Gregory.

11247 | AYN 17

Lionel Bellairs

Serial Alvis owner (qv 12066, 13089, 13691 and 14858 for bio).

11255 | WP 5642

Morgan Motor Company

Established in 1910 as producers of a charismatic three-wheeled car, the Morgan family would naturally have a need for four-wheeled vehicles as well. Falling into this category would be an Alvis 12/50 model (qv 6695), a couple of Rolls-Royces, and this Alvis Speed 20 saloon of 1934. Just over a year later, Morgan would commence production of a four-wheeled sports model, the 4/4, which has continued in a variety of forms to the present day.

11263 | AYH 577

Lancefield coachworks

This was a remarkable works-sanctioned, one-off development of the SB Series Speed 20, extending the wheelbase to 11 feet (perhaps using the side rails of the Crested Eagle model). An early example of 'streamlining,' it would incorporate the novel 'Parralite' construction, which Lancefield Coachworks completed for a customer in Rotherham.

The design of this vehicle precipitated much coverage in the motoring press, particularly in *The Automobile Engineer* of July 1934, and in the *Motor* of May 22, 1934, page 690, where the correspondence correctly predicted, "Seeing it simply convinces that this type of body will come quite soon."

11266 | AXW 807

Lord Amherst

Jeffery Amherst, 5th Earl of that name (December 15, 1896-January 4, 1993), was educated at Eton and Sandhurst, served WWI with the Coldstream Guards and WWII in the Middle East, retiring with rank of Hon Wing Commander (1942). A much-travelled individual, the result of which is his autobiography, *Wandering Abroad,* published in 1976 by Secker and Warburg, ISBN 13 978-0436017209.

11271 | ATU 991

Motor Sport

Photograph in *Motor Sport* issue of April 1951, *Character Cars.*

11282 | AYN 892

Iliffe Publications Ltd

Featured in *Autocar*'s popular series, *Talking of Sports Cars,* no 137, issue of January 29, 1943.

11288 | AYN 15

Duke of Westminster

The 5th Duke of that name, Robert Grosvenor (April 24, 1910-February 19, 1979) was educated at Sunningdale, Harrow and Sandhurst. Served WWII, becoming a Major-General with the North Irish Horse and duly accorded DSO, TD, JP, DL. Served as Member of Parliament for Fermanagh and South Tyrone between 1955 and 1964 and as Lord Lieutenant of Fermanagh between 1977 and 1979. The Grosvenors have always been one of Britain's richest (and philanthropic) families, their portfolio including most of London's Mayfair district. Small wonder, therefore, that the London Alvis agent, Charles Follett, based in Mayfair, was asked to supply11288. Previously owned an SA Speed 20 model (qv 10112).

11295 `BGH 572`
John Profumo CBE, MP
Profumo (January 30, 1915-March 9, 2006) was the 5th Baron of that name, and was educated at Harrow and Oxford. He served in WWII with the Northamptonshire Yeomanry, retiring with the rank of Brigadier. He was twice a Member of Parliament, firstly representing Kettering between 1940 and 1945, and Stratford-upon-Avon 1950 to 1963, rising rapidly to become Secretary of State in Harold Macmillan's administration. It was at about this time that he formed a brief liaison with Christine Keeler, who was also having an affair with Russian diplomat Yevgeny Ivanov. These events precipitated much controversy at the time, destabilising the Government, from which Profumo resigned. For the remainder of his life he devoted himself to charitable work, as the chief fundraiser for Toynbee Hall – an East London charity. The 'Profumo Affair' has spawned a number of documentaries, a film, a stage production, and a biography. For further reading, *Honeytrap* by A Summers and S Dorril 1987. Also, Christine Keeler's autobiography *The Truth at Last,* 2001.

11298 `ANE 269`
A F Rivers-Fletcher
One of three Alvis cars given the 'special' treatment by Rivers (qv 11859 and 14459 for bio and the others).

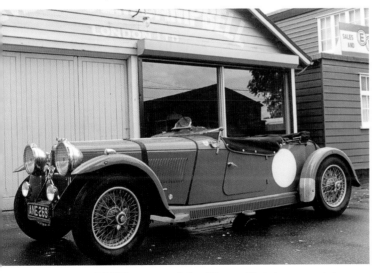

11298 – one of the Rivers-Fletcher specials, seen here, most appropriately, at Brooklands. (Courtesy Ernest Shenton collection)

11301 `FS 9596`
RAC Rally 1935
An entry in the above event by T W McCallum, who would later be associated with a 4.3-litre model (qv 14810), which he used in RAC and RSAC events.

11307 `ABJ 597`
Samuel Wragg
One of three famous brothers involved in the training and riding of racehorses. All three were Alvis owners (qv 8860 and 10847). Samuel's career high points were wins in the Oaks and the Derby.

11323 `YS 200`
Motor Sport
Featured in *Motor Sport* issue of April 1956 in a Chiltern Cars advert.

11333 `KY 7036`
Norman D Routledge
A legendary name in vintage motoring circles, Norman was an acknowledged authority on the Bullnose Morris, Brooklands Rileys, and matters Alvis. He was also an inveterate special builder of which the above is but one. Unusually retaining its four-door body, it was endowed with numerous handling improvements, and a 4.3-litre engine to boot. Re-registered with the mark LYG 922, it performed well in sprint events (qv Firefly 10787 for more on Routledge).

11346 `BLB 794`
Sir Reginald Verdon-Smith
Sir Reginald Verdon-Smith (November 5, 1912-June 2, 1992) was educated at Repton, and at Brasenose College, Oxford, graduating in Law. However, whilst a career in that profession would normally have beckoned, he was tempted to join the 'family' firm, that being the Bristol Aeroplane Company. There followed other senior directorships with Rolls-Royce and Lloyds Bank, but probably his most significant achievement was when, as chairman of the British Aircraft Corporation, he was a prime mover at the time of Concorde and Tornado developments.

For another Alvis/Bristol connection, see 13158, the 4.3-litre model purchased by Sir George Stanley White.

SILVER EAGLE SF

1933 to 1934
200 cars

11351-11450	100
11701-11800	100

Consisting of:
Holbrook saloons numbered variously
  between 2772-2869 — 10
Cross & Ellis tourers numbered
  variously between
  471-713 — 100
  and 4001-1065 — 65
Cross & Ellis tourers numbered
  variously between 53559-53567 — 5

Originally conceived as a 'Firefly Sixteen,' with a development car chassis 10301 built, and a preliminary announcement made in the press, when production began the name had been changed to 'Silver Eagle.' The basic engineering design and format is identical with the Firefly, the various body styles offered being interchangeable with, and numerically sequenced alongside that model. The only significant difference is the front chassis crossmember, which is located slightly further forward on the SF, to accommodate the two extra cylinders. The radiator location and the fractionally longer bonnet are the main recognition points.

Chassis numbers
11351-11450
(Silver Eagle SF – first batch)

Chassis	Reg	Chassis	Reg	Chassis	Reg
11351	KV 6333	11366	AFY 16	11382	-
11352	US 5219	11367	LJ 9358	11383	-
11353	-	11368	KV 7437	11384	BLW 736
11354	FS 7635	11369	JR 1131	11385	BMD 690
11355	KV 7435	11370	KY 6397	11386	BPH 847
11356	-	11371	OC 9999	11387	TJ 5368
11357	KY 6398	11372	-	11388	KV 8003
11358	JR 1404	11373	ANU 182	11389	-
11359	KV 7579	11374	CRF 275	11390	-
11360	VY 5684	11375	-	11391	RG 4426
11361	VY 5049	11376	OC 9999	11392	JB 4767
11362	AXE 247	11377	-	11393	-
11363	NJ 4348	11378	AYY 620	11394	-
11364	AYN 208	11379	-	11395	US 6671
11365	-	11380	US 5114	11396	-
		11381	-	11397	OD 9375

Chassis	Reg	Chassis	Reg	Chassis	Reg
11398	-	11416	-	11434	KY 6999
11399	-	11417	-	11435	-
11400	-	11418	JU 3802	11436	-
11401	-	11419	US 6101	11437	YS 191
11402	-	11420	-	11438	-
11403	-	11421	ANU 880	11439	-
11404	US 5619	11422	-	11440	KY 7069
11405	-	11423	-	11441	-
11406	-	11424	NJ 3456	11442	DG 9197
11407	-	11425	EW 8326	11443	-
11408	-	11426	-	11444	US 6440
11409	-	11427	AVK 577	11445	-
11410	FG 9474	11428	AVK 580	11446	-
11411	AYN 312	11429	US 6102	11447	-
11412	-	11430	JP 2	11448	-
11413	-	11431	-	11449	-
11414	KY 7038	11432	-	11450	-
11415	AOB 156	11433	-		

11371 — **OC 9999**
Frank Hallam
Birmingham Alvis agent and well-known competition driver Frank Hallam drove this car in the 1934 RAC Rally.

11376 — **BLB 795**
Temple Press Ltd
An early promotional example of the new Silver Eagle model, 11376 was used by the publishers of weekly magazine *Motor* for a full road test in the issue of February 26, 1935, pages 137 to 138.

Chassis numbers
11451-11615
(Firefly SB – second batch)

Chassis	Reg	Chassis	Reg	Chassis	Reg
11451	JV 2563	11474	WS 897	11498	FS 9000
11452	-	11475	WJ 9164	11499	KV 7573
11453	FG 9194	11476	US 5031	11500	-
11454	YG 6247	11477	KV 8301	11501	DG 8684
11455	UN 7207	11478	KV 8190	11502	-
11456	-	11479	FM 8508	11503	APP 193
11457	-	11480	VV 3815	11504	-
11458	-	11481	-	11505	BLG 390
11459	ANC 617	11482	KV 8159	11506	ANU 655
11460	MG 3044	11483	AAD 317	11507	-
11461	-	11484	AEL 27	11508	-
11462	MJ 3533	11485	ATU 537	11509	KV 7571
11463	DG 8929	11486	VN 6054	11510	-
11464	-	11487	-	11511	NV 3786
11465	-	11488	-	11512	MJ 4198
11466	TJ 4662	11489	BPC 998	11513	-
11467	-	11490	KV 8826	11514	-
11468	FS 9129	11491	-	11515	ET 8126
11469	US 4683	11492	JR 1706	11516	AYR 943
11470	-	11493	KV 7572	11517	-
11471	-	11494	PI 6714	11518	-
11472	GV 2429	11495	TJ 6555	11519	-
11473	FS 8653	11496	BU 8000	11520	ADH 726
		11497	BGX 82	11521	AYV 912

11522 - - - - - -	11554 - - AYX 487	11586 - - - - - -
11523 - - KV 8825	11555 - - AWA 479	11587 - - UN 8386
11524 - - - - - -	11556 - - AWA 480	11588 - - - - - -
11525 - - - AEL 28	11557 - - AYR 679	11589 - - - - - -
11526 - - -JK 3704	11558 - - - - - -	11590 - - AVO 131
11527 - - KS 6187	11559 - - ARA 212	11591 - - - - - -
11528 - - - - - -	11560 - - UG 9933	11592 - - BLY 279
11529 - - BPF 917	11561 - - -WS 582	11593 - - - - - -
11530 - - -AYN 50	11562 - - AYV 918	11594 - - ADU 373
11531 - -AXX 601	11563 - - - - - -	11595 - - ARB 380
11532 - - KV 9002	11564 - - - - - -	11596 - - - - - -
11533 - - AYL 499	11565 - - ARA 356	11597 - - AOG 26
11534 - - LV 8400	11566 - - UP 9202	11598 - - ARA 679
11535 - - AYV 913	11567 - - - - - -	11599 - - - - - -
11536 - - - - - -	11568 - - - - - -	11600 - - - - - -
11537 - - - - - -	11569 - - -JS 4653	11601 - - - - - -
11538 - - - - - -	11570 - - - - - -	11602 - - - - - -
11539 - - - - - -	11571 - - - - - -	11603 - - - - - -
11540 - - - - - -	11572 - - -WS 699	11604 - - - - - -
11541 - - AYV 916	11573 - - EK 9991	11605 - - - - - -
11542 - - - - - -	11574 - - BLG 392	11606 - - SH 4553
11543 - - KV 9007	11575 - - - - - -	11607 - - ADU 428
11544 - - - - - -	11576 - - -AYA 62	11608 - - BLB 796
11545 - - BLG 274	11577 - - - - - -	11609 - - ALE 669
11546 - - UN 7529	11578 - - AFY 781	11610 - - - - - -
11547 - - - - - -	11579 - - - - - -	11611 - - BLP 154
11548 - - FM 6877	11580 - - - - - -	11612 - - - - - -
11549 - - US 6877	11581 - - -TJ 7476	11613 - - - - - -
11550 - - - - - -	11582 - - AYY 754	11614 - - ADU 97
11551 - - UN 7589	11583 - - - - - -	11615 - - AUG 569
11552 - - KV 9275	11584 - - AUF 951	
11553 - - KV 9116	11585 - - -TJ 7064	

11572: Seen in a competition situation when quite new. (Courtesy Alvis Archive Trust)

11572: The much-rallied W A Scott-Brown Firefly tourer. (Courtesy the late Donald Cowbourne, himself the author of a number of historic car competition books)

11555 AWA 479 / 80

11556 AWA 480 / 79

Sheffield Police

A pair of four-cylinder patrol cars for a regular Alvis customer. The record does not show precisely which registration number applied to which chassis (qv 11707 and 11710 for the Silver Eagle patrol cars supplied at the same time).

11558
Col RH Ballantine-Dykes

Born 1881, died 13th January 1949, served in WWI and was awarded the DSO in 1917, and later an OBE. In 1926 he was appointed DC to King George V, and served as Lord Lieutenant of Cumberland from 1944 until his death.

Chassis numbers
11616-11700
(Crested Eagle, TD, TE – third batch)

Chassis Reg		
11616 - - PV 1220	11619 - - EX 3439	11623 - - - - - -
11617 - - VD 3743	11620 - - - - - -	11624 - -AHW 311
11618 - - - - - -	11621 - - - - - -	11625 - - ADU 690
	11622 - - - - - -	11626 - - - - - -

11627 - - ATO 111	11663 - - UN 7972	11699 - - - - - -
11628 - - ALJ 324	11664 - - BEH 582	11700 - - -JB 6311
11629 - - KG 4789	11665 - - CG 8956	11616 - - PV 1220
11630 - - - - - -	11666 - - - - - -	11617 - - VD 3743
11631 - - - - - -	11667 - - ARB 508	11618 - - - - - -
11632 - - BLB 149	11668 - - GR 1568	11619 - - EX 3439
11633 - - - - - -	11669 - - - - - -	11620 - - - - - -
11634 - - - - - -	11670 - - - - - -	11621 - - - - - -
11635 - - -JR 1597	11671 - - - - - -	11622 - - - - - -
11636 - - - - - -	11672 - - - - - -	11623 - - - - - -
11637 - - KV 9274	11673 - - ARW 296	11624 - - -AHW 311
11638 - - - - - -	11674 - - KY 9016	11625 - - ADU 690
11639 - -AWK 577	11675 - - BTW 318	11626 - - - - - -
11640 - - - - - -	11676 - -BTW 318	11627 - - ATO 111
11641 - - - - - -	11677 - - - - - -	11628 - - ALJ 324
11642 - - FM 8786	11678 - - - - - -	11629 - - KG 4789
11643 - - - - - -	11679 - - BBH 865	11630 - - - - - -
11644 - - ET 8288	11680 - - - - - -	11631 - - - - - -
11645 - - - - - -	11681 - - - - - -	11632 - - - - - -
11646 - - WP 6621	11682 - - - - - -	11633 - - - - - -
11647 - - - - - -	11683 - - - - - -	11634 - - - - - -
11648 - - - - - -	11684 - - US 9828	11635 - - -JR 1597
11649 - - - - - -	11685 - - - - - -	11636 - - - - - -
11650 - - - - - -	11686 - - - - - -	11637 - - KV 9274
11651 - - US 7343	11687 - - - - - -	11638 - - - - - -
11652 - - - - NZ	11688 - - - - - -	11639 - -AWK 577
11653 - - AYA 522	11689 - - - - - -	11640 - - - - - -
11654 - - LV 9597	11690 - - - - - -	11641 - - - - - -
11655 - - YS 1130	11691 - - - YS 578	11642 - - FM 8786
11656 - - -TJ 7393	11692 - - ATT 881	11643 - - - - - -
11657 - - - - - -	11693 - - BNU 551	11644 - - ET 8288
11658 - - - - - -	11694 - - - - - -	11645 - - - - - -
11659 - - ARE 573	11695 - - - - - -	11646 - - WP 6621
11660 - - -AHP 6	11696 - - - - - -	11647 - - - - - -
11661 - - - - - -	11697 - - - - - -	11648 - - - - - -
11662 - - BBH 605	11698 - - - - - -	11649 - - - - - -

11650 - - - - - -	11666 - - - - - -	11682 - - - - - -
11651 - - US 7343	11667 - - ARB 508	11683 - - - - - -
11652 - - - - - NZ	11668 - - GR 1568	11684 - - US 9828
11653 - - AYA 522	11669 - - - - - -	11685 - - - - - -
11654 - - LV 9597	11670 - - - - - -	11686 - - - - - -
11655 - - YS 1130	11671 - - - - - -	11687 - - - - - -
11656 - - - TJ 7393	11672 - - - - - -	11688 - - - - - -
11657 - - - - - -	11673 - - ARW 296	11689 - - - - - -
11658 - - - - - -	11674 - - KY 9016	11690 - - - - - -
11659 - - ARE 573	11675 - - BTW 318	11691 - - - YS 578
11660 - - - AHP 6	11676 - - - - - -	11692 - - ATT 881
11661 - - - - - -	11677 - - - - - -	11693 - - BNU 551
11662 - - BBH 605	11678 - - - - - -	11694 - - - - - -
11663 - - UN 7972	11679 - - BBH 865	11695 - - - - - -
11664 - - BEH 582	11680 - - - - - -	
11665 - - CG 8956	11681 - - - - - -	

11641
Raja of Nayagarh
Krishna Chandra Singh Mandhata (1911-1983) ruled from December 7, 1918 to August 15, 1947. He collected his Crested Eagle in person from Charles Follett in July 1934.

ARB 508
11667
11677
Motor show exhibits
A pair of Crested Eagle saloons specially prepared for the late 1934 show season, 11667 by Charlesworth, for London Olympia, and 11677 by Mayfair for Glasgow's Kelvin Hall.

11641: The Raja of Nayagarh collects his new Crested Eagle from the Charles Follett showroom. (Courtesy Bob Merrill and Wayne Brooks)

This Crested Eagle is one of several vehicles converted to armoured car use by the King's Lynne Home Guard (Brancaster Division) c1941. Others included two Ford V8s and a Railton. Not specifically apportioned, but from the few styling clues still visible, almost certainly from the 11616 to 11700 batch. Captain Mainwaring of *Dad's Army* fame would surely have been delighted to have had this device at Walmington-on-Sea.

11636
Cheshire County Police
Too big, one supposes, for regular patrol work, and more likely allocated to official or custodial purposes.

Chassis numbers
11701-11800
(Silver Eagle SF – second batch)

Chassis	Reg				
11701 - - - - - -	11734 - - KV 9219	11768 - - KG 4596
11702 - - KY 7275	11735 - - WS 1500	11769 - - - - - -
11703 - - BLG 374	11736 - - - - - -	11770 - - WP 6681
11704 - - OD 9739	11737 - - AFC 215	11771 - - - VJ 6367
11705 - - - - - -	11738 - - US 6879	11772 - - ADU 98
11706 - - US 6439	11739 - - US 7041	11773 - - AEL 507
11707 - - AWA 47-	11740 - - YG 7905	11774 - - AYN 212
11708 - - KV 9006	11741 - - - AYA 65	11775 - - KY 9276
11709 - - WV 5709	11742 - - - - - -	11776 - - WV 6121
11710 - - AWA 47-	11743 - - - - - -	11777 - - US 8001
11711 - - OD 9658	11744 - - ATA 188	11778 - - - - - -
11712 - - - - - -	11745 - - CRF 866	11779 - - - JY 4112
11713 - - US 6824	11746 - - - - - -	11780 - - - - - -
11714 - - AFC 191	11747 - - - - JP 79	11781 - - KY 7697
11715 - - - - - -	11748 - - ARA 835	11782 - - - - - -
11716 - - - - - -	11749 - - - - - -	17783 - - ARA 792
11717 - - - WS 619	11750 - - US 7152	11784 - - KY 7791
11718 - - - VJ 6361	11751 - - - - - -	11785 - - BNO 735
11719 - - AOC 481	11752 - - - - - -	11786 - - YG 8537
11720 - - - ATA 7	11753 - - - RJ 2980	11787 - - - - - -
11721 - - - - - -	11754 - - AVO 44	11788 - - AWB 151
11722 - - BMG 10	11755 - - AOH 643	11789 - - LV 9599
11723 - - AOB 777	11756 - - - - - -	11790 - - VG 6754
11724 - - KV 9276	11757 - - - - - -	11791 - - - - - -
11725 - - AYT 707	11758 - - NV 4163	11792 - - KY 7891
11726 - - - - - -	11759 - - KV 9666	11793 - - KV 9734
11727 - - - - - -	11760 - - HH 7453	11794 - - - - - -
11728 - - - - - -	11761 - - BHT 517	11795 - - - - - -
11729 - - - - - -	11762 - - AOF 264	11796 - - - - - -
11730 - - - - - -	11763 - - - - - -	11797 - - - - - -
11731 - - - - - -	11764 - - - JB 4623	11798 - - YG 9422
11732 - - KY 7401	11765 - - KY 7698	11799 - - AUA 665
11733 - - KY 7400	11766 - - ATA 377	11800 - - RV 5535
	11767 - - - - - -	

BLG 344
11703
Dr L T Pollard
Featuring in the book *Back in Five Minutes*, by

11866 - - - - - -	11870 - - - - - -	11874 - - MJ 5851
11867 - - BGK 242	11871 - - - - - -	11875 - - - - - -
11868 - - AUA 498	11872 - - -JY 4329	
11869 - - AAT 637	11873 - - -JY 4889	

William G Coffin, which is a history of the Cheshire town of Malpas during the 1940s and 1950s, 11703 was delivered to the local GP Dr Pollard, but mostly driven by his chauffeur, Ernest Challinor. Book published by the author, ISBN 0-9540654-0-9.

11707 `AWA 477/8`

11710 `AWA 478/7`

Sheffield Police

A pair of six-cylinder patrol cars for a regular Alvis customer. The record does not show precisely which registration number applied to which chassis (qv 11555 and 11556 for the Firefly patrol cars supplied at the same time).

11752

Mayoral car: City of Belfast

Lord Mayor of Belfast at the time of this car's despatch was Sir Crawford McCullagh, and its actual delivery was covered in a feature in the magazine *Autocar*, issue of August 3, 1934.

11800 `RV 5535`

Peter Wheeler

The former chairman of TVR Cars also owned a TA 21 model (qv 25116) and a TD 21 (qv 26170 for bio).

11805 `APP 639`

Lord Birkett KC MP PC

Distinguished lawyer, also owned a 4.3-litre model (qv 13649 for bio).

11837 `JB 4572`

Squire Car Manufacturing Company

Just prior to the production of exclusive and much lauded Squire sports car, the company took delivery of 11837, a Cross & Ellis tourer.

11843 `BGK 250`

Earl of Inchcape

Also later owned a TD 21 model (qv 26447 for bio).

11845 `BGK 243`

Ed Herrmann

Herrmann (July 21, 1943-December 31, 2014) was a very tall (6 feet, 5 inches) character actor, and appeared in numerous productions on both the large and small screens, typically *Gilmore Girls, The*

Chassis numbers
11801-11875
(Speed 20 SB – third batch)

Chassis	Reg				
11801 - - SY 6269	11822 - - RV 5318	11844 - - - - - -
11802 - - KV 9667	11823 - - BLP 197	11845 - - BGK 243
11803 - - KV 9665	11824 - - BLP 156	11846 - - AWA 912
11804 - - - - - -	11825 - - - - - -	11847 - - - - - -
11805 - - APP 639	11826 - - - - NL	11848 - - WP 6635
11806 - -BGW 603	11827 - - - - AUS	11849 - - AUF 814
11807 - - - - - -	11828 - - - - - -	11850 - - BGN 436
11808 - - JW 5032	11829 - - -JV 2902	11851 - - DG 9628
11809 - - -TJ 5666	11830 - - - - - -	11852 - - ADU 374
11810 - - FP 2739	11831 - -AKW 456	11853 - -BMG 889
11811 - - US 6878	11832 - - - - - -	11854 - - NV 4356
11812 - - TG 7893	11833 - - - - - -	11855 - - - - - -
11813 - - - - - -	11834 - - BLH 193	11856 - - - - IND
11814 - - - - - -	11835 - - - - - -	11857 - - MG 3460
11815 - - - - - -	11836 - - - - -DK	11858 - - NG 7644
11816 - - - - - -	11837 - - -JB 4572	11859 - - - - - -
11817 - - - - - -	11838 - - - - - -	11860 - - VY 5631
11818 - - YG 7777	11839 - - - - - -	11861 - - AHY 112
11819 - - WO 8608	11840 - - KV 9964	11862 - - AWB 244
11820 - - - - - -	11841 - - RN 3489	11863 - - - - - -
11821 - - BGO 87	11842 - - ADU 477	11864 - - - - - -
	11843 - - BGK 250	11865 - - - - - -

11805: The ex-Lord Birkett Vanden Plas Saloon. (Courtesy Ernest Shenton collection (top) & John Worrell)

Wolf of Wall Street, and *The Aviator*. Also made commercials for Dodge Automobiles.

11848
Cyril Posthumus
A prolific motoring writer, Posthumus (1918-1992) was also an accomplished maker of models, and 11848 was one of his subjects. His work in this sphere was written up in the January 31, 1947 issue of *Autocar*, by none other than S C H (Sammy) Davis – no mean Alvis driver himself. This car has also featured in the 1979 television adaptation of the Daphne du Maurier novel *Rebecca*, starring Jeremy Brett and Anna Massey. Also appeared on a glossy calendar production at about the same time.

11856
Rajah of Bhopal
Notable member of an Indian dynasty, with many European connections, and with family history traceable to the France of Napoleonic times. For further reading on this angle, a book, *Le Rajah Bourbon* by Prince Michael of Greece, ISBN 978-2-7096-2922-5, can be recommended.

The Rajah's car was a drophead coupé, numbered 3246 in the Vanden Plas records, and supplied through Charles Follett, the London agent.

11859
A F Rivers-Fletcher
Originally a standard Cross & Ellis tourer delivered in Birmingham, this is one of three Alvis cars given the 'special' treatment by Rivers. The original registration mark is not known, 'LSV 193' being allocated much later by DVLA. The other two specials are 11298 and 14459 (bio).

11869 **AAT 637**
Hull City Police
A typically-specified tourer for this East Yorkshire Force.

Chassis numbers
11876-11882
(Firefly SB – third batch)

Chassis	Reg				
11876 - -	BG 2738	11879 - - - - - -		11883 - - - - - -	
11877 - -	AUA 664	11880 - - - - - -		11884 - - - - - -	
11878 - -	AVO 424	11881 - -	ADU 475	11885 - -	WP 9064
		11882 - -	ADU 429		

11878 **AVO 424**
Movie car
Emanating from the final batch of ten Firefly models to be produced, some of which piloted the 13.2hp engine intended for the imminent Firebird model, 11878 would have its special moment when it was feature in the 1954 movie *A Prize of Gold*, starring Richard Widmark and Mai Zetterling.

SPEED 20 SC

1934 to 1936
289 cars

11886-12135	250
12736-12774	39

Consisting of:
Charlesworth saloons numbered variously between 13389-13680	131
Charlesworth coupés numbered variously between 13397-13672 including 2 f/h conversions	34
Charlesworth two-seater roadster	1
Vanden Plas saloons, coupés, tourers numbered variously between 3254-3374	69
Cross & Ellis tourers numbered variously between 30305-30331	27

Remainder: independent makers

The Speed 20 line had been an undoubted success in a competitive sector of the market, and it was thus necessary to keep ahead when the increasing weight of ever more desirable coachwork tended to limit performance. The answer with the SC model was to enlarge the engine by lengthening the stroke to 110mm, thus keeping the 19.82hp rating, and increasing the main bearing sizes by 5mm at the same time. The chassis was stiffened with extra bracing at the front, which also served as engine bearers, and the steering layout was simplified. The massive transverse leaf front suspension was retained, but made slightly softer. Though first and foremost a sports/touring car, the SC continued to have competition potential especially evident in the example stripped out and raced by Charles Follett (qv 11962). Finally, and not really a discernible recognition point, the wheelbase was a mere 1in longer when compared to the preceding SB type.

Chassis numbers
11886-12135
(Speed 20 SC – first batch)

Chassis	Reg	Chassis	Reg	Chassis	Reg
11886	BNB 905	11944	YG 9320	12003	YS 1358
11887	BLL 105	11945	- - - - - -	12004	WD 9226
11888	BGT 583	11946	BYK 196	12005	-SS 4057
11889	BLB 791	11947	- - - - - -	12006	ALJ 657
11890	BYP 295	11948	ARU 240	12007	MG 3686
11891	- - - - - -	11949	- - - - - -	12008	AER 610
11892	- - - - - -	11950	ARB 849	12009	-OU 123
11893	- - - - - -	11951	- - - - - -	12010	AUS
11894	- - - - - -	11952	ARW 763	12011	BXR 402
11895	AHP 4	11953	BNC 2	12012	- - - - - -
11896	BLB 798	11954	BLU 360	12013	- - - - - -
11897	WV 6566	11955	AJO 12	12014	AUS
11898	- - - - - -	11956	- - - - - -	12015	AUS
11899	SN 6529	11957	- - - - - -	12016	AHP 776
11900	- - - - - -	11958	-JR 2776	12017	- - - - - -
11901	ALJ 210	11959	-AUG 11	12018	ATT 527
11902	ALJ 159	11960	BLX 272	12019	- - - - - -
11903	SH 4942	11961	BCD 365	12020	BAE 915
11904	- - - - - -	11962	BLN 769	12021	-VJ 7154
11905	CXU 906	11963	AWK 92	12022	- - - - - -
11906	- - - - - -	11964	BYF 325	12023	BYR 928
11907	- - - - - -	11965	-AFJ 213	12024	BXK 464
11908	BYL 926	11966	- - - - - -	12025	WF 7375
11909	- - - - - -	11967	- - - - - -	12026	JW 7000
11910	BKN 622	11968	- - - - - -	12027	J
11911	BLB 793	11969	ATV 560	12028	- - - - - -
11912	OW 7888	11970	BLM 750	12029	KS 6503
11913	- - - - - -	11971	- - - - - -	12030	YS 378
11914	BXR 858	11972	JX 2363	12031	BNU 409
11915	- - - - - -	11973	FW 5549	12032	-JR 2147
11916	BLE 894	11974	AAR 333	12033	KY 9874
11917	- - - - - -	11975	CG 9974	12034	ARW 293
11918	BLF 777	11976	KY 8639	12035	ARW 83
11919	BMV 7	11977	BOJ 623	12036	CJJ 60
11920	- - - - - -	11978	AKB 583	12037	- - - - - -
11921	BLK 550	11979	- - - - - -	12038	-AWJ 12
11922	BLH 194	11980	AKB 588	12039	RN 4004
11923	WS 2486	11981	BUC 204	12040	RN 4041
11924	-YS 22	11982	AAD 727	12041	BNB 888
11925	- - - - - -	11983	- - - - - -	12042	- - - - - -
11926	BLX 277	11984	AHP 597	12043	AUS
11927	AKB 255	11985	- - - - - -	12044	WS 3403
11928	BYF 322	11986	AHP 774	12045	PV 1916
11929	AON 623	11987	- - - - - -	12046	SB 4662
11930	- - - - - -	11988	- - - - - -	12047	- - - - - -
11931	- - - - - -	11989	AWE 637	12048	YS 641
11932	- - - - - -	11990	WP 7792	12049	WD 9131
11933	- - - - - -	11991	-TJ 8126	12050	BVX 91
11934	BXN 11	11992	AJO 999	12051	BMB 784
11935	AWB 925	11993	AUS	12052	WV 7848
11936	BLF 699	11994	ALJ 652	12053	ARU 291
11937	E	11995	-ARU 25	12054	CEV 514
11938	- - - - - -	11996	US 9809	12055	BXB 721
11939	BUV 276	11997	BLP 153	12056	AKD 309
11940	BLE 892	11998	AOM 191	12057	AVE 98
11941	BHX 129	11999	WD 8752	12058	- - - - - -
11942	- - - - - -	12000	- - - - - -	12059	RD6437
11943	- - - - - -	12001	HF 4608	12060	-JY 5234
		12002	- - - - - -	12061	BHT 469

Chassis	Reg	Chassis	Reg	Chassis	Reg
12062	- - - - - -	12087	AVE 305	12112	AVC 936
12063	- - - - - -	12088	-JT 3188	12113	- - - - - -
12064	-JC 2525	12089	NG 9747	12114	BYF 323
12065	RN 4048	12090	AVP 246	12115	BYX 232
12066	BYF 326	12091	ARW 436	12116	-AVC 80
12067	BKP 564	12092	- - - - - -	12117	- - - - - -
12068	-BND 80	12093	- - - - - -	12118	WS 4545
12069	CPL 730	12094	- - - - - -	12119	BYN 970
12070	YS 1035	12095	-AWK 613	12120	AUS
12071	KY 9898	12096	YS 1737	12121	BOF 306
12072	-YJ 2365	12097	ARH 556	12122	AAK 152
12073	- - - - - -	12098	BRA 114	12123	HF 5222
12074	YS 1036	12099	CS 1965	12124	-CJJ 415
12075	BYN 961	12100	-BNW 691	12125	BOA 187
12076	- - - - - -	12101	-AAK 11	12126	BYF 329
12077	BTN 957	12102	CLG 561	12127	- - - - - -
12078	RV 6505	12103	-AWK 614	12128	BYW 965
12079	BXL 835	12104	FV 5983	12129	- - - - - -
12080	-DK	12105	-JU 6665	12130	- - - - - -
12081	BXP 944	12106	-JY 6199	12131	CGH 927
12082	BYY 902	12107	-YS 29	12132	BYF 330
12083	- - - - - -	12108	YS 2383	12133	- - - - - -
12084	AKF 203	12109	AUS	12134	AAK 436
12085	BWA 543	12110	- - - - - -	12135	- - - - - -
12086	CNU 29	12111	ADE 579		

11888 BGT 583

London Motor Show 1934

As the third chassis of the new SC series to leave the factory, and the first of the saloon types to be bodied by Vanden Plas, 11888 was an exhibit at the Olympia Show of 1934, along with its sports tourer version on 11896. Naturally, there was much press coverage at the time, and the above saloon was covered in *Motor,* issue of December 18, 1934.

11890 BYP 295

Major Oscar M Guest MP

Oscar Guest (August 24, 1888-May 1958) was twice an MP, initially for the Loughborough constituency. Between 1935 and 1945, however, he was elected to the London seat of Camberwell NW. His car had a very distinctive one-off fixed head coupé body by Lancefield. This must have cut quite a dash at the time, in the short trip from his home in Cleveland Sq W2 to the House of Commons.

11895 AHP 4

Sir Charles R H Wiggin TD DL JP

Sir Charles (March 21, 1985-September 16, 1972) was educated at Eton and Trinity College Cambridge. He served in WWI, and was mentioned in despatches, and also served in the Staffordshire Yeomanry (Colonel), became 3rd Baron Wiggin, and was High Sheriff of Warwickshire in 1942, and later still Deputy

11928: A highly interesting pair of photographs, showing both before and after the ingenious Morris Minor bonnet tailpiece conversion. (Courtesy Ernest Shelton collection)

Lieutenant for that County. Lady Wiggin also had an Alvis TJ 12/50 model, chassis 8996 (page 59).

11923 · WS 2486
Professor Norman Dott
Distinguished neurosurgeon, and freeman of the City of Edinburgh. Later owned a 4.3-litre model (qv 14810 for bio).

11928 · BYF 322
Competition car
Originally a coupé bodied by Vanden Plas, this car was skilfully converted postwar by shortening the chassis and endowing it with a 4.3-litre engine. The tail panel, sourced from a Morris Minor, recreates the Alvis 'ducksback' styling of the '20s. Often conducted to good effect by the late Stoke-on-Trent jeweller Ron Buck, the car is indecently fast but more at home on sprints and tests than on circuits.

11930
Alec Waugh
Educated at Sherborne School, Alec Waugh (July 8, 1898-September 3, 1981) was a novelist, chiefly remembered these days for his *Island in the Sun*

11941: This most unusual device actually started life as Betty Streather's 1934 rally car, seen here rebodied postwar by John Grocott. His design may have been influenced by the Embiricos Bentley or by Gabriel Voisin. (Courtesy Alvis Archive Trust)

of 1955, and its subsequent influence upon reggae in general, and the career of Harry Belafonte in particular. Waugh is also said to have invented the concept of the cocktail party.

11935 · AWB 325
Alonso Burdall
For many years the confection Burdall's Gravy Salt was considered to be an essential adjunct to culinary success, especially in the North of England, centred on its Sheffield base. The product disappeared from sale about 2002, but has had its recipe revived in the form of Uncle Roy's Old Fashioned Gravy Salt, and Old Jake's Gravy Sauce.

11941 · BHX 129
Betty Streather
Following ownership of an SA Speed 20 (qv 10057), Betty Streather bought the above car, campaigning it successfully in the 1935 and 1936 RAC Rallies. The car was subsequently acquired by the surgeon (and talented engineer) John Grocott, of Stoke-on-Trent, who re-bodied it in a very individual fixed-head coupé format. Miss Streather continued her Alvis ownership much later on with a Series II TD 21 (qv 26991).

11964 · BYF 325
Countess Helle Frijs
The Countess (November 9, 1886-July 19,1974) was apparently one of four charismatic sisters, and a cousin of Baroness Blixen, who wrote the novel *Out of Africa*. She clearly had a taste for fast cars, also owning an Alfa Romeo RL. Could she indeed

12423    **VS 2780**

Greenock Police

A patrol car for this Scottish force.

12430   **ARW 82**

Chivers Ltd

A company car for the Devizes, Wiltshire-based firm, notable producers of a whole range of jams and other preserves.

    Previously owned a 12/50 (qv 3893).

12484   **AWK 67**

W H Charnock

Harry Charnock (1902-1959) was educated at Lancing College and St John's College Cambridge, and will ever be known as 'The Motoring Poet' for his erudite and amusing commentaries about vehicle and related events. Owner of very many vintage and classic cars, his Silver Eagle special on chassis 12494, always referred to as 'Rumbold' has survived him and is in regular use. For further reading, *Harry Charnock's Motoring Verse* can be heartily recommended, ISBN 1-899743-02-2.

12484: This is a view of 'Rumbold,' the Silver Eagle special immortalised by renowned motoring poet W H Charnock. (Courtesy Ernest Shenton collection)

Chassis numbers
12486-12585
(Firebird SA – second batch)

Chassis	Reg		
12486	- - - - - -	12490 - - ARU 380	12495 - - - - - -
12487 - - BNB 476	12491 - - AKC 999	12496 - - ARU 83
12488 - - GR 1601	12492 - - - - - -	12497 - - YS 1618
12489 - - KY 9974	12493 - - - - - -	12498 - - RN 4040
	12494 - - - - - -	12499 - - AWJ 564

12500 - - TH 5445	12529 - - - - - -	12557 - - AJH 791
12501 - - AWK 95	12530 - - ED 9000	12558 - - -SS 4182
12502 - - HS 8167	12531 - - WV 7633	12559 - - - - - -
12503 - - VH 7443	12532 - - KY 9855	12560 - - BND 669
12504 - - ARW 433	12533 - - WS 4124	12561 - - -SS 4182
12505 - - -TJ 9495	12534 - - - - - -	12562 - - AKV 173
12506 - - - - - -	HVC 218	12563 - - -AVC 78
12507 - - - - - -	12535 - - YS 1463	12564 - - -JV 3986
12508 - - -TJ 8868	12536 - - FV 6903	12565 - - AWK 816
12509 - - - - - -	12537 - - KY 9727	12566 - - - - - -
12510 - - AWK 91	12538 - - YS 3344	12567 - - - - - -
12511 - - - - - -	12539 - - BDH 832	12568 - -AWK 817
12512 - - -JR 3188	12540 - - AAK 929	12569 - - -BDU 57
12513 - - SR 9363	12541 - - WS 4314	12570 - - -BDU 56
12514 - - APX 182	12542 - - - - - -	12571 - - - - - -
12515 - - - - - -	12543 - - BXE 997	12572 - - - - - -
12516 - - BXE 995	12544 - - -JV 3671	12573 - - -VJ 7515
12517 - - -FA 5719	12545 - - BXN 742	12574 - - - - - -
12518 - - - - - -	12546 - - - - - -	12575 - - BRR 222
12519 - - -JU 5976	12547 - - AUO 591	12576 - - - - - -
12520 - - -JL 2237	12548 - - YS 1953	12577 - - - - - -
12521 - - AFG 349	12549 - - BFC 700	12578 - - - - - -
12522 - - COU 939	12550 - - YS 2172	12579 - - AVC 456
12523 - - - - - -	12551 - - VY 6667	12580 - - -JR 3348
12524 - - - - - -	12552 - - - - - -	12581 - - ATB 507
12525 - - - - - -	12553 - - - - - -	12582 - - AHP 634
12526 - - YS 1692	12554 - - YS 1864	12583 - - AVC 237
12527 - - - - - -	12555 - - FV 6202	12584 - - BKC 980
12528 - - - - - -	12556 - - DGJ 416	12585 - - - - - -

12530   **ED 9000**

Warrington Borough Police

A patrol car for this Lancashire force.

12533   **WS 4124**

The Stone Of Scone Raid

Readers of a certain age may recall the widely reported incident where an audacious group of Scottish Nationalists removed the iconic 'Stone' from its resting place beneath the Coronation Chair in Westminster Abbey. A number of vehicles were involved in the execution of this well-planned operation including a Ford Eight, an Armstrong Siddeley, and the above. Some years ago, I was lucky enough to be able to trace the leader of the group, a law student at the time of the incident, and subsequently a distinguished Scottish QC, and am indebted to Ian Hamilton for helping me to put the meat on the bones of this story. The actual 'heist' took place on Christmas Eve 1950, and those keen to know more of the not unworthy motives of those concerned are referred to Ian's book, *Taking of the Stone of Destiny*, Lochar Press, ISBN 0948403-24-1.

12546

Stirling Police

A patrol car for this Scottish force.

12558

SS 4182

East Lothian Police
An open patrol car supplied to this Scottish force.

12560
BND 669

Manchester City Police
An open patrol car supplied to this north of England force.

12562
AKV 173

Keith Piggott
Horse trainer and jockey, father of the even more famous Lester Piggott. Also owned a 12/70 model (qv 15642) and a TA 21 model (qv 24615 for bio).

12571
Ayr Police
A patrol car for this Scottish force.

Chassis	Reg		Chassis	Reg		Chassis	Reg
12687	DUA 730		12704	ATJ 961		12721	- - - - - -
12688	- - - - - -		12705	NV 6258		12722	- - - - - -
12689	CGW 692		12706	DT 6636		12723	- - - - - -
12690	- - - - - -		12707	CWA 21		12724	BVO 76
12691	YS 5010		12708	- - - - - -		12725	- - - - - -
12692	JU 9385		12709	- - - - - -		12726	ATE 20
12693	CNU 519		12710	BPO 6		12727	- - - - - -
12694	- - - - - -		12711	ADG 592		12728	YS 5692
12695	- - - - - -		12712	- - - - - -		12729	BRW 982
12696	- - - - - -		12713	WS 6850		12730	JU 8185
12697	AKU 970		12714	CLB 320		12731	BWM 80
12698	JV 4954		12715	- - - - - -		12732	BDU 60
12699	GR 2465		12716	VY 8530		12733	- - - - - -
12700	- - - - - -		12717	VH 8490		12734	- - - - - -
12701	- - - - - -		12718	JX 3482		12735	- - - - - -
12702	FA 6050		12719	CUM 616			
12703	BDU 922		12720	BHP 932			

Chassis numbers
12586-125735
(Silver Eagle SG – third batch)

Chassis	Reg		Chassis	Reg		Chassis	Reg
12586	GV 3836		12619	AVP 772		12653	- - - - - -
12587	- - - - - -		12620	- - - - - -		12654	BHP 898
12588	WS 3420		12621	- - - - - -		12655	- - - - - -
12589	AKU 802		12622	AWY 328		12656	KG 6466
12590	UN 8142		12623	KY 4727		12657	- - - - - -
12591	- - - - - -		12624	- - - - - -		12658	AKW 139
12592	ADD 788		12625	YS 2400		12659	BCE 1
12593	- - - - - -		12626	- - - - - -		12660	BOC 694
12594	BAU 497		12627	- - - - - -		12661	XS 3861
12595	- - - - - -		12628	VJ 7500		12662	- - - - - -
12596	- - - - - -		12629	- - - - - -		12663	- - - - - -
12597	- - - - - -		12630	- - - - - -		12664	BCE 497
12598	- - - - - -		12631	- - - - - -		12665	- - - - - -
12599	- - - - - -		12632	BDU 676		12666	ACY 292
12600	- - - - - -		12633	E		12667	ATC 611
12601	- - - - - -		12634	- - - - - -		12668	VJ 8767
12602	WS 4128		12635	AVC 668		12669	BPP 710
12603	YS 1771		12636	- - - - - -		12670	- - - - - -
12604	BYX 234		12637	AAH 432		12671	- - - - - -
12605	BVC 7		12638	AVC 987		12672	- - - - - -
12606	- - - - - -		12639	BBJ 624		12673	- - - - - -
12607	- - - - - -		12640	HH 8529		12674	WS 6646
12608	BXR 854		12641	- - - - - -		12675	CEL 766
12609	- - - - - -		12642	AKV 741		12676	WS 7696
12610	AVC 994		12643	BWA 74-		12677	AKV 743
12611	BAU 841		12644	AAX 183		12678	BDU 53
12612	- - - - - -		12645	- - - - - -		12679	CGW 692
12613	BBJ 306		12646	BWA 74-		12680	BDF 721
12614	ZA		12647	VV 3971		12681	BOH 265
12615	JM 1924		12648	- - - - - -		12682	YS 5025
12616	AWK 815		12649	- - - - - -		12683	- - - - - -
12617	AVC 79		12650	AKV 174		12684	AUS
12618	- - - - - -		12651	BOJ 814		12685	- - - - - -
			12652	FF 4429		12686	YS 4651

12605
BVC 7

12610
AVC 994

Alvis works cars
Two special projects of July 1936 here, 12605 being a unique works van, and 12610 being a drophead coupé presented by T G John to his daughter.

12628
VJ 7500

Bulmer's Cider Ltd
A staff car for the well-known Hereford-based cider maker. Later purchased a TD 21 model (qv 26876), and preceded by a 12/50 TE bought second-hand (qv 4434).

12635
AVC 668

Temple Press Ltd
Staff car for the publisher of the weekly magazine *Motor*.

12643
BWA 743/4

12646
BWA 744/3

Sheffield Police
Pair of patrol cars. The record is not clear about which registration number was with which chassis. A third car, being a Speed 20 saloon was supplied to the Sheffield force at the same time (qv 12746).

12661
XS 3861

Paisley Police
A patrol car for this Scottish force.

12721
R A (Rab) Butler MP
12721 preceded Rab Butler's ownership of a TE 21 model (qv 27168 for bio).

Chassis numbers
12736-12774
(Speed 20 SC – second batch)

Chassis	Reg						
12736	- - - IRQ	12749	- - WS 5868	12763	- - YS 3708
12737	- - BVO 886	12750	- - - - - -	12764	- -CGH 922
12738	- - AVC 457	12751	- - -NJ 6996	12765	- - CLA 328
12739	- - AVC 458	12752	- - - - - -	12766	-CGW 691
12740	- BUO 265	12753	- - -JR 3792	12767	- UD 7087
12741	- - BYF 327	12754	- - - - - -	12768	- ANX 325
12742	- - BNF 107	12755	- - ATC 486	12769	- BWB 950
12743	- - - AUS	12756	- - BYT 878	12770	- - - - - -
12744	- - - - - -	12757	- -VJ 7845	12771	- - - - - -
12745	- - AAK 438	12758	- - EZ 1906	12772	- - GY 7177
12746	- - BWA 745	12759	- -FA 5995	12773	- - - - - -
12747	- - -JR 3477	12760	- -CMA 812	12774	- -CXX 624
12748	- -CTW 615	12761	- CGH 928		
		12762	- - - - - -		

12736
King of Iraq
Uniquely-bodied as a special tourer by Cross & Ellis, 12736 was despatched to Baghdad in January 1936. It has remarkably survived the ravages of climate and political unrest and was last recorded in the custody of the Royal Garages, Amman, Jordan, and thence under restoration in the UK.

12746

Sheffield Police
In July 1935, the Sheffield force took delivery of this 'prestige' Speed 20 saloon, together with a pair of Silver Eagle patrol cars (qv 12643 and 12646).

12756
Competition car
Originally a Vanden Plas-bodied coupé, post-WWII, it was converted to racing use and campaigned by J Brydon, with a body by Wragg and fitted with a 4.3-litre engine.

12760
Fodens Ltd
The Alvis marque was much-favoured by the Cheshire-based commercial vehicle manufacturer (qv 13641 and 14676).

CLA 328

12765
Guy Griffiths
Research confirms that Griffiths, doyen of motoring and motor-racing photography (and proprietor of Alton Garage), was the third owner of 12765. Born June 6, 1915-July 12, 1999, he served in WWII and was taken prisoner. The first owner of 12765 was a Lt-Col Nesbitt, and the self-explanatory Capt Tindal-Carill-Worsley, who would later marry Alvis competition driver Dorothy Stanley-Turner (qv 13656 and 23804).

The considerable Guy Griffiths Collection survives, based in Brighton. Details: 01435 813961, and info@guygriffiths.co.uk

SPEED 20 SD

1935 to 1936
149 cars

12775-12783	9
12784/85 (see text)	2
12986-13085	100
13286-13325	40

Consisting of:

Charlesworth saloons numbered variously between 13683-14014	97
Charlesworth coupés numbered variously between 13684-13825	9
Vanden Plas, saloons coupés and tourers numbered variously between 3413-3485	24
Cross & Ellis tourers numbered variously between 30329-30346	12
Cross & Ellis coupé one only: 13818	1
Remainder: independent makers	

With engineering changes mainly confined to a flatter petrol tank and a wider scuttle casting, the final version of the Speed 20 series trickled through to the agents and coachbuilders with little, if any, publicity. Ideas were already in hand for a replacement. The tenth and eleventh chassis within the SD designation were lengthened to an 11ft wheelbase in order to accommodate experimental eight-cylinder engines of 4.4-litres, but these, which might have found favour in an upmarket situation, were not sanctioned for production, this area would be covered by the imminent 3.5-litre model. That engine, however, was tried successfully in a one-off 25.63hp SD (qv 13315) an obvious precursor of the notable Speed 25 series (qv 13326-on).

Chassis numbers
12775-12785
(Speed 20 SD – first batch)

Chassis	Reg	14952 - - - - - -	14956 - - - - - -
14949 - - - - - -		14953 - - ETD 580	14957 - - - - - -
14950 - -DWK 999		14954 - - - - - -	14958 - - - - - -
14951 - - - - - -		14955 - - HRE 729	14959 - - EVC 653

12779
Paris Saloon 1935

Until the contribution of Graber occurred, continental coachwork on Alvis chassis was comparatively little known, so 12779 is a notable exception, being specially built by Vanvooren for the Paris Salon, and sold to an M Bouregon on the day of opening. It is astonishing indeed that somehow the car escaped the attention of the occupying forces in France during WWII, and it fortunately passed into the caring hands of that distinguished motoring journalist Serge Pozzoli (March 23, 1915-July 12, 1999). It is not widely known that almost a decade earlier Alvis Ltd had commissioned a body from Vanvooren, which was

12779: Subtly different from its Charlesworth contemporaries, this is the one-off Vanvooren coupé. (Author's collection)

fitted to 12/50 chassis 4431 and returned to the UK, but sadly no image of this car appears to have survived.

12780
CNB 277
George Formby OBE

This famous entertainer's second Alvis, following an SC Speed 20 (qv 12069) and to be followed by Speed 25 SC (qv 14653 for bio).

12780: The unique Lancefield-bodied SD series Speed 20 saloon, ex-George Formby. (Courtesy Dr B J Nield)

13777
BKV

13778
SN 7595
13779
London and Glasgow Motor Shows 1936

A trio of Silver Crests prepared by the works for the 1936 show season, marking the introduction of this model. The trio comprised one each of the advertised availability of four-light saloon, six-light saloon, and drophead coupé. The coupé (13778) survives at the time of writing.

12784
AHP 775
12785
Works development car

About the time of the transition between the SC and the SD series Speed 20 models, two notable variants were devised whereby the SD chassis was lengthened by eight inches at the business end (so that standard-type coachwork could be used), and two special eight-cylinder blocks were cast, using 80mm bores (up from 73mm), giving a rate of 31.74hp, and a cubic capacity of 4423cc. The earlier

12860 - - WS 7082	12869 - - -JY 7239	12878 - - CKO 545
12861 - - CMB 694	12870 - - CLM 153	12879 - - BHP 223
12862 - - - - - -	12871 - - EZ 1058	12880 - - - - - -
12863 - - - - - -	12872 - - WF 8472	12881 - - - - - -
12864 - - CUA 795	12873 - - CMB 969	12882 - - YS 6564
12865 - - AKW 48	12874 - - - - - -	12883 - - BAO 697
12866 - - BHP 256	12875 - - WN 9287	12884 - - - - - -
12867 - - - - - -	12876 - - VH 8733	12885 - - - - - -
12868 - - - - - -	12877 - - CLW 55	

12785: Although no images have survived of the pair of SD 20-based straight-eight saloons, the engine from one of them did, and was used by Chalenor-Barson to power one of his several specials, which is seen here. (Courtesy Wayne Brooks)

was designated for designer Captain Smith-Clarke's personal use, the latter for T G John. Neither survived for very long in their original form, but engine 13235, ex 12785, would find its way into one of the specials constructed by Chalenor-Barson, which survives to this day.

Chassis numbers
12786-12885
(Firebird SA – third batch)

Chassis Reg		
12786 - - BYX 231	12810 - - - - - -	12835 - - BTV 111
12787 - - - - - -	12811 - - ANP 489	12836 - - NV 7949
12788 - - FV 6535	12812 - - CUF 850	12837 - -BWK 260
12789 - - BRA 447	12813 - - AKY 278	12838 - - - - - -
12790 - - WS 5877	12814 - - -BDU 54	12839 - - BHP 541
12791 - - - - - -	12815 - - -BDU 59	12840 - - - - - -
12792 - - - - - -	12816 - - - - - -	12841 - - BDU 414
12793 - - AVC 995	12817 - - - - - -	12842 - - - - - -
12794 - - - - - -	12818 - - -NJ 7348	12843 - - - - USA
12795 - - AVC 236	12819 - - BUO 980	12844 - - -BLJ 697
12796 - - AKU 138	12820 - - BOH 264	12845 - - EW 9232
12797 - - - - - -	12821 - - - - - -	12846 - - PV 2678
12798 - - TL 4757	12822 - - -JR 3849	12847 - - BDU 798
12799 - - - - - -	12823 - - - - - -	12848 - - BYB 987
12800 - - AKV 175	12824 - - DBB 127	12849 - - - - - -
12801 - - AUB 674	12825 - - WS 7386	12850 - - - - - -
12802 - - SU 3113	12826 - - - - - -	12851 - - BFY 982
12803 - - - - - -	12827 - - CUB 310	12852 - - CWE 640
12804 - -BHW 765	12828 - - -BDU 58	12853 - - - EZ 879
12805 - - YS 6370	12829 - - - - - -	12854 - - BKC 524
12806 - - WS 5375	12830 - - - - - -	12855 - - BDU 675
12807 - - -ATD 83	12831 - - - - - -	12856 - - VN 8178
12808 - - WS 6134	12832 - - UN 9306	12857 - - ANG 606
12809 - - - - - -	12833 - - -JV 4873	12858 - - VY 7777
	12834 - - WS 6463	12859 - - - EZ 865

Chassis numbers
12886-12985
(Crested Eagle TF, TG – first batch)

Chassis Reg		
12886 - - AWK 96	12919 - - HS 8505	12953 - - CVO 478
12887 - - - - - -	12920 - - ET 8933	12954 - - BDU 415
12888 - - AJH 757	12921 - - - - - -	12955 - - - - - -
12889 - - WP 8936	12922 - - - - - -	12956 - - - - - -
12890 - -AWK 615	12923 - - GV 3599	12957 - - UN 9303
12891 - - AAK 141	12924 - - - - - -	12958 - - ASP 424
12892 - - AKF 860	12925 - - BYX 439	12959 - - - - - -
12893 - - -JB 6631	12926 - - -JU 8178	12960 - - - - - -
12894 - - WS 4774	12927 - - -ATC 50	12961 - - - - - -
12895 - - AVC 670	12928 - - - JP 898	12962 - - - - - -
12896 - - YS 5757	12929 - - - - - -	12963 - - WS 7373
12897 - - AWU 90	12930 - - DT 7348	12964 - - BHP 663
12898 - - BXR 853	12931 - - - - - -	12965 - - - - - -
12899 - - - - - -	12932 - - BDU 157	12966 - - AAX 741
12900 - - WS 5019	12933 - - - - - -	12967 - - HH 8636
12901 - - - - - -	12934 - - DPK 683	12968 - - UN 9173
12902 - - WP 9102	12935 - - - - - -	12969 - - CLH 898
12903 - - YS 2686	12936 - - - - - -	12970 - - - - - -
12904 - - - - - -	12937 - - - - - -	12971 - - - - - -
12905 - - AVC 238	12938 - - - - - -	12972 - - -JT 4400
12906 - - - - - -	12939 - - - - - -	12973 - - BHP 221
12907 - - - - - -	12940 - - BCV 284	12974 - - - - - -
12908 - - - - - -	12941 - - - - - -	12975 - - - - - -
12909 - - NV 5456	12942 - -BWK 117	12976 - - - - - -
12910 - - YS 7384	12943 - - - - - -	12977 - - - - - -
12911 - - YS 2887	12944 - - -JK 6029	12978 - - BAD 720
12912 - - - - - -	12945 - - - - - -	12979 - - BRW 457
12913 - - CS 2972	12946 - - - - - -	12980 - - - AUS
12914 - - AVC 996	12947 - - - - - -	12981 - - UN 9304
12915 - - - - - -	12948 - - YS 4775	12982 - - -CJJ 414
12916 - - - - - -	12949 - - UN 8719	12983 - - - - - -
12917 - - BAT 680	12950 - - - - - -	12984 - - DGY 755
12918 - - - - - -	12951 - - - - - -	12985 - - -JU 8178
	12952 - - - - - -	

12964 `BHP 663`

Sir Rudolph Dymoke White MP
Sir Rudolph (June 11, 1888-May 25, 1968) was MP for Fareham from 1939 to 1950. Later also owned another Crested Eagle model (qv 13249). Post-WWII, 12964 passed into the hands of actor Derek Carpenter, who may be recalled for his appearances in that once popular television soap series *Crossroads*. A photograph of 12964 in a pleasant rural setting can be seen in magazine *Autocar*, issue of August 14, 1953, page 203.

12969

CLH 898

Sir Christopher J W Farwell
Prominent high court judge (1877-1943). There is a portrait of him in the National Gallery.

Chassis numbers
12986-13085
(Speed 20 SD – second batch)

Chassis	Reg				
12986	- - YS 4049	13019	- - BWE 97	13053	- - YS 7020
12987	- - AKV 928	13020	- - CLF 393	13054	- - BOV 463
12988	- - - - - -	13021	- - -JY 7385	13055	- - AOD 397
12989	- - - - - -	13022	- - RV 8078	13056	- CTU 892
12990	- - DUL 120	13023	- - BHP 662	13057	- - AOD 786
12991	- CRW 804	13024	- - BON 900	13058	- - BER 441
12992	- - - BYA 11	13025	- - ACR 164	13059	- - YS 7148
12993	- - CLX 947	13026	- - CXM 95	13060	- - BDD 436
12994	- - CXM 97	13027	- - - - GBJ	13061	- - CUU 88
12995	- - - - - -	13028	- - BDU 921	13062	- - BRW 99
12996	- - BFY 855	13029	-CKM 490	13063	- - CAU 104
12997	- - CXM 99	13030	-CGW 698	13064	- - - - - -
12998	- - - - - -	13031	- - CYX 655	13065	- - -JY 7620
12999	- - - - - -	13032	- - VY 7447	13066	-DNW 938
13000	- - - CGF 5	13033	- - CTA 772	13067	- - CHU 721
13001	- - - - - -	13034	- - BDU 796	13068	- - BOX 521
13002	- - BAA 898	13035	- - BHP 224	13069	- - -VJ 8757
13003	- - - - - -	13036	- - CVC 118	13070	- - DYE 166
13004	- - - - - -	13037	- - YS 7302	13071	- BRW 455
13005	- - VV 4516	13038	- - EZ 1047	13072	- - WS 3944
13006	- - CUB 307	13039	- - BHP 225	13073	- - BRW 40
13007	- - SR 9939	13040	- - DPU 146	13074	- - PV 3139
13008	- - BKU 874	13041	- - BHP 661	13075	- - NV 7374
13009	- - - - - -	13042	- - BHP 540	13076	- - YS 9341
13010	- - - - - -	13043	- - - - - -	13077	- - CXM 94
13011	- - WS 7223	13044	- - - YJ 3272	13078	- - CXV 28
13012	- BYF 861	13045	- - BWJ 251	13079	- - CNE 952
13013	- - CLT 472	13046	- - BHP 222	13080	- DMX 829
13014	- - APW 750	13047	- - GR 2812	13081	- - AKY 408
13015	- - CLT 473	13048	- - BHP 539	13082	- - HF 5964
13016	- - - - - -	13049	- - -JP 1400	13083	- - -JT 5070
13017	- - AKU 514	13050	- - - - - -	13084	- - COB 561
13018	- - SV 1077	13051	- - - - - -	13085	- -BWK 778
		13052	- - -CNE 41		

12988

12990

DUL 120

Olympia Show 1935

A pair of exhibits, both Vanden Plas-bodied, 12988 a two-door saloon, and 12990 a tourer.

13001

Lord Inverclyde
13001 preceded his ownership of an SC Speed 25 model (qv 14645 for bio) and followed that of an SA Speed 20 model (qv 10026).

13004

John James Joass
Notable Scottish architect, later owned 4.3-litre model (qv 13182 for bio).

13011

WS 7223

Sir George Burton CBE, DL
A serial Alvis owner (qv 8765, 9834, 1334, 13501, 14630, 25870, and 27382 for bio).

13018

SV 1077

Cornercroft Ltd
Cornercroft Ltd, a prominent Coventry company used this car in one of its advertising promotions. The company, with their 'ACE' trademark, supplied the number plates for very many Alvis works-registered cars. For other examples of Alvis/Cornercroft usage there was later a 12/70 (qv 15719) and a TA 21 (qv 24677).

13011: Serial Alvis owner the late Sir George Burton, pictured here with his SD series Speed 20 saloon (with a 4.3-litre engine). (Courtesy Alvis Archive Trust)

13018: Cornercroft Ltd of Coventry was one of the Alvis company's loyal component suppliers, as evidenced in this 1935 advertisement.

13025

ACR 164

Mike Cairnes

Originally a standard Charlesworth-bodied saloon, it was, postwar, turned into a successful competition car by Mike Cairnes, a racing driver and one-

13025 is one of the Mike Cairnes' specials seen in typical 'paddock' setting. (Courtesy Ernest Shenton collection)

time Alvis agent. It later passed into the hands of another racing driver, M Gatsonides in Holland, whose company is perhaps now better known as the developer of the speed camera.

13034

BDU 796

Pressed Steel Corporation Ltd

A company car to the well-known Oxford-based supplier of pressings and complete bodies to a host of British manufacturers.

13046

BHP 222

RAC Rally 1936

Part of the Alvis team entry for the 1936 event, 13046 was driven on this occasion by *Autocar*'s A G Douglas-Clease. The other works entry was 13020, driven by Charles Follett.

13054

BOV 463

John George Haigh

Otherwise known as the acid bath murderer, Haigh placed a deposit on 13054 using the insurance money from his previous Lagonda, which somewhat mysteriously had been declared stolen but was found below the cliffs at Beachy Head in July 1948. At this time, he was a resident at London's Onslow Court Hotel where he befriended another resident, Olivia Durand-Deacon, who would become his sixth victim. One day she accepted an invitation to view Haigh's 'workshop' at Crawley, where she was shot,

13054: Though of grim quality, this image is indispensable as it the only one known to the author of serial killer John George Haigh's (the acid bath murderer) Speed 20. Photo retrieved from a television screen by Lesley Thomas. The car, however, is a twin to 13018.

and her remains disposed of in an acid bath, leaving no trace save for dental parts – which would be his undoing. Haigh's morbid life story has generated a plethora of articles, books and media programmes, making his car the most notorious Alvis of all time. For further reading I recommend two books, *Haigh, the Mind of a Murderer* by Arthur La Bern, and *The Acid Bath Murders* by David Briffett. David, former editorial director of *The West Sussex County Times*, I especially thank for providing the information which finally helped me to identify the exact car.

13061 CUU 88
14th Earl of Winchilsea
Guy Montagu George Finch-Hatton (May 28, 1885-February 10, 1939) was also Viscount Maidstone. There is another Alvis connection here in that his daughter Daphne married racing driver Whitney Straight, who owned a Silver Eagle model (qv 7903).

13066 DNW 938
Canon G S Pink
At the time of owning 13066, Canon Pink was based at Lincoln Cathedral where, it is understood, he specialised in liaising with local business and employment. Previously owned a 12/70 model, 15568.

3.5-litre

1935 to 1936
13086-13147
62 cars

Supplied as 'chassis-only' to various makers, so no 'catalogued' version.
At least 11 such took up this option, including:
Mulliner, Arnold, Bertelli, Charlesworth, Freestone & Webb, Gurney Nutting, Lancefield, Mann Egerton, Martin & King (Australia), Mayfair, and Vanden Plas

At the heart of this new model lay a major development in the company's six-cylinder engine, now with seven main bearings and cluster valve springs. The model was only ever envisaged as a subject for coachbuilders' individual designs and thus it was that the chassis chosen was a derivative of the SD Speed 20, stretched to a 10ft 7in wheelbase. Some of the designs used were quite exotic, almost French in style. Increase of weight was ever a problem in these circumstances, addressed by an even larger version of this engine, thus creating the 4.3-litre model (qv 13156-on) whilst the 3.5-litre engine was continued in a further derivative of the SD Speed 20, thus creating the Speed 25 model (qv 13326-on).

Chassis numbers
13086-13147
(3.5-litre SA – one batch)

Chassis	Reg				
13086	- - AKV 927	13109	- - - - - -	13133	- - - - - -
13087	- - CGN 160	13110	- - BDU 800	13134	- -BWK 116
13088	- - - - - -	13111	- - DEV 700	13135	- - CWB 305
13089	- -CGW 693	13112	- - BWE 815	13136	- - CRA 794
13090	- -CGW 700	13113	- - CLH 766	13137	- - WF 9009
13091	- - BWE 98	13114	- -BOM 222	13138	- -JU 9326
13092	- - BDU 888	13115	- - BRU 498	13139	- -BWK 657
13093	- - BDU 156	13116	- - - - - -	13140	- - AFS 301
13094	- -CGW 699	13117	- - CXE 368	13141	- - CYV 603
13095	- - WS 8552	13118	- - BTU 333	13142	- - - - - -
13096	- - -CJJ 416	13119	- -JY 7124	13143	- - CYP 343
13097	- - -JD 5942	13120	- - BDU 999	13144	- - BVC 217
13098	- - YS 6653	13121	- - - - - -	13145	- - - - - -
13099	- - - - - -	13122	- - CUU 1	13146	- - BOR 70
13100	- - -JB 9000	13123	- - CLJ 405	13147	- -UJ 8587
13101	- - - - - -	13124	- - - - - -	13148	- - - - - -
13102	- - - - - -	13125	- - - AUS	13149	- - - - - -
13103	- - EY 5333	13126	- - CXL 154	13150	- - - - - -
13104	- - - - - -	13127	- - - - - -	13151	- - - - - -
13105	- - - - - -	13128	- - ANP 307	13152	- - - - - -
13106	- - - - - -	13129	- - -NJ 8646	13153	- - - - - -
13107	- - CXM 98	13130	- - - - - -	13154	- - - - - -
13108	- - BPO 152	13131	- - - - - -	13155	- - - - - -
		13132	- - PV 3000		

13086 AKV 727
Alvis works car
The very first 3.5-litre model to be produced, it immediately became a press car, figuring in a road test conducted by *Motor*, and published in the issue of February 4, 1936, pages 10 to 12.

13087 CGN 160
The second 3.5-litre model made, and an exhibit at the 1935 Olympia Show. Subsequently an entry in the 1936 RAC Rally, driven by J L Sears. Photo of both lodged at the National Motor Museum.

13089
Lionel Bellairs
Aviator and serial Alvis owner (qv 12066, and 14858 for bio).

13104
Runciman family

13105
Henken Widengren
A Swedish racing driver (June 20, 1920-November 3, 1989), he was very much an Anglophile, living much of his life in Bournemouth, and previously owning the second SA Speed 20 made (qv 9268). Both cars were bodied by Bertelli, and indeed it was with A C Bertelli that Widengren finished fifth at Le Mans in 1932 in an Aston Martin.

   Prior to bodying, 13105 had been a chassis exhibit at the 1935 Olympia Show.

13105: the stirring lines of Henken Widengren's third Alvis, with coachwork by Bertelli.
(Courtesy Alan Stote)

DEV 700
13111
Evelyn Roylance Rolt
Evelyn Rolt took delivery of this unique Mayfair-bodied coupé deville, some two years after the death of her husband, a distinguished military man. It was her grandfather, Andrew Barclay Walker who endowed the now famous Walker Art Gallery to the City of Liverpool. She deserves to be famous in her own right as being the mother of racing driver Tony Rolt, who, with Duncan Hamilton won the 1953 Le Mans race in a C-type Jaguar. There exists an equestrian portrait of Evelyn (1884-1941) in oil on canvas by one Lionel Edwards, dated 1926. For other Rolt family Alvis connections (qv 2854 and 3850).

13116
Maharaja of Mayurbhanj
Pratapchandra Bhanj Deo (1901-1968) reigned from 1928 to 1947.

13116: "One careful owner?" (And several who were not?) The Maharajah of Mayurbhanj's car, seen here prior to a painstaking restoration.
(Courtesy John Fasal)

CUU 1
13122
T B Andre Ltd
Company car of the well-known automobile component manufacturer, particularly of telescopic shock-absorbers.

NJ 8646
13129
Miss K Slattery
Miss Slattery, of Newick, Sussex used her new Gurney-Nutting-bodied Alvis in some competitive events during 1936, notably being the joint Concours winner at Bexhill that year. Report and photographs of her with the car appeared in *Motor* magazine, July 7 and 14, 1936, pages 1018 and 1070.

PV 3000
13132
Charles Whitfield King
Second only perhaps to Stanley Gibbons Ltd in the field of purchase and sale of philatelic items, the walls of part of the Whitfield King premises at Morpeth House, 99 Lacey Street, Ipswich, were decorated with stamps, in lieu of wallpaper.

BWK 116
13134
Watanabe
Japanese business man Watanabe had journeyed

13147: The very last 3.5-litre model constructed was to the order of Sidney Guy.

Quality is timeless.

As a pioneer of contract hire Swan National Leasing is proud of its reputation.
Swan National Leasing has the ambition to achieve and maintain the highest standard of service in motorcar management into the 21st century.
By offering the finest range of quality services encompassed by "CoverDrive", the business drivers choice.

By innovation demonstrated through continuous technological advancement and new product concepts such as "Tax Saver", the Contract Purchase Scheme.
By speed of response through the Regional Businesses placing customer service teams closer to you for the fast reaction you need from people you know.
By pride in performance from Swan National Leasing personnel who are determined to be the best.

SWAN NATIONAL LEASING

Swan National Leasing, High Street, Newbridge, Gwent, NP1 4XE. Tel: 0495 247110. A member of T.S.B. Group.

13147: The last 3.5-litre model made was used in a Swan National Leasing advertising campaign. It is seen here with (inset) first owner Sidney Guy.

to England in 1936 with a view to purchasing a Railton, but changed his mind and ordered this Alvis, using it for a Continental holiday before taking it back to Japan. It survived WWII and was,

for a while, converted to run on Jeep wheels and tyres when the originals became unavailable. The car subsequently came into the hands of motoring journalist Shotaro Kobayashi, who has restored it to running order albeit with a tourer body replacing the by then defunct original saloon one.

This replacement body was specially constructed by Rod Jolley to be a replica of the Sir Henry Birkin Alvis racing car (qv 9900).

13137   WF 9009
Lord Hotham CBE DL JP
Henry Frederick Hotham, 7th Baron, of Dalton, North Yorkshire (August 13,1899-November 18, 1967), was educated at Winchester College and Sandhurst. He previously owned a Silver Eagle (qv 8318).

13140   AFS 301
General J Ogilvie Shepherd

13147   UJ 8567
Sidney Guy
After a career with Sunbeam, Guy (October 31, 1884-September 1971) left to form his own company which would become known world-wide mainly in the field of commercial vehicles, though it is sometimes forgotten that some cars were made in the early days – notably an advanced V8 model. 13147 is the last of the 62 3.5-litre models made, and was Sidney Guy's personal car. Trust a fine engineer to appreciate the product of another. Postwar, 13147 has featured in an advertisement for Swan National Vehicle Leasing.

Chassis numbers 13148-13155 were not used.

4.3-litre

1936 to 1940
c166 cars

13156-13185	30
13636-13655	20
14296-14345	50
14799-14871	
(less 6, enemy action)	66

Consisting of:

Charlesworth saloons randomly numbered between 14014 and 14902	70
Charlesworth DHCs 14145 and 14883	2
Vanden Plas: 20 saloons, 5 DHCs,	13
tourers randomly numbered between 3488 and 3686	20
Remainder: individual makers	

Arguably the company's most prestigious model ever, the 4.3-litre had its origins in the 3.5-litre model, built only to order in 1935 and 1936. From this was inherited the 10ft 7in wheelbase length chassis, used for the more commodious derivatives, but now, in addition there was a 'short chassis' version at 10ft 4in, shared with the Speed 25 and more usually applied to the sportier versions, not least of which was the legendary Vanden Plas tourer. This has a truly incredible survival rate, with, after 80 years, all of the bodies surviving, and 12 out of the 13 chassis made. The massive independent front suspension by transverse leaf was used for all the 4.3-litres, as was the remarkable all-synchromesh gearbox. A 'dry-sump' version of this engine was also made, and deployed in some 200 examples of the firm's armoured cars.

Chassis numbers
13156-13185
(4.3-litre SA – first batch)

Chassis	Reg
13156 - -	BKV 161
13157 - - - -	AUS
13158 - -	CYX 658
13159 - - - - - -	
13160 - -	DLT 589
13161 - -	CHP 919
13162 - - - - - -	
13163 - -	EML 461
13164 - - -	EJJ 663
13165 - -	BKV 318
13166 - -	DLM 995
13167 - -	AGB 214
13168 - - - - - -	
13169 - -	BKV 508
13170 - - - - - -	
13171 - -	BNG 1
13172 - -	AGD 638
13173 - - - - - -	
13174 - -	DRR 91
13175 - - - -	AUS
13176 - -	DMA 435
13177 - - - - - -	
13178 - -	BRM 958
13179 - -	DLU 444
13180 - -	DLK 524
13181 - -	CDU 633
13182 - - - - - -	
13183 - -	EWA 69
13184 - -	BDU 824
13185 - - -	VA 12

13156

Iliffe Publications Ltd
The first 4.3-litre, used for promotional work including submission to *Autocar* for a full road test, featured in the issue of April 23, 1937, page 781.

13158

Sir George Stanley White
Born 1882, he will forever be associated with the history of the Bristol Aeroplane Company. Following mentoring by several pioneer aviators of the day, he became managing director of the Aircraft Works in 1911, and played a major part in the development of aerial photography which would be so important in achieving supremacy in WWI. He continued to serve the company as joint deputy chairman until 1955, but still continued to attend work every day until his death in 1964 at the age of 82. The automotive connection would continue, however, in that his son would co-found the reformed Bristol Car Company in 1960, along with Tony Crook.

13160   DLT 589
Olympia Show 1936
Specially prepared by the works for the above exhibition, 13160 was subsequently sold to one Harry Rich of Camborne, Cornwall – a serial Alvis owner who also had the ex Charles Follett SC Speed 20 competition car (qv 11960) and the ex-Edwin Foden 4.3-litre (qv 13641). A photograph of this collection appears in *Autocar* of December 9, 1938.

13171   BNG 1
Welsh Rally 1937
Driven by one E H Barclay on the above event. At various times this car has also carried the registration marks UJ12, and UDB 90.

13182
John James Joass
'JJJ,' as he was known (1868-May 10, 1952) was a distinguished Scottish architect, winning the Pugin Prize in 1892, and being involved in the design of a whole host of memorable buildings such as Colchester Town Hall, the Mappin and Webb store, and the Ably Trinity Church in London's Kingsway. He was also a very keen yachtsman, turning his hand to the design of at least one such vessel.

Previously owned a Speed 20 SD model (qv 13004).

Chassis numbers
13186-13285
(Crested Eagle, TF, TG – second batch)

Chassis	Reg		
13186 - -	BRW 606	13188 - - - - - -	13191 - - - - - -
13187 - -	BOX 800	13189 - - BTU 883	13192 - - - - - -
		13190 - - BDD 758	13193 - - - DRF 62

13194 - - PV 3284	13225 - - NV 7170	13256 - - ABK 10
13195 - - ABC 456	13226 - - BVC 661	13257 - - CFS 68
13196 - - ATJ 467	13227 - - - - - -	13258 - - BFM 446
13197 - - BWK 40	13228 - - - - - -	13259 - - - - - -
13198 - - - - - -	13229 - AKY 279	13260 - - - - - -
13199 - CTO 206	13230 - - - - - -	13261 - - AAY 499
13200 - - - - - -	13231 - - - - - -	13262 - - CDU 437
13201 - - JT 6554	13232 - BLV 615	13263 - - COU 656
13202 - DRE 791	13233 - - UJ 7366	13264 - - FHK 359
13203 - - JY 7937	13234 - - - - - -	13265 - - - - - -
13204 - - - - - -	13235 - - - - - -	13266 - DWM 781
13205 - BDD 658	13236 - - - - - -	13267 - CRW 968
13206 - BVC 100	13237 - - - - - -	13268 - - BBN 505
13207 - CRB 215	13238 - - CYR 340	13269 - EXC 849
13208 - PV 3321	13239 - - - - - -	13270 - VY 9661
13209 - CYR 787	13240 - - ACA 446	13271 - BPW 505
13210 - - - - - -	13241 - AVF 990	13272 - DRW 362
13211 - - JN 7556	13242 - ASF 505	13273 - - - - - -
13212 - DRE 792	13243 - BVC 469	13274 - - - - - -
13213 - YS 7971	13244 - BSG 657	13275 - CTB 333
13214 - VL 8491	13245 - - - - - -	13276 - - - - - -
13215 - VN 9666	13246 - - - - - -	13277 - FVU 837
13216 - - - - - -	13247 - - - - - -	13278 - EXH 782
13217 - - - - - -	13248 - BVC 833	13279 - - - - - -
13218 - BVC 172	13249 - BVC 596	13280 - COR 14
13219 - - - - - -	13250 - - JP 1675	13281 - BVE 102
13220 - - - - - -	13251 - - JU 9725	13282 - - - - - -
13221 - GV 4373	13252 - BYD 960	13283 - - JR 6392
13222 - - - - - -	13253 - - - - - -	13284 - BBN 450
13223 - - - - - -	13254 - - - - - -	13285 - - - - - -
13224 - - - - - -	13255 - CRW 243	

The expedition enjoyed the support of Rotary International. Following its return, given the numerous and prominent alterations, it would have been impossible to sell it as a standard Crested Eagle and it was broken up near Colchester. A detailed account of the preparations involved appeared in the *Wimbledon Borough News* of August 27, 1965.

Chassis numbers
13286-13325
(Speed 20 SD – third batch)

Chassis	Reg				
13286 - - UD 7810		13299 - - CLJ 548		13313 - BWK 779	
13287 - BWK 767		13300 - DGW 591		13314 - BTC 481	
13288 - BWR 744		13301 - BWK 780		13315 - CYP 329	
13289 - BWK 663		13302 - BDK 325		13316 - CAR 823	
13290 - CFY 222		13303 - ERF 656		13317 - EPK 958	
13291 - CRB 622		13304 - DGW 600		13318 - DLK 525	
13292 - - JB 9535		13305 - VV 5739		13319 - BVE 305	
13293 - - JV 4852		13306 - AWP 649		13320 - BSF 637	
13294 - VY 8223		13307 - CJH 446		13321 - CTD 934	
13295 - BZ 4152		13308 - DPN 539		13322 - DLT 583	
13296 - DLK 529		13309 - DGW 599		13323 - DLK 522	
13297 - - NJ 9585		13310 - DUL 112		13324 - - AJF 294	
13298 - DLK 528		13312 - - EPA 48		13325 - BKV 317	
		13311 - DGW 597			

13249 BVC 596

Sir Rudolph Dymoke White MP

Replacing his previously-owned Crested Eagle (qv 12964 for bio).

13267 CRW 968

Grimsby Corporation

Originally part of the works Press fleet, 13267 was despatched to Grimsby where it would perform duties as that town's mayoral car. As such, its original mark was immediately replaced by the Mayoral 'AJV 123' which stayed with it until January 1955, when, upon the supply of a new mayoral vehicle, the Alvis was re-registered yet again with the mark 'FEE 414.'

13271 BPW 505

Trans-Africa Expedition 1965

An ambitious journey undertaken by two young Wimbledon men, David Belilious and Ian Woolsey, driving from London to Cape Town, through 16 countries and covering some 14,000 miles. The car had been most carefully prepared by Wimbledon automobile engineer H J Whistance, who in the past had been employed by Sir Malcolm Campbell.

13310 DUL 112

Hon C J Lyttleton

At the time when the above name was registered on the works Guarantee Card for 13310, Charles John Lyttleton (August 8, 1909-March 20, 1977) would have been well known as an accomplished cricketer. Educated at Eton and Trinity College Cambridge, he played for the university, and later for Worcestershire, where he was captain between 1936 and 1939. He served during WWII with the Expeditionary Forces in France. There would have been no reason to update the works record to the fact that in 1949 he became the 10th Viscount Cobham, KG, GCMG, GCVO, TD, PC, DL, and later still in 1957 the 9th Governor General of New Zealand.

13315 CYP 329

Brigadier R Heathcoat-Amory MC

Roderick H-A (January 30, 1907-July 21, 1998) was educated at Eton, and the Speed 20 SD purchased by him was immediately exported to India. The car is unique in that it was specially fitted from new with the 25.63hp engine, and was thus a precursor of the production Speed 25 model. Upon return from India, the car was delivered to the family seat of Knightshayes Court, near Tiverton, Devon which is now a National Trust property.

13325 BKV 317

John Thompson Motor Pressings Ltd
Famous Wolverhampton-based company, supplier of chassis frames to a large number of manufacturers. Maybe this company car was in part payment of an order.

SPEED 25

1936 to 1940
391 cars

13326-13385 SB	60
13656-13675 SB	40
14346-14495 SB	150
14549-14689 SC	141

Consisting of:
Charlesworth saloons numbered
  variously between 14036-14748   246
Charlesworth DHC numbered
  variously between 13826-14879   62
Charlesworth tourers numbered
  variously between 14811-14820   8
Cross & Ellis tourers AS 136
  (prototype), then 31001-31039   39
Remainder: independent makers

The first appearance of the 25.63hp engine had actually been in the special order only 3.5-litre model from July 1935 (qv 13086-on). It was inevitable that this advanced unit would in due course find its way into other models, and indeed one such engine was tried out in a Speed 20 SD saloon (qv 13315). This led to the phasing out of the SD series, and the birth of the charismatic Speed 25. Unlike the 3.5-litre car, the Speed 25 was very much a 'catalogued' product, with Charlesworth covering some two-thirds of the production – in saloon, coupé and tourer guises. The type still remained available in chassis form to such as Vanden Plas, Mayfair, and Lancefield. The Charlesworth tourers were actually built on Cross &

Ellis frames left over when the latter firm had gone into liquidation.

Chassis numbers
13326-13385
(Speed 25 SB – first batch)

Chassis	Reg				
13326	- - DLH 732	13346	- - -UJ 9113	13367	- - BVC 834
13327	- - DLR 673	13347	- - - - - NZ	13368	- - BAK 932
13328	- - - DLX 8	13348	- - DLT 586	13369	- - CDD 415
13329	- - DLT 676	13349	- - AGD 250	13370	- - WG 5676
13330	- - - - - -	13350	- COM 861	13371	- - EPL 392
13331	- - BKV 509	13351	- - DWJ 738	13372	- - BDG 237
13332	- - - DVK 1	13352	- - DLB 128	13373	- - CXJ 410
13333	- - EZ 6020	13353	- - AGD 253	13374	- - DLD 563
13334	- - BKV 278	13354	- - - - - -	13375	- - - DXK 4
13335	- - AGB 202	13355	- -DXU 166	13376	- - - - - -
13336	- DNB 759	13356	- DLM 303	13377	- CWM 212
13337	- -CYB 68	13357	- - -JK 6446	13378	- - BDG 287
13338	- - AAP 309	13358	-DGW 592	13379	- - CWJ 663
13339	- - YJ 4268	13359	-DGW 594	13380	-DKX 756
13340	- - CKC 775	13360	- - AYR 678	13381	- - - - - -
13341	- - DLH 162	13361	- - ECD 644	13382	- - - - - -
13342	- -DMA 205	13362	- - CXJ 203	13383	- - AGG 945
13343	- - ASG 309	13363	- - CPO 214	13384	- - -EPJ 457
13344	- - CKC 771	13364	- - -JP 2000	13385	- - DTA 265
13345	- - COL 639	13365	- - RN 5387		
		13366	- - DLK 207		

13326 DLH 732

Works development car
This, the very first Speed 25 model to be made, bore the prototype Cross & Ellis body of the four-door tourer type, which would be a significant part of production for the next four years. Its first owner was Humphrey Legge, who had served as a commander in the Royal Navy in WWI, and became chief constable of Berkshire in 1932. Later still, he

13326: The very first Speed 25 made was acquired postwar by the surrealist painter Alfred Landesman. (Courtesy Wayne Brooks)

became 8th Earl of Dartmouth. Another owner of note was the motoring journalist Jerry Ames. The car was privately exported to the United States where it became the property of the surrealist painter Alfred Landesman, who apparently traded some of his paintings to a dealer, in order to obtain the car.

13328 DLX 8
Turk Murphy
Jazz band leader and trombonist. Owned two other Alvis cars (qv 14659 and 14803 for bio).

13334 BKV 278
Sir George Burton CBE DL
A serial Alvis owner (qv 8765, 9384, 13011, 13501, 14630, 25870, and 27382 for bio). This car also featured in some of Alvis Ltd's advertising during 1936.

13343 ASG 309
Iliffe Publications Ltd
Autocar's issue of May 17, 1957, page 686, carries an account of a 1500-mile holiday trip to Eire in 13343, carrying four-up, their luggage, and a large dog. That the mission was successfully accomplished in a 20-year-old car with 117,000 miles on the clock, at an average of 18.8 miles per gallon, speaks volumes for the longevity of the type. The car used still exists.

13346 UJ 9113
Major Arthur Quilton
Replaced 13346 with an interesting TA 14 model (qv 22500).

13365 RN 5387
Sir Alexander Korda
Sir Alexander Korda, (September 16, 1893-January 23, 1956) was a Hungarian who became a British citizen in 1936. Prolific movie producer of over 70 such between 1917 and 1955, one of which, *The Third Man*, of 1949, starred another Alvis owner, Michael Rennie (qv 14856). Son, Peter Vincent Korda, also favoured Alvis, a TC 21/100 (qv 25606).

13365: This photo, taken from the now out of print biography by Paul Tabori (Oldbourne, 1959), shows Sir Alexander Korda in conversation with Orson Welles and Vivien Leigh on the set of *Anna Karenina*.

13380: The remarkable Bickerstaffe Woods Speed 25: a unique Alvis in that it utilised parallel-action sliding doors, believed originally to be a James Young patent, but applied here by Bertelli. (Courtesy Alan Stote)

13380 DKX 756
Arthur Bickerstaffe Woods
Woods (August 17, 1904-February 2, 1944) was a most interesting character who had initially studied medicine, but dropped out and joined an acting troupe. He appeared in the 1934 RKO movie *Lost Patrol* alongside one Boris Karloff, but really excelled as a producer of many films, typically *They Drive by Night* of 1938. He had also obtained an aviator's certificate on August 7, 1932, and subsequently entered service, but was killed when his Mosquito collided with a Wellington over Emsworth, Hampshire. There are those that believe that had he lived, he would have gone on to be numbered amongst the greats, such as Alfred Hitchcock.

Chassis numbers
13386-13435
(Silver Eagle SG – fourth batch)

Chassis	Reg				
13386 - - -	DPF 1	13402 - -	BER 949	13420 - -	BHP 226
13387 - - - - - -		13403 - - - - - -		13421 - - - - - -	
13388 - -	PV 2786	13404 - -	WS 8528	13422 - -	HH 8544
13389 - -	YS 5691	13405 - -	-UJ 7084	13423 -	-BWK 662
13390 - -	BCV 999	13406 - - - - - -		13424 - -	AWY 73
13391 - - - - - -		13407 - -	YS 5239	13425 - -	SY 5827
13392 - - - - - -		13408 - -	YS 5240	13426 - -	YS 6173
13393 - -	CEH 835	13409 - -	YS 5241	13427 - - - - - -	
13394 - -	BRU 333	13410 - -	MJ 9550	13428 - - - - - -	
13395 - - - - - -		13411 - -	RD 8402	13429 - - - - - -	
13396 -	-AKW 356	13412 - - - - - -		13430 - - - - - -	
13397 - - - - - -		13413 - -	CBH 953	13431 - -	BU 9274
13398 - - - - - -		13414 - -	BHP 257	13432 - -	YS 8583
OOF 428		13415 -	-CVM 616	13433 - - - - - -	
13399 - - - - - -		13416 - -	COB 382	13434 - -	AWY 458
13400 - -	CLT 475	13417 - -	CNU 617	13435 - -	VL 7870
13401 - - - - - -		13418 - - -	YJ 3548		
		13419 -	-BWK 115		

13390 BCV 999

Rosewarne family

A prominent Cornish family based near Hayle had a series of Alvis cars, which included the taking over of racing driver the Earl of Cottenham's Speed 25 (qv 14457) following his untimely death in 1943. There was also a Crested Eagle (qv 10687) and a TA 21 (qv 23987).

Rosewarne Manor still survives today as a restaurant and conference venue.

13407 YS 5239

13408 YS 5240

An impressive line-up of some of the many Rosewarne family cars. The Silver Eagle SG is at the centre, with, to its right: 13390, then 14457 (qv). (Courtesy Wearne and Rosewarne families)

13409 YS 5241

Glasgow City Police

A fleet of three identically-specified patrol cars for a force that was a frequent customer of Alvis Ltd.

13434 AWY 458

Karl Hardaker

Businessman, and popular proprietor of the Sunstreet Printing Company of Keighley, Yorkshire, Karl allowed 13434 to be used in that popular television series *It Shouldn't Happen to a Vet*. Amusingly, Karl never had any difficulty in remembering his car's chassis number, as it was the same as his birthday, 13/4/34.

The late Karl Hardaker, born April 13, 1934 with his SG Silver Eagle, chassis 13434.

Chassis numbers
13436-13485
(Firebird SA – fourth batch)

Chassis	Reg				
13436 - -	BAD 329	13452 - - - - - -		13469 - -	SN 7287
13437 - -	BCE 720	13453 - -	YS 8312	13470 - - -	JB 9650
13438 - -	-BTB 52	13454 - -	YS 7259	13471 - -	YS 7896
13439 -	BRH 454	13455 - -	BTU 418	13472 - - -	BRW 9
13440 -	BRU 379	13456 - - - - - -		13473 - - - - - -	
13441 - -	-UJ 6760	13457 - -	BRW 8	13474 - - - - - -	
13442 - - - - - -		13458 - -	ATF 446	13475 - - - - - -	
13443 - - -	BER 59	13459 - - - - - -		13476 - - - - - -	
13444 -	BRU 333	13460 - - - - - -		13477 - -	YS 8291
13445 - -	VN 8501	13461 - - - - - -		13478 - -	WS 9435
13446 - -	HS 8930	13462 - -	DUB 795	13479 -	-BWK 656
13447 - -	YS 6909	13463 - - - - - -		13480 - -	BDD 744
13448 - -	VN 8503	13464 - -	WS 8667	13481 - - - - - -	
13449 - -	VN 8502	13465 - -	BRW 456	13482 - - -	JS 5204
13450 -	-AKW 455	13466 - -	DRF 437	13483 - - - - - -	
13451 - - - - - -		13467 - -	CUB 312	13484 - -	-BWK 281
		13468 - - -	JY 8017	13485 - -	CWA 889

13445 **VN 8501**

13445 **VN 8503**

13445 **VN 8502**

North Riding Constabulary
A fleet of three identically-specified patrol cars for this Yorkshire force, based at Northallerton.

13478 **WS 9435**

William Grant Ltd
Noted whisky distillers, and for the use of its George Grant, 13478 would shortly be joined by another Alvis (qv 14623 for bio).

Chassis numbers
13486-13585
(Silver Eagle SG – fifth batch)

Chassis	Reg	Chassis	Reg	Chassis	Reg
13486	- - - - - -	13519	- - BHP 899	13553	- - - - - -
13487	- - - - - -	13520	- - CXE 184	13554	- - - - - -
13488	- - BYB 600	13521	- - BRU 944	13555	- - WS 9618
13489	- AFM 523	13522	- - -CLV 98	13556	- - CNF 149
13490	- - - - - -	13523	- - - - - -	13557	- - BVC 438
13491	- - WS 7833	13524	- - - - - -	13558	- - VY 8282
13492	- BON 800	13525	- - - - - -	13559	- - - - - -
13493	- EZ 2145	13526	- - - - - -	13560	- - AKY 651
13494	-BWK 769	13527	- GR 2960	13561	- BDD 696
13495	- - - - - -	13528	- CWA 440	13562	- -COH 769
13496	- - - - - -	13529	- CRR 147	13563	- - - - - -
13497	- - - - - -	13530	- - - - - -	13564	- - - - - -
13498	- - SX 4318	13531	- - AUE 590	13565	- - - - - -
13499	- - - - - -	13532	- ANP 900	13566	- CUF 907
13500	- - - - - -	13533	- YS 8328	13567	- - - - - -
13501	- -DHK 916	13534	- AKY 277	13568	- -JS 5298
13502	-BWK 259	13535	- - -G 911	13569	-AWD 612
13503	- - - - - -	13536	- WF 9197	13570	- -JY 8645
13504	- ANP 479	13537	- -JL 3399	13571	- BVC 444
13505	- YS 7599	13538	- WS 9298	13572	- - - - - -
13506	-DMA 106	13539	- AFM 781	13573	- DRF 775
13507	- DT 7176	13540	- - - - - -	13574	- DUB 181
13508	- - - - - -	13541	- CUB 311	13575	- EMF 138
13509	- BWJ 879	13542	- CYU 505	13576	- DTN 689
13510	- AFS 504	13543	-BWK 341	13577	- - - - - -
13511	- CRA 889	13544	-BWK 661	13578	- BVC 44
13512	- DBB 128	13545	- BVC 41	13579	- BDF 404
13513	- VH 9545	13546	- - - - - -	13580	- - - - - -
13514	- BG 4518	13547	- COA 210	13581	- VY 8518
13515	- DTW 3	13548	- - - - - -	13582	- - - - - -
13516	- - - - - -	13549	- BOD 187	13583	- -YJ 3970
13517	- FW 7453	13550	- BRK 501	13584	- DGJ 361
13518	- DT 9724	13551	- CYU 444	13585	-CWE 150
		13552	-DNW 974		

13501 **DHK 916**

Sir George Burton CBE DL
A serial Alvis owner (qv 8765, 9384, 13011, 13334, 14630, 25870, and 27382 for bio).

13501: One of the very many Sir George Burton cars. (Author's collection)

13507 **DT 7176**

Doncaster Police
A patrol car for this South Yorkshire county borough's force.

13561 **BDD 696**

Mercury House Publications
One of this group's titles was *Car Mechanics*, where, in the issue of August 1962, 13561 appeared.

13577
Sir Steven Bilsland KT MC
Steven Bilsland (September 13, 1892-December 10, 1970) was educated at St John's College Cambridge, and was head of the Glasgow bankers of that name. He was also chairman of the Scottish National Trust.

13583 **YJ 3970**

Dundee Constabulary
A patrol car for a regular customer of the Alvis factory.

13585 **CWB 150**

Sheffield Police
A patrol car for a regular customer of the Alvis factory.

Chassis numbers
13586-13635
(Firebird SA – fifth batch)

Chassis	Reg	Chassis	Reg	Chassis	Reg
13586	- - - - - -	13602	- - UN 9943	13619	- - - - - -
13587	- - BRW 983	13603	- - DRF 705	13620	- - YS 9775
13588	- - AOD 659	13604	- -BWK 434	13621	- - - - - -
13589	- - AFS 427	13605	- - -BVC 46	13622	- - AKY 925
13590	- - - - - -	13606	- - CRB 363	13623	- - - - - -
13591	- - - - - -	13607	- - BVC 216	13624	- - CUF 909
13592	- -BWK 768	13608	- - -BVC 43	13625	- - BVC 468
13593	- -BWK 342	13609	- - - - - -	13626	- - BVC 439
13594	- - COA 208	13610	- - BVC 215	13627	- - AGD 312
13595	- - FW 8046	13611	- - AFS 427	13628	- - CYX 653
13596	- - - - - -	13612	- - -BVC 42	13629	- - BFG 442
13597	- - CKA 130	13613	- - CRB 859	13630	- - BTE 33
13598	- - DLD 859	13614	- - BVC 443	13631	- - - - - -
13599	- - YS 9763	13615	- - YS 9543	13632	- - DLH 528
13600	- -BWK 655	13616	- - FW 8106	13633	- - - DGC 7
13601	- - - - - -	13617	- - WS 9990	13634	- - - - - -
		13618	- - - - - -	13635	- - GS 6656

13601
Montague Burton Ltd

With the slogan 'The Tailor of Taste,' outfitters Montague Burton once had a presence on Britain's high streets which numbered in excess of 500 stores. The main factory, however, was based in Leeds, where 13601 was delivered in June 1936. Ten years later, the firm enjoyed a boom, with the supply of 'de-mob' suits to returning military personnel. The original registration mark of this car has not yet been established, but for some reason it was re-registered as MUB 726 when it left the firm's service in April 1949.

13635 **GS 6656**
Pattullo Family

With a history going back to 1840, this well-known Scottish farming family based at Eassie Farm, Glamis, Angus, have specialised in the production of asparagus, directly supplying high-class restaurants throughout the country. Their sea kale is also a sought-after product. This Firebird tourer purchased by them just before Christmas 1936 is actually the very last Firebird made. Many years later they would purchase one of the exceptionally rare Willowbrook-bodied TC 108/G models.

Chassis numbers
13636-13655
(4.3-litre SA – second batch)

Chassis	Reg	Chassis	Reg	Chassis	Reg
13636	- - AYS 692	13637	- - - ETA 1	13639	- - ASF 458
		13638	- - FGF 384	13640	- - DUL 601

Chassis	Reg	Chassis	Reg	Chassis	Reg
13641	- - - ERF 7	13646	- - CVP 537	13651	- - EFC 34
13642	- - - - - -	13647	- - DLT 822	13652	- - CDU 699
13643	- - DXP 180	13648	- - CHP 81	13653	- - - - - -
13644	- - ACO 112	13649	- - DPP 59	13654	- - CRW 294
13645	- - FMP 888	13650	- - CHP 597	13655	- - ASG 22

13637
Lord Carrington

Full title, Peter Alexander Rupert Carrington, KG, GC, MP, CH, MC, PL, DL was born June 6, 1919 and died July 9, 2018.

He served under six prime ministers: Churchill, Eden, Macmillan, Douglas-Home, Heath, and Thatcher. Upon leaving Westminster politics he became the sixth Secretary-General of NATO. 13637 was at least his third Alvis (qv 10945 and 14396). He wrote an autobiography called *Reflect on Things Past* published by Collins 1988.

13641
Edwin Richard Foden

A familiar name in the production of commercial vehicles, Edwin Foden (1876-1950) applied his personal number plate when taking delivery of 13641. These initials would also appear upon a separately branded line of 'ERF' trucks. Foden lived in Blackpool, and upon acquiring a Bentley, put ERF 7 on that, with the Alvis being re-registered as FV 9383. A photograph of the car in this latter form appears in *Autocar*, issue of December 9, 1938.

He also owned a Speed 25 model (qv 14676).

13649 **DPP 59**
Lord Birkett KC, MP, PC

Norman Birkett – 1st Baron Birkett – (September 6, 1883-February 10, 1962) was educated at Barrow-in-Furness Grammar School and Emmanuel College Cambridge, rising to president of the Cambridge Union Society in 1910. A pleasant task during his year in that office was that of welcoming Theodore Roosevelt on his visit to Cambridge. There followed a most notable career in law, being called to the Bar in 1913, and being created Judge of the Kings Bench Division in 1941. In between, he served twice as a Liberal Member of Parliament – Nottingham East 1923-24 and 1929-1931. Mostly remembered as British Judge at the Nuremberg Trials following WWII. More recently, having promulgated a spirited defence of the public's right to access to Ullswater, their Yacht Club, in gratitude, still awards a Lord Birkett Memorial Trophy. Previously owned a Speed 20 SD model (qv 11805).

13650 | CHP 597
Iliffe Publications Ltd
Used by *Autocar* in its *Used Cars on the Road* series, numbered 63 in the issue of December 11, 1953. When new, this car, first owned by Douglas Brock, had attended the tenth Car Mart Golf meeting, and a photograph of it at that event appears in the issue of *Motor*, July 6, 1937, page 1010.

13652 | CDU 699
RAC Rally 1937
Originally part of the works press fleet, 13652 was initially deployed on the 1937 RAC Rally, driven by *Autocar*'s technical editor A G Douglas-Cleave. It was later used on the Welsh Rally, this time driven by H E Symons. When some six months old, it was sold to squadron leader Denys Gilley, of Torquay, by which time it could be considered as fully 'run-in.'

Chassis numbers
13656-13695
(Speed 25 SB – second batch)

Chassis	Reg	Chassis	Reg	Chassis	Reg
13656	- - -BVC 45	13669	- - EHK 549	13683	- - CHP 82
13657	- - BVE 630	13670	- - EZ 5228	13684	- - - - - -
13658	- - DLL 210	13671	- - - - NZ	13685	- - MG 5174
13659	- - -DUL 60	13672	- - DNA 266	13686	- - - FPE 11
13660	-DKX 618	13673	- - BKV 277	13687	- - ASF 446
13661	- - DKC 731	13674	- - DLA 913	13688	- - DXT 95
13662	- - - - - -	13675	- - ASF 461	13689	- - DLT 584
13663	- - - FPE 6	13676	- - - - - -	13690	-DMB 688
13664	-DUM 978	13677	- - EGT 686	13691	- - - - - -
13665	- - - - - -	13678	- - BDG 662	13692	- - CDU 823
13666	- - -AJF 477	13679	- - CDU 822	13693	- - - - - -
13667	- - HS 9608	13680	- - - - - -	13694	- - - - - -
13668	- - CKD 944	13681	- - -DFY 66	13695	- - EBB 723
		13682	- - DLT 587		

13656 | BVC 45
Iliffe Publications Ltd
The publisher of *Autocar* figure prominently in the Alvis story, being a frequent borrower of the marque's products. One of the more strenuous exercises was when 13656 was taken on a 2000-mile trip to the South of France and back, fully reported in the issue of February 26, 1937. Most interestingly, upon leaving Boulogne on the southbound

13656: From the collection of the late Ernest Shenton, who once owned the car, this photograph emanates from *Autocar* files, when the magazine used it for a continental tour in 1936.

journey, the travellers were joined on part of the way by a certain Miss Dorothy Stanley-Turner, in an MG, who would later make a significant contribution to Alvis lore (qv 14867, 23804, and 23831).

13656 would leave the Alvis Press fleet in May 1937, when it was sold without warranty to the Cheshire County Police. Sometime thereafter it lost its distinctive 'BVC 45' registration mark, and was re-allocated 'TRE 180.'

13659 | DUL 60
Robert Sandeman
Aviator Robert Hugh Malcolm Sandeman was born June 18, 1908 into an affluent stockbroking

family and was educated at Malvern College and in Switzerland. He became a senior partner in the firm in 1936, coinciding with the start of his interest in flying. He purchased in February 1937, directly from de Havilland, a Hornet Moth G-AETC (8109). There is a fascinating account of Robert's solo flight to India in the Moth Club's Journal *Enterprise* (no 105 of 1999). Robert had purchased Alvis 13659 at almost exactly the same time as the Moth, and when he married in April 1940, took the car to France for his honeymoon. Sadly, the German invasion at this time precipitated the couple's hasty return by ship, leaving the Alvis behind, where it was most likely commandeered. In wartime service, Robert joined RAF Ferry Command, flying Catalinas, but was killed November 12, 1942 at Mulgrave, Nova Scotia, hitting a rescue vessel which had cut across his path when landing.

13661 **DKC 731**
Liverpool City Police
A patrol car for the Liverpool force, and the newest (and largest) of its 1937 squad, which included one each of Ford V8, Lagonda, MG, Riley and Wolseley, plus a pair of 'waterfall' Triumph Dolomites.

13668 **CKD 944**
Sir John Brocklebank
With a history going back to 1785, and a Whitehaven shipyard that operated until 1865, Brocklebank was a shipping line whose later ships were built at Harland & Wolff. The cargo part of the business was based in Liverpool, and there were subsequent mergers involving the Anchor Line, Wells Line, and Cunard. There is much Brocklebank Line history at the Liverpool Museum.

13685 **MG 5174**
Francis de Wolff
Well-known actor Francis de Wolff (January 7, 1913-April 18, 1984) worked with such notable contemporaries as Errol Flynn, Sean Connery, Gregory Peck, and Orson Welles. His credits include appearances in *Treasure Island*, *The Avengers*, *The Paul Temple Mysteries*, *Maigret*, and, on radio, took part in the very first *Dick Barton, Special Agent*, which became an extremely popular series.

13691
Lionel Bellairs
Notable aviator and serial Alvis owner, previously owned Speed 20 (qv 13084) and later a 4.3-litre (qv 14858 for bio).

Chassis numbers
13696-13701
(Crested Eagle, TK – one batch)

Chassis	Reg				
13696	- - ACA 829	13698	- - - - - -	13701	- - - - - -
13697	- - - - - -	13699	- - CRW 241		
		13700	- - DT 8705		

Chassis numbers 13702-13745 were not used.

Chassis numbers
13746-13775
(Crested Eagle, TA, TB – first batch)

Chassis	Reg				
13746	- - - - - -	13756	- - MG 5065	13767	- - - - - -
13747	- - CRO 689	13757	- - EML 943	13768	- - CRW 900
13748	- - CXJ 224	13758	- - DKO 971	13769	- - - - - -
13749	- - DXX 55	13759	- - CDU 662	13770	- - - - - -
13750	- - - - - -	13760	- - CBJ 362	13771	- - FV 9393
13751	- - - YJ 4255	13761	- - EKR 137	13772	- - COP 226
13752	- - - - - -	13762	- - DS 2084	13773	- - DBH 921
13753	- - -EPJ 454	13763	- - ETW 394	13774	- - CDU 438
13754	- - SN 8048	13764	- - DXR 270	13775	- - - - - -
13755	- - DLH 847	13765	- - - - - -		
		13766	- -BWU 323		

13753: In Gilbert and Sullivan parlance, this Crested Eagle really was 'the very model of a modern major general.' (Courtesy the late Tim Harding)

13753   EPJ 454

Major-General Sir Edward Northey

Edward Northey, GCMG, CB, JP (1868-1953) was a remarkable military man whose career would fill a volume in itself. He was educated at Eton and Sandhurst and commissioned in the Kings Royal Rifle Corps. He saw active service, participating in the battles at Ladysmith, Mons, and Ypres. He rose rapidly through the Army's meritocracy, becoming ADC to King George V in 1915, Governor of Kenya in 1920, and High Commissioner of Zanzibar in 1922. He was present at the Coronation of King George VI in 1937. He resided for much of his life at Woodcote House, and those desirous of knowing more about him are directed to www.epsomandewellhistoryexplorer.org.uk. Thus, in 'Gilbert and Sullivan' parlance, 13755 was truly the very model of a modern major-general.

Previously owned a TG 12/50 model, bought second-hand in January 1930 (qv 4719).

13759   CDU 662

Lancashire County Constabulary

This Crested Eagle was the chief constable's official car. The force was also using a Speed 25 model as a patrol car at about the same time (qv 14394).

13759 was evidently well-used before its sale as 'used' to Lancashire, as it had been supplied to Temple Press Ltd for an appraisal, which appeared in *Motor*, issue of March 9, 1937, page 229.

SILVER CREST

1936 to 1940
420 cars

13776-13875	100
13896-14295	300
16149-16170	20

Consisting of saloons:

Holbrook four-light 4000-4255	256
Holbrook six-light 4521-4596	75
Cross & Ellis DHC 1501-1557	57
Charlesworth DHC 14792-14804	12
Remainder (prototype, Martin Walter, Maltby, Vanden Plas, etc)	20

Evidently somewhat disenchanted with his role in the eponymous company formed with his brothers Fred and Frank, following the merger with Daimler and BSA, George Lanchester left to work for Alvis in 1936, there devising a successor to the popular Silver Eagle. This time both 16.95hp (TF) and 19.82hp (TH) were offered. These engines, whilst having the same bore and stoke as other models in the Alvis range, were quite different, with improved casting techniques now allowing crankcase and block to be combined. Independent suspension was used at the front – a divided version of the by then familiar transverse leaf layout. Thus it was possible to move the engine fractionally forward, affording more general passenger accommodation. Fair to say that in the Silver Crest the emphasis was more 'touring,' than 'sporting.' George Lanchester's second design of this period was the 12/70 (qv 16149-16170, page 154), a four-cylinder car using some engine parts in common with the 19.82hp Silver Crest.

Chassis numbers
13776-13875
(Silver Crest TF, TH – first batch)

Chassis	Reg	Chassis	Reg	Chassis	Reg
13776	- - BWK 909	13810	- - - - - -	13843	- - KS 7448
13777	- - BKV 395	13811	- - - - - -	13844	- -DMB 194
13778	- - SN 7595	13812	- - -ABK 60	13845	- - - - - -
13779	- - - - - -	13813	- - - - - -	13846	- - AGE 142
13780	- - ASC 703	13814	- - BTE 534	13847	- - AJB 300
13781	- - AGB 268	13815	- - - - AUS	13848	- - - - - -
13782	- - - - - -	13816	- - - - - -	13849	- - CRU 660
13783	- - CS 5702	13817	- - - - - -	13850	- - - - - -
13784	- - - - - -	13818	- - -JS 5500	13851	- - - - - -
13785	- - JX 5349	13819	- - - - - -	13852	- - PV 4214
13786	- - - - - -	13820	- - DXB 609	13853	- - ERF 150
13787	- - CRU 170	13821	- - DLT 631	13854	- - - - - -
13788	- - ZA 9602	13822	- - - - - -	13855	- - ABK 620
13789	- - - - - -	13823	- - GR 3766	13856	- - - SO 1
13790	- - - - - -	13824	- -DMB 194	13857	- - - - - -
13791	- - - - - -	13825	- - CAH 19	13858	- - DAT 232
13792	- - CFJ 555	13826	- - BAH 958	13859	- - - - - -
13793	- - - - - -	13826	- - BAH 958	13860	- - ASR 411
13794	- - -CRU 81	13827	- - VS 3390	13861	- - - - - -
13796	- - - - - -	13828	- - - - - -	13862	- - - - - -
13797	- - - - - -	13829	- - - - - -	13863	- - CRW 899
13798	- - JM 2495	13830	- - EPU 478	13865	- - FRE 458
13799	- - - - - -	13831	- - DLK 530	13866	- - - - - -
13800	- -AMR 865	13832	- - - - - -	13867	- - GR 5810
13801	- - DTA 487	13833	- - - - - -	13868	- - DRB 430
13802	- - - - - -	13834	- - - - - -	13869	- - DXA 137
13803	- - ABK 500	13835	- - ASF 457	13870	- - CFM 219
13804	- - CVO 236	13836	- - CRU 418	13871	- - EPU 616
13805	- - -DLT 4	13837	- - - - - -	13872	- - AGE 768
13806	- - ABK 395	13838	- - CDU 824	13873	- - - AUS
13807	- - - - - -	13839	- - DXA 834	13874	- - - - - -
13808	- - APM 554	13840	- - - - - -	13875	- - EBB 725
13809	- - - - - -	13841	- - BKU 842		
		13842	- - -YJ 4555		

13777 BKV 395

13778 SN 7595
13779

London & Glasgow Motor Shows 1936

A trio of Silver Crests, prepared by the works for
the 1936 show season, marked the introduction
of this model. The trio comprised one each of the
advertised availability of four-light saloon, six-light
saloon, and drophead coupé. The coupé (13778)
survives at the time of writing.

13812 ABK 60

Winifred Pink

Winifred Pink was a well-known competition driver
during the 1920s, especially at Shelsley Walsh,
originally driving an Aston Martin there in 1924,
but in 1927 changing to an Alvis (qv 5219), and
winning the Presidents Cup. The following year
she won the 1.5-litre class with a time of 68 seconds
– a performance witnessed by Prime Minister
Stanley Baldwin, who was amongst the spectators.
Ten years later, having retired from competitive
driving, she bought this somewhat more staid
Silver Crest.

13865 FRE 458

Iliffe Publications Ltd

Whilst most would not regard the Silver Crest as
a sports car, this did not apparently prevent this
example's inclusion in *Autocar*'s *Talking of Sports
Cars* issue no 137, of January 29, 1943.

Chassis numbers
13876-13895
(Crested Eagle TA, TB – second batch)

Chassis	Reg				
13876 - - DXA 356	13882 - - DDU 316	13889 - - -ADY 41
13877 - - CFS 658	13883 - - - - - -	13890 - - - - - -
13878 - - BOU 592	13884 - - - - - -	13891 - - - - - -
13879 - - - - - -	13885 - - - - - -	13892 - - BBN 529
13880 - - - - - -	13886 - - -JT 9826	13893 - - CTT 169
13881 - - DND 953	13887 - - BET 777	13894 - - -CYC 61
	13888 - - DTE 771	13895 - - - - - -

Chassis numbers
13896-14295
(Silver Crest TF, TH – second batch)

Chassis	Reg				
13896 - - - - - -	13901 - - - - - -	13907 - - - - - F
13897 - - JX 5133	13902 - - - - - -	13908 - - - - - -
13898 - - - - - -	13903 - - FMP 481	13909 - - - - - -
13899 - - -JG 9090	13904 - - VV 6209	13910 - -AMO 988
13900 - - ANJ 522	13905 - - - - - -	13911 - - CHP 84
	13906 - - - - - -	13912 - - -JT 7979

Taken in 1937, at the time the Silver Crest was entering series production, this works photograph shows a cheerful team of employees at London's Great West Road services station. Of particular interest is the figure seated front row on the far right. This is Sam Kydd (1915-1982) who, from 1946, would take up acting, featuring in over 200 movies, and around 1000 plays. Autobiography: *For You the War is Over* (ISBN: 0-05974-005-6).

13913 - - - - - -	13982 - DXW 740	14051 - - - - - -	14120 - - FAE 620	14179 - - - - - -	14238 - - - - - -
13914 - - - - - -	13983 - - - DFJ 3	14052 - - - - - -	14121 - - - - - -	14180 - - ELH 949	14239 - - DTF 812
13915 - - ASG 676	13984 - - - - - -	14053 - - - - - -	14122 - - HD 6703	14181 - - - - - -	14240 - - JFC 888
13916 - - CWK 6	13985 - - CTB 840	14054 - - -JP 3097	14123 - - CKV 976	14182 - - FKO 374	14241 - - -EAD 2
13917 - - - - - -	13986 - -CWK 372	14055 - - - - AUS	14124 - - CBK 80	14183 - - BS 6420	14242 - - ABX 488
13918 - - DKR 544	13987 - - - - - -	14056 - - - - - -	14125 - - DTB 767	14184 - - - - - -	14243 - - FEL 759
13919 - - - - - -	13988 - - - - - -	14057 - - - - - -	14126 - - - - - -	14185 - - ELN 300	14244 - - - - - -
13920 - - DEL 269	13989 - - AYS 179	14058 - DWM 316	14127 - - EEL 912	14186 - - DYA 433	14245 - -DWK 445
13921 - - ASG 834	13990 - -CWK 963	14059 - - CKU 998	14128 - - EKO 565	14187 - -DRW 495	14246 - - EVC 503
13922 - - CHP 83	13991 - - ADR 1	14060 - - GUB 609	14129 - - - - - -	14188 - - - - - -	14247 - -DWK 821
13923 - - DAL 269	13992 - - ACJ 445	14061 - - AHS 409	14130 - APM 872	14189 - - ELL 488	14248 - - HPU 902
13924 - - -YS 123	13993 - - VY 9737	14062 - - - - - -	14131 - - EYE 939	14190 - - - - - -	14249 - - EDU 90
13925 - - - - - -	13994 - - - - - -	14063 - - - - - -	14132 - - - - - -	14191 - - - - - -	14250 - - - - - -
13926 - - - - - -	13995 - - CTT 905	14064 - - - - - -	14133 - - EXC 846	14192 - - CKU 94	14251 - - - - - -
13927 - - FPC 605	13996 - - VL 9691	14065 - - HH 9499	14134 - - - - - -	14193 - - ACL 912	14252 - - FBH 308
13928 - - CVC 160	13997 - - AFN 261	14066 - - BYG 714	14135 - - -JP 3364	14194 - - - - - -	14253 - - DKV 523
13929 - - - - - -	13998 - - BAP 880	14067 - - DTB 850	14136 - - FWA 38	14195 - -CUO 571	14254 - - BHS 17
13930 - - FMP 835	13999 - - -EJ 5325	14068 - - BGE 854	14137 - - - - - -	14196 - - - - AUS	14255 - - - - - -
13931 - - TK 9571	14000 - - BYG 225	14069 - - CWP 429	14138 - - GS 7696	14197 - - CS 7766	14256 - - BPM 494
13932 - - - - - -	14001 - - SN 7999	14070 - - - - - -	14139 - -DRW 699	14198 - - - - - -	14257 - - - - - -
13933 - - AVL 264	14002 - - - - - -	14071 - - - - - -	14140 - - - - - -	14199 - - BGE 61	14258 - - FRA 640
13934 - - CRW 36	14003 - -CWK 857	14072 - - CKV 243	14141 - - AAV 725	14200 - - ELR 81	14259 - - - - - -
13935 - - VD 7910	14004 - - BUS 235	14073 - -DRW 208	14142 - - - - - -	14201 - - FZ 3	14260 - - FYU 448
13936 - - - - - -	14005 - - - - - -	14074 - - CVE 399	14143 - - - - - -	14202 - - ARV 770	14261 - -GWB 856
13937 - -BKW 446	14006 - - - - - -	14075 - - -EAT 5	14144 - - ELE 849	14203 - - - - - -	14262 - - FLC 935
13938 - - CDF 761	14007 - - - - - -	14076 - - DDU 830	14145 - -DWK 880	14204 - - GPB 833	14263 - - - - - -
13939 - - CRW 242	14008 - - EHU 9	14077 - - GHK 285	14146 - - BYS 764	14205 - - BSF 374	14264 - - CKY 389
13940 - - ENU 778	14009 - - -JR 8131	14078 - - - - - -	14147 - - BGD 283	14206 - - GPD 959	14265 - - ERU 653
13941 - - COT 212	14010 - - - - AUS	14079 - - - - - -	14148 - - FJO 378	14207 - - EPT 838	14266 - - FLA 647
13942 - - - - - -	14011 - - -CVC 2	14080 - - - - - -	14149 - - BKY 997	14208 - - GL 6402	14267 - - - - - -
13943 - - RC 5097	14012 - - - - - -	14081 - - - - - -	14150 - - - - - -	14209 - - - - - -	14268 - - - - - -
13944 - - - - - -	14013 - - ELL 476	14082 - - BGG 589	14151 - - - AUS	14210 - - - - AUS	14269 - - -JR 9006
13945 - - - - - -	14014 - - FGJ 802	14083 - - - - - -	14152 - - ELH 948	14211 - - BGG 590	14270 - - HPE 313
13946 - -DYW 264	14015 - - ERA 688	14084 - - EMB 356	14153 - - BUS 379	14212 - - DHP 67	14271 - - - - - -
13947 - - - - - -	14016 - - AVY 900	14085 - - - - - -	14154 - - - - - -	14213 - - - - - -	14272 - - - - - -
13948 - - HF 6944	14017 - - - - - -	14086 - - - - - -	14155 - - EMA 470	14214 - - - - - -	14273 - - - - - -
13949 - - -JT 7388	14018 - - EUU 660	14087 - - -BYS 65	14156 - - ETT 389	14215 - - EUU 656	14274 - - AST 603
13950 - - - EIR	14019 - - - - - -	14088 - - DUP 739	14157 - - - - - -	14216 - - EOL 917	14275 - - FZ 3814
13951 - - - - - -	14020 - - - - - -	14089 - - VS 3669	14158 - - ENU 795	14217 - - DHP 773	14276 - - DKU 496
13952 - -CRW 805	14021 - - - - - -	14090 - - BGA 902	14159 - - - - AUS	14218 - - - - - -	14277 - - FLX 192
13953 - - - - - -	14022 - - - - - -	14091 - - AUN 530	14160 - - - - - -	14219 - - CDL 428	14278 - - GRF 745
13954 - - CAO 937	14023 - - - - - -	14092 - - ELD 669	14161 - - - - - -	14220 - - - - - -	14279 - - - - AUS
13955 - - -FA 6761	14024 - - -JE 3674	14093 - - -FFJ 781	14162 - - BCX 222	14221 - - LMC 891	14280 - - BPM 961
13956 - - -JS 5505	14025 - -CKW 977	14094 - - BTD 72	14163 - - - ZA	14222 - - - - - -	14281 - - CUY 660
13957 - - AYS 208	14026 - - AUN 149	14095 - - CAB 623	14164 - -CWR 685	14223 - - CN 8675	14282 - - FYP 530
13958 - -CWK 121	14027 - - - - - -	14096 - - - - - -	14165 - - -JN 9865	14224 - - EAL 622	14283 - - FGJ 810
13959 - - - - - -	14028 - - - - - -	14097 - - CKV 461	14166 - - - - AUS	14225 - -CBM 260	14284 - - - - - -
13960 - - BGA 451	14029 - - - - - -	14098 - - - - - -	14167 - - -ELJ 194	14226 - - DAK 69	14285 - - FRA 641
13961 - - - - - -	14030 - - BUE 127	14099 - - CS 8909	14168 - - CKV 895	14227 - - DHP 223	14286 - - - - - -
13962 - - - - - -	14031 - - - - - -	14100 - - - - - -	14169 - - DOP 728	14228 - - BGG 715	14287 - - FYU 447
13963 - - CHP 598	14032 - - - - - -	14101 - - ENU 647	14170 - - BHR 790	14229 - - GS 8024	14288 - - - - - -
13964 - - - - - -	14033 - - CVC 159	14102 - - GKK 554	14171 - GMX 711	14230 - - DAO 168	14289 - - - - - -
13965 - - GR 4192	14034 - - -CVC 4	14103 - - - C 1196	14172 - - - - - -	14231 - - XS 4845	14290 - - FAL 768
13966 - - - - - -	14035 - - - - - -	14104 - - ACJ 810	14173 - - - - - -	14232 - - - - - -	14291 - - ELV 867
13967 - - EZ 7888	14036 - - ACX 985	14105 - - - - - -	14174 - - GL 5419	14233 - - DPX 777	14292 - -DKV 690
13968 - - -FA 6745	14037 - - RC 5429	14106 - - CVE 721	14175 - - - - - -	14234 - - ENE 41	14293 - - EDU 179
13969 - - EZ 7888	14038 - - - - - -	14107 - - BUS 492	14176 - - - - - -	14235 - - HD 6693	14294 - - VS 3927
13970 - - CWK 5	14039 - - - - - -	14108 - - CKV 752	14177 - - - - - -	14236 - - DSM 639	14295 - - - - - -
13971 - - BUE 45	14040 - - BKY 379	14109 - - EWJ 234	14178 - - - - - -	14237 - - - - - -	
13972 - - - - - -	14041 - - CSP 114	14110 - - CKV 141			
13973 - -CWK 614	14042 - - DYX 709	14111 - - EVC 689			
13974 - - HS 9925	14043 - - DTV 821	14112 - - - - - -			
13975 - -CWK 122	14044 - - - - - -	14113 - - DPX 650			
13976 - - - - - -	14045 - - CKV 462	14114 - - - - - -			
13977 - - DYO 415	14046 - - DLJ 167	14115 - -CWK 166			
13978 - - - - - -	14047 - - - - - -	14116 - - GPG 911			
13979 - - CTT 792	14048 - - - - - -	14117 - - BYS 174			
13980 - - - - - -	14049 - - DKB 848	14118 - - EBH 937			
13981 - - - - - -	14050 - - FUG 20	14119 - - - - - -			

TK 9571

13931
Col H Pomeroy-Bond DL

A delightful one-off small limousine with division,
13931 was built by Cross & Ellis to the order of
Dorset's then Deputy Lieutenant, and a well-known

local figure. It's worth mentioning that he had joined the Dorchester bench of Magistrates in 1915, where a senior member at that time was that noted chronicler of Dorset life, novelist Thomas Hardy OM. Bond had previously owned a Silver Eagle model (qv 9079).

14033 CVC 159
Temple Press Ltd
Motor-featured road test car – issue of December 28, 1937, page 987.

14089 VS 3669
Greenock Police
One of three of this force's Silver Crests (qv 14294 and 16164).

14122 HD 6703
Dewsbury Police
A patrol car supplied to this Yorkshire force.

14128 EKO 565
Sir Eustace Borrowes
An Irish Peer (1866-1939), the 11th Baronet, then living in Hythe, Kent, his Silver Crest had one of the unusual four-door convertible bodies, usually electric in operation, that coachbuilder Maltby/Redfern of Folkestone developed for quite a number of British, and indeed American car chassis. Ingenious, but somewhat ungainly in the smaller applications of the design, of which this was one.

14178
London Motor Show 1937
An Olympia Show exhibit.

14186 DYA 433
Dr Howard Alexander Bell
Howard Bell (1888-1974) was born at Wrington, Somerset, studied medicine at Cambridge, and in due course returned to Wrington where he served as a GP for over thirty years. He had served in WWI with the RAMC and survived the battle of Passchendaele in 1917. It is for his hobby, however, that he will be best remembered. That hobby was fly-fishing, spending much time at the

nearby Blagdon water. He devoted a lifetime to the study of fish, their movements and habitats, and the manufacture of artificial flies. Never a man to seek out publicity or recognition of his work, his observations have proved of incalculable value to anglers ever since. The reader is thus referred to the book *Reservoir Trout Fishing* by Adrian V W Freer (Bell's biographer) published 2010 by Crowood Press. Dr Bell's Silver Crest saloon (which still survives), was used for many trips to Scotland in furtherance of his hobby.

14194
Raja of Khetri
Raja Shri Sardar Singh Bahadur (March 16, 1920-February 23, 1987) was educated at Montreux, Mayo College, and Corpus Christi College Cambridge (MA Cantab). He was called to the Bar in 1941 and became the Indian Ambassador to Laos in 1959. Leaving no obvious heir, he created the Khetri Trust in 1985 for the furtherance of education in his native country.

14195 CUO 571
Salmons (coachbuilder)
One of coachbuilder Salmons lines (later Tickford), was the insertion of a fully roll-back top into the roof panel of four-door saloons of a number of different makes, leaving the doors and their apertures unaltered. The only known Salmons conversion of a Silver Crest Holbrook saloon, 14195 was supplied to a Dr Dixey of Barnstaple.

14207 EPT 838
Durham Police
One of a pair of Silver Crests for the Durham force. For the other (qv 16165). For other pertinent Durham force deliveries at this time (qv 14384), a Speed 25 tourer for patrol use, and 14628, also a Speed 25, but a saloon specifically allocated for the Chief Constable's use.

14231 XS 4845
Paisley Police
A patrol car for this Scottish force.

14251
London Motor Show 1938
One of the Olympia Show exhibits of that year.

There is a mystery in that whilst Alvis works' records note it as being bodied by Van den Plas, it does not show up in the Vanden Plas record, though their numbers 3653, 3654, and 3655 mention Alvis Ltd, but 'not executed.'

14328 - - ELK 366	14334 - - - - IND	14340 - - DON 313
14329 - - - - AUS	14335 - - - - IND	14341 - - - - AUS
14330 - - EGP 759	14336 - - ETT 576	14342 - - ETC 542
14331 - -DRW 763	14337 - - -ELH 6	14343 - -FGW 409
14332 - - - - - -	14338 - - EWA 255	14344 - - CTX 9
14333 - DOM 655	14339 - -CKW 479	14345 - - EWJ 411

14254 — BHS 17
Scottish Motor Show 1938
This was one of the Kelvin Hall Exhibition cars in that year, on the J H Galt stand.

14259
Sir Sidney Sitwell

14261 — GWB 856
Bachelors Ltd
A household name in tinned foods, especially peas, this long-established Sheffield Company became part of Unilever in 1943. 14261 was actually sourced from the Norwich Alvis agent, where it had been in stock for quite a few months.

14262 — FLC 935
Viscount Ashbrook
Desmond Lowarch Edward Flower (July 9, 1905-December 5, 1995), 10th Viscount Ashbrook KCVO, MBE, JP, DL, RA, TA. An Irish Peer, he was educated at Eton and Balliol. Served during WWII in the Royal Artillery, becoming Major. Seat, Arley Hall, Cheshire.

14294 — VS 2927
Greenock Police
One of three of this force's Silver Crests (qv 14089 and 16164).

Chassis numbers
14296-14345
(4.3-litre SA, SC – third batch)

Chassis Reg		
14296 - - CKV 642	14306 - - - - - -	14317 - - EGT 51
14297 - -BWX 480	14307 - - FEV 355	14318 - - DTB 221
14298 - - EXK 80	14308 - - DXB 608	14319 - - UD 8768
14299 - - - - - -	14309 - - EXT 637	14320 - - -AJY 33
14300 - DXW 737	14310 - - -AJU 2	14321 - - ELT 382
14301 - - DUL 113	14311 - - ELH 941	14322 - - DXJ 496
14302 - - - - - -	14312 - -DYW 300	14323 - - -SS 4747
14303 - -DXU 870	14313 - - - - AUS	14324 - - - - AUS
14304 - -DOK 253	14314 - - - - AUS	14325 - -CWK 534
14305 - - DUL 111	14315 - - ABT 322	14326 - - DOE 899
	14316 - - DYW 68	14327 - - CCE 980

14298 — EXK 80
Erwin Goldschmidt
Goldschmidt must have cut quite a distinctive figure as an undergraduate at Christ Church College, Oxford, with this brand new 4.3-litre convertible, uniquely bodied by Abbey. However, having been born in 1917 into a highly influential and wealthy German-Jewish family, he was used to such luxuries, having been presented with, as a child, one of those Type 52 miniature Bugatti cars by his father. Goldschmidt Senior was an avid collector of fine works of art, which would be seized when the Nazis came to power, but which Erwin would be mostly successful in recovering some years later. He moved to the USA in 1941, enrolling in the army and serving in the OSS. A career in motor racing followed, commencing with a Type 327 BMW, and notably winning the Watkins Glen Grand Prix in a Cadillac-engined Allard. In 1954, Wolverhampton manufacturer Cyril Kieft would build a special De Soto-engined sports-racing car for Goldschmidt, possibly precipitated by that make's success at Sebring that year.

14308 — DXB 608
Dr Lancelot Ware
Co-founder of MENSA, and a serial Alvis owner. Above is one of six (qv 10708 – Crested Eagle; 11523 – Firefly; 12023 – Speed 20 SC; 20977 – TA 14; 22510 – TA 14). Bio is under 10708.

14313 — AUS

14314 — AUS

14324 — AUS
Victoria Police (Australia)
A set of three vehicles which were sent out in 'chassis-only' form, to be bodied by local makers. There was also a later, standard car for the same force (qv 14806).

14316: Colonel Philip Reed Adair, DFC,
USAF with his Offord-bodied 4.3-litre.
(Courtesy Ernest Shenton)

14316 `DYW 68`
Col Philip Reed Adair USAF
Phil Adair (April 15, 1920-May 13, 2017) was a
WWII Ace fighter pilot in the China/Burma/
India theatre with the famed 'Burma Banshees.'
Numerous decorations including Silver Star, Legion
of Merit, DFC, and a Presidential Unit citation.
Became a USAF test pilot, and later was attached to
NATO in Brussels. Owned 14316 from 1969 until
his death.

14319 `UD 8768`
Monte Carlo Rally 1938
An entry by J H Edwards Moss and J Robert Moss.
Competition no 22.

14320 `AJY 33`
Universal Greetings Ltd
This card manufacturer used 14320 in one of its
promotions. Its reference number is 282 5OT B237-
5 and 2357-3. This car is, of course, the very first
of the iconic shortchassis Vanden Plas tourers, and
as such underwent a degree of development work,
having a despatch number somewhat later than its
immediate peers. Sold when some six months old
to a customer in Plymouth. Copies of the card may
still be available upon enquiry.

14328 `ELK 366`
RAC Rally 1938 and 1939
Entered in the 1938 event by R A Robertson, 14328
was transferred to W E C Watkinson for 1939.
Watkinson was more usually seen at the wheel
of his Speed 20 SB (qv 10875), which he used in
this event in 1934, 1935, 1936 and 1937. 14328
subsequently underwent a series of structural
alterations, but has gradually been restored to
standard format.

It has a claim to fame in being used in the
filming of the John Le Carré novel *Tinker, Tailor,
Soldier, Spy* where actor Ian Bannen plays the part
of Jim Prideaux. It apparently used the spurious
registration mark 'PLA 41' during part of this
dramatization. For a time also, this car has borne
the mark 'ALV 15,' which has been owned by a
number of Alvis enthusiasts over the years.

14330 `EGP 759`
Iliffe Publications Ltd
14330 features in quite a few of the works publicity
shots, and was loaned to magazine *Autocar*, where
it appeared in an article, issue of April 8, 1938,
page 645. It got into *Autocar*'s hands again with the
wartime *Talking of Sports Cars* series, no 48, issue
of May 2, 1941.

14334 `IND`
Nizam of Hyderabad
Mir Osman Ali Khan (Asaf Jah VII) (April 6,
1886-February 24, 1967) was, in a cover feature of
Times Magazine, February 22, 1937, described as
the world's wealthiest man. His Alvis was one of the
very few Maltby/Redfern four-door convertibles,
with electric hood operation to be fitted on this
marque. Because of the inferior petrols then

14334: The Nizam of Hyderabad's 4.3-litre with
body by Redfern/Maltby.

available in India, a compression plate was fitted, reducing the ratio to just 5.4 to one. Biography, see *The Last Nizam* by John Zubrzycki, published by Pan Macmillan, ISBN 9780330-42321-2.

14335
Maharaja of Kashmir

Hari Singh, GCSI, GCIE, KCVO (September 23, 1895-April 26, 1961) was a member of the Imperial War Cabinet from 1944 to 1946.

14340 DON 313
George Henry Bishop

14340's many owners included Bishop, a sometimes controversial motoring journalist, born March 13, 1917. He served in the Middle East during WWII, retiring as major, and worked ten years for Reuters, as a newsman and motoring correspondent. He was founder/editor of *Car* magazine, and staff writer for *Motor*. Went freelance, contributing to such as *Autoworld*, the BBC, *Car*, *Custom Car*, *Financial Times*, *Guardian*, *On Four Wheels*, *Thoroughbred and Classic Cars*, etc. Another notable owner was Jim Bidwell-Topham, one-time proprietor of the Aintree Grand National Race Course.

14340 was used in the 'Cavalcade of Motoring' during the Lord Mayor's Show of November 1964. At the time of writing, 14340 is owned by the Royal Automobile Club, where it is used as a parade car on official events.

Chassis numbers
14346-14495
(Speed 25 SB – third batch)

Chassis	Reg				
14346	- - - AAJ 16	14364	- - -EUB 54	14383	- - DUL 115
14347	- DXW 733	14365	- - - - - -	14384	- - -CPT 75
14348	- - DLJ 852	14366	- - - - IRL	14385	- - EVX 151
14349	- - - - - -	14367	- - - - - -	14386	- - AWS 298
14350	- - DNA 838	14368	- -JN 8914	14387	- - DUL 118
14351	- -CRW 901	14369	- - - - - -	14388	- - DYU 460
14352	- ABK 792	14370	- - AUS 40	14389	- - DOB 887
14353	- ERF 349	14371	- -AWV 546	14390	- ELY 730
14354	- CWM 154	14372	- - CVP 539	14391	- CSM 868
14355	- EZ 7240	14373	- -CRW 497	14392	- EVX 854
14356	- - FPA 330	14374	- - CCG 92	14393	- -JV 5916
14357	- - DRB 392	14375	- - - JU 1	14394	- -CRW 967
14358	- - DUU 900	14376	- - DNC 754	14395	- - BNX 791
14359	- -JP 2295	14377	- - CNY 117	14396	- - CTT 999
14360	- - - AH 72	14378	- - AUS 630	14397	- ANJ 921
14361	- - - - - -	14379	- - BUE 922	14398	- - AWS 474
14362	- DXU 852	14380	- DXW 738	14399	- - BAX 698
14363	- - - - - -	14381	- CRW 37	14400	- -CRW 902
		14382	- - ETN 433	14401	- - DRH 86

14402	- -CWK 371	14434	- - - BDA 2	14466	- - CKV 868
14403	- - BFS 430	14435	- - - -EGJ 4	14467	- - RN 6636
14404	- -CWK 533	14436	- EKX 786	14468	- - BTM 509
14405	- - DNE 554	14437	- GUG 457	14469	- - DDU 216
14406	- - -BVF 75	14438	-CWK 961	14470	- - BSR 271
14407	- - AYS 138	14439	-CWK 960	14471	- - CKV 64
14408	- - BKY 640	14440	- BG 5953	14472	- - HH 9899
14409	- -CWK 600	14441	- EAE 224	14473	- DLJ 681
14410	- - DYK 428	14442	- ELG 551	14474	- - - - - -
14411	- - EUU 659	14443	-CWK 962	14475	- - - EMB 1
14412	- - - - - -	14444	- DOR 656	14476	- - - AUS
14413	- - - - - -	14445	- BGA 777	14477	- HHA 179
14414	- DYN 959	14446	- CKV 398	14478	- DWK 37
14415	- CKV 753	14447	- - - - - -	14479	- EXK 225
14416	- CDD 789	14448	- -EGT 52	14480	- - - - - -
14417	- ACO 966	14449	- EZ 9247	14481	- DXJ 493
14418	-CWK 858	14450	- - - - NL	14482	- BNJ 160
14419	- - FRE 478	14451	- CVC 312	14483	- FGT 502
14420	-DWK 132	14452	- CVC 310	14484	- BSC 307
14421	- GPC 930	14453	-BWD 544	14485	- BSC 308
14422	- DOH 412	14454	- CTF 163	14486	- BSC 309
14423	- - - -DK	14455	- - CVC 3	14487	- BSC 310
14424	- DKB 637	14456	- ELH 944	14488	-BJF 451
14425	- AUK 845	14457	- CVC 313	14489	- ACJ 797
14426	- APN 255	14458	- UD 8971	14490	- DPO 623
14427	- BUE 137	14459	-EJ 5824	14491	- DDU 315
14428	- ANR 244	14460	- - EGW 8	14492	- DDU 486
14429	- - - - - -	14461	- -JT 8817	14493	- -EGT 58
14430	- DNN 766	14462	- DTD 849	14494	- CKU 28
14431	- DYV 689	14463	- EXW 17	14495	- DHP 772
14432	- -EAE 44	14464	- EGP 837		
14433	-CWK 613	14465	- FGJ 684		

14353 ERF 349
Viscount Newport TD, DL, JP

Born Gerald Michael Orlando Bridgeman (September 29, 1911-August 30, 1981), he was also the 6th Earl of Bradford, was educated at Harrow, and Trinity College, Cambridge and served in the Shropshire Yeomanry, and in the Royal Artillery during WWII, being mentioned in despatches. The former family seat of Weston Park was donated to the nation in 1986 following crippling death duties, and has since hosted a G8 Summit Conference.

14353: Viscount Newport's Speed 25 tourer as bodied by Cross & Ellis. (Courtesy J R Fox)

Viscount Newport had previously owned an SA Speed 20 (qv 9844) whilst 14353 itself was comprehensively written up in the September 2017 issue of *Classic Cars*, pages 78 to 84.

14376 DNC 754
Alberto Morin
American movie actor, also owned a TA 21 coupé (qv 24892 for bio).

14384 CPT 75
Durham Police
Evidently a popular make with the Durham force, 14384 would shortly have as stablemates a pair of Silver Crests (qv 14207 and 16165) and a further Speed 25 specifically for the Chief Constable's use (qv 14628).

14386 AWS 298
Sir William Younger DL
William McEwen Younger (September 6, 1905-April 15, 1992) was educated at Winchester, and Balliol College, Oxford and was knighted in 1964. Younger is of course a household name in the brewing industry, and when the family firm became part of Scottish and Newcastle Breweries, he became its first chairman in 1961.

14392 EVX 854
Essex Police
Supplied specifically for the use of one John

14399: A Speed 25 in 'special' format, as constructed by Olaf Lund. (Courtesy Alvis Archive Trust)

Crockford, 14392 is thought to have been an official car rather than for general patrol use.

14394 CRW 967
Lancashire County Constabulary
A flagship patrol car for a force whose driving school at Hutton, Preston almost rivalled, at one time, the Metropolitan police one at Hendon.

14396 CTT 999
Lord Carrington
See 13637 for bio. Previously owned a Speed 20 SB model (qv 10945).

14399 BAX 698
Michael Woods USAF
Constructed by Olaf Lund from the remains of a Charlesworth-bodied saloon, as a 'special', 14399 was imported into the USA by Michael Woods in 1977 and used as a race car. Michael worked for NASA, and for the Federal Aviation Authority as an airplane crash investigator.

14400 EGJ 186
National Motor Museum
This occasional exhibit at NMM was donated by the Bloomfield family.

14422 DOH 412
Joseph Lucas Ltd
Supplier of electrical equipment to Alvis Ltd, and almost all British makes, 14422 was for Oliver Lucas.

14452 CVC 310
Holden Vintage & Classic
Well-known producer of garage equipment and accessories for the enthusiast, Holden used 14452 to illustrate the sturdiness of its lift. For the current range, visit www.holden.co.uk or ring 01888 488488.

14454 CTF 163
Boston Deep Sea Fisheries Ltd
This company was a regular customer of Alvis Ltd.

This particular car underwent some structural alterations after WWII, and finished up in the capable hands of James Symington, of the well-known wine-producing family in Portugal. It has been used by James to transport that country's late President Soares on a vinery tour.

14452: The Holden Speed 25 saloon in an unusual pose. See text for other Holden product availability.

14454: Here, owner James Symington is seen conducting President Soares of Portugal on a tour of the family vineries. (Courtesy James Symington)

14456 ELH 944

The Four Pennies

Fronted by lead guitarist Fritz-Fryer, this Blackburn-based pop group took its name from that town's Penny Street, and was very popular in the mid-'60s, producing seven singles, four EPs and two albums, all on the Philips label. Its most memorable chart-topper was *Juliet*.

14457 CVC 313

6th Earl of Cottenham

Mark Everard Pepys (May 29, 1903-July 19, 1943) was a prominent figure in Alvis racing teams of the 1920s. He was also a prolific writer on motoring matters. Apart from his novel *Sicilian Circuit,* there were such contributions as *Motoring without Fears* of 1928, *Motoring Today and Tomorrow*, also 1928, and *Steering Wheel Papers*. Arguably his greatest contribution came about in his capacity as Civilian Adviser to the Metropolitan Police Flying Squad,

14457: The Earl of Cottenham's new Speed 25 saloon ready for collection from the factory. (Courtesy Alvis Ltd)

14459: In the passenger seat of the Rivers-Fletcher Alvis special is none other than 'Bunty' Scott-Moncrieff. (Courtesy A F Rivers-Fletcher collection)

Hendon (qv 14611) where he was instrumental in writing *Roadcraft – The Police Drivers Manual* – a most worthy guide which was reprinted many times.

An obituary appeared in the *Motor*, issue of July 28, 1943, page 453, and yes, he was a descendant of Samuel Pepys, the famous diarist.

14459 EJ 5824

A F Rivers-Fletcher

Formerly a Charlesworth-bodied saloon, it was given a new lease of life by racing driver Rivers with a competition-style body. He was a charismatic figure on the motoring scene, having been an apprentice to W O Bentley, riding mechanic to Sir Malcolm Campbell, a friend of a host of drivers and constructors, and a great raconteur and wit, much in demand as a motor club guest speaker. There had been two other Alvis competition cars in his stable, both SB Speed 20 models (qv 11298 and 11859), all painted in what would become known as 'Rivers' blue.

14462 DTD 849

14463 EXW 17

London Motor Show 1938

Both these cars were Olympic Show exhibited. The latter is especially notable, bearing as it does a remarkable Art Deco style body by Lancefield Coachworks.

14479 EXK 225

Temple Press Ltd

Weekly magazine *Motor*, November 15, 1938, pages 699 to 700, carried a report written by Oliver Stewart, giving an owner's experiences of it in some detail. Some 70 years later, *Classic Cars* magazine April 2009, pages 102 to 103, reviewed exactly the same car, being similarly enthused about its many qualities.

14484 BSC 307

14485 BSC 308

14486 BSC 309

14487 BSC 310

Edinburgh City Police

A fleet of four patrol cars of identical high specification. 14485, probably the most prominent survivor, has also featured in the popular television series, *All Creatures Great and Small*.

14488 BJF 451

Robert Wicksteed

Wicksteed Park, near Kettering, Northamptonshire was established in 1921 by philanthropist Charles Wicksteed, and is one of the UK's first ever amusement parks with a range of attractions, of which the narrow gauge railway is one of the better known. Family member Robert Wicksteed was probably better known as the long-time custodian of the famous 'Alvis Racing Car No 1' (qv 2091).

14493 EGT 58

Bishop's Move Ltd

Established in 1854, this firm is well-known for its specialist removal services, be it domestic, or entire museum artefact relocations. Whilst its name is an astute and catchy connection of founder J J Bishop with the game of chess, it is proudly reported by the firm that in 2013, it relocated Archbishop Justin Welby from Durham to Lambeth Palace. At one time, 14493 was a company car of this six-

14493: Just visible here on the door of the Bishop's Move depot is the 'Bishop' logo, see inset version. (Courtesy W V Shields - Bishop family)

generation family business. The booklet *Postcards to my Love*, ISBN 0 86303 443-8, published by Maslands of Tiverton gives an interesting insight into Bishop family history.

Chassis numbers
14496-14545
(Crested Eagle TA, TB – third batch)

Chassis	Reg				
14496	- - DRB 461	14512	- - -JK 7959	14529	- - - - - -
14497	- - CVC 661	14513	- -AWH 860	14530	- - BSC 727
14498	- - HC 9978	14514	- - GYH 715	14531	- - EMA 789
14499	- - EGC 157	14515	- GR 4757	14532	- - - - - -
14500	- - BGA 999	14516	- -BWH 400	14533	- - BBN 540
14501	- - - - - -	14517	- - FUA 440	14534	- - - - - -
14502	- - - - - -	14518	- - BYG 990	14535	- - EXH 783
14503	- - ABA 483	14519	- - - - - -	14536	- - BCY 945
14504	- - -EVU 29	14520	-EOM 222	14537	- -AWH 123
14505	- - HRF 700	14521	- - BBN 534	14538	-DWK 302
14506	- - - - - -	14522	- - FNU 842	14539	- - FRF 303
14507	- - -JV 6377	14523	- - FKH 42	14540	- - - JMC 1
14508	- - BSC 280	14524	- - FKN 421	14541	-BWH 151
14509	- - FTN 608	14525	-CDW 880	14542	- - -EGT 56
14510	- - DGA 76	14526	- EOB 929	14543	- FGO 371
14511	- - ELH 950	14527	- -DLV 80	14544	- - - - - -
		14528	- - GUA 678	14545	- - BBN 461

JV 6377
14507
Captain Oscar Dixon

Served WWI with the 1/5th Battalion Lincolnshire Regiment as Commander A-Company. Dixon's interesting military papers are housed in the Liddle Collection at the University of Leeds. Following military service, in 1925, he took over the by then dilapidated Kenwick Hall, near Louth, Lincolnshire, which had been the seat of the Allenby family, and painstakingly restored it. It has survived as a hotel/restaurant and golfing venue.

DGA 76
14510
Albion Motors Ltd

Renowned manufacturer of a wide range of commercial vehicle, Albion had actually made cars between 1910 and 1913. 14510 was a company car.

14534
Brown Shipley Ltd

With a company history spanning three centuries, private banking group Brown Shipley had its origins in maritime trade when sail was still the norm. In March 1940 the company took delivery of this, one of the largest Alvis cars ever made. Mysteriously, the chassis dated from late 1937, and

was, for this model, uniquely bodied by Windovers as a limousine. It seems to have survived the London Blitz, where BS headquarters were, and still are, and was last registered in 1950.

FGO 371
14543
ENV Ltd

Noted maker of automotive transmission systems, the timing of the supply of this company car to it is especially interesting. Up to this point Alvis Ltd had made its own rear axles, but with the new 12/70 model that had been introduced only a few months earlier, rear axles were 'bought in,' from ENV. This new arrangement would continue for all the four-cylinder cars until the last TA 14 left the production line in 1950. Thus, ENV's company Crested Eagle suggests some form of reciprocal arrangement.

Chassis numbers
14546, 14547, 14548
(12/70 prototypes)

Chassis	Reg		
14546	- -CWK 856	14547 - - CKV 61	
		14548 - - DHP 234	

Chassis numbers
14549-14689
(Speed 25 SC – first batch)

Chassis	Reg				
14549	- - DOV 623	14576	- - -JT 8896	14604	- - CSG 700
14550	- - DDU 485	14577	- - DFY 890	14605	- - FZ 3254
14551	- - EDU 304	14578	- - EYP 938	14606	- -DVC 83
14552	- - EYO 370	14579	- - CKU 680	14607	- FGO 659
14553	- - DDU 152	14580	- - EYP 331	14608	- -CYG 22
14554	- - - - CDN	14581	- - DHP 802	14609	- - GKA 22
14555	- BTM 799	14582	- - - - - -	14610	- - EHN 681
14556	- BGD 920	14583	- - EYP 944	14611	- - FLO 685
14557	- - - - - -	14584	- - ENN 841	14612	- - FXT 312
14558	- - FUB 812	14585	-DRW 914	14613	- - DCE 677
14559	- - FNC 129	14586	- - AVJ 510	14614	- - BBT 700
14560	- - EUF 586	14587	- - EYR 215	14615	- - FLC 538
14561	- DRW 210	14588	-DRW 473	14616	- - FGY 333
14562	- - - - - -	14589	- - EYX 622	14617	- - FGU 656
14563	- - CN 8571	14590	-DWK 359	14618	- - EOL 662
14564	- - CAK 999	14591	- - CKW 91	14619	- - FLW 212
14565	- DRW 211	14592	- - -FLD 19	14620	- - FNB 997
14566	- - GPU 146	14593	- - EG 5089	14621	- - CGB 667
14567	- - HMX 34	14594	- - DHP 772	14622	- - DVC 436
14568	- - -BSG 95	14595	- - EXN 535	14623	- - SE 5000
14569	- ETV 550	14596	- - - EYU 7	14624	- - EXJ 769
14570	- - BDY 231	14597	- - FLO 986	14625	- - EKF 769
14571	- - BGE 988	14598	- -FRA 31	14626	- -EOM 559
14572	- EXH 639	14599	- - EYR 219	14627	- - EVC 570
14573	- - EXH 778	14600	- -FGW 404	14628	- - EUP 333
14574	- - DHP 551	14601	- - - - - -	14629	- - - - AUS
14575	- - DHP 771	14602	- - BDY 202	14630	- - IW 6996
		14603	- - FGJ 808	14631	- - FXP 192

14632 - - FXC 317	14652 - - -JV 7793	14672 - -EWK 378
14633 - - - ARG 7	14653 - - FOB 506	14673 - - LMF 49
14634 - - FLD 316	14654 - - FLX 200	14674 - - DZ 6689
14635 - -DKV 410	14655 - - BPN 205	14675 - - BPN 273
14636 - - DVC 581	14656 - - - CUS 7	14676 - - -DJ 8888
14637 - - ARJ 751	14657 - - - CUS 8	14677 - - EVC 561
14638 - - FDU 517	14658 - - - CUS 6	14678 - - GRB 854
14639 - - - FLP 75	14659 - - - CUS 9	14679 - - EVC 560
14640 - - FNB 989	14660 - - SN 9433	14680 - - GGK 19
14641 - - CS 9233	14661 - - MG 6481	14681 - - - - - -
14642 - - -YJ 6622	14662 - - FLD 850	14682 - - EVC 643
14643 - - FXN 610	14663 - -EWK 345	14683 - - - - - -
14644 - - -EDU 91	14664 - - EHP 551	14684 - - EVC 565
14645 - - BHS 279	14665 - - ERW 547	14685 - - EVC 559
14646 - - EDU 303	14666 - - GHA 469	14686 - - EVC 566
14647 - -DWR 144	14667 - - FYV 643	14687 - - EVC 567
14648 - - HPJ 808	14668 - - - - AUS	14688 - - EVC 568
14649 - - GNA 289	14669 - - DSC 882	14689 - - EVC 564
14650 - - EHP 186	14670 - - EVC 139	
14651 - - -EHP 99	14671 - - - CUS 5	

14551 EDU 304

Works car

One of the most significant exhibits at the 1938 Olympia Motor Show of 1938 was the highly polished Speed 25 rolling chassis. It remained on the works strength for some time and was not bodied until mid-1939.

14570 BDY 231

Sir Paul Newall DL

The 666th Lord Mayor of London, Paul Newall (September 19, 1934-June 28, 2015) was educated at Harrow, Magdalene College Cambridge and served in the Royal Fusiliers. He used the year of his Mayoralty to actively promote the City and its trading links with promotional trips to Japan, South Korea, the Middle East, and the United States. A charming man who radiated authority without pomposity. It has also been said that Paul Newall's mother-in-law, Dame Paddy Ridsdale, who had once worked for Ian Fleming at the Admiralty, served as the model for Miss Moneypenny, in Fleming's James Bond novels. Paul Newall later owned a TA 14 model (qv 21938).

14574 DHP 551

Iliffe Publications Ltd

Autocar's road test car appearing in the issue of June 10, 1938, page 1051, and numbered 1200 in the long-running series.

14589 EYX 622

14596 EYU 7

Love's Labour's Lost

In the year 2000, there was a movie production directed by (and starring) Kenneth Branagh, which migrated William Shakespeare's 400-year-old plot into a 1930s setting. Branagh sought out two Alvis cars for this film's production. It was not until much later that it was discovered by chance that the cars concerned were only seven chassis numbers apart, and must have been on the Alvis production line at the same time. Not only that, they have consecutive body numbers which means that the one must have followed the other through Charlesworth's coachworks. A serendipitous reuniting which the Bard himself would surely have appreciated.

14600 FGW 404

London Metropolitan Police

One of a pair of this model used by Scotland Yard. Other (qv 14611).

14607 FGO 659

London Motor Show 1938

A featured vehicle in the Olympia Show of that year – the last to be held before WWII.

14611 FLO 685

London Metropolitan Police

The Hendon Centre was renowned in its day for the advanced driver training of officers. In 1952, when magazine *Motor* reported on its work in the issue of January 23, there were 15 vehicles ranging from Buick to vintage Bentley for students to learn the varied characteristics of. By this time, 14611 had been transferred from routine patrol duties to join this distinguished operation.

14620 FNB 997

Billy Cotton

Billy Cotton (May 6, 1899-March 25, 1969) was an instantly recognisable radio personality of the 1940s and 1950s, particularly with his BBC Band Shows where he grabbed the attention of listeners with the introductory call of "Wakey Wakey." A notable character, he had flown Bristol fighters during WWII, and had played football for Brentford. Less well known is that he raced, finishing fourth in the 1949 British Grand Prix, driving an ERA. His son, also Bill, maintained the BBC connection, becoming controller of BBC1.

14623 — SE 5000
William Grant Ltd

A household name in the distillation of Scotch whisky, the firm was founded in 1887. In 1939, the then proprietor of this family business ordered this distinctively-registered drophead coupé. He had previously owned a Firebird model (qv 13478).

14627 — EVC 570
Sir Winston Churchill

Not owned by, but used by Britain's wartime Prime Minister on a visit to Army Camps in Yorkshire. 14627 was almost certainly on the strength of the West Riding Police Force at the time.

14627: Taken in Harrogate, probably in 1943, Prime Minister Winston Churchill is about to embark upon a visit to the 15th Scottish Division in this Speed 25 tourer, which was an asset of the West Riding Constabulary's at the time. (Courtesy Mrs L Sharp)

14628 — EUP 333
Durham Police

One of four Alvis cars delivered to the Durham Force as WWII hostilities loomed. This one was specifically allocated for the use of the Chief Constable, Sir George Morley CBE, KPM (November 17, 1873-October 13, 1942. For the others at this time, see 14384 a tourer version of the above Speed 25, and a pair of Silver Crests 14207 and 16165.

14631 — FXP 192
Tony Curtis

Movie actor Curtis would later add a TE 21 model to his collection (qv 27327 for bio).

14632 — FXC 317
Iliffe Publications Ltd

When just 13 years old, 14632 became the subject of *Autocar's* *Used Cars on the Road* series, no 40, in the issue of August 15, 1952, page 1012. Much praised therein, it must have represented a good return on an investment by its first owner, £885 in 1939, £795 asked in 1952.

14638 — FDU 517
Works car

A key vehicle in Alvis car development, being a Speed 25 Vanden Plas two-door saloon which had been mothballed during WWII, and converted from its original transverse leaf front suspension, to an experimental coil layout, and was thus an important stage in what would be its series production form with the introduction of the 3-litre TA 21 model in 1950.

14645 — BHS 279
Lord Inverclyde KStJ

Born John Alan Burns (December 12, 1897-June 17, 1957), he was educated at Eton and the Royal Military College, Berkshire. Served as Lieutenant in WWI and thereafter became aide-de-camp to the Governor of Gibraltar. A keen sailor, he wrote a book *Porpoises and People,* published by Halton and Truscott-Smith in 1930, an account of two nautical expeditions, one to India/Malaya 1924/25, and the other around the Mediterranean in 1929. He served as a Captain in the Scots Guards during WWII, and was onboard RMS Lancastrian when it was sunk during the evacuation of St Nazaire in 1940, but was rescued. Previously owned an SA Speed 20 model (qv 10026) and an SD Speed 20 model (qv 13001).

14653 — FOB 506
George Formby OBE

Born George Hoy-Booth (May 26, 1904-March 6, 1961, Formby was, for many years, Britain's

14656 **CUS 7**

14657 **CUS 8**

14658 **CUS 6**

14659 **CUS 9**

14671 **CUS 5**

Glasgow City Police
An impressive fleet of five of a high identical specification during the tenure of Sir Percy Sillitoe as Chief Constable. After decommissioning, 14659 finished up, postwar, in the hands of the Jazz trombonist Turk Murphy who also owned a 4.3-litre (qv 14803).

14676 **ERF 7**

Edwin Richard Foden
The lorry magnate. Also owned a 4.3-litre (qv 13641 for bio).

14679 **EVC 560**

Works car
One of the last cars to leave the factory as WWII hostilities commenced, 14679 would later be immortalised in one of the popular *Profile* publications, no 11, where it occupies the inside back cover in a colour painting by Walter Wright.

Chassis numbers
14799-14872
(4.3-litre SA, SC – fourth batch)

Chassis	Reg				
14799	- - FKE 361	14812	- - DHP 233	14826	- - - - - -G
14800	- - FLY 803	14813	- - DKV 779	14827	- - AHS 706
14801	- - FLC 984	14814	- - FGO 200	14828	- - - - - -
14802	- DOM 580	14815	- - DDU 153	14829	- -FLP 71
14803	- -DRW 361	14816	- - AHS 585	14830	- -DWK 822
14804	- -ERW 780	14817	- - DFY 798	14831	- -DWK 888
14805	- - - - AUS	14818	- - EDU 53	14832	- - ALV 100
14806	- - - - AUS	14819	- - - ELY 2	14833	- -DHO 690
14807	- - BBL 100	14820	- - BGG 954	14834	- - - - - -
14808	- - ELY 190	14821	- - AUH 872	14835	- - GRF 88
14809	- - VY 7777	14822	- - EOB 567	14836	- -DFS 47
14810	- - BSF 345	14823	- - DHP 224	14837	- -DTX 663
14811	- - EGT 53	14824	- - DGD 1	14838	- -DGD 289
		14825	- -DWK 443	14839	- - EDV 795

14653: A typical image of famous entertainer George Formby OBE, 'at home' in Blackpool. (Courtesy the George Formby Society)

highest-paid entertainer, initially with short songs of a humorous, sometimes risqué format, and then branching into movies. There were hundreds of the former, and dozens of the latter. This most generous level of income allowed him to indulge in a passion for cars of high quality, where his turnover of them was quite brisk, with Rolls-Royce and Bentley topping the list at just under 30, sundry Americana such as Packard, and at least three Alvis, of which 14653 is one, and which for a time resided in a Midlands motor museum.

The others were two SC Speed 20s (qv 12068 and 12780).

14654 **FLX 200**

The Daily Mail
One of this newspaper's staff cars, earmarked for the use of a Mr McKenzie.

14840 - - - ELB 1	14851 - - ERW 915	14862 - - - - - -
14841 - - FHN 478	14852 - - EVC 562	14863 - - - - - -
14842 - - - - - ZA	14853 - - EVC 563	14864 - - - - - -
14843 - - - - - -	14854 - - EY 6990	14865 - - - - - -
14844 - - - - DVB 1	14855 - - - - - -	14866 - - BRV 55
14845 - DGW 598	14856 - - KPC 362	14867 - - EDU 600
14846 - - - - FS 40	14857 - - - - - -	14868 - - - - - -
14847 - - FLO 987	14858 - - FGT 510	14869 - - - - - P
14848 - - AVA 400	14859 - - - - - -	14870 - - EVC 240
14849 - - FNF 45	14860 - - - - - -	14871 - - EVC 477
14850 - - DUP 250	14861 - - FXC 318	14872 - VXI3 JKN

14800: The Lord Brabazon car with subsequent owner Peter Horrobin at the wheel.
(Courtesy P J Horrobin)

14800 FLY 803
Lord Brabazon of Tara

More lengthily known as John Theodore Cuthbert Moore-Brabazon, GBE, MC, MP, PC (February 8, 1884-May 17, 1964) was created baron in 1942. He was an outstanding pioneer aviator, making the first officially recognised aeroplane flight in England on May 2,1909. He was educated at Harrow and Trinity and, it is said, spent some of his holidays working for Charles Rolls. He joined the RFC in WWI, becoming Lt Colonel, and played a major part in the development of aerial reconnaissance photography and being twice mentioned in despatches. He served twice as a Conservative Member of Parliament, for Chatham between 1918 and 1929, and then for Wallasey between 1931 and 1942. Brabazon was quite suitably allowed to obtain the registration mark FLY 1, when it was first issued in 1939, and the mark FLY 803, which was allocated later, was understandably as a result of the original being retained.

14802 DOM 580
London Motor Show 1937

Recorded as being an Olympia Show exhibit, after which allocated to a Birmingham customer.

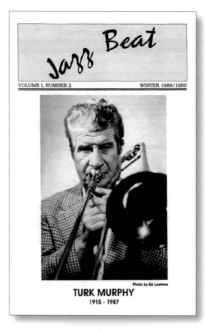

Jazz Beat
VOLUME 1, NUMBER 2   WINTER 1989/1990

TURK MURPHY
1915 - 1987

Famous jazz man Turk Murphy featured on this magazine cover, kindly supplied by Pete Stillwell.

14803 DRW 361
Turk Murphy

Full name, Melvin Edward Alton Murphy (December 16, 1915-May 30, 1987) 'Turk' was a jazz band leader and trombonist who had served in WWII with the US Navy. He made around 40 records, some of which included his pianist and friend Pete Clute, who is known to have taken over one of Turk's Alvis cars. He is also associated with Lu Watters and the Yerba Buena jazz band, and for a time ran a night club known as 'Earthquake McGoons.'

Also credited with owning two Alvis Speed 25 models (qv 13328 and 14659).

14806 EVC 560
Victoria Police (Australia)

Part of a fleet despatched 'down under' (qv 14313, 14314, and 14324 for the others).

14807 BBL 100
Monte Carlo Rally 1949

The sole Alvis competing in this event – entered by Mrs M K Harmon, of Paddington.

14810 BSF 345
Professor Norman Dott

Professor Norman Dott (August 28, 1897-October

10, 1973), to give him his full titles of CBE, MD, FRCSE, FRSE, FRCCC, was made Britain's first professor of neurosurgery in 1932, and had a career so eminent that he was made a Freeman of the City of Edinburgh in 1962. He wrote an autobiography *With Sharp Compassion*, and had previously owned an SC Speed 20 model (qv 11923). The first owner of 14810 had been a wealthy Scottish enthusiast, T W McCallum, who had competed with it in an RSAC Rally. 14810 has also come to prominence as having been one of the subjects of the Franklin Mint model series.

14819 `ELY 2`
RAC Rally 1938
Specially prepared by the works for the above event, 14819 was equipped with some 30 additional features, amongst which were windscreen wipers on the inside of the screen. It was piloted by M Cave-Browne-Cave, also known as an inventor.

14819: The 1938 RAC Rally 4.3-litre car, seen here with its intrepid driver, M Cave-Browne-Cave.

'ELY 2' being appraised by Peter Garnier, far right, then sports editor of *Autocar*, who was, in 1955, on an assignment in Cornwall testing the Lotus IX, XPE 6. (Courtesy the late Harold Lord collection)

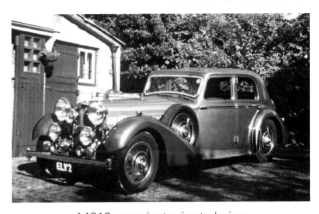

14819 seen just prior to being written off in a postwar accident. (Courtesy the late Harold Lord and Ernest Shenton)

14825 `DWK 443`
Iliffe Publications Ltd
Subject of *Autocar*'s Road Test numbered 1285, in the issue of June 2, 1939, page 951.

14831 `DWK 888`
Sir Percy Sillitoe KBE
14831 was supplied to Sir Percy (May 22, 1888-April 5, 1962) in his official capacity as Glasgow's Chief Constable from 1931 to 1943, and unlike many other cars of this marque purchased by that force, it seems never to have been used for patrol duties, neither was it Glasgow registered, but supplied directly from the works. Sillitoe had a distinguished career, sometimes controversial, with a number of forces such as Kent, and Sheffield, before taking up the Glasgow post. He would later still become Director-General of the national security agency, MI5, and wrote an autobiography, *Cloak without Dagger*, published by Abelard Schuman in 1955.

14845 `DGW 598`
Scottish Motor Show 1938
Following allocation to an Edinburgh owner after the show, 14845 reappeared as the course car at the Bo'ness Hillclimb, May 17, 1947, conducted by Keith Elliott, MD of Alvis agents Galt's of Glasgow.

14856 `KPC 362`
Michael Rennie
An actor, Michael Rennie (August 25, 1909-June 10, 1971) took over 14856 after it had escaped

14856: The Michael Rennie 4.3-litre tourer when owned by Reg Parker. (Courtesy the late Ernest Shenton collection)

14858: Flying ace Lionel Bellair's last Alvis. Its original colour scheme was rather more sober than as here. (Author's collection)

the conflagration of WWII, being fortuitously 'mothballed' and not registered until 1946. Probably his best-known movie is *The Third Man*, in which another Alvis owner, Trevor Howard, also starred (qv 23415). There was also *The Robe* of 1953, and Alfred Hitchcock's *The Day the Earth Stood Still*, where Alvis owner Bernard Herrmann provided the film score (qv 24799).

Also featured, in full colour, on the inside front cover of no 11 of the famous *Profile* publication series. The artist was Walter Wright.

14858   `FGT 510`
Lionel Bellairs

In the late 1920s and early 1930s, private flying was becoming a common activity for those with means, of which Lionel Bellairs was one, having owned an Avro Avian, a Comper Swift, and a Southern Martlet in quick succession. He was also a serial owner of Alvis cars (qv 12066, 13089 and 13691) before taking delivery of the one-off Carlton-bodied 14858. He would not have long to enjoy this impressive car, however, for as war broke out, he

naturally enlisted with the RAF, and it was as Sub Lt 'Skid' Bellairs that he took part in the disastrous 828 Squadron's raid on Luftwaffe positions in Kirkenes (northern Norway), on July 31, 1941, using Fairey Albacores, during the course of which he was shot down.

Also co-drove with Charles Follett in the 1936 RAC Rally – an SD Speed 20, 12783.

14867   `EDU 600`
RAC Rally 1939

This much-photographed Vanden Plas short-chassis tourer was part of the works press fleet, and was well-used, being initially subjected to a full road test by magazine *Motor*, in the issue of May 23, 1939, where maximum speed recorded was 105mph. Shortly afterwards, it was entered in the RAC Rally, earning the premier award for the best open car in the coachwork competition. The driver was Dorothy Stanley-Turner (November 12, 1916-July 8, 1996) – a remarkable individual who had competed at Le Mans in 1937, and was the last woman to win a race at Brooklands, both undertaken in an MG specially prepared by the works, where Cecil Kimber was a friend of her father. She served in WWII, commissioned in the RAF, and appears again in this story with her postwar Monte Carlo Rally exploits in TA 21s (qv 23804 and 23831). 14867 was sold in 1940, then somewhat 'shop-soiled' to W E O'Shei, of the car accessory manufacturer Trico-Folberth, of Brentford.

Chassis numbers 14872-14948 were never completed.

Chassis numbers 14949-14959 (Crested Eagle TD, TE – one batch)

Chassis	Reg			
14949	- - - - - -	14952 - - - - - -	14956 - - - - - -
14950	- -DWK 999	14953 - - ETD 580	14957 - - - - - -
14951	- - - - - -	14954 - - - - - -	14958 - - - - - -
		14955 - - HRE 729	14959 - - EVC 653

14950   `DWK 999`
Darlington Rotary Club

For 1959/60, which had been declared as World Refugee Year, Darlington Rotarians organised a charity auction in order to raise funds. Amongst the 300-plus highly varied donated items was this gift of Crested Eagle 14950 by a Mr Ronald Hodgkins. The car was finally knocked down to a Mrs S Thomas for the princely sum of £92.10s. The auction itself made well over £900 for the cause – twice that which had been expected.

14954
Olympia Show 1938
An exhibit at what would be the last pre-war Motor Exhibition.

14959 EVC 653
Alvis works hack
In the normal course of events, 14959 would have become a stately limousine like most of its immediate peers, but somehow it survived the Blitz on the factory of November 14, 1940, and was, it is believed, initially used as a truck to transport Rolls-Royce Merlin engines between the shadow factories. Postwar, it became the works breakdown truck.

Chassis numbers 14960-15148 were never completed.

12/70

1937 to 1940
746 cars

14546, 14547 and 14548 (prototypes)	3
15149-15508 (SB)	358
15509-15893 (SC)	385

Consisting of:
Mulliner saloons
A42872-A43071	200(SB)
A43072-A43434	363(SC)

Mulliner coupés
A44048-A44195	148

Mulliner tourers
A47786-A47800	15

Whittingham & Mitchel tourers
AT1-AT18	18

Remainder are 'chassis-only'

The second of George Lanchester's designs for Alvis Ltd (qv 13776 et seq for the Silver Crest, his

first). It occupied the slot in the company's range previously occupied by the Firebird, and whilst having the same engine size, this was an altogether different unit, improved casting techniques having now combined the block and crankcase. The new model was shorter, narrower, lighter, more powerful and consequently more 'nimble.' Much of this had been brought about by using some 'bought in' components including a front axle from Alford and Alder, the rear from ENV, steering from Marles, and brakes from Bendix-Cowdrey. Rudge Whitworth 17-inch centre-lock wire wheels endowed a distinctly sporting appearance, as did Mulliner's tasteful coachwork (originally intended for a Bentley). Competition potential was quickly realised with the supply of a racing chassis to Gerry Dunham – a formula which had proved very popular to this day with various special builders appreciative of the model's fine handling characteristics.

Chassis numbers
15149-15508
(12/70 SB – one batch)

Chassis	Reg	Chassis	Reg	Chassis	Reg
15149	- - - - - -	15183 - -	EXW 30	15218 - -	ELH 947
15150 - -	CVE 507	15184 - - -	GBJ	15219 - -	CAX 91
15151	- - - - - -	15185 - -	GR 5926	15220 - -	EZ 9645
15152	- - - - - -	15186 -	FKM 540	15221 - - -	AUS
15153 - -	BZ 5550	15187	- - - - - -	15222 - -	EG 4770
15154	- - - - - -	15188	- - - - - -	15223 - -	JT 8953
15155 -	GMX 653	15189	- - - - - -	15224 -	- - - - -
15156 -	BGE 446	15190 - -	JM 3605	15225 - -	AVG 55
15157 -	DLJ 905	15191 - -	BET 207	15226 - -	DYA 537
15158	- - - - - -	15192 -	- - - - -	15227 - -	EKN 295
15159	- - - - - -	15193 - -	CKV 754	15228 -	GTW 532
15160 -	CKV 397	15194 - -	XG 5545	15229 - -	EYU 824
15161	- - - - - -	15195 -	- - - - -	15230 -	FNU 530
15162 - -	GV 5880	15196	- - - - - -	15231 - -	EFM 197
15163 -	CAX 223	15197 - -	FAL 209	15232 - -	ERA 767
15164 -	EY 6420	15198 - -	ANV 782	15233 - -	AYJ 156
15165 - -	FNU 40	15199 -	CKY 187	15234 - -	HB 5478
15166	- - - - - -	15200 - -	SY 6382	15235 - -	FNU 157
15167	- - - - - -	15201 - -	EZ 9591	15236 -	- - - - -
15168 - -	ECD 773	15202		15237 - -	CGD 513
15169	- - - - - -	15203 -	- - - - -	15238 - - -	AUS
15170	- - - - - -	15204 - -	CKV 867	15239 - -	EUU 653
15171	- - - - - -	15205 - -	FUB 928	15240 -	GWL 272
15172 -	FGW 398	15206 - -	CBM 636	15241 -	- - - - -
15173 - -	ELL 484	15207 - -	CER 768	15242 - -	EGT 55
15174 - -	CGA 699	15208 - - -	AUS	15243 - -	DDV 638
15175	- - - - - -	15209 - -	FEH 511	15244 - -	BWS 818
15176	- - - - - -	15210 - -	ELT 459	15245 - -	JK 7665
15177 - -	GBB 978	15211 - -	EKO 270	15246 - -	GS 7714
15178	- - - - - -	15212 -	- - - - -	15247 -	- - - - -
15179 - -	FFJ 780	15213 - -	PV 5550	15248 - -	ETV 766
15180 - -	AJG 719	15214 - -	CKV 869	15249 - -	FGO 191
15181 - -	BLB 222	15215 - -	APN 300	15250 - -	DPO 909
15182 - -	SX 4744	15216 - -	CKV 896	15251 - -	BSF 617
		15217 - - -	BSF 4	15252 - -	CTF 273

Chassis	Reg	Chassis	Reg	Chassis	Reg
15253	FRA 336	15323	DDU 832	15393	- - - - - -
15254	CTF 274	15324	AUS	15394	DRW 761
15255	CTF 271	15325	EUU 652	15395	- - - - - -
15256	- - - - - -	15326	EKR 400	15396	DRW 913
15257	EKA 777	15327	DDU 831	15397	- - - - - -
15258	- - - - - -	15328	- - - - - -	15398	JR 7985
15259	CTF 272	15329	AFR 351	15399	BMO 57
15260	ELL 477	15330	DSM 476	15400	EFJ 156
15261	EWB 632	15331	- - - - - -	15401	AAV 382
15262	EMB 297	15332	ARV 948	15402	- - - - - -
15263	EP 7157	15333	FZ 2589	15403	- - - - - -
15264	CUO 594	15334	DDU 834	15404	RG 9468
15265	AUN 530	15335	BWN 557	15405	JMY 524
15266	DRO 117	15336	- - - - - -	15406	KS 8116
15267	DDU 215	15337	CVE 292	15407	- - - - - -
15268	IW 6252	15338	DHP 803	15408	- - - - - -
15269	BGE 855	15339	EYE 935	15409	EUD 468
15270	DRW 167	15340	EEL 573	15410	DTC 309
15271	IB 7489	15341	JI 7975	15411	EYL 653
15272	- - - - - -	15342	CAX 663	15412	BG 6905
15273	EMB 524	15343	- - - - - -	15413	CVE 777
15274	DHP 801	15344	AEW 995	15414	- - - - - -
15275	GRE 786	15345	- - - - - -	15415	DWM 314
15276	- - - - - -	15346	ELR 512	15416	- - - - - -
15277	CKV 977	15347	AUH 890	15417	DWK 305
15278	COT 490	15348	- - - - - -	15418	DRW 762
15279	JT 8448	15349	BSG 949	15419	BJB 167
15280	AEW 971	15350	EXW 498	15420	JR 8446
15281	- - - - - -	15351	CH	15421	EHN 255
15282	DSM 515	15352	- - - - - -	15422	JV 7014
15283	DHP 550	15353	- - - - - -	15423	JR 8447
15284	DDU 833	15354	- - - - - -	15424	DWK 131
15285	- - - - - -	15355	- - - - - -	15425	DWK 482
15286	- - - - - -	15356	DRW 168	15426	FNU 656
15287	CWT 365	15357	EKA 888	15427	AVY 355
15288	- - - - - -	15358	- - - - - -	15428	AUJ 597
15289	AUS	15359	DFJ 978	15429	BWS 910
15290	CER 919	15360	- - - - - -	15430	DWK 36
15291	ELL 481	15361	- - - - - -	15431	AUS
15292	DYB 955	15362	EWJ 716	15432	- - - - - -
15293	BCA 375	15363	- - - - - -	15433	- - - - - -
15294	CUO 653	15364	ETV 300	15434	CGA 19
15295	EUW 652	15365	FVK 913	15435	FGO 82
15296	BFY 457	15366	ABX 669	15436	EKD 458
15297	- - - - - -	15367	DRW 760	15437	FKJ 610
15298	- - - - - -	15368	DRW 209	15438	FLG 645
15299	- - - - - -	15369	GNO 41	15439	CN 8827
15300	EUU 651	15370	BYS 333	15440	DDF 182
15301	CAX 233	15371	BCO 68	15441	FRA 636
15302	SN 8463	15372	JR 8121	15442	DWK 446
15303	DNK 708	15373	JR 8369	15443	CSG 999
15304	APN 788	15374	- - - - - -	15444	DYC 971
15305	AUS	15375	DRW 473	15445	DWK 558
15306	DOP 922	15376	- - - - - -	15446	DWK 481
15307	EMB 308	15377	EKD 707	15447	GTW 392
15308	BYS 162	15378	DRW 474	15448	FMA 602
15309	DLV 295	15379	EEL 373	15449	DPT 665
15310	HH 9898	15380	DRW 698	15450	- - - - - -
15311	- - - - - -	15381	CKU 230	15451	HPA 659
15312	CDG 844	15382	- - - - - -	15452	CDV 719
15313	AUT 286	15383	EXT 638	15453	CDV 756
15314	HMF 200	15384	- - - - - -	15454	CS 8659
15315	EXH 781	15385	ETU 551	15455	ERU 385
15316	DHP 68	15386	- - - - - -	15456	- - - - - -
15317	AFE 385	15387	DFY 951	15457	CGB 397
15318	EUU 654	15388	DRW 496	15458	- - - - - -
15319	- - - - - -	15389	AFE 800	15459	WG 7957
15320	- - - - - -	15390	ENN 165	15460	ST 9944
15321	BRV 664	15391	- - - - - -	15461	JS 6020
15322	AUN 797	15392	JR 8364	15462	FTO 120

Chassis	Reg	Chassis	Reg	Chassis	Reg
15463	CGD 27	15479	FTO 700	15495	GHT 220
15464	ERR 583	15480	GKJ 529	15496	FOE 744
15465	- - - - - -	15481	- - - - - -	15497	- - - - - -
15466	DKV 522	15482	FXK 311	15498	DCY 77
15467	FLD 314	15483	BRV 402	15499	FYR 374
15468	EDU 54	15484	KMG 168	15500	HVK 284
15469	- - - - - -	15485	FUU 700	15501	DGB 624
15470	- - - - - -	15486	HHK 555	15502	- - - - - -
15471	- - - - - -	15487	FXC 210	15503	EWK 928
15472	ABW 250	15488	EG 5478	15504	BHS 924
15473	- - - - - -	15489	FXR 195	15505	DKW 134
15474	FUF 210	15490	- - - - - -	15506	GGC 330
15475	FTO 666	15491	- - - - - -	15507	BWF 822
15476	HEV 740	15492	FXV 562	15508	GGC 326
15477	DWR 421	15493	EWK 343		
15478	- - - - - -	15494	FYV 985		

15172: A very early 12/70, bodied in the Vanden Plas tourer style by Cross & Ellis.

15172 — FGW 398

A specially commissioned body on a very early 12/70 chassis 15172 was an attempt to replicate in miniature the highly desirable Vanden Plas body style fitted to the Alvis 4.3-litre short chassis tourers. The result is in perfect scale, and would easily confuse the uninitiated from a short distance away. The builder of this device was not Vanden Plas itself, but Coventry's Cross & Ellis. Sadly a one-off, but it made another tourer, similar, but without the prominent swage lines (qv 15334).

15173 — ELL 484
Iliffe Publications Ltd

This was the first Whittingham & Mitchel body of a run of 18 such, originally commissioned by Alvis agent Hugh Anderson. It had quite a busy life as a demonstrator, and was loaned to weekly magazine *Autocar* to become the subject of one of its full road test features, no 1176 in the issue of March 4, 1938.

15218 — ELH 947
Monte Carlo Rally 1938 And 1939
An entry by H M Balfour on both occasions.

In the 1938 event, Balfour would have finished much higher in the listings but for losing an hour, chivalrously assisting his countryman, Sir W Carmichael-Anstruther and his Ford, to extricate themselves from a ditch. Balfour previously owned a Firebird model (qv 12277).

15223 JT 8953

15252 CTF 273

15254 CTF 274

15255 CTF 271

15259 CTF 272

Brig-Gen H W Cobham CMG, DSO
A fleet of four patrol cars supplied to the Preston Borough force, but curiously registered with a Lancashire County Council mark rather than the 'RN' of Preston Borough.

15260 ELL 477

RAC Rally 1939
The third Whittingham and Mitchel tourer body to be built on a 12/70 chassis, it was an entry by W J Watson.

15334 DDU 834

Welsh Rally 1938
Entered by H Symons, who had competed with a 4.3-litre in the previous year's event. 15334 was fitted with a one-off tourer body by Cross & Ellis, which was similar to, but not identical to, a commissioned tourer by the same maker (qv 15172).

15336
Newry Police
Patrol car supplied to this County Down force.

15343
Cadbury Ltd
Company car of the well-known confectionery producer, at its Bourneville, Birmingham base.

15345
Nestle Ltd
Company car of the well-known confectionery producer, at its Surrey base.

15397
A W L'Estrange-Fawcett MC
Arthur Wellesley L'Estrange-Fawcett (1894-1961) was educated at Corpus Christi College, Cambridge and served in WWI, being commissioned in the Gloucestershire Regiment, and was mentioned in despatches July 24, 1917 for conspicuous gallantry. Postwar he would become a notable screenwriter and film producer, working for Gainsborough Pictures. Of his more memorable 'signings,' both in 1931, would be a young Charles Laughton in *Down River* about to embark on a notable Hollywood career. Also, Lupino Lane in *No Lady* – a member of the talented and numerous acting family, who had just returned from the USA.

15405 JMY 524

John Magnus Peterson
In 1945, 'Jock' Peterson, then a master at Eton College, took over the ownership of 15405. In 1950, he moved on to Shrewsbury School as headmaster, where later a TA 21 would be acquired (qv 25114 for bio).

The painting of 15405, by one G Cartwright, is set in the environs of Kings College Cambridge, where many Eton boys subsequently transferred to.

15442 DWK 446

Gladys Maud Ripley
Acclaimed singer of her day, contralto Gladys

15405: A painting of mysterious origin, by one G Cartwright, of John Magnus Peterson's 12/70 (qv 25114). (Courtesy the Alvis Archive Trust)

Ripley (July 9, 1908-December 21, 1955) specialised mainly in opera and oratorio. She worked with conductors Sir Adrian Boult, Sir Malcolm Sargent, Sir Thomas Beecham, Serge Koussevitzky and Wilhelm Furtwangler, and appeared on record albums that featured the music of Elgar, Handel, Mendelssohn, Purcell, Verdi and Wagner.

15446   GL 6260

Sidney Adolph Horstmann

The second Alvis of former car manufacturer Horstmann of Bath (qv Firebird 12362 for bio, and 15748, another 12/70).

Chassis numbers
15509-15893
(12/70 SC – one batch)

Chassis	Reg
15509 -	DKW 412
15510 - - -	ANL 2
15511 - - - - - -	
15512 - -	FYM 538
15513 - -	FYV 645
15514 - -	FZ 7316
15515 -	FYX 976
15516 -	BRG 267
15517 - -	FZ 7483
15518 - -	FHN 710
15519 -	DWK 303
15520 - - - - - -	
15521 - -	AVA 829
15522 -	DWK 304
15523 - - - - - -	
15524 -	DWK 483
15525 - - - - - -	
15526 - - - - - -	
15527 - - - - - -	
15528 - - - - - -	
15529 - -	DS 2206
15530 - -	FUF 835
15531 - -	FLA 105
15532 - - - - - -	
15533 - - - - - -	
15534 -	DAA 405
15535 -	DWK 556
15536 - - - - - -	
15537 - -	AUJ 635
15538 - -	CBL 34
15539 -	DWK 484
15540 -	BJY 642
15541 -	DWK 557
15542 - - - - - -	
15543 -	FMA 666
15544 - - -	JR 7984
15545 -	DWK 625
15546 -	GL 6260
15547 -	GVK 195
15548 -	FGF 413
15549 -	DWK 624
15550 - -	DPT 656
15551 - -	DPT 657
15552 -	DWK 447
15553 - -	FZ 2973
15554 - -	CFS 438
15555 - -	EYX 621
15556 - -	CCR 535
15557 - -	CNX 570
15558 - -	JPF 356
15559 - -	GL 6393
15560 - -	GGC 804
15561 -	EOM 196
15562 - - - - - -	
15563 - -	AJG 356
15564 - -	UD 9890
15565 - -	GKE 737
15566 - - - - - -	
15567 - -	AWH 99
15568 -	DWM 546
15569 - - -	DVC 8
15570 - - - - - -	
15571 - -	EYY 825
15572 - -	FGF 385
15573 - -	GR 6097
15574 - -	EYX 624
15575 - -	CWS 539
15576 - - -	IL 3021
15577 - - - - - -	
15578 - -	ST 9895
15579 - -	EYD 731
15580 - - - - - -	
15581 - -	FLC 772
15582 - -	FGT 505
15583 - - - - - -	
15584 - - - - - -	
15585 - -	GNU 72
15586 - -	DSM 915
15587 - -	WD 5050
15588 - -	CVF 457
15589 - -	GUA 669
15590 - -	DNX 307
15591 - - - - - -	
15592 - - - - - -	
15593 - -	CVE 905
15594 - - -	DVC 9
15595 - -	GS 8456
15596 - - - - - -	
15597 - -	DVC 82
15598 - -	DTC 870
15599 - -	BBT 40
15600 - - - - - -	
15601 - - - - - -	
15602 - -	ENY 638
15603 - -	AUJ 810
15604 - - - - - -	
15605 - - - - - -	
15606 - -	FBH 622
15607 - -	PV 5550
15608 - -	CGG 594
15609 - -	BHS 620
15610 - - -	BJG 62
15611 - -	FWE 252
15612 - -	DVC 348
15613 - -	FGT 509
15614 - -	DVC 434
15615 - -	DVC 439
15616 - -	FKN 877
15617 - - - - - -	
15618 - -	CBK 507
15619 - -	GV 7487
15620 - - - - - -	
15621 -	FGW 325
15622 - -	EKD 222
15623 - - - - - -	
15624 - -	GR 7494
15625 - - - - - -	
15626 - -	DVC 582
15627 - - - - - -	
15628 - -	DTD 836
15629 -	DVC 84
15630 - - - - - -	
15631 - -	CGB 542
15632 - -	DCJ 49
15633 - -	EG 5094
15634 - -	GRF 809
15635 - -	BG 7181
15636 - -	AUX 580

Chassis	Reg
15637 -	GVW 157
15638 - -	CDW 68
15639 - -	BWF 176
15640 - -	FMA 125
15641 - -	FMA 806
15642 -	BMO 303
15643 - -	BNJ 429
15644 - -	AST 358
15645 - - - - - -	
15646 - -	DNG 281
15647 -	CWY 766
15648 -	CNM 977
15649 - -	VV 8332
15650 - -	BZ 6575
15651 - -	DGA 303
15652 - -	EYA 334
15653 - - -	Z 9208
15654 - - - - - -	
15655 - -	GNB 160
15656 - - - - - -	
15657 - -	FLD 313
15658 - -	FLD 311
15659 - -	HPD 749
15660 -	CDW 515
15661 - -	HPE 511
15662 - - - - - -	
15663 - - - - - -	
15664 - - - - - -	
15665 - - - - - -	
15666 - -	AHH 545
15667 - - - - - -	
15668 - -	CGD 607
15669 - -	DVC 534
15670 - - - - - -	
15671 - - - - - -	
15672 - -	HJO 333
15673 - - - - - -	
15674 - -	AFX 222
15675 - -	EFD 239
15676 - -	BFE 301
15677 - -	CDV 998
15678 - -	EFY 834
15679 - - - - - -	
15680 - -	FLM 862
15681 - -	EYA 141
15682 - -	DKV 778
15683 - -	CSF 434
15684 - -	CSC 818
15685 -	CTM 656
15686 -	FKC 775
15687 - -	BHS 148
15688 - - - - - -	
15689 - - - - - -	
15690 - -	BNJ 779
15691 - -	HPG 857
15692 - -	BCJ 547
15693 - -	HRE 230
15694 - - - - - -	
15695 - -	HRE 904
15696 - -	HRE 981
15697 - - - - - -	
15698 - -	FLE 729
15699 - - - - - -	
15700 - -	BDP 80
15701 - -	CWS 282
15702 - -	FLD 318
15703 - -	ETE 244
15704 - - - - - -	
15705 - -	EDU 257
15706 - - - - -	CS
15707 - - - - -	CS
15708 - -	FLM 19
15709 - -	FZ 4838
15710 - - -	AST 99
15711 - -	CS 9619
15712 - -	FTO 763
15713 - -	HNW 478
15714 - - - - - -	
15715 - -	FZ 5078
15716 - -	EDU 180
15717 - -	SB 5990
15718 - -	SB 5991
15719 - -	EDU 236
15720 -	KMF 236
15721 - - - - - -	
15722 - -	DKV 661
15723 - -	FLF 766
15724 - -	DKV 662
15725 - -	CMJ 228
15726 - -	CGG 553
15727 - -	EOV 880
15728 - - - - - -	
15729 - -	CSG 248
15730 - - - - - -	
15731 - -	CUS 572
15732 - -	DAK 114
15733 - - - - - -	
15734 - -	EHP 34
15735 - - - - - -	
15736 - -	EFY 584
15737 - -	EDU 664
15738 -	COD 176
15739 - -	EHP 251
15740 - -	HNW 149
15741 -	IW 6799
15742 - -	FHN 287
15743 - - - - - -	
15744 -	GWA 671
15745 - - -	YJ 6916
15746 - -	DFS 644
15747 - -	BBT 702
15748 - -	GL 7007
15749 - - -	FXF 30
15750 - -	FZ 5927
15751 - -	BVH 360
15752 - -	EYB 332
15753 - -	FYV 967
15754 -	DWX 435
15755 -	DWT 215
15756 - -	EYC 159
15757 -	IW 6848
15758 - -	EHP 552
15759 - -	SN 9075
15760 - -	FRH 42
15761 - -	EHP 403
15762 - -	JRE 712
15763 - -	CTR 607
15764 - -	EHP 824
15765 - -	FUW 444
15766 - - - - - -	
15767 - -	CUS 524
15768 - -	CWS 17
15769 - -	EHP 823
15770 - -	BJY 827
15771 - -	FZ 6662
15772 - -	CWS 573
15773 - -	ETG 259
15774 - -	FXV 300
15775 - - - - - -	
15776 - -	GAU 216
15777 - -	ETC 580
15778 - -	EG 5675
15779 - -	FXR 740
15780 - -	ETG 430
15781 - -	EHP 402
15782 - - - - - -	
15783 - -	ERW 10
15784 - -	DGA 149
15785 - -	DWW 868
15786 - - - - - -	
15787 - -	JPA 207
15788 - -	DFS 611
15789 - -	FYE 384
15790 - - - - - -	
15791 - -	CCO 28
15792 - - - - - -	
15793 - - -	AUS
15794 -	EWK 261
15795 - - - - - -	
15796 - -	ETG 508
15797 - -	BVJ 203
15798 - -	FYE 797
15799 - -	DED 123
15800 - - - - - -	
15801 - -	ERW 546
15802 - -	BDT 564
15803 - -	FYY 343
15804 - -	DGB 755
15805 - -	FYX 971
15806 - -	GAU 610
15807 - -	GS 9459
15808 - -	FYY 636
15809 - - - - - -	
15810 - -	BWF 592
15811 - - -	BRD 2
15812 - -	FYV 977
15813 - -	DGB 82
15814 -	LHX 220
15815 - -	FZ 7080
15816 - - - - - -	
15817 - -	DGD 137
15818 - -	JNW 156
15819 - -	JV 8286
15820 - -	JX 8098
15821 - -	DED 124
15822 - -	DFS 238
15823 - - - - - -	
15824 - -	BFR 869
15825 - -	FYX 972
15826 - - -	UI 3713
15827 - - - - - -	
15828 -	DBM 519
15829 - - - - - -	
15830 -	DOU 496
15831 - -	JBB 135
15832 - -	BHS 897
15833 - -	EWK 719
15834 -	BRG 83
15835 - -	DGB 84
15836 - -	EY 6959
15837 - -	FYV 642
15838 - -	DOU 446
15839 - -	BUT 792
15840 - -	FYX 979
15841 - - -	JEV 76
15842 - - - - - -	
15843 - -	BPY 695
15844 - -	GNB 49
15845 - -	FYX 987
15846 - -	GGC 479

20514 - - - - - - B	20584 - - KHY 566	20654 - - - - - -	20724 - - XS 6106	20794 - - - - - -	20864 - MNW 436
20515 - - - - - B	20585 - - LRA 885	20655 - - GZ 6178	20725 - - HUR 347	20795 - - JWJ 440	20865 - - EX 6167
20516 - - - - - B	20586 - - BFK 756	20656 - - - FCJ 20	20726 - - GDU 784	20796 - - - AUS	20866 - - - - NZ
20517 - - - - CH	20587 - MML 558	20657 - - DUT 406	20727 - - HBJ 650	20797 - - - AUS	20867 - - CNL 324
20518 - - - - - B	20588 - - KUB 663	20658 - - MPL 23	20728 - - EUX 55	20798 - - - - - -	20868 - - ETR 217
20519 - - - - - B	20589 - - - - G 1	20659 - - HVF 353	20729 - - - - B	20799 - - - - B	20869 - - - ZA
20520 - - - - - B	20590 - - - - - B	20660 - - MML 559	20730 - MML 554	20800 - - - AUS	20870 - - - - CH
20521 - - - - - B	20591 - - - - - B	20661 - - DFR 170	20731 - - FYG 441	20801 - - - - - -	20871 - - - - - -
20522 - - - - - B	20592 - - LNU 928	20662 - - - - - -	20732 - - - - - B	20802 - - JMB 92	20872 - - ACP 440
20523 - - JVC 611	20593 - - KTV 718	20663 - - KBH 177	20733 - - - - - -	20803 - - - - - -	20873 - - CBN 855
20524 - - DDP 931	20594 - - BHL 88	20664 - - NPD 968	20734 - LEH 374	20804 - CUD 819	20874 - - - - - -
20525 - - - - - B	20595 - HXJ 911	20665 - - - - - -	20735 - LKO 112	20805 - - - - - -	20875 - - - - - -
20526 - - - - - B	20596 - - EBL 282	20666 - - HTC 932	20736 - MJO 302	20806 - LJO 690	20876 - - - - CH
20527 - FWS 576	20597 - - - - - B	20667 - - - - - -	20737 - - JTO 73	20807 - - - AUS	20877 - - - - - -
20528 - - - - - B	20598 - - FSF 697	20668 - - - - - -	20738 - - - - - -	20808 - HVR 202	20878 - - DJ 9757
20529 - - ANH 47	20599 - - GHP 314	20669 - - - - - -	20739 - - KTF 24	20809 - - - - - -	20879 - - - - - -
20530 - - - - - B	20600 - - - - - -	20670 - - LPD 14	20740 - KLH 455	20810 - HOE 762	20880 - FKV 619
20531 - - - - - B	20601 - - - - - B	20671 - - - EJF 41	20741 - JAH 915	20811 - - - - - -	20881 - EX 6071
20532 - - - - - B	20602 - - FWS 962	20672 - - HVR 368	20742 - - - - - -	20812 - DUT 424	20882 - HCD 955
20533 - - - - - -	20603 - - - - - B	20673 - - - - - -	20743 - - - CH	20813 - HAH 265	20883 - - - NZ
20534 - - - - - -	20604 - KUM 154	20674 - - - ZA	20744 - - - CH	20814 - - - AUS	20884 - - - - - -
20535 - - - - - B	20605 - - LUB 450	20675 - - - - - -	20745 - EVJ 125	20815 - HVO 401	20885 - EG 7479
20536 - - - - - B	20606 - - KRB 680	20676 - MRA 215	20746 - GFD 889	20816 - MRB 602	20886 - ERP 941
20537 - - JUE 560	20607 - - EVJ 112	20677 - - EUS 629	20747 - ATS 396	20817 - - HLV 31	20887 - - - - - -
20538 - GRU 220	20608 - - GNX 427	20678 - HUO 346	20748 - GPW 837	20818 - - HEL 82	20888 - - HXJ 73
20539 - GKV 30	20609 - HUR 418	20679 - - - - - -	20749 - JTV 569	20819 - FVB 591	20889 - FKV 600
20540 - FDA 748	20610 - FVE 609	20680 - JC 8859	20750 - HRO 840	20820 - ANH 444	20890 - - - - - -
20541 - HVR 126	20611 - - ANH 433	20681 - GVF 517	20751 - - JTV 52	20821 - HDU 160	20891 - JWJ 562
20542 - - CVG 55	20612 - - GVF 569	20682 - JAU 401	20752 - - - - - B	20822 - - CVG 54	20892 - GNP 780
20543 - JYF 895	20613 - - JNB 847	20683 - FVC 303	20753 - LJO 129	20823 - HUR 201	20893 - - - - - -
20544 - GRU 645	20614 - - - - - -	20684 - - - - - -	20754 - - - - - -	20824 - CCL 998	20894 - HAH 192
20545 - B	20615 - OMP 100	20685 - - - - - -	20755 - - - - - -	20825 - EX 6172	20895 - - - - - B
20546 - - - - - B	20616 - - - - - -	20686 - TMG 120	20756 - GNG 180	20826 - ARC 314	20896 - DRX 564
20547 - FOU 650	20617 - - - - - B	20687 - MEH 618	20757 - FVC 866	20827 - - GFG 40	20897 - BJL 746
20548 - - - - - B	20618 - - LNU 61	20688 - - - - - -	20758 - - - - - -	20828 - - - - ZA	20898 - ECA 123
20549 - - HVF 2	20619 - - - - - B	20689 - - BRN 28	20759 - FGY 401	20829 - JYW 289	20899 - JWJ 441
20550 - - - - - -	20620 - - - - - B	20690 - HNG 159	20760 - - - - - -	20830 - EN 8985	20900 - - - - - -
20551 - - - - - -	20621 - - - - - B	20691 - JMB 933	20761 - - - - - -	20831 - KLG 275	20901 - FYG 442
20552 - - - - - -	20622 - - - - - -	20692 - MNU 560	20762 - EX 6139	20832 - JTO 808	20902 - - - - - -
20553 - - - - CH	20623 - - JXM 901	20693 - - JLF 504	20763 - FVC 865	20833 - - - - - -	20903 - JXK 506
20554 - KAU 137	20624 - - HNK 326	20694 - - - - - -	20764 - - - - - -	20834 - - - - - -	20904 - FA 9509
20555 - - - - - -	20625 - - LPE 800	20695 - - LRB 608	20765 - - - - - -	20835 - HAH 883	20905 - DDR 775
20556 - - TMH 10	20626 - - JUR 827	20696 - - - - - -	20766 - - - CH	20836 - JPO 487	20906 - - FSP 73
20557 - KVT 719	20627 - MEH 396	20697 - HOD 765	20767 - EBD 949	20837 - - - - - -	20907 - - - ZA
20558 - - - - - B	20628 - - LPF 914	20698 - - MHK 56	20768 - - - - - -	20838 - - EOU 1	20908 - - - - - -
20559 - - - - - B	20629 - - FWU 271	20699 - MEH 534	20769 - FVC 867	20839 - FSC 648	20909 - - - - - -
20560 - - - - - B	20630 - - - - - B	20700 - - - - - -	20770 - - - - - -	20840 - JMB 333	20910 - FGB 463
20561 - - - - - B	20631 - GDF 814	20701 - - CFV 193	20771 - LRB 167	20841 - HVM 649	20911 - - - - B
20562 - - - - - B	20632 - - - - - B	20702 - - FSF 66	20772 - FA 8690	20842 - JWJ 528	20912 - - - - - -
20563 - - - - - -	20633 - GVF 297	20703 - FYG 392	20773 - NNU 290	20843 - JRR 111	20913 - - - - - -
20564 - - JWJ 563	20634 - - - - - -	20704 - EVJ 704	20774 - - - - - -	20844 - ACP 144	20914 - LJO 213
20565 - - - - - B	20635 - KHU 350	20705 - - - - - -	20775 - - - ZA	20845 - GNP 651	20915 - - - - - -
20566 - GAC 289	20636 - LPE 845	20706 - ACW 12	20776 - FWW 384	20846 - FKV 291	20916 - EU 8432
20567 - - - - - -	20637 - - - - - B	20707 - MML 556	20777 - DRP 267	20847 - FYG 445	20917 - - - - B
20568 - FSC 979	20638 - - - - - -	20708 - MNU 171	20778 - KUM 691	20848 - JWB 883	20918 - CVG 541
20569 - HVR 127	20639 - - - - - B	20709 - HTJ 538	20779 - - FSP 23	20849 - - JGJ 832	20919 - - - - - -
20570 - - - - - -	20640 - HNF 908	20710 - - - - - -	20780 - SMG 165	20850 - JKA 898	20920 - - - ZA
20571 - CVA 777	20641 - - - - - B	20711 - - - - - -	20781 - - - - - B	20851 - - - - - -	20921 - - - ZA
20572 - HYP 238	20642 - HKF 353	20712 - ACH 200	20782 - JWB 998	20852 - JYO 851	20922 - EKW 576
20573 - JLP 344	20643 - JKB 113	20713 - HKF 354	20783 - - - - - B	20853 - LNU 743	20923 - - - - - -
20574 - KBH 879	20644 - - - - - -	20714 - LNW 707	20784 - - - - - B	20854 - ANH 744	20924 - DPN 958
20575 - - - - - B	20645 - EAY 374	20715 - - - - - -	20785 - JAL 158	20855 - UMK 234	20925 - JHN 273
20576 - - - - CH	20646 - - - - - -	20716 - - - - CH	20786 - CRD 375	20856 - BCH 299	20926 - - KWE 7
20577 - - - - CH	20647 - FCJ 246	20717 - ANH 545	20787 - - - ZA	20857 - - - - - -	20927 - - - - - -
20578 - - - - - B	20648 - - - - - -	20718 - - - - - -	20788 - HXP 523	20858 - HTD 287	20928 - - - - - -
20579 - - - - - -	20649 - - JAL 109	20719 - HG 9547	20789 - NHX 95	20859 - - - - - -	20929 - - - - P
20580 - - - - - B	20650 - LPF 537	20720 - - - - - -	20790 - - - - - -	20860 - FSC 101	20930 - CBN 859
20581 - - - - CH	20651 - MML 560	20721 - BRN 29	20791 - JFM 166	20861 - - - - - -	20931 - DUX 274
20582 - - - - CH	20652 - - - - - -	20722 - FWW 861	20792 - ANH 10	20862 - - - - - -	20932 - GHP 766
20583 - - - - - -	20653 - DNT 825	20723 - GAC 197	20793 - - - AUS	20863 - - - - - B	20933 - - - - B

20934 - - HXV 790	21004 - - - - - -	21074 - - - - - -	21144 - - - KZ 409	21214 - - - - - -	21284 - - - - - -
20935 - - JMA 636	21005 - - - JYF 892	21075 - GHP 409	21145 - EDT 373	21215 - - - JTB 98	21285 - CVY 988
20936 - - - - - B	21006 - - EN 8983	21076 - FGA 671	21146 - - - - - -	21216 - - MJO 765	21286 - - - - - -
20937 - - - - - B	21007 - GDU 707	21077 - - - - - -	21147 - - - - - P	21217 - - - BRN 24	21287 - HVU 628
20938 - LBB 269	21008 - FAK 679	21078 - HYD 666	21148 - - - - - S	21218 - - - - - -	21288 - - - - - -
20939 - - - - - -	21009 - MFC 566	21079 - DRX 712	21149 - - - - - -	21219 - - - - - B	21289 - KHW 351
20940 - KUG 924	21010 - GVF 787	21080 - FA 8687	21150 - - ZH 335	21220 - - ZH 918	21290 - - JTD 66
20941 - FUY 879	21011 - JTV 459	21081 - KMA 852	21151 - - - - - -	21221 - KHW 339	21291 - JTE 826
20942 - CFE 736	21012 - - - - - -	21082 - LWA 274	21152 - - LAU 58	21222 - LPG 939	21292 - - - - - -
20943 - - - - - B	21013 - - - IRL	21083 - - GBM 1	21153 - FSF 583	21223 - - - - - -	21293 - JLX 905
20944 - - - - - -	21014 - - - AUS	21084 - FFH 450	21154 - - - - - -	21224 - - - - - -	21294 - KHA 967
20945 - HPX 550	21015 - GVF 786	21085 - EWF 999	21155 - - ZH 413	21225 - - - - - B	21295 - - - - - -
20946 - - - - - -	21016 - LRB 990	21086 - - - - - -	21156 - JTV 901	21226 - - DRP 89	21296 - EKY 430
20947 - - - JGJ 36	21017 - JWJ 564	21087 - MPH 110	21157 - - - - - -	21227 - - - - - S	21297 - - - - - -
20948 - - - - - B	21018 - JAL 201	21088 - LPF 895	21158 - JNB 823	21228 - GWR 830	21298 - - TMV 4
20949 - - - FSP 21	21019 - JP 5859	21089 - JGK 176	21159 - EKY 425	21229 - GKV 749	21299 - - - - - -
20950 - - - - - -	21020 - JGH 536	21090 - GER 815	21160 - GAX 700	21230 - - - - - B	21300 - JLF 506
20951 - - - - - -	21021 - LRB 768	21091 - EUK 600	21161 - - - - - -	21231 - - - - - -	21301 - - JYF 57
20952 - EKW 942	21022 - - - - - -	21092 - - - - - B	21162 - CHW 109	21232 - - - IRL	21302 - - - USA
20953 - GVF 535	21023 - FVE 321	21093 - - - - - B	21163 - - - - - -	21233 - - JTC 38	21303 - - - - - -
20954 - - - - - P	21024 - - - - - -	21094 - - - - - -	21164 - - - - - -	21234 - - - - - P	21304 - - - - - -
20955 - EYS 730	21025 - CVD 942	21095 - CFK 506	21165 - FVJ 576	21235 - - - - - -	21305 - - - - - -
20956 - ACP 935	21026 - DHS 500	21096 - - - - - -	21166 - - - - - -	21236 - ZE 1904	21306 - - - - - -
20957 - FWP 883	21027 - - - - - -	21097 - - - - - -	21167 - - - - - S	21237 - KWA 69	21307 - SMV 224
20958 - FSC 939	21028 - GAO 985	21098 - - - - - -	21168 - - - - - -	21238 - - - - - -	21308 - CHH 590
20959 - - - - - -	21029 - - - - - -	21099 - DDY 45	21169 - - FKW 3	21239 - - - JJJ 662	21309 - - - - - -
20960 - PV 7909	21030 - - - - - -	21100 - JUL 110	21170 - - - - - S	21240 - FNM 876	21310 - - - - - -
20961 - GAK 305	21031 - MFC 70	21101 - - - - - -	21171 - - - CH	21241 - - - JTU 96	21311 - FGB 673
20962 - - - - - -	21032 - JMB 786	21102 - - - - - -	21172 - JGU 769	21242 - - - IRL	21312 - EWK 827
20963 - DHS 189	21033 - GAA 787	21103 - KWE 503	21173 - FSF 929	21243 - LNW 112	21313 - - - - - S
20964 - JWJ 442	21034 - - JTJ 425	21104 - JTV 600	21174 - ZH 1898	21244 - KTJ 906	21314 - - - - - -
20965 - - - - - -	21035 - - - - - -	21105 - EKW 993	21175 - GDV 709	21245 - - - - - -	21315 - - - AUS
20966 - - - - - -	21036 - CFX 573	21106 - - - - - -	21176 - - - - - -	21246 - DJY 396	21316 - - - - - P
20967 - - - - - -	21037 - - - - - P	21107 - LUA 207	21177 - - ZH 394	21247 - NFC 504	21317 - - - - - -
20968 - - - EUN 6	21038 - LNW 703	21108 - - - - - -	21178 - JTV 572	21248 - - - - - -	21318 - KWJ 224
20969 - KHY 466	21039 - GHP 559	21109 - EKY 122	21179 - CWH 761	21249 - GDV 991	21319 - HOL 194
20970 - - - - - -	21040 - - - - - B	21110 - JDT 412	21180 - - - - - P	21250 - GRW 782	21320 - - - - - S
20971 - MHK 53	21041 - - - - - -	21111 - CWH 110	21181 - - - - - -	21251 - GUY 260	21321 - LHA 170
20972 - - - JTF 96	21042 - LRA 660	21112 - LNW 737	21182 - - - - - -	21252 - - - - - -	21322 - - - - - -
20973 - - - - - -	21043 - HTF 567	21113 - HOU 120	21183 - EBL 837	21253 - - - - - -	21323 - DPN 862
20974 - HFJ 249	21044 - JYP 378	21114 - - BRN 26	21184 - GNB 392	21254 - - - JJJ 665	21324 - - - - - -
20975 - GAB 843	21045 - ACP 487	21115 - - - - - -	21185 - - - - - -	21255 - HNG 708	21325 - JP 6892
20976 - - - - - -	21046 - JMB 787	21116 - - - - - -	21186 - - - - - -	21256 - GRW 298	21326 - - - - - -
20977 - NRE 912	21047 - - - - - -	21117 - - - - - -	21187 - - - - - S	21257 - - - IRL	21327 - DRP 787
20978 - DUT 824	21048 - - - IRL	21118 - LPK 719	21188 - HBJ 910	21258 - FKW 197	21328 - EKY 480
20979 - - - - - -	21049 - JYP 379	21119 - HUR 206	21189 - - - - - -	21259 - - - - - -	21329 - LUB 589
20980 - ACP 110	21050 - - JGJ 39	21120 - - - - - -	21190 - MPC 96	21260 - - - - - -	21330 - CJR 122
20981 - - - - - S	21051 - HUF 909	21121 - JGU 763	21191 - EKY 894	21261 - KAU 258	21331 - DFN 300
20982 - GHP 187	21052 - DNJ 863	21122 - - - - - -	21192 - LUB 956	21262 - - - - - B	21332 - WI 2298
20983 - FGB 452	21053 - - - - - -	21123 - - - - - -	21193 - - - - - -	21263 - - - - - B	21333 - - - IRL
20984 - - - - - -	21054 - GCE 514	21124 - GWY 951	21194 - - - - - -	21264 - - - - - B	21334 - HD 8212
20985 - - - EVG 1	21055 - - - - - -	21125 - FWP 583	21195 - EAJ 875	21265 - - - - - B	21335 - - - - - -
20986 - - - - - -	21056 - CVY 687	21126 - - - - - -	21196 - DBW 524	21266 - - - - - B	21336 - - - - - -
20987 - KAU 237	21057 - HUF 860	21127 - - - - - -	21197 - HLV 518	21267 - - - - - B	21337 - GWX 444
20988 - - - - - -	21058 - - - - - -	21128 - ANH 350	21198 - EO 8629	21268 - HVF 187	21338 - FDT 857
20989 - - - - - -	21059 - - - - - -	21129 - - - - - -	21199 - HAA 276	21269 - JKR 312	21339 - FGD 666
20990 - HVF 987	21060 - DWH 22	21130 - SMX 267	21200 - AEE 527	21270 - ZH 1014	21340 - - - - - -
20991 - FDT 262	21061 - GCE 515	21131 - JTD 892	21201 - - - - - -	21271 - - - - - S	21341 - MUG 790
20992 - ACP 109	21062 - - - - - -	21132 - JMB 935	21202 - - - - - -	21272 - GOR 871	21342 - - - - - B
20993 - CWH 762	21063 - - - - - P	21133 - EYS 962	21203 - DRX 993	21273 - DRP 786	21343 - - JJJ 668
20994 - - - - - -	21064 - - - - - -	21134 - - - - - -	21204 - DTP 361	21274 - - - IRL	21344 - - AEP 3
20995 - FFY 605	21065 - - - - - -	21135 - EKY 363	21205 - - - - - -	21275 - - - - - -	21345 - - - AUS
20996 - FOT 459	21066 - JGW 160	21136 - - - - - -	21206 - GNX 127	21276 - JLN 528	21346 - - - - - S
20997 - - - - - -	21067 - - - - - -	21137 - LPJ 365	21207 - JGU 767	21277 - - - IRL	21347 - - - IRL
20998 - CVG 119	21068 - EJU 748	21138 - - - - - -	21208 - - ZH 995	21278 - - - - - S	21348 - - - - - P
20999 - - - - - -	21069 - JMB 788	21139 - JCD 528	21209 - KAH 269	21279 - - - - - -	21349 - CJG 500
21000 - - - - - -	21070 - LRA 325	21140 - - - - - B	21210 - - - - - -	21280 - JLN 525	21350 - KWE 387
21001 - GDU 495	21071 - - - IRL	21141 - CHM 823	21211 - - - IRL	21281 - - - - - P	21351 - FWK 865
21002 - - - - - -	21072 - FBT 71	21142 - EJU 580	21212 - - ZH 629	21282 - - - IRL	21352 - - - - - -
21003 - - - JNB 44	21073 - JLF 510	21143 - - - - - -	21213 - - - IRL	21283 - - - - - -	21353 - - - - - -

21354 - - KTF 189	21424 - - - - - -	21494 - - LUA 383	21564 - - JUR 184	21633 - -KLM 931	21703 - - JYL 703
21355 - - -JTJ 702	21425 - - - - - -	21495 - - - - - -	21565 - - JLO 573	21634 - DPN 300	21704 - - - - - -U
21356 - - - - - -	21426 - - JTD 582	21496 - - ORE 769	21566 - - - - - -	21635 - - FBC 184	21705 - - - - - -
21357 - LUA 783	21427 - - - - - -	21497 - - - - - -	21567 - HOM 368	21636 - - - - - -	21706 - - MPA 155
21358 - - - - - -	21428 - - - JAD 88	21498 - - FTM 857	21568 - EJU 702	21637 - LHY 772	21707 - - ESA 352
21359 - - - - - -	21429 - - - - - -	21499 - - - IRL	21569 - CVG 695	21638 - GDT 268	21708 - - LUB 414
21360 - - - - - -	21430 - - - FDT 1	21500 - - - - - -	21570 - JLW 680	21639 - -JLP 156	21709 - - - - - -
21361 - - - - - -	21431 - - - - - -	21501 - LPK 298	21571 - DRV 645	21640 - FCR 159	21710 - - FJW 200
21362 - - - - - -	21432 - - - IRL	21502 - DVH 24	21572 -HDD 224	21641 - FGG 363	21711 - - - - - -
21363 - - - AUS	21433 - - - IRL	21503 - JLU 897	21573 - MVW 167	21642 - -JLP 349	21712 - - - - - -
21364 - - - - - -	21434 - ZH 5263	21504 - - - - - -	21574 - JLN 530	21643 - - - - - -	21713 - - -HVF 50
21365 - - - - - -	21435 - - - IRL	21505 - FDA 755	21575 - LPL 572	21644 - LUB 356	21714 - - FGE 774
21366 - MNO 800	21436 - - -FWF 57	21506 - -JP 6445	21576 - - - - - -	21645 - -JLP 350	21715 - - - IRL
21367 - JNA 998	21437 - - ZH 2897	21507 - - - - - -	21577 -KWB 547	21646 - JAH 263	21716 - - JYR 755
21368 - ZH 1376	21438 - - DVY 278	21508 - - - IRL	21578 - KAU 215	21647 - - - AUS	21717 - - - - -B
21369 - - - IRL	21439 - - HDD 54	21509 - EG 8246	21579 -HON 224	21648 - - - - - -	21718 - - GVC 481
21370 - ZH 1736	21440 - - - IRL	21510 - - - - - -	21580 - - MZ 28	21649 - CVG 659	21719 - - -MZ 595
21371 - - - - - S	21441 - FDA 858	21511 - JYH 498	21581 - EDT 882	21650 - -MNU 852	21720 - - - - ET
21372 - - - - - S	21442 - ANH 782	21512 - HFJ 787	21582 - - - - - -	21651 - CVL 544	21721 - - GVC 437
21373 - - - - - -	21443 - - ZF 608	21513 - ZH 2656	21583 - JUL 109	21652 - RRF 698	21722 - - DVH 653
21374 - ANH 725	21444 - CVG 542	21514 - ECO 106	21584 - - - - - -	21653 - EAV 548	21723 - - JYP 372
21375 - - - - - S	21445 - -HDG 250	21515 - KPP 198	21585 - HEL 797	21654 - ACM 256	21724 - - GVC 967
21376 - HDV 936	21446 - - - - - -	21516 - JYC 941	21586 - -MPD 800	21655 - - - - - -	21725 - -MRA 361
21377 - BRN 394	21447 - ZH 1121	21517 - DBK 920	21587 - -DDN 292	21656 - - - AUS	21726 - - - - ET
21378 - GWW 243	21448 - FMJ 320	21518 - JLN 522	21588 - EAW 125	21657 - - - - - -	21727 - - - - - -
21379 - - JTJ 646	21449 - - JTF 34	21519 - - - - - -	21589 - JPO 257	21658 - - - AUS	21728 - - - - ET
21380 - ZE 2023	21450 - - - - - -	21520 - HOL 795	21590 - - - - - -	21659 - MPA 574	21729 - - - IRL
21381 - ZH 1257	21451 - - - - - -	21521 - - - - - -	21591 - LRB 440	21660 - - - - - -	21730 - GVC 503
21382 - DRD 660	21452 - - - - - -	21522 - EG 8320	21592 - - MZ 10	21661 - CVG 593	21731 - - - - ET
21383 - - - IRL	21453 - - - - - -	21523 - - - - - -	21593 - LPK 299	21662 - - - - - -	21732 - - - AUS
21384 - - - - - S	21454 - -EJF 843	21524 - - - - - -	21594 - CUD 874	21663 - JYR 349	21733 - - - - - -
21385 - - - IRL	21455 - EBL 777	21525 - - - - - -	21595 -HSM 670	21664 - DDB 507	21734 - - - - - -
21386 - GWW 425	21456 - MJO 100	21526 - -FWF 24	21596 - FOD 554	21665 - JKB 503	21735 - - - - - -
21387 - - - - - -	21457 - - - IRL	21527 - FWS 170	21597 - - - - - -	21666 - - - - ET	21736 - - ZH 6121
21388 - - - IRL	21458 - - JLY 26	21528 - KHY 562	21598 -HFM 934	21667 - - - - - -	21737 - FAM 164
21389 - FAK 707	21459 - GCG 729	21529 - KKJ 978	21599 -EWV 574	21668 - DRV 164	21738 - - EI 4676
21390 - - - - - -	21460 - - - - - -	21530 - GNX 413	21600 - - - - - -	21669 - LRB 702	21739 - -KMB 419
21391 - SMX 881	21461 - SL 3171	21531 - AFB 474	21601 - -JYF 897	21670 - JLH 228	21740 - - - AUS
21392 - - JAH 83	21462 - FGE 113	21532 - CWH 212	21602 - DVH 149	21671 - - - ET	21741 - FOD 434
21393 - CVL 447	21463 - - - - - -	21533 - GCG 144	21603 - JLW 677	21672 - - - ET	21742 - HBJ 813
21394 - - - - - -	21464 - ZB 7592	21534 - - - AUS	21604 - - - - - -	21673 - KAU 734	21743 - - - JM 2
21395 - -TI 4528	21465 - AHN 727	21535 - - - - - -	21605 - LUA 851	21674 - - - AUS	21744 - - - - - -
21396 - - - - - -	21466 - -CHH 608	21536 - - -JP 6741	21606 - JML 948	21675 - - - AUS	21745 - - - - -B
21397 - - JTE 380	21467 - - - GBJ	21537 - JDV 478	21607 - JDV 913	21676 - CWH 358	21746 - - FWM 99
21398 - - - - - -	21468 - -EMO 478	21538 - JLN 529	21608 - - - - - -	21677 - IX 2000	21747 - - - - -B
21399 - LVT 346	21469 - - - - ET	21539 - - FMJ 63	21609 - - - - - -	21678 - MJO 646	21748 - - - - - -
21400 - - - - - -	21470 - GNP 515	21540 - - - - - -	21610 - - - - - -	21679 - KPP 615	21749 - - - - - -
21401 - KHY 441	21471 - - - - - -	21541 - FGG 936	21611 - KPP 428	21680 - - - - ET	21750 - - - - - -
21402 - EBL 510	21472 - - - AUS	21542 - - - AUS	21612 - - - - - -	21681 - - - - ET	21751 - - - - -B
21403 - - - - - -	21473 - - -AI 7377	21543 - JLX 901	21613 - KHY 839	21682 - - -HLJ 2	21752 - - - - ET
21404 - LUA 208	21474 - -KWB 378	21544 - - - - - -	21614 - - - - - -	21683 - - JYF 59	21753 - - - - - -
21405 - - - - - -	21475 - GWK 351	21545 - - - - - -	21615 - FAK 259	21684 - HDD 319	21754 - - - - -B
21406 - - JYF 52	21476 - - - - -B	21546 - LTN 874	21616 - - EJB 51	21685 - DBN 184	21755 - EBD 666
21407 - - - IRL	21477 - - - -FM	21547 - ZE 2375	21617 - MVW 829	21686 - GVC 268	21756 - JLW 673
21408 - - - IRL	21478 - EVJ 795	21548 - - - - - -	21618	21687 - ZH 6191	21757 - - - - -B
21409 - ZE 2146	21479 - GVC 289	21549 - GWK 798	- - - - - AUS	21688 - - - - - -	21758 - JLW 678
21410 - KTB 883	21480 - - - - - -	21550 - - - - - -	21619 - LVK 199	21689 - DCK 566	21759 - - JLU 90
21411 - JKA 785	21481 - JLX 909	21551 - JNN 300	21620 - -HEL 22	21690 - CTY 467	21760 - - - - - -
21412 - IH 6536	21482 - - - - - -	21552 - - - IRL	21621 - - - - BR	21691 - -JP 6764	21761 - SH 8273
21413 - DRP 508	21483 - - - - - -	21553 - - -JNB 2	21622 - JDV 850	21692 - DRD 400	21762 - - - - - -
21414 - ZE 3776	21484 - - - - - -	21554 - - - - - -	21623 - JYL 705	21693 - -JLT 157	21763 - - - - - -
21415 - - GBJ	21485 - - - - - -	21555 - JLU 85	21624 - PV 8350	21694 - FCJ 520	21764 - GVC 739
21416 - FWS 672	21486 - PV 8349	21556 - - - - - -	21625 - MVW 776	21695 - - - - - -	21765 - - - - - -
21417 - ZH 2036	21487 - HOM 74	21557 - JLO 576	21626 - FDA 998	21696 - - - - - -	21766 - - - AUS
21418 - HAD 862	21488 - HEL 559	21558 - - - - - -	21627 - - - - - -	21697 - - - - -U	21767 - - - - - -
21419 - - - IRL	21489 - - - - -B	21559 - - - - - -	21628 - -DRV 14	21698 - - - - - -	21768 - - - - - -
21420 - JLU 894	21490 - JLN 523	21560 - LUA 209	21629 - FWF 333	21699 - -KWE 779	21769 - ECO 282
21421 - MPF 298	21491 - JDV 302	21561 - MTW 982	21630 - - JYF 60	21700 - CWH 866	21770 - - - - - -
21422 - - - - - -	21492 - -KHN 115	21562 - ZH 5282	21631 - JYL 707	21701 - - - - ET	21771 - CVG 737
21423 - - EET 504	21493 - MTW 803	21563 - - -JYF 896	21632 - - - - - -	21702 - - - - - -	21772 - - - - - -

21773 - - DCL 172	21843 - - DDN 598	21913 - -GBM 732	21983 - - ENR 832	22053 - - - - AUS	22123 - - - - - -
21774 - - FBC 374	21844 - - - - - -	21914 - - - - - -	21984 - - -JYF 891	22054 - - FUS 887	22124 - - HAO 720
21775 - - - - - -	21845 - - MPB 163	21915 - - GOU 685	21985 - - HBJ 991	22055 - - JYO 394	22125 - - KKP 263
21776 - - - AUS	21846 - - CWH 878	21916 - - - - - -	21986 - - - - - -	22056 - - CWH 835	22126 - - JPX 555
21777 - - - - - -	21847 - - - - - -	21917 - - AGL 646	21987 - - - APO 1	22057 - -MNU 730	22127 - - LUG 837
21778 - - LAE 547	21848 - - CCK 213	21918 - - LWA 683	21988 - - - AUS	22058 - - MPB 315	22128 - - JFM 520
21779 - - - - - -	21849 - - - - - -	21919 - - LUM 523	21989 - - JRO 888	22059 - - JYD 666	22129 - - DRV 723
21780 - - - - - -	21850 - - - - - -	21920 - - - - - -	21990 - - - - - -	22060 - - GBM 493	22130 - - LHT 665
21781 - - - - -CH	21851 - - GHO 66	21921 - - - - - -	21991 - - - - - -	22061 - - GKV 945	22131 - - - - - NL
21782 - - - - - -	21852 - - HAC 713	21922 - -KMB 679	21992 - -GHO 816	22062 - - - - - -	22132 - - KWJ 384
21783 - - JUL 104	21853 - - - - - -U	21923 - - HAB 473	21993 - - - - - -	22063 - - ACN 946	22133 - - GOR 222
21784 - - KPP 900	21854 - - - - - ET	21924 - - - - - -	21994 - - - - ET	22064 - - - - - -	22134 - - HHP 135
21785 - MVX 963	21855 - - - - - -	21925 - - KTJ 158	21995 - - - - - -	22065 - - GVC 943	22135 - - JYL 709
21786 - - - - - -	21856 - - - - - -	21926 - - - - - -	21996 - - KWJ 218	22066 - - - - - -	22136 - - LUG 795
21787 - - KTF 234	21857 - - - - ET	21927 - - - - - -	21997 - - - - ZA	22067 - - -JP 6985	22137 - - - AUS
21788 - - - - - -	21858 - - - - -HK	21928 - - - - - -	21998 - - CPR 844	22068 - -GWD 265	22138 - - HLJ 855
21789 - -EJB 500	21859 - - FHR 620	21929 - - LWA 498	21999 - - JYD 447	22069 - - GFS 878	22139 - - JYL 708
21790 - - AKS 600	21860 - - GSC 187	21930 - - LUM 921	22000 - - LHT 400	22070 - - - JYF 54	22140 - - FKU 230
21791 - - - - - -	21861 - - SY 8780	21931 - - -LWA 31	22001 - - JUR 934	22071 - - FKU 112	22141 - - DHM 77
21792 - -NPB 76	21862 - - - - - -	21932 - - - - - -	22002 - - PRE 606	22072 - - - - - -	22142 - - HDU 412
21793 - - - - - -	21863 - - - - - -	21933 - - JYL 701	22003 - - EY 8866	22073 - - EG 8655	22143 - - HDU 879
21794 - - - - -CH	21864 - - HWR 612	21934 - -MUA 790	22004 - - JUL 103	22074 - - - - - -	22144 - - - - - -
21795 - - JKD 647	21865 - - KPT 873	21935 - - - - - -	22005 - - PRE 700	22075 - - - - ZA	22145 - - JYM 532
21796 - - LAE 519	21866 - -NWL 137	21936 - - LUM 921	22006 - - JUL 106	22076 - - ECO 727	22146 - - FBE 121
21797 - KKM 621	21867 - - LDH 923	21937 - - JYP 373	22007 - - - - - -	22077 - - AVV 207	22147 - - NPU 126
21798 - - - - - -	21868 - - GOR 965	21938 - - -KGF 83	22008 - - MZ 1544	22078 - - - - - -	22148 - - - - -U
21799 - - - - - -	21869 - - DDN 603	21939 - - KWJ 522	22009 - - GKV 922	22079 - - AVV 295	22149 - - JVC 702
21800 - - JLX 904	21870 - - - - - -	21940 - - - - - -	22010 - - - - - -	22080 - - JOD 309	22150 - - - - -U
21801 - - JTE 565	21871 - - KDU 550	21941 - - - - - -	22011 - -CHH 780	22081 - - -JYF 894	22151 - - - - -U
21802 - -KWE 187	21872 - - NHK 55	21942 - - NJO 341	22012 - - - - - -	22082 - - KTO 999	22152 - - EUJ 350
21803 - - - - - -	21873 - - - - - -	21943 - - KGC 532	22013 - - - - - -	22083 - - LBH 811	22153 - - - - TR
21804 - - JCD 480	21874 - - - - - -	21944 - - FJU 489	22014 - - -EJB 955	22084 - -KKO 499	22154 - - - AUS
21805 - -KWE 186	21875 - - - - - -	21945 - - JYU 527	22015 - - SMX 530	22085 - - EDR 434	22155 - - FHR 500
21806 - - - AUS	21876 - - FDT 255	21946 - - - - - -	22016 - - JYR 751	22086 - - - JYF 53	22156 - - AKS 880
21807 - - - - - -	21877 - - - - - -	21947 - - KWJ 396	22017 - - - - - -	22087 - - KDE 82	22157 - -JYW 75
21808 - -KMA 280	21878 - - KWJ 573	21948 - - LWB 268	22018 - - JYR 348	22088 - - - USA	22158 - -CHH 863
21809 - - - - ET	21879 - - KGC 540	21949 - -MNU 652	22019 - - - - - -	22089 - - - -FVJ 1	22159 - - EUJ 961
21810 - - KAU 999	21880 - - - - - -	21950 - - NHK 880	22020 - - MPE 927	22090 - - DRV 714	22160 - - - - -S
21811 - - - - - -	21881 - - -JLY 507	21951 - - - - - -	22021 - - ATS 230	22091 - - - - - -	22161 - - GWP 487
21812 - - - - - -	21882 - - - - - -	21952 - - - AUS	22022 - - FEW 737	22092 - - GDA 250	22162 - - HG 9906
21813 - - - - - -	21883 - - - - - -	21953 - - -KGF 84	22023 - -GWD 336	22093 - - -JTF 603	22163 - - JYR 758
21814 - - MPA 653	21884 - - MHU 156	21954 - - CRS 788	22024 - - HDF 319	22094 - - MPC 974	22164 - - - - - -
21815 - - - AUS	21885 - - FUT 286	21955 - -GWD 456	22025 - -GWY 599	22095 - - JYD 890	22165 - - - - - -
21816 - - ECO 532	21886 - - FGG 835	21956 - - MZ 1334	22026 - - GGA 44	22096 - - - JYF 56	22166 - - JYR 350
21817 - - - - - -	21887 - -EMO 134	21957 - - - - - -	22027 - - - - - -	22097 - FWM 243	22167 - - FBE 541
21818 - - JXR 118	21888 - - - - - -	21958 - - JOM 679	22028 - - KKB 296	22098 - - - - - -	22168 - - - - - -
21819 - - -JLP 820	21889 - - DEA 777	21959 - - KWJ 687	22029 - - - - - -	22099 - - - - - -	22169 - - - - - -
21820 - - - AUS	21890 - - HAO 893	21960 - - MPH 48	22030 - - - - - -	22100 - - - - - -	22170 - - NFC 579
21821 - - HAO 314	21891 - - EMO 13	21961 - - - - - -	22031 - - DRV 614	22101 - - - - - -	22171 - - - -U
21822 - - - - ET	21892 - -LHW 410	21962 - - - - - -	22032 - - CCK 54	22102 - - -JYF 899	22172 - - LHU 123
21823 - - FOD 897	21893 - - ACP 846	21963 - - FDT 370	22033 - - NFC 357	22103 - - NFC 571	22173 - - - - - -
21824 - - JYR 341	21894 - - - - - -	21964 - - CVL 852	22034 - - -JOD 44	22104 - - - -JNE 7	22174 - - - - -S
21825 - - ASN 727	21895 - - KAL 517	21965 - - GER 484	22035 - - HDU 880	22105 - - HOP 810	22175 - - -JP 7096
21826 - - JUF 999	21896 - - - - - -	21966 - - - FUS 46	22036 - - - NL	22106 - - - - - -	22176 - - LUM 233
21827 - - FED 585	21897 - - - - - -	21967 - - GKV 475	22037 - -GWY 866	22107 - - HOV 279	22177 - - -DCL 25
21828 - - - - - -	21898 - - MHT 36	21968 - - JYD 214	22038 - - JYE 909	22108 - -EDW 845	22178 - - JYM 533
21829 - - MPE 759	21899 - - - - - -	21969 - - CVG 821	22039 - - - - - -	22109 - - KWJ 702	22179 - - - - ET
21830 - - -JFJ 286	21900 - - AJX 117	21970 - - - - - -	22040 - - - - - -	22110 - - NPF 810	22180 - - - - ET
21831 - - - - - -	21901 - - LHU 453	21971 - - KGC 533	22041 - - JKD 750	22111 - - JOC 369	22181 - - KTV 218
21832 - - ENR 448	21902 - - FUN 200	21972 - - FCJ 681	22042 - - JYH 578	22112 - - GGA 462	22182 - - MPD 359
21833 - - KHN 751	21903 - - HRU 95	21973 - - KGC 531	22043 - - KTA 513	22113 - - - - - -	22183 - - - - -S
21834 - - -DVY 27	21904 - - JYP 371	21974 - - - - - -	22044 - - JYH 524	22114 - - - - - -	22184 - - JYR 757
21835 - - LVK 959	21905 - - - JYF 58	21975 - - JXL 910	22045 - - JND 429	22115 - - JNE 277	22185 - - KTV 660
21836 - - - - - -	21906 - - - - - -	21976 - - LUG 441	22046 - - - - - -	22116 - - JYL 828	22186 - - JYR 754
21837 - - LWB 679	21907 - - ECX 830	21977 - - FCR 817	22047 - - GOR 40	22117 - -KHN 529	22187 - - GGA 157
21838 - - GGB 904	21908 - -GNM 275	21978 - - - - - -	22048 - - NNO 57	22118 - - JYV 671	22188 - - SL 3297
21839 - - -DVY 28	21909 - - LUM 522	21979 - - -FFU 28	22049 - - JYV 678	22119 - - GYG 673	22189 - - FCY 603
21840 - - KWJ 158	21910 - - - - - -	21980 - - - - - -	22050 - - CVG 910	22120 - - JKD 711	22190 - - GWP 581
21841 - - -SS 6900	21911 - - - IRL	21981 - - - AUS	22051 - - - - - -	22121 - - JYP 376	22191 - - HHP 602
21842 - - GBT 560	21912 - - HHP 318	21982 - - -DVH 536	22052 - - -JP 7037	22122 - - - AUS	22192 - - GDA 318

22193 - - BCF 634	22263 - - JNF 359	22333 - - - - - -	22403 - - - - - -	22473 - - FBE 618	22543 - DVH 908
22194 - - - - - -	22264 - - FKU 612	22334 - - - - - -	22404 - - KTB 569	22474 - - GGB 876	22544 - HRW 379
22195 - - - - - -	22265 - - GBT 669	22335 - - JYN 992	22405 - - EBX 826	22475 - - JYW 173	22545 - - - - - -
22196 - - DHM 16	22266 - - - KLE 20	22336 - - ATS 427	22406 - - - - - -	22476 - - FWM 523	22546 - LUM 918
22197 - - - - - -	22267 - KHN 962	22337 - - GBT 632	22407 - - - - - -	22477 - - GSC 543	22547 - DBN 149
22198 - - OFC 142	22268 - - FBE 282	22338 - - KKR 726	22408 - - KLM 51	22478 - MPG 672	22548 - PRF 865
22199 - - DVY 22	22269 - KHN 692	22339 - - - - - -	22409 - MRA 860	22479 - - EAP 961	22549 - - - - - -
22200 - - - - CDN	22270 - TMH 118	22340 - - JM 7781	22410 - - - - - -	22480 - - LWA 696	22550 - - - - - -
22201 - - - - - U	22271 - - GGA 330	22341 - - - - - -	22411 - - - - - -	22481 - HHP 893	22551 - ENJ 153
22202 - - - - - P	22272 - - HDF 950	22342 - - - - - S	22412 - GGA 800	22482 - - - - - -	22552 - KGC 535
22203 - - - - - S	22273 - - CJR 313	22343 - - - - - S	22413 - - - - - -	22483 - - - - - -	22553 - LPP 57
22204 - - KGC 539	22274 - - - - - -	22344 - - - - - S	22414 - KTV 949	22484 - - - - - -	22554 - - - - - -
22205 - GNM 265	22275 - - - - - -	22345 - - - - - S	22415 - NTW 254	22485 - GGB 116	22555 - DFE 336
22206 - - JYM 540	22276 - - - LWA 49	22346 - - - - - S	22416 - KYA 884	22486 - - - - - -	22556 - MPH 926
22207 - - JYP 377	22277 - - - - - -	22347 - - - - - S	22417 - GNM 510	22487 - FKU 935	22557 - FDT 943
22208 - - KWJ 621	22278 - - - - - -	22348 - - - - - E	22418 - MEH 762	22488 - LHU 789	22558 - KAL 83
22209 - - MPF 500	22279 - - - - - U	22349 - - - - CH	22419 - FDT 820	22489 - LHU 788	22559 - - - - - -
22210 - - FTR 232	22280 - - JYP 380	22350 - - - - - S	22420 - JYU 529	22490 - NWL 465	22560 - - - - S
22211 - - ENV 467	22281 - - EUT 425	22351 - - FVJ 316	22421 - DFN 858	22491 - JYW 754	22561 - EBK 303
22212 - - EDR 172	22282 - - - - - S	22352 - - - - - S	22422 - KYA 949	22492 - FKU 897	22562 - GNM 596
22213 - - - - - -	22283 - - - - - -	22353 - - KAR 305	22423 - - - - - -	22493 - GBT 853	22563 - LHW 320
22214 - - CJR 394	22284 - - JYU 523	22354 - MPG 104	22424 - - - - - -	22494 - - - - - -	22564 - JYW 293
22215 - - - - NZ	22285 - - - - - S	22355 - - EUJ 470	22425 - LUM 524	22495 - - JC 9550	22565 - JOF 198
22216 - - - - - -	22286 - - - - RA	22356 - HWR 564	22426 - - - - - -	22496 - DCL 128	22566 - - - - - -
22217 - - JYM 535	22287 - - - - - S	22357 - - KMN 18	22427 - JPW 524	22497 - FBD 283	22567 - - - - - -
22218 - - KWJ 385	22288 - - NFC 817	22358 - - DVY 338	22428 - - - - - -	22498 - - JTJ 654	22568 - LND 702
22219 - - KTU 255	22289 - - - - - -	22359 - - KTT 112	22429 - - - - - -	22499 - DBA 997	22569 - CHH 991
22220 - - - - GR	22290 - - KKR 509	22360 - - - - - U	22430 - KGC 538	22500 - GOT 524	22570 - NWL 223
22221 - HRW 622	22291 - - CCK 568	22361 - - - - - -	22431 - - JP 7345	22501 - - - - - -	22571 - GJW 366
22222 - - - - - -	22292 - - - - - -	22362 - - - - - S	22432 - - - - - -	22502 - - - - - -	22572 - FKW 77
22223 - - - - - -	22293 - - JYO 582	22363 - - - - - S	22433 - JYU 528	22503 - - - - - -	22573 - LUM 919
22224 - - - - - S	22294 - - CRS 945	22364 - - FKU 649	22434 - - - - - -	22504 - KLE 486	22574 - - - - - -
22225 - - - - - S	22295 - - - KLP 12	22365 - - - GFH 39	22435 - - - - - -	22505 - JKF 854	22575 - KLE 487
22226 - - - - - S	22296 - - KLE 743	22366 - - - - - S	22436 - HHP 866	22506 - - - - - -	22576 - GDA 919
22227 - - - - - -	22297 - - LKJ 100	22367 - - - - - U	22437 - - - - - -	22507 - FCY 830	22577 - FVJ 555
22228 - - FTR 347	22298 - - - KLE 16	22368 - - DRS 224	22438 - NWL 130	22508 - - - - - -	22578 - FKW 9
22229 - - - - - S	22299 - - DFE 370	22369 - GTM 160	22439 - MPF 900	22509 - - - - - -	22579 - - - - - -
22230 - - - - - S	22300 - - KLT 911	22370 - - KBP 553	22440 - - JFJ 431	22510 - KAR 551	22580 - - - - - -
22231 - - GSC 117	22301 - - KLE 746	22371 - - - - - S	22441 - - - - - -	22511 - FWN 36	22581 - - - - - -
22232 - - JFJ 379	22302 - - OPU 438	22372 - - GSG 639	22442 - EBK 146	22512 - - - - - -	22582 - FRY 395
22233 - - - - - E	22303 - - JFK 314	22373 - - - - - S	22443 - KTA 631	22513 - AGL 384	22583 - - - - S
22234 - - - - - S	22304 - - - JTF 601	22374 - - JYV 280	22444 - KTU 415	22514 - HHP 704	22584 - - - - - -
22235 - - KTA 138	22305 - - - - ET	22375 - - - - - -	22445 - JYU 530	22515 - - - - GR	22585 - KYB 391
22236 - - - - - E	22306 - - - - - -	22376 - - - - - -	22446 - JM 7850	22516 - - - - - -	22586 - GVE 459
22237 - HDG 142	22307 - FWM 461	22377 - KLL 115	22447 - RZ 3011	22517 - PFC 604	22587 - DBN 196
22238 - - JUR 944	22308 - - JYR 346	22378 - - - - - -	22448 - HRT 831	22518 - - - - ET	22588 - HRM 284
22239 - - JP 7059	22309 - - - - - -	22379 - - JVM 77	22449 - JVF 378	22519 - MVT 154	22589 - LWA 635
22240 - - JP 7052	22310 - - KYA 543	22380 - GSC 463	22450 - - - - U	22520 - JUF 211	22590 - - - - - -
22241 - - EBK 140	22311 - - - - - -	22381 - FKU 687	22451 - JNG 979	22521 - JPW 390	22591 - LPP 526
22242 - - NFC 820	22312 - - EUT 537	22382 - MGP 576	22452 - - - - U	22522 - - - - - S	22592 - DFR 600
22243 - - - - - -	22313 - HWR 126	22383 - LHU 449	22453 - JKV 791	22523 - - - - - S	22593 - GOT 955
22244 - CWH 754	22314 - HWO 109	22384 - - - - - -	22454 - JYU 522	22524 - FTR 562	22594 - - - - - -
22245 - - GGA 153	22315 - NWL 539	22385 - FKU 669	22455 - - - - S	22525 - - - GBG	22595 - - - - - -
22246 - - - - - -	22316 - - GSC 450	22386 - LWA 132	22456 - JYU 526	22526 - - - - - -	22596 - AEP 677
22247 - - DBA 930	22317 - - GGA 709	22387 - - - - - -	22457 - - - - - -	22527 - DVH 910	22597 - DUD 136
22248 - MRA 536	22318 - - DRD 72	22388 - KBP 161	22458 - - - - - -	22528 - - JP 6441	22598 - DCL 200
22249 - - FEW 860	22319 - - - - S	22389 - - - - - -	22459 - NTW 729	22529 - HNX 63	22599 - - - - - -
22250 - - - - - -	22320 - - JYR 342	22390 - - - - - -	22460 - LWA 434	22530 - - - - - -	22600 - GGB 709
22251 - - - - - -	22321 - - - - P	22391 - - GSP 98	22461 - LKE 526	22531 - - - - - -	22601 - JOF 447
22252 - - - - - -	22322 - - - - - -	22392 - GDA 626	22462 - - - - - -	22532 - - - - - -	22602 - - - - - -
22253 - - GBT 560	22323 - - - - ET	22393 - LHW 764	22463 - LKE 618	22533 - HGA 284	22603 - MNW 672
22254 - - JYU 524	22324 - - - - CDN	22394 - GVE 193	22464 - HHP 703	22534 - - - - - -	22604 - - JTJ 573
22255 - - JYM 664	22325 - - - - - -	22395 - - - - - -	22465 - LWA 372	22535 - DVH 909	22605 - CJR 766
22256 - - - - - -	22326 - - - - ET	22396 - HAC 795	22466 - HDG 469	22536 - - - - - -	22606 - DBN 401
22257 - - - - - -	22327 - - - - - -	22397 - ERX 161	22467 - LHU 844	22537 - - - - - S	22607 - ERX 293
22258 - - CTK 489	22328 - - - - - -	22398 - - - - - -	22468 - TMH 670	22538 - GOT 769	22608 - - - - - -
22259 - - ERP 237	22329 - LUM 920	22399 - - - - - -	22469 - JP 7158	22539 - - - - - -	22609 - LKE 973
22260 - - - - - -	22330 - HUY 175	22400 - - - - S	22470 - JPO 900	22540 - - - - - -	22610 - JP 7526
22261 - - DVY 425	22331 - KLO 319	22401 - - - - S	22471 - JC 9377	22541 - - - - - -	22611 - NVW 865
22262 - - AVV 533	22332 - GSP 100	22402 - - - GBZ	22472 - GSC 519	22542 - JYW 555	22612 - - - - - -

22613 - - - - AUS	22683 - - LHN 444	22753 - -TMX 156	22823 - - CCK 962	22893 - - -JP 7436	22963 - -OHK 500
22614 - - - - - -	22684 - - - - - -	22754 - - - - - -	22824 - - JOH 609	22894 - - PV 9160	22964 - - - - - -
22615 - - GSF 248	22685 - - - - - -	22755 - - - - AUS	22825 - - LKK 463	22895 - FMW 424	22965 - - - - - -
22616 - - GGB 929	22686 - - AJV 806	22756 - - - - - -	22826 - - - - - -	22896 - - DCL 460	22966 - - MBH 39
22617 - - - - - -	22687 - - - - - -	22757 - - - - - -	22827 - - LWB 660	22897 - - AEP 911	22967 - - BEB 22
22618 - - -KGF 81	22688 - - - - - -	22758 - - JAD 240	22828 - - - - - -	22898 - - KNN 218	22968 - - - - - -
22619 - - DVH 908	22689 - - - - - -	22759 - - - - - -	22829 - - KLH 473	22899 - - AJV 972	22969 - - - - - -
22620 - - - - - -	22690 - - EBK 673	22760 - - - - - -	22830 - - JPW 835	22900 - - CRN 42	22970 - - - - - -
22621 - - EUX 277	22691 - - -KLE 14	22761 - - MUA 57	22831 - - DBN 523	22901 - - ENJ 818	22971 - - KLO 314
22622 - - - - - -	22692 - - - - - -	22762 - - - - - -	22832 - -MPK 194	22902 - - KYC 463	22972 - - ARC 949
22623 - - - - - -	22693 - - KTT 902	22763 - -MPH 929	22833 - - - - - -	22903 - - - - - -	22973 - - LKK 959
22624 - - LHN 327	22694 - - - - - -	22764 - - - - - -	22834 - - FFU 394	22904 - - - AUS	22974 - - - - - -
22625 - - GEW 61	22695 - - GVB 143	22765 - - - - - -	22835 - - - - - -	22905 - - DVY 999	22975 - - LDE 140
22626 - - -KGF 85	22696 - - - - - -	22766 - FWM 669	22836 - -FOW 328	22906 - - KLM 59	22976 - - - - - -
22627 - - - - - -	22697 - - - - - -	22767 - - - - - -	22837 - FMW 160	22907 - - HAA 62	22977 - - LHY 540
22628 - - - - - -	22698 - - DCL 363	22768 - - GGD 268	22838 - - OEV 316	22908 - - ERX 888	22978 - - KLO 317
22629 - - DRG 212	22699 - - EDR 801	22769 - - - - - -	22839 - - PV 9132	22909 - HWK 709	22979 - - LWB 955
22630 - - - - - -	22700 - - KYB 861	22770 - - KTT 858	22840 - - - - - -	22910 - - LHY 104	22980 - - DFE 723
22631 - - - - - -	22701 - - HRU 679	22771 - - FFU 228	22841 - - MUA 334	22911 - - - - - -	22981 - - MUB 34
22632 - - DBN 398	22702 - - - - - -	22772 - - JVU 839	22842 - - KLH 479	22912 - - - - - -	22982 - - - - - -
22633 - - DBN 270	22703 - - JPW 630	22773 - - GDK 630	22843 - -MVT 549	22913 - -OHK 372	22983 - - DCL 510
22634 - - - - - -	22704 - -TMX 282	22774 - - - - - -	22844 - - MPK 7	22914 - - - - - -	22984 - - - - - -
22635 - - - - - -	22705 - - - - - -	22775 - - GGD 442	22845 - - HAX 691	22915 - - KYC 574	22985 - - LMA 590
22636 - - - - - -	22706 - - ATS 600	22776 - - ERX 543	22846 - - DBN 518	22916 - - - - - -	22986 - - -FKY 43
22637 - - KLO 316	22707 - - JOF 875	22777 - - LWB 212	22847 - - LHN 572	22917 - - GSF 874	22987 - - - - IND
22638 - - - - - -	22708 - - LMA 203	22778 - - HWK 269	22848 - - -JXJ 268	22918 - - -JXJ 701	22988 - - ERP 685
22639 - - GGD 280	22709 - - -KLE 19	22779 - - - - - -	22849 - -KLM 479	22919 - - GWF 774	22989 - - - - - -
22640 - - - - - -	22710 - -NWL 542	22780 - - - GCJ 55	22850 - - - - - -	22920 - - FKW 842	22990 - - - - - -
22641 - FMW 796	22711 - - - - - -	22781 - - EDR 844	22851 - - - - - -	22921 - HWK 667	22991 - -DHH 190
22642 - - - - - -	22712 - - - - - -	22782 - - LAU 798	22852 - - GJW 464	22922 - - - - - -	22992 - - GCJ 200
22643 - - KFM 21	22713 - - - - - -	22783 - - - - - -	22853 - - -DNL 24	22923 - - - - - -	22993 - - DBN 611
22644 - - - - - -	22714 - - - - - -	22784 - -MTN 604	22854 - - JFJ 806	22924 - - - - AUS	22994 - - LWE 287
22645 - - ENJ 333	22715 - - - - - -	22785 - - GDK 600	22855 - - KKA 315	22925 - - - - - -	22995 - - - - - -
22646 - - - - - -	22716 - - LKK 692	22786 - - - - - -	22856 - - - - - -	22926 - - - - - -	22996 - - NPA 880
22647 - - GWF 113	22717 - - - - - -	22787 - - -KYC 77	22857 - - NNU 141	22927 - - - - - -	22997 - - DNL 365
22648 - - FMR 935	22718 - - - - - -	22788 - - DBN 420	22858 - -GTM 960	22928 - - - - - -	22998 - - DBN 674
22649 - - - - - -	22719 - - KLE 749	22789 - - - - - -	22859 - - LWB 577	22929 - - - - - -	22999 - - -KLP 11
22650 - - -KGF 87	22720 - - KTT 668	22790 - - - - - -	22860 - - - - - -	22930 - HWW 997	23000 - - MPL 559
22651 - - - - - -	22721 - - KLT 917	22791 - - - - - -	22861 - - DRS 348	22931 - - - - - -	23001 - - NJO 502
22652 - - KJH 413	22722 - - - - - -	22792 - - - - - -	22862 - - KTB 895	22932 - - GSF 893	23002 - -KMN 864
22653 - - - - - -	22723 - - - - - -	22793 - - FAY 596	22863 - - KLM 53	22933 - - - - - -	23003 - - KNK 529
22654 - - DCL 307	22724 - -GTM 175	22794 - -NWL 800	22864 - - - - - -	22934 - -MUA 354	23004 - - - - - -
22655 - - EG 8945	22725 - - DBN 418	22795 - - - - - -	22865 - - JAD 439	22935 - - JVF 460	23005 - - - - - -
22656 - - EDR 577	22726 - - - - - -	22796 - - KLE 770	22866 - - EG 9165	22936 - - - - - -	23006 - - - - - -
22657 - - KTE 489	22727 - - - - - -	22797 - -KLM 261	22867 - - EDR 962	22937 - - - - - -	23007 - - - - - -
22658 - - PV 8974	22728 - - ASN 859	22798 - - HTX 777	22868 - - - - - -	22938 - - DFE 644	23008 - - JDD 194
22659 - -LHW 448	22729 - - - - - -	22799 - - - - - -	22869 - - - - - -	22939 - - EJY 213	23009 - - FDM 544
22660 - - - - - -	22730 - - DHS 781	22800 - - JOH 493	22870 - - OEV 561	22940 - - ECX 363	23010 - - LMA 658
22661 - - DHH 45	22731 - - JOH 148	22801 - - ENJ 543	22871 - - - - - -	22941 - - FAV 169	23011 - - KNA 307
22662 - -FKW 269	22732 - - EET 597	22802 - - - - - -	22872 - -KLM 939	22942 - - - - - -	23012 - - EJY 395
22663 - - - - - -	22733 - - - - - -	22803 - - - - - -	22873 - - - - - -	22943 - - OHK 95	23013 - - - - - -
22664 - - LWA 826	22734 - - - - - -	22804 - -FKW 607	22874 - - - - - -	22944 - -MPK 599	23014 - - - - - -
22665 - - GDT 103	22735 - - - - - -	22805 - - - - - -	22875 - - - - - -	22945 - - LMA 59	23015 - - KYC 965
22666 - - - - - -	22736 - -FOW 203	22806 - - DCL 376	22876 - - - - - -	22946 - - GJW 708	23016 - - GDT 482
22667 - -HRW 820	22737 - - - - - -	22807 - - - - - -	22877 - - - - - -	22947 - - JOK 606	23017 - - EPM 314
22668 - - -JP 7346	22738 - - KLE 742	22808 - - FSC 101	22878 - - - - - -	22948 - - - - - -	23018 - - GGE 941
22669 - - GSF 399	22739 - - - - - -	22809 - - - - - -	22879 - - LKK 991	22949 - - -JXJ 694	23019 - - ATS 833
22670 - - - - - -	22740 - - KLE 744	22810 - MNW 998	22880 - - GSF 619	22950 - - - - - -	23020 - - DFX 883
22671 - -LHW 810	22741 - GOW 326	22811 - - - - ET	22881 - - LAU 809	22951 - - - - - -	23021 - - FKY 146
22672 - -MVT 345	22742 - - GSF 169	22812 - - - - ET	22882 - - ERX 774	22952 - - - - - -	23022 - - KDV 441
22673 - -FKW 309	22743 - - AJX 472	22813 - -MTN 751	22883 - - -DST 18	22953 - - GDT 339	23023 - -MVK 413
22674 - - MPJ 901	22744 - - - - - -	22814 - - FFU 297	22884 - - JVF 221	22954 - - PV 9199	23024 - - - - - -
22675 - - - - - -	22745 - - - - - -	22815 - - - - - -	22885 - -FKW 765	22955 - - - - - -	23025 - - - - - -
22676 - -NWL 793	22746 - - - - - -	22816 - - FOW 98	22886 - - ERP 135	22956 - - - - - -	23026 - - JVF 649
22677 - - GGD 159	22747 - - KBP 808	22817 - - - - - -	22887 - - - - - -	22957 - -HAX 816	23027 - - - - - -
22678 - - LPP 463	22748 - - GGD 67	22818 - - JOK 136	22888 - - - - - -	22958 - - LHN 659	23028 - - - - - -
22679 - - KLE 488	22749 - - - - - -	22819 - - KYC 153	22889 - - LWB 593	22959 - - DCL 500	23029 - - - - - -
22680 - - FVJ 694	22750 - -MRB 480	22820 - - JVU 957	22890 - - MUA 353	22960 - - NJO 313	23030 - - SV 1638
22681 - HWK 437	22751 - - - - - -	22821 - - GSF 543	22891 - - - - - -	22961 - - - - - -	23031 - - GMJ 492
22682 - - HAB 180	22752 - - LWB 43	22822 - - LWB 277	22892 - - KLM 58	22962 - -GDK 684	23032 - - - - - -

23033 - - DBN 752	23103 - - HD 8679	23173 - - EPM 745	23243 - - - - - -	23313 - - EVY 117	23383 - OMD 858
23034 - - - - - -	23104 - - - - - -	23174 - - - AYJ 47	23244 - - DJT 363	23314 - MHN 265	23384 - - - JP 7718
23035 - NNU 492	23105 - - GUK 99	23175 - - - - - -	23245 - - DVG 226	23315 - - - - - -	23385 - - LWJ 307
23036 - - SO 8780	23106 - - - - - -	23176 - KOD 497	23246 - - - - - -	23316 - - - - - -	23386 - - - - - -
23037 - - - - - -	23107 - - - - - -	23177 - - - - - -	23247 - - DBN 823	23317 - - LWJ 171	23387 - - NBB 501
23038 - - ADJ 812	23108 - - KLT 912	23178 - - EG 9473	23248 - - - - - -	23318 - FEW 482	23388 - HBT 397
23039 - - PV 9298	23109 - GCJ 360	23179 - - - JRT 43	23249 - KYX 743	23319 - GUS 458	23389 - - - - - -
23040 - LWE 200	23110 - LMA 886	23180 - - - - - -	23250 - - - - - -	23320 - - - - - -	23390 - BNH 322
23041 - LHN 254	23111 - GSG 695	23181 - LMB 235	23251 - GWS 260	23321 - - - - - -	23391 - - - - - -
23042 - HAA 658	23112 - - - - - -	23182 - ETP 330	23252 - OWL 725	23322 - - - - - -	23392 - JAO 603
23043 - RRF 629	23113 - DNL 541	23183 - - KLY 47	23253 - HKV 456	23323 - HUY 228	23393 - PV 9612
23044 - KKB 77	23114 - DFE 820	23184 - GSG 983	23254 - - - - - -	23324 - - - - - -	23394 - LKR 483
23045 - JOL 674	23115 - NJO 738	23185 - DUD 958	23255 - KPX 458	23325 - GHR 788	23395 - - AUS
23046 - - - - - -	23116 - KLP 620	23186 - - - - - -	23256 - SRE 420	23326 - KND 557	23396 - MKX 152
23047 - FMW 927	23117 - - - - - -	23187 - FFW 211	23257 - - - - - -	23327 - BCP 142	23397 - ONO 694
23048 - HBT 279	23118 - KYD 571	23188 - MUG 90	23258 - NPD 503	23328 - HBM 510	23398 - GDT 855
23049 - - - - - -	23119 - HWO 404	23189 - DRD 777	23259 - - - - - -	23329 - LKM 928	23399 - DNL 987
23050 - FKY 134	23120 - FAW 810	23190 - - - - - -	23260 - - - - - -	23330 - - KUL 98	23400 - SRE 893
23051 - LWE 244	23121 - - - - - -	23191 - - - - - -	23261 - KAH 757	23331 - - - - - -	23401 - - - - - -
23052 - DCL 596	23122 - FKY 318	23192 - - - - - -	23262 - - - - - -	23332 - KYN 299	23402 - OFC 302
23053 - - JP 7558	23123 - MUB 721	23193 - HKV 220	23263 - LTT 475	23333 - - - - - -	23403 - GYS 39
23054 - ONO 962	23124 - - KLY 44	23194 - - - - - -	23264 - JAO 508	23334 - KXA 963	23404 - - - - - -
23055 - - - - - -	23125 - EJY 506	23195 - MHN 62	23265 - - - - - -	23335 - EN 9876	23405 - - - - - -
23056 - DFE 826	23126 - EPM 474	23196 - MUB 722	23266 - JRW 399	23336 - FWN 879	23406 - - - - - -
23057 - EDN 173	23127 - GGG 750	23197 - - - - - -	23267 - GAK 890	23337 - MPP 579	23407 - - - - - -
23058 - FBL 250	23128 - LWE 693	23198 - KAH 526	23268 - AGR 161	23338 - - - FJB 88	23408 - - JP 7717
23059 - HWX 277	23129 - HCG 305	23199 - KPX 68	23269 - PV 9454	23339 - DNL 987	23409 - EDP 200
23060 - - - - - -	23130 - KNB 562	23200 - KXO 647	23270 - - - - - -	23340 - - - - - -	23410 - KTJ 359
23061 - - - - - -	23131 - FWN 613	23201 - HCE 742	23271 - - - - - -	23341 - HHO 101	23411 - - - - - -
23062 - EPM 325	23132 - - - - - -	23202 - HRK 333	23272 - GFY 467	23342 - - - - - -	23412 - KXA 966
23063 - KDV 556	23133 - KYD 569	23203 - - - - - -	23273 - - - - - -	23343 - NPH 590	23413 - HHO 92
23064 - - - - - -	23134 - EJY 735	23204 - - - AUS	23274 - JDG 351	23344 - NPE 600	23414 - FKY 988
23065 - - DFV 91	23135 - - - - - -	23205 - ECX 661	23275 - FNV 437	23345 - - - - - -	23415 - KXA 962
23066 - LKN 222	23136 - KLY 935	23206 - BFB 183	23276 - NNW 664	23346 - NPC 645	23416 - - - - - -
23067 - MZ 5715	23137 - - - - - -	23207 - MUG 204	23277 - HDA 563	23347 - LUO 148	23417 - HER 345
23068 - - - - - -	23138 - - - - - -	23208 - LWE 709	23278 - KYL 693	23348 - - - - - -	23418 - LTT 538
23069 - HWD 252	23139 - NEH 18	23209 - - - - - -	23279 - - - - - -	23349 - EVH 314	23419 - CRN 540
23070 - - - - - -	23140 - FWV 162	23210 - - - AUS	23280 - - - - - -	23350 - - - - - -	23420 - - - - - -
23071 - HWX 236	23141 - GDT 617	23211 - - - - - -	23281 - - - AUS	23351 - EDN 690	23421 - - - - - -
23072 - FAW 518	23142 - NPB 983	23212 - MUB 723	23282 - - - - - -	23352 - - - - - -	23422 - BEE 474
23073 - - - - - -	23143 - KLY 42	23213 - - - - - -	23283 - FAP 126	23353 - - - - - -	23423 - - - - - -
23074 - - - - - -	23144 - - - - - -	23214 - - - - - -	23284 - KYL 692	23354 - - - - - -	23424 - EVY 126
23075 - - - - - -	23145 - - KLY 46	23215 - - KUL 91	23285 - MHW 623	23355 - DNL 729	23425 - LWJ 893
23076 - HWO 56	23146 - - - - - -	23216 - KLY 933	23286 - JRM 372	23356 - - JS 8577	23426 - JOX 143
23077 - - - - - -	23147 - KLY 934	23217 - - - - - -	23287 - - - - - -	23357 - JDU 404	23427 - - - - - -
23078 - JVF 919	23148 - KLY 936	23218 - KLY 931	23288 - MLG 447	23358 - - - - - -	23428 - JHP 820
23079 - - - - - -	23149 - KLY 41	23219 - - JP 7662	23289 - LYC 156	23359 - - - - - -	23429 - GAK 659
23080 - - - - - -	23150 - - - - - -	23220 - - - - - -	23290 - HFS 433	23360 - SS 7336	23430 - - - - - -
23081 - HWD 311	23151 - OTW 720	23221 - KUL 99	23291 - HDT 355	23361 - KND 286	23431 - - - - - -
23082 - MUB 35	23152 - - - - - -	23222 - HKV 563	23292 - - - - - -	23362 - FPY 235	23432 - - JP 7878
23083 - FKY 252	23153 - - - - - -	23223 - SRE 349	23293 - KYL 687	23363 - - - - - -	23433 - KYN 302
23084 - - - AUS	23154 - - - - - -	23224 - EET 990	23294 - KVM 762	23364 - JRW 170	23434 - - - - - -
23085 - - KLP 19	23155 - - - - - -	23225 - BEE 355	23295 - - - - - -	23365 - GCJ 768	23435 - - AUS
23086 - - - - - -	23156 - - - - - -	23226 - - - - - -	23296 - KFJ 474	23366 - HBM 515	23436 - HBT 555
23087 - KYD 973	23157 - - - - - -	23227 - AUS	23297 - - - - - -	23367 - - - AUS	23437 - JDF 460
23088 - EG 9402	23158 - GFY 79	23228 - KLY 939	23298 - - - - - -	23368 - - - - - -	23438 - FJB 287
23089 - - - - - -	23159 - - - - - -	23229 - KOA 360	23299 - - - - - -	23369 - - - - - -	23439 - MUM 110
23090 - EY 9160	23160 - - KYP 87	23230 - - - - - -	23300 - - - AUS	23370 - JDU 258	23440 - MHW 140
23091 - LWE 416	23161 - - - - - -	23231 - LRL 889	23301 - EJY 763	23371 - LYA 557	23441 - - - - - -
23092 - JMO 681	23162 - HRK 360	23232 - - - - - -	23302 - KRR 486	23372 - KUU 379	23442 - - - - - -
23093 - - - - - -	23163 - UMK 115	23233 - - - - - -	23303 - KUL 97	23373 - - - - - -	23443 - - - - - -
23094 - JOM 316	23164 - DHH 310	23234 - DBN 822	23304 - JDD 672	23374 - MHW 494	23444 - DS 2893
23095 - KLT 913	23165 - HKV 352	23235 - JAC 648	23305 - ECX 730	23375 - DWH 307	23445 - ECT 108
23096 - FWV 155	23166 - DRG 742	23236 - FVN 762	23306 - LWJ 266	23376 - KUU 375	23446 - NPJ 780
23097 - - - - - -	23167 - JON 358	23237 - MHT 118	23307 - KOD 933	23377 - GDK 922	23447 - - - AUS
23098 - JEL 876	23168 - DRG 648	23238 - MBH 949	23308 - OVW 152	23378 - NPD 933	23448 - DJT 739
23099 - - - - - -	23169 - - - - - -	23239 - - - - - -	23309 - HOR 600	23379 - - - - - -	23449 - LDE 749
23100 - - - - - -	23170 - - - - - -	23240 - - - - - -	23310 - EDN 438	23380 - - - - - -	23450 - JRW 111
23101 - HCE 472	23171 - GCJ 525	23241 - LWE 805	23311 - - JDU 20	23381 - JOP 624	23451 - - - - - -
23102 - KDV 945	23172 - - - - - -	23242 - FKY 650	23312 - - FNT 94	23382 - KUU 378	23452 - - - - - -

23453 -	23623 SGP	23693 TRE 928	23763 LYD 995	23779 BJE 503	23795 JKV 775
23454 -	23624 SGP	23694 KYP 89	23764 LPT 888	23780 KYX 970	23796 -
23455 -	23625 -	23695 MWB 671	23765 -	23781 JKV 790	23797 FJY 184
23456 -	23626 -	23696 -	23766 GBG	23782 -	23798 -
23457 PNO 289	23627 -	23697 -	23767 BJE 478	23783 -	23799 -
23458 ACW 859	23628 -	23698 -	23768 -	23784 EBN 72	23821 GKY 405
23459 -	23629 GFY 833	23699 -	23769 -	23785 -	23822 KHP 520
23460 BFB 777	23630 -	23700 KUF 39	23770 -	23786 OPF 824	23823 EBN 519
23461 FCO 154	23631 -	23701 -	23771 -	23787 LLB 66	23824 LXH 812
23462 LWJ 682	23632 MPP 836	23702 FUT 941	23772 HOU 762	23788 JAX 853	23825 NWA 753
23463 -	23633 KYO 798	23703 -	23773 LOD 404	23789 ORB 207	23826 -
23464 -	23634 NUA 532	23704 LTE 171	23774 JVC 610	23790 -	23827 LXH 811
23465 EF 9142	23635 MWB 202	23705 LAL 787	23775 -	23791 -	23828 -
23466 MWA 478	23636 -	23706 EHS 386	23776 LKC 164	23792 -	23829 -
23467 KXN 872	23637 AUS	23707 KOF 918	23777 LGX 775	23793 JKV 792	23830 -
23468 -	23638 FMO 467	23708 LAH 45	23778 OPE 915	23794 -	
23469 EG 9780	23639 SE 7273	23709 HVE 474			
23470 BNH 420	23640 LGF 825	23710 -			
23471 BCE 1	23641 DVL 699	23711 DHH 881			
23472 -	23642 -	23712 SM			
23473 -	23643 FMO 585	23713 NUB 112			
23474 NHW 4	23644 FDR 110	23714 KBJ 732			
23475 LTV 531	23645 GVJ 649	23715 DRS 542			
23476 ERV 131	23646 LNK 429	23716 -			
23477 DWH 497	23647 -	23717 F			
23478 -	23648 -	23718 DCK 564			
23479 -	23649 KVR 207	23719 KYX 744			
23480 -	23650 -	23720 -			
23481 KPX 846	23651 GAW 295	23721 HWF 732			
23482 GCJ 992	23652 DTY 669	23722 FF 7788			
23483 -	23653 DHH 689	23723 -			
23484 -	23654 -	23724 HGE 16			
23485 -	23655 -	23725 GKU 754			
23486 GAK 166	23656 -	23726 -			
23487 -	23657 BNH 727	23727 GVJ 919			
23488 -	23658 -	23728 LGK 55			
23489 KOB 860	23659 -	23729 KAD 281			
23490 FCO 815	23660 -	23730 -			
23491 PNO 63	23661 -	23731 DWH 923			
23492 DVL 450	23662 AHC 516	23732 -			
23493 HGB 702	23663 -	23733 DWH 890			
23494 NL	23664 -	23734 EFE 96			
23495 S	23665 -	23735 JRM 990			
23496 S	23666 -	23736 EVY 831			
23497 -	23667 SM	23737 LGF 832			
23498 -	23668 -	23738 -			
23499 MTA 577	23669 JDG 706	23739 OJO 969			
23600 DTY 699	23670 GCA 661	23740 -			
23601 NNU 263	23671 VHX 49	23741 -			
23602 DVL 620	23672 KYO 90	23742 -			
23603 -	23673 -	23743 KLJ 154			
23604 -	23674 -	23744 JVC 394			
23605 -	23675 -	23745 FRX 259			
23606 MWA 966	23676 GKU 524	23746 LYD 717			
23607 -	23677 KFJ 644	23747 PFC 263			
23608 LPT 966	23678 RHK 256	23748 LNN 832			
23609 JP 7879	23679 -	23749 -			
23610 HWF 494	23680 -	23750 KOJ 796			
23611 -	23681 -	23751 JKV 899			
23612 -	23682 -	23752 -			
23613 -	23683 PTW 162	23753 -			
23614 TRE 673	23684 JWK 936	23754 LGC 847			
23615 -	23685 -	23755 EVH 880			
23616 -	23686 -	23756 NUB 936			
23617 GKU 91	23687 TRF 898	23757 LPO 1			
23618 -	23688 PTW 812	23758 NHN 444			
23619 -	23689 -	23759 LKH 3			
23620 EJG 121	23690 JWK 271	23760 MWE 828			
23621 -	23691 -	23761 MWE 465			
23622 -	23692 -	23762 -			

20528   **B**

Le Mans 24 Hours 1949

Of the first 30 TA 14 chassis built when production commenced in 1946, 18 went, without any bodies – to Belgium, to the agent Sincau of Brussels. 20528 was one of these, which finished up in the atelier of one L Eggen, who had the ambition to make a competition sports out of it. Indeed, it ran a number of low key events, quite reliably, and with a variety of bodies, the ugliest of which resembled one of the pre-war 'tank' Bugattis. An entry for the 1949 Le Mans race, it expired at lap 32 with bearing trouble. There is a possible explanation: spirited driving on early TA 14's on right-hand bends can produce the odd momentary rattle as the oil pump gulps air instead of oil. A situation especially likely if the full one and a half gallons are not present. The incident mentioned above may well have been the catalyst that resulted in extra baffles being incorporated in the sump castings of later cars. 20528 is unquestionably a direct ancestor of the

20528: The unsuccessful Le Mans competition TA 14 in one of its several forms. (Courtesy Alvis Archive Trust)

20528: This interesting photograph by Eileen Goddin is one of a model of the TA14 Le Mans car, which is on display at the Le Mans museum.

Belgian-designed TB 14 sports model first seen at the Earls Court Motor Show in 1948, (qv 22568). For the interesting life of the first 'production' TB 14, see 23500.

20573   JLP 344
6th Baron Grantley
Full title: Richard Henry Brinsley Norton (1892-1954).

Interestingly, this car is the very first Mulliner saloon (numbered M1) to be built, and figures in a photograph much seen, of the first three saloons about to be despatched to the main London, Glasgow and Belfast agencies, significantly on November 14, 1946 – six years to the day that a Blitz had destroyed much of the factory. Brooklands of Bond Street retained it as a demonstrator for a considerable period, using it in events like the Lord Mayor's Show, and not registering until 1948. So long, in fact, that a letter found in the works records asks what has become of it? Brooklands' reply briefly states: "We have now allocated this car to Lord Grantley, and hope you will find this satisfactory."

20573 was later to feature in *Autocar*'s *Used Cars on the Road*, January 18, 1957.

20674
Lt Col Cecil Eric Hunt-Davis
This, only the fifth Mulliner saloon to be released, was the company's first postwar export to the African continent, where the Lieutenant Colonel was stationed at the time, having previously served with Australian Forces and fought at Gallipoli. His son, Brigadier Sir Miles Hunt-Davis, would, many years later, become PPS to that distinguished Alvis owner, Prince Philip, Duke of Edinburgh (qv 26600).

20***   LPL 271
Jack Hawkins CBE
For biographical details refer to the Hawkins TA 21 model (qv 24627).

A considerable mystery surrounds the Hawkins TA 14 which was used in the Launder and Gilliat crime movie, *Fortune is a Woman*, where Jack plays a tenacious insurance investigator. The car concerned seems, for all intents and purposes, to be a standard production Tickford drophead, but its registration number well precedes the time of that particular version's announcement. There are two possible explanations: one – that this chassis originally bore a cheap 'woody' body which was re-bodied by Tickford under a tax break concession valid at the time; or two – it is actually a Richard Mead body, the early versions of which were constructed on Tickford frames, which had been intended for its version of the MG VA model had WWII not intervened. We may never know.

20839   FSC 648
William Whitelaw MP
Or more fully: The Rt Hon Viscount Whitelaw KT CH, MC DL (August 28, 1914-July 1, 1999). He was educated at Winchester, and at Trinity College, Cambridge. A distinguished military career followed, and in peacetime an entry into politics, becoming the Conservative member from 1955 for Penrith and the Borders, and representing that constituency for 28 years. He held office under four prime ministers: Harold Macmillan, Alec Douglas-Home, Edward Heath and Margaret Thatcher.

Book: *The Whitelaw Memoirs* published by Aurum Press, 1989. ISBN 978-1854100283.

20972   JTF 96
Arthur Holt MP
Liberal Arthur Holt (August 8, 1914-August 23, 1995) represented the Bolton West constituency from 1951 to 1964, becoming Chief Whip for

1962/63, and Party President 1974/75. 20972 is the first of his four known open Alvis cars, and is the first 'production' drophead coupé to be built by Tickford on the TA 14 chassis. When the TA 21 model was announced, Arthur Holt had an early Tickford version of that as well (qv 24***). In 1954, a TC 21/100 Tickford succeeded the TA 21 (qv 25413) and finally in 1960 a TD 21 Park Ward (qv 26346) would replace the TC 21/100.

20977 NRE 912
Dr Lancelot Ware

Co-founder of MENSA, and a serial Alvis owner. Above is one of six (qv 10708 – Crested Eagle; 11523 – Firefly; 12023 – Speed 20 SC; 14308 – 4.3-litre; 22510 – TA 14).

20998 CVG 119
Kay Petre

Kay Petre (May 10, 1903-August 10, 1994) had a full name of Kathleen Coad Defries and originated from Canada. She was a notable character on the racing circuits until an accident in 1937 curtailed that career.

Thereafter, she took to motoring journalism and is credited with designing certain fabrics for the Austin Motor Company.

Now, whilst it has never been proven that she actually owned 20998, she was certainly associated with the publicity surrounding it, being the first example of a new fixed head coupé style designed

by Duncan Industries. Kindred to this were some highly misleading reports in the national press of the day implying that three manufacturers – Alvis, Daimler and Healey – would be going into mass production using the same body shell. The truth was far more mundane. Duncan's stylish coach-built body would readily fit the Alvis TA 14, Daimler's DB 18, and Healey's Riley-engined 'four,' the difference in wheelbase being merely at the business end. Thus the actual 'mass production' merely amounted to two Daimlers, 30 or so Alvis, and about 40 Healey. There is also the rumour of a single Bentley.

21021 LRB 765
Rolls-Royce Ltd

It remains a mystery why Rolls-Royce Limited should purchase the product of a rival. Evaluation perhaps? It was allocated to their Mr Swift.

21110 JUL 110
Iliffe Publications Ltd

In 1951, *Autocar* started a new series, *Used Cars on the Road*, but not with as much detail as the main weekly road tests. 21100 was the very first car to kick off this series, appearing in the issue March 30, page 388.

21169 FKW 3
Jack Straw MP

Former Labour Member of Blackburn, serving

20998: Although she never actually owned it, racing driver Kay Petre was associated with much of the publicity surrounding the first Duncan-bodied TA 14. (Courtesy Alvis Archive Trust)

21169: Seen here on a general election campaign trail is former home secretary Jack Straw with a woody version of the TA14. No rusting at these hustings. (Courtesy Newsquest)

between 1979 and 2015, Jack Straw, born August 3, 1946, borrowed this TA 14 'woody' for one of his earliest campaign trails, by which time it had lost its short registration mark, to be replaced by EWA 293 B. Straw served as a Cabinet Member in both the Tony Blair and Gordon Brown administrations, and has been a Home Secretary and Foreign Secretary. He wrote a book called *Last Man Standing*, published by Macmillan, 2012. ISBN 978-1447222750.

Straw is, not unnaturally, a Blackburn Rovers supporter (qv 26717 and 26721 for another Alvis connection).

21177
Iliffe Publications Ltd

Around 1958/1960, 21177 was a staff car for the magazine *Autocar*, and had been bought in from Performance Cars Ltd, Brentford for a four-part series called *Buying and Restoring a Car*. These would appear in the issues of January 2 and 9, 1959, and January 29, 1960, and are a useful adjunct to TA 14 ownership. A little-known fact is that about this time, and also on *Autocar*'s strength, was that now much-collected artist Gordon Horner (1915-January 2006), who did a sepia sketch or two of this very car, one of which, showing it by the shore of Loch Maree, Ross and Cromarty, to which this writer took a particular shine. Just

21177: Artist: the late Gordon Horner perfectly captures the fine lines of Mulliner coachwork. The location of this piece c1959 is by the side of Loch Maree, Ross and Cromarty.

before he died, I managed to trace Gordon, then in retirement in Sussex, and ask him if I could use this piece for a Christmas card. Gordon amusingly replied in the affirmative, as *Autocar* had never paid him for it anyway.

21189
Sir Louis Greig KBE, CVO

Sir Louis Greig (November 17, 1880-March 1, 1953) had been a surgeon, stockbroker and a confidant of three monarchs: George V, Edward VIII and George VI. The biography of this remarkable man, entitled *The King Maker*, has been written by his grandson Geordie Greig, editor of *The Mail on Sunday*, to whom I am indebted for this inclusion. ISBN 13-978-1444730258. Any who

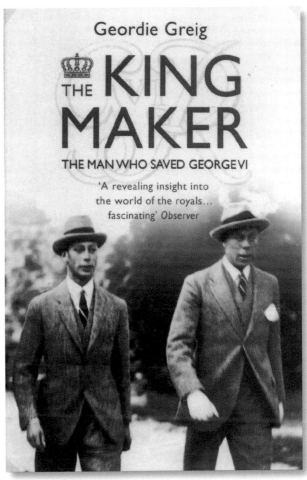

Geordie Greig, editor of the *Daily Mail*, has written a remarkable biography of his grandfather, Sir Louis Greig, owner of TA 14 21189. The cover of the book shows Sir Louis with the future King George VI.

(Courtesy Geordie Greig)

enjoyed the movie *The King's Speech* will find this book a natural follow-on.

21366 — MNO 800
Tom Driberg MP

Thomas Edward Neil Driberg May 22, 1905-August 12,1976), later ennobled as Baron Bradwell, was educated at Lancing College and Christ Church, Oxford. He was twice a Parliamentarian, representing Maldon from 1942-1945 and Barking from 1959-1974. Ever a controversial figure, he initiated the 'William Hickey' column of the *Daily Express* and was a prime mover in the Campaign for Nuclear Disarmament. His unusual friendships would generate criticism, not least of which was his socialising with the Kray twins. He wrote some ten books, one of which summarised his crossword puzzles prepared for *Private Eye*. Of these, his autobiography, *Ruling Passions,* published by Jonathan Cape, ISBN 0-365-04369-X, must be considered the most definitive further reading.

21421 — MPF 298
Donald Monro

A name more usually associated with the Invicta marque, Donald Monro constructed a sports car on this chassis, hoping to achieve some competition potential by reduction of weight. The car was written up in *Autocar*'s popular series *Talking of Sports Cars* number 354 in the issue of March 26, 1954. A cowl replaced the traditional Alvis grille, and with front wings that appear to have originated with a Citroën

21421: This is Invicta specialist Donald Monro's interpretation of what a TA14 tourer should look like. (Courtesy Iliffe Publications)

Light Fifteen, the car looked quite rakish. Donald's daughter, Shirley, would later assist in racing one of the Rivers-Fletcher Alvis cars (qv 11859).

21458 — JLY 26
Archie Scott-Brown

Racing driver and son of an Alvis dealer, Archie was born in Paisley on May 13, 1927, and died in an accident at the Spa circuit May 19, 1958. His TA 14 is especially interesting in that it was unique in being specially fitted with a side-valve Ford V8 engine that, in standard form, would give some 20bhp more than the original Alvis four, giving it a performance not far short of the contemporary standard Allard that used the same engine, examples of which were plentiful and inexpensive after WWII.

For further reading see *Archie and the Listers* by Robert Edwards, published by Haynes. ISBN 1-85260-469-7.

21475 — GWK 351
Practical Motorist

In the absence of a full workshop manual for the TA 14, the very detailed articles published in the issues of *Practical Motorist* for February, March, April and June 1959 are arguably the best technical guide ever written about the model. For the preparation of these features, 21475 was borrowed from the London Service Department of Alvis Ltd. The author was one S E Field.

21512 — HFJ 787
Steele-Perkins family

Son of an Exeter doctor, Crispian Steele-Perkins, born December 18, 1944, is a virtuoso, acclaimed worldwide, of the trumpet, and has amassed a private collection of over 100 wind instruments, often used for education purposes. Crispian has written to me enthusiastically with memories, particularly holidays in Ireland with the two Alvis cars. Crispian's credentials are considerable: educated at Copthorne, Marlborough, and the Guildhall, then playing with such distinguished ensembles as the Sadlers Wells Theatre, the London Gabrieli, the Amsterdam Baroque, the King's Consort, and indeed many others.

Naturally, his discography is quite extensive, and thereto his website www.crispiansteeleperkins.

com is to be recommended. There is also his book: *Trumpet* in the Yehudi Menuhin Music Guides, published by Kahn & Averill, 2006, ISBN 978-1-871082-69-2. For the 'other' S-P Alvis (qv 23677).

21536 JLN 529
Countess Szechenyi
Gladys, Countess Szechenyi was the second of that name, being the third daughter of Gladys Vanderbilt (American Heiress) and Laszlo Szechenyi, a Hungarian Count. This second Countess (August 18, 1913-1978) married Christopher Finch-Hatton, 15th Earl of Winchilsea, in 1935, but they divorced in 1945. By the time the Alvis was delivered to her London address in November 1947, she had thus reverted to her maiden name as above.

21630 JYF 60
Valay Industries Ltd
Once a very familiar name in the field of automobile cosmetic products, 21630 was, for a time, the company car.

21631 JYL 707
Gen Sir George Erskine
A fuller description reads: Sir George Watkin Eben James Erskine (August 23, 1899-August 29, 1965) GCB, KBE, DSO (and indeed many others, including honours from Belgium, Luxembourg and the USA). He began a military career at Sandhurst and joined the Kings Royal Rifle Corps. He served both in WWI and WWII, notably with the 7th Armoured Division, and in widely spaced theatres of war too numerous to mention here. His peacetime service is equally notable, being Aide-de-Camp to Queen Elizabeth II, and Lt Governor of Jersey from 1958 to 1965.

21577 KWB 547
E Paramore Ltd
21577 preceded a TA 21 (qv 24043) as the company car of this well-known tool manufacturer.

21591 LRB 440
Sir Ernest Shentall JP
Shentall Ltd was a family firm which operated

a chain of some 50 grocery shops around the Chesterfield district in the 1940s. Ernest, born 1861, had been a moving force in the business and had risen to become Mayor of Chesterfield in the years 1913 to 1919.

21743 JM 2
Sir John Moores
Sir John Moores (January 25, 1896-September 25, 1993) was an entrepreneur and philanthropist, exemplified in his connection with the Littlewoods Pools and retail empire. Gave his name to the Liverpool John Moores University. He was also chairman of Everton Football Club on several occasions. The mark 'JM2', obviously retained, and a replacement, 'NKC 512', applied in 1952.

21938 KGF 83
Sir Paul Newall
Lord Mayor of London – 1993/1994. Biog under his previously-owned Speed 25 model (qv 14570).

22001 JUR 934
Rod Hull
The entertainer used 22001 in one screening of an *Emu's Christmas Show*.

22023 GWD 336
Joseph Lucas Ltd
Allocated to one of Alvis Ltd's major component suppliers, possibly as part of a reciprocal arrangement. There had been a precedent, with the supplying of a Speed 25 model in 1937 (qv 14422).

22068 GWD 265
Girling Products Ltd
Allocated to Girlings as a company car, a photograph of 22068 appears on the cover of one of the firm's published *Brake Manuals*.

22110 NPF 810
Ken Smeeton
The ingenious Alvis Works Manager, in what appears to have been a private enterprise, succeeded in marrying together a brand new Alvis

TA 14 chassis with an unused Vanden Plas tourer body, which had been mothballed during the war, and would otherwise have been fitted to the 4.3-litre short chassis model. Very appealing, but sadly believed now lost.

22121 | JYP 378
Earl of Gainsborough

Anthony Gerard Edward Noel (October 24, 1923-December 29, 2007) became President of the Rural District Council Association of England and Wales. Will most probably be best remembered for his efforts to oppose the reorganisation of local councils. (Redcliffe-Maud Report, and the subsequent Local Government Act of 1972).

22204 | KGC 539
Harold von Kluber

von Kluber (September 6, 1901-February 14,1978) hailed from Potsdam and was a highly esteemed physicist and astronomer, and could be described as a disciple of Albert Einstein, who had been born not all that far away at Ulm. After WWII, he journeyed to England in furtherance of his original research and became assistant director of the Solar Physics Laboratory at Cambridge, which is where 22204 was mainly in use, as part of his other interest – in classic cars.

22290 | KKR 509
Eros Films Ltd

Founded in 1947 with headquarters in London's Wardour Street, the company history can be traced back to 1920 with a chain of cinemas built up by the brothers Hyams – Philip, Sydney and Michael – which were sold out to British Gaumont in 1928. Bankruptcy befell Eros in 1961, but not before the production and distribution of such notables as *The Man who Watched Trains go By* and *The Sea Shall not have Them.*

22377 | KLL 115
Withold Gracjan Kawalec

Born in Wilno, Poland, Kawalec (November 17, 1922-December 24, 2003) became active in the Polish resistance movement, was captured by the Russians and joined the Polish unit in Palestine. He participated in the fighting at Tobruk, but

22500: Major Arthur Quilton was conspicuously successful in obtaining the lapsed TA 14 registration number from Devon County Council to add the finishing touch to his TA 14. (Courtesy Alvis Archive Trust)

made it to England, where he joined the RAF. In the immediate postwar period he studied sculpture at the Nottingham College of Art, working mostly in alabaster. His work is now much prized and examples of it can be seen in institutions at Sydenham, Basford and Crediton.

22500 | GOT 524
Major Arthur Quilton

The resourceful Major Quilton, upon replacing his Alvis Speed 25 (qv 13346) with a TA 14, succeeded in persuading the Devon County Council to re-issue the lapsed mark 'TA 14' to it.

22510 | KAR 551
Dr Lancelot Ware

Co-founder of MENSA, and a serial Alvis owner. Above is one of six. (qv 10708 – Crested Eagle; 11523 – Firefly; 12023 – Speed 20 SC; 14308 – 4.3 -litre; 20977 – TA 14). Biog is under 10708.

22568 | LND 702
Alvis Works Development Car

Exports of the TA 14 model to Belgium were comparatively numerous when production started in 1946, and were mostly in 'chassis only' form. One such chassis was tastefully bodied as a two-seater roadster by the Brussels company F J Bidée, and caused quite a stir at the first Salon that it was exhibited. This reaction caused Alvis Ltd to consider a limited production run, and development work was entrusted to the Surrey firm of King and Taylor Ltd, and a running chassis numbered 22568 was supplied to them. It would appear that body formers, maybe even a complete car were brought over from Belgium to facilitate this. The resulting prototype was exhibited at the 1948 Earls Court Motor Show – red in colour and featuring such niceties as cocktail cabinet in the voluminous doors. Maybe the only car which has ever been exhibited at Earls Court twice, it was back in 1949, now white but with re-positioned headlights of the sealed beam type, to conform with USA lighting regulations. (A similar alteration was done on the Morris Minor for the same reason). Alvis Ltd kept the car until the latter part of 1950 when it was sold as 'shop-soiled' to the Manchester agent, when it was well over two years old. The lucky 'first' owner was one Geoff Godber-Ford, who used it to trailer his pair of Norton trials bikes to events.

22674 MPJ 701
Roy Raymonde
Remarkable cartoonist (1929-2009) who was taught the craft by none other than the great Ronald Searle. Worked for the magazines *Playboy* and *Punch*, and for the *Sunday Telegraph*. Some of his originals are housed in the V&A, and others in the British Cartoon Archive.

22829 KLM 58
Movie car
Used in two movies. During its sojourn in the Isle of Man, where it had to be re-registered with the TMN 49 mark, it was pictured with comedian Norman Wisdom, who was also a resident of the Island.

23116 KLP 620
Peter Cavanagh
Cavanagh (October 31, 1914-February 23, 1981) was an actor, but more famously, a comedy impressionist who was much in demand on radio. He quickly became known as 'The Voice of Them All.'

23116: Impressionist and broadcaster Peter Cavanagh with his TA 14 Carbodies coupé outside BBC's broadcasting house. (Courtesy Alvis Ltd)

23126 EPM 474
Frank Wootton OBE
Frank Wootton (July 30, 1911-April 21, 1998) has been justifiably described as one of the greatest aviation artists of all time, being appropriately appointed as Official Artist to the Royal Air Force. His work is widely collected and largely continues in the genre left by F Gordon Crosby. Especially relevant to this discourse is his exciting depiction of Alvis owner Douglas Bader (qv 25554) bailing out from a stricken Hurricane. In another less-known montage of 1953, Wootton incorporated the colourful tax disc of EPM 474. Wootton also wrote two successful books aimed mainly at the junior market: *How to Draw Aircraft* and *How to Draw Cars.*

23284 KYL 692
Inspector Morse
23284 featured in the mystery entitled *Ghost in the Machine* from the popular series based on Colin Dexter's well-known character. Released January 4, 1989.

Incidentally, Colin Dexter himself once addressed a gathering of 300 Alvis owners, in the most appropriate location of Keble College, Oxford, July 7, 2001.

23378 NPD 933
Carlton Cards Ltd
A commission from artist Robert G McHugh, in Carlton's Stone Gallery series featured 23378, with the registration number digits 'adjusted' by

23378: Robert G McHugh's painting done for Carlton Cards Ltd. See text for possible availability.

A memorable role of actor Trevor Howard was in the 1945 David Lean film *Brief Encounter*. The image is from the publicity material of the Carnforth Station Heritage Centre (01524 735165), where most of the action took place.

the artist. It is certain that 23378 was the subject, however, because as far as we know, it was the only TA 14 Carbodies convertible to have been built with quarterlights in the doors. Copies of this charming card may still be available from Carlton. Its reference numbers are: EHMA 13424-1 and 64962-2. The restoration of 23378 was covered in much detail in the February 1986 issue of *Practical Classics*, pages 50-54.

23415   KXA 962
Trevor Howard

Trevor Howard, (September 29, 1913-January 7, 1988) was an actor who appeared in over 70 movies, such as *The Third Man*, *Mutiny on the Bounty*, and probably best-remembered of all, *Brief Encounter*.

Further reading: *Trevor Howard, A personal Biography* by Terence Pettigrew, published by P Owen 2001. ISBN 978-0720611243. Recommended as it includes a photograph of Howard with the TA 14.

23467   KXN 872
Fortnum & Mason

Often referred to as HM The Queen's grocers, 23467 was one of the cars of this company – long-established at no 181 Piccadilly, and with a history going back to the year 1707.

23623   MXR 85
Revd Lt Col Edward Ord TD

Distinguished Roman Catholic Army Chaplain, Edward Ord (August 2, 1908-March 6, 1984), was ordained in 1932, becoming Chaplain HM Forces when WWII broke out, serving initially with 8th Battalion DLI. In 1942, he saw service with the 8th Army in the Western Desert, was present at the Salerno landings and the bitter battle for Monte Casino, being mentioned in despatches for devotion to duty. In postwar service he was posted to Singapore in 1949, and 23623 was allocated to him at that point. He and the Alvis returned to the UK in 1952. This accounts for the anachronistic registration mark, being more contemporary with the TA 21 period.

23677   KFJ 644
Steele-Perkins family

23677 was the replacement for an earlier TA 14 (qv 21512 for bio).

23500: The first production TB 14 model was used by Edward Ward (Viscount Bangor) on a fact-finding tour of the USA, and was specially loaned by John Parkes. Unfortunately distorted images are from Ward's books by kind permission of his daughter, Hon Lalla Ward, actress.

23757 **LPO 1**

London Philharmonic Orchestra

A delivery to Alvis agents Caffyns of Eastbourne, the TA 14 23757 was serendipitously allocated the mark 'LPO 1,' quite routinely by West Sussex County Council. This remained with it until 1964, when a retention was applied for and the car re-registered as 930 FBX. The mark attracted the attention of the London Philharmonic Orchestra, and was subsequently transferred to another Alvis: a TF 21 model (qv 27411).

TB 14

1950
23500-23599
100 cars

APM Sports
1001-1099   100

Chassis	Reg	Chassis	Reg	Chassis	Reg
23500	-23599	23532	ERG 1	23566	GKW 940
23500	JVC 458	23533	SM	23567	GUN 432
23501	AUS	23534	SGP	23568	BSN 499
23502	-HK	23535	RL	23569	AEC 421
23503	AUS	23536	LGX 770	23570	-LFJ 212
23504	AUS	23537	GBZ	23571	EFE 671
23505	AUS	23538	CDN	23572	
23506	-T	23539	PE	23573	OEH 819
23507	AUS	23540	CDN	23574	ECL 123
23508	-T	23541	KLJ 518	23575	HUS 384
23509	AUS	23542	MTV 550	23576	MTV 824
23510	IND	23543	LLK 799	23577	GWM 437
23511	AUS	23544	OEH 564	23578	AHG 355
23512	B	23545	HSG 97	23579	HYS 615
23513	GKW 294	23546	BVV 423	23580	HUS 214
23514	NUG 803	23547	JP 8870	23581	
23515	MZ 9788	23548	GAV 444	23582	EDB 677
23516	NAF 1	23549	SM	23583	RPU 584
23517	NHT 11	23550	MWJ 469	23584	LND 570
23518	LLF 999	23551	ORB 244	23585	
23519		23552	SGP	23586	HYS 187
23520	-CH	23553	EFR 698	23587	EHS 844
23521	GBZ	23554		23588	ECL 265
23522	S	23555	USA	23589	ONW 119
23523	S	23556	BDJ 239	23590	LXA 453
23524	S	23557	MTD 6	23591	HWS 43
23525	IND	23558	JGB 659	23592	
23526	FBK 732	23559	MFM 563	23593	NPP 631
23527		23560	NUM 517	23594	
23528	KNY 819	23561	KTG 373	23595	LKF 888
23529		23562	JGB 444	23596	LXU 529
23530	DHE 252	23563	OPG 249	23597	LVM 186
23531	SM	23564	HUS 471	23598	JGB 56
		23565	LXA 451	23599	

Having origins in one of the very first TA 14 chassis exported to Belgium in 1946 and bodied as a streamlined roadster by F J Bidée in Brussels, a car was exhibited at the Brussels Show and there caught the eye of the Alvis management who thought that the production version might make sense. Bidée sent over a set of body formers to the Surrey firm of King & Taylor Ltd, to whom Alvis had already supplied an appropriate chassis (no 22568). The result was exhibited twice: at Earls Court in 1948 and 1949, on the latter occasion having grown built-in headlights, whereas the initial version had these mounted behind the grille.

The production versions, exactly 100 in number, were constructed in Coventry by A P Metalcraft Ltd, and begin to filter out in the early months of 1950. These were built on normal TA 14 chassis, standard except for the addition of an extra carburettor, and an axle ratio from 4.875 to 4.3 to one.

23500 **JVC 458**

Alvis works Press Car

As the very first of the hundred production models of the Fourteen Sports Tourer (qv 22568 for the prototype), 23500 was naturally at the forefront

235**: An as yet unapportioned TB 14 was owned by actor James Mason and used, along with his Rolls-Royce Silver Cloud, in his advert promoting the Studebaker Hawk, seen here in 1961.

White's *On Top of Old Smokey*, which mountainous feature was traversed during the Alvis trip.

235**
James Mason
Actor James Mason's Alvis TB 14, preceded by a dozen years or so, his purchase of a TD 21 model (qv 26766). His TB 14 is featured in the background of Mason's 1961 advertisements for Studebaker, with its Gran Turismo Hawk.

235**
Weymouth Operatic Society
Instances of motor vehicles actually appearing on stage during a production are comparatively rare, and health & safety regulations would probably preclude it these days. Such an exception was the use, by the above society, of an Alvis TB 14 in its 1958 production of Emmerich Kalman's operetta: *The Gipsy Princess*, which was reviewed in the *Dorchester Echo* of June 17. Interestingly, a much earlier example of this unusual practice also involved an Alvis. This occurred when *Mr Cinders* was in the middle of a run at the Adelphi Theatre. Charles Follett is known to have supplied an eye-catching two-tone 12/50 beetleback (and maybe others if someone took a fancy to the 'lead' car and bought it). The dates of the Adelphi run were February 11 to July 13, 1929.

of sales promotions. An interesting story attached to this is that when Alvis chairman John Parkes got to hear of a fact-finding expedition about to be undertaken in the USA by the BBC's eminent correspondent Edward Ward, he generously shipped 23500 for Ward's use. Thus it is that the car is mentioned in his book *I've Lived like a Lord* (ISBN 07180 7799, published by Michael Joseph). Edward Ward (November 5, 1905-May 8, 1993), later to become the 7th Viscount Bangor, had worked for Reuters before joining the BBC in 1937 and was taken prisoner of war by the Italians at Tobruk. A propensity for being in the right place at the right time saw him covering the Japanese surrender in 1945, Indian Independence, and the 1956 Hungarian uprising. The USA tour of the Alvis, accompanied by wife-to-be Marjorie Banks, is covered, fascinatingly, in another book: *The US and Us* published by Allan Wingate in 1952. Interestingly, when Ward became a castaway on Roy Plomley's *Desert Island Discs* radio show August 28, 1961, one of the pieces chosen was singer Josh

TA 21

1950 to 1953
23803-25119 and 25323-25332
1317 cars

Consisting of:

Mulliner saloons numbered M2000 to M3000 larger rear window from M2500	1000
Mulliner experimental saloons SP611 & SP689	2
Mulliner un-numbered	2
Tickford coupé T 20001 to 20300	300
Tickford un-numbered	1
Graber various 623, 625, 626, 627, 628, 629, 643, 644, 651	9
Unrecorded cars (experimental & sectioned show chassis)	3

Chassis	Reg
23803 - -	JWK 290
23804 - -	KDU 439
23805 - -	NPP 743
23806 - - -	Peru
23807 - -	LYY 893
23808 - - -	AUS
23809 - -	KHP 575
23810 - -	EBN 546
23811 - - - - - -	
23812 - - - -	NL
23813 - -	KHP 574
23814 - - - - -	B
23815 - - - - -	S
23816 - - - -	SM
23817 - - - -	NL
23818 - - - - - -	
23819 - - - -	NZ
23820 - - - -	NZ
23831 - -	KHP 576
23832 - - - -	NZ
23833 - - -	AUS
23834 - - - -	NZ
23835 - - - -	NZ
23836 - -	AUS
23837 - - - - -	B
23838 - -	AUS
23839 -	WHX 137
23840 - - -	AUS
23841 - - - -	CH
23842 - - -	AUS
23843 - - - - -	B
23844 - -	LOF 613
23845 - - -	NL
23846 - -	LOB 541
23847 - - - -	HK
23848 - - -	CDN
23849 - - - -	S
23850 - - -	NL
23851 - - - - -	S
23852 - - - - -	S
23853 - - - - -	S
23854 - - - - -	S
23855 - - - - -	S
23856 - - - -	CO
23857 - - - - -	S
23858 - - - - -	S
23859 - - - - -	S
23860 - - - - -	S
23861 - - -	CDN
23862 - - -	SGP
23863 - - - - -	S
23864 - - -	AUS
23865 - - -	SM
23866 -	KRW 546
23867 - - - -	S
23868 - -	OUB 300
23869 - - -	AUS
23870 - - - -	S
23871 - - -	CH
23872 - - -	CH
23873 - - -	AUS
23874 - - -	CH
23875 - - -	AUS
23876 - - - - -	S
23877 -	MUO 912
23878 - - - - -	S
23879 - - -	AUS
23880 - - - - - -	
23881 - - - -	CH
23882 - -	ZL 4549
23883 - - - -	NL
23884 - -	FPN 342
23885 - -	KWD 142
23886 - -	LXY 878
23887	
23888 - -	LXU 596
23889 - -	EHH 100
23890 - -	FPN 991
23891 - -	FRV 775
23892 - - -	CDN
23893 - - - - -	S
23894 - - - - -	S
23895 - - - - -	S
23896 - - - - -	S
23897 - - - - -	S
23898 - -	HAK 313
23899 - - - -	S
23900 - -	JWO 888
23901 -	MKB 519
23902 -	NEW 86
23903 - -	JFS 796
23904 -	NTO 315
23905 - - - - -	E
23906 - - - -	CH
23907 - - -	NL
23908 -	KWK 909
23909 - - - - -	S
23910 - - - -	NZ
23911 -	GCO 500
23912 - - - - -	S
23913 -	HBC 637
23914 - - - -	USA
23915 - - - -	NL
23916 -	KVC 38
23917 - - - - -	S
23918 -	CNH 184
23919 - - - - -	S
23920 -	SPU 625
23921 - - - - -	S
23922 -	OHN 736
23923 - - - - -	S
23924 - -	GJB 846
23925 - -	JVE 174
23926 - - - - -	S
23927 - - - - -	S
23928 - -	PBB 57
23929 - - - - -	S
23930 - - - - - -	
23931 -	FVY 505
23932 -	APV 142
23933 -	Rhodesia
23934 - - - -	RL
23935 -	JGD 280
23936 - - - - -	S
23937 - - - - -	S
23938 - -	JP 9025
23939 -	LXY 882
23940 -	JMJ 141
23941 - - -	AUS
23942 -	HVJ 700
23943 -	ERG 718
23944 - -	LAD 10
23945 -	KNP 205
23946 -	LYW 484
23947 -	ECK 301
23948 - - - - - -	
23949 -	HFY 192
23950 -	JWF 936
23951 -	EVL 460
23952 - - -	KVC 1
23953 - -	PPE 592
23954 - -	JOR 804
23955 - -	GMO 20
23956 - -	JDA 858
23957 - - - -	CH
23958 - - - -	CH
23959 - - - -	CH
23960 - -	LEL 674
23961 -	HOW 856
23962 - -	PPF 903
23963 -	LXY 889
23964 -	LXY 883
23965 -	MDV 814
23966 - - -	AUS
23967 -	MDV 889
23968 -	ECL 819
23969 -	MRO 907
23970 -	NMN 280
23971 -	EWH 147
23972 - - - - -	F
23973 -	OUB 718
23974 - - - -	CH
23975 -	KDT 206
23976 - - -	USA
23977 -	MYD 888
23978 -	KVC 347
23979 -	HAW 414
23980 -	NFM 382
23981 -	LYW 476
23982 -	STW 490
23983 -	LYW 477
23984 -	JGD 411
23985 -	LXY 874
23986 -	LXY 890
23987 -	OAF 306
23988 -	FRV 571
23989 - -	JFS 677
23990 -	NWE 227
23991 -	KDG 815
23992 - - - - - -	
23993 -	LOH 743
23994 - -	JGD 829
23995 -	LYW 480
23996 -	FUH 491
23997 -	OAE 385
23998 -	HAK 607
23999 -	LYW 479
24000 -	AJK 269
24001 -	HBC 883
24002 -	MNN 809
24003 -	OZ 3671
24004 -	EWH 142
24005 - - - - - -	
24006 -	BSN 769
24007 - -	JP 9078
24008 -	RFC 846
24009 -	LYW 482
24010 - -	JGD 4
24011 -	KRM 788
24012 -	RWL 25
24013 -	MGO 478
24014 - -	LLJ 157
24015 -	MGK 589
24016 -	HAK 641
24017 -	HCA 333
24018 -	MKC 450
24019 -	PBB 235
24020 - -	JGG 24
24021 -	CEE 710
24022 - -	LWY 487
24023 - -	JFH 216
24024 - - - - - -	
24025 - -	FDP 777
24026 -	OHN 891
24027 -	SVW 68
24028 -	MGC 496
24029 -	CFB 896
24030 -	JVE 432
24031 -	JCR 405
24032 -	PRB 321
24033 -	JOT 175
24034 -	EY 9900
24035 -	TNN 789
24036 -	AFL 670
24037 -	AJC 617
24038 -	JGD 849
24039 -	MGC 499
24040 -	LFJ 864
24041 -	MOD 88
24042 -	PPG 960
24043 -	NWE 548
24044 -	VRF 438
24045 -	LAC 621
24046 -	SH 9425
24047 -	CNH 276
24048 -	LOK 101
24049 - -	PPJ 29
24050 -	ECL 980
24051 -	JGG 419
24052 -	KBT 370
24053 -	MGC 514
24054 -	LRT 405
24055 -	HVJ 796
24056 - - -	AUS
24057 -	KEW 177
24058 - - - - - -	
24059 - -	BEJ 188
24060 -	AFL 754
24061 -	ECK 349
24062 -	MGC 502
24063 -	MGC 519
24064 -	KKV 796
24065 - - - - -	F
24066 -	JJW 505
24067 -	NYA 333
24068 -	MGN 713
24069 - - - - -	P
24070 -	FRV 888
24071 -	HAC 379
24072 -	KKV 790
24073 -	BSN 835
24074 - -	JSC 7
24075 -	WHX 697
24076 - -	BEJ 197
24077 -	MUR 635
24078 -	LHP 232
24079 -	LNY 671
24080 - -	LUF 33
24081 -	LXJ 194
24082 -	MGC 516
24083 -	NYA 888
24084 -	MNN 578
24085 -	MGC 517
24086 -	MLT 888
24087 -	GDR 50
24088 -	JGE 394
24089 -	MGK 567
24090 -	SVX 600
24091 - - -	IRL
24092 - -	LDU 786
24093 - - - - - -	
24094 - - - -	CL
24095 - -	ECK 394
24096 -	MGK 569
24097 - - -	AUS
24098 - - -	AUS
24099 -	HCY 530
24100 -	NTV 405
24101 -	HFY 328
24102 -	EHV 934
24103 -	MGY 308
24104 - - -	JCJ 1
24105 -	EWH 310
24106 - - -	JSC 23
24107 -	LDU 59
24108 - - - -	HK
24109 -	MGC 511
24110	MOD 693
24111 -	OUG 392
24112 - - - - - -	
24113 - -	BHF 103
24114 -	OAE 870
24115 - - -	AUS
24116 -	JGE 449
24117 -	MFU 811
24118 -	MGK 581
24119	OUM 167
24120 -	MGK 568
24121 -	PPH 815
24122 -	MGP 933
24123 -	GET 651
24124 -	MGJ 551
24125 - - - -	CL
24126 -	LDU 430
24127 -	JVE 751
24128 -	OHU 40
24129 -	EWH 640
24130 -	CU 5700
24131 -	MVA 659
24132 - -	LXJ 77
24133 -	HCA 472
24134 - -	HRY ...
24135 -	LNX 280
24136 -	MPX 331
24137 - -	JSC 162
24138	MGW 129
24139 -	EHH 412
24140 -	MRR 476
24141 -	HHR 870
24142 -	LCD 992
24143 -	FRD 500
24144 -	MGK 579
24145 -	LNX 250
24146 -	NYA 850
24147 -	MKD 646
24148 -	NYA 800
24149 -	OHT 370
24150 -	MGP 935
24151 - - - - - -	
24152 -	NWJ 608
24153 - - - - - -	
24154 -	MGK 572
24155 -	JGE 596
24156 -	LZ 3030
24157 - - - - - -	
24158 -	FVY 712
24159 -	TEV 96
24160 -	JCR 747
24161 - - - -	NZ
24162 -	MKH 940
24163 -	MGK 580
24164 -	MGK 578
24165 -	LRT 648
24166 -	HMR 800
24167 -	HMR 44
24168 -	EVL 815
24169 -	MGP 932
24170 -	MND 471
24171 -	PHN 41
24172 -	KDT 507
24173 -	LLJ 444
24174 -	OUG 775
24175 -	LOL 919
24176 - -	JTR 96
24177 -	MOD 900
24178 -	PHN 278
24179 -	HCA 536
24180 - - -	AUS
24181 -	MGK 586
24182 -	MGK 584
24183 -	MGK 582
24184 -	KCE 66
24185 - - - - - -	
24186 -	MGY 591
24187 -	NMN 507
24188 -	TNO 353
24189 -	RNU 149
24190 - -	LDU 1
24191 - - -	SGP
24192 -	ODH 763
24193 -	NWJ 143
24194 -	CNH 481
24195 -	OKE 738
24196 -	MGP 927
24197 -	JJW 501
24198 -	JP 9138
24199 -	MNG 896
24200 -	ASY 53
24201 -	PBB 951
24202 -	GDR 293
24203 -	HKU 212
24204 -	GBK 211
24205 -	HNT 195
24206 -	MPW 112
24207 -	JSP 999
24208 - - - - - -	
24209 -	JSC 777
24210 -	AHG 971
24211 -	KWY 56
24212 -	JUS 413
24213 -	MGP 931
24214 -	FRD 600
24215 -	RWL 194
24216 -	LHP 273
24217 - - - - - -	
24218 -	LHP 983
24219 -	LOL 278
24220 - - - - - -	
24221 -	JFH 345
24222 - - - - - -	
24223 -	DT 1283
24224 -	NYB 165
24225 -	PPK 803
24226 -	HRY 363
24227 - - -	AUS
24228 -	ETA 1
24229 -	HKU 304
24230 -	NWJ 236
24231 - - -	AUS

24232 - - - - - -	24302 - - JGG 786	24372 - - JUS 142	24442 - - - - USA	24512 - - GFN 330	24582 - - -JSC 406
24233 - GMO 919	24303 - - - - AUS	24373 - - MJJ 774	24443 - - HTT 561	24513 - OHM 717	24583 - - LWD 821
24234 - - MLY 914	24304 - - FHJ 618	24374 - - HFY 640	24444 - - -EJL 106	24514 - - - - - -	24584 - - HUJ 768
24235 - - - - AUS	24305 - - LRW 56	24375 - - CKS 256	24445 - - -JCJ 489	24515 - - -JCJ 727	24585 - -MXF 135
24236 - - - - AUS	24306 - -XMF 200	24376 - - - - NZ	24446 - - MLT 905	24516 - - HJU 496	24586 - ZO 1222
24237 - - LHP 348	24307 - - NYB 699	24377 - -MUU 446	24447 - - - IRL	24517 - - NNK 897	24587 - - KGA 486
24238 - - - - AUS	24308 - - - AUS	24378 - - PEH 994	24448 - - JUS 628	24518 - - PVT 424	24588 - - - AUS
24239 - - - - AUS	24309 - - MLT 901	24379 - -KNM 263	24449 - - MLT 908	24519 - - JOW 115	24589 - -MXF 142
24240 - - - AUS	24310 - - - AUS	24380 - - PEH 966	24450 - - - - SGP	24520 - - - - - -	24590 - - - - -D
24241 - - - AUS	24311 - - - AUS	24381 - - - JSF 62	24451 - - - USA	24521 - -MUU 444	24591 - - BDX 50
24242 - - - - AUS	24312 - - MLY 913	24382 - - MJJ 775	24452 - - OAU 144	24522 - CVV 91	24592 - MXK 924
24243 - - - AUS	24313 - -OMA 797	24383 - - JUS 627	24453 - - APV 821	24523 - ORL 22	24593 - ERN 292
24244 - - LOL 665	24314 - - - AUS	24384 - - GDR 777	24454 - - LAO 551	24524 - - LRU 485	24594 - AFA 900
24245 - - LHP 279	24315 - - KAA 252	24385 - - PTN 834	24455 - - EVG 410	24525 - -MUU 445	24595 - - - USA
24246 - -HKU 430	24316 - - MLT 896	24386 - - MLT 902	24456 - - LDD 617	24526 - - HYF 807	24596 - - NUO 15
24247 - - - - - -	24317 - - KCE 769	24387 - - - - - -	24457 - - MLY 911	24527 - - FFE 483	24597 - - - USA
24248 - -MXF 133	24318 - - -JYS 397	24388 - - JUK 150	24458 - -TTW 656	24528 - - LTG 777	24598 - - - USA
24249 - - - - AUS	24319 - - - AUS	24389 - - - - NZ	24459 - - GRX 417	24529 - - - USA	24599 - - - - NZ
24250 - - OZ 4644	24320 - - KBT 451	24390 - -HKU 882	24460 - - LUF 456	24530 - LS 5532	24600 - MOE 857
24251 - -BCM 576	24321 - - MLT 899	24391 - - -JP 9382	24461 - - MLY 916	24531 - - KER 100	24601 - -MXF 127
24252 - - - - AUS	24322 - - KAA 154	24392 - - HJU 197	24462 - - OHW 349	24532 - - TVX 428	24602 - CKS 656
24253 - -MGP 942	24323 - - - - SGP	24393 - - LDD 639	24463 - -UML 866	24533 - - - SGP	24603 - - USA
24254 - - - - NZ	24324 - - -RPB 71	24394 - - AEC 933	24464 - - BEG 362	24534 - - - JSG 80	24604 - - - USA
24255 - - - AUS	24325 - -OKK 613	24395 - -OHU 841	24465 - - -JYS 546	24535 - - AJK 737	24605 - - - USA
24256 - KCE 369	24326 - - MAC 334	24396 - - MLV 212	24466 - - JUS 848	24536 - - RPF 392	24606 - - - USA
24257 - - LRW 99	24327 - - PTN 723	24397 - - JUS 875	24467 - -PNW 333	24537 - - -JYS 899	24607 - LDF 435
24258 - - - - - -	24328 - - MLT 898	24398 - - MLY 910	24468 - - LUF 595	24538 - - - FBN 2	24608 - -MXF 128
24259 - - - AUS	24329 - - - - NL	24399 - - MLT 897	24469 - -OFM 393	24539 - - LOX 801	24609 - -MXF 132
24260 - - LHP 438	24330 - - JGG 956	24400 - - MLT 894	24470 - - MLY 907	24540 - - KGA 342	24610 - - - SGP
24261 - - LON 200	24331 - - -JSC 868	24401 - - LTG 138	24471 - - I.O.Man	24541 - - - AUS	24611 - - - USA
24262 - - - AUS	24332 - - CSS 274	24402 - -OWA 169	24472 - HKW 165	24542 - -MOB 235	24612 - KCG 999
24263 - - - - AUS	24333 - - - - G 1	24403 - - JUS 522	24473 - -GBO 615	24543 - HMW 920	24613 - LDT 223
24264 - - PEH 847	24334 - - - AUS	24404 - - GBK 882	24474 - - LOV 707	24544 - - OAU 558	24614 - - - USA
24265 - - MJJ 761	24335 - - MLT 887	24405 - - MLY 40	24475 - -MUU 448	24545 - - - -HK	24615 - GDP 515
24266 - - LHP 568	24336 - - SO 9874	24406 - - MLY 906	24476 - - HKW 353	24546 - -MXF 129	24616 - - USA
24267 - - - AUS	24337 - - - AUS	24407 - - OHW 201	24477 - -PNW 860	24547 - -MXF 131	24617 - - - USA
24268 - - MFJ 142	24338 - - HRY 722	24408 - - OPP 972	24478 - - LWD 257	24548 - - -JP 9584	24618 - PHN 974
24269 - KWX 806	24339 - - MLY 924	24409 - - OUM 298	24479 - - -JS 9636	24549 - - KGA 159	24619 - FFE 544
24270 - - LHP 622	24340 - -EWH 759	24410 - -MUU 447	24480 - - OTO 813	24550 - - KBT 904	24620 - MXH 77
24271 - - - AUS	24341 - - - AUS	24411 - - - - - P	24481 - - MLY 928	24551 - - JUK 950	24621 - CNN 566
24272 - - EVG 167	24342 - - RPC 604	24412 - - - - NL	24482 - - FFR 706	24552 - - LWK 943	24622 - -KTM 260
24273 - - - - - -	24343 - - MJJ 763	24413 - - MLT 910	24483 - - - SGP	24553 - -MUU 456	24623 - MAC 20
24274 - -MGP 944	24344 - - MLY 107	24414 - - - - NZ	24484 - - - SGP	24554 - -MUU 450	24624 - EVG 734
24275 - - GRP 790	24345 - - UML 809	24415 - -EWH 722	24485 - - NYC 585	24555 - -MUU 458	24625 - KGA 571
24276 - - - - - A	24346 - - OUM 760	24416 - - LWK 226	24486 - -MGY 591	24556 - - - - - -	24626 - ZO 1230
24277 - - LHP 889	24347 - - JGG 950	24417 - - -JP 9507	24487 - - SFC 299	24557 - - RPE 243	24627 - -MXF 130
24278 - - - - - P	24348 - -EWH 570	24418 - - JUS 526	24488 - - OZ 5689	24558 - - MFJ 592	24628 - FCK 505
24279 - - - - NL	24349 - -EWH 721	24419 - - OHW 205	24489 - - HUJ 259	24559 - - MXK 600	24629 - HKW 959
24280 - - - SGP	24350 - - MJJ 768	24420 - - TPU 585	24490 - - - USA	24560 - - MNF 256	24630 - - - SGP
24281 - - - - NL	24351 - - - AUS	24421 - - MLT 895	24491 - - LWK 925	24561 - -OWB 195	24631 - OHY 435
24282 - - - SGP	24352 - - FFE 141	24422 - - OKL 973	24492 - - - SGP	24562 - - HZ 5299	24632 - PAE 343
24283 - - - - SM	24353 - - UNT 631	24423 - - RPA 509	24493 - - RPB 608	24563 - - MLV 934	24633 - KGA 536
24284 - - - AUS	24354 - - - - SM	24424 - - MLY 915	24494 - -MUU 442	24564 - MXM 976	24634 - LKV 838
24285 - - - - NZ	24355 - - MND 93	24425 - - RRA 158	24495 - - -JYS 205	24565 - - JSG 111	24635 - FHS 324
24286 - - PPK 570	24356 - - - AUS	24426 - -OWA 368	24496 - - -JSF 935	24566 - - OAU 606	24636 - MAC 303
24287 - - - - AUS	24357 - - - AUS	24427 - - -RPD 76	24497 - - PVK 189	24567 - - - - - B	24637 - -MXF 141
24288 - -MGP 947	24358 - - KAA 546	24428 - - FVH 481	24498 - - MLV 650	24568 - - - CDN	24638 - MOC 499
24289 - - LON 885	24359 - - - AUS	24429 - - KDT 907	24499 - -MUU 451	24569 - - - AUS	24639 - - -JUJ 200
24290 - - -JP 9310	24360 - -EWH 723	24430 - - CNH 795	24500 - - - - NL	24570 - -MUU 443	24640 - LKV 226
24291 - -MGP 946	24361 - - MLT 903	24431 - - JTR 666	24501 - - - - NL	24571 - -MXF 133	24641 - -MXY 208
24292 - - APV 603	24362 - - - - - -	24432 - - ERS 372	24502 - - MLY 927	24572 - -MUU 463	24642 - MAC 785
24293 - -MGP 945	24363 - -EWH 641	24433 - - -EJL 140	24503 - -KNM 701	24573 - - - AUS	24643 - -DFB 50
24294 - - BCW 45	24364 - - JUS 888	24434 - -MLW 999	24504 - -MUU 457	24574 - - RPF 356	24644 - KER 508
24295 - - JVB 869	24365 - -MGP 949	24435 - - LRU 441	24505 - -MUU 454	24575 - -MXF 123	24645 - - - USA
24296 - - MJJ 758	24366 - - JUS 770	24436 - - PHN 562	24506 - - PVK 232	24576 - - GDN 635	24646 - NRO 572
24297 - - HFY 431	24367 - -MKF 625	24437 - - OZ 5585	24507 - - LOX 74	24577 - - KGA 419	24647 - PVK 612
24298 - - MJJ 757	24368 - - RJO 270	24438 - - HMW 465	24508 - -EWH 873	24578 - - - AUS	24648 - KUY 666
24299 - -LRW 257	24369 - - JUS 527	24439 - - - IRL	24509 - - MUW 655	24579 - - OMN 83	24649 - OAU 913
24300 - - - HHS 7	24370 - - MJJ 769	24440 - - JUS 941	24510 - -MUU 441	24580 - MXK 542	24650 - - - USA
24301 - - RPA 675	24371 - - SV 1824	24441 - - - - NL	24511 - -MUU 462	24581 - - - AUS	24651 - - - USA

24652 - - LKV 341	24722 - MXM 987	24792 - - - - - -	24862 - - - - - F	24932 - - - - USA	25002 - -MKV 707
24653 - - LKV 342	24723 - MXM 992	24793 - - GCX 121	24863 - - KJW 209	24933 - - OAL 221	25003 - -MVC 778
24654 - - HNR 152	24724 - -MXY 207	24794 - - PAE 969	24864 - - MXJ 361	24934 - - NGO 643	25004 - - FES 221
24655 - - -KGB 36	24725 - - JOW 807	24795 - -MXY 216	24865 - - ODU 863	24935 - - JAK 445	25005 - - NEL 707
24656 - - - - USA	24726 - -MYT 604	24796 - - HKY 490	24866 - - JBD 694	24936 - - NVF 930	25006 - - SPH 641
24657 - - HNR 734	24727 - - -KSP 83	24797 - - - SL 549	24867 - - JAK 216	24937 - - PWA 506	25007 - - PWJ 926
24658 - - - KMJ 1	24728 - - - - USA	24798 - - - - USA	24868 - - LWU 837	24938 - - VHK 637	25008 - - NLO 945
24659 - - - - USA	24729 - - - - USA	24799 - - - - USA	24869 - - HET 555	24939 - -LWW 758	25009 - - - - NZ
24660 - - - - USA	24730 - - - - -MA	24800 - - - - USA	24870 - - - - CDN	24940 - - -SS 7777	25010 - MWK 329
24661 - - - - USA	24731 - -MXY 214	24801 - - - - USA	24871 - - - - USA	24941 - - PPP 816	25011 - - NNC 756
24662 - - - - USA	24732 - - OZ 7413	24802 - -UTW 377	24872 - - NOD 687	24942 - MWK 197	25012 - - - - - J
24663 - - MVM 222	24733 - MXM 988	24803 - - - - USA	24873 - -MYT 606	24943 - - NUV 748	25013 - - NJJ 582
24664 - MXM 991	24734 - - LEW 70	24804 - - XRE 883	24874 - - PUG 318	24944 - - DS 3324	25014 - - NLF 557
24665 - -OWB 793	24735 - - OKT 20	24805 - MNX 639	24875 - - UVX 54	24945 - - - - NZ	25015 - - PMB 545
24666 - - EHH 815	24736 - - CJE 236	24806 - - PAF 451	24876 - - KGE 341	24946 - -PKM 749	25016 - - -JFY 439
24667 - - - JSR 39	24737 - - HBL 575	24807 - -MYY 506	24877 - -MYT 615	24947 - - GVH 254	25017 - - PTU 128
24668 - -MXF 144	24738 - - FHE 412	24808 - - CVV 409	24878 - - NVF 222	24948 - - - - NZ	25018 - - -HTP 69
24669 - - - - SGP	24739 - -MDU 325	24809 - -MYO 800	24879 - - OWJ 716	24949 - - - - - J	25019 - - - - USA
24670 - JSG 324	24740 - -MVU 927	24810 - - CU 5949	24880 - - - USA	24950 - -NGO 634	25020 - - - - -U
24671 - - HFY 905	24741 - - CJV 840	24811 - - - HJ 134	24881 - - - - USA	24951 - -LWX 995	25021 - - - - USA
24672 - -MXY 210	24742 - - - - - -	24812 - -UTW 231	24882 - - BDX 688	24952 - -NGO 659	25022 - - - - USA
24673 - - KGA 943	24743 - - -JP 9697	24813 - -NGO 647	24883 - - KOT 775	24953 - - - - NZ	25023 - - - AUS
24674 - MXM 978	24744 - - GFN 720	24814 - - GRD 777	24884 - - LAB 141	24954 - - - SGP	25024 - -FWH 672
24675 - - - - USA	24745 - - HKY 502	24815 - - RHN 313	24885 - - NGO 631	24955 - - - - - -	25025 - - RZ 399
24676 - - - - USA	24746 - - - - SGP	24816 - -MVU 379	24886 - - BHC 516	24956 - -NXH 490	25026 - - RTO 313
24677 - - LKV 220	24747 - - -FFV 60	24817 - - -KJW 10	24887 - - - - USA	24957 - - CTS 559	25027 - - - NZ
24678 - - - - USA	24748 - - KDA 664	24818 - - KGD 743	24888 - - - - USA	24958 - - NEL 576	25028 - - JKU 737
24679 - - FBN 210	24749 - - KGD 123	24819 - - GRD 156	24889 - - NGO 635	24959 - -YMF 233	25029 - - CU 6104
24680 - - KGA 894	24750 - -MDU 723	24820 - -MYT 605	24890 - - GSF 893	24960 - - SBB 520	25030 - - - USA
24681 - - MXM 984	24751 - -OWE 372	24821 - - KFS 246	24891 - -NVM 400	24961 - - BEN 496	25031 - - NUV 593
24682 - -MDU 537	24752 - -MXY 215	24822 - - - - - -	24892 - - - - USA	24962 - -NXU 305	25032 - - NUV 943
24683 - - PUA 949	24753 - - MFJ 865	24823 - - - - USA	24893 - - BHF 473	24963 - -NVM 357	25033 - - BHC 767
24684 - - - - USA	24754 - - JWS 391	24824 - - - - USA	24894 - - LBM 720	24964 - - - NZ	25034 - - JPY 733
24685 - -MXY 211	24755 - - FBN 481	24825 - - - - USA	24895 - - NLF 931	24965 - - -KCA 82	25035 - - TPB 272
24686 - - - - USA	24756 - - -GRV 82	24826 - - - - USA	24896 - - MWK 136	24966 - - - - USA	25036 - -NLM 475
24687 - -MXY 345	24757 - -MHP 464	24827 - - -BEJ 848	24897 - - FRG 276	24967 - - AEF 789	25037 - - BEN 808
24688 - - MXM 982	24758 - - -PPP 38	24828 - - BCW 619	24898 - - KOU 466	24968 - - NXJ 781	25038 - - NLT 886
24689 - - GJY 682	24759 - -KOR 788	24829 - - KFS 150	24899 - - - - USA	24969 - - GVH 157	25039 - - - - - J
24690 - - XRE 297	24760 - - XRF 420	24830 - - - - -MA	24900 - - - - USA	24970 - - - USA	25040 - - PWJ 603
24691 - - RPH 225	24761 - - MOH 136	24831 - - PAF 163	24901 - - - NZ	24971 - - KTR 979	25041 - - NLV 333
24692 - - OYA 169	24762 - - -SPC 61	24832 - - SPC 297	24902 - -MAD 713	24972 - MWK 180	25042 - - - - USA
24693 - - MDU 11	24763 - - OUR 15	24833 - - - - - -	24903 - - KFS 536	24973 - - KOU 454	25043 - - - - USA
24694 - -MXP 636	24764 - - JWS 210	24834 - - OZ 8310	24904 - - SPD 730	24974 - - - - NZ	25044 - - - - USA
24695 - - MXM 981	24765 - - MOK 469	24835 - -MVC 600	24905 - - - - - J	24975 - - - - - J	25045 - - - - USA
24696 - - LKV 792	24766 - - VS 5643	24836 - -HDW 610	24906 - - MGK 56	24976 - - - AUS	25046 - - - - USA
24697 - - KZ 7103	24767 - - PUB 582	24837 - - CJX 641	24907 - - NGT 482	24977 - - - - - J	25047 - -ODU 336
24698 - - LKV 986	24768 - - - - SGP	24838 - -MYT 611	24908 - - HJB 193	24978 - - TPB 495	25048 - - - - - -
24699 - - MAD 61	24769 - - - - USA	24839 - - - - USA	24909 - - - 1909 E	24979 - - PWJ 979	25049 - MWK 198
24700 - - SFC 673	24770 - - MOH 495	24840 - - - - USA	24910 - - MWU 88	24980 - -RUM 385	25050 - - - - USA
24701 - -EHH 823	24771 - - GKJ 727	24841 - - HKY 669	24911 - VXW 805	24981 - - NUV 935	25051 - - TPD 548
24702 - - - - CDN	24772 - MNX 418	24842 - - SPA 466	24912 - - MUF 515	24982 - OWK 117	25052 - - LBY 140
24703 - -NNG 791	24773 - - -FCL 61	24843 - -MOL 282	24913 - - - - USA	24983 - -PMV 742	25053 - - - AUS
24704 - - - - USA	24774 - - - - USA	24844 - - -OTE 52	24914 - - - NZ	24984 - - VHK 618	25054 - - - - - F
24705 - - CVV 362	24775 - - HBU 513	24845 - - MUE 79	24915 - -NGO 641	24985 - - NLC 473	25055 - - LER 834
24706 - -UHK 620	24776 - - - - USA	24846 - -MHP 448	24916 - - NLO 959	24986 - - -NJJ 568	25056 - - NYF 325
24707 - - SE 7496	24777 - -MDU 317	24847 - - - - USA	24917 - - UPA 954	24987 - MOX 367	25057 - -OOD 143
24708 - - NKB 700	24778 - - KGB 897	24848 - - - - USA	24918 - - - - NZ	24988 - - - - - J	25058 - - OLN 594
24709 - - - - USA	24779 - - - - USA	24849 - - - - USA	24919 - MON 647	24989 - - KVB 332	25059 - - RTC 639
24710 - - - - USA	24780 - - - - - -	24850 - - - JAJ 366	24920 - - - - USA	24990 - MWK 720	25060 - -JAV 648
24711 - - - - USA	24781 - - - - -CH	24851 - - - - SGP	24921 - - -SA 13	24991 - - -NJJ 589	25061 - - CEP 999
24712 - - - - USA	24782 - - - - USA	24852 - - HAP 100	24922 - - CBR 919	24992 - -YTW 484	25062 - - KVJ 145
24713 - - PAE 269	24783 - -MDU 725	24853 - - PPK 108	24923 - - -NJJ 579	24993 - - - - NZ	25063 - - LGD 497
24714 - - LKV 717	24784 - -MXY 229	24854 - - HWM 363	24924 - MWK 110	24994 - - PVT 873	25064 - - FVG 895
24715 - - UNO 43	24785 - - - - USA	24855 - - MWD 35	24925 - - - - CDN	24995 - - - - -DK	25065 - - OHP 784
24716 - - MEL 457	24786 - - GPM 454	24856 - - HBO 84	24926 - - - - USA	24996 - -PUM 455	25066 - - NDU 207
24717 - - - -G 211	24787 - - - - -CH	24857 - -MYT 619	24927 - - KJW 677	24997 - -VNO 273	25067 - - GRA 11
24718 - - LTX 556	24788 - - HUN 723	24858 - - SJO 662	24928 - - - - CDN	24998 - - NLO 643	25068 - - OKC 836
24719 - BDX 279	24789 - -MVU 115	24859 - - MRW 153	24929 - - JHR 412	24999 - - TWL 454	25069 - - NDU 51
24720 - MXM 996	24790 - - CEP 767	24860 - - - - - -	24930 - - LS 5671	25000 - - LGA 863	25070 - - NXU 296
24721 - - BHC 300	24791 - - KWF 838	24861 - - - - CDN	24931 - - - - USA	25001 - - NDT 203	25071 - - JNV 900

25072 - - PWE 885	25091 - - - 5033 H	25110 - - SPL 613
25073 - 901 AMM	25092 - - - - NZ	25111 - -ORW 653
25074 - - - OFJ 38	25093 - - KSC 825	25112 - - CEG 844
25075 - -OXU 496	25094 - - NDU 899	25113 - - MCE 30
25076 - -MVC 877	25095 - -429 AML	25114 - MUX 590
25077 - - -KBC 50	25096 - - OVC 662	25115 - -OGY 954
25078 - NUV 862	25097 - - PWB 440	25116 - NYU 817
25079 - MFG 66	25098 - - BHC 701	25117 - -NXU 307
25080 - - - - -DK	25099 - - JUX 717	25118 - -OLH 113
25081 - -NXV 727	25100 - - - SNW 9	25119 - BDA 223
25082 - - TPF 607	25101 - -NWR 364	25323 - -NYK 791
25083 - - OLV 204	25102 - - - - - J	25324 - - - - NL
25084 - - - MDA 7	25103 - - NDU 138	25325 - -OXU 191
25085 - WMX 959	25104 - - LWY 927	25326 - - - USA
25086 - - NDU 751	25105 - - - - CDN	25327 - - OLF 747
25087 - - - - - -	25106 - - - AUS	25328 - - -PWJ 70
25088 - SPL 217	25107 - NUV 939	25329 - - - - NZ
25089 - - - - -CH	25108 - - NDU 205	25330 - - MSF 909
25090 - - LUS 383	25109 - - - - - J	25331 - -NXV 622

All new from stem to stern (with the exception of the gearbox internals), this design mainly emanated from the drawing board of Willie Dunn, with Chris Kingham developing an especially sturdy six-cylinder, seven bearing engine, which would serve the marque well for the next seventeen years. Coil springs were used at the front, following experiments with one such application to Speed 25 chassis 14638. Salisbury provided the rear axle (instead of ENV) and Lockheed the brakes (instead of Girling). The angle of the chassis tapering aft of the A-post remained the same as in the TA 14 in order to accommodate a derivative of the by now familiar Mulliner saloon body shape. This itself was now of quite significant construction – using a series of aluminium castings bolted together to replicate the ash frame of the original design. Tickford retained the ash frame, however, for the coupé version. The first saloon was consigned to Geneva in March 1950 for the official announcement. A new era was now under way.

23804 KDU 439
Monte Carlo Rally 1951
Entered by Dorothy Stanley-Turner WRAF, accompanied by Commander P S Wilson, AFC, and Commander H C N Goodhart RN. This was the second production TA 21 model.

After this quite successful expedition (it finished 32nd in a quite large field) it returned to the works press fleet, and would reappear when it was submitted to *The Motor* for a punishing Continental Road Test, which appeared in the issue of January 16, 1952.

23804: A pre-production TA 21 on the 1951 Monte Carlo Rally with Dorothy Stanley-Turner and crew. (Courtesy Alvis Archive Trust)

23809 KHP 575
Iliffe Publications Ltd
23809 was already getting on for two years old when it was submitted to *Autocar* for one of its full weekly Road Tests, which appeared in the issue of February 15, 1952. It had, however, by then been fitted with the latest production updates, including, most importantly, the twin carburettor set-up.

23831 KHP 576
Monte Carlo Rally 1952
Entered by Dorothy Stanley-Turner, accompanied by Commander P S Wilson and Air Commodore Tindal-Carill-Worsley.

23952 KVC 1
HM Foreign Office
Thought to have been allocated to Swedish Duties.

24043 NWE 548
F Paramore Ltd
Whilst not as large a company as its main competitors Record and Stanley, this company produced a similar range of products like carpenters' planes and engineering vices under the

The hotel has been coaxed skilfully into the 21st century—without losing the sense of history or place that for more than a hundred years has attracted people from all walks of life and corners of the globe.

23871: The fourth TA 21 Tickford to be constructed was used by the Orient Express company in the promotion of its hotel, Caruso Belvedere, at Ravello. (Courtesy Belmond Hotels)

'PARAMO' brand name. 24043 replaced an earlier company Alvis – a TA 14 (qv 21577).

24162 FFE 141
Sir Basil Parkes
Fishing magnate, with operations at Fleetwood and Grimsby.

24186 MGY 591
Jack Hylton
Famous bandleader Jack Hylton (July 2, 1892-January 29, 1965) was as accomplished in entrepreneurial activities as he was musically. As early as 1931, he had collaborated with Igor Stravinsky on the production of his seldom-aired opera buffa, *Mavra*. Jack is, however, more usually associated with the popular music scene, and the production of best-selling records. After a contract with HMV, he transferred to and became a director of the Decca record label. One source credits him with 'discovering' Shirley Bassey.

24276 OLP 17
HM Foreign Office
An embassy car, allocated initially to Vienna, then transferred to Washington.

24312 MLY 913
Tulip Rally 1954
This was a private entry by Trevor Boothroyd, with works support, which included Alvis employee Ron Walton. The Walton memoirs of his time at Alvis Ltd make a fascinating and informative read. Entitled *Young Ron – an Alvis Experience*, published by Dart Valley Press, Buckfastleigh.

24324 RPB 71
Simon Rigge
Simon Rigge's education commenced at Tonbridge School, and continued at Oriel College, Oxford. Following experience in the publishing field, initially with Purnell's (qv 26728) and with *The Observer*, he transferred to Time-Life Books, overseeing an impressive catalogue. In 1979, Rigge established his own company: Sheldrake Press, which has gone from strength to strength, specialising in books on history, architecture, design, travel, cookery, etc, many of which Simon has written himself. Too numerous to mention all here, but the website – www.sheldrakepress.co.uk – will produce full details.

24326 MAC 334
Lord Leigh
John Piers Leigh, 5th Baron Leigh of Stoneleigh, would, in 1951, commission from Tickfords a special fixed head coupé version of its TA 21, which was catalogued officially only as a convertible. It had attractive lines with overtones of the Healey and Humber bodies that Tickford was making at the same time. Lord Leigh had previously owned a 12/70 model (qv 15557).

24383 JUS 627
Charles Chicheley Plowden
Botanist and respected member of the Royal Horticultural Society, and author of *A Manual of Plant Names* published by Allen Unwin in 1970, and twice reprinted: ISBN 978-000-458-0087.

Retired to the Lake District, where he ran a pub: The Royal Oak, at Cartmel. Previously owned a Silver Eagle model (qv 12720).

24416 **LWK 226**
Monte Carlo Rally 1953
Entered by Dorothy Stanley-Turner, her co-drivers were Nancy Mitchell and Rosemary Fotheringham-Parker.

24454 **LAO 551**
Marianne Faithfull
Iconic singer of the sixties, Marianne produced substantial discography: singles, LPs and EPs. Born December 29, 1946, she has an autobiography, *Faithfull*, published by Little, Brown & Co. ISBN 978-031627-3244.

24493 **RPB 608**
Baron Lyle
Born Charles Ernest Leonard Lyle (July 27, 1882-March 6, 1954), he was educated at Harrow and Trinity College, Cambridge, knighted in 1923, a baronet in 1932 and acceded to the title in 1945. He will be remembered as 'the Sugar King,' brought about by the merger of A Lyle & Company with Henry Tate Ltd in 1921. He was the force behind opposition to the proposed nationalisation of the sugar industry initiated by the then Labour government. The cartoon character 'Mr Cube' was ubiquitous at this time. A talented sportsman also, he competed in the Men's Singles at Wimbledon

The once ubiquitous cartoon character 'Mr Cube' was the invention of Baron Lyle (of Tate & Lyle) in order to promote the sugar industry.

in 1922, 1923, 1924, and duly became chairman of the Lawn Tennis Association in 1932. Also elected to Parliament on three occasions: 1918-1922, 1923-1924 and 1940-1945, a different constituency on each occasion.

24487 **SFC 299**
Iliffe Publications Ltd
24487 was featured in *Autocar*'s occasional *Used Cars on the Road* – number 125 in the series.

24499 **MUU 451**
Nigel Balchin
Nigel Balchin (December 3, 1908-May 17, 1970) was a prolific author and screenplay writer. After graduating from Peterhouse, Cambridge, he started writing alongside his consultancy and civil service positions, sometimes using the pseudonym 'Mark Spade.' During WWII, he rose to the rank of Brigadier. There were at least 15 novels and 17 screenplays, plus other books of a technical nature, some of which leant on his experience as a psychologist. Of the novels, probably best known is *Mine Own Executioner* of 1945, later made into a film, and of the screen plays *The Man who Never Was* – a war story that won a BAFTA award in 1956.

24501 **NL**
Pia Beck
Once described by Oscar Peterson as 'the best jazz pianist in the world' (and he should know), Pia Beck (September 18, 1925-November 20, 2009) produced many albums, singles and EPs. There is an autobiography, in Dutch, called *The Pia Beck Story,* published by Tiebosch. ISBN 90-6278-782-7.

24537 **JYS 899**
Rod Jolley
Michelangelo of sheet metal, Hampshire coachbuilder and restorer, Rod produced a remarkable sprint/road-going sports car from an otherwise terminal TA 21 saloon. Not for the faint hearted.

24546 **MXF 129**
Simoniz Ltd
Purveyor of a wide range of automotive cleaning

24537: The fearsome Rod Jolley competition car was originally a standard TA 21 saloon. (Courtesy Ernest Shenton collection)

That Michelangelo of sheet metal, Rod Jolley is pictured in 1989, receiving an award for an FTD with the even faster Alvis Giron special, in the Weston speed trials. (Courtesy Alvis Archive Trust)

products, Simoniz used 24546 in one of its prominent advertisements.

24560 MNF 256
Beware of Children
Dually released, also with the *No Kidding* title, this movie of 1960 starred Leslie Philips, Irene Handl, Joan Hickson, and 24560.

24576 GDN 635
Terry's of York Ltd
The well-known chocolatiers had its company TA 21 specially finished in brown. When replaced by a

TE 21 in 1965 (qv 27317), a similarly appropriate hue was applied to that as well.

24615 GDP 515
Keith Piggott
Jockey and horse-trainer, and father of the even more famous Lester Piggott, Keith Piggott was born in 1904 and remained active in the sport until his death at the age of 89. Previously owned an Alvis 12/70 model (qv 15624) and prior to this, a Firebird model (qv 12562).

24616 USA
Carmen Miranda
Although there is some doubt as to whether or not she actually owned it, Carmen Miranda's promotion of the TA 21 Tickford coupé in transatlantic advertising was conspicuously successful, with 65 of a total of 300 of this model being sold stateside. She was born February 9, 1909 and was originally a milliner. She shot to fame with songs usually in the samba genre, appeared in some 30 movies between 1933 and 1955, and made over 100 record singles. She died tragically young on August 5, 1955 of a heart attack, at merely 46.

24616: The United States Alvis importer used singer and actress Carmen Miranda to promote the TA 21 Tickford convertible. (Courtesy Alvis Ltd)

24627 MXF 130
Jack Hawkins CBE
At one time judged Britain's most popular actor, Jack Hawkins (September 14, 1910-July 18, 1973) specialised in the military, or 'stiff upper lip' role. This would apply to his own life when, having

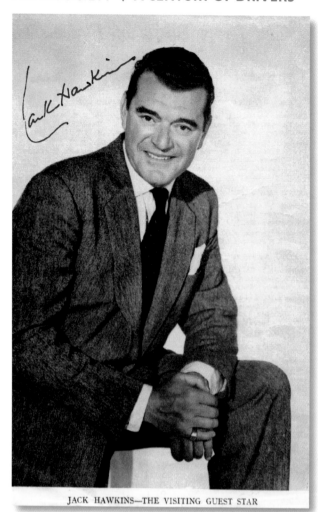

JACK HAWKINS—THE VISITING GUEST STAR

Actor Jack Hawkins. The autographed photo is from a theatre programme belonging to the author's late aunt.

contracted cancer of the larynx, he continued to work, sometimes with his voice dubbed by other actors. Nevertheless, he starred in over 80 movies, to popular acclaim. Insofar as Alvis is concerned, *The League of Gentlemen* of 1960 (nothing to do with the eponymous television series of 1999 to 2002) has to be mentioned, being a crime movie involving the aforesaid 24627 (with its number plate changed in some shots to a spurious VGJ 347). Hawkins was no stranger to Alvis use, having deployed a thus far unidentified TA 14 Tickford drophead coupé in the 1957 *Fortune is a Woman*, where he plays an unrelenting insurance investigator. An autobiography, published after his death, is worthy of note. This is *Anything for a Quiet Life* ISBN 978-08128-17089.

24658 KMJ 1

Gerry Dunham

Raced at Silverstone by the long-time Luton Alvis agent, Dunham used the high ratio back axle on this occasion, that up to this point had only been standard on the TB 21 model. Some time later, Dunham moved the registration mark KMJ 1 on to a TC 21/100 (25704), whereupon 24658 became TRO 135.

24662 USA

Tony Curtis

Curtis replaced 24662 with a TE 21 (qv 27327 bio).

24677 LKV 220

Cornercroft Ltd

Well-known Coventry-based manufacturer of car accessories such as number plates and wheel discs, under the above name and also the ACE brand, the company used 24677 in its advertising. Alvis Ltd did a lot of business with Cornercroft and, indeed, there had been a similar precedent involving the use of a Speed 20 SD (qv 13018) in 1936. In-between these two dates, Cornercroft would acquire a 12/70 as a company car (qv 15719) in 1939.

24696 LKV 792

Sir Alec Issigonis CBE, FRS

Being engaged by Alvis Ltd to design an all-new 3½-litre V8 passenger car, 24696 was the first company car allocated to Issigonis during his time there. The other was also a TA 21 (qv 25065 for bio).

24736 CJE 236

Denholm Elliott

Elliott (May 31, 1922-October 6, 1992) was educated at Malvern College and served in the RAF, but was shot down in action, survived and became a prisoner of war. There were at least 120 screen appearances, the most memorable being *Indiana Jones and the Raiders of the Lost Ark*.

24782 USA

MGM Picture Corporation

Why Elliott Morgan of Metro-Goldwyn-Mayer

specifically ordered this Tickford drophead coupé to be delivered in primer, on June 7, 1952, remains a mystery.

24799 USA
Bernard Herrmann

A musical child prodigy in the mould of Mozart, Saint-Saens and Prokofiev, Benny, as he liked to be called (June 29, 1911-December 24, 1975), had won a prestigious prize for composition at the age of 13. He subsequently studied under Percy Grainger, and at the Julliard School, and is best known for his movie scores, of which there were over 50, under directors such as Orson Welles, Alfred Hitchcock and Martin Scorsese between 1941 and 1975. Conducting was also one of his many accomplishments, often championing the music of lesser-known composers. It is only fairly recently that the real worth of Benny's more serious music, like the Symphony and the Piano Concerto, is at last being more widely recognised,

A hugely important figure in 20th century music, this CBS photograph shows a comparatively young Bernard Herrmann, and was kindly supplied especially for this book by Mrs Norma Herrmann. The image probably dates from about the time of his *Citizen Kane* score. Such memorables as *Psycho* and the author's favourite *North by Northwest* would follow.

with the individuality and orchestration typical of the genius that he was. Of the many movies, *North by Northwest* must especially be mentioned, not least because it starred another Alvis enthusiast, James Mason, who owned a TB 14, and a TD 21 (qv 26766). Herrmann also wrote the score for *The Egyptian,* which starred Edmund Purdom – another TA 21 owner (qv 25020).

24831 PAF 163
Freeman-Sanders Co

Probably unique in Alvis sales orders in having been specifically ordered without an engine, 24831 was delivered to Arthur Freeman-Sanders at his Penzance works. The reason for this is intriguing, Arthur being a diesel engine expert previously employed at Listers. Diesel engines for passenger cars were far from common at the time, and even less so in six cylinder format. The Alvis was one of two development cars (FS 2) in the project, the other (FS1) being a Studebaker Dictator. With only 55bhp on tap compared with the TA 21's 93, it would have been no fireball, but was, from reports, far more refined than others of that ilk. There is no record of Alvis Ltd ever having expressed any interest in taking up the idea itself, although many years earlier it had conducted experiments with a Gardner oil engine in a Speed 20 SB.

Freeman-Sanders' pioneering work would be more widely recognised with his work on the popular Ferguson tractor engine.

24859 MRW 153
Works development car

On the sales demonstration fleet, press car, and raced at Silverstone by Gerry Dunham. Has also been twice re-registered: as SXG 956, and later 8247 JH.

24891 NVM 400
The Hotspur Press

An iconic and highly visible Manchester landmark, Medlock Cotton Mill dates from the early 19th century, but was taken over by the Percy brothers for their printing purposes and re-named the Hotspur Press. 24891 was delivered to then proprietor G A Ashcroft, in April 1952. When that business closed it became a venue for artists and musicians, and gave its name to a rock band. More recently it had been occupied by squatters, since evicted. For the connection of 'Hotspur' and 'Percy' brush up your Shakespeare.

24892 USA
Alberto Morin
Never a star-billing actor, unlike some of his contemporaries, Alberto Morin (December 26, 1902-April 7, 1989) had a very lengthy Hollywood portfolio, appearing in well over 200 movies between 1928 and 1988, such as *Two Mules for Sister Sarah*, alongside another acknowledged auto buff Clint Eastwood. Morin was not new to Alvis ownership, having previously owned a Speed 25 model (qv 14376).

24892: Hollywood actor Alberto Morin with his Tickford TA 21, after taking an award at a California car club event c.1961. (Courtesy Alvis Archive Trust)

24964 NZ
Kenneth Burward-Hoy
Distinguished virtuoso of the viola. Replaced 24964 with a TD 1 model (qv 26446).

25020 USA
Edmond Purdom
A hugely successful actor, Edmond Purdom (December 19, 1924-January 1, 2009) worked with

Mario Lanza on the widely acclaimed production of *The Student Prince*. Even more worthy of mention is his role in *The Egyptian* for which Alvis owner Bernard Herrmann (qv 24799) wrote the film score.

25032 NUV 943
Saunders Roe Ltd
Saunders Roe was, of course, a key player in the development of Christopher Cockerell's hovercroft designs, the prototype of which employed an Alvis radial aircraft engine. The supply of this car to them would seem to indicate some kind of reciprocal arrangement.

25036 NLM 475
RAC Rally 1954
Driven in the above event by Jacobs, who was the proprietor of the then well-known Times Furnishing Company. Co-drivers were Lawrence and Turner.

25050
George Reeves
US actor Reeves, born January 5, 1914, died June 16, 1959 in a mysterious shooting incident. He made well over 50 appearances in a variety of roles, but is probably best remembered for his portrayal of Superman in the TV series from 1951 to 1958.

One of his first appearances was in the 1939 *Gone with the Wind,* but the star billing on that occasion was taken by Alvis owner Leslie Howard. See 12069, a Speed 20 SC.

25065 OHP 784
Sir Alec Issigonis CBE, FRS
The second TA 21 allocated to Issigonis during his time at Alvis Ltd, and re-allocated to Salisbury Transmissions, maker of rear axles for all the production 3-litres, after his departure. For the preceding Issigonis TA 21 and bio see 26496.

25114 MUX 590
John Magnus Peterson
In the book *City on the Hill* by David Gee, Greenbank Press, ISBN 978-0-9523699-8-1, the author makes reference to having been given a lift to Henley in an Alvis car belonging to the headmaster

Chassis	Reg			25130 - - - - USA	25141 - - - - USA
25120 - - KYS 921				25131 - - - - USA	25142 - - FAG 710
25121 - MXM 997				25132 - - - - - ZA	25143 - - KVJ 520
25122 - - - - USA				25133 - - - - - NZ	25144 - - OYE 804
25123 - - - - - - S				25134 - MOC 775	25145 - - - - USA
25124 - - JSG 195				25135 - - - - AUS	25146 - - - - USA
25125 - - - PZ 729				25136 - LWK 942	25147 - - LDT 525
25126 - - - - USA				25137 - - LVC 536	25148 - - RTC 127
25127 - - - - AUS				25138 - - - - -MA	25149 - - - - USA
25128 - - - - USA				25139 - -OKT 143	25150 - MXM 986
25129 - -MXF 137				25140 - HKW 397	

An old Salopian, John (Jock) Magnus Peterson, a great intellectual and sportsman would return to Shrewsbury school in 1950 as headmaster. The portrait of him has been specially made available for this book through the good offices of Dr Richard Case, and Dr David Gee of the school.

of Shrewsbury School. Due to the excellent records at Red Triangle, it has now been established beyond doubt that Peterson, who was head from 1950 to 1963, owned 25114. 'Jock' Peterson (1902-1978) had, prior to this, been a master at Eton College from 1945 to 1950. Whilst there he had owned an Alvis 12/70 model (qv 15405).

25116   NYU 817
Peter Wheeler
Once part of the car collection of the late TVR Cars chief, 25116 was one of three such. The others were a Silver Eagle (qv 11800) and a TD 21 (qv 26170 bio).

TB 21

1950 to 1954
25120-25150
31 cars

APM Sports prototype (XX1)	1
then 1101-1130	30

As was the case with the TA 14 model, it was the intention to offer a two-seater roadster version on the new 3-litre chassis. The prototype, and Earls Court Show exhibit, was the only one to incorporate the flat, fold-down windscreen of the TB 14 model, the production versions having a vee-type screen. Flexible side screens were now beginning to go out of favour on a car of this type, and the works experimented with a drophead coupé derivative on 25137, and even a four-seater version was under consideration. In the event, however, only 31 examples of the TB 21 were produced. Mechanically, they are identical with the parent TA 21 model save for a raised final drive ratio of 3.77 to one, and the use of a single SU carburettor.

25120   KYS 921
Motor Show Exhibit
This car, the prototype TB 21 with A P Metcraft's test body XX1 had started life as a 'mule' mounted on TA 21 chassis 23806 in order to make the 1950 Earls Court Show of October in time. Whilst on the works stand, it was photographed with two notable

The prototype TB 21 sports at the Earls Court Motor Show in October 1950. Actress/singer Petula Clark is having its delights explained to her. (Courtesy Alvis Ltd)

visitors on Press Day. The first was HRH Princess Margaret. The other visitor to 'Downtown' Earls Court on that day was actress and singer Petula Clark (born November 15, 1932). Petula would go on to sell over 68 million records and would thus never have to "... sleep in the subway," as in one of her more memorable lyrics. Interestingly, one of her earliest stage impersonations was that of Carmen Miranda, who, a couple of years later, would be associated with Alvis sales promotion in the USA, centred on a TA 21 Tickford coupé (qv 24616). Pet Clark would have a further association with Alvis when she drove a 12/50 Duckback in the 1969 version of the movie *Goodbye Mr Chips* (qv 2571).

25132 MDU 332
M J McGuinness

A particularly exciting life has been led by 25132, whose life began registered in Coventry by the works, under the Home Delivery Export Scheme, and duly despatched to Kenya and bought by McGuinness from John Revill in 1974. This was a time of civil unrest in that country, of which McGuinness wrote as follows: "My reason for buying the Alvis was not purely for it's aesthetic qualities, for while my family resided in Salisbury, I had established my headquarters in Bindura and was forced to use the frequently ambushed connecting road. The Alvis was, in my view, the ideal vehicle for this purpose; she was heavy, had a good ground clearance, a top speed in the nineties, and with the hood and windscreen down, gave an excellent field of fire for the 'cut down' Russian RPG which lay beside me on the passenger seat. That vehicle travelled everywhere, and never gave one moment's trouble, be it on farm roads or tarmac."

25144 OYE 804
Vic Hyde

American entertainer Vic Hyde, an automobile enthusiast if ever there was one, had an eclectic taste in vehicles ranging from a Messerschmitt KR 200 to a GM Futureliner bus – one of only twelve made. Hyde (1913-2006), when he played the London Palladium, used to attend meetings of the Morgan Three-Wheeler Club at the King of Belgians pub. Always much in demand, Hyde performed with Liberace, Frank Sinatra, Bob Hope

and Johnny Cash. He also performed for HM The Queen, and for at least three US Presidents: Truman, Eisenhower and Ford. A further Alvis was later added to the Hyde collection, purchased from Efrem Zimbalist Jr. This was a TC 21/100 (qv 25703).

TC21 & TC21/100

1953 to 1955
25151-25300 and 25333-25908
726 cars

Consisting of:
Mulliner saloons
  M3001-M3150 + revised body   150
  M3151-M3600   450
Tickford coupés
  AL1-AL 100   100
Graber (various)   26
  654-661 inclusive
  668-674 inclusive
  676, 677, 678,
  681-686 inclusive
  695, 700

Chassis	Reg				
25151	- - PYB 119	25180	- - NVU 248	25210	- - PAT 122
25152	- - ODU 854	25181	- - - S 9031	25211	- - KAK 284
25153	- - NXH 532	25182	- - - RHT 2	25212	- - RMB 799
25154	- - NVU 432	25183	- MDT 739	25213	- - - - AUS
25155	- - JDW 166	25184	- MKV 835	25214	- - GBN 653
25156	- - OLV 878	25185	- - ODU 291	25215	- - PPO 408
25157	- - - - GBG	25186	- - RTC 513	25216	- - RUA 796
25158	- - -TRA 50	25187	- - NXU 298	25217	- - KAK 270
25159	- - JRP 588	25188	- - ODU 213	25218	- - NLJ 177
25160	- - KGD 954	25189	- - SE 303	25219	- -PKC 24
25161	- - OKC 59	25190	- - HVD 271	25220	- - - - NZ
25162	- - NDU 206	25191	- - PKA 340	25221	- - - WEV 89
25163	- - NAO 612	25192	- - NOJ 327	25222	- - - - - -
25164	- - HAP 108	25193	- -JBL 258	25223	- - -JJB 919
25165	- - RTC 513	25194	- - PWE 363	25224	- - - - 4953 H
25166	- - - - -	25195	- - OGY 968	25225	- - OAT 666
25167	- - - - AUS	25196	- - LFS 274	25226	- - FHH 421
25168	- - NXT 933	25197	- -LGG 23	25227	- - NDD 244
25169	- - - - - -	25198	- - KBC 580	25228	- - - JFY 35
25170	- - - - NZ	25199	- - LGB 679	25229	- - - - NZ
25171	- - - - - S	25200	- - NTX 78	25230	- MNP 964
25172	- - NXU 300	25201	- - NVR 31	25231	- - - - NZ
25173	- - - - NZ	25202	- -OOD 162	25232	- - FHL 393
25174	- - PTJ 640	25203	- NOK 856	25233	- - - - NZ
25175	- - - - NZ	25204	- - ONB 33	25234	- - LWF 555
25176	- - - AUS	25205	- -JKW 90	25235	- - LWF 762
25177	- - HTP 818	25206	- - KAK 700	25236	- MKV 458
25178	- - NXA 894	25207	- - RKL 915	25237	- - ODV 182
25179	- - JVN 505	25208	- - - - NZ	25238	- - - - NZ
		25209	- - - - NZ	25239	- NVM 177

25240 - - - - NZ	25342 - - TKX 49	25412 - -OXX 892	25482 - - OYE 822	25552 - - HHV 70	25622 - - -PHP 61
25241 - - - - NZ	25343 - - NBT 315	25413 - - STE 326	25483 - - NHP 521	25553 - - OXJ 584	25623 - - PHP 251
25242 - - RUA 797	25344 - - OEH 564	25414 - - JBO 671	25484 - - OLY 124	25554 - - OYU 979	25624 - - PXR 822
25243 - -MKV 990	25345 - -HCX 981	25415 - - OYE 795	25485 - OXM 585	25555 - - OYE 808	25625 - - PDU 970
25244 - - - - NZ	25346 - - - - NZ	25416 - - WMJ 861	25486 - OXM 586	25556 - - PGH 336	25626 - KKW 735
25245 - - - JWK 6	25347 - - UBB 295	25417 - - - - NZ	25487 - - DSN 204	25557 - - JTP 480	25627 - - -PGJ 3
25246 - - - - NZ	25348 - - -UPG 37	25418 - - - - NZ	25488 - - NHP 781	25558 - - LUT 140	25628 - - RKD 181
25247 - -RHU 966	25349 - - LBC 432	25419 - OWK 792	25489 - - FSD 396	25559 - - TLG 239	25629 - - - - -
25248 - - LMJ 235	25350 - - CFL 133	25420 - - NNP 538	25490 - GWH 191	25560 - - OYR 363	25630 - - 900 DRE
25249 - - -XJW 66	25351 - - NDF 847	25421 - - OLY 129	25491 - - PDX 260	25561 - - - RZ 777	25631 - - -JJG 150
25250 - - - - NZ	25352 - OOM 500	25422 - - NHP 520	25492 - - - - CH	25562 - - LAM 711	25632 - - PYR 329
25251 - - - - NZ	25353 - - - - AUS.	25423 - - OYE 791	25493 - - MSP 800	25563 - - UBH 18	25633 - - PWK 39
25252 - - LOY 909	25354 - - ORU 10	25424 - - OXU 486	25494 - - 218 BML	25564 - - - - NZ	25634 - - - - NZ
25253 - -NXH 532	25355 - - - - NZ	25425 - - OLY 139	25495 - - 382 BMF	25565 - - POB 486	25635 - - TNN 690
25254 - - - - CH	25356 - -MER 709	25426 - - - - F	25496 - - OLY 132	25566 - - STT 444	25636 - - LVJ 545
25255 - - JSU 357	25357 - - - AUS	25427 - -367 BMX	25497 - OXW 687	25567 - - - - CH	25637 - KKW 920
25256 - - - - NZ	25358 - - NHP 990	25428 - - NHP 851	25498 - - GCL 970	25568 - - PGH 323	25638 - - - AUS
25257 - - - S 9352	25359 - -JWM 883	25429 - - PGH 333	25499 - - OLY 131	25569 - - DTS 894	25639 - - DS 3508
25258 - MWT 999	25360 - - -OLT 19	25430 - - NHP 487	25500 - - - - F	25570 - - RPO 820	25640 - - THU 884
25259 - - RUG 39	25361 - - - - NZ	25431 - -OYW 921	25501 - DXW 684	25571 - - OAO 553	25641 - - - - F
25260 - - - JNR 40	25362 - - - - CH	25432 - - - - CH	25502 - - DSN 300	25572 - - VPE 4	25642 - - PKV 166
25261 - - TJO 282	25363 - - HFV 220	25433 - -MGA 200	25503 - - TLG 495	25573 - -OOX 500	25643 - - VJO 900
25262 - - CU 6333	25364 - -JWM 882	25434 - - OLO 402	25504 - - EEE 750	25574 - - PDX 251	25644 - - - AUS
25263 - -MGG 864	25365 - - - AUS	25435 - - OLF 759	25505 - - GVS 608	25575 - - - LJF 2	25645 - - - AUS
25264 - - KSG 957	25366 - - - - NZ	25436 - - ONE 898	25506 - - OKV 67	25576 - - UEH 600	25646 - - SN 6631
25265 - - LMJ 726	25367 - - - AUS	25437 - - PUO 772	25507 - -PDU 29	25577 - - KVA 185	25647 - - PYU 995
25266 - - PYB 777	25368 - - - AUS	25438 - - RHJ 980	25508 - - - GBJ	25578 - - PNA 508	25648 - - LAJ 892
25267 - - - - DK	25369 - - - - NZ	25439 - - UPD 295	25509 -TNW 767	25579 - - KUT 2	25649 - - - NZ
25268 - - - - NZ	25370 - - RWJ 975	25440 - - - CH	25510 - OXU 490	25580 - - LVJ 200	25650 - - OWF 2
25269 - - - - NZ	25371 - - - CH	25441 - - MUS 632	25511 - - OGE 428	25581 - - PGH 345	25651 - - PUE 769
25270 - - SNW 888	25372 - -OON 918	25442 - -HBW 266	25512 - - OYE 829	25582 - KKW 883	25652 - - - - NZ
25271 - -KWS 136	25373 - - STR 649	25443 - - - - NL	25513 - - - - CH	25583 - - PDU 543	25653 - - -16 DRF
25272 - - - AUS	25374 - - PVF 848	25444 - - - - NZ	25514 - KKU 683	25584 - - NWY 71	25654 - - - - CH
25273 - - - J 201	25375 - -MCG 981	25445 - OWK 605	25515 - - JTP 362	25585 - - STV 888	25655 - - - - NZ
25274 - - - - NZ	25376 - - - CH	25446 - - OLX 506	25516 - - JRX 478	25586 - - VJO 888	25656 - - NCG 171
25275 - - CSN 840	25377 - -ORW 517	25447 - - - - CH	25517 - PKF 846	25587 - - RFJ 175	25657 - - PLH 392
25276 - - LWF 979	25378 - MWP 231	25448 - - SUB 544	25518 - VTD 200	25588 - - GWH 937	25658 - - VPJ 861
25277 - -RKO 284	25379 - OXW 300	25449 - - - AUS	25519 - - KNR 60	25589 - - KAV 928	25659 - -PNF 95
25278 - - - - NZ	25380 - - MWP 65	25450 - - PPX 323	25520 - - OYE 833	25590 - - KDL 892	25660 - - RNC 996
25279 - - ONA 290	25381 - - UPJ 720	25451 - -546 BMC	25521 - - KNR 999	25591 - - PXD 249	25661 - - - - NZ
25280 - - - - NZ	25382 - - - - NZ	25452 - - - PPX 3	25522 - - OLY 134	25592 - - PNB 686	25662 - - PHP 959
25281 - - - - NZ	25383 - - ECP 689	25453 - - PUO 888	25523 - - - - CH	25593 - - - CDN	25663 - - PLH 423
25282 - - - - NZ	25384 - - ECP 356	25454 - - ONF 199	25524 - - SKP 678	25594 - - GTK 152	25664 - - - - NZ
25283 - - - - CH	25385 - -MTM 1	25455 - - OYE 824	25525 - - PGH 311	25595 - - - - NZ	25665 - - - RPW 5
25284 - - - - CH	25386 - OXM 585	25456 - - MJW 353	25526 - - JRD 500	25596 - - - - NZ	25666 - - - - NZ
25285 - -OOD 464	25387 - -OON 194	25457 - - SAE 881	25527 - VWL 927	25597 - - GAG 477	25667 - - - - NZ
25286 - - SUB 110	25388 - - - - NZ	25458 - - MBY 333	25528 - - TUB 574	25598 - - LSG 950	25668 - - NRK 25
25287 - - - - DK	25389 - - GVG 48	25459 - - OLN 333	25529 - -PGU 13	25599 - -PLH 11	25669 - - -YRA 34
25288 - - -DJX 99	25390 - -KKU 157	25460 - - ONE 444	25530 - - PGH 343	25600 - - FBV 481	25670 - - TWB 810
25289 - - PWJ 774	25391 - OWK 252	25461 - - - - F	25531 - JWM 885	25601 - - OCD 714	25671 - - PLH 428
25290 - - NYU 808	25392 - - TUB 252	25462 - - - - NL	25532 - - SBP 255	25602 - - PLH 396	25672 - -MBC 583
25291 - - GCL 107	25393 - - OVC 582	25463 - - - - - F	25533 - - ECP 666	25603 - - PRW 150	25673 - - 215 FRE
25292 - MWW 217	25394 - - UBB 156	25464 - - - - - S	25534 - - OXJ 77	25604 - - NGA 193	25674 - HBN 828
25293 - - GM 6150	25395 - - - - NZ	25465 - -KMR 853	25535 - - - - -	25605 - - KFY 752	25675 - - - - NZ
25294 - - - - NZ	25396 - - OYP 779	25466 - - SCV 112	25536 - - - - F	25606 - - TPP 995	25676 - - - - NZ
25295 - - PYC 400	25397 - YVW 198	25467 - - GEE 300	25537 - - OCD 87	25607 - - JUH 21	25677 - - VPG 678
25296 - - - - NZ	25398 - - SKP 498	25468 - - - CDN	25538 - - PLL 765	25608 - - OTX 704	25678 - -RPT 50
25297 - -LGG 89	25399 - - - - NZ	25469 - - - - NL	25539 - - PGH 312	25609 - GWH 937	25679 - - STA 180
25298 - - OYO 199	25400 - -KKU 803	25470 - - ONF 213	25540 - - - AUS	25610 - - SWJ 275	25680 - - PNE 258
25299 - - TNN 598	25401 - - - - -	25471 - -MGD 152	25541 - - RKA 540	25611 - - -ECN 59	25681 - - - - F
25300 - - - - NL	25402 - - CEJ 950	25472 - - FCH 926	25542 - - PFD 577	25612 - - PXR 105	25682 - - - - NZ
25333 - - - - NZ	25403 - - - STO 9	25473 - - -MSP 2	25543 - VJO 329	25613 - - PGH 344	25683 - -PWK 602
25334 - - PZ 3146	25404 - - - - NZ	25474 - - SUM 766	25544 - - MUS 800	25614 - - VPE 389	25684 - -WPD 734
25335 - - - - NZ	25405 - -MWJ 567	25475 - - YDV 906	25545 - - GRG 515	25615 - - - NZ	25685 - - ENH 777
25336 - - - - NZ	25406 - -MJW 567	25476 - -XVX 310	25546 - - - NL	25616 - - PGH 318	25686 - - KKY 251
25337 - - UPK 272	25407 - - - - -	25477 - - OLY 130	25547 - - - USA	25617 - - - - - -	25687 - - LFY 361
25338 - - OXJ 536	25408 - -KWN 426	25478 - - NGD 287	25548 - - OYE 803	25618 - - - - NZ	25688 - - - - NZ
25339 - - POF 477	25409 - -OXU 493	25479 - - OWD 160	25549 - - KNV 543	25619 - - -LJF 100	25689 - - RBJ 504
25340 - - PGH 348	25410 - - - - NZ	25480 - - UPG 161	25550 - - LSG 371	25620 - - - - NZ	25690 - - - - NZ
25341 - - - - AUS	25411 - -MOT 851	25481 - - OYO 514	25551 - - TPP 359	25621 - - KFY 843	25691 - - TUG 618

25692 - - TUG 57	25762 - - JPN 593	25831 - - WEH 444		25901 - - YFC 940	25904 - - XBH 173	25907 - - SGF 642
25693 - - RUB 997	25763 - - PRU 666	25832 - - RDU 467		25902 - - WUA 893	25905 - - - SFJ 493	25908 - - UTT 220
25694 - - NUS 151	25764 - - URL 111	25833 - - OMJ 123		25903 - - RKV 59	25906 - NWK 949	
25695 - - - - NL	25765 - - - PLM 9	25834 - - - HRS 80				
25696 - - - - NZ	25766 - - 922 BTW	25835 - - WNE 339				
25697 - - - - AUS	25767 - - MJA 324	25836 - - MNT 212				
25698 - - PLH 422	25768 - - PXD 250	25837 - - OGE 575				
25699 - - PLM 983	25769 - - SPO 7	25838 - - RON 798				
25700 - - LAK 583	25770 - - WPC 56	25839 - - RFJ 838				
25701 - - - - AUS	25771 - - - - CH	25840 - - DFA 677				
25702 - - - - NZ	25772 - -680 DMK	25841 - - NVE 759				
25703 - - - USA	25773 - - HRG 341	25842 - - RLX 367				
25704 - - - - - -	25774 - - PTX 254	25843 - - RLT 784				
25705 - - MVB 345	25775 - - - - - F	25844 - - PGA 155				
25706 - - KJB 800	25776 - - JPM 665	25845 - - RNF 669				
25707 - - - - NZ	25777 - - THY 691	25846 - - RRU 118				
25708 - - VBB 205	25778 - - ETS 420	25847 - - - - - -				
25709 - - PYR 356	25779 - - - - NZ	25848 - - LFY 509				
25710 - - MBE 486	25780 - - - - NZ	25849 - - NSR 696				
25711 - - 383 BTW	25781 - - WAE 470	25850 - - RLT 803				
25712 - - - - CH	25782 - - LKU 857	25851 - - RGO 957				
25713 - - MSR 20	25783 - - - - NZ	25852 - - NZ 7443				
25714 - - - AUS	25784 - - - - NZ	25853 - - OWP 460				
25715 - - PLH 412	25785 - - UTF 964	25854 - - PYG 344				
25716 - ONM 262	25786 - - - RNB 78	25855 - - - BJP 775				
25717 - UNW 485	25787 - - KRD 9	25856 - - - - CH				
25718 - - - - CH	25788 - - - - - F	25857 - - PWU 312				
25719 - - PNF 778	25789 - - PYR 346	25858 - - SHP 642				
25720 - - LPY 911	25790 - - UUG 385	25859 - - TDU 810				
25721 - - - - NZ	25791 - - - - CH	25860 - - TNN 789				
25722 - - - - NZ	25792 - - - - CH	25861 - - TTT 592				
25723 - - JCX 333	25793 - - - - CH	25862 - - JTY 376				
25724 - - WHN 23	25794 - KRX 701	25863 - - FNH 891				
25725 - - - - NZ	25795 - - PXR 115	25864 - - TUO 976				
25726 - - MSC 181	25796 - CJK 364	25865 - - - YPB 5				
25727 - MWO 896	25797 - - PYR 349	25866 - - VAU 666				
25728 - - PXD 262	25798 - - PYR 357	25867 - - PCR 647				
25729 - - - - NZ	25799 - - - NBC 8	25868 - - OAX 561				
25730 - - - - NZ	25800 - - SYL 434	25869 - - VAU 425				
25731 - - - - NZ	25801 - - LKU 200	25870 - - RVR 851				
25732 - - PLJ 666	25802 - - LNR 838	25871 - - WBH 800				
25733 - - - - NZ	25803 - - OYG 159	25872 - - 182 GMV				
25734 - - - - NZ	25804 - - TBP 242	25873 - - - - CH				
25735 - - - - NZ	25805 - - RLH 341	25874 - - UYB 651				
25736 - - - - NZ	25806 - - UWE 242	25875 - - RLO 320				
25737 - WPC 360	25807 - - - GBG	25876 - - VWB 503				
25738 - UNW 863	25808 - - UKT 693	25877 - - RWK 542				
25739 - - - - - F	25809 - - NVB 590	25878 - - UDE 860				
25740 - - - - - F	25810 - - RNC 400	25879 - - RLT 798				
25741 - PSM 987		25880 - - FGL 23				
25742 - WPD 180	25811 - - SPX 280	25881 - - RYK 137				
25743 - 481 BYH	25812 - - LKU 382	25882 - - - - - -				
25744 - - PXR 99	25813 - - VHT 117	25883 - - DFA 904				
25745 - - - - NZ	25814 - - SXL 205	25884 - - WNW 844				
25746 - - - - NZ	25815 - -OWU 427	25885 - - WLG 42				
25747 - VPG 993	25816 - - - - CH	25886 - - VWJ 898				
25748 - - - NZ	25817 - - UUG 969	25887 - - SNA 550				
25749 - - - NZ	25818 - - - - -	25888 - - 462 ETW				
25750 - - DSN 838	25819 - - - - CH	25889 - - SLC 616				
25751 - - - - NZ	25820 - - HAG 20	25890 - - YPD 331				
25752 - - - NZ	25821 - - LBL 357	25891 - - - - CH				
25753 - KBO 766	25822 - - 785 FHK	25892 - - RYK 129				
25754 - 564 ERE	25823 - -NWK 404	25893 - - - - - -				
25755 - PXR 138	25824 - - PUF 99	25894 - - ORK 200				
25756 - KDP 499	25825 - - HCL 709	25895 - - WNW 182				
25757 - UUB 190	25826 - - KJN 200	25896 - - - UZ 488				
25758 - TYR 992	25827 - - RNF 668	25897 - - RYK 144				
25759 - PDX 187	25828 - - PUF 778	25898 - - RYK 139				
25760 - UUA 358	25829 - - OUY 593	25899 - - SGF 639				
25761 - PXL 625	25830 - - RGH 535	25900 - -OOR 353				

The TC21/100 (ie 100mph model) is, in its most advanced form, generally perceived to embody all the later features of wire wheels, bonnet scoops, concealed hinge doors (saloon), high compression head and the 3.77 axle. In real terms, however, it was a case of using up old stock, and individual specifications can differ quite considerably. The basic chassis design, overall dimensions and cylinder block remained the same as the preceding TA 21 model. The eagle-eyed reader may spot the apparent absence of the chassis numbers 25301 to 25322 from the listings. This is because this particular series existed in engine form only, being the units supplied to Healey's at Warwick for use in its G-series Sports Convertible.

25325 `OXU 191`
Woodrow Wyatt MP

A colourful and sometimes controversial figure, Wyatt (July 4, 1918-December 7, 1997) joined the BBC *Panorama* team, had a popular column, *The Voice of Reason*, in the *News of the World*, and became Chairman of the TOTE. He wrote two autobiographies: *Into the Dangerous World*, 1952, and *Confessions of an Optimist*, 1985.

25385 `MTM 1`
J W E Banks

J W E Banks, he of the Peterborough company that manufactured 'KONI' shock absorbers, campaigned 25385 in the Monte Carlo, Alpine and Tulip Rallies during 1954.

25413 `STE 326`
Arthur Holt MP

Serial owner of three other Alvis cars: TA 14 (qv 20972 for bio), TA 21 (qv 24***) and a TD 21 (qv 26346).

25536 `F`

Liège-Rome-Liège 1954

The photograph, kindly supplied by Laurent Le Point, shows Jean Guichet driving 25536 in a typically spirited fashion during the above event. He was not placed, but just a year later, in 1964, he

25536: "On pleasure bent?" Jean Guichet on the 1954 Liège-Rome-Liège rally. (Courtesy Laurent Le Pont)

25598: The Douglas-Home TC 21/100 at a Scottish event when fairly new. The accompanying 12/50 is 4834.

would win the 24 hour Le Man's Race in a Ferrari, partnered by Nino Vaccarella. He had hoped to repeat this success the following year, when his co-driver then was Mike Parkes, son of J J Parkes, Alvis Ltd's managing director, but had to retire due to gearbox problems.

25554 — OYU 979

Group Captain Sir Douglas Bader
Or, to give him his full title: Group Captain Sir Douglas Robert Stuart Bader, CBE, DSO, DFC and bar, FRAeS, DL (February 21, 1910-September 5, 1982). Having lost both his legs in a flying accident in 1931, Bader fought back, regaining his licence to fly and distinguishing himself with an impressive tally of kills before being captured and becoming a prisoner of war until 1945. His life story was chronicled in the best-seller by Paul Brickhill, *Reach for the Sky*. ISBN 1-55750-222-6, published by Odhams in 1954, and made into a successful movie with Kenneth More as Bader. There was also Bader's own book on the Spitfire and Hurricane, *Fight for the Sky,* published by W S Cowell, 2004: ISBN 0-304-35674-3. Bader's quest for mobility applied to fast cars as well as aircraft. Such disabilities as suffered by Bader would normally have confined the driver to an invalid carriage, but in the early 1950s Automotive Products Ltd was developing its semi-automatic 'Manumatic' system, and an early version of this was fitted to Alvis TC 21/100 25554 – the first delivery of such a system to a member of the public. Bader went on to own three other Alvis: see 25978, 26655, 27024.

25598 — LSG 950

Henry Douglas-Home
Younger brother to the rather better known former Prime Minister Sir Alec Douglas-Home, Henry (November 21, 1907-July 18, 1980) was an ornithologist and broadcaster. Part of his time at school was contemporaneous with 'James Bond' creator Ian Fleming.

25606 — TPP 995

Peter Vincent Korda
Son of the famous film producer/director Sir Alexander Korda, Peter (born 1921) was probably influenced by his father's choice of an Alvis Speed 25 model (qv 13365).

25608 — OTX 704

London-Peking 2000
Arguably one of the most widely-travelled Alvis cars ever, this device was the one most ably piloted to second place in the above event by Chris Denham and Ron Bendall. A television series followed entitled *Slow Blokes to China,* as did an entry in the hardly less arduous 'Inca Trail.' More detail may be available from Denham Productions in Plymouth (01752 345444).

25647 — PYU 995

Iliffe Publications
25647 featured as number 168 in this journal's

25608: One of the most travelled Alvis cars of all time: Chris Denham's TC 21/100. (Courtesy Alvis Ltd)

occasional series *Used Cars on the Road*. It had been supplied for this purpose by well-known Alvis specialist Gatehouse Motors.

25699 · PLM 983
Lady Caroline Freud

Perhaps better known to most as the novelist Caroline Blackwood, and part of the Guinness family, Caroline (July 16, 1931-March 14, 1996) had a life seemingly every bit as eventful as some of the characters she wrote about. As a result of an introduction by 'James Bond' writer Ian Fleming, she met artist Lucien Freud, son of the famous Sigmund. They duly married, and honeymooned in Paris, where they were entertained by another quite well-known artist, one Pablo Picasso. Particularly relevant to this Alvis discourse is Blackwood's book *The Last of the Duchess*: ISBN 978-06794-39707, published by Pantheon. This is, of course, a biography of the Duchess of Windsor. The Windsors' Alvis TE 21 is covered separately (qv 27259).

25703 · USA
Efrem Zimbalist Jr

Star of well over 100 productions – stage, and the large and small screen – Efrem Zimbalist (November 30, 1918-May 2, 2014) was an instantly recognisable figure. Memorable appearances include: *77, Sunset Strip*, *The FBI*, and *Maverick*. Wrote a book: *My Dinner of Herbs,* 2004, Limelight Editions: ISBN 978-0-87910-988-2. Sold 25703 to the American entertainer Vic Hyde, who already had a TB 21 model (qv 25144).

25739 · USA
Christine Todd Whitman

A prominent US Republican politician, Christine (born September 26, 1946) was the 50th Governor of New Jersey: 1994-2001, and held the Environmental Protection Portfolio in the G W Bush administration. Published a book: *It's My Party Too*, 2005, Penguin Press.

25741 · PSM 987
A Murder of Quality

25741 appeared in this 1991 television adaptation of the John Le Carré novel (ISBN 0978-0743-431682). It wasn't the first time that an Alvis had appeared in a Le Carré adaptation, as a 4.3-litre was used in *Tinker, Tailor, Soldier, Spy* (qv 14328).

25755 · PXR 138
Graeme Garden OBE

Due in no small part to a painstaking restoration by former Park Ward employee, the late John Holder, 25755 has figured prominently in a variety of productions. Television presenter Graeme Garden (born February 18, 1943) gave it the most obvious usage when making a documentary about the A6 Trunk Road that runs from London to Carlisle, visiting a host of interesting locations en route, where it proved to be a worthy and reliable steed. There were also appearances in the television play *Princess Daisy* of 1983, and similarly, *Paradise Postponed* of 1986 starring Annette Crosbie. 25755 was also the subject of a postcard – one of a series emanating from the J Arthur Dixon Company and the Quadrant Picture Library. The former was taken over by the John Hinde Company after Dixon's demise, so maybe

25755: The Graeme Garden/John Holder TC 21/100 featured on a picture postcard. See text for possible availability.

25798: The TC 21/100 of Sir Nicholas Sekers. The driver here, however, is the late Eric Williamson, who kindly supplied the photo.

copies of this fine representation are still available from them.

PYR 349
25797
Lord Melchett
Born Julian Alfred Edward Mond (January 6, 1925-June 1973), he served in the Fleet Air Arm in 1942 and acceded to the title as the 3rd Baron in 1949. In due course he became chairman of the British Steel Corporation. In 1989, BSC would buy out Alvis-supporting Walkersteel (qv 26717 and 27621).

PYR 357
25798
Sir Nicholas Sekers
Born December 12, 1910 in Hungary, Sekers came to England, founded the West Cumberland Silk Mills in 1938, specialising in the production of parachute fabric, but postwar had progressed to fashion fabrics as new artificial materials became available. Clearly a man of great culture, he founded the Rosehill Theatre at Whitehaven and also became a board member of the Glyndebourne Opera company, the London Philharmonic Orchestra and the Royal Shakespeare Company. Then, like Edward Ward, Viscount Bangor (qv 23500), he featured as a castaway on an episode of *Desert Island Discs* (Broadcast April 22, 1968). Died January 23, 1972 in Czechoslovakia.

RLH 341
25805
Sir Thomas Armstrong
Sir Thomas (July 15, 1898-June 26, 1994) was

a highly respected musician who had served in France during WWI. Organist, conductor and adjudicator, he became Principal of the Royal Academy of Music from 1955 to 1968. He had been both a pupil and a friend of the composer Ralph Vaughan-Williams. One of Sir Thomas' last appearances, at the age of 91, was on an episode of *Desert Island Discs* hosted by Sue Lawley, July 21, 1989.

25900: The late Michael McNair-Wilson MP, With his much cherished, very late Mulliner saloon. (Courtesy Alvis Archive Trust)

25850 RLT 803

F W Woolworth & Co Ltd

This Woolworth company car was succeeded by another Alvis: a TD 21 (qv 26505).

25900 OOR 353

Sir Michael McNair-Wilson MP

Sir Michael (October 12, 1930-March 18, 1993) represented the Newbury constituency between 1974 and 1992. Newbury, of course, is an area much favoured by Alvis-owning horse trainers and jockeys (qv 26637).

TC 108/G

1956 to 1958

25909-25945

37 cars

Consisting of

Willowbrook saloons

001-015 prefixed, '56 or '57 (year) — 15

Graber (various)

691, 692, 693, 694, 696, 697, 698, 699, 702, 703, 705, 706, 708, 709, 710, 711, 712, 714, 715, 716, 719, 720 — 22

Chassis	Reg				
25909	20 KMG	25918	CH	25928	DEK 385
25910	DJS 600	25919	YWA 333	25929	CH
25911	CH	25920	CH	25930	CH
25912	543 ALG	25921	CH	25931	9 JGC
25913	UDU 59	25922	CH	25932	BYE 1
25914	YNK 922	25923	CH	25933	WDU 434
25915	CH	25924	CH	25934	CH
25916	CH	25925	TLL 394	25935	VDV 720
25917	CH	25926	XYB 560	25936	CH
		25927	TGA 629	25937	CH

15 months elapsed between the departure from Holyhead Road of the last TC21/100 25908, and the first TC 108/G 25909. This unfortunate situation had come about because Standard-Triumph had bought out the Mulliner coachwork facility, hence no more TC21/100 saloons and, in a double blow, Tickfords had been taken over by the Aston Martin/Lagonda group, hence no more dropheads either. The solution was long drawn out and fell short of expectations. Graber of Berne had been taking small numbers of Alvis chassis since

1946, and the results had been much admired. So it was then that Graber was commissioned to complete two development cars: 25858 and 25859, and the body formers to go with them. The latter were sent to Willowbrooks in order to initiate series production of the type. The resulting model, whilst much acclaimed from an aesthetic and performance point of view, did not result in volume and, indeed, Service Records of the period abound with instances of quality control issues. Somewhat strangely, rather more of the type were bodied quite successfully in Switzerland, than in the UK. Alvis Ltd began to look elsewhere for some continuity.

25909 20 KMG

Vactric Ltd

This, the first TC108/G (with the second Willowbrook body) was allocated to the then well-known manufacturer of vacuum cleaners and such like appliances. Less well-known is that Vactric also specialised in aircraft control systems – another aeronautical connection to Alvis products.

25914 YNK 922

Abel-Smith Family

This, the first Willowbrook body (on the sixth chassis), was delivered to the family seat of Woodhall Park, Hertfordshire in February 1957. Originally prominent in banking, which had started with the Smith Bank in the 1780s (sold to National Provincial, and later still being absorbed by National Westminster), the family have produced several Members of Parliament and two High Sheriffs of Hertfordshire. There were also Royal connections. Interesting newsreel footage exists from a programme about the late Princess Margaret which shows the late Group Captain Peter Townsend using the Abel-Smith car 25914 in what appears to be the environs of Kensington Palace.

25938 9 VMG

Development Car

With a build date of November 6,1956, 25938 is authenticated from works as having originally been designated a TC 108/G, and had a Willowbrook body (by elimination, number 14 or 15). There is a mysterious two-year gap in its life before it was allocated to Park Ward Ltd, for development

25941: The Graber-bodied TC 108/G of an epic escape story. (Courtesy Alvis Archive Trust)

purposes, where this body was removed. Graber had sent over to Park Ward a prototype shell which would in due course lead to the production TD 21. This was allocated Park Ward's number: 18000. Now officially re-designed as a TD 21 in works nomenclature, it was not actually road registered in its new form until June 1959 – well after TD 21 production had commenced. Due to company mergers etc, 25938 was actually in the ownership of Rolls-Royce Ltd for a while.

25941 | CH |

Ralph Schwarz

In arguably one of the most epic Alvis journeys of all time, and widely reported in the international press at the time, it was in August 1969 that a remarkable event took place. The resourceful Swiss Ralph Schwarz, contrived to smuggle his East German fiancée out of the country, concealed within a specially made false petrol tank with ventilation holes. A temporary four gallon one provided the means to proceed. Ralph still owns the car after all these years, but it has now reverted to a standard pattern petrol tank, the life-saving ersatz one having become an exhibit in a Berlin Museum.

TD 21

1958 to 1962
25946-26730
785 cars

Consisting of:

Park Ward saloons

18000 (prototype on chassis 25938)	1
18001-18500	500
18801-18870	70

Park Ward coupés

18501-18680	180

Graber (various)

721-755 inclusive	35

Chassis	Reg			
25946	WRW 633	26001 - - - - - CH	26057 - - - - E 417
25947	- - WYE 556	26002 - - - - TM 2	26058 - - RKY 644
25948	- WRW 891	26003 - - - 3367 UA	26059 - - - EC 1000
25949	- - 2458 UA	26004 - - WVC 902	26060 - - - 1279 WJ
25950	- - - - - -	26005 - - WTM 696	26061 - - WYE 564
25951	- XDA 500	26006 - - AGM 123	26062 - - UKV 564
25952	- WUW 850	26007 - - 165 FAO	26063 - - - - CDN
25953	- WWK 398	26008 - - - - - CH	26064 - - - XLE 35
25954	- - JSN 210	26009 - - - - - CH	26065 - - 1818 DA
25955	- XRW 752	26010 - WXY 999	26066 - YOM 615
25956	- - - VUS 47	26011 - - - - - NL	26067 - - 1453 WJ
25957	- VXK 920	26012 - YOB 700	26068 - - - UHJ 22
25958	- 710 DKC	26013 - RKU 550	26069 - - - XLE 45
25959	- 670 HPH	26014 - - LJV 500	26070 - - 185 GKN
25960	- RKY 456	26015 - 745 CWW	26071 - - - - CDN
25961	- VXK 917	26016 - 282 BUO	26072 - - WLY 95
25962	- XRW 74	26017 - AGM 161	26073 - AGM 123
25963	- WXF 44	26018 - - XVR 7	26074 - 9779 AC
25964	- 7000 OI	26019 - 329 KPB	26075 - AGM 460
25965	- -176 JPF	26020 - - - YAO 2	26076 - 177 JEH
25966	- WAB 200	26021 - -909 BBJ	26077 - - - - - -
25967	- - - XND 7	26022 - - WLY 89	26078 - - VCE 769
25968	- GM 9999	26023 - - 118 GDA	26079 - - - - - CH
25969	- 1292 SM	26024 - 714 DYD	26080 - - - - - CH
25970	- 810 HPL	26025 - - 3808 UA	26081 - - - - - CH
25971	- - - - - CH	26026 - - 6260 AH	26082 - SDW 408
25972	- - - - - CH	26027 - XVC 534	26083 - - - - CDN
25973	- - - - - CH	26028 - - 52 KPD	26084 - - - - - - B
25974	- 140 BKF	26029 - PNL 123	26085 - 534 WMV
25975	- - - SV 848	26030 - LJV 818	26086 - - - - - B
25976	- XON 111	26031 - -299 GMA	26087 - - - - USA
25977	- YDA 600	26032 - GCC 866	26088 - - - USA
25978	- WUL 200	26033 - TAY 568	26089 - - 7157 UA
25979	- - - - CH	26034 - ORC 600	26090 - 562 AXB
25980	- 2273 DA	26035 - - WYR 8	26091 - UVJ 939
25981	- WXP 629	26036 - - 14 GJH	26092 - - 1 ALV
25982	- 9999 BP	26037 - WYH 100	26093 - 658 LPF
25983	- - - 2 PO	26038 - - 1700 DA	26094 - -XLE 41
25984	- SJU 777	26039 - - 1 TMV	26095 - YOV 400
25985	- 5928 WE	26040 - - - NS 27	26096 - -XLE 38
25986	- XDU 472	26041 - PNJ 504	26097 - YWX 276
25987	- - - - - B	26042 - - - CDN	26098 - - XLE 50
25988	- 190 DKC	26043 - - - CDN	26099 - - YBM 33
25989	- - WXL 3	26044 - - - CDN	26100 - - AS 3100
25990	- - - O 78	26045 - - - CDN	26101 - - - Y 28
25991	- - - - - B	26046 - - - CDN	26102 - XXH 870
25992	- - 55 BTA	26047 - ORC 303	26103 - YWY 61
25993	- XDU 976	26048 - XWF 11	26104 - 8729 UA
25994	- WLY 99	26049 - WLY 73	26105 - - 4442 N
25995	- WXO 777	26050 - 498 WPH	26106 - 234 FTV
25996	- WLC 550	26051 - SVY 710	26107 - 454 AYV
25997	- SJV 232	26052 - MEE 300	26108 - YDU 841
25998	- VSC 110	26053 - WOU 10	26109 - YLC 297
25999	- 2389 UA	26054 - -9464 TJ	26110 - MGR 666
26000	- - - - CH	26055 - XKV 656	26111 - YLC 288
		26056 - 868 KTC	26112 - TKG 206

26113 - - - - - -	26183 - - YLC 287	26253 - - VJN 550	26323 - MNH 777	26393 - - 520 AXU	26463 - - - AKB 3
26114 - - - 4677 N	26184 - - 641 DRT	26254 - - - 1011 W	26324 - - 569 AXB	26394 - - 5338 HP	26464 - - 480 BBP
26115 - -XXH 862	26185 - - 137 FEE	26255 - - YXK 99	26325 - - 700 AXV	26395 - - 4626 DG	26465 - -614 CYW
26116 - - OCF 783	26186 - - OCF 783	26256 - - -666 HP	26326 - - - 9 GRR	26396 - - 680 MMB	26466 - -WUT 888
26117 - - YHP 464	26187 - - YVC 452	26257 - - 788 GTV	26327 - - 3648 AZ	26397 - - 705 AYP	26467 - - CGM 70
26118 - - 2992 DA	26188 - -AGM 844	26258 - - - 1 KKJ	26328 - - - - - -	26398 - - 5850 HP	26468 - - - - - -
26119 - - -XLE 47	26189 - - 5467 HP	26259 - - -XLE 32	26329 - - TKY 850	26399 - - - - - -	26469 - - -105 NC
26120 - - TKG 470	26190 - - 3445 NG	26260 - - - JW 96	26330 - - 584 GTG	26400 - - UKU 800	26470 - -908 DNM
26121 - - 336 LPK	26191 - - VBD 777	26261 - - 369 NPF	26331 - - 2410 UG	26401 - - 404 COJ	26471 - -888 KWL
26122 - - 6454 KH	26192 - - JLO 239	26262 - - - - HS 1	26332 - - PGH 333	26402 - - 511 AXU	26472 - - YUN 10
26123 - -XXH 875	26193 - -BGM 130	26263 - - FGC 177	26333 - -BGM 769	26403 - - WAY 25	26473 - - 345 KTV
26124 - - MJV 590	26194 - - YLW 872	26264 - - YXA 18	26334 - - - 3800 K	26404 - - 3675 CZ	26474 - - 90 BGX
26125 - - AGM 600	26195 - - NEW 56	26265 - -BGM 310	26335 - - -21 FLK	26405 - - 572 SPC	26475 - - 2 HBJ
26126 - - 165 YMP	26196 - - SH 191	26266 - - 3949 PE	26336 - - -81 RPA	26406 - - 518 AXU	26476 - - 150 TRA
26127 - - YLW 883	26197 - - VAM 375	26267 - - 300 KLG	26337 - - - - -CH	26407 - - 5647 HP	26477 - - 2858 NC
26128 - - - -7 JLG	26198 - - 4167 DU	26268 - - - C 6790	26338 - - - - -7 UM	26408 - - 765 TPK	26478 - - - BR 15
26129 - - YBT 888	26199 - - 1636 VW	26269 - - - - -CH	26339 - - OSN 478	26409 - - 285 BGN	26479 - - 2434 TF
26130 - -533 YMG	26200 - - 7767 RE	26270 - - - - -CH	26340 - - 500 CZ	26410 - - -28 APX	26480 - - WZA 999
26131 - - RCH 112	26201 - - 1478 NT	26271 - - 1250 HP	26341 - - 519 AXU	26411 - - -UZA 78	26481 - - 288 BGN
26132 - MIF 769	26202 - - PD 1227	26272 - - 1436 HP	26342 - - 1866 NB	26412 - - 6289 HP	26482 - - -JB 3945
26133 - - AGM 666	26203 - -556 EMO	26273 - - - IND	26343 - - 7675 HP	26413 - - 6059 HP	26483 - - 8240 HP
26134 - - -866 JPP	26204 - - -1 GHW	26274 - - YLW 890	26344 - - 3261 MC	26414 - - 4493 WX	26484 - - XVJ 143
26135 - - -90 FTV	26205 - - - -740 K	26275 - - YND 77	26345 - - - - -CH	26415 - - 6509 HP	26485 - - FCZ 220
26136 - - XYE 711	26206 - - -1 GHW	26276 - - - -72 AZ	26346 - -RWH 514	26416 - -WRP 409	26486 - - 289 BGN
26137 - - 660 FYB	26207 - - - - -CH	26277 - - 272 LPP	26347 - - -EXS 28	26417 - - - 6720 K	26487 - - - RJ 516
26138 - - 6000 WJ	26208 - - YLC 295	26278 - - YLC 298	26348 - - VUT 520	26418 - - 701 AYP	26488 - - 290 BGN
26139 - - - 10 ELV	26209 - -VWN 897	26279 - - LOK 33	26349 - - 3051 VX	26419 - - 6951 HP	26489 - - 457 CUY
26140 - - 777 JMB	26210 - - 4718 UB	26280 - - 4958 VW	26350 - - 5101 K	26420 - - 448 AYY	26490 - - 319 EPW
26141 - - - DMB 1	26211 - - 9317 PK	26281 - - YXA 23	26351 - - 221 RPA	26421 - - 36 MTU	26491 - - - - - NZ
26142 - - 5432 WJ	26212 - - - JB 329	26282 - - -KER 39	26352 - - 333 JHY	26422 - - - 6234 K	26492 - - - -JD 38
26143 - - - 77 JLG	26213 - - 2283 TR	26283 - - 889 BOB	26353 - - 507 AXU	26423 - - - BDP 6	26493 - - 2856 NC
26144 - -XXH 876	26214 - - - JB 296	26284 - - 557 AXB	26354 - - - - - NZ	26424 - - 677 HRY	26494 - - 3174 HN
26145 - - 5610 RE	26215 - - - - GBJ	26285 - - 552 AXB	26355 - - -YRY 62	26425 - - 6350 AZ	26495 - - - JB 776
26146 - - VCJ 67	26216 - - RJA 200	26286 - - YLW 885	26356 - - 402 RPG	26426 - - 2202 VF	26496 - - KNT 72
26147 - - 340 MPA	26217 - - 856 NPB	26287 - - - GBJ	26357 - - DS 244	26427 - - 7184 HP	26497 - -EJB 282
26148 - - 640 LTF	26218 - - NGS 199	26288 - - 551 AXB	26358 - - PRG 403	26428 - - 913 BLW	26498 - - - 6 COP
26149 - - 5432 WJ	26219 - - GWE 20	26289 - - RJR 775	26359 - -WCA 145	26429 - - - YVA 30	26499 - - ZW 7316
26150 - - 34 MPF	26220 - - 4000 NX	26290 - - 505 AXV	26360 - - - - USA	26430 - - - - -CH	26500 - - XVN 800
26151 - - 600 KKY	26221 - - YLC 300	26291 - - 666 BBM	26361 - - - - NZ	26431 - - 266 BGN	26501 - - 7477 AD
26152 - - - UWV 1	26222 - - - 165 HP	26292 - - 640 PPH	26362 - - 5482 VX	26432 - - 702 AYP	26502 - - - - -CH
26153 - - 1917 NA	26223 - - - E 57	26293 - - - GBJ	26363 - - YZ 9599	26433 - -KHS 88	26503 - - - - -CH
26154 - - NGS 499	26224 - - 6499 DA	26294 - - 570 BYT	26364 - - - -CH	26434 - - 51 BYM	26504 - - 8335 MV
26155 - - 7997 VC	26225 - - 463 HTO	26295 - - 553 AXB	26365 - - - - -CH	26435 - - 1144 VF	26505 - - 282 BGN
26156 - - 367 PPB	26226 - - 208 SPA	26296 - - 6844 HP	26366 - - 101 RPP	26436 - - 343 TFM	26506 - - JRM 666
26157 - -930 AXM	26227 - - - - - -	26297 - - 659 EUO	26367 - -777 RMA	26437 - -421 MPO	26507 - - 901 ARY
26158 - - 3969 DA	26228 - - 770 NPK	26298 - - 564 AXB	26368 - - 3266 MC	26438 - - ESC 777	26508 - - 257 TPC
26159 - - - NYW 1	26229 - - 333 NKX	26299 - - - - -CH	26369 - - 501 AXU	26439 - - 7067 PG	26509 - - 8707 HP
26160 - - 600 AAO	26230 - - 1680 BT	26300 - - - - -CH	26370 - - - - -HK	26440 - - 314 EPW	26510 - - TWB 990
26161 - -YWK 887	26231 - - VCJ 810	26301 - - 507 AGB	26371 - - 1466 BY	26441 - - - 3 BGN	26511 - - 278 BGN
26162 - - - 50 EV	26232 - - 760 AWP	26302 - - 292 HTO	26372 - - 3720 NB	26442 - - 8629 MU	26512 - - - SH 732
26163 - - RNL 383	26233 - - 7070 DA	26303 - - 651 PPF	26373 - - 724 BYK	26443 - - MFL 885	26513 - -DTW 100
26164 - -YWK 258	26234 - - -663 HP	26304 - - 278 OTB	26374 - - 600 FPY	26444 - - 2332 WA	26514 - - 4659 JH
26165 - - SKY 299	26235 - - VYN 860	26305 - - 917 MKX	26375 - - 4454 AD	26445 - - - - -MF	26515 - - YXA 868
26166 - - 4800 DA	26236 - - - 9 GRR	26306 - - -VSG 60	26376 - -575 GWE	26446 - - LGL 370	26516 - - 555 FCH
26167 - - 5949 UB	26237 - - - - -CH	26307 - - 497 AXU	26377 - - - USA	26447 - - - - -MF	26517 - - 721 HLF
26168 - - KKS 577	26238 - - - - -CH	26308 - - HB 4531	26378 - - 7503 HX	26448 - - 704 AYP	26518 - - - GW 84
26169 - - - - - -	26239 - - - - -CH	26309 - - 180 KDH	26379 - -WBO 444	26449 - - 619 CLM	26519 - - 4649 CD
26170 - - YLC 293	26240 - - - - -CH	26310 - - 1501 VF	26380 - - - 6568 D	26450 - - 555 AXB	26520 - - 4027 UM
26171 - - 237 GTV	26241 - - - - -CH	26311 - - 325 BGX	26381 - - 510 AXU	26451 - - 10 KTO	26521 - - 110 RPP
26172 - - 6244 RE	26242 - - - - -CH	26312 - -BGM 707	26382 - - 915 AXX	26452 - - DXS 898	26522 - - - - -CH
26173 - -XXH 869	26243 - - 6336 UB	26313 - - 508 AXU	26383 - - TRC 462	26453 - - - - -CH	26523 - - - - -CH
26174 - - 4440 DA	26244 - - YLW 880	26314 - - HEC 250	26384 - - 509 AXU	26454 - - 9965 MK	26524 - - -40 BUU
26175 - - 136 NPE	26245 - - NEE 717	26315 - - 305 AUM	26385 - - - 6240 K	26455 - - CGM 68	26525 - - -87 ARY
26176 - - YLC 299	26246 - - - - GBJ	26316 - - - 7 AXK	26386 - - - 7142 IJ	26456 - - - NH 61	26526 - - 103 RKX
26177 - - - EC 222	26247 - - URD 111	26317 - - - GBJ	26387 - - 592 CAO	26457 - -AOI 1700	26527 - - 8141 PE
26178 - - - - -CH	26248 - - - VFS 2	26318 - - XAY 154	26388 - - - AYA 1	26458 - - LGL 595	26528 - - - -PJR 1
26179 - - - - -CH	26249 - - VCJ 910	26319 - - - SJB 1	26389 - - - CY 17	26459 - - TPM 300	26529 - - 84 BGX
26180 - - NS 4982	26250 - - - 684 JH	26320 - - 4708 W	26390 - - DCW 92	26460 - - TEL 780	26530 - - HP 1446
26181 - - 6161 DA	26251 - - 982 KGE	26321 - - 8440 DA	26391 - - 4514 UG	26461 - - 6935 UG	26531 - - -88 TPD
26182 - - 293 CTR	26252 - - YXE 459	26322 - - 400 LKE	26392 - - 707 AYP	26462 - -WZA 203	26532 - - -YET 86

26533 - - 94 BGX	26599 - MCW 295	26665 - - 8148 UM
26534 - - 974 BXB	26600 - - - OXR 1	26666 - - 811 HYV
26535 - -693 CYW	26601 - - 70 BYM	26667 - - 3100 ED
26536 - - 287 BGN	26602 - - - SHY 1	26668 - - 900 CYK
26537 - - -277 RW	26603 - - YCJ 987	26669 - - YOO 219
26538 - - JDH 993	26604 - - - - CH	26670 - - 7928 NE
26539 - - 3598 NF	26605 - - - - CH	26671 - - -99 DLC
26540 - - 304 BXD	26606 - - 3008 WD	26672 - - -97 DLC
26541 - - TJA 661	26607 - - - AKL 4	26673 - -765 MTO
26542 - - 1900 WD	26608 - - 786 CUV	26674 - - 601 YNN
26543 - -WTL 414	26609 - - 454 TBH	26675 - - 6621 RW
26544 - - 609 HYR	26610 - - 809 CLL	26676 - - 6221 RW
26545 - - WH 350	26611 - - - 1 ALV	26677 - - 4323 VC
26546 - - 977 BXB	26612 - - 794 CUV	26678 - - 468 YPA
26547 - - XVJ 168	26613 - - XVY 755	26679 - - VFY 240
26548 - - 4379 NC	26614 - - 6394 PE	26680 - - 108 DLC
26549 - - YCE 500	26615 - - - - USA	26681 - - 6446 RW
26550 - - 4755 WA	26616 - - 789 CUV	26682 - - 125 VBH
26551 - - VZ 9666	26617 - - -985 ND	26683 - - 6549 RW
26552 - - 8275 DU	26618 - - 55 BYM	26684 - - JEX 55
26553 - - 23 CUT	26619 - - - - - -	26685 - - - JEL 55
26554 - - RCF 530	26620 - - - HH 48	26686 - - YSF 777
26555 - - 104 TPL	26621 - - 7455 WY	26687 - - 700 DPO
26556 - - XVJ 820	26622 - - 787 CUV	26688 - - 891 CYK
26557 - - 56 DOF	26623 - - 796 CUV	26689 - - 6687 RW
26558 - - WUJ 616	26624 - - - -EE 90	26690 - - - DGM 2
26559 - - - - - CH	26625 - - 56 BYM	26691 - - -44 CYR
26560 - - 735 BYK	26626 - - 3848 CZ	26692 - - - - - -
26561 - - - - - -	26627 - - -538 NOT	26693 - - - PZC 29
26562 - - - - -CH	26628 - - 5000 ND	26694 - - 232 EXN
26563 - - 607 BRY	26629 - - 4569 RW	26695 - -RMA 154
26564 - - 89 BGX	26630 - - 801 CUV	26696 - - 231 EXN
26565 - - 1021 RW	26631 - - 798 CUV	26697 - - 144 FCG
26566 - - VKU 990	26632 - - 903 CYK	26698 - - 9477 JW
26567 - -CGM 333	26633 - - 2636 ND	26699 - - MM 132
26568 - - 744 BYK	26634 - - 65 BYM	26700 - - 887 CYK
26569 - - 670 CLN	26635 - -KHD 102	26701 - - 799 NOJ
26570 - - - FC 101	26636 - - NBF 771	26702 - - 1681 VC
26571 - - RJT 111	26637 - - 856 CLJ	26703 - - SBF 300
26572 - - - - -CH	26638 - - 800 CUV	26704 - - 673 BYL
26573 - - - - CH	26639 - - 9274 DU	26705 - - 665 CJF
26574 - - SHS 697	26640 - - - - -CH	26706 - - STK 360
26575 - - 23 BUW	26641 - - 28 VWL	26707 - -226 DXO
26576 - - 740 BYK	26642 - - - - -CH	26708 - 666 MWL
26577 - - - DO 43	26643 - - - RJV 1	26709 - - YJG 229
26578 - - 880 KNY	26644 - - MB 1054	26710 - - 235 EXN
26579 - - 863 LYB	26645 - - 66 BYM	26711 - - YSG 190
26580 - - - - -ZA	26646 - - YRC 641	26712 - - 556 BWB
26581 - - - - REE 8	26647 - - - -AJG 3	26713 - - DS 6441
26582 - -500 BYW	26648 - - -24 CLF	26714 - - 8078 RW
26583 - - 731 BYK	26649 - - LC 3705	26715 - - 7935 RW
26584 - - 282 PKL	26650 - - -JT 1000	26716 - - SEE 380
26585 - - -53 HYP	26651 - - 9777 HA	26717 - - 866 WTF
26586 - - 8649 NC	26652 - - - - -CH	26718 - - - WJW 3
26587 - - - - A 188	26653 - - 4767 RW	26719 - - 1626 UK
26588 - - - 2288 CZ	26654 - -36 CUB	26720 - -WKY 898
26589 - - 700 EOC	26655 - - - 27 CLF	26721 - - 867 WTF
26590 - - 738 BVK	26656 - - 306 PPO	26722 - - 222 TKP
26591 - - 822 CLM	26657 - - 664 CPX	26723 - -125 VKX
26592 - - 9175 DU	26658 - - 802 CUV	26724 - - 674 DLD
26593 - - 737 BYK	26659 - - 509 ANW	26725 - - 905 CYK
26594 - - 741 BYK	26660 - - 104 DLC	26726 - - 119 EXB
26595 - - 449 TBH	26661 - - TMS 593	26727 - - 7731 RW
26596 - - 966 HYF	26662 - 788 CXW	26728 - - 136 ELT
26597 - - 8973 DU	26663 - - 892 CYK	26729 - - -744 BAJ
26598 - - - MS 21	26664 - -208 DXO	26730 - - - - -CH

After a frustrating fallow period of some two years, the Alvis car is back in production. The Park Ward contract, with its access to that firm's 300-ton ERCO stretch press, brought about a reduction in price compared with the labour-intensive construction of the preceding Willowbrook body. The first TD 21s actually use up stock intended for the TC 108/G, and indeed, it is not until chassis 25971 that the improved 'six port' head begins to be fitted, and likewise, disc front brakes only appear as standard from chassis 26077. A 'bought-in' Austin gearbox (not universally liked) replaced the Alvis unit (dating from 1937). Also disliked was the umbrella-type handbrake, and this was soon discontinued. Park Ward used a slightly differing number system between saloon and coupé. Many years later, a perceived increase in demand for the latter has led to a number of saloons being 'decapitated' and converted with varying degrees of success. Reference to the body numbering guide on page 193 will confirm originality, or otherwise.

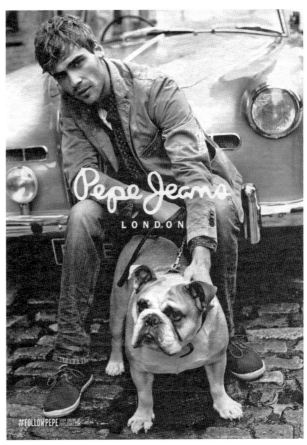

An as yet unidentified TD 21 deployed in a Pepe Jeans advertisement. An example of the starter dog fitment!

25955 **XRW 75**

De Havilland Propellers Ltd

One of many Alvis cars allocated by the works to companies with which it had aeronautical or supplier connections.

25978 **WUL 200**

Group Captain Sir Douglas Bader

Bader's second Alvis, replacing TC21/100 (qv 25554 for bio). Succeeded by: 26655, another TD21, and 27024, a TE 21).

25986 **XDU 472**

Motor (**Temple Press Publications**)

Motor, in its road test feature, number 4/60, in the issue of February 3, 1960, pages 15 to 18, selected 25986 for its detailed analysis. 25986 also appeared in a contemporary issue of the monthly *Country Life*.

25994 **WLY 89**

Ordeal by Innocence

Prolific novelist Agatha Christie's arguably most memorable character is that of Miss Marple. There have been many versions of her detective work: on radio, the stage, and the large and small screens. 25994's appearance relates to an interpretation of about 2007.

26002 **TM 2**

Humphrey Whitbread

Of the well-known brewing family, Humphrey Whitbread was appointed High Sheriff of Bedfordshire in 1962. The distinctive registration mark was naturally retained by the Whitbreads, and the car has subsequently been recorded as AEW 540 A, and more recently as 941 UXF.

26025 **3808 UK**

Heartbeat

Featuring rural life in 1960s Yorkshire, this television series ran to over 350 episodes between 1992 and 2009. The producers were quite astute in avoiding any anachronisms in the selection of vehicles, of which 26025 is a timely example.

26059 (EC 1000): Humorist Frank Muir's first Alvis car, as purchased from one Eric Cant, hence the registration number. Photo kindly supplied especially for this book by current owner Charles Van Ingen.

26027 **XVC 534**

Iliffe Publications

Used in *Autocar*'s road test, numbered 1747, and in the issue of October 16, 1959, pages 380-383.

26059 **EC 1000**

Frank Muir CBE

Frank Muir's first (of three) Alvis, and purchased from one Eric Cant, hence the registration number. Subsequently re-registered as: 975 JGC. For bio see 27389, together with 26824 for the 'middle' car.

26066 **YOM 615**

ATCO

Supplied to the Pugh family, well-known manufacturer of a whole range of lawn mowers, 26066 was painted specially in the company's distinctive shade of green. Worth mentioning too is that for a short time ATCO was actually a car manufacturer itself. Just prior to WWII, about 200 examples of the ATCO Trainer were produced. This was a little vehicle of dodgem proportions, designed to give some controlled driving experience to the under-16 age group.

26078 **VCE 769**

Big Fry

This once ubiquitous television commercial featured 26078.

26107 454 AYV

Endeavour

A spin-off from the popular Colin Dexter 'Inspector Morse' books, 26107 appeared in one such episode starring Jenny Seagrove.

26134 866 JPP

R W D (David) Marques

Famous Rugby Union International and multiple Alvis owner: (qv 27470 for bio and also 14566).

26149 5432 WJ

Iliffe Publications

Though not as detailed as *Autocar*'s main weekly road tests, there was the occasional *Used Cars on the Road* series also. 26149 would feature as the subject of number 192 of this, in the issue of June 15, 1962.

26164 YWK 258

Air Commodore F Rodwell Banks

An unsung hero of two world wars, 'Rod' Banks (March 22, 1898-May 12, 1985) initially joined the Royal Navy in 1914, serving in the Caspian Sea at the time of the Russian Revolution. Between the wars his almost obsessional research into fuels, and particularly their octane rating, would benefit speed kings like Cobb and Seagrave, but more importantly the Schneider Trophy aircraft which were the antecedents of the Spitfire. WWII saw Rod Banks at the Aeroplane and Armament Experimental Establishment, which is where his rank of Air Commodore was awarded. Earning a host of academic qualifications too numerous to

26164: Air Commodore Francis Rodwell Banks, who rendered notable service in both World Wars.

26170: An Alvis example from the late Peter Wheeler's collection of classic cars.

mention, plus military honours from France, the USA, and Imperial Russia, Banks took on a number of consultancies, one of which was with Blackburn Aircraft, which is how 26164 came to be allocated to him. The pioneer aviator Robert Blackburn was, of course, himself a serial Alvis enthusiast: see 9863, 10855 and 12097 for Speed 20s of SA, SB and SC types respectively.

For further reading: The Rod Banks autobiography, *I Kept no Diary*, published by Airlife, ISBN 0-950-4543-9-7.

26170 YLC 293

Peter Wheeler

Peter Wheeler (February 29, 1944-June 11, 2009) was a successful entrepreneur who had bought the TVR Car Company in 1981. An avid collector of interesting motor cars, of which the above is one of three of the marque duly purchased, the others being a Silver Eagle (qv 11800) and a TA 21 (qv 25116). It is worth mentioning that the very first TVR, from the Trevor Wilkinson days, was an Alvis Firebird model. (See: Firebird).

26171 237 GTV

Earl of Shrewsbury

The 21st Earl (1914-1980) obtained this car via the Nottingham agents. The original seat of the Earls of Shrewsbury was Alton Towers, now a theme park.

26174
4440 DA
Brewster Mason
Actor Brewster Mason (August 30, 1922-August 14, 1987) was a member of the Royal Shakespeare Company and also appeared in many movies, such as *Quatermass* and *The Dam Busters*. An accident curtailed his stage career somewhat and led to an increase in his radio work.

26174 has also been re-registered with the mark: DBY 606 B.

26184
641 DRT
Fisons
The company car of the well-known industrial group specialising in fertiliser products. See also numerous reference to serial Alvis owner Sir George Burton, who was Fisons' MD for many years.

26208
YLC 295
Pie in the Sky
26208 featured in this popular television series which ran between 1994 and 1997. It starred Richard Griffiths and Maggie Steed.

26213
2283 TR
Don Pedro Colley
An American actor born August 30, 1938, Colley has appeared in well over 20 movies and television series. Worth mentioning are: *The Dukes of Hazzard, Beneath the Planet of the Apes, Cagney and Lacey, Starsky and Hutch* and *Herbie Rides Again*.

26252
YXE 459
John Osborne
A famous playwright, John Osborne (December 12, 1929-December 24, 1994) has a huge canon of works to his name, where perhaps *Look back in Anger* and *The Entertainer* spring most readily to mind.

26265
BGM 310
Rt Hon David Steel MP
Now Lord Steel of Aikwood KT, KBE, PC and born

March 31, 1938, David Steel entered Parliament as member for Roxburgh, Selkirk and Peebles in a 1965 by-election. Became leader of the Liberal Party in 1976, and entered the Lords in 1997. Steel is also an enthusiast for the Rover P5.

26281
YXA 23
Lord Glenconner
Perhaps better known to some of us of a certain age as the Hon Colin Tennant (December 1, 1926-August 27, 2010), he was educated at Eton and served as a Lieutenant in the Irish Guards before proceeding to New College, Oxford. He bought and developed the island of Mustique, where the late Princess Margaret was a frequent visitor. Acceded to the title in 1983.

26294
570 BYT
Kim Gardner
Noted musician Kim Gardner (January 27, 1948-October 24, 2001) has made or contributed to over 30 albums. Bass guitarist with The Thunderbirds (later Birds), he has worked with Eric Clapton, Rod Stewart and Bo Diddley.

26298
564 AXB
Laurence Vaughan-Williams
Highly qualified barrister, with practices on the mainland and on the Isle of Man. Member of Lincoln's Inn, Isle of Man Law Society, Commercial Bar Association and The Institute of Directors. A returning officer to the Manx Parliament. Previously a TC 21/100 owner (qv 25719).

26336
81 RPA
AB Picture Corporation
In business from 1927 to 1970, the above company had many screen successes, not least of which were *The Dam Busters* of 1954, and *Ice Cold in Alex* of 1958, the latter starring Alvis enthusiast Harry Andrews: TD 21 (qv 26814) and TE 21 (qv 27182).

26346
RWH 514
Arthur Holt MP
Serial owner of three other open Alvis cars: a TA 14 (qv 20972 for bio), a TA 21 (qv 24***), and a TC 21/100 (qv 25413).

26365
Count Charles de Limur
The brief biography of the remarkable Charles de Limur will be covered later (qv 27474). 26365 was a standard Park-Ward bodied model purchased from the London agents and used in England. Charlie once told me of an amusing incident, being mistaken for HRH Prince Philip, when driving through Windsor Great Park in this car. For HRH's similar car see 26600. Eventually 26365 was traded in to Herrman Graber against the TF 21 27474, and Graber somewhat re-modelled the TD 21 before passing it on.

266 BGN
26431
Moss Bros'
The first Moss Bros' 3-litre. Replaced by a TE 21 (qv 27251).

5101 K
26350
London's Burning
This was a television series, where 26350 appeared in episode 3 of series 5. The car would later make an appearance in *A Rather English Marriage*, which starred Albert Finney, Tom Courtenay and Joanna Lumley.

DCW 92
26390
Haynes Publishing
Unfortunately for Alvis owners, never a subject for one of Haynes most worthy manuals, this TD 21 is an exhibit in the company's Motor Museum. Its

That 'king of skiffle,' music legend Lonnie Donegan. Further recommended reading is Donegan's biography *The Skiffle Craze* by Mike Dewe (Planet ISBN 978-090518855), to whom this image is believed credited.

registration mark is somewhat anachronistic to the car, having apparently originated on a Daimler in 1954.

2332 WA
26444
Lonnie Donegan
Prime mover in that musical phenomenon known as 'skiffle,' Lonnie Donegan (April 29, 1931-November 3, 2002) had a host of hit numbers, such as *Have a Drink on Me* and *Rock Island Line*. Some had a humorous angle, as with posing the question: "Does your chewing gum lose its flavour on the bed post overnight?"

30 AYO
26447
Earl of Inchcape
Kenneth William James Mackay (December 27, 1917-March 17, 1994), the third Earl, was educated at Eton and Trinity College Cambridge, and served during WWII with the 27th Lancers, attaining the rank of Major. In civilian life he was a well-known shipping magnate and had numerous other directorships, including the companies Burmah Oil and BP.

614 CYW
26465
Hammond Innes
A famous and prolific novelist (July 15, 1913-September 6, 1998), several of the his novels were turned into movies, typically, *Campbell's Kingdom*, *Wreck of the Mary Deare*, and *The Doppelganger*. At some stage, the registration mark (original) above was lost, and a replacement, 777 VBJ, applied.

90 BGX
26474
Araldite Ltd
26474 is the car once featured in adhesive manufacturer Araldite's adverts.

2858 NC
26477
R P (Bob) Girardi
Born November 18, 1961, Bob Girardi is a novelist specialising in mystery themes. Falling into this category would be his *Madeleine's Ghost*, *The Pirate's Daughter*, and *Vaporetto 13*.

26487 RJ 516

The Iron Maiden

A movie of 1962 starring Michael Craig, Jim Dale and Joan Simms. Another familiar face in the credits, in a minor role, was Sam Kydd, appearing with his son Jonathan. Sam would have been quite at home having 26487 on the set, as he was actually employed by Alvis Ltd as an engineer at its London Service Centre. For those who like to be exact in these matters, the 'Iron Maiden' was a Fowler traction engine (number 15657) whose registration number FX 6661 can clearly be discerned. This is very much a movie for aircraft buffs as well.

26493 2856 NC

Z-Cars

26493 made an appearance in an episode of the above – a popular television series based in and around Liverpool.

26505 282 BGN

F W Woolworth & Co Ltd

The company car of the once ubiquitous high street retailer. Preceded by a TC 21/100 (qv 25850).

26591 822 CLM

British Aircraft Corporation

Allocated to BAC on June 8, 1961, 26591 is yet another of the many connections Alvis shares with the aeronautical industry.

26592 9175 DU

HM Foreign Office

Allocated to the Foreign Office, presumably for embassy duties, the registration mark was allocated by Coventry City Council under the Home Delivery Export Scheme.

26600 OXR 1

HRH Prince Philip, Duke of Edinburgh

Built to special order, and replacing HRH's previous Lagonda, 26600 bristles with special equipment too numerous to mention in detail. Only three of the Park Ward bodied cars have featured the much deeper windscreen evident in the photograph. The car is kept at Sandringham, is in good order and gets an occasional outing.

26610 809 CLC

Martini and Rossi

This very long-established international company is especially noted for its vermouth and sparkling wines. 26610 was the company car of its London operation. The company has also sponsored motor racing teams from time to time, notably Ferrari and Williams. There was a merger with Bacardi in 1993.

26620 VTK 536

Inspector Morse

26620 appeared in the episode entitled *Dead on Time* and had previously been used in an ITV series *Under Suspicion*.

26637 856 CLJ

Trainer

Filmed appropriately near Newbury, this television series ran to some 23 episodes during 1991 and 1992 and starred David McCallum and Susannah York. 26637 had unfortunately lost its original registration mark by the time filming had commenced, so it appears as KSV 954 on screen.

This was far from being the first time that the paths of Alvis and horse-racing had merged, for the marque was favoured by such well-known jockeys as George Duller (qv 5622) Sir Gordon Richards (qv 8163) and Harry Wragg (qv 8860).

A 'real-life' Newbury horse trainer, Keith Piggott, father of the famous jockey Lester, had two Alvis cars: the first a 12/70 (qv 15642), later replacing it with a TA 21 (qv 24615).

26655 27 CLF

Group Captain Sir Douglas Bader

Douglas Bader's third Alvis (qv 25554 for bio, 25978 and 27024).

26664 208 DXO

Kenneth Burward-Hoy

A highly-esteemed string virtuoso, especially on the viola, Kenneth is equally at home on the classical music scene as with more popular genres. He has contributed to no fewer than 55 records alongside such notables as Sarah Vaughan, Quincey Jones, Steven Sondheim and Harry Connick Jr. Previously owned a TA 21 model (qv 24964).

26675

Professor Roger Warwick

A distinguished professor of anatomy at Guy's Hospital Medical School, Roger Warwick had been looking for a TD 21 to buy second-hand, and just had to have this one when he saw his initials on the number plate. The plate was naturally retained later on, whereupon 26675 was re-registered as 762 HYR. The car was originally on the Alvis works sales department fleet.

26713 DS 6441

Andy Stewart

The Scottish entertainer December 20, 1933-October 11, 1993, enjoyed considerable vogue at one time and was compere of the series *The White Heather Club*. His recording hits included: *The Green Hills of Tyrol* and the humorous *Donald Where's Your Troosers?*

26717 866 WTF

26721 867 WTF

Jack Walker

Jack Walker (May 19, 1929-August 17, 2000) was a highly successful businessman, making his fortune in steel and ploughing back much of it into his favourite football club – Blackburn Rovers – which he actually owned from 1991 until his death. His company, Walkersteel, which he started in 1951, was sold to the British Steel Corporation in 1989. The two cars are a matching pair, only one of which is believed to have survived. Not only did Jack Walker have a road near to the Ewood Park Stadium named after him, but there is also a ten-foot high statue of him by James Butler on the club site.

26728

Purnell's Encyclopaedia

An interesting story is told about this car by Alan Smith, managing director of Tophams

Singer Andy Stewart. Illustration from contemporary Stewart promotional material.

Picture Library. In mid-1962 Alan had taken a job representing Purnell, the encyclopaedia publishers, and was expecting to be allocated something like a Ford Anglia as a company car. Alan's boss, Wilf Harvey, had enquired, seemingly jokingly, what sort of a vehicle the company should be using for this type of work. Alan had observed that he had always admired the 3-litre Alvis. To his surprise, not to mention future comfort, one was in stock at the agents Brooklands of Bond Street, and was immediately requisitioned for the purpose.

26730 CH

Baron von Pallandt

Full name Frederik Jan Gustav Floris was the 'Frederik' half of the popular singing duo Nina and Frederik. Baron von Pallandt (May 14, 1934-May 15, 1994) was murdered at Puerta Talero in the Philippines the day after his 60th birthday, by pirates trying to steal his boat.

26730 is the last Series 1 TD 21 made and was an export to Switzerland.

Singing duo Nina and Frederik are seen here looking over a TD 21 drophead at a motor show. They went on to purchase 26730, which was the last series one made.

TD 21 II

1962 to 1963
26731-27015
285 cars

Consisting of:
Park Ward saloons
18871-19067   197
Park Ward coupés
18681-18733   53
Mulliner Park Ward saloons
9001-9014   14
Mulliner Park Ward coupés
9501-9505   6
Graber (various)
756, 757, 758, 759, 760, 761, 762, 763,
764, 765, 766, 767,768, 769, 771   15

Chassis	Reg		
26731 -	- 555 TKO	26736 - - OFL 917	26742 - - 5193 VC
26732 -	- XAK 430	26737 - - UZC 311	26743 - - 4282 VC
26733 -	- OJC 428	26738 - - - NBU 1	26744 - - - JB 845
26734 -	- 3333 NE	26739 - - - AHJ 1	26745 - - 397 VPP
26735 -	- - 2 FOO	26740 - - -94 DLC	26746 - - - 620 FN
		26741 - - 8279 RW	26747 - - 117 HYN

26748 - - 1848 NE	26818 - - 142 ELT	26888 - -EGM 515
26749 - - 603 UVT	26819 - - 932 GOJ	26889 - - 630 GYS
26750 - - 4363 NF	26820 - - JSH 185	26890 - - -30 FLK
26751 - - 9695 RW	26821 - -909 CWB	26891 - - 749 FBC
26752 - - 807 WK	26822 - - 9978 VM	26892 - - - - AUS
26753 - - 5642 XJ	26823 - - HCU 505	26893 - - 3935 VM
26754 - - 4293 UN	26824 - - 4722 BH	26894 - - 1246 PK
26755 - - -880 KV	26825 - - - MF 61	26895 - - - -CH
26756 - -212 DXO	26826 - - 3251 TD	26896 - - - 84 FLY
26757 - - 500 GBP	26827 - - 135 HYN	26897 - - 429 FLD
26758 - -4947 JN	26828 - - 78 HYK	26898 - - 250 EXN
26759 - - 508 CAY	26829 - -130 XBH	26899 - - 14 PJH
26760 - 213 DXO	26830 - - 203 DXO	26900 - - 79 FLY
26761 - DZD 838	26831 - - YZ 9599	26901 - - - 888 KF
26762 - 900 MJO	26832 - 9250 MX	26902 - - -583 EJB
26762 - - - -NS 27	26833 - 700 TKT	26903 - - 297 CAY
26764 - -205 WBH	26834 - - -74 EXB	26904 - - 8468 VC
26765 - 4040 WF	26835 - - 669 FPO	26905 - - SZD 422
26766 - 1004 WK	26836 - - 2358 DF	26906 - - 705 FGC
26767 - 8192 RW	26837 - - 7773 NF	26907 - - 430 FLD
26768 - - - - NZ	26838 - -3474 WK	26908 - - MLF 719
26769 - 117 DLC	26839 - - 3 DYR	26909 - -MZD 781
26770 - 32 FXM	26840 - PSN 308	26910 - - 895 CRP
26771 - 229 EXN	26841 - 138 ELT	26911 - - - PKS 2
26772 - 575 EPO	26842 - 480 YPP	26912 - - 216 ENV
26773 - 601 EBP	26843 - 4317 VC	26913 - - 86 GOR
26774 - 122 XBH	26844 - 5085 VC	26914 - - UES 145
26775 - - - - -CH	26845 - 9815 DD	26915 - - 2576 VT
26776 - - - -CH	26846 - - - - -CH	26916 - - YXJ 265
26777 - - - -CH	26847 - 873 EWB	26917 - - -232 KX
26778 - 200 RYC	26848 - 2794 VC	26918 - - 7833 VM
26779 - 154 ELT	26849 - PMG 70	26919 - -781 MUP
26780 - FSS 659	26850 - - 94 FLY	26920 - - 239 EXN
26781 - 5998 VC	26851 - 961 XTX	26921 - - 436 FLD
26782 - 760 XPH	26852 - 8999 PK	26922 - - 364 NDV
26783 - -DGM 888	26853 - 159 ELT	26923 - - 842 ECH
26784 - -200 DXO	26854 - TVG 666	26924 - - 817 FGU
26785 - - - -CH	26855 - - -18 FLK	26925 - - 7708 VC
26786 - 1005 WK	26856 - 370 GCG	26926 - - 900 DNV
26787 - - - AA 28	26857 - - - -CH	26927 - - XHS 323
26788 - -325 GBM	26858 - - - -CH	26928 - - - - -
26789 - WWH 747	26859 - - - -CH	26929 - - -25 FLK
26790 - 28 BNW	26860 - -144 GOK	26930 - - 789 CUK
26791 - 804 TKP	26861 - -NME 370	26931 - - 248 EXN
26792 - 2162 VC	26862 - - -63 GLB	26932 - - 7040 BH
26793 - -204 DXO	26863 - 808 EYY	26933 - - - -CH
26794 - 439 FLD	26864 - 2341 KD	26934 - - 256 EPY
26795 - -205 DXO	26865 - 969 CMO	26935 - - - - -CH
26796 - 6054 VC	26866 - 189 CWW	26936 - - -99 FLY
26797 - 1347 DF	26867 - REE 222	26937 - - 3969 VT
26798 - 260 DRY	26868 - VCL 400	26938 - -766 GWA
26799 - -861 PBJ	26869 - - LJ 222	26939 - - 9389 VC
26800 - WDB 194	26870 - -74 FLW	26940 - - - -CH
26801 - - 14 VC	26871 - 8777 UK	26941 - - 6855 PE
26802 - - - 3 EWJ	26872 - - - DS 4	26942 - - 997 WJH
26803 - 296 YPP	26873 - -643 EXD	26943 - - 999 EYP
26804 - - - - -NL	26874 - 919 LOD	26944 - - 635 SHU
26805 - 3929 UK	26875 - HC 8694	26945 - - 3532 ET
26806 - 2203 WK	26876 - 4188 VC	26946 - - -271 FJF
26807 - 8348 NE	26877 - WCF 281	26947 - - XBN 511
26808 - - - -CH	26878 - 1979 PK	26948 - - RJX 824
26809 - - - - -CH	26879 - YXJ 666	26949 - - 598 HYL
26810 - -216 DXO	26880 - 6348 VC	26950 - - 8978 BH
26811 - MUM 21	26881 - - 1 ALV	26951 - XWM 655
26812 - -PNW 621	26882 - 8665 KV	26952 - - -13 DBC
26813 - 9370 VM	26883 - -JCS 660	26953 - - 8052 BH
26814 - - -148 VC	26884 - 5085 VC	26954 - - 2602 KW
26815 - - - - - -	26885 - 6747 BH	26956 - - 600 KW
26816 - 155 ELT	26886 - 3300 NX	26957 - - 836 GBC
26817 - EP 1000	26887 - 4189 VC	26958 - - -21 FLK

26959 - - 780 DKG	26978 - - - - CH	26997 - - - - Y 28
26960 - - UGR 499	26979 - - - - CH	26998 - - 9505 PG
26961 - - WAG 47	26980 - - 182 GBC	26999 - - 667 CLJ
26962 - - 1999 KX	26981 - - 996 KEA	27000 - - 2398 KV
26963 - - 982 FNW	26982 - - 8611 DF	27001 - - - 2 YKM
26964 - - FGM 303	26983 - - -328 KV	27002 - - 11 FYW
26965 - -700 GNW	26984 - - -65 GLB	27003 - - VVG 600
26966 - - NCC 140	26985 - - 3126 KV	27004 - - FGM 828
26967 - - 145 KPP	26986 - - - -BIB 9	27005 - - 248 GUA
26968 - - 2771 KV	26987 - - 919 DDA	27006 - - - 89 FLY
26969 - -835 GYW	26988 - - ORC 600	27007 - - YBW 684
26970 - - - - AUS	26989 - - 25 FXM	27008 - - VJW 404
26971 - - 355 GBC	26990 - - 3434 VR	27009 - - 2688 KV
26972 - - 5002 RU	26991 - - -24 DRL	27010 - - 423 HYP
26973 - - VLC 444	26992 - - 992 HYU	27011 - - 2958 KV
26974 - - 888 SJH	26993 - - 1333 KV	27012 - - 6211 PF
26975 - - - - USA	26994 - CML 444A	27013 - - XHS 939
26976 - - - WEE 2	26995 - - - - -CH	27014 - - - WBR 6
26977 - - 222 JOV	26996 - - YCV 57B	27015 - - 328 EVJ

Considered by many to be the best of the Park Ward era cars, on account of its unstressed engineering refinement and especially tidy frontal arrangement, where new apertures served the dual purpose of the new spotlight mountings and air intakes. Mechanically, Dunlop disc brakes all round were found preferable to the former Lockheed disc and drum arrangement. Newly optional was a five-speed ZF gearbox, infinitely better than the previous Austin-Healey unit with its somewhat vague action. Mid-way through the production of the Series II, there was a merger between the Park Ward and H J Mulliner coachbuilding firms, resulting in a change to the Alvis body numbering system. Confusingly (and illogically) it is the later cars that have the lower (MPW) numbers, but the above listing explains the correct chronological sequence.

26734 `3333 NE`

Manchester City Police

26734 was supplied to the above force on February 21, 1962. It was presumably for the use of the chief constable, as it would not have looked well in panda car livery. Also: '999 NE' might have appeared too obvious.

26735 `2 FOO`

Sir Robert McAlpine Ltd

Although Sir Robert McAlpine himself, 1847-1934, famous for founding the internationally-known construction company, was long-deceased by the time 26735 was constructed, it was the company car of that organisation.

26752 `807 WK`

Harold Brooks-Baker

Actually American-born, Harold Brooks-Baker (November 16, 1933-March 5, 2005), from his earliest days, recovering from polio as a child, developed what has been called an obsession with genealogy in general, and the British aristocracy in particular. This anglophile took up residence in England, and in due course became managing director of Debrett's Peerage (relinquished upon a takeover), and also editor of Burke's Peerage. Infusing himself into the type of lifestyle personified by the novels of Henry James, F Scott Fitzgerald and Dornford Yates, Brooks-Baker later derived a viable income by selling obscure baronies and titles to the wealthy. The single-mindedness of his research would, however, occasionally upset Buckingham Palace. He wrote no books himself, but for further reading there is nothing better than the article by Sarah Duguid in *The Mail on Sunday* of March 13, 2005, p42/43, a larger-than-life biography which could provide the basis for a most entertaining movie.

26755 `880 KV`

Forever Green

Often featuring in this television series and starring John Alderton and Pauline Collins, running from 1989 to 1992, 26755 started life as a works delivered car. By the time of the television series it had lost its short, distinctive number and had been re-registered as ALA 901 A.

26758 `4847 JN`

Nicholas Parsons CBE

This was Nicholas' first Alvis, to be followed by a TE 21 (qv 27232 for bio).

26767 `8192 RW`

Iliffe Publications

An *Autocar* road test (number 1887) featured 26767 in the issue of August 10, 1962.

26783 `DGM 888`

Classic Car Weekly

Featured in the December 12, 1990 issue of the above, along with (qv 26847).

26766

 1004 WK

James Mason

An extremely popular movie actor with over 120 such to his credit, James Mason (May 15, 1909-July 27, 1984) was born in Huddersfield. He was educated at Marlborough and Peterhouse, Cambridge. His career is peppered with Alvis influences, starting with a role given to him in 1933 by Sir Alexander Korda, who would presently purchase a Speed 25 (qv 13365). Also, in two of the Mason movies, both of 1959 – *North by Northwest* and *Journey to the Centre of the Earth* – the music score was provided by Bernard Herrmann, a TA 21 owner (qv 24799). Unsurprisingly, Mason was called upon to do commercials, including a well-known one for Studebaker, where his previously-owned TB 14 Alvis can be seen in the background.

26799 **861 PBJ**

Lord Benjamin Britten OM, CH

A British composer, Benjamin Britten (November 22, 1913-December 4, 1976) was born in Lowestoft. His Life Peerage was only awarded in the last year of his life. Often a controversial figure, he was taught composition by Frank Bridge, and Britten's sometimes lauded orchestration was actually due in large part to the influence of that great percussionist James Blades. There are many biographies, amongst which is that by Michael Kennedy, published by J M Dent, ISBN 0-460-02201-6, which is worthy of consideration.

Britten is probably the only Alvis owner to feature upon a coin of the realm, being the Centenary fifty-pence piece, of which around 5 million were minted in 2013. Here, I have discounted the prototype coins prepared for the reign of Edward VIII (qv 27259). Only about 49 examples were struck, but none circulated due to the abdication crisis. These are confined to the Royal Mint Museum.

26814 **148 VC**

Harry Andrews CBE

Originally a works-registered car, actor Andrews replaced 26814 with a TE 21 (qv 27182 for bio). 26814 was subsequently re-registered under XSK 535.

26799: The Benjamin Britten car seen leaving the Red House. (Courtesy Alvis Archive Trust)

As far as is known, Benjamin Britten was the only Alvis owner to feature upon a circulated coin of the realm, in 2013, with a minting of 5.3 million.

(Courtesy Alvis Archive Trust)

26824 **4722 BH**

Frank Muir CBE

Frank Muir's second Alvis (qv 26059, and 27389 for bio).

26831 **YZ 9599**

David W Laing

David Laing has spent a lifetime arranging concerts and festivals in a wide variety of locations and, says David, the prestigious-looking TD 21 has on a number of occasions come in handy for chauffeuring musicians between venues. David tells me that there is a groove in the underside of 26831's dashboard which was caused by Paul Tortelier's fibre-glass cello case. One of several Alvis with musical connections.

26876 **4188 VC**
Bulmers Cider

Initially works-registered and used originally for demonstration purposes, 26976 was in due course allocated to H P Bulmer & Co Ltd, the renowned Hereford cider maker. It was there that it was re-registered with the Hereford Mark: 166 EVJ.

The company had much earlier bought a Silver Eagle model (qv 12628), and even earlier than that, a second hand 12/50 TE (qv 4434).

26830 (Courtesy the late sculptor Bryan Parkes)

26830 **203 DXO**
Bryan Parkes

Bryan was a notable sculptor with many commissions to his credit, nationally and internationally, working from his studio in Welwyn. Especially worthy of mention is his mask of Albert Einstein of 2006, received to critical acclaim and described as a 'hollow face illusion.' Coincidentally, Bryan was the nephew of long-time Alvis Ltd's chairman, John J Parkes.

26847 **873 EWB**
Popular Classics

26847 was featured in the October 1989 issue of the above and would, not long after, re-appear in *Classic Car Weekly* – the issue of December 12, 1990.

David Laing's saloon with distinguished company at the Romney, Hythe and Dymchurch railway.
(Courtesy Alvis Archive Trust)

26894 **1246 PK**
Rear Admiral Sir Morgan-Giles MP

To give him his full title, Sir Morgan Charles Morgan-Giles DSO, OBE, GM, DL, MP, was born June 19, 1914 and died May 4, 2013, just a few days short of his 99th birthday. He was a most colourful character, both in his distinguished naval service, and in the House of Commons, where he represented Winchester from 1964 to 1979. His full biography is too great to reproduce here, but it is worth mentioning that for a time he was commanding officer of HMS Belfast – a familiar

tourist attraction moored in the Thames between Tower Bridge and London Bridge.

26926 **900 DNV**
Boon

Featured in the television series of that name, starring Michael Elphick.

26962 `1999 KX`

The Big Sleep

The classic 1946 Humphrey Bogart movie *The Big Sleep* underwent a remake in 1978, this later version starring Robert Mitchum and Sarah Miles. 26962 also figured quite prominently.

26980 `182 GBC`

Classic Car Mart

26980 figured in a major feature in this periodical, issue of November 2003.

26964 `FGM 303`

Sir Paul Newall

Born September 17, 1934, Paul Newall became the 666th Lord Mayor of London for 1993/94. He used his mayoral year largely in trade-promotional trips abroad, especially to the Far East and the USA, after which he returned to his job as a stockbroker with Lehman Brothers. It has been said, incidentally, that Sir Paul's mother-in-law, who had worked for Ian Fleming at the Admiralty during WWII, served as the model for Miss Moneypenny in the Bond novels. The above TD 21 has been preceded in Paul Newall's ownership by a TA 14 (qv 21938) and a Speed 25 (qv 14570). He died July 28, 2015.

26984 `65 GLB`

Perfect Scoundrels

This was a popular ITV series which ran for quite a few episodes between 1990 and 1992. It starred Peter Bowles and Brian Murray, but it has not been possible to isolate which episodes 26984 also starred in.

26991 `24 DRL`

Betty Streather

Betty Streather's name was once a familiar one on the car rallying scene during the 1930s, where one of her mounts was an Alvis Speed 20 (qv 10057). In her later years, she purchased the above late model TD 21, but from correspondence that has come to light at Red Triangle, there were some warranty problems with the car when it was new.

27006 `89 FLY`

Gordon Fraser

Gordon Fraser (February 26, 1911-June 27, 1981) was educated at Oundle, St John's, Cambridge and Sandhurst, serving in WWII in North Africa with the Intelligence Corps. He became a household name on two counts: his eponymous 'gallery' and, of course, for the company he founded, producing distinctive greeting cards. The latter business was acquired by Hallmark Cards in 1993. Some of the original Gordon Fraser are held at Bedford and some at the Victoria and Albert Museum.

TE 21

1963 to 1965
27016-27369
354 cars

Consisting of:

Mulliner Park Ward saloons	
9015-9259	245
Mulliner Park Ward coupés	
9507-9601	95
Graber (various)	
772, 773, 774, 775, 776, 777, 778, 779,	
780, 781, 782, 783.	12

Chassis	Reg			
27016	- - - 3101 KV	27043 - - - ABC 333B	27071 - - - XJV 222
27017	- - - 3100 KV	27044 - - - 77 VNK	27072 - - - - - ZA
27018	- - - 3102 KV	27045 - - - 46 HLW	27073 - - FPE 297B
27019	- - - TFL 205	27046 - - -756 UCV	27074 - - BAY 341B
27020	- - AWE 202B	27047 - - - EMY 9B	27075 - -AGM 666B
27021	- - 600 ECE	27048 - - - 1084 PP	27076 - - - - - ZA
27022	- - - - ALF 63	27049 - - - 527 CBY	27077 - - - 5060 PP
27023	- - - - 7 GYE	27050 - - - - - -CH	27078 - - - 8061 GZ
27024	- - - 36 GLR	27051 - - - - - -CH	27079 - - BLE 376B
27025	- - 898 HWE	27052 - - - 5075 KV	27080 - - - 33 HYF
27026	- - - MHJ 674	27053 - - - - JJJ 774	27081 - -CTW 238B
27027	- - 4600 KV	27054 - - - 4604 VU	27082 - - 7568 VU
27028	- - 8662 VR	27055 - - -340 VYD	27083 - -CJF 440B
27029	- - - - EJ 25	27056 - - - 838 GYW	27084 - - - - -CH
27030	- - - - - -CH	27057 - - APB 181B	27085 - - - - - -CH
27031	- - - - - -CH	27058 - - - 592 EUK	27086 - - AAU 200B
27032	- - - 64 FRX	27059 - - - 360 VPP	27087 - - BWA 333B
27033	- - 1819 VU	27060 - - - -11 HLF	27088 - - BKK 909B
27034	- - 404 EDA	27061 - - - 8646 HA	27089 - - BTY 119B
27035	- - 833 GYW	27062 - - - XCF 850	27090 - - ASG 673B
27036	- - 4413 KV	27063 - - - AAY 150	27091 - - AWY 825B
27037	- -AMA 157B	27064 - - - -29 HLF	27092 - - AUC 553B
27038	- - 8674 KX	27065 - - -8447 KW	27093 - - CLG 892B
27039	- - - 575 FKG	27066 - - - 972 HUB	27094 - - - 1950 EH
27040	- - 831 GYW	27067 - - - 812 KUE	27095 - - AUC 555B
27041	- - - 799 ERC	27068 - - CLL 681B	27096 - - DPU 766B
27042	- - - 8675 KX	27069 - - BMA 444B	27097 - - AUW 66B
		27070 - - - XJL 967	27098 - - - - 995 XJ

27099 - - AUC 560B	27169 - - - BOY 200	27239 - FWA 333C	27309 - - FDA 222C	27329 - - HAP 300D	27349 - - LGN 595D
27100 - - - -JF 9276	27170 - - DJU 939C	27240 - - EDU 422C	27310 - - JUC 944D	27330 - - - GLW 8C	27350 - - JUU 555D
27101 - - AUC 570B	27171 - - ABR 742B	27241 - - CRY 862C	27311 - - -MME 7C	27331 - - KBN 212F	27351 - - JXE 147D
27102 - - AKX 675B	27172 - - AVC 105B	27242 - - EFH 200C	27312 - - - - - - ZA	27332 - - - - - - -	27352 - -NBH 949D
27103 - - AUC 568B	27173 - - CLA 408B	27243 - - - - PXD 1	27313 - - DUB 840C	27333 - - GUA 845D	27353 - GWK 878D
27104 - -BGM 830B	27174 - - AAF 900B	27244 - - EWJ 323C	27314 - - EHJ 525C	27334 - - FHP 599C	27354 - - JYL 872D
27105 - - AWS 553B	27175 - -DKX 152B	27245 - - CRS 768C	27315 - - FDU 751C	27335 - - GXE 580C	27355 - - - DS 259
27106 - - - 20 GDA	27176 - - BJW 679B	27246 - - - - - -CH	27316 - - EFL 655D	27336 - - KYB 243D	27356 - -FGM 525D
27107 - - - - XLA 2	27177 - - CGJ 775B	27247 - - - - - -CH	27317 - - DDN 547C	27337 - - PHV 730E	27357 - GWK 743D
27108 - - AYT 593B	27178 - - DLY 720C	27248 - - DYY 630C	27318 - - -GJJ 860C	27338 - - JLB 127D	27358 - - WLG 42
27109 - - -718 TTT	27179 - - FGG 582C	27249 - - CNC 144C	27319 - - HWR 710C	27339 - - OOO 505D	27359 - - - LXN 1
27110 - - 351 GMO	27180 - - AKS 491B	27250 - - FYX 381C	27320 - - - -9700 IB	27340 - -CWL 485C	27360 - - - -JZI 434
27111 - - CLN 173B	27181 - -AWK 801B	27251 - - AVG 434C	27321 - - FDU 752C	27341 - - GBC 230D	27361 - - JUU 456D
27112 - - AYT 602B	27182 - - CGJ 779B	27252 - - ERW 797C	27322 - - GGJ 137C	27342 - - EFH 200C	27362 - - -KJJ 717D
27113 - - - 2738 RA	27183 - -CYX 140C	27253 - - COB 77C	27323 - - GLX 568C	27343 - - MWE 90D	27363 - - GRT 161D
27114 - - DDU 482B	27184 - -AWK 803B	27254 - - CCT 105C	27324 - - - FHP 6C	27344 - - HRC 690D	27364 - - GUV 667C
27115 - - - XCL 666	27185 - - CGJ 778B	27255 - - EYE 827C	27325 - - GGY 687C	27345 - - HDM 333C	27365 - -GDD 232D
27116 - - - YEE 645	27186 - -AWK 802B	27256 - - FDA 222C	27326 - - - - 1 ALV	27346 - - HRC 689D	27366 - - - - DS 4
27117 - - ADA 726B	27187 - - GPA 152C	27257 - - GYV 153C	27327 - -DKV 627C	27347 - - NYP 221E	27367 - - PGH 706E
27118 - - ACY 509B	27188 - - - CNE 7C	27258 - - FHP 601C	27328 - - HNJ 156D	27348 - -HWK 652D	
27119 - - - 3540 XJ	27189 - - CLA 418B	27259 - - -FJF 887D			
27120 - - DVH 197B	27190 - - DOC 70C	27260 - - - JDF 63C			
27121 - - CLL 540B	27191 - - AVC 999B	27261 - - - BCK 8C			
27122 - - - 6951 HP	27192 - -CYX 129C	27262 - - CWS 33C			
27123 - -DMA 355B	27193 - - EDU 379C	27263 - - - -WCT 7			
27124 - - CLR 256B	27194 - - EKX 774B	27264 - -CYX 136C			
27125 - - YKT 320B	27195 - - AXJ 951B	27265 - -FWK 774C			
27126 - - -416 CKR	27196 - - - - - - -	27266 - - FKE 315C			
27127 - - EPU 757B	27197 - - CNR 997B	27267 - - FYX 385C			
27128 - - AHR 430B	27198 - - CGJ 774B	27268 - - FDU 753C			
27129 - - BBH 588B	27199 - - CLE 485B	27269 - - ERC 950C			
27130 - - - BJJ 811B	27200 - - - -JTW 29	27270 - - GWB 22C			
27131 - - BGU 897B	27201 - - CLA 410B	27271 - - EBD 455C			
27132 - - -BJF 114B	27202 - - CLA 414B	27272 - - - OEY 404			
27133 - - BXD 333B	27203 - - CLA 416B	27273 - - DLX 858C			
27134 - - BNT 333B	27204 - - - OZH 11	27274 - - -LLG 55C			
27135 - - - XVG 63	27205 - - - EBB 50C	27275 - - DVJ 358C			
27136 - - -100 BKD	27206 - -LHK 160C	27276 - - ELL 965C			
27137 - - ANH 294B	27207 - - BAE 567B	27277 - - BUA 653C			
27138 - - DPC 148B	27208 - - BNF 697C	27278 - - FWJ 500C			
27139 - - - NEW 56	27209 - - GGJ 140C	27279 - - ELL 951C			
27140 - - CBA 239B	27210 - - - DYS 4C	27280 - - EVC 155C			
27141 - - BLE 394B	27211 - - CLE 855B	27281 - -DRH 400C			
27142 - - - - - NL	27212 - - CLC 770B	27282 - - - - 2 CDE			
27143 - - - - -CH	27213 - - JTD 839B	27283 - - DVJ 446C			
27144 - - BGJ 860B	27214 - - ELL 962C	27284 - - - CRB 11			
27145 - - BDA 300B	27215 - - ATS 237C	27285 - - ENJ 100C			
27146 - - DVH 183B	27216 - -EWD 679C	27286 - - ELL 969C			
27147 - - - 39 WHT	27217 - - EDU 115C	27287 - - FRC 622C			
27148 - - BLU 109B	27218 - - BRR 150C	27288 - - BTS 394C			
27149 - - BLU 112B	27219 - - EUY 840C	27289 - -CNH 333C			
27150 - - BDA 674B	27220 - - - DAU 9C	27290 - - GDT 363C			
27151 - - BDA 526B	27221 - - CWD 66C	27291 - - EWH 28C			
27152 - - BLU 114B	27222 - - CYX 125C	27292 - - KWA 88D			
27153 - - - - 4700 D	27223 - CGM 666C	27293 - - - FRY 8D			
27154 - - ARW 40B	27224 - -CYX 130C	27294 - - FPW 525C			
27155 - - - - REE 8	27225 - -DOR 933C	27295 - - -JWT 71C			
27156 - - 796 KUM	27226 - - FYX 172C	27296 - - - - - -CH			
27157 - - BUK 343B	27227 - - CGM 616C	27297 - - - - - -CH			
27158 - - AKE 777B	27228 - - CBB 462C	27298 - - -XZH 444			
27159 - - BYY 222B	27229 - - - CIO 617	27299 - - CVR 489C			
27160 - - - 8213 KR	27230 - -LWH 128C	27300 - - -GAP 44C			
27161 - -AWK 232B	27231 - - - 26 NOD	27301 - - JPH 185C			
27162 - - - -JA 1000	27232 - - JUD 931D	27302 - - FRB 201C			
27163 - - ASY 195B	27233 - - BGL 444C	27303 - -KPW 294C			
27164 - - ARW 900B	27234 - - ELL 962C	27304 - - FDU 630C			
27165 - - ARW 899B	27235 - - GBH 600C	27305 - - HWJ 222C			
27166 - - - - HR 22	27236 - - NLG 618C	27306 - -CUM 546C			
27167 - - CGJ 777B	27237 - - EDU 2C	27307 - -CUM 749C			
27168 - -GVW 242B	27238 - - CYX 139C	27308 - - FDA 505C			

This upgrade of the 3-litre was both technical and cosmetic, both at the business end. Under the bonnet, further revisions to the cylinder head, which included increasing the diameter of both inlet and exhaust valves by 2mm, coupled with tidier manifolding and larger diameter exhaust pipes collectively, contributed to a useful 13.5 per cent power increase: now 130bhp@5000rpm. Outside, the front wing leading edge was fractionally raised in order to accommodate a pair of vertically-stacked headlights, albeit of a slightly smaller diameter than before. This new arrangement rendered superfluous the previous spotlight cum air intakes of the TD 21 series II, hence there was a revival of the horizontal slots first seen on the TD 21 Series I. Another (less obvious) recognition point is the appearance of a rear seat centre arm rest. Also, the five-speed ZF gearbox, initially optional on the series II, now becomes the standard fitment.

The last two TE-designated chassis frames were never officially bodied, but returned to the stores. It is highly probable that one of these would become the basis of the 'Burns' special, and the other to repair an accident-damaged car.

27024 **36 GLR**

Group Captain Sir Douglas Bader
27024 was Bader's fourth and last Alvis, an association which had started in 1954 (qv 25554 for bio, 25978, and 26655).

27053

Course Car, British Grand Prix 1993
This event took place at Silverstone, July 11, 1993.

27024: The hurricane mascot on Group Captain Douglas Bader's TE 21 is seen here being inspected by none other than HRH Prince Philip (qv 26600). (Courtesy Alvis Archive Trust)

27053: Seen here in use as a course car at the 1993 British Grand Prix. The passengers are A de Cesaris, and V Katayama.

The illustration shows racing drivers Andrea de Cesaris and Ukyo Katayama being driven round the circuit. Both were on the Tyrrell-Yamaha team at the time, but did not draw any points on this occasion.

27064 **29 HLF**

The Curious Gardeners
This was, of course, a popular BBC television series from 2001, which was presented by Guy Cooper and Gordon Taylor. A sequel in book form was to follow, published by Headline: ISBN 978-0747236146.

27100 **JF 9276**

John Fenwick
John Fenwick is he of the many department stores which bear his name.

27064 (29 HLF): This TE 21 received much exposure when used in the television series *The Curious Gardeners*, which was followed by a book.

27100: With John Fenwick, here is David Michie, the long-time service manager of Alvis Ltd, and founder of Red Triangle. (Courtesy Alvis Ltd)

27102 **WPR 805 B**

Michael Aspel OBE
A very well-known radio and television presenter, Michael Aspel was born January 12, 1933 in Battersea, where he went to Emanuel School, but was evacuated to Chard when war broke out. National Service followed in the Kings Royal Rifle Corps plus some unremarkable jobs before breaking into media. People will have their own recollections of Michael's very many presentations, but probably *This is your Life*, *Antiques Roadshow* and having hosted 'Miss World' no less than 14 times, will most readily spring to mind.

27144 BGJ 808 B
Nic Fiddian-Green
Born 1963 and educated at Eton and the Chelsea College of Art, Nic is a notable sculptor, specialising in the reproduction of horses' heads, which have appeared in a great variety of sizes and have been much in demand in both public and private locations at home and abroad. He also wrote an autobiography: ISBN 978-0956756800.

27128 AHR 430 B
Richard's Things (movie)
This was a production of 1980 starring Liv Ullman, in which 27128 also appeared.

27160 8213 KR
Malcolm McDowell
A hugely talented actor who has appeared in around 170 movies, Malcolm Taylor McDowell was born in Leeds, June 13, 1943. Of these, *A Clockwork Orange* of 1971 is probably the one which springs most readily to mind. There is, however, another Alvis connection where, in *The Artist* of 2011, one scene is set to Bernard Herrmann's music which accompanied Hitchcock's *Vertigo*. Herrmann, of course, was a long-time owner of TA21 Tickford drophead coupé (qv 24799).

27161 AWK 232 B
Sir Norman Bettison QPM
Formerly chief constable of the West Yorkshire police force, Norman Bettison, born January 3, 1956, had witnessed the Hillsborough football tragedy as a spectator and became involved in the controversy that followed it. He set out his story in his book *Hillsborough Untold*, published by Biteback in 2016: ISBN 978-178590089.

27168 GVW 242 B
R A (Rab) Butler MP
To give him his full title, Richard Austen Butler, Lord Butler of Saffron Walden, KG, CW, PC, DL, (December 9, 1902-March 8, 1982) was an MP from 1929 to 1964. He held numerous offices in various Conservative Governments including Chancellor, Foreign Secretary, Home Secretary and finally,

RAB: the late Richard Austen Butler MP. A former deputy prime minister. (Courtesy Elliott & Fry, public domain, via Wikimedia Commons)

Deputy Prime Minister. He is generally credited as being the main architect of the 1944 Education Act. Further reading is his book *The Art of the Possible* (1971), published by Hamish Hamilton, ISBN 978-024 1020074. Not generally known is that Rab Butler had previously been an Alvis owner, purchasing a Silver Eagle model new (qv 12721).

27182 CGJ 779 B
Harry Andrews CBE
With some hundred or so movies to his credit, actor Harry Fleetwood Andrews (November 10, 1911-March 6, 1989) cut an instantly recognisable figure whatever the role, be it Roman, Shakespeare or galactic. The adventures with an Austin Ambulance will be remembered in *Ice Cold in Alex* of 1958. 27182 had been preceded in Andrews' ownership by a TD 21 (qv 26894). It is worth mentioning at this juncture that the 1978 remake of the 1946 Humphrey Bogart classic *The Big Sleep,* in which Andrews also starred, used another TD 21 (qv 26962) but there is no record of him owning this one.

27207 BAE 567 B
Professor Robert Laughlin
First delivered to a company in Bristol, 27207 had

Anthropologist professor Robert Laughlin. (Courtesy Harvard University Archive)

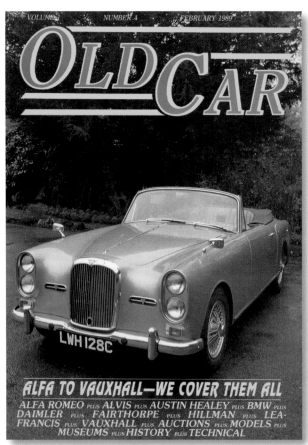

Often seen on the small screen, this image of 27230 comes from the now defunct *Old Car* magazine.

an unremarkable history until 1972, when it caught the eye of a Professor Robert H Laughlin and was exported to the USA. Originally intending to be a poet, Laughlin took a BA at Princeton, but took up anthropology, studying at Harvard (earning an MA in 1961 followed by a PhD in 1963). Bob Laughlin's area of study concerned the Mayan civilisation in Mexico, becoming a world authority on the subject, writing a number of related books including: *The People of the Bat* (ISBN 978 0874745900), *Beware the Great Horned Serpent* (ISBN 978 0942041194), *The Ch'ol Maya of Chiapas* (ISBN 978 0806147024), and especially *The Great Tzotzil Dictionary of San Lorenzo Zinacantán*, so small wonder that the letters TZOT appeared on the US number plate of Bob's Alvis.

In later life, Bob Laughlin became Curator Emeritus of Maya Studies at the Smithsonian Institution. A remarkable contributor to world anthropology, without whose astonishing 'dictionary' later researchers would have found their work much harder.

27209   GGJ 140 C
John Aldridge RA
A noted artist, especially in the fields of oil painting and wallpaper design, John Aldridge (July 26, 1905-May 3, 1983) was educated at Uppingham, and Corpus Christi, Oxford. In wartime, he served with the British Intelligence Corps and after hostilities ended, took up a post teaching in the Slade.
He is much remembered for his quite informal exhibitions at Place House, Great Bardfield, Essex.

27230   LWH 128 C
Kingdom (with Stephen Fry)
It was quite some time after being featured as the

cover car on a number of the now defunct *Old Car* magazine, that 27230 was adopted for the television series *Kingdom*, where Stephen Fry plays the part of a country solicitor.

No stranger to the big screen either, 27230 also featured in the 2007 movie *When Did You Last See Your Father?*, based on a story by Blake Morrison and starring Jim Broadbent and Colin Firth.

27232   JUD 931 D
Nicholas Parsons CBE
Born October 10, 1923, Nicholas – a charming, unassuming man with a quite remarkable career in radio, television and movies, has a versatility of talent that is unlikely to be equalled. Ever an enthusiast for the Alvis marque, 27232 had been preceded by a TD 21 (qv 26758). One morning, quite a few years ago now, I was astonished to get a telephone call from him, asking if I could locate the current owner of his formerly owned

27232: The second Alvis of television personality the late Nicholas Parsons, who kindly supplied this photo.

27259: 'Lost' for some 30 years, the Duke of Windsor's TE 21 turned up and has now been restored. Following some detailed sleuthing by the author, it has also been reunited with its original registration number. (Courtesy Mike Fitkin)

27259: As far as is known (unless a reader can advise otherwise) the uncrowned King Edward VIII (later, Duke of Windsor) was the only Alvis owner to feature on a postage stamp.

TE 21. This I managed to do, and we kept in occasional contact ever since, especially during the preparation of *Alvis Three Litre in Detail* Herridge and Sons.

For further reading, the Parsons autobiography *The Straight Man,* published by Wiedenfeld and Nicolson 1984, can be heartily recommended. ISBN -978-02978-12395.

27251 — AVG 434 C
Moss Bros
Company car of the famous London gentleman's outfitters. For the use of Monty Moss and preceded by a TD 21 (qv 26431).

27259 — FJF 887 D
King Edward VIII (Duke of Windsor)
Reigning briefly from January 30, 1936 until December 11 of the same year, the Duke of Windsor (June 23, 1894-May 28, 1972) was a car enthusiast of eclectic tastes. Alvis 27259 was sourced separately and privately from the Leicester agents Francis Motors, rather than being a direct factory order. It was duly despatched to the Windsors' home in Paris, where it remained until some time after Wallis Simpson's death on April 24, 1986. Somewhat later still the car found its way back to the UK, where it was re-registered as a routine import, and the significance of its origin was lost. Only in 2016 did the evidence of its original registration number come to light, with which it has now been reunited.

27261 — BCK 8 C
Mike Winters
Mike Winters (November 15, 1930-August 26, 2013) was one half of that once hugely popular comedy duo, along with his brother Bernie. Together they were responsible for the 1977 book *Shake a Pagoda Tree.* Further reading by Mike himself is *The Sunny Side of Winters*, a 2010 publication by J R Books.

27285 — ENJ 100 C
Mick Fleetwood
Mick Fleetwood was the eponymous part of the popular group Fleetwood Mac, formed in 1967 and subsequently responsible for a whole string of hits that would eventually total in excess of 100 million discs. Other members at various times included

27285: Former editor of *Germania* magazine, the late Rex Harvey is pictured here with the 'Fleetwood Mac' car. (Courtesy Rex Harvey)

John McVie, Stevie Nicks and Lindsay Buckingham. Alvis 27285 was subsequently acquired by the late Rex Harvey, a long-time editor of the well-known philatelic magazine *Germania*.

FRY 8 D
27293
Mike McCartney
Mike (brother of Beatle Paul) is one third of the trio that made up the popular Liverpool-based group The Scaffold. The others were the poet Roger McGough and John Gorman. There were a number of hits, of which *Lily the Pink* was probably the most successful, earning them a gold award. There is also an interesting book from Mike entitled, unsurprisingly *Liverpool Life*, published by Garlic Press, ISBN 1-90499-07-6.

DDN 547 C
27317
Terry's of York
The noted chocolatiers, perhaps unsurprisingly, ordered this car finished in a tasteful shade of brown.

DKV 627 C
27327
Tony Curtis
Curtis, born June 3, 1925 (as Bernard Schwartz),

was a remarkable movie actor, with versatile performances in over 100 films, but his career declined as a result of a battle with alcoholism, etc. He was also a talented painter. His movie of greatest interest to car enthusiasts was arguably *Monte Carlo or Bust*, of 1969. He died September 29, 2010. Suggested reading is *Tony Curtis, The Autobiography,* published by William Morrow, ISBN 978-0-688-09759-2. He previously owned a Speed 25 model (qv 14632). Alvis 27327 was also owned for a time by actor/comedian Dick Shawn (December 1, 1922-April 17, 1987). It is reported that Shawn actually died on stage, but the audience initially declined to leave, believing what they had observed was a pratfall.

RLD 717 E
27382
Sir George Burton CBE, DL
Born April 21, 1916, George Burton would become a noted industrialist and a long-time chairman of Fison's. Educated at Charterhouse, and Weimar, he started at Fison's in 1934. He was commissioned in the Royal Artillery from 1939 and served in North Africa, Sicily, Italy and Austria, returning to Fison's when hostilities ceased. He ranks as one of the most serial of Alvis drivers, owning a variety of models which are separately enumerated: see 8765, 9384, 13011, 13334, 13501, 14630, and 25870). He died in January 2010.

TF 21 1965-1967

27370-27475
106 cars

Consisting of:
Mulliner Park Ward saloons	
9260-9339	80
Mulliner Park Ward coupés	
9602-9621	20
Graber (various)	
784, 786, 790, 791, 793, 794	6

Chassis	Reg				
27370	- - - - - CH	27377	- - POO 777D	27385	- - - HAP 100
27371	- - NAB 719D	27378	- - DBY 193D	27386	- - DWL 666D
27372	- - FVC 895D	27379	- - - - DS 45	27387	- - EKW 800D
27373	- - FVC 896D	27380	- - -GHP 16D	27388	- - GRW 60D
27374	- - - - - GF 6	27381	- - -GES 816E	27389	- - - 9065 MW
27375	- - FVC 897D	27382	- - RLD 717E	27390	- - OPC 425D
27376	- - RLY 813C	27383	- - - WDH 38	27391	- - KOY 301D
		27384	- - KLR 245D	27392	- - GFS 999D

27393- - - ENC 1D	27424- - -JRW 445E	27445- - - CAN 896D
27394- - LDT 253D	27425- - - - XLE 9	27446- - - - MCA 5
27395- - EFG 967D	27426- - KUK 101D	27447- - - 4141 PH
27396- - - PLN 31E	27427- - NPF 915D	27448- - GKV 109D
27397- - HDV 149D	27428- - HHH 645E	27449- - BRE 477D
27398- - HNR 660D	27429- - -JRW 446E	27450- - -JRW 594E
27399- - LPO 790D	27430- - HDL 750E	27461- - -JOE 248E
27400- - - - HJM 2	27431- - KBU 413D	27462- - -PLA 212E
27411- - KLE 422D	27432- - - - -M 116	27463- - - FJT 12D
27412- - LAD 584E	27433- - GVC 861D	27464- - MPM 517F
27413- - GCD 222D	27434- -PMM 790E	27465- - KHO 999E
27414- - -LWP 75D	27435- -GGM 424D	27466- -WKX 488E
27415- - CAN 972D	27436- - GKV 832D	27467- - -JUB 777E
27416- - GVY 500D	27437- - PGH 733E	27468- - KUG 757E
27417- - HCR 202D	27438- - - - - CH	27469- - GGR 963E
27418- -GOW 292D	27439- - - - NYW 1	27470- - -LCT 329F
27419- - CAN 873D	27440- - RLC 767E	27471- - PCH 317F
27420- - -DJC 256D	27441- - KYT 970D	27472- - SLM 167F
27421- - -JDU 916E	27442 - PLB 816E	27473- - - - - CH
27422- - - KYF 7D	27443- - - - -BH 80	27474- - - - - CH
27423- - - -FIO 170	27444- - - JOJ 202E	27475- - - - - CH

27389 was the late humorist Frank Muir's third Alvis, and depicted here is the cover of his autobiography.

Virtually indistinguishable from its TE 21 predecessor from a short distance away, one has to move a little closer to take in the differences. Inside, the instruments are now set in a binnacle directly in front of the driver, reviving an idea first espoused back in 1958 on the prototype TD 21 25938. Raise the bonnet and now visible is an additional HD6 SU carburettor. This, coupled with an increase in the compression ratio from 8.5 to 9.0, has raised power output to 150bhp, though at the slightly reduced 4750rpm level. Thus the top speed is now just on 120mph. Even less obvious is a very minor alteration to the rear spring anchorages to allow the fitment of a fractionally wider half-elliptic spring.

Whilst production of the catalogued Mulliner Park Ward TF 21 had been officially signed off in September 1967, three further chassis found their way to Graber in Switzerland to be bodied there, with the very final example, 27475, being accepted by its lucky first owner early in 1968.

27389   9065 MW
Frank Muir CBE

Arguably one of the greatest humourists of all time, Frank Muir (February 5, 1920-January 2, 1998), together with his writing partner Denis Norden, impacted on the UK's entertainment scene in no small way, and the connections are too numerous to list in full, but typically *Take it From Here*, numerous quiz shows and commercial voice-overs, as with the Cadbury's Fruit and Nut Case one. For further reading, his *Oxford Book of Humorous Prose* can be recommended (1990), and especially his autobiography *A Kentish Lad* (ISBN 978-0552-

7602 94), published in 1997 by Corgi Books. An obvious Alvis enthusiast, Frank had previously owned not only a TD 21 (qv 26059 – a Series I) but also another TD 21 (qv 26824 – a Series II). Any one of the three might have been the subject of the advertisement that he placed upon parting with, "This car has been solely used for transporting retired clergymen to Evensong, and has been nightly sponged down with a light hock."

27411   LP0 1
Harold Radford Ltd

This small but highly specialised London coachbuilder is probably best remembered for its 'Countryman' estate design, mostly seen on the Bentley Mk VI chassis, though one of them was specially commissioned for the second Alvis 3-litre

27411: The extended boot aperture is immediately obvious here. (Author's collection)

27446: Adam Gilchrist with a rolled Veedon Fleece carpet. Could a seductive Cleopatra be about to emerge from it? (Viz George Bernard Shaw's *Caesar and Cleopatra*, act III.) (Courtesy Adam Gilchrist)

prototype, 3L2. The TF 21 shown, 27411, was another special commission, this time from one Edward Farr, a keen fisherman who needed fold-down rear seats and a dropped boot aperture to accommodate his rods. This was a highly practical conversion and might have been considered for production had the TF 21 been continued. The car was originally registered with the mark KLH 472 D, and has also used the mark LPO 1 (emanating from an Alvis TA 14 23757 and also associated with the London Philharmonic Orchestra), before bearing the current PBY 75D. Radfords would also have a hand in the experimental Alvis GTS design, based on Rover P6 underpinnings – now an exhibit at Gaydon.

27446 TYF 346 F
Adam Gilchrist
After a career that had commenced at Sotheby's, Adam started his own company, Veedon Fleece, in 1993, specialising in the manufacture of individually-designed carpets and rugs of the highest quality, and often to a specified reproduction pattern. Examples of Adam's work may be found in a number of stately homes. The materials concerned are mainly sourced from Nepal, where by the use of advanced factory methods, Adam is also credited with curtailing the exploitation of child labour in that part of the world. He is an avid Alvis (and Bristol) collector. 27446 has also been recorded with the registration mark MCA 5.

27470 LCT 329 F
R W D (David) Marques
Born December 9, 1932, David Marques had a distinguished sporting career between 1956 and 1961, and is considered a giant of Rugby Union. He played with many teams. Educated at Tonbridge School and Cambridge University (with National Service in the Royal Engineers in between) Marques was capped 23 times for England and was also noted with British and Irish Lions, Oxford and Cambridge, and particularly Harlequins. The TF 21 was preceded by a TD 21 (qv 26134) and even earlier by a Speed 25 (qv 14566). He died September 29, 2010.

27474 USA
Count Charles de Limur
Perhaps one day someone will write a full biography of a quite remarkable individual. Born in Paris, on March 23, 1923, into an aristocratic French family, Charlie, as he liked to be known, was sent to the Summerfield Preparatory School, St Leonard's-on-Sea, Sussex, where a contemporary pupil was the future Prince Rainer III of Monaco. Another pupil at this time was Cecil, son of Sir Dennistoun Burney, inventor. Charlie clearly remembered one of the ungainly Burney cars appearing at Summerfield (qv 7273).

Later moving to the United States, Charlie continued his education at Andover and Amhurst,

214

subsequently, in WWII, enlisting as an ambulance driver, serving in 1942/44 with the First Free French Division in North Africa under Field Marshal Bernard Montgomery. He then returned to the United States and became a riveter, building Liberty ships. He became an American citizen in 1949. There followed a highly successful career in banking (Chase and Crocker National) and thereby the means of indulging his impeccable tastes, be it with paintings, books, French ceramics, Venetian glass, etc, and even producing his own exquisite Chardonnay from his Napa Valley winery from 1986. Cars were also a passion, including the purchase of a Graber-bodied Bugatti Type 57 (chassis 57447), and, with an adroit sense of timing, the Alvis TF 21, 27474, also bodied by Graber (no 791), which left the Swiss atelier exactly 30 years to the day after the Type 57 had done.

Another typically cultured gesture was the use of a Constantin Kluge painting for the winery's bottles. Golf was also a passion, as was his collection of 78rpm mainly jazz records. Indeed, Benny Goodman was numbered amongst his personal friends. His TF 21 had been preceded by a TD 21 (qv 26365), which was used in England. Charlie died in San Francisco on April 12, 2004, but his cultural influence will be long remembered.

27474: A quite typical gesture of the late Count Charles de Limur was the commissioning of a Constantin Kluge painting as a label for his exquisite chardonnay, a bottle of which, seen here, was presented by him to the author.

Appendix

▼

Alvis humour

This was freelance artist, the late Gordon Horner's cartoon of the famous BIlly Cotton. It was reprinted in *Thoroughbred and Classic Car*, issue of August 1977 (qv 14620, p143).

From the Australian magazine *Alvibatics*, a take on the Alvis-Rover merger of 1965.

It is not unknown for the Alvis car to be on the receiving end of police attention (qv 13054). However, this brilliant cartoon by Alan Marsh offers a more amusing aspect. (Courtesy Alvis Archive Trust)

There were very many Alvis police car sales, a fact acknowledged in this Works ad, echoing a similar one by Shell Petroleum. Politically incorrect today?

The famous motoring cartoonist Apsley (Tony Phillips-Smith) penned this view of the author's researches in February 2012, after an appreciative commission from the board of the Alvis Owner's Club. (Author's collection)

Bunion, in archaeologist's guise, seems less than enthusiastic here at the unearthing of a Silver Eagle radiator. A George Martin original, kindly donated in 1982, by PA Features, Fleet Street.

"If ye find anything on this carr which doesn'ae rattle, then throw it awa 'caus it doesn' ae belong to it."

– from *Alvibatics*, the apocryphal story of a Scotsman selling his old TA 14 to an impecunious student.

On an Alvis wedding car, paraphrasing chapter 15 of St John's gospel: "Greater love hath no man than he polish four 72-spoke chrome wire wheels for a friend" (a quote from John Oliveira).

Another memorable Apsley cartoon was his take on Prince Philip's well-known TD 21 (q.v. 26600), seen here. For further examples of Apsley's witty work (largely Alvis-based) look no further than the book *Apsley and Old Cars* (978-1-9160090-0-4, Surrenden Press, 2019)

Parodying a situation quite familiar to owners of one particular Alvis model, the subtitle to this familiar bronze might read: 'Samaritan returning lost hub cap to a TA 14 owner.'

"Pirates are not confined to Penzance, nor hams to Parma"

– the author, upon club's management.

Autograph and caption of the late comedian Al Read. At one time the words "Right Monkey" were painted on the bonnet of his Speed 20 'March' Tourer, AXA 137 (qv 10869).

"Have you ever tried the de ville position?"

– the late Hazel Buck.

The Coventry Job? "You were only supposed to blow the bloody doors off!"

Also from Veloce Publishing –

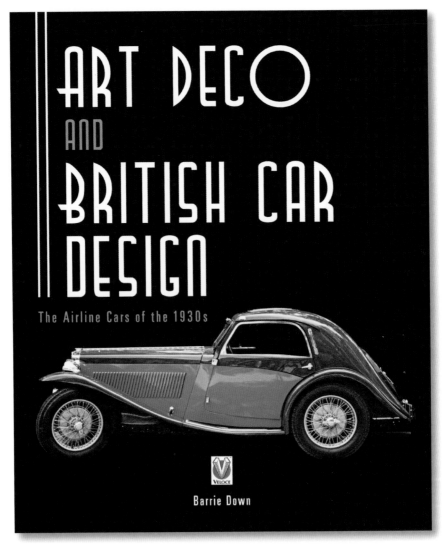

A study of the Art Deco styling elements of streamlined car designs, describing their development, commonality, and unique aeronautical names. It also portrays British streamlined production cars made between 1933 and 1936. This unique account of a radical era in automotive design is illustrated with both contemporary and colour photographs.

ISBN: 978-1-787116-22-1
Paperback • 25x20.7cm • 144 pages • 215 colour and b&w pictures

For more information and price details, visit our website at www.veloce.co.uk
• email: info@veloce.co.uk • Tel: +44(0)1305 260068

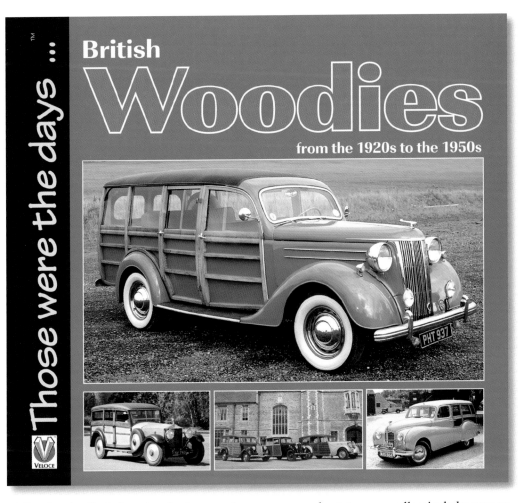

Those were the days ...™

British Woodies

from the 1920s to the 1950s

VELOCE

Wooden-bodied shooting brakes, station wagons and estate cars, collectively known as Woodies, were the original SUVs (sports utility vehicles). While they were initially created for a specific purpose, their versatility, adaptability and load-carrying abilities meant that they quickly found favour with British buyers from all walks of life. In their heyday, they were built on virtually every make of car and light commercial chassis, and could be seen on every road in Britain. Sadly, today they are a rarity due mostly to the fact that their wooden bodies were not built to last – and most didn't! Thousands were built by hundreds of coachbuilders, both large and small, and with the passage of time it may never be possible to record all of their details with any accuracy. The work of hundreds of small coachbuilder firms is highlighted and illustrated with 99 rare and previously unpublished photos of these wooden wonders.

ISBN: 978-1-84584-169-0
Paperback • 19x20.5cm • 96 pages • 89 colour and b&w pictures

For more information and price details, visit our website at www.veloce.co.uk
• email: info@veloce.co.uk • Tel: +44(0)1305 260068

Also from Veloce Publishing –

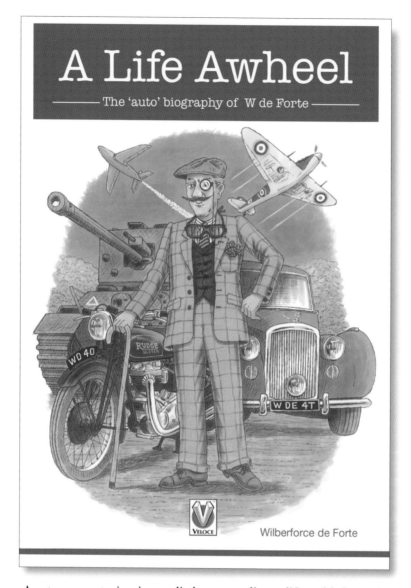

A veteran motoring journalist's extraordinary life, told through delightfully eccentric stories and charming diary extract. This unique book is packed with fascinating stories about classic cars and motorcycles, set in a bygone world, and properly fixed in time. (Fiction)

ISBN: 978-1-845848-44-6
Paperback • 21x14.8cm • 288 pages • 5 b&w pictures

For more information and price details, visit our website at www.veloce.co.uk
• email: info@veloce.co.uk • Tel: +44(0)1305 260068